1915 Steven
birth
60 & 98
130 definition
of humour
Benchley 141
MB 213 - letter
Hugh Capp -
NB also 220-1
religion 234
also 238

# THE LETTERS OF
# STEPHEN LEACOCK

SELECTED AND EDITED BY DAVID STAINES
WITH BARBARA NIMMO

**OXFORD**
UNIVERSITY PRESS

# OXFORD
UNIVERSITY PRESS

70 Wynford Drive, Don Mills, Ontario M3C 1J9
www.oup.com/ca

Oxford University Press is a department of the University of Oxford.
It furthers the University's objective of excellence in research, scholarship,
and education by publishing worldwide in

Oxford    New York

Auckland    Cape Town    Dar es Salaam    Hong Kong    Karachi
Kuala Lumpur    Madrid    Melbourne    Mexico City    Nairobi
New Delhi    Shanghai    Taipei    Toronto

With offices in

Argentina    Austria    Brazil    Chile    Czech Republic    France    Greece
Guatemala    Hungary    Italy    Japan    Poland    Portugal    Singapore
South Korea    Switzerland    Thailand    Turkey    Ukraine    Vietnam

Oxford is a trade mark of Oxford University Press
in the UK and in certain other countries

Published in Canada
by Oxford University Press

### Library and Archives Canada Cataloguing in Publication

Leacock, Stephen, 1869–1944.
[Correspondence. Selections]
The letters of Stephen Leacock / selected and edited by David Staines with Barbara Nimmo.
Includes index.
ISBN-13: 978-0-19-540869-0
ISBN-10: 0-19-540869-1

1. Leacock, Stephen, 1869–1944—Correspondence.    2. Authors, Canadian (English)—
20th century—Correspondence.    I. Staines, David, 1946–    II. Nimmo, Barbara, 1909–    III. Title.
PS8523.E15Z48 2006        C818'.5209        C2006-900873-6

Cover and text design: Brett J. Miller

1  2  3  4 – 09  08  07  06

This book is printed on permanent (acid-free) paper ∞.
Printed in Canada

# TABLE OF CONTENTS

# PREFACE

Humanist and humorist, educator and economist, professor and pundit, Stephen Leacock (1869–1944) devoted his life to education, first through his classrooms (at Upper Canada College in Toronto and later at McGill University in Montreal), then through his writings on history, economics, and political science, and finally—and perhaps most enduringly—through his many volumes of humour. 'Humour is essentially a comforter,' he maintained, 'reconciling us to things as they are in contrast to things as they might be.'

In his own time Leacock was the most famous Canadian author both at home and abroad. He was the most celebrated humorist in the English-speaking world from about 1910 until at least the late 1920s. Sales of his books of humour as well as his textbooks and studies were phenomenal. In 1906, for example, he published *Elements of Political Science*, which was translated into nineteen languages; this textbook remained its author's greatest moneymaker.

When Leacock arrived in Montreal in 1901, he appreciated the city's intellectual excitement, and he threw himself with gusto into all the activities of his chosen profession. He chaired the Department of Political Science and Economics at McGill from 1908 until his retirement in 1936. For McGill, despite his deep anger and resentment over his forced retirement, he had lasting regard. And although he would never boast of his abilities in the French language, he was completely bilingual, writing and speaking in French with ease.

Like many of his contemporaries, Leacock employed the written word as the chosen vehicle for his thoughts. 'Thinking is writing,' he once remarked. 'Read all the current magazines and then recognize that thinking is writing. If you can't think you can't write.' Elsewhere he observed: 'Good writers know that to write well is to think well. Bad writers think that all that is necessary is to think well of themselves.'

Writing occupied all of Leacock's time: more than sixty books, monographs, and pamphlets, not to mention thousands and thousands of articles and lectures of varying degrees of length and seriousness. The secret of his remarkable writing style is good conversation, good talk, filled with ideas and information and humour. With so many publishing avenues for his articles in Canada, the United

States, Britain, and other Commonwealth countries, Leacock had ample space for his good conversation.

Leacock did not invest a great deal of time in letter-writing. When the occasion demanded, he wrote passionate letters, many of these on academic questions; he was a devoted nationalist, for example, who would speak out strongly in his letters against the importation of foreign professors when there were good Canadian graduate students going without jobs. He wrote some long and personal letters, especially to his beloved mother. On the other hand, there are no letters to his closest friends, to his wife Beatrix, to his best friend, René du Roure, or to Mary Little. 'Talking', he wrote in one letter, 'is so much better than letters.' There are, however, extensive letters to his niece Barbara Ulrichsen, afterwards Barbara Nimmo, and to Fitz Shaw when distance separated them. And there was his intimate circle of friends, including B.K. Sandwell and J.A.T. Lloyd from his Upper Canada College days, and his many publishers who became his close friends, beginning with John Lane in 1910.

Almost all of Leacock's letters are handwritten. Leacock frequently wrote his letters with pen and ink on ruled paper. His favourite writing papers consisted of the unused parts of McGill University examination books, which were ideal for this purpose because they were ruled on one side, they were letter-size, and nobody wanted them. All of the letters printed in this collection have been reproduced in their entirety; if they were subsequently typed, I have favoured the original version. A line through a word or words means that this passage was crossed out in the original letter. Brackets [ ] signify that the text within them—in most cases a letterhead—was not a written part of Leacock's letter. Parentheses ( ) around a date indicate that I have added the date for the sake of clarity or consistency. Parentheses in the closing signature to a letter are Leacock's own: this was one of the ways he sometimes signed his name.

*The Letters of Stephen Leacock* contains more than eight hundred letters Leacock wrote from his early years until the day he went into hospital for his final battle with throat cancer. Gathered from libraries and personal holdings in Canada, the United States, and Britain, they offer the closest glimpse possible of Leacock's life as it progressed through the years.

*The Letters of Stephen Leacock* began more than fifteen years ago when Barbara Nimmo and I started preparing a volume of correspondence of her Uncle Stephen. She began to transcribe some letters in her possession, and I wrote to many people and many libraries to find out if they had letters. Mrs Nimmo's sudden death in 1993 ended our happy but short collaboration. Her daughter Nancy Winthrop aided my searchings, as have her own daughters, Beth Brown and Cindy Winthrop.

Ralph Curry's *Stephen Leacock: Humorist and Humanist* (1959) was the first biography of Leacock; I am grateful to Professor Curry and his wife Gwen for their support of this project. David M. Legate's cantankerous *Stephen Leacock* (1970) and Albert and Theresa Moritz's serious *Leacock: A Biography* (1985, revised as *Stephen Leacock: His Remarkable Life*, 2002) testify to Leacock's enduring fame.

Alan Bowker's edition of *The Social Criticism of Stephen Leacock: The Unsolved Riddle of Social Justice and Other Essays* (1973, revised 1996) and *On the Front Line of Life: Stephen Leacock—Memories and Reflections, 1935–1944* (2004) reveal Leacock's continuing quest for progress and social justice. I am indebted to Alan Bowker for his careful reading of this collection of letters; he spared me several inaccuracies.

Vishnu R.K. Chopra's 1975 McGill doctoral dissertation, *Stephen Leacock: An Edition of Selected Letters*, his account of seventy letters, provided valuable details about some of Leacock's correspondents. Carl Spadoni prepared *A Bibliography of Stephen Leacock* (1998), a complete account of Leacock's massive achievement, and I am indebted to him for his timely answers to many questions.

Friends in Orillia on Lake Couchiching deserve heartfelt thanks for their hospitality and many kindnesses, especially Jean Dickson and J.A. 'Pete' McGarvey, and the directors of the Leacock Home, including Ralph Curry, Jay Cody, Craig Metcalf, and Fred Addis. Likewise friends on Lake Simcoe include Mary Letitia Brown, Peter Sibbald Brown, and Peter Gzowski. In Montreal I acknowledge the aid of David McKnight, Richard Virr, and Bruce Whiteman of the McGill University Library, and I appreciate the helpful kindness of John and Judy Mappin and Terry Mosher. In Ottawa I am grateful to my colleague Gerald Lynch for his enthusiasm for this edition. In Toronto I have profited from the fine support of William H. Latimer. And in the United States I am grateful for the generosity and support of Peggy Smith, her husband Dr E. Kenneth Smith, and their daughter Susan Carney.

At Oxford University Press I am grateful to Richard Teleky, who first signed up this edition, to William Toye, who long ago read and commented on the letters that had been assembled thus far, and to Eric Sinkins, who has guided the book through the press with gracious patience and understanding.

Last but not least, I acknowledge with love the constant support of Noreen Taylor, including her ability to decipher the indecipherable.

# ACKNOWLEDGEMENTS

*The Letters of Stephen Leacock* gratefully acknowledges the following institutions and libraries:

The Robert Benchley Collection in the Howard Gotlieb Archival Research Center, Boston University, Boston, Massachusetts, for the letters to Robert Benchley

The Gallery of History, Inc., for the letters to Mrs Wainwright

The Houghton Library, Harvard University, Harvard, Massachusetts, for the letters to Houghton Mifflin and its staff

The Stephen Butler Leacock Archives, Leacock Museum National Historic Site, Orillia, Ontario (Fred A. Addis, Curator) for the letters to Lord Atholstan; the *Atlantic Monthly*; the Bank of Canada; R.W. Bardwell; W.M. Birks; Mr Blum; V.C. Clinton-Baddeley; John Home Cameron; W.T. Condor; W.N. Defoe; Russell Doubleday; H.L. Draper; John Drinkwater; James Eakins; R.T. Ferguson; Eugene Forsey; Gordon Glassco; Mr Greenway; H.A. Gwynne; Mrs R.B. Hamilton; Home University Library; W.A. Irwin; Hugh Kelly; John Kelly; Tina Kelly; Vernon Knowles; William Kaye Lamb; Mr Larkin; Tresham Lever; J.A.T. Lloyd; E.G. McCracken; J.E. McDougall; J.B. MacLean; Magistrate of Brockville; Mr Markel; Daniel C. Marsh; Marie Meloney; Andrew Miller; Montreal Trust Company; Napier Moore; John Murray; Mr Napier; *North American Review*; Kenneth Noxon; Mr Olley; *Orillia Packet and Times*; Dorothy Parker; Dorothy Purdell; *Queen's Quarterly*; Real Estate Department, Canadian Pacific Railway; Paul Reynolds; G. Eric Reid; Herbert T. Shaw; Fred Smith; G.L. Smith; Mrs Smith; Henry M. Snevily; Charles Spearman; George Stewart; J.R. Tanguay; Arthur B. Thompson; Town of Orillia; Traffic Department, City Hall, Montreal; Caroline Ulrichsen; Charles Vincent; Thomas H. Wilson; William Dudley Woodhead; Walter Yust; and for the letters to Edward Beatty (Nov. 1934, 21 Nov. 1934, 7 Nov. 1935, 11 Dec. 1935, 21 Jan. 1937, 4 Feb. 1937); Robert Benchley (4 Jan. 1935); Thomas B. Costain (2 Sep. 1922, 2 Jun. 1941, 22 Dec. 1941, 7 Feb. 1942,

26 May 1942, 7 Jun. 1942, 6 Jul. 1942, 12 Aug. 1942, 26 Aug. 1942, 6 Oct. 1942, 8 Oct. 1942, 16 Oct. 1942, 28 Oct. 1942, 6 Nov. 1942, 19 Nov. 1942, 5 Dec. 1942, 2 Mar. 1943, 12 Aug. 1943, 25 Aug. 1943); Percy Cudlipp (24 Jan. 1937, 2 Apr. 1937); Frank Dodd (23 Jan. 1923, 1 Feb. 1923, 11 Nov. 1924, 12 Feb. 1925, 26 Mar. 1925, 14 Mar. 1930, 22 Jan. 1935, 30 Oct. 1935, 23 Nov. 1936, 5 Dec. 1936, 2 Jan. 1937, mid-Jan. 1937, 20 Apr. 1937, 29 Aug. 1939, 4 Apr. 1940, 7 Aug. 1941, 3 Dec. 1941, 18 Feb. 1943, 9 Mar. 1943, 26 Feb. 1944); Hugh Eayrs (2 Jan. 1931, 14 Mar. 1932); P.P. Howe (2 Apr. 1937; 14 Jun. 1937; 25 Oct. 1937; 18 Nov. 1937); John Lane Company (5 Feb. 1936); Charles Leacock (21 Feb. 1915, 10 Apr. 1932, 23 Jan. 1940, 9 Aug. 1940, 27 Aug. 1941); Peter Leacock (1874, Jan. 1876, 28 Jun. 1884); Rosamond Leacock Edwards (23 Jan. 1942); Stephen Leacock, Jr (4 Dec. 1934); A.E. Morgan (13 Feb. 1936); and Basil W. Willett (9 Jan. 1932)

Rare Books and Special Collections Division, McGill University Library, Montreal, Quebec, for the letters to all McGill academic and administrative staff (with the exceptions noted in the immediately preceding and immediately following notes) and the letters to Lyndon E. Abbott, Mr Blodgett, Dora Hood's Book Room, Dr Alton Goldbloom, Earl Grey, Sam Gundy, James Keddie, John Kettelwell, Louis Kon, W.D. Lighthall, E.V. Lucas, Dorothy Duncan MacLennan, Archibald MacMechan, Lucien Montreuil, Cleveland Morgan, Robert B. Pattison, S.B. Putnam, Grace Reynolds, Mr Schofield, Barbara Whitley, and Charles Leacock (13 May 1920)

Osler Library, McGill University, Montreal, Quebec, for the letters to Dr Charles F. Martin and Mrs Martin

William Ready Division of Archives and Research Collections, McMaster University Library, Hamilton, Ontario, for the letters to Frank Dodd (26 Mar. 1925, 28 Feb. 1930); Hugh Eayrs (23 Sep. 1926, 5 Dec. 1929, 13 Feb. 1930, 14 Apr. 1930, 24 Jun. 1930, 16 Dec. 1930, 2 Jun. 1931, 21 Feb. 1932, 17 Sep. 1934, 25 Aug. 1936); W. Wallace Goforth (9 Sep. 1926); Raymond Knister (29 Oct. 1931); and Macmillan of Canada (9 Aug. 1930)

The National Library of Canada, Ottawa, Ontario, for the letters to Peter Leacock (24 Sep. 1875, 4 Jan. 1886) and Henry Sibley Johnson

Orillia Public Library, Orillia, Ontario, for the letters to Gerald Christy (20 Jan. 1923); Harry C. Clarke; Harold Hale; Agnes Leacock (22 Apr. 1907); Miss Low (20 Sep. 1937); and J. Beverley Robinson

Princeton University Library, Princeton, New Jersey, for the letter to F. Scott Fitzgerald

Queen's University, Kingston, Ontario, for the letters to Peter McArthur, Lorne Pierce, and B.K. Sandwell

University of Reading, Reading, England, for the letters to Alf Bryn; Sigrid Enghardt; P.P. Howe (25 Oct. 1937); John Lane (22 Jul. 1910); Mr Sherard; and Basil W. Willett (9 Jan. 1926, 25 Jan. 1926, 27 Jan. 1926, 4 Oct. 1930)

Harry Ransom Humanities Research Center, The University of Texas at Austin, for all the letters to Walter A. Johnson, John Lane, and Basil W. Willett from 17 Jul. 1910 to 18 May 1924 with the exception of the letter to John Lane (22 Jul. 1910) noted in the preceding citation; Thomas B. Costain (11 Dec. 1941, 7 Jun. 1942, 1 May 1943); Leonard Moore (2 Jan. 1923); Christopher Morley (21 Jan. 1924, 9 May 1924); and Secretary of the P.E.N. Club (19 Apr. 1923)

Robarts Library, University of Toronto, Toronto, Ontario, for the letters to W.C. Bell and Alfred Tennyson DeLury

E.J. Pratt Library, Victoria University in the University of Toronto, Toronto, Ontario, for the letters to Pelham Edgar and Helen Edgar

The letters to W. Wallace Goforth (2 Nov. 1936), Carl Goldenberg, W.J. Healy, Francis Paget Hett, Agnes Emma Leacock (with the exception of the one noted above), Daisy Leacock, George Leacock, Lillian Leacock, Margaret Leacock, Mary Leacock, Stephen Leacock, Jr (with the exception of the one noted above), Adelaide Hett Meeres, Barbara Nimmo, Donald Nimmo, Mrs Herbert T. Shaw, Barbara Ulrichsen, and Colonel Scott Williams are reprinted with permission from private sources.

*To the Memory of*

BARBARA NIMMO
1909–1993

and

MARY STAINES
1906–1990

# CHAPTER 1

## STEPHEN LEACOCK
# THE EARLY YEARS

## 1869–1907

Stephen Leacock was born on 30 December 1869, 'exactly the middle year of Queen Victoria's reign', as he commented in *The Boy I Left Behind Me*. His birthplace was Swanmore, 'a hamlet and parish on "Waltham Chase" in Hampshire'. For many years, he explains, he believed he had been born in Swanmore, 'a suburb of Ryde in the Isle of Wight, and as I know that my grandfather lived near Ryde, I moved my birthplace into that suburb.' Some doubt arose, and so he contacted and received a reply from a solicitor at Ryde who had conducted the Leacock family business for generations. 'He wrote that he thought it extremely unlikely that I was born in such a locality as Swanmore, Ryde. . . . I was led by this to write to the Vicar of Bishop's Waltham, and he sent me back a certificate of my birth and christening at Swanmore Parish Church, and he said that not only was I born in Swanmore but that Hampshire was proud of it.'

The third child—and the third son—of Walter Peter Leacock and Agnes Emma Butler, young Stephen grew up in a family that seemed to be always on the move. At his own mother's instigation, Peter had, along with his brothers and sisters, converted to Catholicism at a young age, yet this new faith shows little impact on him. He secretly married Agnes when he was only eighteen and she was twenty, on 1 January 1867 in the Anglican parish of All Saints' Church, Norfolk Square, London; at the time of their marriage, Agnes was pregnant with the first of the couple's eleven children.

The following March, Peter and Agnes sailed for Natal, the closest port to Maritzburgh, South Africa, where Peter tried to farm a plantation bought for him by his father. The locusts ate up the crops, and the South African climate proved harmful for Agnes, who had suffered a serious concussion as a child. In early 1868 they returned to England with young Thomas James (Jim), born 14 July 1867.

Back in England the Leacocks lived at various times in Swanmore, in Shoreham in Sussex, and in Porchester, while Peter was 'learning farming' in order to be sent to America. Although Agnes was delighted to be back where she could visit her family, Peter, because of his Catholic religion and his secret marriage, was never invited to her home. During these years Agnes bore five more children: Arthur Murdock (Dick) (29 July 1868), Stephen Butler, Charles John (6 December 1871), Agnes (Missie) (15 March 1873), and Edward Peter (Teddy) (6 January 1875).

Stephen describes Porchester as 'the only place of my childhood days in England that I really remember. I lived there for two years (age four and a half to six and a half), and in a sense it still means the England that is England to me.' While the family was living there, his paternal grandfather was consulting the map and picked Kansas because 'at that time the railways only got that far'. But as Stephen explains, the family would never settle in Kansas: 'My father went first, and we were placed in Porchester so that we couldn't get to the Isle of Wight too often. We were ready to go to America when word came that my father's farm in Kansas had been eaten by grasshoppers (they are the same as locusts). This meant delay while my grandfather looked for something farther still. So we waited on in Porchester, and I had altogether six years of an English childhood that I had no right to have under the rules.'

Porchester is the home of Stephen's first four letters, all written to his father while he was abroad, at first in Kansas and afterwards in Toronto. With the failure of the second farm, Peter's father persisted in locating a farm capable of supporting his son and daughter-in-law and their six children. For the third time he established his son, this time on a one-hundred acre tract in Ontario. Peter went ahead to prepare the land for his family—Stephen's third letter acknowledges his father's presence in Toronto—and the family sailed in the spring of 1876 from Liverpool to Montreal on the *Sarmatian*. Although his mother cried as they left England, Stephen was fascinated with the ship that was his new home:

> The *Sarmatian* was one, was practically the last one, of those grand old vessels of the Allan Line which combined steam with the towering masts, the cloud of canvas, the maze of ropes and rigging of a full-rigged three-masted ship. She was in her day a queen of the ocean, that last word which always runs on to another sentence. She had been built in 1871, had had the honour of serving the queen as a troopship for the Ashanti war and the further honour of carrying the queen's daughter to Canada as the wife of the Marquis of Lorne, the governor general. No wonder that in my recollection of her the *Sarmatian* seemed grand beyond belief.

After arriving in Montreal, the family took a river steamer to Toronto, then a train north to Newmarket, where Peter and his hired man met them and drove them in two wagons north to Sutton, a village comprising 'two mills, two churches, and quite a main street, with three taverns'. Stephen's mother, who was, despite her year on the plantation in South Africa, much more accustomed to ordered life, was horrified by the family's new surroundings, and Stephen himself described the farm as 'the damnedest place I ever saw. The site was all right, for the slow slope of the hillside west and south gave a view over miles of country and a view of the sunset only appreciated when lost. But the house! Someone had built a cedar log house and then covered it round with clapboard, and then someone else had added three rooms stuck along the front with more clapboard, effectually keeping all the sunlight out.' Although Stephen's recollections give a bleak impression of the family's lifestyle at this time, it is important to note that the Leacocks had a hired man and three other servants. Nevertheless, farm life was far from easy.

Stephen attended School Section No. 3, Township of Georgina, but when his mother noticed her children losing their Hampshire accents, she decided to teach them at home. She hired a tutor, Harry Park, 'from whom we received, for the next three or four years, teaching better than I have ever had since and better than any I gave in ten years as a schoolteacher'. Stephen's grandfather paid for the tutor, 'for fear, of course, that we might come back home on him'.

Like young boys his age, Stephen read widely and well, his mother having brought to Canada many significant works. Among the books he read as a boy were Charles Dickens's *Pickwick Papers*, his introduction to a writer who would haunt his imagination all his life; all the stories written by Jules Verne; and all the stories then published of Mark Twain, another writer who would have a lasting impact on him.

In 1878 appeared Peter's younger brother, Edward Philip Leacock, Stephen's 'Remarkable Uncle', as his July 1939 essay made apparent in the *Reader's Digest* series 'The Most Unforgettable Character I Have Ever Met'. E.P., as he was called, 'scented Winnipeg from afar, was one of the first in, and at the time of which I speak was piling up a fortune on paper, was elected to the New Manitoba legislature, and heaven knows what'. His own speculative railroad was never more than a letterhead, yet he seduced Peter into following after him in 1880 or 1881 and Stephen's oldest brother later still. The venture was sponsored through the sale of equipment and even livestock from the Leacock farm in Sutton, but as Stephen explains, 'the lean cattle and the broken machinery fetched only about enough in notes of hand (nobody had cash) to pay for the whiskey consumed at the sale.'

Stephen and his two older brothers were now in residence at Upper Canada College, Stephen first attending in January 1882. The following summer, vacationing as always at Sibbald's Point, Agnes decided to rent out the farm for enough to make the payment on the mortgage and move to Toronto on 'the strength of a casual legacy from England that should have been hoarded as capital but was burned up as income'.

During this period, Agnes bore five more children: George (1 March 1877), Caroline (Carrie) (16 August 1878), Maymee (24 November 1880), Rosamond (Dot) (28 May 1884), and Margaret (Daisy) (10 September 1886). These dates confirm that Stephen's father did come home a few times during his sojourn in Winnipeg: he was with the family when Agnes was moving to Toronto in the summer of 1883 and later still when Margaret was conceived.

Agnes moved her large family into a fine house on John Street in Toronto, where she employed two maids and kept a team and carriage. As his letters to his father of 28 June 1884 and 4 June 1886 make clear, Stephen was devoted to both his parents. When his father returned broke from the West in the late summer of 1886, Stephen and his family returned to the farm, and thus began what Stephen would later call 'a shadowed, tragic family life'.

In the fall of 1886, Stephen returned to Upper Canada College, and in the following spring he graduated as head boy. In the summer of 1887, the family situation was severe indeed, and Stephen's own words provide the most complete account of what took place: 'The situation ended by my father leaving home again in 1887. No doubt he meant to come back, but he never did. I never saw him again.' Peter travelled, ending up in Bedford, Nova Scotia, where, under the pseudonym of Captain Lewis, he had another son (who died at seventeen) and passed away at the age of ninety-two on 4 August 1940.[1]

Agnes lived at the farm for another four years, but Stephen's two older brothers, Jim and Dick, 'left home for good, both to the West, Dick into the Northwest Mounted Police and Jim in the wake of my remarkable uncle. That made me—my father being gone—the head of the family at seventeen.' This was a responsibility that Stephen would take seriously for the rest of his life.

In June 1887 Stephen passed the matriculation examinations for entrance into the University of Toronto, and after one year there embarked on his teaching career with a thirteen-week teacher training program at the Strathroy Collegiate Institute in Strathroy, Ontario. He then applied for jobs everywhere, finally obtaining, through the agency of his former tutor Harry Park, a position at Uxbridge High School, a mere eighteen miles south of his mother's farm. With his monthly pay of $59.33 he could afford a modest livelihood as well as contributions to his mother's income. Thus, in 1889 he began his support of his mother, which continued throughout her life.

That fall, Leacock renewed his affiliation with Upper Canada College by accepting a position as assistant master in modern languages. Classroom duties occupied him until three o'clock, and afterwards he took classes to complete his bachelor's degree at the University of Toronto. He graduated in 1891.

With his BA in hand, Leacock received a promotion at Upper Canada College: second modern language master and assistant house master in residence. The following year he became first modern language master. It was during this period of teaching that he tried his hand at the writing of humorous sketches, succeeding admirably with such works as 'ABC: or, The Human Element in Mathematics', 'My Financial Career', and 'The Awful Fate of Melpomenus Jones'. And at this time, too, he was promoted to senior house master, the highest ranking faculty appointment at Upper Canada College.

---

1  For further information see Elise Churchill Tolson, *The Captain, The Colonel, and Me (Bedford, NS, since 1503)* (Sackville: The Tribune Press, 1979), pp. 210–14.

Leacock, however, was not content with secondary school teaching, even at the prestigious Upper Canada College. He aspired to complete his doctorate, and in his choice of university to pursue his doctoral studies he was deeply influenced by Gordon Laing, a fellow graduate of Toronto in 1891. Laing, after his graduation, had begun to study law and had obtained a teaching position at Whetham College, British Columbia. Two years later, he had gone to Johns Hopkins University, where he had earned his PhD in classics in 1896. His first academic position had been as a lecturer in Latin literature at Bryn Mawr College. When Laing accepted an instructorship in Latin at the University of Chicago in 1899, Leacock decided to leave Upper Canada College to join him; he borrowed $1500 from his mother and went to the University of Chicago, where he and Laing were roommates for the academic year of 1899–1900:

> I had selected Chicago because of the arrival there on the staff (1899) of Dr. Gordon Laing. He and I had been fellow students, Damon and Pythias,—or is it Scylla and Charbydis,—at Toronto. He beat me at graduation by thirty seconds. He had taken classics,—an even heavier load of it. But he had stuck to it, attended Johns Hopkins, studied at Rome and Athens, dug excavations, read inscriptions, wrote papers,—in short never let on that he didn't really know anything and kept it up for fifty successful years.[2]

For Leacock, the University of Chicago 'was an *alma mater* indeed: it led me on through a few stringent years to all the good fortune and success that I had the luck to get later.'[3] And two members of the faculty especially interested him. The first was Dr Judson:

> His method of lecturing, a forward advance with pauses of casual questions, struck me as so good that I stole it and never used any other. Later on when he was President I had the honour of knowing him very well by reason of the marriage of his daughter with Dr. Gordon Laing.[4]

The second was Thorstein Veblen, the renowned economist, whose *Theory of the Leisure Class* was published in 1899. Leacock admitted to being 'deeply impressed by him':

> He had no manner, no voice, no art. He lectured into his lap with his eyes on his waistcoat. But he would every now and then drop a phrase with a literary value to it beyond the common reach. In the first lecture I heard, he happened to say, 'Hume,

2 'My Recollection of Chicago', *My Recollection of Chicago and the Doctrine of Laissez-Faire*, ed. Carl Spadoni (Toronto: University of Toronto Press, 1998), p. 4.
3 Ibid.
4 Ibid., pp. 5–6.

of course, aspired to be an intellectual tough.' That got me, and kept me; the art of words is almost better than truth, isn't [it].[5]

In 1898 or 1899 Stephen met his future wife, Beatrix Hamilton, at a tennis game in Orillia. Her grandfather, Henry Pellatt, had a large summer home near Orillia named Southwood, where Beatrix and her mother, Mrs R.B. Hamilton, frequently spent their summers. Beatrix, or Trix as her friends called her, was physically commanding with extensive amateur stage experience. Because of her theatrical commitments, Stephen and Beatrix were married in the actors' church, 'The Little Church Around the Corner' in New York City, on 7 August 1900, and they had an apartment in Chicago as their first home together.

It was during this time that Henry Neville Sanders, a lecturer in classics and Sanskrit at McGill University, suggested to Leacock that he apply to McGill for a lectureship in political economy; Leacock, in fact, had applied for the position even before he was married. On 21 January 1901, he entered Room 5 in Arts Hall to deliver his opening lecture. For three years Leacock followed the pattern of teaching at McGill and then moving to Chicago for the spring semester. His lectures were in both history and political science, focusing on the general theories of political science and on the history of the British Empire. Once he was awarded his doctorate in economics, on 16 June 1903, he was appointed to the full position of lecturer at McGill.

During the next four years Leacock established himself as a first-rate academic scholar and teacher. His textbook *Elements of Political Science* (1906) proved to be throughout his lifetime his biggest money-maker; translated into nineteen languages, it filled a desperate need in the marketplace. In addition to the scholarly articles he also wrote at this time, he published a work combining political science and history, *Baldwin, Lafontaine, Hincks: Responsible Government* (1907), which commanded a privileged position in the twenty-volume Makers of Canada series, edited by Duncan Campbell Scott and Pelham Edgar and published between 1903 and 1908. In 1906 he was raised to the rank of associate professor.

During his early years in Montreal, Leacock engaged in a number of activities that fostered his writing of humour. In 1902, for example, he became a member of the Pen and Pencil Club, an exclusive, all-male organization where Leacock frequently presented addresses. His first one, 'Opening a Bank Account', was probably an adaptation of 'My Financial Career'. Members of this club included the painter Robert Harris, John McCrae—later famous as the author of 'In Flanders Fields'— and Andrew Macphail, professor at McGill in the history of medicine and destined to become a close mentor to Leacock. And as early as 1906 Leacock, already a distinguished scholar, was assembling his comic pieces for a projected book of humour.

5    Ibid., p. 6.

*To his father, Peter Leacock*          (1874)

My dear Dadda

I thank you for the letter, mama has hurt her hand so wriite for her. I am 5. we each had crackker at tea I send you am almanac.

Mamas hand is straped on a board and it is no use There is to be a Xtmas tree at the school on the 8th We shall go

> Your affec
> Stephen

*To Peter Leacock*                    Portchester
                                      Ja (1875)

My dear Dadda

I thank you for the book. Jim has a young Xtmas tree We have got a new Baby he was born on the 6th We very often go into Fareham

> Your affec Son
> Stephen

*To Peter Leacock*                    Sep$^{t}$. 24th/75

My dear Dadda

I am glad Toronto is a nice place. My cat is grown up to be a Mother cat and has got 2 little kittens

> your affec$^{e}$ Son
> Stephen

*To Peter Leacock*                    (1876)

My dear Dada

Edward is vaccinated he is just like me on Monday we went to a grand tea party at Mrs Bakers

> Your affec
> hoping

## *To Peter Leacock* June 28/84

My dear father,

The little ones all started for the lake this afternoon; they went this morning but they missed the train. The party were 8 in all, carrying about 10 trunks and some ½ dozen dogs & cats; In order not to be late they went to the station about an hour early, and, true to their orders not to go on to the platform, they sat patiently in the car for the best part of an hour before the train started. Of course they forgot some of their luggage. Miss Wilson headed the young Israelites and Miss Bertha made an able second. There will be probably be a notice about in to-morrow's mail headed "Departure for happy hunting grounds" or something of that sort. Do you remember the fuchia which you got for mother at a butcher's shop on Queen st? There are 76 buds on it now & the Italian primroses & violets are doing well. I got some checkers down town and Mother & I played three games; I beat her in all of them, but she says it was only because she got stupid at the last, or the baby cried in the middle, or she thought that king was a common, or something of that sort.

Mother wants me to tell you that it was not the children's fault that they missed the morning train, as they were all up at half past four, in fact they hardly slept at all, and their trunk had been packed about a week before.

Mother was out in the yard for the first time yesterday and had all the pleasure of beating me in a game of croquet; she put in down in her diary (at least its very likely) in red letter capitals.

Yr affec<sup>e</sup> son
Stephen. B. Leacock

## *To Peter Leacock* January 4, 1886.

My dear Father
Mother has been very sick from taking too much medicine but Dr Strange was here today and saw here and gave her some new medicine instead of the old. She seems better tonight and ask– me to write to you: it would be better if you could come down. Flora arrived all right this morning. Baby is quite well.

Your affec. son
Stephen B. Leacock

*To his sister, Rosamond Leacock*[1]    U.C. College
                                        May 2 1895

My dear Dot

It is quite a long time since I have written to you, isn't it? We are having beautiful weather here quite like summer. Has the ice all gone out of the lake yet? Tell me all the news: are the little Hetts better now? Give my love to Addie.[2] I hope that the Alderman is well. Dick was here for a few days last week but he has gone to Milton. Give my love to everybody. We are having cricket and tennis here: I am writing to mother by this same mail

                                        your affec^te brother,
                                        Stephen B Leacock

1  Dr Rosamond Mary Butler Leacock (1889–1949) was a physician at the Hospital for Sick Children in Toronto. She later married Harry D. Edwards; they had no children.
2  John Roland Hett married Letitia Martyn Sibbald, the daughter of Captain Thomas Martyn Sibbald; they were the occupants of Eildon Hall, Sibbald's Point, Ontario. They had many children, including Francis Paget and Adelaide (Addie).

*To his mother, Agnes Leacock*    (May 2, 1895)

D^r Mother,

Teddy has a job at Brampton. It will be rather tough for him there at first and, as I know no one there, I thought it might be a good idea for you to write to Mrs Cayley and say that he has gone there and ask her to get Mr Cayley to drop a line to the English Church clergyman there & get him to look Teddy up, if he (Mr Cayley) knows the clergyman. Say that you dont know anybody in Brampton & are afraid that it will be pretty lonely for Teddy there. Old Cayley will write to the other Good Man whether they know one another or not. Be sure to do it Teddy goes to church regularly so knowing the clergyman will cost him nothing in attendance—The man may have noticed him any away. Please dont forget to do this—I had no idea that Teddy was here looking for work until the day George came. Sent note to Gundley (150) and $1 interest—I suppose you covered the other fifty with a cheque. No news—love to all (which is <u>few</u> now)—you & the Alderman & Dot must feel lost—No, I am not coming home for the 24th as I intend to go to Milton and Brampton and see how Teddy and George are getting along—Tell Dot I am sorry to scribble over her letter[1]

                                        Your loving son
                                        Stephen B. Leacock

1  This letter has been written on the back of the letter to Leacock's sister Rosamond of the same date, and the final sentences had to be scribbled on the side of the letter to his sister.

## *To Agnes Leacock*                    May 27th 95

My dear Mother

I got the letter from Dot, and yours today—There is nothing much in it to answer but I will scribble a line or two to you to pass the time, as I am in night study. I will try and find a book such a Dot asks for, but I am afraid it will be hard, or tell Dot that if she really wants a play badly I have no doubt I could write her one. Does she want it written in verse or in in prose? Sad or droll? She has only to speak. God bless her, where does she mean to stay when she comes down to Toronto? here? or at Miss Brayley's or where? But I dont want her to come unless I am reappointed here; otherwise I need all my money. We know nothing yet of the future of the college Much talk in all directions but nothing done yet. You are much wiser not to come down to Toronto: I am glad about your head but you must of course be very careful of yourself. Are not those palpitations you are troubled with very likely caused by the nerves and not from there being thing the matter with the heart itself? A low nervous condition always acts upon the heart, and can only be remedied indirectly by having lots of rest and air, and quiet. I am sure that your tranquil mornings must do you good: it gave me quite a pang of homesickness when you spoke of the Alderman coming home with a rush full of news. I could just imagine it and for the moment felt as if I <u>could</u> tolerate the little Alderman with some pleasure for about five minutes. The weather here has been very cold and unpleasant lately; I have been very busy indeed, examining as usual at the University and have not been at all well. I have been taking a tonic, beef iron and wine. Have you ever tried it? Would you like me to send you some up? How is Charlie getting along? Do you remember that jolly wedding that the Bird concocted last year,—got them to go in for it, all in a hurry at ~~the~~ a supper party? The thing terminated the other day in a tragedy—The two hadn't enough money, man hadn't constant work—both took to drink—went on sprees together—finally he brought home a big jar of whisky one day and they had a huge spree for 3 days—At the end of it, he was found dead in a corner of the room, lying on the floor with his head jammed into a corner & the woman in bed too drunk to know that he was dead. They buried him and at the funeral the Bird in a sad suit of black walked in front, chief of the mourners—which I think the most profoundedly humorous thing the bird ever did. Give my love to Mrs Hett. I hope all her crowd are well.

Your affec Son
Stephen B Leacock

P.S. This is the first letter that ever passed between us not provoked by business.

# To William Peterson, Principal, McGill College[1]

Jan 17 1900

Principal Peterson
McGill College
Montreal

Dear Sir—

Mr Sanders of your faculty writes me that there is a possibility of a lectureship being shortly established at McGill in Political Economy—In such an event I should like to apply for the position. I am at present doing Post Graduate work in the department of Political Economy at Chicago University—I did not take political economy as an undergraduate at Toronto: the course was not yet founded. Previous to coming here I did five years of private study and did enough graduate work to easily be admitted to graduate school here—In my undergraduate course at Toronto I took classics and Modern Languages. I graduated in 1891. My standing in my course was very good. I took the first proficiency scholarship on entering the university: did not write the first year exam: was first in first class in Modern Languages (scholarship) and second in first class in Classics at the end of my second year: was first in first class in Modern Languages at the end of my third year: in the final exam$^n$ in Modern Languages the ranking was alphabetical in the classes.

I am asking the Professors here to write to you as to my competency to undertake the work. Of course it would not suit me very well to leave Chicago just at present as it would involve dropping the work I have in hand, but I presume there is no intention on your part of engaging anyone until the autumn—My present degree is B.A., but I believe it would be quite possible for me if I came to Montreal to arrange to presently get my degree of Ph.D. from Chicago. I am thirty years of age. This is my first year at Chicago.

Yours sincerely,
Stephen Leacock

P.S. In the event of an appointment, I could, if necessary, come to see you personally to make arrangements as to courses to be given and so forth.

1   Edinburgh-born William Peterson (1856–1921) graduated from the University of Edinburgh with first-class honours in classics. After completing his post-graduate work at Oxford, he returned to the University of Edinburgh to teach classical languages. He became principal of Dundee College (1882–95) before going to McGill as principal in 1895. He was knighted in 1915. In January 1919 he suffered a stroke that left him an invalid; he resigned from McGill the following April and departed for England.

## *To William Peterson*                    Jan 18–1900

Principal Peterson
McGill College
Montreal

Dear Sir.

In my letter to you of yesterday in regard to a position at McGill in Political Economy, I should have referred you to Professor Caspar Miller, and D$^r$ Veblen of this University. I have done most of my work with them, and thought it better to ask you to write to them for full information instead of merely asking them for the usual testimonial

Yours faithfully
Stephen Leacock

## *To William Peterson*                    Graduate Hall
University of Chicago
May 5–1900

Principal Peterson
McGill University
Montreal

Dear Sir

I am just in receipt of your letter of the third instant. In answer I may say that I am taking Political Science in connection with my work in Economics. My work in Political Science both before Xmas and at present, has been entirely with Professor Judson, the head professor of the department—I expect to continue my courses with him next year. I should be most happy to make application for such a temporary position as you speak of as it would work very well with my course here. I believe it is customary here to allow temporary work in higher teaching in one's own department to count as part of a graduate course. With many thanks for your courteous letter

Yours sincerely
Stephen Leacock

## *To William Peterson*

Principal Peterson
McGill University
Montreal

Dear Sir:—

I beg to acknowledge the receipt of your letter of June the 9th. In reply to it I may say that I should, in the event of my coming to Montreal, be most happy to give any help I could to students wishing it out of lecture hours. In the matter of remuneration, the arrangement suggested would be entirely satisfactory to me. In case of your having anything further to communicate to me, my address from June 20, until Sep 28 will be, Orillia, Ontario: after that I hope to return to Chicago.

Yours sincerely
Stephen Leacock

## *To William Peterson*

[The University of Chicago]
23 Graduate Hall
April 1. 1903

Principal Peterson
McGill University

Dear Sir,

The chair in Political Economy in the state university of Arkansas has fallen vacant. The President has written to the Department of Political Economy here to nominate a man and the Department (Prof Laughlin) has nominated me. Both the professor of economics now leaving Arkansas to take a post at Leland Stanford, and his predecessor were appointed in this same way on the nomination of Professor Laughlin. There is therefore a very reasonable probability that I shall be appointed to the position. I am taking the liberty in writing to President Buchanan of the University of Arkansas to refer him to you in regard to my teaching qualifications.

I thought it well also in view of your conversation with me of last week to let you know of my application. I understand that the appointment will be made in the course of a month or so. Should I therefore receive an offer from Arkansas it will hardly be possible for me to hold the position open for myself long enough to be able to correspond with you in regard to what you might care to do in the matter.

May I ask whether you see your way under these circumstances to offer me an increase in salary? I have arranged to go up for my doctors degree next month and I presume that if I succeed n taking it, this also might be offered as a claim on a higher salary.

Yours sincerely
Stephen Leacock


## To William Peterson

[The University of Chicago]
23 Graduate Hall
April 10 1903

D$^r$ Peterson
Principal: McGill University
Montreal

Dear Sir

I am in receipt of a letter from Dean Walton of April 6$^{th}$ in which he tells me that you will be able to promise me a salary of two thousand dollars in the event of my coming back to McGill, provided that I do work in the summer session. I shall be very happy to return on those terms. The details of the work I am to do will depend, I suppose, on the particular requirements of the time. I hope however that it will mean as little increase in any historical work as possible as I am anxious to be identified as far as may be with the department of Economics and Political Science.

Yours sincerely
Stephen Leacock


## To William Peterson

[The University of Chicago]
23 Graduate Hall
April 28. 1903

Principal Peterson
McGill University
Montreal

Dear Sir

I beg to acknowledge the receipt of your letter of the 22$^{nd}$ in reference to the ratification of my appointment at McGill. I may say in reply that I am quite sensitive of the fact that I have received most favorable treatment at McGill both in reference to the present increase in my salary and in having been enabled to complete my course here by twice leaving Montreal before the close of the session. I shall be only too happy to feel that I am now returning to a permanent position on the staff and have no intention of applying for or seeking any other position. With apologies for the delay in my answer which was due to a temporary illness,

> Yours sincerely
> Stephen Leacock

## To William Peterson

Orillia Ontario
April 22 1905

Principal Peterson
McGill University
Montreal

Dear Sir,

I received a week or two ago a letter from Miss Carey Thomas suggesting that I should apply for the professorship of Economics now vacant at Bryn Mawr by the resignation of Professor Keasly. Miss Thomas implied in her letter that, when her leisure served her, she intended to write to McGill to make inquiries about my work: I presume that this might mean that she would write to you.

The position she is offering only carries with it a salary of $2000 and as the cost of living at Bryn Mawr is very high it has no material advantages over the position I now occupy, except of course that I might later on have an honorable place among the gentlemen Miss Thomas has dismissed. I wrote to her and declined to apply. I thought it better to let you know of this in order that, in the event of Miss Thomas writing to you, you should not suppose that the matter was of my seeking.

> Yours faithfully
> Stephen Leacock

## *To William S. Booth*

McGill University
May 2 '04

W<sup>m</sup> S Booth Esqre[1]
Houghton Mifflin
Boston

Dear Sir

I am in receipt of your most courteous letter of April 22—I shall be most happy to submit to your inspection the book I am engaged on. Just at present I have undertaken a lot of extra work, so I fear I shall not have much of my book done before next Xmas.

But I shall be most happy to send you all, or a part of it, as soon as completed.

Yours sincerely
Stephen Leacock

1   William S. Booth was an editor at Houghton Mifflin, Boston, Massachusetts.

## *To Canon Green*[1]

Montreal
Oct 19 1905

My dear Canon Green

We are simply <u>delighted</u> with the pictures, all of which are to go in our drawing room as my wife says they are much too good for my study. Beatrix is enchanted with the marine picture: we have taken it at once to be framed by Morgan & Co and they are putting on it a very wide plain black frame with gilt rim between the frame and the picture and no mat: they said a mat would be a mistake. We went there because there is a man there who really knows pictures and on whose taste we can rely. This first picture is to be ready on Saturday and if we like it I shall at once send the others to the same place.

I really cannot express to you how pleased we are with the pictures and how much we appreciate your kindness. I am myself especially taken with the view of the Severn river: the coloring is really beautiful and yet I am sure quite truthful. I think you have quite succeeded in expressing the effects you were aiming at in the sketch of the frowning rocks over the river: the successive distances of the background are finely brought out and in the foreground the <u>sheen</u> of the water is admirable. I hope that if you are in Montreal this winter you will come to see ~~your~~ us and be able to judge how the pictures look when framed.

Yours very sincerely
Stephen Leacock

1   Canon Richard W. Green (1848–1934) came to Orillia from Toronto in 1888 to become the rector of Saint James' Anglican Church for the next twenty-three years. An eloquent preacher, a devoted adherent of the Christian faith, and a distinguished painter, he was president of the Orillia Branch of the Church of England Temperance Society.

*To William Peterson*                    McGill University
                                         Montreal
                                         Jan 16 1906

Principal Peterson
McGill University

Dear Sir

I wish to ask for an increase of five hundred dollars in salary. It is somewhat difficult for me to advance my claims to such an increase without appearing to sound my own praises and to estimate very favorably the value of my work to the University. I hope therefore that you will pardon what would otherwise appear a very egotistical letter.

I think that I may however claim that during the five years I have lectured at the University, my work has been a success. My classes have been largely attended and I am certain that the constant preparation and thought I have put upon my lectures have not been without result.

I have also acquired additional qualifications for the post I occupy by obtaining since my appointment to it the degree of Doctor of Philosophy, granted to me magna cum laude by the University of Chicago. I have moreover completed a book of some 300 pages on the Theory of Political Science which is now in the press, being published by Houghton Mifflin & Co of Boston. In addition to this I have written a number of articles on political and economic topics connected with Canada, and have been and am constantly engaged in literary work and special research such as it is profitable to a University that the members of its staff should undertake.

On the other hand I cannot refrain from saying that I find my present salary inadequate for my reasonable needs. During my first two years of lecturing at McGill I received one thousand and fifteen hundred dollars as my two years salary. In this period I got badly into debt and have remained in a position of chronic financial embarrassment. The result is that, agreeable as is my work at the University my private life has been an uninterrupted succession of overdue accounts, protested notes and legal proceedings for debt. Nor do I under present conditions see any reasonable prospect of relief. To make provision for past debts and for future contingencies, to pay my ordinary household expenses and to provide even for that thin decency conformable to the position of a lecturer is beyond the compass of my present salary.

I trust that you will pardon my writing in so personal a strain; I thought it wiser to acquaint you with the plain facts of my position. It is not however because I am in debt that I am asking for an increase in pay. It is because I think I am worth it.

I am most anxious to remain in Canada and at McGill. With each succeeding year I find my work more interesting and I should much wish to feel that for success and advancement in life I need not look beyond the bounds of my own university. The branch of study with which I am connected offers a wide field, and in this country and at this moment a field of peculiar attractiveness. I think that very much can be done at McGill by making Colonial History and Government and those political problems of Canada which excite so much public attention, an object of special study and peculiar consideration. If we are the leading university of Canada we ought to stand before the Canadian public as a place where the young men of the country can receive a special training in those things that most concern the public life of the Dominion. To such work as this I should be only happy to devote myself, but I should wish to come to it single minded and freed from the continuous worry of financial embarrassment.

Yours faithfully
Stephen Leacock

## To William Peterson

McGill University
Jan 31 1906

Principal Peterson
McGill University

Dear Sir

A matter of some disagreement has arisen between Professor Flux and myself which I think proper to report to you.[1] Professor Flux has informed me that he is not satisfied with my present courses in the fourth year and proposes to change them. He says that as they now stand they involve my teaching matters of an economic character. He lays before me the following alternative: either my fourth year courses must only be offered to students who have taken Professor Flux's work in the third year, or, other courses must be prescribed of a character not involving economic topics. Professor Flux has suggested as fourth year courses Colonial Administration and the History of Political Theory.

I have already acquainted Professor Flux with my views on the matter. I think the courses as now given quite satisfactory: I had 18 students of last year's fourth years, and 14 of the present class. All of these were optional. I have never heard any of them complain that they found the lectures difficult to understand for want of preliminary instruction by Professor Flux. Nor have I heard complaints

---

1    Alfred William Flux (1867–1942) taught in the Department of Political Economy at McGill University from 1902 until 1908.

of any kind from any quarter except from Professor Flux who has not attended my lectures. The courses I now give deal with the actual legislation of modern government. The titles are clumsy but the subject matter is useful, interesting and, I think, well adapted to the wants of our students. I enclose a schedule of the courses, and the notes from which the lectures are delivered can be submitted to you in full if you desire.

On the other hand the courses that Professor Flux wishes to submit are not, in my opinion, nearly so useful to our students. Colonial Administration, divested of such topics as Tariffs, Railroads etc becomes a highly specialised course constituting a study in law rather than Political Science. The History of Political Theory is a subject on which I gave lectures to a small class some years ago: I found it quite unsatisfactory, too advanced & too specialised for ordinary students and of infinitely less value to them than what I now give.

Under present conditions the students who take my work in the fourth year belong to one of three categories: –

1. Honour Students in Economics (of which there have been none for two years)
2. Honour Students in History
3. Continuation Students who take the courses as ordinary continuation of the work done with me in the ~~fourth~~ third year.

Last year this last category contained 17 of the 18 students. This year ~~they~~ it contains 7 of the 14 the rest being the honor history class. The adoption of Professor Flux's first alternative whereby my class would be open only to his ex-pupils would leave me with few or no students. The adoption of the second alternative would require the students to take courses which I think of far less value to them than the present.

Professor Flux tells me that the authority in the matter rests with him and I have answered that in that case discussion between us is idle

I regret very much to trouble you with this matter: I find it necessary to do so since otherwise the altered courses will be inserted next month in the new calendar.

Yours faithfully
SL

## To Paul Samuel Reinsch[1]

[McGill University
Montreal]
June 29 '06

Professor Paul. S. Reinsch,
PanAmerican Delegation
State Department
Washington, D.C.

Dear Sir

It will give me great pleasure to come to Providence next Xmas and take part in the formation of a colonial institute in connection with the Political Science Association. I shall be most happy to read a paper on <u>Responsible Government in the British Colonial System</u>. I am just completing a book on 'Baldwin LaFontaine and Hincks' (Makers of Canada Series. Morang & Co) with a subtitle Responsible Government. This has occasioned my getting access to a lot of stuff in the Canadian Archives Department from which I can make a useful paper. The point of it is to show that the idea of self-government came from the colonies not the mother country: that Lords Sydenham, Metcalfe, Stanley, John Russell & Even (Lord Grey did not contemplate the grant of the present system and in their despatches instructions etc were at much pains to prove its impracticality. If this is too historical a subject, I should be pleased to read a paper on The Present Crisis in the British Colonial System: that sounds rather like a newspaper heading but I mean by it the proximate development of inter-imperial relations. I've been making some speeches on it in Canada and am vastly interested in it all. There is a fine field in the realm of <u>Colonial History & Politics</u> still only partly explored, and I am delighted to hear that your association, of which I shall be happy to become a member, intends to do something in this direction.

Pray Excuse a letter indecorously long.

Yours sincerely
Stephen Leacock

---

1   Paul Samuel Reinsch (1865–1925), Professor of Political Science at the University of Wisconsin, was a United States delegate to the Pan-American Conferences of 1906 and 1910. In 1913 he left his professorship to become American Minister to China, resigning this position in 1919.

*To Houghton Mifflin*                    [McGill University
                                          Montreal]
                                          Nov. 2 1906

Messers Houghton Mifflin & Co.

Dear Sirs

Many thanks for letter of Oct 26 and cheque for $76\frac{90}{100}$, representing sales of
<u>Elements of Political Science</u> till Oct 1 1906. Considering the scope of the book,
this seems very satisfactory

At the present moment I am busily engaged in proofreading, notemaking,
index making etc for a book I have just completed for the Makers of Canada
Series Morang. & Co. Toronto. It seems to involve such a lot of odd work that
it may keep me busy till the end of the winter.

After that I shall get to work at once on a book I am anxious to submit to
your house. It deals with <u>Poverty</u> and the question of its persistence in spite of
industrial advance and labor saving machinery. I want to write it for the <u>public</u>,
not for the professoriate: I have no use for cryptographic economics: that sort of
speculation has been written to death and ~~only~~. The professors read one anothers
books and the public pays no attention.

But I will write you later about the book. I would sooner publish it with
your house than anywhere else but it may not be in your line as it is not to be
an educational book

Very sincerely
Stephen Leacock

*To Agnes Leacock*                       Dec 30 1869
                                          Dec 30. 1906

My dear Mother

I was so glad to her from Beatrix that you were looking ever so well and
that your rooms seem ~~very~~ comfortable. Your move to Toronto seems to have
been a success. I got back from Providence this morning, very tired. My trip was
a great success and the paper I read on Canadian government was apparently
considered very good. I met all the leading American authorities on Political
Science and on the strength of my book was received with open arms and
elected to a seat on the Executive Council of Political Science Association of
America,—a title which sounds as grandeloquent as the official positions of the
Pickwick Club.

I told Beatrix to tell you how fast I am getting on and how very
wonderfully clever I am but she said you were not interested in it—However,—

today is my birthday. I am 37 years old,—almost grown up. Tell Daisy to write me all the news in full and explain to me her prospects and what she is going to do. Please ask her also to go to the Toronto public Library or The Reference Branch of it and ~~fir~~ ask for the back numbers of the Canadian Magazine and hunt up two or three little things I wrote. They are called:—

1 Hoodoo McFiggin's Chritmas

2 The Poet Answered

and there may be a third, I cant remember. They appeared somewhere in the years 1897 or 1898. When found, either, buy me back numbers at the office of the Magazine, or if that is not possible, have me type written copies made, or copy them herself in ink and I will have them type written. If she will do all this I will giver her <u>one dollar</u> cash and ten dollars on the publication of the book of which these sketches form part. Only tell her not to delay. I hope to publish it this summer but I am not sure whether I can get a publisher or not. Bx tells me you all had Xmas dinner at the Grand Union: it must have been a funny experience for <u>you</u>. Would you care to come down here for a fortnight or so? I suppose not—we cant afford the railroad fare among us? I expect to be in Toronto on the morning of Saturday Jan 26th: I am to speak at the Banquet of the Society of Canadian Authors that night and shall probably stay over till Sunday night or leave on the Sunday morning train. I am invited to one or two places but if I can have Daisy's dog-coop for the night and breakfast with you in the morning I should prefer it. I am sending you a New York paper with a thing I wrote in it.

Your loving son
Stephen Leacock

## To William S. Booth

[McGill University
Montreal]
Dec 31 1906

Dear Mr Booth.

Herewith I send you a type written copy of the preface of the Book of my collected sketches. From it you may perhaps gather an idea of the plan and nature of the volume. I hope to send you in about three or four weeks the sketches themselves. I have copies of very few of them but am getting ~~them~~ type written copies prepared from back files of papers and magazines. If you should accept them ~~then~~, the matter of illustrating them or not, lies in your discretion. My personal opinion inclines against it. The dignified kind of humour which these sketches are supposed to represent is perhaps better without illustration. But I leave that to you. One might suggest that a photogravure of ~~the matter is~~

an Equestrian Statue of the author surrounded by the Houghton Mifflin firm, might be inserted at the back of the book.

Wishing you a very Happy New Year.

Yours sincerely
Stephen Leacock

## PREFACE

A good number of Many of the sketches which form the present volume have already appeared in print. Others of them are new. Of the reprinted pieces "Melpomenus Jones", "Policeman Hogan", "A Lesson in Fiction" and many others were contributions by the author to the New York "Truth". The "Boarding House Geometry" first appeared in "Truth" and was subsequently republished in the London "Punch" and in a great many other journals. The sketches called "The Life of John Smith" and "Society Chit Chat" appeared in Puck. "The New Pathology" was first reprinted in the "Toronto Saturday Night" and was subsequently republished by the London "Lancet" and by a Breslau newspaper in the form of a German translation. The story called "Number Fifty-Six" is taken from the Detroit "Free Press". "Hoodoo McFiggin's Xmas" and one or two shorter sketches appeared as contributions to the "Canadian Magazine". "My Financial Career" was originally contributed to the New York "Life" and has been frequently reprinted. The wide circulation which some of the above sketches have enjoyed has encouraged the author to prepare the present collection.

The author desires to express his sense of obligation to the proprietors of the above journals who have kindly permitted him to republish the contributions which appeared in their columns.

McGill University,
Montreal, 1907.

# CHAPTER 2

## STEPHEN LEACOCK
# THE CECIL RHODES
# TRUST TOUR

## 1907–1908

'The time has come; we know and realize our country,' wrote Stephen Leacock in *Greater Canada: An Appeal*, which was published in March 1907. 'We will be your colony no longer. Make us one with you in an Empire permanent and indivisible.'

Leacock had long been an advocate of a new imperialism that would place Canadians on an equal footing with the people of Great Britain. He believed it was time for Canada to wake up to its new calling, not as an independent country nor as united with its neighbour to the south, but as a fully committed and integral member of the British Empire, with imperialism involving the recognition of a wider citizenship. This form of imperialism, according to Leacock, would put to rest the notion of Canada as a mere colony: 'I, that write these lines, am an Imperialist because I will not be a Colonial. This Colonial status is a worn-out, by-gone thing. The sense and feeling of it has become harmful to us. It limits the ideas, and circumscribes the patriotism of our people. It impairs the mental vigour and narrows the outlook of those that are reared and educated in our midst.'

Leacock's convictions about the necessity of a new role for Canada in the Empire were gaining strength around this time, and he began to express these views both in writing and in lectures. In early 1906, for example, he gave six 'university extension lectures', arranged by the May Court Club in Ottawa and given under the auspices of McGill University. His passionate advocacy of a reorganized British Empire as a federation of equal nation-states formed the substance of these six lectures, delivered every second Friday from 12 January to 23 March. Leacock capped the lecture series on 2 April at the Canadian Club in Toronto, where he delivered a talk entitled 'The Imperial Crisis'.

Leacock's ideas garnered the attention—and the support—of Earl Grey, who had attended Leacock's final two Ottawa lectures. The active and popular governor general was impressed by Leacock's popularity as a lecturer on the

British Empire and asked him to undertake a world lecture tour on behalf of imperial unity under the sponsorship of the Cecil Rhodes Trust, named for the British-born diamond magnate and former prime minister of Cape Colony in southern Africa. Aware of Leacock's teaching commitments at McGill, Grey wrote to the university's principal, William Peterson, asking for a two-year leave of absence for the professor. He also enlisted the support of George Parkin, Leacock's principal at Upper Canada College and then organizing secretary for the Rhodes Scholarship Trust, who had undertaken a similar journey to Australia and New Zealand on behalf of the Imperial Federation League five years before he became principal.

McGill's board of governors approved a one-year leave of absence for Leacock and agreed to pay his expenses during the trip. The Rhodes Trust made a cash contribution, and the governor general himself offered to make up any differences between these sums and the actual costs.

On 27 April Leacock and his wife embarked from Halifax on the SS *Victorian*. His original plan called for a series of lectures in England, followed by lectures in Australia, New Zealand, and South Africa, and a return home through British Columbia, the newly formed provinces of Alberta and Saskatchewan, and the Maritimes. Although the Canadian portion of the tour did not materialize, Leacock realized all his plans for England, Australia, New Zealand, and South Africa.

In England, in addition to delivering his lectures and meeting with the authorities of the Cecil Rhodes Trust, Leacock undertook a variety of vacationing tours, including a weekend with Rudyard Kipling at his country home, Bateman's, in Sussex. After stopping in Paris for a few days 'for my wife's shopping', he continued on to Australia, New Zealand, and South Africa.

The trip was a triumph: all of Leacock's lectures were received enthusiastically, there were many splendid dinners and receptions, and the lecturer was able to make even some of his most difficult topics palatable by means of diverting and amusing digressions. But while Leacock was rightly enjoying his immense popularity as a lecturer, his thoughts still rested with his homeland. In April, as he was leaving for Halifax, he wrote to his mother: 'Personally I would rather be going to Lake Cou[chi]ching than round the world.' And in a letter dated 30 May he tells her: 'I am awfully anxious to get a *place*; if the little point is not too wet I'd like it. If it is not obtainable then the Hughes point. . . . The more I see of foreign parts the less I think of them compared to Canada.' His surviving letters to his mother—especially his letters from South Africa, which had demanded his mother's presence shortly after her marriage—offer a rare glimpse of Leacock writing personal letters.

Leacock's awareness of his family's history—albeit brief—in South Africa may have intensified his strong reaction to the vestiges of the Boer Wars, which pitted descendents of Dutch and Huguenot settlers (the Boers) against British colonial administrators. The British overcame the Boers in the second Boer War, which had ended in 1902—only years prior to Leacock's visit—in large part because of their use of concentration camps, where inhabitants of the country-side in the colonies of Natal and Transvaal had been imprisoned. Leacock's sym-pathies are clearly with the Boers, and his disdain for the tactics of 'plutocrats and tyrants . . . carried on as ruthlessly as the wars of an Asiatic conqueror' could only have reinforced his views of the necessity for Canada to find a more secure and independent position within the British Empire.

When Leacock returned to McGill in the fall of 1908, he was appointed William Dow Professor of Political Economy; at the same time he became chair of the Department of Economics and Political Science, a position he would hold until his retirement in 1936. His annual salary was then $3,500, which he sup-plemented by $500 by giving special lectures each year. In the same year he bought his summer home in Orillia, Ontario, and thus began his pattern of spending summers and holidays in Orillia and winters in Montreal.

## To Earl Grey, Governor General of Canada[1]

McGill University
Montreal.
25th March/07

Your Excellency

Since our conversation of yesterday, I have naturally devoted a good deal of thought to the subject under discussion. I foresee difficulties which had not occurred to me on the spur of the moment and should like to submit to Your Excellency a somewhat modified plan.

The difficulties lie in the matter of organization. There being no league, association or organised body to make the necessary arrangements for hiring premises, advertising, gathering an audience &c., it is difficult to see how this can properly be done. Mere correspondence with persons likely to be interested would perhaps result in failure. nor should I feel at all confident of my own ability to go forth to organise and make arrangements for the addresses as I went along. It would not indeed be the kind of work that I should care to undertake. Moreover the question of premises, notices, advertising would involve a constant and considerable expense.

It has therefore occurred to me that the scheme might be modified so as to assume the following form. The lectures should be given as extension lectures (no exact term for what I mean presents itself) offered by McGill University at

---

1    Earl Grey (1851–1917) was a devoted imperialist who saw his appointment as Canada's ninth Governor General (1904–11) as an opportunity to forge stronger links of empire.

the instigation of the Rhodes Trust and delivered all round the empire in the colonial universities and educational institutions. Under this arrangement the very ground-plan of the idea, the sending out of a lecturer by a great colonial university as a sort of temporary loan, to sister institutions to aid in a work in which the sentiments of all should be interested seems to me eminently in accord with the ideas of the founder of the Rhodes Scholarships.

The lectures might be many or few at each place: given as a short course, or as a series of addresses in two or three successive nights, &c., according as the peculiar situation of each place might dictate. Where places were near together, two or three colleges or institutions might be embraced in the lectures at the same time. The lectures would deal with the general range and class of subjects that lie under what might be called Imperial Development and Organization: they would contain much that is historical, much that is analytical and a good deal of fair and open discussion of present problems. If I gave them I should not think it well to make them merely elementary and expository. I should want to put into them, while keeping a purely academic tone, a good deal of analytical discussion of the meaning and growth of modern democracy and its relation to the imperal conception, and of topics on a sufficient high plane to hold the attention of educated men. I should aim at capturing the interest of the leading minds of the community. All of this would involve academic rather than polemic treatment. But there might and ought to be, nevertheless, a guiding thread of thought,—a presentation of the growth and meaning of imperial unity, an appeal for earnest and intelligent co-operation in the future problems of the Empire.

Some suitable title might be found for the enterprise, the Cecil Rhodes Lectures on Imperial Organisation, or something of the sort and the part taken by McGill University put into sufficient prominence to give it due credit.

Under this scheme organisation would be quite easy. Circular letters sent out from McGill would announce the lectures to the other colleges and institutions: the latter would merely be called upon to supply premises and gather audiences.

The financial method of procedure I should suggest should be as follows:

1. The Rhodes Trustees to pay the salary of the lecturer. If I were to be the lecturer I should think £500 (five hundred pounds per annum) a proper remuneration.
2. The organisation university (let us say McGill University) to pay the expenses (transportation, hotels, &c.) of the lecturer. I should think it possible to get railway passes.
3. The local universities supply premises and make announcements.

In this shape there is something very definite and simple about the scheme. I should think, too that it could be carried out within twelve months, at any rate as a first essay. After that another University and another man might follow.

I do not know whether it would be possible for me to do it, I mean, whether the necessary arrangements can be made, but I should think that somebody can be found either here or elsewhere who could be sent out on these terms. The project is one which would create such wide interest and reflect such high credit upon the University that might undertake it, that I should naturally like to see McGill University the first to make the attempt.

> I am,
> Your Excellency's obedient
> Servant,
> Stephen Leacock

## To William S. Booth

[McGill University
Montreal]
April 16 '07

W. Booth Esqre
Houghton Mifflin

Dear M<sup>r</sup> Booth.

Will you please do something for me. I am leaving Canada next week to make a lecture tour round the world (for the trustees of the Cecil Rhodes estate)

Your firm owes me whatever royalties are due on sales of my book since October 1, 1906, the date of their last payment.

Will you kindly get them to make up the account to date and forward the sum due it without delay as I am naturally anxious to straighten out all my accounts & payments before I sail.

I write to you in this personal, pleading strain as a means of preventing delay.

> Yours very sincerely
> Stephen Leacock

## To Agnes Leacock

McGill
Monday April 22. 1907

Dearest Mother
I find it impossible to come home to say goodbye before sailing. As I am to leave Halifax on Saturday April 27 and am to speak in St John N.B. on Thursday it cant be managed. I am awfully sorry. I only finished my college work this morning and have to spend tomorrow at Ottawa. But as a matter of fact I am not going away for very long. If all is well we expect to be back in New York in February of next year. I am writing to Dot in reference to

some business details. Personally I would rather be going to Lake Couching than round the world. I hope you will be all right while I am away

> With best love
> Your affectionate son
> Stephen Leacock

P.S.

An answer to this can easily reach me addressed S.S. <u>Victorian</u>. Allan Line. Halifax. After that address me in care of the <u>Canadian Commissioner London</u> England. Things will be forwarded from there.

P.S.

What about your brother in Australia Will you write him that I am coming. Can you send me a photograph of yourself to take with me?

## To Agnes Leacock[1]

> [Bridges and Reversible Falls,
> St. John, N.B.]
> Thurs. April 25. 1907

We reached here at noon today. I speak here tonight and go on to Halifax by the night train. My route has been altered since I wrote. I go from London to South Africa. My address is always, care of, The Rhodes Trust. Seymour House, Waterloo Place London. W. Both send our love.

> Stephen.

1   This communication comes in a postcard with a picture of the bridges and reversible falls in Saint John.

## To Agnes Leacock

> [Halifax Hotel
> Halifax, Canada]
> Sat April 27 [190]7

Dear Mother

Just a few lines to say goodbye. So many thanks for the handkerchiefs and especially for marking them: the same for the socks. I send you a bunch of papers in regard to my speeches here and at St John. They have been terrific successes

> love to all &
> goodbye
> Stephen Leacock

P.S. Tell Daisy I was delighted to get her letter and am writing her.
P.P.S. please clip the papers & keep clipping

Probable Route

| | | |
|---|---|---|
| Leave Halifax | April 27 | 1907 |
| Arrive London | May 5 | 1907 |
| Leave England | "    15–20 | 1907 |
| Reach Sydney | July 1 | 1907 |
| Leave Australia | Oct 1 | 1907 |
| Reach New Zealand | "   6 | 1907 |
| Leave New Zealand | Nov 6 | 1907 |
| Reach Cape of Good Hope | Dec 1st | 1907 |
| Leave  "   "   "   " | Jan 1st | 1908 |
| Reach New York | Feb 1 | 1908 |
| (Pass viâ Toronto) | | |
| Reach Vancouver | Feb 6 | 1908 |
| Lecture in British Col. | Feb 6–March 1st | " |
| Lecture in North West | March 1st–April 1st | " |
| Lecture in Maritime Provinces | April 1 May 1st | 1908 |

## To Agnes Leacock

[Seymour House
Waterloo Place, S.W.]
May 11

My dear Mother

I send you in this some wildflowers from Sussex. You will value them doubly when I tell you that they were picked for you by Rudyard Kipling at his house. I stayed at his house at Burwash in Sussex. He gave me a pipe. This in haste. We expect to sail on the <u>Macedonia</u> (leaves Southampton on May 24). We catch it a few days later overland at Marseilles. We go to Freemantle West Australia arriving there on June 25 and stay 2 weeks Then on to Auckland New Zealand arriving about July 25. Address as above. Love to all. great haste

Your affecte son
Stephen Leacock

## To Agnes Leacock

[Cranston's Waverley Hotel,
Southampton Row, W.C.
London,] May 17 [190]7

Dear Mother

Just a few lines. hope all well at home. I am getting on finely. Spoke at a big meeting yesterday—great success—had lunch with Mr Balfour, also present Mr Alfred & Mrs Lytlleton, Lord & Lady Jersey, Mr & Mrs Deakin I have met a lot of people—am getting very thick with the Tariff reform party. They are hot dogs. Enclosed an article from <u>Morning Post</u>. If I wish to I can speak here next year in the interests of the Unionist party all over the place Politics over here is a great game and this is the market for brains. Had lunch at the Cecil's today— met the Bishop of London & a "bunch" of Lords—I rush about all day—speak at Oxford tomorrow—Balfour & Lyttleton very nice to me—no doubt would forget me tomorrow There is no doubt that if I like to chuck up things in Canada I could next year I could fit in somewhere here: but I have no intention of doing it. Too much work.

Am expressing George's clothes Much love to all. We sail from Marseilles to West Australia by the <u>Macedonia</u> on May 31—Shall be all next week in France. Went to tea with Belle & Dora. not seen Cousin Tom.


## To William Peterson

[Hotel Louvois
Place Louvois
Paris]
May 24 [190]7

Principal Peterson
McGill University
Montreal

My dear Dr Peterson

I beg to acknowledge with many thanks your letter of May 10 and enclosed banker's draft for £250. I will let Mr Boyd know of this payment as I believe he write out to Canada in regard to sending back the 1000 sent out there.

We are staying a few days here for my wife's shopping, on the way to Marseilles whence we sail next week on the Macedonia for Fremantle, West Australia: there we stay two weeks and then go to Auckland, arriving about July 25th and remaining in New Zealand till the end of August. Mr Deakin told me that he thought I had much better go to New Zealand first and keep Melbourne and Sydney till later.

I sent you under separate cover an article of mine in the Morning Post.[1] I spoke at the <u>Victoria League</u> and in the Examination rooms Schools at Oxford before very good audiences. I made it very clear to the Rhodes Trustees, at a meeting, that McGill University, as such, had no official connection with my present tour and that, as far as the University was concerned, I was simply a professor on leave of absence. On the card of invitation issued by the Victoria League, I was put down as Extension Lecturer of McGill: but I took occasion in

1  'After the Conference. John Bull and His Grown Up Sons', *Morning Post* (London), 17 May 1907, p. 7.

speaking (quite obiter and in connection with a jest) to state that I was not there in that capacity. I thought it better to be very definite on that score as I find the Trustees appear anxious to have their only connection with me a financial one. Their attitude and that of Dr Parkin towards my tour has been pretty much as you expected.

I saw your boy at Oxford; he is looking awfully well and seemed in very good spirits. At lunch at All Souls one of the Fellows told me that told me that he was a very old friend of yours and asked me to send remembrances when I wrote: unfortunately, I dont know his name.

I saw a great many people in London: went to lunch with Mr Balfour. stayed in the country with Rudyard Kipling and saw a great deal of Jebb, Fabian Ware (Editor, Morning Post) and Amery of the Times.

> With kind regards
> Yours sincerely
> Stephen Leacock

## To Agnes Leacock

> [Hotel Louvois
> Place Louvois
> Paris]
> Sunday May 26

My dear Mother

We are in Paris. Leave here for Marseilles on Wednes. or Thursday and sail from there on the 31st of May by the P. & O. Macedonia.

We've now been over a month at this batting round,—hotels, steamers trains, tips, porters, money, money, I'm sick of it already. I forget when I wrote last. I spoke in London & in Oxford. There seems to be no news. I wish I was at the Lake. Paris is very lovely but Orillia is much livelier and (joke for George). I expect to be back on Feb 1st 1908

> love to all
> y.a.s. Stephen Leacock

You can address an answer to this, c/o The Bank of New Zealand, Auckland. or no, on second thoughts it would go just as quickly by way of the trust Rhodes trust—or yes I dont know. try it anyway mark the letter Keep till called for c/o Bank of New Zealand Auckland New Zealand
After that of course write only c/o Rhodes Trust

## *To Agnes Leacock*

[Grand Hotel de Genève
Marseille]
Thurs. May 30

Dr Mother

Just leaving here for Australia. We go on board the <u>Macedonia</u> tonight & sail tomorrow. She is an enormous boat, looks like half a dozen hotels floating together. Both well. had ten days in Paris & 1 day here in Marseilles  Will write from Egypt  love to all

Your affec son
Stephen Leacock

P.S. We expect according to reckoning to be back anywhere after February 1st 1908. Tell Charlie I am awfully anxious to get a <u>place</u>; if the little point is not too wet I'd like it. If it is not obtainable then the Hughes point. On either of those, he may, subject to ratification by me make an offer. And I'd like him to try & do something about it this summer so that I can take up the place next spring. The more I see of foreign parts" the less I think of them compared with Canada. And I want a place of my own

love
SBL

## *To his sister Margaret[1], his brother George[2], and Agnes Leacock*

[S.S.] Macedonia
Tuesday June 4 1907

My dear Daisy & George & Mother.

This is written up at the top end of the Mediterranean: we are getting near Port Said (pronounced like the word "side") which is at the entrance of the Suez Canal. That sounds very romantic and far away but there is really nothing more in it than in approaching Washago. George will understand The following definitions:—

(1) Mediterranean Sea: blue ink with white soap suds.

(2) P & O. Liner: large ~~dev~~ steam devil box, filled with sleeping cupboards

(3) Passengers—dogs

(4) Suez Canal—sand ditch

   etc   etc

1   Margaret Lushington Leacock (1886–1962) married William Edward Burrowes; they lived in Belleville, Ontario, and had five children.
2   George David Young Leacock (1877–1958), Stephen's favourite brother, was twice married, first to Ethel who died, then to Mary Thomson, a nurse who took care of the dying Ethel. Both marriages were childless.

Apart from such definitions, this steamer might be thought interesting: it is a huge affair with a saloon that holds about 200 people. On this trip there are only about 80 passengers, I mean firstclass passengers, some go to Egypt, some to Aden at the other end of the Red Sea where they "change" for Bombay, some to Colombo in Ceylon, (change for China & Japan) some to West Australia, others to East Australia (one weeks voyage from West Australia) and the few rest to New Zealand. Of course the Anglo Indians are the Kings  Opposite me at table are two Egyptians, or Turkish Egyptians, one is called <u>Mustapha el Tunsi</u> and the other Tewfik el Something Else. Mustapha is just the same as Lex Kay painted browner and Tewfik would do right as he is for bartender at the Daly House. Mustapha talks only Arabic and damn little of that being too rich to talk. Tewfik is by way of improving himself and talks what he considers English: he says he has "gone at London this the three times". Tewfik has never seen snow. He asked about the snow at Montreal, How deep, he said, twenty feet? Yes I said from twenty to twenty-five. He pondered awhile and then said How many <u>inches</u>? About nine or ten I told him. Then he asked if it was "cold, yes?"—I said, Well I tell you Tewfik its the kind of cold you dont feel, you get to like it, it has a bracing stimulating effect so that one gets to thoroughly enjoy it: "I understand," Tewfik said gravely, "I understand", <u>not work</u>". Tewfik and Mustapha get off this afternoon at Port Said where they take the train "to go at Cairo,"—which Tewfik says, is "five hours of go"

— — — — —

Being on board ship is mere damn foolishness. I'd as soon be shut up in a little pen with a railing, beside a mill damn—Today the hot weather is beginning. They have put big white fans in the saloon. These are swung up & down over the tables by black & yellow devils called Lascars. Lascars wear red turbans blue flowing coats and white trousers and brown feet. They talk god knows what. Everybody dresses for dinner and in the evening there is music and dancing on deck; this is not nearly as good as any ordinary floor space. The steamer goes all day and all night, it shakes with its machinery but as far as the waves are concerned, it might as well be standing on grass. Bugles blow, and gongs ring and bells sound, fools gather little tickets for lotteries and pools, idiots throw ~~coat~~ coits and shove disks up & down the deck and waiters (called stewards) run up & down with beef tea—all of which is the most damn tiresome foolishness I was ever "into".

They play cricket on deck with nets up to stop the ball: they are just the "lads" that can play, too, these young English boys going out to India. I find that "an English officer", means simply a <u>boy</u> with a little fluff of mustache on his face, and that a general or a colonel or Administrator, means, as Frank Toogood would say, a "man of about me own age". All English people talk English. My Heavens, one gets sick of it. You hear people say—"When's lench?" "lench? in about an ah," and after a cricket match they say, "Did you <u>hyah</u> the <u>skaw</u>?" The

Australians talk more as we do. I dont know any of the people at all well. But there are three men at my table, Anglo Indians, that seem very interesting. They govern about 3 million people each, more or less

— — — — —

We stay, or rather to be English I should say, we "sty" at Port Said about 8 hours. As it is very hot this will be a "baw". Then we go for about 14 <u>ahs</u> through the Canal and then down the <u>Red Sea</u> (<u>3</u> days). Thats what surprises one over here to find the distances so long; for instance London to Marseilles by steamer is about the same as Liverpool to New York—the Mediterranean takes 6 days, and, as I say the Red Sea nearly 4. We dont leave this boat till <u>June 26</u> when we are "<u>doo</u>" at Fremantle West Australia We stay there till (about) July 10th and then go on in the <u>Himalaya</u> (P & O.) and arrive at Sydney (about) July ~~19~~ 17th, change ships & reach Auckland New Zealand about <u>July 25th</u>. I am going to try to get a trinket or rag for the girls at Port Said but feel pretty sure that I cant get anything "suitable" (joke

I'd forgotten that Charlie is at home. Say, Charlie, see if you can find out about buying land on Lake Couchiching. I've no use for Sutton. I'd like the Little point or Hughes Point or even further up. I'll pay ½ cash.

x x x x x x x x x x

Next year we must start building

— — — — — — — — — —

I get so damned sick of travelling. Its only fit for people of Daisy's age. However,—"I will now close". Watch me do it.

> Your loving son & brother
> Stephen Leacock

P.S. I'll write from Aden if I can & from <u>Colombo</u> anyway. After that you'll hear nothing for a long time as West Australia is far & mails fewer

## To Agnes Leacock

[S.S.] Macedonia
Friday June 7

Dear Mother

We are now half way down the Red Sea (which by the way is bright blue), between Suez and Aden: the Red sea is one thousand three hundred miles long & 300 miles broad. Last night & today it has been hot, too hot to write much but I wanted to be sure of sending off a letter from Aden. The thermometer is over 90° and that is fairly cool weather. Port Said & the Canal are awfully interesting. We had a day at Port Said, a red hot place built on the sand and inhabited by Egyptians and Arabs, narrow streets awfully smels and villainous looking people. The canal goes 90 (ninety) miles with the desert each side of it just a wilderness of sand blowing to and fro: in the distance mirages—very wonderful—just like the bible. I bought you an Egyptian shawl at Port Said but after a desparate hand to hand struggle with the Egyptian post office found I couldnt send it. All the Egyptians wear Red fezzes. We went into an Arab Mosque. They put huge straw shoes on us so that our feet should not defile the floor. Eastern people are awful,—squalid, rotten, villainous. I got a necklace of with Egyptian stones (very expensive) for Daisy. I will get it sent from Colombo if I can. We have still 20 days to West Australia. It was very interesting to see the continental mail come on at Port Said (it had come in a special fast boat via Brinidisi in Italy & was transhipped) 3000 bags of it. They hired 72 Egyptians to carry the bags on. Each bag called off by an officer as it passed. The Egyptians went in an endless chain round and round and at each end of the line an old Arab squatted and handed to each man a tally stick to carry with him and took it away from him at the other end when he handed over the letter bag. The carrying lasted for an hour and a half because each bag had to have its name read and they came from all over the world & went to all over the east. An officer called them out "Italy-Bombay"—New York-Canton"—Holland-New Zealand" and so on and so on and another officer called out Right! and checked them off on a list—all this in the early morning, 6 o'clock. The two steamers anchored side by side in the canal with a double gang way between & the string of Egyptians coming and going. After it was over all the Egyptians were sent overboard down a flight of steps hung over the side and searched at the foot of the steps by the Egyptian police—after which they were put into boats & rowed to the landing stage of the port about 100 yards or so—the save time & get them off quickly, they jammed them into the boats like sardines—I counted 34 in one little boat the size of Rapley's —— The boat is rolling, so my writing shakes— I wish you could see me in my white suit & panama hat—looks quite Oriental —"She" also wears white but looks foolish

I must say I shall be mighty glad to get home again and tell Charlie I am very keen about buying a little place—its my greatest ambition in life.

Tell George, (he will be glad to hear it) that one gets used to being at sea and lose all fear that the boat will "uptip". Yet it seems strange in the middle of the night to step out on deck & see the boat roaring away through the blackness, full pelt with foaming black and white waves hissing about it—not a soul in sight— few dim lights here & there—dead quiet except for the throb of the machinery 30 feet below—I think Mr Green could preach a very good sermon on it and show that if we could all see the foam about us more clearly etc.

The Anglo-Indian people leave at Aden. It will seem like parting with all my oldest friends. I dont take to the Australians at all—After Aden we have six days across the Indian Ocean: it is the worst time of year, the time of the "monsoon" with terrific storms, waterspouts, lightnings and waves forty feet high—all of which I dont mind a particle—the boat is rolling too much to write—I observe the sea is rising and the lower of heaven falling in the darkening waters of the deep—perhaps I spoke too soon about not minding. I take it back.

There will be quite gap between this letter and the next. The next will be posted from Colombo on or about the <u>16th of June</u> and should reach you about the 12th of July—I have met one of the nicest fellows, about my own age, I ever struck—He's in the artillery and is going up to central Baloochistan for years to be stationed at Quetta—There is no doubt that when these English fellows are nice they're the salt of the earth—but its strange to realize that of all of us on the boat hardly any two go to the same place—all over the map—Hong Kong, Siam, Penang and they take it all as a matter of course—years of exile in hot damnable places—say goodbye to their mothers & wives and children, and <u>off</u> they go with their little leather portmanteaus covered with labels and their weekly Times and English pipes and all the rest of their outfit. They are a great people—but be damned if I'd want to do it—India must be simply awful. The Anglo Indians say that in India people "bar" (that means to have no use for) Rudyard Kipling and consider he gives a quite wrong impression of Indian life

Goodbye, love to all Tell Daisy to write

Stephen Leacock

## To Margaret Leacock

[S.S.] Macedonia
Friday June 14

Dear Daisy,

Very many thanks for your long letter which I did not get but which is no doubt somewhere on its way

We are now in the Indian Ocean whose proper name is Hot Ink Pot of Hell. Tomorrow we hope to reach Ceylon. Just after I wrote my last letter the hot weather began. The Red Sea was awful. Wet stuffy heat, the air damp with it impossible to move or sleep or think or read,—thick, hot, damp oppressive heat—The perspiration runs off your body in streams, your little mouth gasps for air and your yellow eyes roll to the brassy sky for relief—After the Red Sea comes Aden built among sand and rock with the crater of a dead volcano overlooking it and desert all round it—hotter than ever—not a tree in sight—not a blade of grass, low houses built on the sand with red tile roofs—big ones and little ones—in these live the British soldiers 2000 of them & the Resident and staff and shipping people and coal people—and in huts live foreign devils of all sorts, skinny Arabs and Somalees from the coast of Africa, black as coal dust.

Here the steamer anchored and the Indian passengers changed to the other steamer waiting to take them to Bombay. A great flock of little boats came out with niggers & Arab boys & Somalees and chattering like hell; with these big barges for cargoes into the barges we unloaded five million dollars in gold sovereigns, going out to India. They pack it in boxes about as strong as biscuit boxes, and raise it out of the hold and over the side in huge baskets hoisted by a crane, each box held five thousand pounds and about ten made a basket full— they sling it up and down like dirt—and a lot of jabbering niggers are put on the barge to stack it in piles—when the gold goes up and down they all clap their hands in unison and sing Somalee chants like Au Christee minstrels—you throw them pennies from the deck (40 feet above them) and they scramble or fight for the pennies and when they get them a head Arab takes them away— The niggers try to put the pennies in their mouths or make out they've fallen over board—when they get the barge full a couple of very clever niggers come buzzing along with a tug and hitch on to it. it looks so funny to see them as they only wear turbans and an old carpet round their middle—jabbering like the devil and running their little tug up and down and bunting into things while a naked captain gives orders to a naked deckhand and shouts to a naked engineer—all the tugs have awnings over them—every thing in the east has an awning or it couldnt lives—every now and then a special boat comes along rowed by 8 or ten niggers, all the oars wallopping ~~ab~~ away in a go as you please fashion and the boat as big and heavy as a sawlog and in the back of it a man in white clothes with a white cigarette and a white helmet and white boots—he's one of the European population come off to visit the ship, a quarantine officer, or officer of a ship in harbor or an officer of one of the regiments. After the gold the niggers loaded in silver; this was in ingots each about the size of a loaf of bread—Aden seems the most awful hole in the world. Since Aden we have had 5 days of the Indian Ocean over which blows a thing called the Monsoon wind which would wither up a burdock if it touched it—It is so hot that the people sleep on deck, gasping for air even at that—the cabins are like fiery furnaces and the sun is red hot at five in the morning—your clothes stick to your skin—and yet, can you credit it—these silly people dress for dinner every night & swelter in solemn black, not that they like but ~~if they stopped dressing for dinner~~ they are nearly all Australians now and ~~ev~~ if they stopped dressing for dinner it would look as if evening dress came to an end when the Indians got off—of course the Anglo Indians think themselves far superior to the Australians

I posted a letter from Aden—to mother—this I hope to post in Colombo— The ship is still rolling so it is hard to write very plainly. Imagine eating your dinner like this.

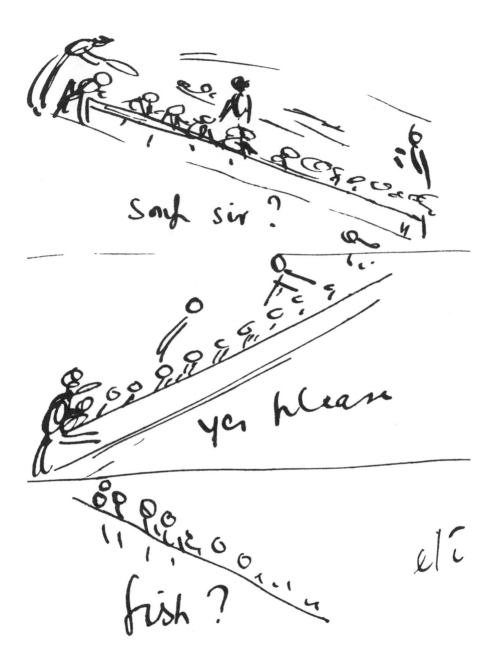

or reading like this

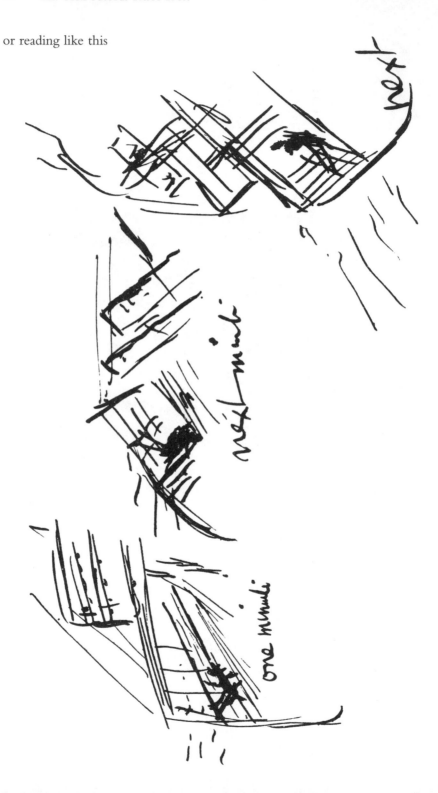

I'm afraid you cant make of these pictures but try this

Chess on board ship

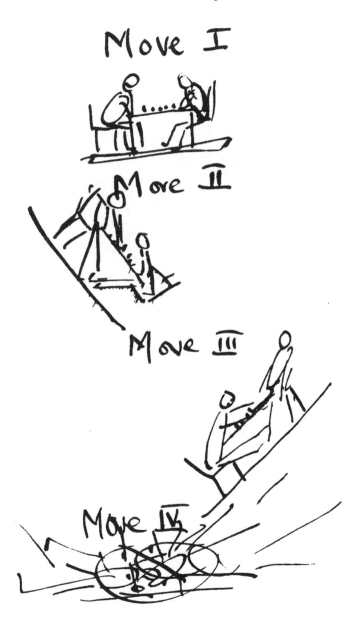

I must now close

>       love to all
>       Yr affec brother
>       Stephen Leacock

## To Agnes Leacock

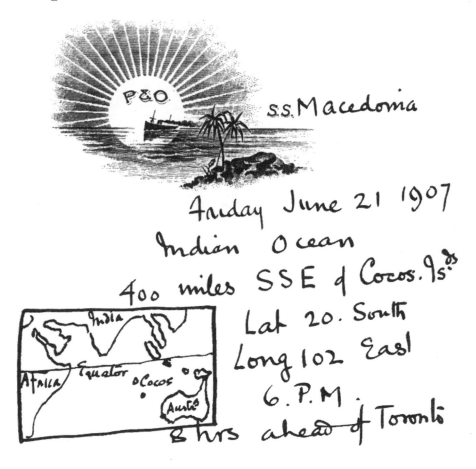

P&O

s.s. Macedonia

Friday June 21 1907

Indian Ocean

400 miles SSE of Cocos. Is^ds

Lat 20. South

Long 102 East

6. P.M.

8 hrs ahead of Toronto

India

Equator    o Cocos

Africa

Austa

Dear Mother

We are getting slowly nearer to West Australia. Hope to land on Tuesday next. We got on the boat on May 30 & expect to get off on June 25. Yesterday we passed the Cocos Islands. Just the place for Charlie. Right out alone in the Indian Ocean. Thickly wooded coast seemed about 10 miles long for each of the two big islands—yellow sand—surf booming all along, palm trees: no sign of life.

Today is midwinter in the southern hemisphere. Even here in lat 20 where it is only just cool. At this time of year (Dot) the sun is directly over head in lat 23

North which is nearer you than us. This part of the Indian Ocean is very lovely. No storms—at night while moonlight—no waves, only a long heaving swell. The ship moves at night with a hissing sound between two broad bands of white foam soft as wool. Today it blew a little, but not really enough. I am tired of the voyage. Also of the prospect of speaking. shall cut it down. Tell Charlie he must be sure to be available for next summer. I'll supply all expenses and he shall have a proper share of possession in the land & house we build. We can arrange that .. Tell Daisy to write. All she can. It will be a great pleasure to get home news. We shall be mighty glad to get back. So sorry I am no use to you financially just now. Dont know what, if any, money I'll have on return. Will add a line before posting.

y.l.s.
y.l.b.
s.b.l.

## To his brother Charles Leacock[1]

[S.S.] Himalaya
July 14 1907

Dear Charlie.

This is at sea, between Adelaide and Melbourne off the South East Coast of Australia. It takes from Saturday afternoon till Monday morning to sail from Adelaide to Melbourne although it only looks a few hundred yards on the map. The enclosed picture is a view of the city of Perth, West Australia, as seen from the other side of the river. What rather spoils the idea of it, when you know it, is that the river is only 2 feet deep all across, a distance of about 3/4 of a mile. We went ashore at Adelaide yesterday, the ship being anchored in the harbor which has practically no shelter so that the ships cant come into the wharf. Adelaide is just the same as any other place: it has about 160,000 people in it. The weather was reported to be a "cold snap" (this month is mid winter in Australia) but it was hardly cold enough to wear an overcoat. People in Adelaide never see such a thing as ice or snow. Last night in the smoking room they were talking about cold and some one said to me "how cold have you seen it in Canada", I said (quite truthfully) that I had known it thirty degrees below zero in Montreal one day last winter. A man at the other side of the table said, Well I've seen it forty." I said, "Where?" and he said, "In Canada I come from Canada," so I said, "I suppose that was out west," and he said,—no it was up beside Lake Simcoe, near a little place called Lefroy where I used to live" . . . . . . . . Also, when we were in Perth we met a Mrs Ridsdale whose name used to be Miss Irwin and who came from Barrie. She is about 50 to 60. She heard that we were from Canada and came over to call on us and talked of Barrie

---

1  Charles John Gladstone Leacock (1871–1951) was a professional engineer and an employee of Ontario Hydro. In and out of the Whitby Asylum at his own instigation, he managed on his own with intermittent help from his brothers. He never married.

and the Lake and Sutton and the Andersons and Sibbalds and all the people of 30 years ago with the pathetic interest known only to those who live in exile. She had heard no news of Sutton for years and years: knew of Mrs Roderick's death but of nothing since. So I had to tell her all the news and who had died and who had married and who had moved away. I never can remember just what Sutton people are dead, so I thought it best to be on the safe side and killed them off with an unsparing hand. I thought it was better that Mrs Ridsdale should hear the worst and get it over rather than go on in uncertainty for years and years. I am afraid I left the village pretty well depopulated . . . . . . . . . . . . . . We reach Melbourne tomorrow July 15, stay 36 hours and reach Sydney on Thursday, July 18, get the New Zealand Steamer on Saturday July 20 and hope to reach Wellington N.Z. on Wednesday 24th. After that we stay in N.Z. till the end of August.

Love to all at home
y. affec. brother
Stephen

## To Agnes Leacock

[Grand Hotel Wellington
Wellington, New Zealand]
July 24 [190]7

My dear Mother

I was delighted to get your letter of May 22, written from the Grange and at the same time one from Charlie written from the Daly House May 22 and two from Dot of May 19 and May 22 respectively. These were the first letters we have had since leaving Marseilles.

Tell Dot that her business dealings are satisfactory. Tell Charlie I was much pleased to get his letter and ask him to try to get prices on the Little Point and on Hughes, or a 99 years lease price on Hughes. I am very anxious to buy land when I get home

We got here at noon today after a bad voyage. Beatrix never left her bunk from leaving Sydney harbour till this morning. This (Wellington) is a queer looking place. You come through the gap between the North & South Islands with high mountains on each side and then the steamer is headed straight in among the cliffs and round a corner and you come to Wellington built in a sort of cup with mountains all round it. There is just room for the business part of the town at the foot and the rest of the houses climb up the side of the mountain. Charlie would have thoroughly enjoyed the voyage: the last two days the wind blew dead ahead and the bows of the ship went high in the air and then splashed down with a roar into the sea and great clouds of spray, regular sheets of it came, flying over the ship. Our cabin was right in the bows so we got all the motion that was going. I felt sick all the way over though I was actually seasick & missed no meals. We expect to stay in this town about three or four weeks and in New Zealand altogether about five weeks: very sick of moving & travelling and after this last trip we dread the voyage to the Cape. The Orillia Lacrosse team, or are they Canadian, are playing over in Sydney this week. last week they were in Queensland. I dont think we shall run across them. This job (between ourselves) is not half the fun you might think. One gets so sick of moving about & strangers and in Australia & N.Z. there are no great wonders to see.

I've been addressing my letters to Daisy and am grieved not to hear from her.

Once a month or so there is a mail this way viâ Vancouver and when you can catch it it is quicker to write to us direct. We expect to leave Australia for the Cape on or about Nov 15th (I write a further line tonight giving exact dates) so that any letter that can reach us before then & can catch the Vancouver-Sydney mail had better come this way. Address care of the <u>Union Bank of Australia</u> Sydney. N.S.W. but for anything of great importance write also in duplicate the other way

I'll add a line tonight. I post also by this mail a letter to Daisy written on the Moeraki.[1]

1    The rest of this letter does not survive.

## To Houghton Mifflin

Wellington
New Zealand
Aug. 31. 1907

Messers Houghton Mifflin & Co.
Boston

Dear Sirs

Until further notice will you please pay to my sister <u>Rosamund Leacock</u> care of Mrs R.B. Hamilton, 349 Sherbourne St, Toronto, any remittances that may be due to me upon my Elements of Political Science.

Yours truly
Stephen Leacock

Permanent address
McGill University
Montreal

## To Agnes Leacock

[F.C. Faber's
Rutland Hotel
Wanganui,] N. Z.
Thurs. September 12 1907

Dear Mother

We are here on our way to Auckland. I spoke here last night. We sail from New Plymouth to Auckland tonight. There is no railway. I speak at Auckland on Thursday, we go to Rotorua for over Sunday & sail for Sydney on Monday Sep ~~13~~ 16 reaching there if all is well Sep 16. As far as I know our movements are:

| | |
|---|---|
| Sep 16–Nov. 1. | in Sydney |
| | Union Bank of Australia |
| Nov 1–Nov 15 | – Melbourne |
| Nov 15–Dec 15 | – At Sea |
| Dec 15–Feb 1 | – South Africa |
| Feb 1–21 | – At Sea to England |
| March–4 to 10 | reach home |

in haste
love to all
S.L.

## To Agnes Leacock

c/o Union Bank of Australia
Sydney N.S.W.
Sep 26

My dear Mother

I was surprised not to get any letters from home when we arrived here 3 days ago. Have heard nothing since Dot's letter of the end of June in regard to her expenses: I sent her £20 in a draft which should reach her early in October.

We hope to sail from here on the <u>Geelong</u> Blue Anchor Line for South Africa on October 18. The boat stops 4 days at Melbourne and 4 at Adelaide and reaches Durban in the middle of November; we go up to the Transvaal, or I do, for a month. Beatrix will perhaps stay in Natal as Ry fares in South Africa are very high. It cost £7-15 to Johannesburg from Durban & return. Then in the middle of December we hope to sail from Durban to Cape Town on the <u>Commonwealth</u> (same line), stay there a month and in the middle of January leave for London on the <u>Wakool</u> (same line), due in London on February 11th 1908: from there we go at once viâ Liverpool & New York to America.

We've not seen the Palmers yet but hope to in a day or so: Mr Palmer lives in North Sydney across the harbour. Sydney is a magnificent place beside it the Canadian cities look like villages. It has 520,000 people in it. The harbour is wonderful and is full of all kinds of shipping, British French German Japanese and coastal boats and always 3 or 4 warships. Write in answer to this, care of the <u>Standard Bank of South Africa</u>, Durban Natal as the Trust people I find are a little mixed as to proper dates of postage and letters chase us round. I address the University here on Monday and other gatherings later, but not many as the time is short. We shall be very glad to start homewards: it will make the time seem shorter to be moving towards home.

I am awfully anxious to buy a small place on Lake Couchiching next spring: I shall try to have enough money for the land next year and live on it in tents and shacks for next summer & build on a large house the year after. I want to have if I can at least 10 acres, a sort of small farm, room for a very large garden, an orchard, and a field for root crop hen feed & so on. I shall keep hens and a cow as to a horse I dont know: it needs so much land to feed it off. I must get Charlie to go into it with me and have the place big enough for him to have a cottage of his own on it if he cares to: he might not like to merely share in the house. When I get it really going Charlie can work it all the year round and when I am ready I will retire to it. The first difficulty is to get the land (I am pretty sure of the money if all is well). I think favorably of Hughes Point. Wherever it is, I'd like you and the girls to come to it next summer: there will be tents provided and a wooden kitchen and wooden shanty bedrooms for you and for Beatrix & me: the hard ground for Daisy, who have never answered my letters. When I build my house I shall make it very plain but at the same time very large. I mean to plant a good avenue of trees leading up to it. In a few years with hard work it will begin to look fine. After it has been up two or three years I shall brick it with white brick and put in lattice windows in the place of its original ones and tiles instead of shingles on the roof. Then by adding a sun dial, a yew hedge a rook and three wall flowers it will become a charming English place. I am tired of cities and people: it is a case of "goodbye proud world I'm going home," as the poet said when he skooted to the woods.

I was commissioned to write a hymn of praise (in prose) on New Zealand for the first issue of <u>The Dominion</u> a new paper that started life on the first <u>Dominion Day</u> (Sep 26 yesterday).[1] (I suppose you know N.Z. is a Dominion now. I got two guineas for it and think it pretty good. Tell me how you like it. Love to all

Your affecte son<br>Stephen Leacock

1　'The Imperial Aspect. "A Group of Mighty States"', *Dominion* (Wellington, New Zealand), 26 September 1907, page 8.

## *To Agnes Leacock*

Sydney. New South Wales
Oct 4 1907

My dear Mother

I enclose herewith an article I wrote for the first number of the <u>Dominion</u> issued on the first <u>Dominion Day</u> of New Zealand. Please keep it as I have no other copy. I sent you also under separate cover a little book of views of Sydney.

We went over to see the Palmers at North Sydney across the harbour yesterday. Mr Palmer is all right again after his operation. We saw one of the daughters called Kathleen who is something like Dot. I am going to have lunch with Harrington Palmer tomorrow and go to a cricket match. The Palmers have a very pretty house in large grounds with fine trees and roses. They are quite out of touch with any English connection (except Dr Charlie) and are straight out Australians.

This is a wonderful and magnificent city, the London of the Antipodes as Sydney Mackenzie would call it (George will tell you who he is). When I think of Toronto and Montreal beside Sydney, I "laff". The Botanical Gardens here are beyond description: I keep wishing you could see them: azaleas as big as a house and flowering shrubs, palm trees and tropical plants all growing like tangled weeds out of doors

I've been working night and day on my new book <u>The Outer Empire and Imperial Unity</u>: I hope to finish it by the end of next April; Ive done about 45,000 words now. I see that my book on Baldwin and Lafontaine is out and that the Canadian reviews think very well of it.

I do hope Dot's not working too hard: often I am worried about her: if she is in danger of breaking down, be sure to make her stop working. I'm so afraid her lungs might be affected by the sedentary life.

I gave an address to the University here and shall probably do the same at Melbourne and Adelaide but in South Africa dont expect much opportunity to talk. I may perhaps go to Chicago University next spring or summer to give a special course of lectures: but I dont know. I think I mentioned in my last that we sail on the <u>Geelong</u> Blue Anchor Line Oct 18 to Durban (Natal), thence a month later (S.S. Commonwealth) to Cape Town, thence a month later S.S. <u>Wakool</u> to London, thence to New York where we hope to arrive about Feb 20th–25th 1908 if all is well.

It seems so funny to have the weather get hotter and hotter as October goes on & to hear people talk of the awful heat of <u>January</u> and the hot north and the <u>cold</u> south also to be out of sight of the <u>dipper</u> and North Star and to see the Southern Cross instead. It looks like this. Two stars point to it and it lies on its side with 5 (visible) stars in it. It doesn't amount to much.

Love all
Thank Daisy letter
S.L.

*To Agnes Leacock*                          S.S. Geelong
                                            At Sea
                                            Melbourne to Adelaide
                                            Oct 24 1907

My dear Mother

Just rec'd before leaving from Melbourne today your letter of Sep 5 and Daisy's included both written from the Grange: made me quite wish to be "home" wherever home is. Much shocked to learn~~ed~~ of Mr Stevenson's death, mingled with the gay commentary of Daisy's letter of sailings, picnics & parties, it suggested sad reflections upon the vanity of life.

We've just spent five days in Melbourne. I gave a speech. Mr. ~~Da~~ Deakin the prime minister gave a lunch for me at the Parliament house—himself, 6 or 7 of the Cabinet & the Dean of the Law faculty of the University: quite an honour. But I am glad to come away. We stay over in Adelaide 3 days, I speak there and then "Ho for Durban", 20 days trip. We have the most delightful boat ever built, a monstrous drowsy old thing with broad decks all sunshine and huge cabins with old fashioned furniture, hardly any passengers, about 25 in all, fine food of just the kind I like, (~~roast~~ cold roast beef & good eggs & bottled beer & plain things, no frills and fancies like the P and O—I have laid in a big stock of books mostly old fashioned books mixed with works of devotion and homilies suitable to the deep peace of the Southern ocean. You can form no idea of the charm of the Southern Seas here when it is calm—a cloudless sky, and a deep sense of drowsiness on the waters with only the hum of the engine to punctuate without disturbing it. It's the first real peace we have known since we left: and after Adelaide my speaking (which I dislike now all the glamour being off it) is practically over as I shall not do much, perhaps none, in South Africa. I wrote Charlie a long letter last mail about my "farm": I shall see to it at once on my return: I have lots of work in sight for next year and so can afford to buy. I am so sorry you wont accept my hospitality for the summer, but perhaps while it is still in the making the place wouldn't be comfortable enough for you. I want about ten acres if I can get it so as to have lots of room for an orchard and paddock etc as well as a garden.

Kathleen Palmer came to see us off at Sydney: I am afraid that Mr and Mrs Palmer didn't take the faintest interest in us: nor did the old man ask a single question about you. He seems to be of that egotistical type that "gramp" is and only talks about himself. Charlie Palmer is very different and very friendly. We are so glad to leave Australia: sick to death of it and of the blow–blow–blow of the Australians.

With love to all. Tell Daisy Ill write later

                                            Your affecte son
                                            Stephen Leacock

## *To Agnes Leacock*

The Marine Hotel
Durban. Natal.
Nov. 18 1907

Dearest Mother

I was so glad to get a bundle of letters from you today when we arrived here in Durban. I had been thinking of you as we came into the harbour this morning with heavy mist and rain shrouding the hills and the big swell of the Indian Ocean booming up in white clouds upon the sand,—I mean thinking of your being here forty years ago—the ocean and harbour, the sea side of it look I suppose about about the same: The Bluff is there still with bright green trees running up to the top of it: to the light house and signal station: when the war was on, the light house man ~~used~~ was in league with the boers and used to signal to them the arrival of the ~~big~~ ships: it was found out and they shot him for it in the market place here—where the sand beach was along which you walked to the hotel is now the Parade embanked with stone from the sea and with the hotels along the waterfront, palm trees along it and flowering shrubs, and up and down it Zulus hauling rickshaws. I will be certain to post you views of it all tomorrow—We were glad to get ashore: we had lived in the boat a month reckoning from Sydney out, and from the last port, Adelaide, South Australia, 2 weeks and 5 days. Across the Australian Bight (which is 4 days) we had heavy weather with the wind roaring in the rigging at night and the the ship creaking and straining at every sea: it was a fine sight to watch the great seas come roaring over the forecastle head as the ship plunged into them sixty feet deep—then after that two weeks of ideal weather, dozing on deck, or playing baseball (I taught them) for exercise, and in the evening sitting in the smoking room with whiskeys & water and tales of hairbreadth adventures in Canada. Sometimes after midnight I used to go up on the Bridge with the officers and watch the dim sea chase past the ship, all still except for the dull throb of the engines and all dark except for a odd light or two here or there and the lanterns up in the forestay above the crowsnest.—Its a long long voyage across, 6000 miles more or less from port to port. —The ship leaves tomorrow to go on for Cape Town & London and we are sorry to say goodbye to the people; they seem like old friends. It is so strange on these boats to meet people from all parts, Australians, English South Africans, hardly any two from the same place—But what impresses me most of all the way the ships find their way, days & days, miles and miles, with the dark of night and the drift of currents and tides and then on such a day they say, tomorrow we ought to sight the coast of Africa—I got up early this morning & stood on deck watching for the coast: there was a great drive of mist on the water with a long black swell running under it, and presently out of it grew a dim shape that the sailors said was the Durban bluff—most wonderful it seems to me.

— — —

We expect to stay here a few days: then to Martizburgh for a few days. There Beatrix will probably stay while I go to the Transvaal viâ Ladysmith. I have introductions to Boer leaders and hope to get some idea of things—So glad Dot got the money all right and more glad still to hear that she was well. Tell Charlie I will answer his letter in a day or so: I was delighted to hear from him This place is full of Kaffirs Zulus and Hindoos. There are 100,000 hindoos in Natal. We sat and watched a hindoo juggler on the stone balcony of the Hotel facing the sea: there were a lot of us off the boat and we gave him about 1/6 each so that he'll be rich for life

Best love to all

Your affectionate son
Stephen Leacock

*To Agnes Leacock*                         [Imperial Hotel
                                           Maritzburg, Natal]
                                           (November 24, 1907)

Sunday Nov 14—I continue this at Maritzburg. I am posting you views of Durban & of this place which I have bought but they wont reach you till the mail after this (one week later). The large square ones are views of 'Old Durban', meaning about 25 years ago, but probably much more like the town of your time than the present. Maritzburg in the photos looks very different from the reality, with a false appearance of grandeur: in reality is just a big straggling brick village, set in a cup of the hills with trees and flowers all among it. Most of the houses on the main street (Church St) are later than your time but I noticed a ~~go~~ white stone presbyterian church dated 1852. I cant get a photoh of it. It looks like this:

Its a little place, very low & all proportioned. We walked in the cemetery this morning and among the tombstones I saw that of Rev James Green Dean of Maritzburg born 1821 <u>died 1906</u>: was Dean from 1849–1906. Didnt he christen Jim? Near him is his eldest daughter Mrs Lionel Scott. Later Mrs Tucker twice married died 1889. There a two Miss Colensos living here Still children in your time now angular masculine old maids of from 50 to 60. This place seems utterly dead. Indeed all of South Africa is dead since the war. We stay here a week. I am to give an address ~~a wee~~ next Friday. Then I leave Beatrix here and go to the Transvaal for a fortnight, staying over a day at Ladysmith on the way. I got Dots letter for which many thanks. Assure her from me that when I get home no one will ever hear me mention my travels   love to all: I enclose a fragment to Charlie

S.L.

### To Agnes Leacock

[Transvaal Hotel
Pretoria]
Dec 6 [190]7

Dear Mother

This is written, as you see, from Pretoria. I think even Dot's hard mind would be touched with a sense of interest attaching to this place. It sits in a hollow of the hills: a huge open square, a market place, low one story houses, mule cars and ox carts. Near by here is ~~Krun~~ Krugers house, one story, with french windows opening on the verandah, the "Stoep" as they call it where he use to sit. Cedar & cypress trees stand in front of the house. A little further up the street is cemetery where his grave is—with a big ugly black monument. About him are the tall head stones of the Fathers of the republic thus—

Doesn't it seem sad? But the old man has a fine crop of our soldiers to keep him company: line upon line of them with graves in regular military lines, a last parade. They lie in hundreds, each with a dagger-shaped cross of ~~white~~ iron, pained white, for a headstone, carrying the name, the regiment and date, no more. All parts of the empire lie together, you read on one, Norfolk regiment, on the next New South Wales Infantry, the next Canadian mounted rifles and so on, line after line. But the Pretoria Cemetery is only one of many. You see them all along the Natal Railway line in the open veldt. In Ladysmith, where I stayed a day There are 3000. Here I think about 1000. On the tops of the hills about Pretoria there still stand Krugers big forts of earth and stone and along the line between here and Johannesburg big stone block houses with no windows, only loopholes for the artillery. The war here of course is still a thing of yesterday: and the two races are about as far apart as ever.

. . . . . I stayed at Johannesburg a week. Its a big place with skyscraper buildings, innumerable gold mines that look like vast sawmills with smoke stacks and corrugated iron roofs and in front of each a ~~a~~ pile of dumped out earth as big as a cathedral. I had lunch with the Commissioner and dined one night at the house of a Rand magnate, a white palace better than anything I saw in London, with a troop of noiseless Asiatic servants. . Last Sunday I went out to Krugersdorp (25 miles west of Jo'burg) and walked over the ground of Jameson's battle in the Raid. On the way up from Natal I saw the Tugela battle field, very peaceful green grass & little thorn bushes on the plain, the river with an iron bridge and behind it the sudden rise of the big hills that gave the Boers their position. I think even Dot would have been interested in the little stone monument among the grass a couple of hundred yards from the river that marks the spot where Lieu. Roberts was killed when they tried to save the guns. Close to the bridge is <u>Colenso</u>, just a way station, with Kaffir craals near by and a few yawning niggers. Ladysmith is a little poky dusty place, dreariness itself——Well, I must stop. I expect to go back to Maritzburg on Sunday. This is Charlies birthday. Is he 41 or 56, I forget. Tell him I have pretty well finished the plans of the summer cottage

> love to all. y aff son.
> Stephen

## To Agnes Leacock

[Marine Residential Hotel
Sea Point South Africa]
Jan 3 [190]~~7~~8

Dear Mother

No particular news. Hope Maymie and the little boy are all right. Having lovely weather here, tennis, swimming etc, seems much more suitable to Xmas than snow & ice. Hope you had a good family gathering for Xmas day. Our latest plans are to sail ~~from~~ for N.Y. via <u>Atlantic Transport Line</u> S.S. Minnetanka, <u>Feb 20</u>, but not certain: we might catch the Adriatic a week earlier. This is just a line to wish you happy new year. I had dinner the other night with Dr Jameson (of the Jameson Raid). He lives in Cecil Rhodes' famous house Groot Schuur al Rondebosch in the suburbs of Cape Town

love to all
Stephen Leacock

## To Agnes Leacock

[Marine Residential Hotel
Sea Point South Africa]
Jan 15 [190]8

Dear Mother

Just got your letters of Nov 30 & Dec.3. referring to Daisy's exam, Maymie's baby and other things. If Daisy doesn't pass it doesn't matter. She doesn't need to work. No news in particular. We leave here on Sunday via S.S. <u>Wakool</u> for London: arrive Toronto about the 1st of March. Weather here beautiful summer weather but not hot in any oppressive way except on odd days. I have learned many thinks in South Africa, especially about the war. I think it one of the most accursed things that was ever done. Just imagine Old Mr Slate Secretary Reitz fought with his <u>nine</u> sons along side of him, seven Krugers fought, and in one of the last battles General Botha's little boy of 10 years old rode beside him when they charged on the English guns and <u>took them</u>: the Boers had had no food at all for <u>48 hours</u> before that battle. In the concentration camps 20,000 women & children died. What do you think of women huddled into tents with the corpses of their children sometimes two days old in the tent with them. I know of a mother who made a coffin for her little ~~childen~~ out of the sides of biscuit boxes and tried to bury it herself in the sand. Yet these same people sent word out to their husbands never to surrender. While this was happening here, drunken fools shouted in London and Toronto the celebration of <u>Mafeking</u> and <u>Pretoria</u>: It was one huge crime from start to finish, organised and engineered by a group of plutocrats and tyrants and carried on as ruthlessly as the wars of an Asiatic conqueror. And that is the <u>British Empire</u>! That imperialism! However,—no use worrying you about it. Must close love to all

y.a.s.
SBL

## To Agnes Leacock

[Thackeray Hotel,
Great Russell Street,
London.]
Fri. Feb 14 '08

Dear Mother

We have just arrived here safely after a wonderfully fine passage of three weeks & three days from Cape Town—calm all the way. We expect to sail on the 27th by the <u>Minneapolis</u> (Atlantic Transport Line) for New York: Due to arrive there about Feb 7th. not sure if I go to Toronto first or Montreal. Got your letters up to Jan 21: also Charlie's: tell him I hope to conclude arranging for buying land as soon as I come. he need supply no cash. I have enough. You to the Grange for this year. Very good. Got Dots letter. All right if she fails. Perhaps better. Work too hard. Love to all.

y.a.s.
Stephen Leacock

## To Agnes Leacock

[S.S. Merion]
Mon. Feb 24

Dr Mother,

This from Queenstown—find this boat is slower than we thought—probably reach Philadelphia about Thursday or Friday of next week. from there telegraph to Mrs Hamilton—arrange with her to tell you—probably arrive in Toronto on Friday or Saturday morning (March 6 or 7)—Phila<sup>a</sup> train (Lehigh Valley) gets in at 10 in the morning We shall be on the Philad<sup>a</sup> sleeper if any one meets us—We had [···] dock at Liverpool [···] to start—awful gales—no steamers left Liverpool —not even Mauretania—last night—big storm—first I've seen—(very dreadful) —"all except Alum were terribly sick"—likely to be rough all the way over— boat very very steady, nearly 12,000 tons—B. very sick last night—glad we weren't on small boat. Have [···]¹ <u>no one</u>: enclosed cheque for Dot, case of accident

yr affecte son
Stephen Leacock

1   These three small omissions are the result of a tear in the letter.

## To William Peterson

c/o Mr Henry Pellatt
349 Sherbourne St
    Toronto
Monday March 9 '08

Principal Peterson
McGill University
Montreal

My dear Dr Peterson

My wife and I reached Toronto in safety on Saturday, having come from London via Philadelphia. I am writing to Lord Grey by this mail to inform him of my return and to give him some account of my tour in South Africa.

Unless there are any special circumstances which may necessitate my coming down to Montreal, I should prefer not to do so: this, of course, merely as a matter of personal economy. As far as I understand it the arrangement of my work for next year is quite simple. I presume I am to take it up where I left off:—taking the Railroad Department work of the 3rd and 4th years in the Science Faculty, and in Arts the third and fourth year political science as before. This gives me a total of twelve lectures a week. I suppose that I am not needed this year as an Examiner for the Matriculation Examinations. I expect to spend the next five or six months here working in the libraries and later on to go to the country for the summer.

Yours faithfully
Stephen Leacock

## To the Editor
## North American Review

[McGill University]
Oct 29 1908.

The Editor
The North American Review
Franklin Square. N.Y

Dear Sir

I hope the accompanying article may be suitable for publication in your Review. It is based on first hand sources. I spent last winter in S. Africa in the course of a tour of the British Empire which I made under the auspices of The Cecil Rhodes Trust and McGill University for the purpose of delivering public lectures on Imperial Development. I consequently had every opportunity of meeting the leaders of both parties.

If the article is of no use to you, I should be obliged if you would send it back as soon as possible, as it will not keep.

Very sincerely
Stephen Leacock

# CHAPTER 3

## STEPHEN LEACOCK
# HUMORIST

## 1909–1915

Stephen Leacock's career as a humorist began in earnest in 1906, when he gathered together his humorous pieces that had appeared in magazines and periodicals, packed them up, and mailed them to Houghton Mifflin, his textbook publisher, to see if they would be interested in publishing the collection. They wrote back confirming their lack of interest.

This turned out to be but a minor setback. Early in 1910, George Leacock, Stephen's younger and favourite brother, looked over the comic pieces one evening and thought that they were ready for publication. The next day he consulted with the Gazette Printing Company; he paid fifty dollars on account to the company, which agreed in turn to pay five cents a copy to George as publisher and two cents a copy to Stephen as author. Shortly thereafter, Leacock reimbursed his brother, assuming full responsibility for this publishing endeavour.[1] The entire edition of 3,000 copies sold out in two months, making Leacock a modest profit of $230.00.

---

1  In a letter to Harold Hale, dated 30 August 1951, George Leacock reminisced:

the first book Stephen published was 'Literary Lapses'. In fact, I was in Stephen's house one evening in Montreal years ago and he was showing me a lot of the manuscripts that he had written and I said, 'Stephen, why don't you publish these', and he said, 'Allright, why don't you', and I gathered up the stuff and if memory serves me rightly after all these years, I took them down to a firm called the 'Montreal News Company' to a man called Tangway or some such name. Stephen of course was then unknown as a writer and he said he could put them up in a small edition selling at .35¢, which would cost about .27¢, leaving an extra .08¢. So I told Stephen that I would be the publisher and take .05¢, and he could have .02¢ a copy. We laughed over the thing, as I think we were going to have to invest some $500.00 for the first edition.

After I left Montreal on one of my business trips, as at that time I was travelling out of Montreal to the John Foreman Company, Stephen wrote me and enclosed his cheque for $50.00, and said, 'George, I thought you might be stuck, and I'll take the responsibility for this deal,' and that left me out of the deal.

By sheer coincidence, the British publisher John Lane was visiting Montreal on business and chanced to buy a copy of *Literary Lapses* at a newsstand for reading on his return voyage to England. Immediately after finishing it he cabled Leacock that he would like to bring out the book in a regular trade edition; Leacock cabled back: 'I accept with thanks.' And thus began their long careers as publisher and author, as well as devoted friends.

*Literary Lapses*, published in 1910, marks the beginning of Leacock's distinguished career as a humorist. With only a very few exceptions, he would publish a volume of humour every year until his death. Thus, the following year, Leacock published his second comic volume, *Nonsense Novels*, which consisted of ten short parodies of many kinds of novels and particular authors, including mathematical theorems and travel brochures, Arthur Conan Doyle and Walter Scott. *Nonsense Novels* met with the same kind of immediate success that *Literary Lapses* had found. Leacock the humorist was capturing attention throughout the English-speaking world.

A former student of Leacock's at Upper Canada College, B.K. Sandwell, played a significant role in Leacock's career as a humorist. In 1909 Sandwell, the drama editor of the Montreal *Herald* and soon-to-be associate editor of Montreal's *Financial Times*, had been approached by Leacock for his opinion about publishing a collection of humorous pieces. Sandwell had advised against it, pointing out that such a comic collection could only harm Leacock's professional reputation. Of course, *Literary Lapses* was successfully published in spite of Sandwell's recommendation, and just two years later it was Sandwell who approached Leacock to discuss the latter's writing. In late 1911 he arranged a meeting with Leacock and Edward Beck, the managing editor of the Montreal *Star*. The result of their talk was 'the only really large-scale commission that Leacock ever received for a fictional job to be done for a purely Canadian audience. I do not know what the figure was,' Sandwell recalled, 'but it was probably not large enough to have interested him a few months later when he was swamped with commissions from American magazines and syndicates; but in 1912 it was adequate and he had a wealth of material which was not so suitable for his American buyers and which he was delighted to have a chance of using.'[2]

*Sunshine Sketches of a Little Town*, his sympathetic series of sketches of the foibles and follies of a thinly disguised Orillia, Ontario, first appeared as a series of twelve separate articles in the *Star* from 17 February until 22 June. Following their successful serialization there, they were gathered together with only a few changes and published as a book two months later. *Sunshine Sketches of a Little Town* has established itself as one of the major works of Canadian literature, and yet its central town of Mariposa, so close to Sherwood Anderson's Winesburg, Ohio, and Thornton Wilder's 'Our Town', boasts a cast of characters who engage

2    B.K. Sandwell, 'How the "Sketches" Started', *Saturday Night* (23 August 1952): p. 7.

in the pastimes, vocations, and shenanigans of people all over the world. As one scholar has written, the book 'should have been and should be, outside as well as inside Canada, the uniquely beloved work in the Leacock canon because its account of people and their ways is a very funny, very warm-hearted Canadian or Ontario version of humanity as it was in almost any small town in the Western World.'[3]

Following the publication in 1913 of *Behind the Beyond and Other Contributions to Human Knowledge*—another comic volume, which would go through six printings in its first five years—came *Arcadian Adventures of the Idle Rich* (1914), a book Leacock had been contemplating as early as November 1912. A companion volume to *Sunshine Sketches of a Little Town*, it exposed the falseness of life in the metropolitan centres. Set in the United States, it moved away from the good-humoured irony of *Sunshine Sketches* to sharp-edged satire on hypocrisy and greed. *Moonbeams from the Larger Lunacy*, published in 1915, was Leacock's sixth volume of humour in as many years.

During this time, Leacock also continued his scholarly work. In addition to completing a variety of articles and reviews, he was honoured to write the first, second, and twentieth volumes of a new series, 'The Chronicles of Canada'. *The Dawn of Canadian History* told the story of Canada's First Nations; *Adventures of the Far North* gave an account of the early explorers' search for the Northwest Passage; and *The Mariner of St Malo* presented a study of Jacques Cartier's place in Canadian history. Although they had probably been in preparation since his 1907 success with his historical book on Baldwin, Lafontaine, and Hinks, the three volumes appeared together in 1914.

Leacock became active in politics in 1911, when he was appointed a member of the Fleming Electoral Reform Commission of Quebec. Always calling himself a Conservative, he was perturbed by the Liberal proposition of reciprocity with the United States. During the 1911 federal election campaign Leacock stumped his East Simcoe riding, which included Orillia, on behalf of a Conservative candidate; the riding, though traditionally a Liberal riding, elected a Conservative. So, too, he campaigned in Brome in the Eastern Townships for the Conservative candidate, who became the only Conservative Member of Parliament elected from Quebec in that year. He also wrote anonymous pamphlets on behalf of a group of Toronto businessmen opposing reciprocity.

Leacock's horror at the events of the First World War is always evident in his letters to his British publisher, John Lane. On 24 August 1914, shortly after the outbreak of the war, Leacock wrote: 'As to England I suppose that in this time of stress and anxiety we must not expect too much. We need a thumping big victory before we can turn our mind to smaller things.' The following year, he

3   Douglas Bush, 'Stephen Leacock', *The Canadian Imagination: Dimensions of a Literary Culture*, edited by David Staines (Cambridge, MA: Harvard University Press, 1977), p. 143.

wrote again: 'We are all in a wild passion of indignation over the Lusitania. Recruits are springing out of the ground' (13 May 1915). Leacock sent copies of his books to soldiers' hospitals and conveyed similar requests to Lane himself.

In a letter to Lane dated 20 July Leacock commented: 'The war looks gloomy enough just now but I am hoping that we shall soon have better news.' Leacock's initial optimism concerning the outcome of the war is evident also in 'In the Good Times After the War', the closing story of *Moonbeams from the Larger Lunacy*, which is identified in an initial footnote as 'An extract from a London newspaper of 1916'. The setting of the story is the British House of Commons in 1916: there is a long and humorous discussion of Home Rule in this post-bellum period, and there is 'a real fine moving picture show of the entrance of the Allies into Berlin'. Leacock clearly envisioned, or hoped for, a swift end to the brutal conflict raging in Europe.

For Leacock, the most significant event of these years was the birth of his son, on 19 August 1915. As Stephen's mother wrote:

> a great event has taken place. My first Leacock grandchild was born on the 19th of August, Stephen's boy. He and Beatrix have been married a long time and this longed for child has taken up all my thoughts of late. I hope very soon to see him; at present he and his mother are in the maternity hospital, and it's not much use for me to go to Montreal till they get home to Cote des Nieges, as one can see so little of people in hospital, but Stephen writes often of the boy and he's a chip off the old block I'm sure—like Stephen and my father. He is to be called Stephen Lushington.[4]

Agnes's commentary is dated 5 September, eighteen days after the birth. Beatrix and her new son were still in the hospital, and though Leacock's description to his mother of the birth—'He had a close run for his life as he had decided to throw himself into the world wrong end first'—suggests some inkling of future problems, Leacock rejoiced unreservedly, as the events of the war were pushed to the background by his happiness at the birth of Stephen Jr.

4    From Agnes Leacock's commentary; see Appendix.

## To J.R. Tanguay[1]

165 Cote des Neiges Road
Montreal
Feb 3 1910

The Manager
Montreal News Co

Dear Mr Tanguay.

Pursuant to our recent conversation I propose to place with you for sale 3000 copies of my book <u>Literary Lapses</u> now being manufactured by the Gazette Co.

It is understood that you are to pay me 23 cents each for the books sold, and that they are to be put on the retail market at 35 cents. I am to pay you 3 cents a pound for such books as you send out and are returned to you unsold. I will also supply you with 200 paper placards and 100 placards in cardboard to be used as advertisements in stores and book stands.

You will make payment to me of my share of receipts ~~thre~~ at intervals of three months after the first receipts of the copies from the printer, the first payments being made at the end of three months, the second at the end of six months, the third at the end of nine months and a fourth and final payment at the end of a year when the unsold books shall be returned and our transactions closed.

This agreement of course has no reference to any future edition or to copies of the book over 3000, nor does it carry with it any monopoly of sale.

Yours sincerely
Stephen Leacock

1   J.R. Tanguay was the cashier at the Montreal News Company.

## To Harold Hale[1]

165 Cote des Neiges Road,
Montreal, March 25, 1910.

Harold Hale, Esq.,
Orillia, Ont.,

Dear Harold,—

I am going over to Europe this summer and shall not be able to come to Orillia, and would like to rent my little place there if possible. As you know, it

1   Harold Hale (1874–1963) joined his father, George Hale, at a young age in the publishing of the *Orillia Packet*, later to become *The Orillia Packet and Times*. His association with the newspaper spans 65 years from printer's devil to editor. Maintaining a high standard of ethical journalism, he was also an intense historian who helped preserve both written history and historical sites. He maintained a good friendship with Stephen Leacock throughout his life.

has a shanty on it with furniture and cooking things etc. The shanty is, of course, no good; I say it in all humility, but at any rate it would make a first class camping place, and the point itself is delightful. I was wondering whether you would care to try to find me a tenant for it. I will rent the place for the summer for $40.00, and if you rent it for me I will give you $5.00 commission on doing so. Advertising in the Packet would not cost you anything and might find a tenant. Can you tell me anything about the C.P.R. expropriating part of my property.

It is quite likely that I am to go to Bracebridge to address a Canadian Club there. If so I will drop off at Orillia and talk to the Orillia club.

Very sincerely,
Stephen Leacock

## To John Lane[1]

McGill University
July 17 1910

John Lane Esqre
The Bodley Head
Vigo St
London

Dear Sir

I am much obliged to you for your letter of July 5th and your cable of the 16th in regard to the publication of my <u>Literary Lapses</u> I cabled today an acceptance of your offer to publish giving me fifteen per cent royalty (15%). My own edition will soon be sold out. Can you quote me a price per thousand sheets for sending me out yours, ready for me to bind here? I might, with profit to both of us, cut out my Canadian Edition. I presume that you will put the book on the United States market as well. I have some other humorous stuff on hand of which I should like to discuss with you: it is being syndicated in bits here and in the States but I hold the copyright.

In the meantime I am delighted to think that my book will appear in England under such good auspices.

Very sincerely
Stephen Leacock

1   In 1887, John Lane (1854–1925) co-founded, with Elkin Mathews, The Bodley Head, a small publishing firm initially involved in the antiquarian book trade. The two men broke up at the close of September 1894, and the firm became John Lane–The Bodley Head. As well as being a business associate, Lane became a close friend of Stephen Leacock.

## To John Lane

McGill University,
Montreal, July 22nd. 1910.

John Lane, Publisher,
The Bodley Head,
London.

Dear Sir:—

I duly received your cable asking for proof read copy of Literary Lapses and for additional material. I am sending you the book under separate cover and also additional material as follows—

I.   Article–How to make a million dollars.
II.  Article–Aristocratic education.
III. Article–The passing of the poet.
IV.  Article–A Christmas Letter.
V.   Article–A Study in still life.

These will come to you in two or more separate envelopes as they have to come from different places.

Very faithfully,
Stephen Leacock

## To John Lane

Gerard Hotel
West 44 St New York
Aug 9. 1910.

John Lane Esqre
The Bodley Head
Vigo St
London

Dear Mr Lane.

I beg to acknowledge your letter of July 27 which was forwarded to me here. I shall be very glad to make such arrangements as will prevent my Canadian edition from interfering in any way with your book. Perhaps it will be best to let the copies that are left of it (only a few hundred, I think) get sold out, and then replace it by an edition made from your sheets and sold at the same price as yours.

I am afraid that I have not yet sent you enough matter: if you write or cable to me for more, mentioning the number of thousands of words needed to fill your form, I will gather and send the material with as little delay as possible. Meantime I enclose herewith a number of poems, some in type and some in type-writing, under the heading Today in History. They were written for Canadian consumption, and hence the topics are in many cases local in character. At present the series is syndicated, serialized I think you call it, in

Canada by a Montreal concern, but I should like very much to get an arrangement for doing such work for an English house. The terms I get here are 75 per cent of the gross receipts, the Syndicate having to incur all the trouble of placing the matter. It is not sold here in the shape of blocks or matrixes but is printed only for greater ease of inspection and use by the purchaser. I should be very glad to begin, as from any convenient date, supplying the matter in lots of 2 weeks or a month at a time. I was at first a little uncertain as to the best length and form of verses to use and hence the variation in the specimens, enclosed, but I am inclined to believe that they should not be shorter than 20 or longer than 50 lines. We sell them here to daily papers which print one each day. It has occurred to me also, that several of them such as the ones marked with a star, can be removed from their particular setting in the calendar and converted into short poems of general application, either by a mere change of title or, at any rate, by a very slight variation of the opening lines.

If you would think it a good plan to sandwich some of them into <u>Literary Lapses</u>, pray do so. The copyright is mine. On the other hand it might be a better plan to try to make up a little book of verse by itself. I have no idea of the capacity of your market for absorbing comic poetry. I send you also a poem called <u>Vanitas</u> which was published in Canada and the United States a fortnight ago. I have it in mind to do more on the same plan, possibly a series dealing with the Vanities of Life, and imprinted with that resigned and not entirely cheerless melancholy which is the stock in trade of the professional humorist.

I have also some other stuff of a different range (though purporting to be humorous) in the form of essays. I have been meaning to add two or three more to them to make enough for a book. At the present moment I have no copies of them by me but on my return to Montreal in the course of a week or so, I will post them to you and see what you think of them. I have been doubtful whether to publish them as they stand, (with new, similar ones added) under such a title as <u>American Essays</u> or to recast the material and to make of them a book in chapters. The unwritten, or rather the only partly-written ones, deal with Democracy, Morality and, I think, Women.

About one half of the stories in <u>Literary Lapses</u> were copyrighted in the United States, by <u>Puck</u>, <u>Life</u>, and more than either of these by a defunct weekly called <u>Truth</u>  I obtained leave to republish. Nothing in the book was ever published serially in Great Britain. I hope that you will pardon so long a letter. The interest which you have been good enough to show in my work is my excuse for going so fully into details.

Yours very faithfully
Stephen Leacock

P.S. Please address me at <u>McGill</u> as my stay here is uncertain.

## To John Lane

Orillia Ontario
Aug 19, 1911

Dear Mr Lane

I ought to have written to you sooner to thank you for your good works in connection with my <u>Nonsense Novels</u>, and for much else. A few weeks ago I was in New York and made the acquaintance of Mr Johnson, Mr Cannan & Mr Jones.[1] They were extremely kind to me and I was delighted to find that you have such energetic and able men in charge of your American house.

The manager of the Publishers Press told me a little while ago that he had sent you a cheque for the first 1000 sheets of <u>Nonsense Novels</u>. I may mention, by the way that I am no longer a director of that company.[2]

Very sincerely
Stephen Leacock

1    The three men worked for John Lane in New York. Walter A. Johnson was the managing director of the firm. Jefferson Jones, who had a long history of working with Leacock, was the manager of the firm and stayed on when it was purchased by Dodd, Mead and Company at the end of 1921.
2    See Carl Spadoni, 'The Publishers Press of Montreal', *Papers of the Bibliographical Society of Canada* 24 (1985): 38–49.

## To John Lane

McGill University
Aug 23 1910

Dear Mr Lane.

I have already caused to be sent to you last week articles:—

1) Aristocratic Education
2) Men who Have shaved me

I now send under separate covers papers as follows:—

1) Three Essays (The Apology of a Professor: Literature & Education in America: The Psychology of American Humour): These of course are not suited to publish in Literary Lapses but you will recollect that I wrote in regard to their separate publication

2) Corrected Copy Poem <u>Vanitas</u>. The version here sent was for use in the states and differs from the one already forwarded. I think it the best to use if you decide to put poetry into the book.

3) Poem. <u>A Reader's Lament</u>. To publish this ~~needs~~ in the U.S. needs the consent of <u>Life</u>, a N.Y. weekly paper: It appeared under title <u>The Constant Reader</u> (about 1904 I think)

4. Group of Poems (8) already referred to, taken from <u>Today in History</u> with Headings altered to suit.

5. Article. <u>How to Live to be Two Hundred</u>

I must thank you for your kindness and the trouble you are taking in this matter

> Very faithfully
> Stephen Leacock

## To Margaret Burrowes                                    Oct 27 1910

My dear Daisy—

I am overjoyed to hear of the Baby. I was hoping you'd call him <u>Stephen</u>. I shall use that as his name whether you do or not. I am sending him a present today. You ought to call him Stephen to save the inconvenience of having 2 Billies round the house.

I had just written to Dot  The letter will be in the same mail.

Of course I dont want to be selfish about his being called Stephen: no doubt you & Billy ~~man~~ will call him Billy and quite right too but just for fun I will call him Stephen on my own account

I think I'll send him a Bible first but have not decided: I want to do the thing on the lines of the best precedents.

> with best love to all
> yr affec bro.
> Stephen Leacock

## To John Lane                                    McGill University
                                                   Montreal
                                                   Nov. 7 1911

Dear Mr Lane,

I received last week a bill from your firm for £173. I do not quite understand it: I presume it includes the account for sheets of <u>Literary Lapses</u> ~~and~~ delivered on my order to the account of the Montreal News Co, and for sheets of <u>Nonsense Novels</u> delivered on my order to the Publishers Press.

But the manager of the Publishers Press told me that he had sent you a cheque on this account for about $200.<u>00</u> in or about the first week in August. Is this true? I think I mentioned to you that I am not now connected with the management of the Publishers Press: I resigned because my confidence in it was entirely shaken on learning that my name had been used without warrant as President of the Company. This statement by the way I should like you to regard as confidential. But you will understand that I am anxious to learn whether Mr Epstein's statement that he sent you $200 on the account is true

In any case of course I am responsible for your being paid for the ~~sheets~~ copies of Nonsense Novels.

Very sincerely
Stephen Leacock

P.S. May I say how much I have enjoyed Mrs Lane's delightful book <u>The Talk of the Town</u>.[1] I am sure it will have great success.

1   Anna Lane, *Talk of the Town* (London, New York: John Lane, 1911).

## To William Peterson

McGill University
November 22, 1911.

Dear Mr. Principal,

Professor Keay[1] and I have discussed today, in the most friendly spirit, the difficulty which has arisen in regard to the teaching of the 4th. year Transportation students.

The situation is as follows. The subject of economics forms a part of the programme of the Transportation students of the third and fourth years. In the third year they study the <u>Elements of Political Economy</u> and are placed in the general class for beginners which is made up of themselves, the second year Arts students, and the first year Commercial students. This part of the arrangement appears to give general satisfaction, and Professor Keay is anxious for it to continue. In the fourth year, in order to economize the teaching power of the University, Dr. Hemmeon[2] and I adopted three years ago the plan of putting the science men and the Honour Arts men into a combined class which meets twice a week and studies <u>Transportation Problems</u>. This course is therefore at one and the same time a part of the Arts course in Honours and of the Transportation course. The arrangement is by no means an ideal one and involves a certain, though not very great, sacrifice of the interests of both the Arts men and the science students. In the case of the Arts men, a course of fifty lectures on Transportation is out of proportion to the time they are able to give to other special aspects of Economic Science such as, Tariffs, Labour, etc. In the case of the science men, a disadvantage arises from the circumstances that a part of the work, not very great, is ground they have already covered. This is true, let us say, of the opening portion of the course dealing with the history of the railways and the earlier and simpler aspects of railway legislation. Necessarily, throughout the course, they are less interested and less capable of discussion in matters of theory than the fourth year Art students. I

1   H.O. Keay was professor of transportation in the Facutly of Applied Science at McGill University.
2   Joseph Hemmeon (1879–1963) received his BA (1898) from Acadia, his MA (1904) from Dalhousie, and his PhD (1906) from Harvard, all three degrees in political economy. He joined McGill as a lecturer in 1907 and succeeded Leacock as chair of the department in 1936. He retired from McGill in 1946.

repeat, therefore, that the arrangement is one that is by no means perfect, and that can only commend itself on grounds of economy. Professor Keay informs me that he had hitherto supposed that the course was framed and conducted purely along the lines required by the science students, and that although he was aware of the attendance of the Arts students and had no objection to it as such, he presumed that they were merely adjoined to a science class. Professor Keay and Dr. Hemmeon and I are agreed that we can find means to work out the programme of the present year in a manner more or less satisfactory. But we find it rather difficult to get a basis for permanent operations. Dr. Hemmeon and I do not think that we can in any degree alter the subject matter of the course or the form of its teaching with sacrificing our students in Arts. Professor Keay feels that while he is willing to cooperate with us in tiding over the difficulties of the present year, he would like to see his fourth year students in future receive instruction wholly designed for their particular needs.

Dr. Hemmeon and I would be greatly pleased if an arrangement could be found whereby all special science classes, as such, are removed from our tuition. We should of course should be most willing to admit science students to our Arts lectures, wherever the number of the class or other circumstances are such as to permit it without loss to our own students.

Since the time when the existing arrangement was first made our department has grown considerably in size and activity. We have now 63 students in the Elements of Political Economy, and about 55 in the two third year classes in Political Science and Economic Theory (the so called ordinary courses). In the honour classes, in which there were on an average . . . . students between 1901 and 1907 we have 8 students in the third year and 9 in the fourth. The plain fact is that our time is entirely occupied and more than occupied with the claims made upon it by our own students. I may state, in the interests of frankness, that neither Dr. Hemmeon nor I would be willing, even for special remuneration to give special lectures to the science class. Moreover, if we felt justified, now or later, in asking for an addition to the teaching staff, we should both feel that the work in Arts would be better in the hands of a person trained in Political Economy generally, rather than in those of a railroad specialist. I may add, however, that Dr. Hemmeon and Professor Keay and I all concur in the desire to find an arrangement that will involve a minimum of expense to the University and will satisfy the needs of both faculties.

I must apologize for inflicting so long a letter at this particular time. The situation involves no immediate need of action, and I thought you might like to have this complete statement of the case for consideration at your leisure.

I am
Yours obediently
Stephen Leacock

*To John Lane*                          McGill University
                                        Montreal
                                        November 29, 1911.

Dear Mr. Lane,

This is in answer to your two recent letters regarding an order from the Musson Book Co. of 200 sheets of Literary Lapses, and regarding the account of the Publishers Press.

The Musson Co. were not odering the sheets for me, but I will write them in regard to the matter.

I note according to my account that I am credited with Royalties on 940 (equal 868), Literary Lapses sold in America: the price is put at 3/6 and the royalty at 10 per cent, Is this correct? The price should be $1.25, and the royalty 10 per cent. This would make $108.50, due to me and not £15-3-9-, as in your account.

Re the Publishers Press. I am very sorry to hear that the publishers Press has sent you no payment on Nonsense Novels. As I told you in a previous letter I resigned my connection with that company last August. Since then Dr. Macphail and I and other gentlemen who had allowed our names to go on the board of directors on account of the valuable national services which we thought the company would perform, have been hearing all sorts of rumours as to the position of the company and the incompetence of its management. I mention this to you in confidence as you have dealings with the company apart from my book. I am sorry to say that Mr. Epstein is even charged before the courts with stealing stereotype plate from a rival syndicate. This may or may not be well founded but you will appreciate my reasons in mentioning it to you. I have thus far found it impossible either to get money from the Publishers Press for royalties due to me or to get them to send a remittance to you.

I cannot tell you how deeply I regret having been the means of introducing Mr. Epstein to you. You will I am sure understand that I acted in all good faith. I make myself fully responsible for the Nonsense Novels account, and will write you later as to what I will do with the 1000 in your hands.

                                        Very sincerely
                                        Stephen Leacock


*To John Lane*                          McGill University
                                        [Montreal]
                                        Dec 21 1911

Dear Mr Lane

Mr Epstein of the Publishers Press states that early in December he sent you a cheque to apply on the account of <u>Nonsense Novels</u>.

As I am afraid that this cheque might be as apocryphal as the last one, I should like to know if it has been received and the amount of it

With the compliments of the season

Very sincerely
Stephen Leacock


## To John Lane

McGill University
Montreal
Jan 8. 1912

Dear Mr Lane

Many thanks for yours of Dec 29: I hope that the cheque for $222 will turn out all right. You will be glad to hear that things look much better for the Publishers Press. Through the efforts of some influential shareholders Epstein has been forced to surrender his stock and is now out of the company. An audit is being made and it is likely that some men of prominence and standing here will take hold of the affair. You see the peculiar part of the enterprise was that Epstein had managed to get a number of the most wealthy and influential men in Canada, by playing them off on one another, on to the list of his sleeping shareholders and dummy directors. If you know anybody who is conversant with business in Canada you have only to tell him that the company includes Sir Henry Pellatt (50 shares), the Drummonds, Mr Baumgarten, the late Robert Meighen, Lorne McGibbon, J. W. McConnell, John Hamilton of Quebec etc etc and he will tell you that it ought to be as solid as the bank of Montreal. I have therefore every hope that you will not lose anything from your dealings with the company. There will be a meeting of shareholders on the 25th, which will probably be followed by a reorganisation. I will keep you advised and I do not think that you need be at all anxious about your account

Will you please send me twelve (12) copies of Literary Lapses and charge them to my account.

Very sincerely
Stephen Leacock


Postscript: I forgot to say that I have handed over the agency for Literary Lapses to the Musson Company. They will buy sheets from you and will pay you for the sheets.   S.L.

*To John Lane*                              McGill University
                                            Montreal.
                                            Feb 24 1912

Dear Mr Lane,

    I am glad to say that I have good news of the Publishers Press. At a general meeting of shareholders and creditors on Feb 22, a proposition was made by one of the creditors (Mr Harriss who owns the Canada Metal Co) to take over the concern, Mr Harriss to obtain a block of stock and in return to become liable for all existing debts, the same to be duly scheduled for ratification. The shareholders expressed their consent and the meeting stands adjourned till Feb 29 for the final ratification which I expect will go through. This will mean that you & I as creditors will be fully paid. I am putting in my account for Nonsense Novels (2000 copies, cost price and royalties): if the cheque issued to you in December for $222 is paid that will be deducted. I am also calling attention to your account (I cannot check the figures of it) and having it entered on the schedule of debts. The meeting also consented that the agency held by the Publishers Press for the sale of Nonsense Novels should terminate at once, and that any agencies held by the Publishers Press for the sale of your books, or the books of the John Lane Co of New York should be terminated at once if you so desire (You see, I couldn't have the resolution made to <u>terminate</u> your agency as it would be invalid in that form without your consent) I presume therefore that you will prefer to take steps to call in any balance of your books still in the hands of the Publishers Press and will present your account for copies not returned. I have every hope that all these accounts will be paid up and you will lose nothing.

    Meantime I am communicating with Mr Musson about taking over the 1000 copies of Nonsense Novels which you have with the imprint of the Publishers Press: it is too late to give this agency to Bell & Cockburn without first offering it to Mr Musson as I promised him that I would do so. I shall have his answer in a day or so & will write you at once regarding the disposal of the books (the 1000 copies)

    I send you under separate cover some stories called <u>Sunshine Sketches of a Little Town</u>. They are appearing in the Montreal Star and two or three small Canadian papers: but I have reserved the books rights and the serial rights outside of Canada. I hope to do ten or twelve of these and to make a book of about 50,000 words. So if you would care to serialize them in England or in the United States and then publish them in book form I should be delighted. But I should not care to have them serialized in any way that would delay the publication of the book, nor (you will pardon my mentioning it, just as a matter of business) should I be willing to share the serial rights with you unless it was understood that you were publishing the book. There would be no point in it;

and I know you will excuse my mentioning it. Mr Wilkinson is in communication with me about Bell and Cockburn taking over the Canadian sale of <u>Sunshine Sketches</u>, if you publish it, and he speaks as if he would secure an order for 1500 copies in advance. But I tell him that I ought to get 15 per cent on the Canadian retail price and not merely 10 per cent as in the States. For greater ease of transaction I am sending a copy of this letter and of the Sketches to your New York house, in order that they may be in a position to ~~follow out~~ sell the Sketches in the States etc with a minimum of correspondences

Very sincerely
Stephen Leacock

P.S. I should have acknowledged the receipt of yours of Feb 10

## To John Lane

McGill University
Montreal
Feb 27. 1912

Dear Mr Lane

I have arranged with Mr Musson that he will take over the agency for the Canadian sales of <u>Nonsense Novels</u>, relinquished by the Publishers Press. He is to buy the book from you and it will be charged to him not me. He will also take over from you the 1000 copies of <u>Nonsense Novels</u> in your possession with the imprint of the Publishers Press, and he will pay you for these <u>eleven pence each</u>. Will you please remove them from my account, though of course I am still liable for them if Musson fails to pay. Mr Musson wishes them delivered at once to his <u>London agents</u> who will forward them to Canada. For any copies of Nonsense Novels ordered beyond this thousand, Mr Musson is liable solely

Very sincerely
Stephen Leacock

## To John Lane

McGill University
Montreal
March 2. 1912

Dear Mr Lane

At a meeting of the shareholders of the Publishers Press on ~~March~~ Feb 29, Mr Harriss of whom I wrote before asked for a fortnights delay to look further into the accounts  Meantime Chipman and I will attend to your interests. I am posting you more <u>Sunshine Sketches</u> tomorrow. Would you feel inclined to start printing them at once to save time. Of course I've only written 25,000 words so far and might get stuck or fall ill. But it would help greatly with Canadian sales to put the book on the market in May right after the newspapers are finished with the stuff.

Is there any chance of your coming out here this summer? I wish you could come while the University is "sitting."

Very sincerely
(see postscript)                                          Stephen Leacock

<u>P.S.</u> I enclose a letter to the Musson Co which explains about Literary Lapses & Nonsense Novels. Please dont charge anything to me as the Mussons are supposed to pay direct

## To John Lane

McGill University
Montreal
March 11 1912

Dear Mr Lane.

I have already sent you three <u>Sunshine Sketches of a Little Town</u> namely
    1. The Hostelry of Mr Smith
    2. The Speculations of Jefferson Thorpe
    3. The Marine Excursion of the Knights of Pythias.
I now send you under separate cover No 4. The Ministrations of Canon Drone Most of the next one is also completed so that I have over 30,000 words done. This means that I will have enough for a book as a certainty with even as much as 5 or 6 thousand words more though I hope to do in all about 50 to 60 thousand  I hope, as I said, that you can see your way to going ahead with printing the book and "taking a chance" on my duly delivering the MSS. Mr Wilkinson says that Bell & Cockburn would be willing to make an arrangement with me whereby I would get 15 per cent on Canadian sales (15 per cent of Canadian retail price) provided you would supply them with bound copies or sheets on a similar basis to that with Nonsense Novels.

Very sincerely
Stephen Leacock

## To John Lane

McGill University
March 20. 1912

Dear Mr Lane

I was so sorry to hear that you had not been well and trust that you are quite recovered. It hardly looks at present as if I could join you in New York next month but I shall try to. Do you expect to come to Montreal?

The Publishers Press Business is adjourned again till the 26th. Mr Harriss may not proceed with his tentative offer and in that case the concern will go into liquidation and I do not know how much, if anything the creditors will get.

Re. Sunshine Sketches of a Little Town. I have 35,000 words complete, including Chap V. "The Whirlwind Campaign in Mariposa, which I send you today. My arrangements with Bell and Cockburn are practically complete. They will buy sheets or bound books from you, at whatever price you and they settle, and will pay me a 15 per cent royalty on their Canadian retail price. The copy will, I hope, be all in your hands in another month.

The Musson Company, as I think you know have taken over the agency for Nonsense Novels and Literary Lapses. The 1000 copies of Nonsense Novels with the imprint Publishers Press are to be delivered to their London agent.

I have not received the 12 copies of Literary Lapses ordered: the invoice came & not books except 1 copy by post.

                                                    With kind regards
                                                    Stephen Leacock


*To John Lane*                          McGill University
                                        Montreal
                                        April 3 1912

Dear Mr Lane

     Yours of March 13th & 19th to hand. I'm afraid I sent your reader awfully bad copy: I will now keep the rest of the Sunshine Sketches in hand and send you the whole copy from the start in a revised and corrected form so as to minimize proof reading. I can make it Canadian enough (to English readers) by inserting a sentence or two here and there. I have at present 45,000 words actually written, and it looks as if the whole thing would run to 60,000 though of course you will understand that I wouldn't like to spin it out for the mere sake of words. I should think it likely that I can go beyond 60,000 words without padding & puffing. I quite agree with you about not bothering to try to serialize the stuff in England

                        . . . . . . . . . .

The Publishers Press had gone into liquidation. It's affairs were so tangled that without taking that step there was no certainty about its liabilities. It will now be offered for sale as a going concern and we hope that in this way the creditors may not come off so badly. You forgot to tell me if you are to be in Montreal in

April. If so will you come and stay at my house. My wife and I will be delighted if you can. We leave here in the beginning of May (the 12th) for France so that my address for any letters leaving England after May 1st will be in care of <u>Thomas Cook and Son</u>, Paris.

Very sincerely
Stephen Leacock

*To John Lane*                                        McGill
                                                        Montreal
                                                        April 26

Dear Mr Lane

Yours of April 16 to hand—I am to sail on May 12th and I am so crowded with work between now and then that I am afraid that it will not be possible for me to go to New York but I am hoping to see you here. My wife and I have just sublet our house for the summer so that we shall be in lodgings but my address will be obtainable at McGill. I am disappointed not to be able to have you at my house but you must let me know the probable date of your arrival here if it turns out that you can come to Montreal

I have <u>completed</u> 48,000 words of the <u>Sunshine Sketches</u> and hope to do about 10 or 12 thousand words more but dont feel sure of it. My own feeling is that <u>light</u> literature of this sort should be short and relatively cheap, but I suppose that even 60,000 words is a very short book

With kind regards
Stephen Leacock

*To Walter A. Johnson*[1]                              McGill. May 11 '12

Dear Mr Johnson

<u>Awfully</u> sorry to miss seeing Mr Lane—please tell him so—I am sailing for France tomorrow and will post my MSS from there to London. It fills 53,000 words with an autobiographical preface of 1,000 more.

best regards
in haste
Stephen Leacock

1   See footnote 1, page 65.

## To John Lane

Hotel Vouillemont
Paris
Rue Boissy d'Anglas
May

Dear Mr Lane

I have here with me now the entire MSS of my Sunshine Sketches. It makes 62,500. I hope we can print it with as little delay as possible so as to catch the Canadian summer market early. As soon as I have looked over the MSS (which has been delayed in coming to me) Ill post it to you

Very sincerely
Stephen Leacock


## To Basil W. Willett[1]

c/o Thomas Cook & Son
1 Place de l'Opéra
Paris
June 4 1912

Dear Mr Willett

I am very anxious to get the proofs of my <u>Sunshine Sketches</u> at the earliest possible moment as it will save a lot of time if I can correct them while still here. I only need the galley proof and can leave the rest to you. One day will easily suffice for my reading. I wish to sail on June 15th from Havre. Mr Lane wrote me some time ago (when I offered to send the MSS in sections as completed) that the whole thing could be set up in a week. I hope it will be possible to do this as it would suit my arrangements very well

Will you please hand on the enclosed memorandum for your proof readers

Very sincerely
Stephen Leacock


P.S. In my opinion, the full title <u>Sunshine Sketches of a Little Town</u> ought to appear both outside the book & on the title page.

---

1    An associate of John Lane at the Bodley Head, London, who went on to become a director of the firm.

*To John Lane*                              Hotel Vouillemont
                                            Rue Boissy d'Anglas
                                            Paris
                                            June 10 1912

Dear Mr Lane

Many thanks for your very kind letter, which shows me that you are safely back from your travels.

I quite appreciate what you say about the book (Sunshine Sketches) and still more your evident consideration of my interest. I am glad the price is to be fairly low as I think that humorous stuff ought to be cheap; those who are most willing to buy it are young people with lots of life and fun in them and, as a rule, not too much money. Rich people buy stuff with a gorgeous cover & fine paper, and never read it.

Will you please have them send the proofs to this hotel as I think it will save time to do so. I wish very much that I could have come over to London to see you but I have things to do here and leave, I hope, on Saturday, so that my time is all too short.

I approve very much of a cheap edition of Literary Lapses & Nonsense Novels: the Mussons of course have the Canadian sale of these. I was sorry to find that Mr Musson takes it a little ill that <u>Bell & Cockburn</u> have the new book

                                            with very best regards
                                            Yours sincerely
                                            Stephen Leacock


*To Basil W. Willett*                       [Cranston's Kenilworth Hotel
                                            Great Russell Street
                                            London, W.C.]
                                            Sat m'g Je. 15.
                                            Train to Liverpool

Dear Mr Willett

On thinking it over I would rather not recommend any topic for a picture out of <u>Sunshine Sketches</u> for the jacket. If the man who draws it knows his business I am sure that he would prefer to read far enough into the book to find a subject that strikes him and as as the book is light reading it will not involve any great strain on his brain to read some of it. As soon as he gets what he wants he can stop reading instantly.

I must thank you so much for the very pleasant lunch of yesterday. I fear I trespassed most unconscionably on your time but I was enjoying my talk so much that I did not notice how far on in the afternoon it was.

My kindest regards to Mr Lane

> very sincerely
> Stephen Leacock

## To Walter A. Johnson

McGill University
Nov. 5, 1912.

Dear Mr. Johnson

By all means go ahead and make the arrangements for using the stuff out of my <u>three</u> books in <u>newspapers</u>. I enclose an article of 1100 words called "<u>Familiar Incidents</u>" I. With the photographs". It is the first of a series of about half a dozen that I have promised to do for a new paper that is being founded here; they start to print these articles in December and pay me 2½ cents a word for the Canadian Serial rights (note book rights). I should be awfully obliged if you could sell them in the States too: in any case I send you this one, which is all that I have done.

Mr. Boyden has been writing to me for 2n article and I am going to do a special one for him.

It is very likely that my next book will deal with the <u>Idle Rich</u> and will be called <u>Arcadian Adventures</u> with the <u>Idle Rich</u>. It will probably be in about 12 instalments of 5000 words each (thats only a guess, none of it is written). I can easily dispose of the serial rights here. But perhaps I'd better wait till I have some chapters of it done before I discuss it further with you.

> Very sincerely
> Stephen Leacock.

## To William C. Bell[1]

McGill University
Montreal
April 3. 1913

Dear Mr Bell

I am afraid that my <u>Arcadian Adentures</u> has not yet reached the advertising stage. Hardly any of it is written and in any case it is likely that Mr Walter Johnson (John Lane Co) will arrange to serialise it before book publication. This would take a long time.

But meantime I have other stuff: The American Magazine is to publish in a month or so an imitation play of mine called <u>Behind the Beyond</u>. It is a satire

---

1    William C. Bell was a co-founding partner in Bell & Cockburn, a publishing firm from 1911 to 1914, when 'the stress of war times . . . forced it to the wall'. After Bell & Cockburn ceased operations, Sam Gundy of the Canadian branch of Oxford University Press announced that Bell would join Oxford on 1 January 1915 with 'a splendid opportunity to continue the building up of a fine list for the Canadian reading public'.

on the modern problem play. It contains 7500 words. Mr Johnson is going to publish it either all by itself as a 50 cent book like those of Julian Street[2]—or as a more expensive book, putting with it ~~the~~ other fugitive writings that I have ready. But I feel sure the separate small book is best. I presume that you would like to take this for Canada and perhaps you might care to write Walter Johnson about it.

Next. I wrote last year about 15,000 words in six sketches <u>A Holiday in Paris</u>. I think I'd like you to publish them. They were in Toronto Saturday Night, but as I remember it Saturday night only had serial rights. I've sent for copies to look them over & see what they look like. My impression is that they hardly need any alteration. I promised long ago to send copies to Mr Johnson but I have neglected to do so. But I'd be delighted if you'd take the thing up & get the book ready for the summer market.

Very sincerely
Stephen Leacock

P.S. When are you coming to Montreal?

P.P.S. It is better to use <u>McGill</u> as my address, especially as my house is sub-let for the summer after May 1st

S.L.

2  Chicago-born writer Julian Street (1879–1947) penned a series of travel books and comic studies.

## To Walter A. Johnson

McGill [University]
April 28 '13

Dear Mr Johnson

Very many thanks for yours of last week with check for $93.00. I am awfully pleased that you like the opening pages of the <u>Arcadian Adventures</u>. I hope to send along more but it may be rather slow work—or perhaps very fast, I dont know.

I expect Mr Lane here on May 5th & wrote to him in New York by Saturday's mail

I am sending over to England all the copy for my book ~~which~~ "<u>Behind the Beyond</u>". I see from Mr Bryden's letter that there will be no trouble as to the date of publication, I mean as to interfering with serial publication in the American of stuff that will be in the book. I am so glad that youre taking such trouble over my "works"

Very sincerely
Stephen Leacock

## To John Lane

McGill University
Montreal Nov 5 1913

Dear Mr Lane

I am delighted beyond measure with the appearance of my new book. It is excellent all through & the illustrations delightful.

I dont know just how fast I shall get on with the <u>Idle Rich</u> especially as I have started some different stuff called <u>Afternoons in Utopia</u> which may develop into something. If it begins to do so, I'll send along a bit of it. But in any case I hope to have material enough for a new book a year hence and will certainly follow your advice about the <u>quantity</u> of words in it.

best regards
very sincerely
Stephen Leacock

## To J. A. T. Lloyd[1]

[McGill University]
Nov 28

Dear Lloyd

So many thanks for sending me your book. We have both (my wife & I) read it with great interest. It is certainly a very striking production with plenty of originality about it. I am so glad that you seem to be finding your natural bent instead of having stayed on here among the ranks of us unhappy teachers of the young. When you get time send me a line or two of news of yourself & what work you are doing. I see good old bow-wow now & again & 3H Holmes both much the same as ever: We often speak of you. So too does Stony whom I always try to hunt up when I am in Toronto.

I suppose you never contemplate coming over to this side of the water. If you should do so be sure to let me know as I should like to see something of you.

Yours as ever
Steve Laycock
al
Stephen Leacock

---

1    British novelist and critic John Arthur Thomas Lloyd (1871–1956) worked for a time on the *Toronto Week* and taught at Upper Canada College, where he knew Stephen Leacock. In addition to his many novels, he published books on Poe, Turgenev, and Dostoevsky.

## To John Lane

McGill University
Montreal
Dec 9 1913

Dear Mr Lane

I send the signed contract herewith.

I am delighted with <u>Behind the Beyond</u> and am awfully glad to see thats it is getting such a good reception. The book sellers here tell me that they are doing very well with it

This autumn, I am sorry to say, I have been dreadfully crowded with college work and rather tired out so that I have done hardly any new work but I hope to get busy now in earnest.

I shall very likely be in London next June

Very sincerely
Stephen Leacock

## To Harold Hale

[McGill University
Montreal]
Dec 28    13

Dear Harold

Thanks for the <u>Packet</u> Calendar. It now adorns the faculty room of the Arts Faculty, so that even the professors can keep track of the day of the week

Very sincerely with
the season's wishes
Stephen Leacock

## To Basil W. Willett

McGill [University Montreal]
Dec 30 1913

Dear Mr Willett

I have been rather surprised that my royalties have not yet come to hand and thought it best, in case of accident to send a line.

Royalties are due on <u>Literary Lapses</u> & <u>Nonsense Novels</u> from July 1. 1912 to July 1 1913 (accounts Oct 1. 1913) and on Sunshine Sketches from Jan 1 1913 to July 1 1913 (accounts Oct. 1. 1913).

Judging from last year they are overdue and in these days of suffragettes & Pillar boxes, one gets anxious.

Compliments of the Season
Stephen Leacock

## To Basil W. Willett

McGill University
Feb 2 1914

Dear Mr Willett

Many thanks for cheque for £176—I am glad to hear that <u>Behind the Beyond</u> is going well.

I think it would be better in future in advertising to cut out the <u>Canadian Mark Twain</u>. I see from my clippings that it goes down the wrong way.

I am sending you an article. Will you please see if you can sell it for me, (deducting a commission)

As far as I know the <u>Nineteenth Century</u> have not used my article on American Humour.

I expect to have the whole MSS of my <u>Arcadian Adventures with the Idle Rich</u> ready by Sep 1st

Very sincerely
Stephen Leacock


## To John Lane

McGill University
Feb 28. 1914

Dear Mr Lane

I take shame on myself that you could think I was considering anybody's offer. I have not too forgotten that you found my little <u>Literary Lapses</u>, read it on the steamer and cabled me an offer to publish it.

I am also well aware of how much you have done to circulate my books & promote my interest

If we ever part company it will be because you wish it

What is more to the point is that I have got my <u>Arcadian Adventures with the Idle Rich</u> well started & mean to stay with it

I have done quite a few fugitive pieces this winter, & shall have enough for a bookfull in 1915. I also mean to do a book called <u>The Present and the Past</u> (a set of stories of which I have already one to illustrate the idea that all the familiar faults of today are very ancient. I also mean to do a book called The <u>Annals of Concordia College</u>, applying the Sunshine-Sketches method to university life and professor-dom

By the way an old friend of mine wishes to translate <u>Sunshine Sketches</u> into German. I am willing. Have you any connection with German publishers and how do the rights in the case stand.

I am writing to Mr Shorter & shall send him a sketch or two—My wife & I will be in London late in May or early in June & are looking forward to seeing you

Very sincerely
Stephen Leacock

## To John Lane

[McGill University]
May 6 1914

Dear Mr Lane

Apologies for delay—I was waiting so as to acknowledge the receipt of £222 odd from Mr Bell which was paid this week  I have sent him formal receipts in duplicate as directed. Very many thanks. My wife and I leave tomorrow for Europe. We shall not reach England till the middle of June but I'll write you from Paris. We are both looking forward to seeing you & Mrs Lane

Our address will be c/o Thomas Cook & Son, Avenue de l'Opéra, Paris. They will forward.

with best regards
Stephen Leacock

P.S. I have now completed 43,000 words of <u>Arcadian Adventures</u>.


## To Agnes Leacock

[Hotel St James & D'Albany
Paris]
Sunday . May . 24 1914

Dear Mother.

I got your letter of the 12th (from Orillia) yesterday: awfully sorry to hear that Charlie is not better yet: I had supposed he was getting on all right: of course he neednot bother with any work on arrangements about my cottage. There is nothing there that matters in any case.

We had a rather tedious voyage—nearly two days stopped still for fog—got to Liverpool on the 18th England looks lovely in May. We stay a night in London at the Charing Cross hotel & then down to Dover by the morning train: The hop-country in Kent is beautiful isn't it? We expect to stay here in Paris for another week or two & then I suppose to London (for business) and then to the seaside.  But our address will be all the time c/o Thomas Cook & Son Paris. Everything seems so cheap here after the Canadian Hotels & restaurants

I am so sorry to miss seeing Dot.  I wrote to her from Liverpool. What is the name of the parish where your father was, is it Subarton, or Surbiton, or what?  Also where were you born? & Ill look up the date.

love to all
Y. affe. son
Stephen Leacock

## To Basil W. Willett

[Trouville-Palace
Trouville-sur-mer]
July 6. 1914

Dear Mr Willett

I've struck a difficulty. I find it quite impossible (so far) to get type-writing done here by a competent (English) person. My MSS as I write it wont do for printers. How would it be if I send it over to you & you get it done for me and I will then correct & return it for you to print from. You see, even if my MSS were decent enough for printers to use, I'd still need a second copy for Jefferson Jones.

I will of course pay whatever is the proper rate per thousand words for this class of work

Wouldnt it be well to print now the chapters that you have in hand (they make 43,000 words) and I can read the galley proofs while I am here.

With best regards & with many thanks for your kindness to me in London

Very truly
Stephen Leacock

## To John Lane

[Trouville-Palace
Trouville-sur-mer]
July 9 1914

Dear Mr Lane

I am arranging to sail on the <u>Megantic</u> on July 18th, if I can get suitable accomodation. This is rather sooner than I had expected but, for reasons of family business, I am anxious to reach Canada a little before the first of August, if possible. I wrote last week to Mr. Willett <u>re</u> my MSS of the <u>Arcadians</u> & the impossibility of getting it typewritten here. I will bring it to London and leave it with you although I think it likely that when I leave there will still be a few thousand words to finish,—but very little. We can now take it for granted that the book will contain from <u>sixty</u> to <u>sixty-five</u> thousand words. As the original date assigned in our correspondence (I think viâ Jefferson Jones) was September 1st, I presume it will be alright if the small part that will be unfinished when I sail is sent back from Canada within a week of my landing. I must of course read <u>galley proofs</u> but if these come out pretty well I imagine that I can dispense with reading the page proofs. I should like with your approval to see the book bound in blue of the colour of the enclosed piece of card. My own opinion inclines to three & six as the ~~price~~ best price, which makes it uniform with the others; but in this of course your judgment is better than mine. On the whole I dont think I should like illustrations: I believe the book will go better without them: it needs of course a coloured jacket

I hope to be London on the morning of the 17th & will come to the office & discuss with you or Mr Willett the points I have raised here.

Walter Peter Leacock, father of
Stephen Leacock, 15 July 1877.
(Leacock Museum Archives,
PL–157)

Agnes Emma Butler Leacock,
mother of Stephen Leacock,
1874. (Leacock Museum
Archives, PL–133)

Agnes Leacock (*centre*) with her children (*from left to right*) Edward Peter (Teddy), holding the family dog 'Gyp'), Charles John (Charlie), Stephen Butler, Rosamond (Dot), Caroline (Carrie), Margaret (Daisy), Thomas James (Jim), Maymie Douglas, Agnes Arabella (Missie), and George. Arthur Murdoch (Dick), the second of the Leacock siblings, is not in the photo. (Leacock Museum Archives, PL–334)

Six-year-old Stephen Leacock sits for a portrait with his sister Missie in Shoreham, Sussex, 1876. (Leacock Museum Archives, PL-001)

October 1887 — Aet. 17.

Stephen Leacock, graduate of Upper Canada College, 17 October 1887. (Leacock Museum Archives, PL-005)

Stephen and Beatrix Leacock with their son Stevie outside their Cote des Neiges home in Montreal, 1916. (Leacock Museum Archives, PL–021)

Stephen Leaock, proud father, with his son Stevie in Montreal, Winter 1916. (Photo courtesy Peter Sibbald Brown)

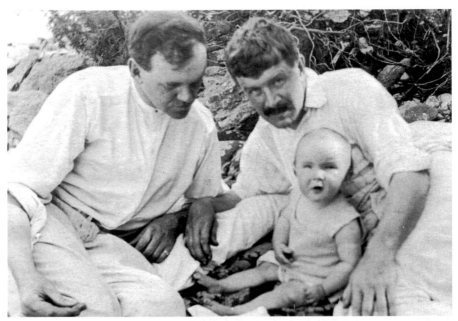

Stephen Leacock and Stevie with Leacock's favourite brother, George, at The Old Brewery Bay, Orillia, 1916. (Leacock Museum Archives, PL-170)

Stephen Leacock Jr with his dog, 1919. (Leacock Museum Archives, PL-113)

Beatrix with 'Paddy' in the sunroom of the Leacock's home at The Old Brewery Bay in Orillia, August 1925. Just four months later she would lose her battle with breast cancer. (Leacock Museum Archives, PL-088)

But I should be obliged if you could send me a line by return to say that the arrangement for delivery of <u>MSS</u> is all right. I fear I couldn't quite finish the book before I leave without undue hurry over it, and yet it would be rather an inconvenience for me to remain longer on this side. I can of course send Jefferson Jones the last piece of MSS in duplicate

I have not yet thanked you, and I cannot adequately, for all your personal kindnesses to my wife & myself in London

Very sincerely<br>
Stephen Leacock

P.S. Will you please tell Mrs Lane that since my wife has read The <u>Champagne Standard</u>,[1] about fifty percent of her conversation begins, "Mrs Lane says . . ."

1    Anna Lane, *The Champagne Standard* (London: John Lane, 1906).

## To John Lane

165 Cote des Neiges Road
Montreal 1914    Aug 24

Dear Mr Lane

Mr Bell sent me £80 making £280 on an account of £286 & odd shillings. I presume that he means to square off the other £6 against my debt to him for copies of my books sent me last week. This is not really a proper thing to do seeing that his own royalty account to me (to July 1st last, is not made up) but in war time it is near enough.

I am glad to hear that Jeff Jones thinks that the book is going well, all considered. I think the book sellers here are very confident of a large Xmas sale. As to England I suppose that in this time of stress and anxiety we must not expect much We need a thumping big victory before we can turn our minds to smaller thing.

I'm sorry I cant see you to say a word of goodbye. Please take over to Mrs Lane our very warmest regards

Very sincerely<br>
Stephen Leacock

## To John Lane

[McGill University
Montreal]
Nov 11. 1914.

Dear Mr Lane

My six copies of the American edition of the <u>Arcadians</u> have duly arrived & I am awfully pleased with the make-up & appearance of it. Unfortunately there is every sign here that the market will be a dull one. No body reads anything. But I hope that the book will do well sooner or later.

Julian Street & his wife are in town—I am doing what I can to make things pleasant for them: the more so as it turns out that he is a cousin of the Streets of Toronto,—old friends of mine.

I am sorry to say that Mr Bell only sent me £200.

Best regards to Jeff Jones

Very sincerely
Stephen Leacock

## To John Lane

[McGill University
Montreal]
Friday Dec 4 1914

Dear Mr Lane

This just a line to wish you <u>bon voyage</u>, if I am fortunate enough to catch you on the Lusitania.

I'm sorry I didn't get a chance to say goodbye in person—

I am sure that any arrangement about ~~the~~ financial matters that suits you will suit me. On general principles I'd sooner not be paid through Bell & Cockburn as I find it slow, and also I have to pay exchange on their cheques as apparently their banker wont let them have cheques paid at par in Montreal (a point which I dont understand as it is a privilege which our banks usually grant to ~~our~~ customers in good standing). If you send me a cheque on London I get now a days par for it, but I suppose you mean that if Bell and Cockburn send you a cheque you can only get something well below par for it.

But anything that suits you will suit me. I hope you will be able to let me know soon how <u>The Arcadians</u> is going in New York and London.

With very best regards to Mrs Lane & yourself

Stephen Leacock

## To John Lane

[McGill University
Montreal]
Dec 12 1914

Dear Mr Lane

I am sorry to say that Bell & Cockburn have not yet paid me my royalties (July 1 1914) nor am I able to get any definite assurance of payment. As I believe you are aware, the firm are in great difficulties. Under these circumstances I am quite sure that you will understand my point of view when I say that I should not wish to have any royalties paid by you through an order on them. This might merely lessen my chance of getting from them what they owe me, which of course will soon include their royalties on my new book.

I am getting most glowing reviews of the Arcadians from all over the States, longer & better than I ever had before

I saw in the papers that your boat was delayed in starting but I hope that in spite of the delay & the gales you are safe at home again

Best regards to Mrs Lane

Very sincerely
Stephen Leacock

## To William C. Bell

[McGill University
Montreal
December 17, 1914]

Dear Mr Bell

I should very much like to see you if you are to be in Montreal soon.

As to the Clarendon press what per cent of royalty would they pay?

(a) on Sunshine Sketches, Behind the Beyond & Arcadian Adventures

(b) if they offer to take over my two ~~new~~ other books (Literary Lapses & Nonsense Novels) next July.

The Arcadians at 20% sounds all right but as to the first two one must in all fairness have regard to the fact that Clarendon Press would be taking these books over as established books without running any of the usual publishers risks.

I dont want to drive a bargain but merely to do what is reasonable all round and I expect to be very largely guided by what you personally say—

But if for example the agent of Doran or any other person presently says, "why if we had known those agencies had fallen we'd have done better than 15%"—I should feel that the Clarendon had "put one over on me."

There is also this to be considered,—suppose I were offered a twenty per cent royalty on Sunshine Sketches and Behind the Beyond on condition that the firms were also given Literary Lapses and Nonsense Novels and the offer of ~~all the~~ whatever other books I may give to John Lane under the existing contract of the Arcadians which calls, I think, for four more ~~books at 20 per cent,~~ on the same terms as Lane has the English rights: these terms I think are 20 per cent with a rise to 25 per cent after so many thousand—

You will see that the matter is a rather important one & worth going in to. The future sales of Sunshine Sketches & Behind the Beyond in Canada will never be very large & I should think that the publishers would rather feel like giving me the higher per cent on those books for the sake of what might come after.

All of this I submit to your best consideration.

Very sincerely
Stephen Leacock

## *To William C. Bell*

[McGill University
Montreal]
Jan 1. 1915.

Dear Mr Bell

I have just sent to Jeff Jones the <u>MSS</u> (about 6,000 words, at a guess) of a little book that I'd like to see published, say, in the form of <u>Mr Sellyer</u> (the thing that Jeff Jones got out in the spring). It is a fanciful study,—in the form of an imaginary gathering,—of the art of Dickens. It is called at present,—

The Mind of the Master
Fiction & Reality in the Art of Charles Dickens

---

A Fireside Fantasy
By
Stephen Leacock

---

But I might alter that to suit it better in book form. Will you please write and ask Jeff Jones to send you a proof as soon as he can and then give him an idea as to how many you could sell. I should think that at 50 cents you could sell a thousand in Canada. Later on if we ever come to publish a set of my works this and other stuff would go into a volume called <u>Literary Studies</u>, or "<u>Essays and Literary Studies</u>

Will you please take this matter up as soon as you can

Very faithfully
Stephen Leacock

## *To William Peterson*

[McGill University
Montreal]
Jan. 18. 1915

Dear Mr Principal—
(Re Outside Examination in Political Economy)

In previous years we have had two papers set by an outside examiner (at $15$^{00}$ a paper, Civil Service rates,—and 50 cents per candidate for answers read). The cost, as a total, was about $55 to $60 per annum.

Dr Hemmeon & I would be reluctant to give up the system which is of great help to our work but would be willing to content ourselves with having the papers <u>set</u> by an outsider (cost $30). Personally I shall pay the rest of the fee (for outside correction) myself; and this gladly, as I know the University must economise this year.

Very truly
Stephen Leacock

## To E. V. Lucas[1]

McGill University
Feb 9 1915

Dear Mr Lucas—

Very many thanks for your letter: I hope that next time I am in London I may hunt you up on my own account (which, when it will be,—to use a Latin form of speech—I do not know)— — —I think that perhaps you are right about the greater freedom of satire allowed to writers on this side of the water from the editorial point of view—: not however from the point of view of the public; as far as they are concerned you (that is <u>one</u>) may get "away with it" or one may not. You can never tell whether they will say in a lazily amused fashion, "how very true", "how extremely entertaining", or whether all of a sudden there will descend on you a dense flock of clergymen, temperance workers, women-rights-women, municipal purity-people and all the whole batallion

* * *

May 11 1917[2]

Dear Mr Lucas.

The above thoughts form only one of many honest & honorable attempts to write to you & thank you for your correspondence & your kindness & the book you sent me on Cricket. Oddly enough the Hambledon Cricket stuff was more appropriate than you could guess. My mothers people (the Butlers) came from there and their house Bury Lodge (now owned by my cousin Captain Thomas Butler) overlooks the little hamlet. So that you may well imagine that rotten as I am as a correspondent I felt, when I received that book, a positive rush of ink to the head.

You are a person who somehow finds times to do five times more things,— and all well done,—than are given to ordinary man to perform. Possibly then you could find time to write two words of forgiveness for my (<u>apparent</u>) rudeness. If you did it might lead to a correspondence terminated only by death,—& even after that printed & sold like that of 'Goethe to Carlyle.

Very sincerely
Stephen Leacock

1  Edward Verral Lucas (1868–1938) was a British man of letters and editor of the correspondence of Charles and Mary Lamb. He wrote books on the painters John Constable
   and Johannes Vermeer. He belonged to the London literati, was a frequent contributor to
   *Punch*, and in 1924 became chairman of the Bethune Publishing Company.
2  This letter is a continuation of the letter of 9 February 1915, which Leacock had never
   completed. On 11 May 1917, he finished the letter by filling the remaining space.

## To Pelham Edgar[1]

[McGill University
Montreal]
Feb 12    1915

Dear Pelham

It turns out that the Daughters of the Empire cannot arrange my meeting—too much else on: would it be possible for you to do what you said. I repeat that of course I pay all my own expenses. It may be that the Anglo French Society would have no use for that kind of entertainment (Reading from My Works). In that case I take no offence. It's only the money I want not the fun of talking. Let me know: my present dates are: ———

| St John | Feb 15 |
| Halifax | — 16 |
| Quebec | March 1 |
| Montreal | "    15 |

I could come to Toronto at any time after March 15 but not later than the end of March: my pass given by the CPR runs out April 1

Very sincerely
T.K.O.
Stephen Leacock

1   Pelham Edgar (1871–1948) was educated at Upper Canada College. He received his BA (1892) from the University of Toronto and his PhD (1897) from Johns Hopkins University. He began his teaching career as a modern-language master at UCC (1892–5), and he was later appointed to the staff of the Department of French at Victoria College, Toronto, in 1897, later transferring to the Department of English, where he served as department head for twenty-eight years.

## To Charles Leacock

McGill University
Feb 21 1915

Dear Charlie—

Would you care to think of going partners with Billy on a small farm, say 50 acres.  If so I can get you the purchase money, I believe, from the Trust at interest. The plan would be, thus—

You borrow the money & buy the farm.

You & Billy as partners rent it from you, at the same rate that you pay for it as interest.

You & ~~Billly~~ Billy put in $500 each to buy stock, horse, machines, etc etc

You both live on it and off it

You could arrange that either one of you could take other work for one month, two months, six months at a time, working out some financial arrangement as to how this can be done.

The cost of the farm would be about $2000—you could get say $1500 from the Trust & pay $90 interest (6 per cent) to the Trust; you would have a $500 mortgage on the farm (at 6 per cent) which would mean a payment of $30 a year: total interest charge on your purchase $120. The rent therefore at which you would let it to yourself & Billy would be $120<u>00</u>

You have now in cash, have you not, about $400 & I owe you $112<u>00</u>

Billy has also cash.

Now is the time to buy. .

I have written to a string of agents & will forward you a long list of farms in a few days. Let me know what you & Billy think of this (general) plan.

y.a.b.
Stephen Leacock

## To John Lane

[McGill University
Montreal]
Feb 25. 1915

Dear Mr Lane

Kindly note enclosed from Miss Greene & my answer, which please forward if satisfactory.

I was sorry to hear you speak so gloomily of the outlook in your last letter especially as I know what a lot it takes to dash your spirits. But one cant help feeling depressed just now

Mr Bell is here and tells me, to my great surprise, that prospects in the Canadian book trade are reviving rapidly and that sales this year are far better than at the opening of last year.

With best regards to Mrs Lane

Very sincerely
Stephen Leacock

## To Basil W. Willett

[McGill University
Montreal]
Apr 7 1915

Dear Mr Willett

Have you not in the office a <u>MSS</u> by my colleague here Professor Cyrus ~~McM~~ Macmillan? It is a set of Canadian legends & folklore stories. <u>I have not seen</u> it but should expect it to be good.

Macmillan is getting anxious over the long delay in getting an opinion as to your publishing it. I should be awfully glad if you would look into the matter. Best regards

> Very truly
> Stephen Leacock

*To John Lane*                                        McGill University
                                                       Montreal
                                                       April 21 1915

Dear Mr Lane

I send you under separate cover the MSS of a volume of verse by Mrs William Redpath (Beatrice Redpath) which I am most anxious to get you to publish.[1] The writer is a young and charming Montreal lady who is just marking her début in literature. I think her work is exquisite, the best stuff in its line that I have seen for a long while and I am most eager to get you to take her up. Nobody else could give her work the kind of introduction to the literary world of London & New York that you can.

I have already sent Mrs Redpath's poetry to Jeff Jones & to Mr Bell.

I know that this is a wretched time to approach a publisher with new material but I feel that Mrs Redpath has a future in front of her & I want to see her numbered in your flock.

She has as yet not put a book title on the Verses: that can be easily done
                                  Chapter II

I send you also two things of my own for sale in England. One is an article on the works of O Henry and though I say it myself its a pretty good article.

The other is a short piece called In the Good Time after the War*. Neither of these things has been offered for sale on this side, being written on the English market.

> Very sincerely
> Stephen Leacock

*P.S. I have been giving Public Readings from my works in Montreal, Toronto and a lot of other places—big success—and I read this after the war as a concluding piece: it goes like hot cakes. But of course it's only suited for English publication. At Toronto I had the biggest theatre in the place full to the roof. I forgot to say that I am doing this for the Belgian relief fund & pay my own expenses

P.S. Since writing this have just received your letter with royalty statement: am awfully pleased at such a good showing —

1    Beatrice Redpath, *Drawn Shutters* (London: John Lane, 1916).

## To John Lane

McGill University
May 13 1915

Dear Mr Lane

Re <u>Dr Macmillans MSS</u>. I thought the best thing to do was to show Dr Macmillan exactly what you said. I strongly advised him to leave the MSS with you till 1916 without your pledging yourself in any way to publish it. ~~but~~ I told him that even if he could find anyone willing to publish it sooner it would be decidedly against his own interest. He will write to you. I was much impressed with what your own reader said about the book. It sounded like the words of a person who knew what he was talking about.

Perhaps I had better repeat that I have not seen a word of the MSS though I should imagine that the work is good: it rests, I know, upon a very solid foundation of preparation of the subject. I am afraid though that I must say that Macmillans name is not well enough known to sell books on. I told him quite frankly that I should have to tell you this.

Dont forget also <u>Mrs Redpaths Verses</u>. That is a very different thing. I have read them myself and am certain of their quality. I may perhaps mention that the Redpath family are among the pillars of Montreal. They gave us at McGill our beautiful building, the Redpath Library. Mrs Redpath's husband is a junior member of the tribe & is not well off but the name is good & needs no introduction in Canada. I have other things to write of too but will put them in a separate letter. We are all in a wild passion of indignation over the Lusitania. Recruits are springing out of the ground.

Very sincerely
Stephen Leacock

## To John Lane

Orillia <u>Ont</u>
<u>June 5. 1915.</u>

Dear Mr Lane

I have just received your letter of May 20 to say that you will publish Mrs Redpath's poetry. I think your offer to give her ten per cent after the first thousand is first rate & in view of the present state of trade & of the fact that Mrs Redpath is only beginning is quite all that one could expect. I am sure she will accept & I have written to her. Her address is <u>43 St Luke St, Montreal</u>. In regard to the Canadian edition I would like to suggest (but only to suggest as I have no right to do more) that Mrs Redpath ought to have her <u>ten per cent</u> on the <u>Canadian sales</u> from the start. Her family is so well known & she has various friends of whom I am one who will use all their efforts to get her book sold. I can do a great deal personally with Toronto Montreal & other papers & would do it perhaps with keener interest if I thought that Mrs Redpath was going to

get a little money out of it from the start. When you meet her on your next visit
you will recognise her singular charm & talent at once. I have been so anxious
to get you to take her up because I know (from personal experience) what wide
influence you can exercise in literary circles in an author's favour.

So many thanks for your kindness about the articles I sent. I enclose an
advertising circular that may interest you. My best regards to Mrs Lane. My wife
and I are looking forward to your next visit

> Very sincerely
> Stephen Leacock

## To W.D. Lighthall[1]

[The Old Brewery Bay
Orillia, Canada]
Je 16 1915

W.D. Lighthall Esqre
Montreal

My dear Lighthall

On behalf of the Committee in charge of the unveiling of the Monument
at Orillia to Champlain (July 1), I am requested to invite you here to read a
poem, or proem, to be composed by you and read as a prelude or preliminary
to the little pageant of the landing of Champlain which forms part of the
proceedings of the day.

I presume that such a prelude would speak of the great work of Champlain,
—but you know more about that than I do. The reading would be supposed to
occupy only four or five minutes

I need hardly say that of course you come as our guest and at our expense.

The invitation is apparently very late because the idea of this prelude in verse
was only suggested yesterday. It was one of the first things proposed by Mr
Mitchell the director of the pageant when he arrived here yesterday.

Will you please <u>telegraph</u> an answer to <u>Mrs Frank Evans</u>, <u>Orillia</u>, and write
to her for any further details you may need.

The affair here is to be on a big scale with great publicity & I am sure you
will be glad to be associated with it

> Very sincerely
> Stephen Leacock

---

1   William Douw Lighthall (1857–1954) was a lawyer and author, holding a range of
government posts in Quebec. Elected to the Royal Society of Canada in 1902, he became
president in 1918–19. He was a novelist, a poet, and an anthologist; his anthology *Songs of
the Great Dominion* (1889) was only the second major anthology of Canadian poetry.

## To W.D. Lighthall

[The Old Brewery Bay
Orillia, Ontario]
Je 20. 1925[1]

My dear Lighthall.

We are all so sorry that you cant take part in the Champlain business. As to Huron relics I am asking my friend Mr Harold Hale, editor of the <u>Orillia Packet</u>, to write you on the matter. I have an idea that there are things to be picked up round Penetang & perhaps here. The Huron mission was on the <u>Wye</u>, was it <u>not</u>? about 30 miles north west of here.

With renewed regrets
Stephen Leacock

1   This letter was written in 1915; Leacock's date is an error.

## To John Lane

Orillia. Ontario. July 10. 1915.

Dear Mr Lane

(Yours of the 25th of June)—I shall be delighted to assist in any way in my power with the Belgian book.

I quite see your point of view as to Mrs Redpath's poems and, on reflection, think the arrangement suggested by you is, in view of the general position of the trade, a most fair one.

As to my new book    { (MOONBEAMS FROM THE LARGER LUNACY }

I have 40,000 words ready (about 20 sketches or more. I have suggested to Jeff Jones that I send him the <u>MSS</u> and that he sends you the stuff in galley proofs. This would be simpler, would it not, than any other way.

I am so glad to hear of Mrs Lane's new book: we all need it and my wife especially, who is a great admirer of Mrs Lane's work, is looking forward to it.

I do hope you are coming to Montreal this October

Delighted to hear good news of Travers[1]: I am writing to him

Very sincerely
Stephen Leacock

<u>P.S.</u> I have on request bought & send about 25 copies of my books to soldiers hospitals: am asked to send some more. Would you be willing to supply them at your cost price instead of the trade price & to forward them as coming from you

1   Ben Travers (1886–1980) was a distinguished British playwright and novelist.

& me jointly. In especial I had a request from the Canadian hospital at Cliveden. We might send 2 copies of each book there. The other address (a general distribution for hospitals man) I've not got at hand but will send on to you if you care to join in the idea

S.L.

## To John Lane

July 20 1915<br>Orillia. Ontario.

Dear Mr Lane

(Yours of July 2)—I must apologize for not having kept you better informed of my plans for an autumn book. I have been in correspondence about it with Jeff Jones for some time and was under the impression that I had written you all about it

With your approval I mean to get out a volume to contain all the different sketches that I have sold to magazines in the last 2 years & that have not yet appeared in book form. They run from 1000 to 3500 words in length and I have enough to make 40,000 words in all. I am proposing to call the book,—

MOONBEAMS

FROM THE

LARGER LUNACY

Even if I had a more sustained and organic book ready I should hesitate to put it on the present rotten market. Jeff Jones thinks that my short stuff (suitable for reading out loud) always finds a good reception and he is most hopeful of the book. Mr Bell has already been booking advance orders and tells me that the trade takes to the title very well. I have suggested to Jones that I send him all the MS and that he sends it to England in corrected galley proof. This will save time & trouble will it not.

I hope that all this will meet your approval.

I also want to bring out as soon as the market is suitable a book called —

ESSAYS

AND

LITERARY STUDIES

It consists of magazine articles on literary topics (not political) & I am sure it will do well enough. This, of course would not count as one of the books covered by our existing contract unless you wished it so, which I presume would not be the case as the contract refers to "works of fiction". I also want to do when I can a volume to be called

THE AMERICAN HUMORISTS

This would include studies of Nathaniel Hawthorne, Benjamin Franklin, James Russell Lowell, Oliver Wendel Holmes, Bret Harte, Mark Twain & some lesser people in groups. It will take me two years to do it.

———————

Also:—

I am doing for the American magazine a new series of burlesque stories the first of which is done & accepted. The editor has no objection to my selling the same stuff in England provided it does not appear prior to its use in the American. I will therefore send you the MS of story no. 1. (The introduction & title of the series have to be different for England from what I use for the States)

———

~~Next~~ If you succeed in disposing of it will you please tell the people who take it that they may <u>cable to me at my expense</u> and I will send ~~No.2~~ <u>Story No 2</u> which would otherwise not get to them in time for use a month after the first. The words Number Two and the name of the magazine will be understood by me as meaning that I am to forward the second story.

If you can't sell them there is no great harm as I ~~am~~ have already sold them to the American.

Next,—as to Mrs Redpath's poetry.

She writes me that she wishes to call her volume <u>Drawn Shutters</u>. & she has just prepared a poem under that name which indicates as it were the keynote of the book,———such thoughts and feelings as come to one's mind when the house is closed against the outside world and the noises from the street come only muffled and indistinct to one's ear. I like the title very much & think it will accord with the vein of melancholy which runs through the ~~work~~ book & which is very characteristic of Mrs Redpath's literary work. I think that this melancholy, ~~sinking~~ deepening at times into morbidity will give to the book something very distinctive and help to make the public take hold of it. I have asked Sir William Peterson (head of McGill & temporary editor of the University Magazine) if I may do for the magazine an article on Mrs Redpath's book. I will also use all the influence I can with the Canadian & New York press.

———

Macphails address which I forgot to give you is Field Ambulance No. 6. Canadian Expeditionary Force. I heard from him last at Shorncliffe. The war looks gloomy enough just now but I am hoping that we shall soon have better news.

So sorry to hear that Miss Fish is indisposed.

with best regards
Stephen Leacock

*To Agnes Leacock*                    165 Cote des Neiges Road
                                      Montreal
                                      Aug 19. 5³⁰ P.M.
                                      1915

My dear Mother

Young Stephen was born at a quarter to three this afternoon. He is a fine big boy, in fact a regular corker, and weighs eight and a quarter pounds. Beatrix had made an error about the date of his birth, but thank Heaven, we left Orillia in time or the journey might have been too much for her. He had a close run for his life as he had decided to throw himself into the world wrong end first. We had the three best men in Montreal and four nurses. Peters told me that without those <u>seven</u> people working at it, there would have been no chance. Beatrix was taken ill at 6 this morning and I drove her over to the maternity hospital. She had a bad time but it is over now & she is resting & doing fine. The baby looks ~~very~~ just like Barbara and little Stephen and me and all the rest. Beatrix was awfully well right up to the end except that she had a bad fall two days ago. But Peters says that the baby is not a premature baby being if anything over developed. Beatrix will have to stay where she is for some time, I dont know how long, two weeks I should think. How soon can you come down? We must take up the arrangements for the christening right away. I want my friend Mr Symonds the rector of the cathedral to do it.

I need hardly say that ~~the~~ your journey down here is of course to be at my expense. If you haven't the ready money wire or write me & I'll send it:

I sent a wire to George today. Will you please tell Charlie and the rest. Teddy is probably still with you . . . I gave the telegraph company one dollar to take the message from Sutton to the Grange: so dont let them charge you for it . . . I could only stay with Beatrix for a little while this afternoon as they wanted her to sleep but I am going over after dinner and we'll see the baby together. I never yet saw a baby that looked so complete, so all-there, so little like a red monkey as Stephen does: indeed he seems to me a most remarkable child. Please ~~right~~ write and tell Carrie that her present hit it just right because it arrived at the very hour that he was born. I'd write to her myself but I have no address. Beatrix wont be able to write for some days. Be sure to let me know right away just how soon you can come, and come as soon as you can.

Your loving son
(Old) Stephen Leacock

P.S. Tomorrow I am going to make my will and appoint trustees, guardians and a staff of godfathers, godmothers, proxies and assistants. We have decided that from the boy's birth there shall be no extravagance over him. We got from Eatons a plain basket for him to sleep in,—there I guess this is as much as is fair to inflict in one dose.

# CHAPTER 4

## STEPHEN LEACOCK
# HUMORIST

## 1915–1920

Intensely patriotic, Stephen Leacock felt enraged as the War continued. He was in constant correspondence with friends and former students overseas, and he became a frequent lecturer for the Belgian Relief Fund. During this time his humorous writings became a weapon he wielded freely against those he felt were responsible for allowing the brutal war to continue.

The opening section of *Further Foolishness: Sketches and Satires of the Day* (1916), appropriately titled 'Peace, War and Politics', contains five stories that touch on many of the issues of the day. While all five stories have laughter as their goal, they also present Leacock's barely concealed attitudes about the Great War and its actors. Leacock's fury with Germany, for instance, is made clear in 'Germany From Within Out', and in 'The White House from Without In'— through extracts from the diary of a president of the Unites States —Leacock draws a not unrecognizable portrait of Woodrow Wilson, who says prayers every morning, retreats to his pigeonhouse at the sound of trouble, and cannot explain why he fails to treat Germany in the same manner as Mexico. The final story of 'Peace, War and Politics' carries Leacock's scathing denunciation of the United States for its inactivity during the war.

The closing essay of the collection, 'Humor, As I See It', turns to the nature of comedy. Arguing that 'the very essence of good humour is that it must be without harm and without malice,' Leacock baits one of his English critics who had disparagingly asked, 'What is there, after all, in Professor Leacock's humour but a rather ingenious mixture of hyperbole and myosis?' After disingenuously agreeing with this sentiment, Leacock outlines a series of poor jokes and anecdotes that fail in spite of being malicious, and he concludes with a resounding defence of comedy that is, for the creator, 'hard, meritorious and dignified'. Then, summoning the two authors—Mark Twain and Charles Dickens—who stand behind his own writing, Leacock concludes: 'Mark Twain's *Huckleberry Finn* is a greater work than Kant's *Critique of Pure Reason*, and Charles Dickens' creation of

Mr. Pickwick did more for the elevation of the human race—I say it in all seriousness—that Cardinal Newman's *Lead, Kindly Light, Amid the Encircling Gloom.* Newman only cried out for light in the gloom of a sad world. Dickens gave it.'

In the same year Leacock published *Essays and Literary Studies,* a collection of eight previously published and more serious pieces. Although humour plays a central role in these essays—they are good-natured and affectionate—they resemble 'Humor As I See It' in tending towards serious discussions of literature and new interpretations of history, foreshadowing future directions in his writing. He also brought out a pamphlet, 'National Organisation for War', which had a first printing of 2,000 copies; it was later re-published for the government with a circulation of a quarter of a million copies.

Throughout 1917 Leacock had been publishing short humorous pieces, which were gathered together under the title *Frenzied Fiction.* But amid all these works of Leacockian nonsense is the half-serious 'Father Knickerbocker: A Fantasy', which shows again that during this time, Leacock's mind was never far from the ongoing global conflict. Leacock's 'fantasy' revolves around the United States committing itself to the reality of the war: 'And I knew that a great nation had cast aside the bonds of sloth and luxury, and was girding itself to join in the fight for the free democracy of all mankind.'

The year that brought an end to the Great War produced no new book from Leacock, though the events of the war continued to occupy his thoughts and inspire his writing. In 1919 he produced *The Hohenzollerns in America,* which features a series of pieces that lambaste the deposed German emperor and his entourage. Included among these is an especially amusing story of a club's efforts to raise money for Belgian Relief; when the first fundraising events have taken place, the 'treasurer was compelled to announce to the Committee a new deficit of two hundred dollars. Some of the ladies of the Committee moved that the entire deficit be sent to the Belgians, but were overruled by the interference of the men.'

In 1919 Leacock accepted an assignment form the *New York Times* to write a six-part series on social justice. Slightly expanded, these were brought together in 1920 as *The Unsolved Riddle of Social Justice,* exploring the ramifications in society of social justice. Still undoubtedly conservative, Leacock argued for a more liberal approach to social problems, advocating social security, minimum wage laws, and a legislated reduction in working hours. In the same year, Leacock published *Winsome Winnie and Other New Nonsense Novels,* a second collection of burlesque novels. His ability to swing from the serious issue of social policy to parodies of fiction demonstrated yet again his versatility not just in writing but in thought.

Throughout this period Leacock continued his demanding schedule as a professor and chair, while remaining unstinting in his dedication to the university. In 1919, for example, he helped to found *The McGill News,* the publication of the Graduates' Society, and became the first chairman of its editorial board; over the next twenty-five years he would support the periodical by contributing original pieces to it. While such contributions were greatly valued at McGill, Leacock began to garner recognition from other institutions as well, receiving honorary degrees from Queen's University in 1919 and from Brown University, Dartmouth College, and the University of Toronto the following year.

In contrast to his busy life as a writer and academic, Leacock's personal life at this time was peaceful and calm, devoted largely to spending time with his new son. Both parents delighted in the hours they spent with young Stephen, though it was during this time that the boy's lack of physical development first caught the Leacocks' attention. That they had no further children perhaps reflects their preoccupation with the unfortunate health of their only child.

## To John Lane                                     August 21 1915

Dear Mr Lane—

(Yours of Aug 5 & Mr Willets of the 6th)—

Please tell Mrs Lane that we've been reading "Maria Again" out loud with great joy. My dictum on the book is that everyone who reads "Maria Again" will want to read "Maria" again and then probably Maria again again.

———————————

Mrs Redpath's poetry. I have sent Jeff Jones two pages of personal material about Mrs Redpath & her family. Her father who was Chief Engineer of the C.P.R. was one of the best known men in Canada. He built the great bridge across the St Lawrence at Lachine. I will get from her today a photograph to send to Jeff Jones & if she can give me two I will send one to you as well. She is, as I mentioned, extremely beautiful and I suppose that even in literature that helps (no doubt I owe a great deal to my own face in the success I have had). But Mrs Redpath is in an even higher class than mine . . . I am arranging with Sir William Peterson that the University Magazine will help along her book, and I hope to get very substantial help from Maclean's Magazine and (Toronto). I happen to be doing some work for them. They have lots of money, a circulation of 45,000 and pay me a higher rate than or as high as the London magazines. The Editor Mr Costain is a very nice fellow & good to do business with. I am sure that I can get him to help boost Mrs Redpath. I can also do much with Saturday Night and of course the Montreal & Toronto daily papers are easy. I am so sorry that you will not be here this autumn. It's a great disappointment to all your friends here and quite apart from that it would have been a great help to my new book & to Mrs Redpath's to have you look over the ground & make suggestions. But Mr Bell tells me that you have so much to do just now that you can hardly get across.

Re My book (for early in 1916—ESSAYS AND LITERARY STUDIES: practically all the material in this has been published in magazines already. For instance the famous or infamous article on American Humour that was in the 19th Century: only it will be revised so that the offending sentences at the end of it about the future of American humour will come out. So I fear there is nothing in this that we can use till it comes in Book form. But the material for the book

### THE AMERICAN HUMORISTS

none of which is yet written might prove usable in magazines. I wonder if Mr Prothero of the Quarterly would stand for some of it. I once did him an article on Reciprocity but it was written in the rush & hurry of Election work and I doubt whether he thought much of it.[1] If you know him & get an opportunity within the next few months would you mention that I am working on a set of literary papers to be called The American Humorists & am wondering what Editor would be interested in having a look at them. They would be serious literary studies but done in an easy vein and would include Hawthorne, Benjamin Franklin, James Russell Lowell, Oliver Wendell Holmes Bret Harte & Mark Twain. (Do you know, I am sure that a book of this sort if well done ought to have a good sale in the United States. People do love the Idea of American Humour. It's like French politeness, & British courage and Scotch whiskey.

But bless me, I am writing away & leaving the largest item of news out.

You will be glad to hear that my wife and I have a little son,—nor so very little either as there are eight and a quarter pounds of him. He was born on August 19, 1915. His name is Stephen Leacock. He is,—I say it of course without prejudice,—in every respect a remarkable boy, and in point of personal appearance he is so like me that over at the Maternity Hospital, where he is living, they can hardly tell us apart.

> Very sincerely
> Stephen Leacock.

P.S. You've done so much to give me publicity I wish you would shed a little on my son. Please put him in the Bodleian. Perhaps it would save time just to cut out the set sentences that I will mark above & transfer them to the Bodleian.

1   'Reciprocity between Canada and the United States', *Quarterly Review* (London) 214, no. 427 (April 1911): 491–508.

## To John Lane

[University Club of Montreal]
Sep 15 1915

Dear Mr Lane

I want to introduce to you through this letter an old college classmate of mine Mr Frederick Armstrong.

He is going over to London next week as the General Manager of the Export Association of Canada, a new and powerful association just formed by our manufacturers.

It would be of decided service to Mr Armstrong if you could give him a card of introduction to one or two of the men on the financial staff of the <u>Times</u>, <u>The Morning Post</u> or any London papers likely to be interested in his work.

They would probably also be interested (especially if on the Tariff Reform side) in meeting Armstrong & hearing what he can tell them of the trade outlook. He has travelled widely and seen a great deal of British overseas trade,—in Russia, S. America & S. Africa. It was on this account that the manufacturers here invited him to take up this work.

I am asking Mr Armstrong to post you this letter in London & to follow it up by a call at the Bodley Head

> best regards
> Stephen Leacock

### To John Lane

McGill University
Sep 22 1915

Dear Mr Lane

Very many thanks for your check for £40-5-6 for which I enclose a receipt, and still more for your extremely generous interpretation of my share, which is more than my due. My wife wants me to express her thanks & mine for your congratulations about our son. He is getting on famously . . . .

We have started in the <u>University Magazine</u> a review of current books (chiefly for books dealing with Canada, with imperial politics & serious, literary, artistic or biographical subjects). We only mean to deal with a limited number & expect to be able to help very greatly the Canadian sale of any book we take up. I would therefore be obliged if you would always let me know just which of the Bodley Head books would best fall into the line of what we want. There is <u>no need to send the books</u> as I think the Oxford Press or Jeff Jones will see to that. Sir William Peterson wrote to both of them.

> Very sincerely
> Stephen Leacock

P.S.
Mrs Redpath has not had her proofs yet. I hope her book is under weigh allright.

### To John Lane

McGill University
Montreal
Oct 12 1915.

Dear Mr Lane

I was most pleased to receive the royalty statement and to see that we are holding our own so well in spite of the depression. I think that we have reason to congratulate ourselves on such a good showing. I must say I begin to fear that the outlook for business for the coming year looks pretty gloomy but in the face of such great national hardship as is being felt and the sacrifices that are being made, any man ought to feel that one is lucky to keep on one's feet at all.

There was an error in the statement, easily verified. The percentage in England on the <u>Arcadians</u> should be 20% not 15%. If Jeff. Jones is to settle with me will you please send him a memorandum on this point.

I was more than delighted with the Bodleian's notice of my son. I am keeping it for him to read later on.

I have not yet seen the new wrapper for <u>Literary Lapses</u> & <u>Nonsense Novels</u>. Jeff. Jones, I suppose didn't send me samples as he probably thought that Gundy or Bell would send them.

I have just been reading Mrs Redpath's proofs. The poems seem to me exquisite. I can give them a good lift in the University Magazine and I hope to arrange to get Mrs Redpath's picture and a special notice of her work in Toronto <u>Saturday Night</u> and in <u>Macleans Magazine</u>. The latter has a circulation of forty thousand. I hope Mrs Redpaths book will be out soon as it ought to do well if it catches the Canadian Xmas market. By the way Mrs Redpaths cousin, a Mrs Allan, who is an artist and an illustrator designed and sent to you a wrapper for the book. I did not see it? Is it suitable and will you be able to use it.?

> Very sincerely
> Stephen Leacock

## To John Lane

<u>McGill</u>
Montreal
Jan 24 1916

Dear Mr Lane

First of all, best New Years wishes to you & Mrs Lane, and my very best thanks for the books: it was awfully kind of you to remember us.

I send back the contract unsigned. In fact I had already written Jeff Jones that 15 per cent is enough, and, equally of course, I shouldn't expect any advance royalty. As soon as Jones explained the matter to me I saw it at once. I am delighted to think that you may be out here at some time this year. But you must come here when the University is in session and when all the people are in town. July & August are almost dead months in Canada as everybody goes to the summer resorts. There are ever so many people here who will want to meet you and I shall want to make my arrangements well ahead. My friend Dean Moyse, the head of the Arts Faculty,—the Devonshire man who met you at dinner the last time,—very often talks of you and "all your works"

I am thinking hard and deep for my autumn book: I ought to have the manuscript in your hands by October 1st, ought I not?

I fear the war outlook is pretty bad,—at least as we see it here: one sees no end.Yet people in England appear to be settling down to it with that wonderful matter-of-fact determination which is the best thing in English character.

> with best regards, and to Mrs Lane,
> Very sincerely
> Stephen Leacock

P.S. Make the Essays contract any way you like. I know that I am always safe in your hands.

P.P.S. Congratulations on the Gainsborough article: it is awfully interesting.

## To Pelham Edgar

165 Cote des Neiges Rd
Montreal
[February 9, 1916]

Dear old Pelham

I am awfully sorry to hear that you've been laid up: hope you are getting on better

I will note the house number & will try to come & occupy that room: I dont know any room I would sooner sleep in. I expect to be in Toronto on Sunday the 20th (passing from Woodstock Ont to New York but I fear it will be only between trains & perhaps not even that as I may only go as far as Hamilton & catch the train there. I am to do a week Feb. 14–20 in East Ontario & Berlin & Woodstock, reading for the Belgian Fund & I have to be in New York for a thing on Monday Evening the 21st I would really hate to reappear in Toronto though it's kind of you to think of it. I get more & more adverse to doing things in public: and in any case I have already Pittsburg, Baltimore & Wellesley (Massachusetts) on my hands & an orgy at Buffalo that I look forward to with dread (—to be paid as an 'entertainer', God help them,—) and altogether, my dear Perfess, I have trouble enough—I am sorry to say,—in the interests of Christian feeling, that I was delighted to read what you said of N———x. My own view exactly.Yet his brother here is one of the decentest men I ever knew.

Funny damn thing here the other night:—a banquet was arranged for Brymner[1] the artist: in congratulation of his C.M.G. Mr Baker of the C.P.R. very kindly placed the C.P.R. Rd station dining room at the disposal of the committee as he said they could do the thing cheaper than the a club. It was the first time the Railway dining room had ever been so used & hence all the staff from the Chef down were on the mettle. They wanted to show that when it came to banquets the C.P.R. could break all records. So they did. But of course

1    William Brymner (1855–1925) was a painter and teacher who, after studying in Paris, was appointed director of art classes at the Art Association of Montreal.

being a <u>station</u> <u>dining</u> <u>room</u>, accustomed to people catching trains, their one idea of efficiency was <u>high speed</u>. Time was everything. Oysters & soup flew through the air. Dish succeeded dish like lightning & the poor little banquet, never a very costly one or elaborate even as planned was over in thirty five minutes. Over its corpse, three or four speeches were made. But as it turned out that all of the speakers were men of few words, each relying on other people doing the talk, the whole banquet which began at 8³⁰ was over at a quarter to ten. The gay revellers were out on the street by ten oclock & the dining, cleaned up, swept, and closed tight within five minutes of their leaving. The whole thing is felt by the Railway to be a triumph of management. They think, with a little more practice, that they'll be able to run a banquet through in about twenty five minutes . . . . . . . . . There is no great news here. My boy is fine . . . I hope to show him to you,—or show you to him,—sometime this spring on the way to Orillia.

I suppose that you & Mrs Edgar feel as depressed and preoccupied over the war as we do here. I never felt it so much before, I mean the aspect of interminable length. There seems damn little light . . . . .

I am also getting old. Are you? I had expected to stay young for ever and always felt as if I had not <u>begun</u> yet and was still planning what I would do when I grew up. Now I find, almost suddenly, that it is nearly over.

I feel like the indignant nigger at the ballot box, who said,—"Is <u>that</u> all? boss, is <u>that</u> all you do?"—And so with life: one asks, "Is <u>that</u> all, boss?"

Best remembrances to you both. I'll try to see you going through Toronto one way or the other: But my mother has been ill & I want what spare time I get to make arrangements to move her down here.

TKO
Stephen Leacock

### To John Lane

Montreal March 27. 1916

Dear Mr Lane,

I must apologize for my delay in sending the enclosed & in answering your letter. I'm afraid I couldn't manage "<u>Canadian Chaps</u>: it's rather out of my line & in any case I have to get a book ready for you by Oct 1st, I have to deliver a <u>play</u> (of which later) by July 1st and I've a lot of public readings to give for the Belgian Fund & on my own account, my college work to do, and a paper to write for the Royal Society of Canada.

I am therefore what we call in temperance circles, "full".

Very sincerely & with best
regards to Mrs Lane
Stephen Leacock

## To John Lane

165 Cote des Neiges Road
Montreal
Apr 22 1916

Dear Mr Lane

Very many thanks for yours of the 6th and the statement. I see we have done far better than a year ago. Yes, certainly Jones & I will settle about the payment. As to the book of Essays I am quite sure that one & the same edition will do for England & the States: indeed I have forgotten just what the variations were. I had understood from Jeff. Jones that there would be two printings. It was no idea of mine. The American edition is out and is admirably made. I am so sorry that I was slow in answering yours of Feb 17th about the <u>Canadian Chaps</u> & sorry that I cant undertake it. But no doubt you have my answer by this time.

I hope to do a <u>novel</u> as my autumn book: that seems to me, on general principles, a wise thing to do

Best regards from my
wife & myself
Very sincerely
Stephen Leacock

## To Henry Sibley Johnson[1]

Prince George Hotel
Toronto
May 29 1916
("<    > Voyage" as we say
in <u>France</u>

My dear Johnson

If I were a natural liar & humbug I would answer your letter in a cool & restrained tone as if the idea of an LL.D. from Princeton were as natural to me as it would be Mr Roosevelt or the Prince of Wales or any of the truly great. But I will be very frank: the mere suggestion of it has thrown me into a dangerous condition of excitability, If, through your efforts, I am lucky enough to get it, I shall never forget it all my life: and, in any case, I thank you really & truly from my heart for the suggestion that you at least would like to see it conferred on me.

I'd be only too flattered to deliver one or two of the lectures as suggested: on that head, (fear nothing)—if I am invited, I will not disgrace you.

Lecturing to university audiences is my <u>forte</u>, just as wax figures were the forte of Artemus Ward. I have lectured to assembled Oxford, with a pulse as even as if I were sitting in a Saloon . . . . .

---

1   Henry Sibley Johnson (1852–1922), a graduate of Princeton University (AB, 1878), held various positions in banking and real estate in Cleveland, Ohio. He was president of the Western Association of the Princeton Club.

I was so sorry not to have seen you in Cleveland. As Kendall perhaps told you, I was only there from dinner time till the middle of the night.

But I hope we shall soon meet again somewhere before we meet never to part in the next world (I feel that we are going to the same place,—wherever it is—Kendall is hardly qualified, they'll want him higher up . . . . .

> best regards
> yours sincerely
> Stephen Leacock

## To John Lane

McGill [University]
[Montreal]
June 12 1916

Dear Mr Lane

Yours of June 1 just in: I am extremely sorry to hear of Mrs Lane's ill health. Please convey to her my sympathy & best wishes.

I note what you say about Mrs Allen's work: no doubt you are right: and certainly these are very bad times to take risks in.

I am, as I told you, working on a play for Mr Maude.

If it gets done & is all right I want to do another at once and write it as a novel at the same time, finishing the novel in time for autumn publication. I have already talked it over with Jeff. Jones. I suppose from your point of view, if I complete the MS by October 1st that is time enough. I shall look forward to seeing you here before then.

Best regards to Lieutenant Ben Travers, if & when you see him, and may God look after the boy & keep him safe for he is well worth it.

> best regards
> Stephen Leacock

I think I asked you the other day about the royalties from Mr Hawtrey. If paid to you keep them till the next statement

## To John Lane

Orillia
Ont.
June 27 16

Dear Mr Lane

Re <u>Germany Within</u> I've written Jeff. Jones & asked him to send the letter to you. I want to ~~tru~~ lengthen the book by including other things with it, all war studies. First, a <u>Diary of the President</u> which was published last month in Vanity Fair. N.Y & made a big hit with Mr Roosevelt: second, <u>The Peacemakers</u>

(revised, with Miss Addams named merely a <u>Lady Pacifist</u> etc etc third, a new piece, still to be written to be called <u>In Merry Mexico</u>. All this under an attractive title & with a gay jacket will sell like a hot bun.

Please let me know what you think—

Very sincerely
Stephen Leacock

## To John Lane                                  July 27 1916

Dear Mr Lane
Re <u>Germany Within</u>. I feel it would be better in the light of what you say, to give up the idea of this book. The pictures are excellent. The article was published this spring in Macleans Magazine Toronto. I asked Jeff. Jones if he could resell it in N.York, It was he, not I, who suggested making a book of it.

Could we revert to the idea of reselling for magazine use? As the thing was printed in Toronto we could accept a cheaper price. I am sending a copy of this to Jeff Jones who can perhaps sell the thing in N.Y also. But if not it doesn't matter.

I want to do a whole book for this autumn but so far none of it is written. It ought to be a novel. In a separate letter I write you re Cyril Maude to invoke your good offices

Very sincerely
Stephen Leacock

## To John Lane                                  July 27 1916

Dear Mr Lane
Could you possibly find time to see Cyril Maude re the Sunshine Sketches play?

The matter is thus. We sold dramatic rights to <u>Michael Morton</u>; the rights if not used to expire early in 1917.

Morton arranged with Mr Maude to write the play. Mr Maude paid Morton £100 down. The MS was completed in February 1915 and sent to Mr Maude who was at that time in America, in fact as it happened in Montreal. On receipt of the MS Mr Maude as per agreement sent Morton another $100. Morton had thus received $200 as advance royalty.

Mr Maude & I read the play in Montreal. It turned out to be, in my opinion, worthless. I arranged with Mr Maude that I would write another play in place of it, and ask no pay for it beyond what I was already to have received under the contract which sold the dramatic rights (2 per cent, less what I have to pay to you, namely at your suggestion 10 per cent of what I get)

I said to Mr Maude that I would complete Act I before he left America (May 1916) & come to N. York & read it to him, and would if Act I was satisfactory complete Acts II, III, & IV by July 1 & post to London.

All this I have done. When I read Act I to Mr Maude, he was delighted with it. On receiving the other acts he sends me the cables which I enclose. From them I gather that he wants to cut Acts III & IV all to bits and substitute stuff to be done, I presume, by Morton. This wont do. Mr Maude objects to my third act because his part in it is subordinated to the others. But as I wrote the play he, (Mr Maude as Jeff Thorpe) is only the stage for ~~3/4 2/3~~ 3/4 of Act I, practically all of Act II, 1/2 of Act III and the whole of Act IV. This is enough.

I imagine also though Mr Maude does not say so that Morton will not consent to ~~take or~~ let my play be substituted for his. But the offer that I made, giving him all the money he would get in any case even if he had written the whole thing, and coupling his name as joint author, seems to me generosity itself. His rights would expire early ~~The~~ in 1917 unless Mr Maude put on his (Morton's) play,—a thing out of the question. ~~The~~ But the question of Morton is complicated by the following fact.

At Mr Maude's suggestion, I wrote (in Montreal at the time of our reading Mortons play) a letter <u>to</u> Mr Maude & intended for him to show, or send, to Morton. This letter asks Morton to consent to a <u>complete revision</u> of the play. In conversation with Mr Maude it was well understood that I was to write a new play, all new.

Will you please see Mr Maude & try to get him <u>either</u> to present my play as it stands, or to give it back to us.

Pray believe me, my play is a glorious thing. We shall get a lot of money for it. But chopped up & defaced as the cables suggest it will be of no account & wont run.

I understand that Mr Maude (whose address is The Garrick Club London) may leave for New York early in August. Pray see him, if possible, without loss of time & will you kindly cable me to Orillia as to what can be done.

Very sincerely
Stephen Leacock

P.S. I am aware that I am asking a great deal in giving you all this trouble but I know no one who can manage these things as you can.

*To John Lane*                         McGill University
                                       Montreal
                                       Sep 24  (1916)

Dear Mr Lane

I fear the enclosed are late. Will you please see that no one loses the little picture of me taken in 1873, & the one of my mother. She is still alive (72 years old), & indeed is a good deal more alive than I am.

                              Very sincerely
                              Stephen Leacock

P.S.

Since writing to you I have got as the title for my new book
                    FURTHER FOOLISHNESS
have written Jeff Jones very fully.


*To Agnes Leacock*                     Thursday Sep 28 (1916)

Dear Mother

Very many thanks for the little book which I am putting in Stephen's library. He is crazy over books,—red ones especially—books, horses and dogs. He begins to understand a great deal now though beyond "dada" & now & again "nana", he says nothing. A man came with a street organ, so I hired him to come into the house and play to Stephen.

By the way an English illustrated paper is writing up a article on me & sent for photographs, so I sent one of Stephen and later, when I could hunt it up, one of you. I am afraid though that yours is will be late as the mail was slow & I was told they must have the copy by October 1st as it is for the November number (The Bookman, London.). But how fine for Hook to be in it. For you of course it is doubtful honour to be put in merely as the mother of your son.

We can easily arrange about your 'residence' at the point later on: I dont know whether my hopes of building will be realised: looks doubtful just now. If I do you could have the present cottage. If not a new one. I'll talk with Charlie about it when I see him. What is the minimum minimum of rooms for your house?

                              Y. affec son
                              Stephen

## To J.A.T. Lloyd

[McGill University
Montreal]
Oct 23/1916

My dear Lloyd—

I was very glad to get your note of Oct 9 (rec'd today) & to hear that you had safely got into the archives. Your sole business now, as I understand it, is to draw the clothes over your head & go to sleep. If you sleep hard enough, you will become in time Curator of the British Museum, in which case you are hardly expected to give any signs of life at all. From that,—provided not a sound is heard from you for ten years or so,—you will be moved up to be Keeper of Queens Mary's Records, or Librarian to the Royal Household. That is practically the same as death.

In other words you have started on a brilliant career as an Archivist and I congratulate you on it. You are, for an Archivist, hopelessly young & irresponsible; but they generally say in that department that a man who enters it must not be judged by his first twenty years service.

. . . . So you saw Douglas Christie! It is years since I've heard from him, directly. I understood that they wouldn't let him go to the front,—not in shape for it—.

. . Yes, Ive have a son (14 months old),—Stephen Lushington Leacock,—a wonderful boy. His picture (if it reached England in time) is to be in the November <u>Bookman</u>

—I saw Peacock here the other day,—now a leading financier: Holmes I see from time to time in Toronto,—unchanged. Jackson vidi tantum or words to that effect.

Best regards, & remembrances
Stephen Leacock, (père)

## To John Lane

McGill University
<u>Nov 30. 1916.</u>

Dear Mr Lane

I was delighted to get the royalty statement with so good a showing. Jefferson Jones & I can arrange the terms of payment.

In the American edition of my new book the matter is arranged as on the enclosed schedule. This gives it unity. I shall be sorry indeed if the copy for this did not reach you. I thought Jones was sending it. If not, it is my fault. In any case by the time you get this it will be too late to alter anything.

I am sorry that your eyes have been troubling you again. Are you careful about the light you sit in: I find by experience that facing a window or a light is bad. In your office, as I remember it (and as I let me hope to see it again soon,) the window light is in your face as you sit.

I am afraid that the cost of paper will be only one of the difficulties that are approaching as I fear that after the war, or even before that, conditions for business will be desperately bad in England. You are fortunate in having such a man as Jefferson Jones at the American end.

With best regards from us both to yourself & Mrs Lane—

Very sincerely
Stephen Leacock


## To John Lane

McGill Univ'y
Dec. 24 1916

Dear Mr Lane.

The compliments of the Season & a Merry Xmas——Mrs Lane's <u>Maria</u>[1] has just come in: looks very tempting: shall read it tonight & write my thanks to her.

The delay in <u>Further Foolishness</u> was my fault altogether. We shall now have time to arrange the material in appropriate sections as in the American edition.

Miss Fish's drawing is simply delightful. What a wonderfully high standard she keeps up (I see her pictures in the illustrated papers each week)

I am printing at my own expense for free distribution 2000 copies of a pamphlet <u>National Organisation for War</u>. I want to ask you if you can get it copied in English papers (no pay to me, of course). I also want to get Lord Northcliffe to take it up. I hear he reads my books: that will do as an introduction. Do you know him—or can you, through friends, get my pamphlet before him.

Very sincerely
Stephen Leacock

1    Anna Lane, *War Phrases According to Maria*, illustrated by A.H. Fish (London, New York: John Lane, 1917).


## To John Lane

McGill
Feb 22 (1917)

Dear Mr Lane

I reënclose the account for clearness sake. "Jeff" was name given by Michael Morton to the Sunshine Sketches play. You have the contract on your records. They were to pay 2 per cent: advance royalty of £50, less Hughes Massies commission. You were good enough to split with me taking only 10 per cent of what they paid as the matter had been done by me and not through you.

The enclosed account is incomplete. The play ran for a week in <u>Montreal</u> after the date indicated here.

This play you will remember was the one written by <u>Morton</u>, not by me. My own was not acted. I failed to make an arrangement with Mr Maude. I ~~am~~ have written to <u>Jeff Jones</u> re printing my play this spring: ~~he will~~ I am asking him to forward you the letter.

As I read our contract made by you with Michael Morton I have the right to <u>print</u> the play. But please read ~~it or~~ the contract for yourself before we do so.

Also, what about taking steps to get from Morton the right to <u>act</u> my play, in case any manager wants it. Will you please see what his attitude is & what can be done.

As I wrote the <u>whole</u> of my play, as as it is not a mere case of selling the rights of the book, will you be content with 10 per cent of the gross receipts from the stage if we succeed in getting it played, it being understood that whatever sum we pay Morton for the release is to be paid out of our royalties before either of us get anything, that is, 90% of it would fall on me and 10% on you.

Is this fair. I really think that my play is fine & ought to bring in a lot of money if we can get it free and get rid of Mortons claim whatever it is.

Very sincerely
Stephen Leacock

## To F. Scott Fitzgerald[1]

McGill Univ
Mar 16    17

Dear Mr Fitzgerald[2]

Your stories are fine. As Daniel Webster said, or didn't say, to the citizens of Rochester, "Go on."[3]

1   F. Scott Fitzgerald (1896–1940) was born in St Paul, Minnesota, and educated at Princeton University from 1913 to 1917. After leaving the university without finishing his degree, he went on to become a distinguished novelist and short story writer.
2   Earlier in the month, Fitzgerald had written to Leacock from the Cottage Club, Princeton University, Princeton, New Jersey:

Dear Mr Leacock
    As imitation is the sincerest flattery I thought you might be interested in something you inspired. The Nassau Literary Magazine here at Princeton of which I'm an editor got out a 'Chaopolitan number', as a burlesque of 'America's greatest magazine'.
    The two stories I wrote 'Jemina, a story of the Blue Ridge mountains, by John Phlox Jr.' and 'The Usual Thing' by 'Robert W. Shamless' are of the 'Leacock school' of humour—in fact Jemina is rather a steal in places from 'Hannah of the Highlands'.
    I'm taking the liberty of sending you a copy—needless to say it increased our circulation & standing in undergraduate eyes.
    Hope you'll get one smile out of it for every dozen laughs I got from the Snoopopaths.
                                        Very appreciatively yours
                                        F. Scott Fitzgerald
3   Daniel Webster (1782–1852), American lawyer, orator, and statesman, was a major political figure of his time. No such quotation exists in his extant writings.

## To John Lane

McGill Univ'y
Mar 16 17

Dear Mr Lane

I am naturally delighted with the <u>Punch</u> thing.

I hope Mrs Lane got my letter. The mails seem so slow and uncertain these days.

Ive just read the proof of Mrs Allans verses "The Rhyme Garden." They seem to me exquisite. They ought to have a great success.

I am so sorry that you have been laid up.

> best regards
> Stephen Leacock

<u>P.S.</u> I am very glad that Lord Northcliffe is printing the pamphlet. The government here,—I think I told you,—are circulating a quarter of a million.

How do you feel about the war? Is it drawing to an end. Or ~~here~~ are there years of it yet. It makes the world a sad place.

> S.L.

## To W. D. Lighthall

Orillia
Ont    Je 14 17

My dear Mr Lighthall

I send you herewith (under separate cover) a catalogue of books for sale that may interest you.  It is the library of my old friend W. S. Jackson[1] now leaving Upper Canada College after 40 years of work.

He is going to England & the books, as you see, are offered at great bargain.

> very sincerely
> Stephen Leacock

1    W.S. Jackson (1854–1947) taught at Upper Canada College from 1877 until 1917.

## To John Lane

McGill Univ'y
Oct 16/17

Dear Mr Lane

I am interested in bringing out to Canada on sick leave a Canadian Soldier by name, <u>Private Albert Reardon</u>, No 49,731, Fourth Canadian Bat$^n$. He has been at the front three years and is now on sick leave for ~~3 months in~~ 2 or 3 months in England. His wife is cook at my house. I have written to Sir George Perley and hope to get the necessary permission for Reardon to come out. His wife has saved up plenty of money & can pay his way out & back but for reasons that I need not state, but which you could easily imagine, it is better not to ~~give~~ send Reardon the passage money. So I have told his wife to write to him and tell him, if he gets his leave for the voyage, to go to the Bodley head where he will get a ~~paid~~ passage bought for him on request.

I should be ever so much obliged if you could have somebody go from the Bodley Head with Reardon when he turns up & buy him a passage out, to cost not more than, say, £10 or thereabouts and charge it to my account with the firm. I am reluctant to give you so much trouble but his wife is an excellent woman and a good cook (I hope you'll taste her cooking before so long) and I want to do all I can for her.

I have a lot of other things to write about but wont put them in this letter.

best regards
Very sincerely
Stephen Leacock

P.S. If Reardon is not in London he will write and ask to have his passage bought for him


*To John Home Cameron*[1]                    [McGill University
                                             Montreal]
                                             Nov 27 1917

My dear Cameron

It is, as you say, a far cry to the late eighties & the early nineties, but my memory is no less tenacious than yours. The question of which you write (the establishment of a <u>Punch</u> in Canada) is a very interesting one. It is a thing I have often thought about,—and so perhaps I am unduly possessed by the difficulties of it. To begin with, it would be awfully hard to reproduce here the kindly human tone of Punch, never partisan and never bitter. I have never seen in it an unkind word. Our public would have to be educated to it, and our writers would have to learn the art of it.

In the next place it is hard for anything to live here without party support, without the tariff or the banks or the motor car business or something extraneous of the sort.

And beyond that the market is small & the public few. The French are left on one side. The polyglots of the West are out of count, and our country shrinks till it become rather less than Lancashire in its number of readers. Nothing Canadian is read across the Border, and nothing Canadian reaches the English public.

---

1  John Home Cameron (1859–1944), professor of French at the University of Toronto, was an authority on Montaigne and Zola; he also published books on French composition and grammar.

All this means that the circulation of such a paper would be extremely limited: it could only get the whole available Canadian circulation by making itself loud, blatant, cheap, filled with <u>leads</u> and <u>dodges</u> and cheap tricks to get circulation Short of doing this it would have to be content ~~with~~ permanently with a quite limited circulation.

All of this would mean that if conducted on a dignified non-partisan basis the paper could not pay its way, & could not possibly pay contributors on a scale to call forth the best stuff.

It would mean therefore that as a business proposition it would be, I should think, very very dubious. Of its national value if conducted on a dignified patriotic basis there would be no doubt. But it would mean a constant loss for somebody and benevolence grows weary.

Especially to be noted is the fact that the kind of copy needed could only be got if it were paid for at good rates. People will contribute a little for love's sake but in the long run free copy will be found to be worth exactly what is paid for it.

To all of which I subscribe myself

Yours sincerely
Stephen Leacock


## To Basil W. Willett

Orillia. Ont.
May 16 1918

Dear Mr Willett

Will you please send a copy of each of my books to Mr W.S. Jackson The Albany, Fondlingbridge, Hants, and charge them to my account. I enclose slips to slips to gum into them. Mr Jackson is an old schoolmaster of mine and a very dear old friend. He was for about thirty five years at Upper Canada College. We all wanted him to accept the principalship last year but he felt that he wanted to go home to England (He came out here as a young man about 40 years ago).

Will you please show this note to Mr Lane, and if, when Mr Jackson is next in London, he comes into the Bodley Head I shall take it as a great personal favour if you can show him any kindness. He has always been a great cricketer & was in his time our best bat in Canada so perhaps if there is still such a thing as cricket you might find the time to take him to a game.

I hope you are not in earnest when you say that they may drag you from the Bodley Head to the trenches. If they take you & Mr Lane the poor authors will starve.

with best regards
Stephen Leacock

## *To Christopher Morley*[1]

Orillia Ontario.
Summer Address
June 16 1918

My dear Mr Morley

Ever so many thanks for your delightful book.

There is a story to the effect that Lord Roseberry wrote to old Sir Henry Parkes, an Australian backwoodsman & statesman who broke out into literature in his old age,—"After reading your book of poems I feel that I know just the kind of man you are."

I can say the same thing to you in a quite other sense & with no ambiguous intent.

Your <u>Shandygaff</u> is the best brew of the sort that I have tasted for a long time. Hitherto when I wanted quiet amusement for a lazy hour and the contact of a cultivated mind, I have had to read my own books. Now I shall use yours.

> Very sincerely
> with many thanks
> Stephen Leacock

1    Christopher Morley (1890–1957), British man of letters and author. His *Shandygaff* (1918) has the revealing subtitle: 'A number of most agreeable inquirendoes upon life and letters, interspersed with short stories and skits, the whole most diverting to the reader'.

## *To John Lane*

Orillia Ont.
(Summer Address)
June 27 '18

Dear Mr Lane

I have written an article, (published in the <u>Bellman</u> of June 15) to show that <u>Edwin Drood</u> was not killed by Charles Dickens.[1] I am asking the editor to send you ten copies and I thought that, as you know everybody in London, you wouldn't mind sending them to the people interested. Sir W. Robertson Nicoll is the leading authority on Edwin Drood & Mr Chesterton has always been much interested.

It's a long, long time since I've seen you. I hope that you are feeling better than when you last wrote.

Jeff. Jones is to come up here for a week end with me and we are planning my next book which is to be a series of stories dealing very gently and harmlessly with the lights & shadows of college life in a small college. But I fear that we cannot get it out till the spring of 1919.

My wife & son join in kindest regards to Mrs Lane & yourself.

> Very sincerely
> Stephen Leacock

1    'Edwin Drood Is Alive', *Bellman* (Minneapolis) 24, no. 622 (15 June 918): 655–62.

## To John Lane

Orillia
Ontario
July 28. '18

Dear Mr Lane.

I have just rece'd yours of the 5th: very glad to hear of your deal with <u>Answers</u>.

I think I am right in saying that second serial rights (right to republish out of the books) in England is at our disposal in regard to all the stories in my books up to and excepting <u>Frenzied Fiction</u>: of these a part were sold outright. As far as all serial rights are concerned, we having only book rights

I think that my arrangement with Vanity Fair (New York) permits us to publish in book form and to sell second serial rights out of the book, after book publication.

But for greater certainty I will get Jeff. Jones to draw up a typed list of all the stories ~~in C~~ and I will add a note to each as to where it was published & when & the state of the rights. He & you & I can then each have copies of this list

I had a very pleasant visit here from Jones over a Sunday: I am glad to see him come up to Canada at last. I have been wanting to get him to Montreal for some time

I was glad to hear from you again. In these anxious days it is nice to get news of ones old friends. It was pleasant to think of you & Brancker running across one another. My wife and my little son join in very best regards to you and Mrs Lane

Very sincerely
Stephen Leacock


## To William C. Bell

Orillia
Wed Sep 11    18

My dear Bill

That Paul Jones book (or rather books) is beautiful Charlie will be here at the end of the week & I'm keeping it till he comes. It's too damn good of you.

My boat is in good shape now. If you are able to slide up here for a day or two of fishing let me know & I'll have everything ready.

best regards
Stephen Leacock

*To John Lane*                                    McGill University
                                                  Montreal
                                                  Jan 16. 1919

My dear Mr Lane

It was awfully kind of you to think of us at Xmas & to send such lovely books. Young Stephen is delighted with his, and has become permanently enrolled among Miss Fish's many admirers (though she is married now is she not & has another name but I forget it)

I hope that you and Mrs Lane had a good Xmas & New Years. The feeling of relief in England must be wonderful.

Jeff. Jones will have written to you of my plans for my new book. The Hohenzollerns of America. We hope to have it out in 6 weeks or so

By the way I want to come over to England in 1920 to lecture (I mean give 'humorous' readings & talks). Can you tell me who are the best people that arrange that sort of thing? I've lectured in all the big cities in the States & here.

                                                  with best regards to Mrs Lane
                                                  Very sincerely
                                                  Stephen Leacock

*To Basil W. Willett*                             McGill University Montreal
                                                  Jan 28 1919

Dear Mr Willett

(Yours of Jan 13th, and one other recent letter, both regarding the Hohenzollerns.

I had asked Jefferson Jones to forward my correspondence on the new book to save writing it all out twice. He has perhaps forgotten to do so. He hopes to have the book in type in about a month & published by March 15; I am sending him the copy & he will send you the galley proofs. This, you will remember, is what we have been doing for some years.

As to Gundy, he has only the contract that I made with him some years ago giving him the Canadian sale of the books contracted for with Mr Lane in 1914. This new book is the last of them. I presume therefore that your arrangements with Gundy will be similar to those of past years: I think he buys his books from your New York company.

I have thought a great deal about what you say as to the title: generally speaking I would never use a mere title of the moment as of course it gets useless. But Jefferson Jones and I both think that there is a good chance of this title hitting the American market just right, and Mr Bell likes it very much. Moreover the advance advertising is now in the hands of the trade & it is too late to change. I only hope I'm right. At the same time I'm much obliged for ~~the~~ your sympathetic discussion.

> With best regards to Mrs Lane
> Very sincerely
> Stephen Leacock

## To Archibald MacMechan[1]                    Feb 7 19

Dear MacMechan

Congratulations on your fine article in the U.M. But the case is even worse that you suppose. All the stuff that you would throw out is only put there to pad the advertisements. A modern paper carries 60% advertising as the "saturation point". It's size is based on how many advertisements it can get. Having got these it then fills in 40% of "literature".

So will you ~~now~~ write an article on How to Kill Excess Advertising. That is the real trouble. Do that & the paper question is solved

> With repeated congratulations
> Yours sincerely
> Stephen Leacock

1   Archibald MacMechan (1862–1933) received his BA (1884) from the University of Toronto and his PhD (1889) from the Johns Hopkins University. He held the Munro Chair in English language and literature at Dalhousie University. He wrote many newspaper articles, especially for the Montreal *Standard*, which led to his *Headwaters of Canadian Literature* (1924).

## To J. Beverley Robinson[1]                    McGill University
                                                 Montreal
                                                 Feb 8. 1919.

My dear Beverley

I want to endorse in the warmest way and to forward in every way in my power your proposal of making an extended lecture tour. Everybody who heard you at your Montreal meetings is most enthusiastic. Your lectures, I think, will do a lot of good in helping to keep before the public at a critical time in our history some of the really vital factors that must be considered in making peace with the Germans or even in entering on a league of nations.

1   J. Beverley Robinson (1885–1954), grandson of Sir John Beverley Robinson, chief justice of Upper Canada, went overseas with the Governor General's Body Guards when the First World War broke out. He transferred to the RFC as a lieutenant, was downed in action, and was taken prisoner. After two-and-a-half years, he escaped from the German camp. After the war he made an extensive lecture tour, describing his experiences in Germany.

The mere intrinsic interest of your lecture as a war story is enough to reward amply the audiences who come to hear you: but I feel that over and above all such interest, your talk will do a most patriotic service to the country.

It has occurred to me that a few lines such as I have written here might be of some small use to you in places where I have a personal acquaintance & where I am known as a lecturer. If this is the case I should be only too pleased if you will send a copy of this letter wherever it may be of any interest or service.

> Very sincerely
> Stephen Leacock

## To Basil W. Willett                                    [Late March 1919]

Your of Feb 19 re title of book. What you say is quite true: the Kaiser might be shot at any minute But in that case ~~the~~ it is not the <u>title</u> that is queered it is the book itself. Jones & I have agreed that it shall not be published if anything of that sort happens while it is in the press. But as about 75 or 80 pages deal with the Hohenzollerns in America we think that the book had better stand or fall in that. In any case it is too late to alter it now as I should not want to publish one and the same book under two titles

After all there are risks & chances in everything. If the book doesn't sell, we cant help it. But I'm sorry that you & Mr Lane dont like the title.

> with best regards
> Stephen Leacock

P.S. Excuse this "scrap of paper" no other in sight.

## To Helen Edgar, wife of Pelham Edgar

> McGill
> Apr 1 19

My dear Helen

I am sorry to say that the Pond lecture people have got my lectures so mixed up & changed this month that I have not been able to arrange about coming to Toronto. I am leaving here for Minneapolis on the 13th & "work back" as they say in Vaudeville circles to <u>South Bend</u> Indiana on the 21st (Monday). ~~They~~ I have to be in Montreal on Thursday morning <u>April 24</u>. The Pond people are to wire me whether I am or am not to lecture on the night of <u>Tuesday 22</u>. If I do: then I couldnt manage Toronto. But if not I could ~~lecture in Toronto~~ leave Indiana in time to lecture in Toronto on Wed Evening Apr 23 & get the late train (if there is still one) to Montreal. But if they want me for Apr 22 in Indiana it is too late. You see I couldn't cut out the Pond lecture without positive loss of money both for me & them.

In any case I fear the 23rd is too much of a rush for you.

Also, I hate very much the idea of people being stung for tickets. I see it in operation here.

I'll write or wire you as soon as Pond lets me know

Ever so many thanks for the present you sent Stephen: he was delighted with it. He is to come out of bed today though not walking yet. Best regards to Pelham.

Very sincerely
Stephen Leacock


## To Alfred Tennyson DeLury[1]

Orillia
Ont. Je 4  '19

My dear DeLury.

I think it altogether likely that there will have to be some new appointments in classics at McGill. Macnaughton goes to Toronto & Rose is, I believe, not coming back to us (he's on active service at present). Billy Chisholm told me about Magee already. So I am sending your letter on to Dean Moyse of the Arts Faculty, Acting Principal of the University. I think that if I were Magee I'd write to Dean Moyse and ask him in a general way about the openings in classics and then if the answer is at all satisfactory go down to Montreal & get Billy Chisholm to have him meet Moyse & Macnaughton, the outgoing professor, at the club in a nice easy way. This kind of thing would put him on the ground first.

Very Sn Leacock

1   Alfred Tennyson DeLury (1864–1951) was a professor of mathematics and dean of Arts (1922–35) at the University of Toronto. He wrote several textbooks on mathematics as well as biographies of astronomers.


## To John Lane

McGill University
Nov 20 '19

Dear Mr Lane.

I was very glad to get your letter of Oct 24, though I regret to hear that the labour outlook is so very unsatisfactory. Jones and I have just signed a contract which I am sure you will find quite satisfactory. It was very good of you to hand over the French translation rights on such favorable terms: I am most anxious to see my friend DuRoure[1] make something out of it. It is hardly likely that I shall,

1   René du Roure was born in Paris about 1880. He graduated *Agrégé des lettres* from the University of France and taught at Laval University in Quebec before joining McGill in 1912. After serving with the French forces during the First World War he returned to McGill and in 1919 became head of the French department, a position he held until his sudden death on 15 October 1940. He was Leacock's closest friend on the McGill faculty.

as DuRoure is to get $1000 before I get anything. On the other hand his work may make a hit & we may both come in on it.

If you have not received the MS of <u>The Unsolved Riddle of Social Justice</u> please cable me at once as it was sent to you long ago.

I have decided not to lecture in England in 1920 as the outlook is too uncertain & Christie[2] offers no fixed guarantee. In fact I might easily <u>lose money</u> on what he offers

I like your suggestion about the <u>Prince of Mariposa</u> but doubt if I shall get round to it as I am awfully busy just now with one thing & another.

> Very sincerely
> Stephen Leacock

2   Gerald Christy was one of England's major literary agents. He joined Leonard Moore in 1912 to create Christy and Moore Ltd. Among his many writers was Winston Churchill.

## To Gerhard Lomer[1]                                    March 13, 1920

Dear Lomer

I enclose a letter from my friend, Mr James Rodgers, the Consul general of the United States, together with documents forwarded by him.  I told Mr Rodgers that I was making the best use of his present by giving the papers to the McGill Library.

> V. Sincerely
> Stephen Leacock

1   Gerhard Lomer (1882–1970) was born in Montreal and graduated from McGill University in 1903. From 1903 to 1907 he taught English and education at McGill. He earned his PhD (1910) in education from Columbia University. In 1920 he was appointed university librarian at McGill, a position he held until his retirement in 1947. In 1954 he published an index to Stephen Leacock's writings.

## To Basil W. Willett                          McGill University,
                                               Montreal.
                                               15 March, 1920.

Mr. Willett,
The Bodley Head
Vigo Street,
London, England.

My dear Mr Willett,

Herewith a short story. Will you please sell it for me? The American rights are sold, but only to a club paper, the Detroit Athletic Club News, the circulation of which will not interfere with anybody.

I am sorry to say that I have had to sever all connection with Mr. J.B. Pond of the Pond Lyceum Bureau. Between you and me and with every avoidance of the law of libel, it is not possible for people to get from Mr. Pond money that is due to them. Jefferson Jones could tell Mr. Lane a great deal about this. You will perhaps remember that arrangements were being made for me to lecture in England in this coming spring. I had to abandon the plan owing to other work, but it is necessary for me to write to Mr. Christy (his name is Gerald Christy, is it not?) the London lecture manager, in order to make him understand that Mr. Pond is not authorised to make any future arrangements in regard to my work. I do not know Mr. Christy's address, and I therefore enclose in this letter the communication that I am sending to him. I shall be very greatly obliged if you will see that it is forwarded, and I think, too, that it might be well if you would file a copy in your office as a matter of record. I think that Mr. Lane might do a very great service to literary people in London, who think of coming to lecture in America, if he would discuss Mr. Pond and his affairs with St. John Ervine, Coningsby Dawson, Hugh Walpole, and others, who have been under the Pond management.

I have other things to write of, but they can stand over for the present. With very best regards both to yourself and to Mr. Lane,

Very sincerely,
Stephen Leacock

## To John Kettelwell[1]

McGill University
Montreal
May 11. 1920

Dear Kettlewell.

I was delighted to hear from you. I suspected that you shared my views on prohibition but I am glad to be assured of it. Life is absolutely <u>rotten</u> in the States just now: I have to go there very often lecturing and I don't see how they stand it.

I like your Hohenzollern jacket very much indeed. My new book is to be a series of burlesque stories of the same kind more or less as <u>nonsense novels</u>. I am asking the N. York house (Lane & Co) to get you to make the jacket. I dont think you need to have any of the actual stories before you to make the jacket. Only 1 story is done yet. It is to appear in Harpers July number. But I have no sure proof of it & anyway I'd sooner have a jacket based on the general idea of <u>Nonsense Stories</u>. I hope you will find the time & inclination to do this

Very best regards
Stephen Leacock

---

1    John Kettelwell was a British book illustrator who flourished in the 1910s and 1920s. He designed an edition of *Nonsense Novels* (1921).

## To Charles Leacock

Dear Charlie

I lecture in S<u>th</u>. Bend, Indiana on Tuesday May 18: leave there on same night at 1.45 a.m. & am due in Hamilton 3.50 p.m. Wed aft & connect there for Orillia to arrive 8.37 p.m.—Please meet me or no perhaps it will be better if you are at the cottage with supper ready. Please get from Charlie Jones a bottle of whiskey as I shall very likely stay a couple of days. I'll write Charlie to give it to you.

I think that I have got the icehouse property but say nothing about it yet. If so I shall build a summer house and I shall be able to give Jones plenty of work. We must open up a new road & as the C.P.R will take 17 feet off the edge of the field.

your a. b.
Stephen Leacock

I've written to see if I can buy Kilgour's boat: not heard from him yet

<u>P.P.S</u> Get Jones if you like to fix up all the flower, or perhaps no wait till I come.


## To Basil W. Willett

McGill Univy
Montreal Oct 4/20

Dear Mr Willett

Gundy sent me the balance of £800 so that I have received in all on the royalties due ~~Oct~~ April 1st & Oct 1st, £150, £800 and by cable to the Royal Bank $911.80. Would you mind sending me a ship-shape account & then we can get straight.

The <u>Bystander</u> has sent me nothing so far. The New York custom is to pay at once on publication. If they have paid you, or are paying you by instalments, please send the money less the commission on to me as paid.

I hope that you have now the full copy of <u>Winsome Winnie</u> I finished all the MSS on Aug 20 but Jeff. Jones's printers were very slow.

What about The <u>Dippers</u>? I want to try to give it a shove here as soon as I can. It is not out yet on this side is it?

My best regards to Mr Lane if he has not sailed yet. I look forward to seeing him here

Very sincerely
Stephen Leacock

## To Basil W. Willett

McGill University
Oct 27 20

Dear Mr Willett

Herewith a story <u>Personal Experiments with the Black Bass</u>. It is sold (first American serial rights) in Detroit, and in Toronto

I hope that you can dispose of it.

Many thanks for the Bystander account (I havent checked it up yet) and the cheque.

Best regards
Stephen Leacock

## To Houghton Mifflin

[McGill University
Montreal]
9 November, 1920.

Dear Sirs,

I write to you to see whether you would think it feasible to get some kind of cooperation as between publishers and authors to obtain better terms from the booksellers.

The point is this.

In connection with discussing the price of my new book (Winsome Winnie and Other New Nonsense Novels) my publishers (John Lane Company, New York) tell me that if the book is sold at $1.50 the bookseller has to have 65 cents, and if the book is sold at $1.75 the bookseller has to have 75 cents. This seems to me too utterly preposterous for words.

In the case of a writer who is as yet quite unknown, I can well understand that such a gigantic sacrifice might have to be made to the bookseller. But where a writer's name is so well known that there is absolute certainty of a sale of many thousand copies (I think that I may say this of myself with all due modesty) the terms exacted seem out of keeping with common sense.

I take for granted that the authors under your management are placed in the same position of disadvantage as I am, and I should like to know whether, in your opinion, it might be possible by some sort of common action to secure better terms.[1]

Very faithfully,
Stephen Leacock

1  Ferris Greenslet of Houghton Mifflin replied at length on 16 November 1922:

It doesn't seem to me that the fact that one writer is easier to sell than another should effect the discount on his books. If he is going to have a book sell at a given store, that store has to buy a larger quantity of his books to begin with, for an increasing interest charge of space occupied, and all other expenses of handling.  As a matter of fact, booksellers expect and receive a larger discount on large orders than they do on small orders, i.e. on 'best sellers' rather than on what are termed in the trade, 'high-toned plugs.' . . . I don't in short, believe that anything can be done short of a complete reorganization of the book trade over the country to shorten discounts of current literature in book form.

## To Houghton Mifflin

[McGill University
Montreal]
Dec 29  20

Houghton Mifflin Co

I sent you today by parcel post the proofs of my Political Science.  All is finished & complete except the lists of books at the ends of the Chapters in Parts II & III.  These I will send separately.  I think it would be best to let me have page proofs but if I don't correct it in time go right ahead.

V. faithfully
Stephen Leacock

# CHAPTER 5

## STEPHEN LEACOCK
# HUMORIST

## 1921–1925

In 1921 Stephen Leacock solicited an invitation from Christy and Moore, literary agents in London, England, for a speaking tour of England under their direction. Eager to travel again to the British Isles, Leacock accepted, provided that McGill University would grant him his second leave of absence in twenty years. McGill agreed to the leave, and Stephen, Beatrix, and Stephen Jr, sailed for England on 14 September aboard the *Metagama*, arriving in London twelve days later.

Over the following three months Leacock gave a total of fifty-one scheduled lectures in England and Scotland. The lectures consisted of two basic talks, 'Frenzied Fiction' and 'Drama As I See It', which Leacock could easily adapt to cover particular authors and themes likely to be well received by the audience he was addressing. Throughout his highly successful tour Leacock maintained the attitude of a raconteur who wanted to share ideas with his eager audiences.

Although Leacock did not publish a book in 1921, the year of his lecture tour, he made use of his experiences abroad in his next book, *My Discovery of England* (1922), in which he discusses his trip to England through a series of pieces ranging widely in both topic and tone, from a humorous account of the carelessness of the immigration officials to an insightful analysis of Oxford University's success as an educational institution.

In 1923 Leacock published two books: *Over the Footlights* marked a return to parody, while *College Days* gathered together pieces he had written for the *Varsity*—the University of Toronto newspaper—and other college magazines. With the war five years since ended, Leacock appeared to be comfortably writing the kind of lighthearted humour 'without harm or malice' typical of his work before his anger over the events in Europe added an element of bitterness to his writing. But in the preface to *The Garden of Folly* (1924), another collection of assorted humorous pieces, Leacock offers some revealing comments about the anguish underlying his sense of humour:

if a man has a genuine sense of humour, he is apt to take a somewhat melancholy, or at least disillusioned view of life. Humour and disillusionment are twin sisters. Humour cannot exist alongside of eager ambition, brisk success, and absorption in the game of life. Humour comes best to those who are down and out, or who have at least discovered their limitations and their failures. Humour is essentially a comforter, reconciling us to things as they are in contrast to things as they might be.

Though Leacock was certainly far from 'down and out', it is fair to say he had experienced some disillusionment in his personal life, particularly with regards to his son. Although Stephen Jr accompanied his parents on his father's lecture tour of Britain, there was increasing concern about the slow progress of his natural development. In the fall of 1923 the assistant dean of McGill's Faculty of Medicine, on Leacock's behalf, sought out the help of a young specialist in pediatrics, Anton Goldbloom, who recalls their meeting in his autobiography:

> He mentioned no names at first but recounted the long story of a child's illness, of unsuccessful treatment and of dissatisfied parents. He then told me that all the formalities of dismissing the attending doctors had already been completed, that the child's father had conferred with him and several of his faculty colleagues and that I had been chosen to take the case over; the father, he said, was Stephen Leacock. I was called the following day and so began a friendship with Stephen Leacock with [sic] lasted until his death. I was fortunately successful in the treatment of his child.[1]

Goldbloom adds about Leacock: 'His intellectual honesty, his facility for clear and humorous expressions and his sheer brilliance intermingled with naïveté and medical credulity impressed me most about him. He had an insight with regard to pediatrics that I would gladly have wished on the antagonists and scoffers in the Faculty of Medicine.'[2]

But Leacock's concern over his son's growth soon paled in the light of the tragedy that overcame his wife. In 1924 Beatrix began suffering a gradual loss of strength and energy. The thought of spending the summer of 1925 in Orillia made her glad that they had this vacation property. The condition persisted, however, and accompanied by her close friend and neighbour, Mrs H.T. 'May' Shaw, she went to her doctor in Montreal in the fall of 1925. She left his office informed that she had breast cancer.

At that time the newest cancer remedy was the lead treatment being offered in Liverpool, England. Within two days of enlisting the support of the renowned physician Dr Blair Bell, a group of four—Stephen and Beatrix, Stephen Jr, and

---

1    Alton Goldbloom, *Small Patients: The Autobiography of a Children's Doctor* (Toronto: Longmans, Green, 1959), pp. 209–10.
2    Ibid., p. 210.

Mrs R.B. Hamilton, Beatrix's mother—set sail for Liverpool, only to learn upon their arrival that there was nothing that could be done to alleviate Beatrix's condition, which had deteriorated rapidly; she was too weak for the specialists either to operate or to start the lead treatment.

Beatrix died in Liverpool on 15 December 1925. Her husband arranged for her cremation and then started home with her ashes, which were buried on 31 December in Saint James Cemetery in Toronto.

### *To Margaret Burrowes*                    Ma 25/21

Dear Daisy

Stephen sends his best thanks for the Easter card.

When you go up to Sutton I wish that you could bring all the children up to us. We have plenty of room. You can take the morning train from Belleville to Oshawa arrive at 10: We will meet you there with the car (we have a new 7 passenger car) & bring you up in 4 hours arriving easily at 2 in the afternoon. We can then take you over to Mothers cottage in the car. I dont know how much time you care to be away from Belleville but if you would like to come in for a few days in June (apart from your later visit) we should be delighted. Let us know. I expect to go through Belleville on the Grand Trunk Day Train (Internl Limited) arriving at 2⁵⁶ on <u>Saturday April 2.</u> Perhaps you could bring the children to the train as before

> y. a. b.
> Stephen Leacock

### *To John Lane*                    Orillia. Ont
June 14. 1921

Dear Mr Lane

I got your letter of the 8th too late to do anything more than telegraph the Club.

Wont you please come up here from Toronto (86 miles) and have a day or two at my country cottage. We are in runing order now & I can put you up very comfortably & give you some good motoring & fishing & a horn of scotch whiskey as often as needed. Please call me up by telephone from Toronto. My number is <u>Orillia .638.</u>

> Very sincerely
> Stephen Leacock

## To Col. Scott Williams

Orillia Ont June 18th–21

Colonel Scott Williams
Camp Borden Ont

Government aviator Frank Mitchell carrying mail from British Columbia fell in the bush near Orillia last night found his way to my house now there under care of Dr Edward Ardagh machine not yet found have telephoned Camp Borden and the person who answered seemed to disclaim all responsibility or interest in the matter shall I telegraph to Ottawa or will you take action in regard to finding the machine disposing of the mail and looking after Mitchell I cannot express too strongly my indignation at the attitude of complete indifference expressed over the telephone

Stephen Leacock

## To John Lane

Orillia. Ont.
Aug 21 21

Dear Mr Lane

I have been hoping against hope to get a book done: but the prospect of it looks poor. What I have been working on is a book of burlesque plays & films (moving pictures) under the title. THE DRAMA AS I SEE IT. I will send you the table of contents & a part of the opening by an early mail

My wife & I sail on the Metagama Sep 17 from Montreal (C.P.R) It will be delightful if you & Mrs Lane can come on that boat too

With very best regards
all round
Stephen Leacock

## To Agnes Leacock

Care of Gerald Christy
The Outer Temple
Strand
London
Thursday Sep 29 1921

Dear Mother

We arrived here safely—very rough for 3 days after leaving—the good fellow was sea sick.

You will see from the clippings that we live in a blaze of publicity. We have been photographed standing sitting & eating. The I send was taken on the platform at Euston Station. I'll send some others. Keep these clippings as I need them: let Charlie see them & keep them.

Tell Charlie to pay any accounts sent from Orillia by Jones & charge them back to me.

> In haste
> Y. affec. son
> Stephen Leacock

P.S. They have made more fuss over me here in five minutes than in New York or Canada in five years.

## To Agnes Leacock

> Oct 10 1921
> Sheffield. Yorkshire
>   but address
> 58 Romney, Westminster
> London

Dear Mother

I got your letter just as I was leaving London this morning for Sheffield. I lectured in Hull & in York last week to very big audiences. The English towns outside of London seem dingy & dirty and third rate & the hotels fuggy and gloomy. I go to Liverpool tomorrow & then to Rugby School. Steevie is very well but as yet has no children to play with—but there are some children of a nearby clergyman that he is going to play with soon. You have no idea the fuss that has been made over me in London. I have been put up at the Athenaeum & the Garrick & the Savile Club where no one gets in. There was a big dinner given for me at The Whitefriars Club & Mr Pettridge the novelist referred to me as having:—"~~crept in with characteristic~~ "with characteristic modesty crept in London unobserved. Nothing but two column notices announced his coming."

But apart from beer, I wouldnt live here for anything. Bx is going to go & see Belle & Dora. I shall see Carrie Palmer in Liverpool but no other relations unless they write to me. I'd like to see Stephen Butler but dont know where he is.

I must now get dressed & go over & lecture here.

> y a s
> Stephen

Tell Charlie again to pay any correct accounts from Jones. Tell him to see at once that Jones puts in the <u>grain seed</u>. Not to wait till spring. Tell him to arrange with Vick to supply it

## *To  Basil  W. Willett*                    10th. October. 1921.

Dear Willett,

In America when I am lecturing I always find it necessary as part of the business to give copies of my books to the Chairmen at meetings, and such people.

By arrangement with the John Lane Company, I always charged these books to them.

I presume that you will only think it proper to allow me to do the same here. I need hardly say that I never include under this heading books books given to people with whom I have any personal connection.

If you acquiesce in this please send a WINSOME WINNIE to Mr. J.H. Edge, Y.M.C.A., Clifford Street, York, and paste in it the enclosed slip.

> Yours very sincerely,
> Stephen Leacock


## *To  Agnes  Leacock*                    58 Romney St
London
Oct 20 '21

Dear Mother

The enclosed is a little bit of English Holly that I cut in a lane in Derbyshire. I have been lecturing every night: lately in London: big crowds everywhere. I lectured at Rugby School & saw Cecil's son John Butler Parry, but I think I told you that already. I expect to see Rosomond Hill at Manchester. Hester Butler turned up at this house yesterday.

Stevie is very well but I dont think that it agrees with him as he cant get any decent outside play. I told you that I saw Aunt Fanny & Carrie a little while ago. We've had our pictures in all the big illustrated papers Steeve takes in quite for granted. Yesterday I lectured at Eastbourne in Sussex The nearest I shall get to Hampshire on my trip: unless I go on purpose.

> Your affecte son
> Stephen Leacock


## *To  Basil  W. Willett*                    Saturday Nov 5. 1921.

My dear Willett,

Thank you very much for your long letter of yesterday & still more for the very reasonable & conciliatory way in which you write.

I heard indirectly yesterday that Mr Lane had concluded the sale of his New York business. Perhaps you will be in a position very soon to let me know if this is true.

> Very sincerely
> Stephen Leacock

P.S. I doubt if it would be quite the thing to autograph books on the terms suggested. In fact I should hardly care to, a point of view which I am sure you share.

## To Agnes Leacock

[St Enoch Station Hotel
Glasgow]
Sunday ~~Dec~~ Nov 27 1921

Dear Mother

I am afraid it's quite a time since I've written to you. For a week past I've been in Scotland. I left Beatrix and Stevie behind in London. I've been in Glasgow Edinburgh Aberdeen, Falkirk, Greenock, Bridge of Allan and back to Glasgow again and I speak here twice more & then to Leeds & then back to London for a day & then back to Sheffield & to Barrow in Furness. A week ago in London I called upon Sir Thomas Butler, went to tea there at 5 oclock on Sunday. He is a small man in height. I had supposed him tall. The two daughters were there, one married with a very clever baby (boy) of 1 year & 2 months. She was just off to Ireland. That same night I went to a dinner party with Sir Chartres Biron, the famous magistrate & met Mr Short the Home Secretary and (what interested me very much) Sir Antony & Lady Hawkins,—that means Anthony Hope who wrote the Prisoner of Zenda & all those books—I liked him very much. I've met among others:—

Rudyard Kipland & Arnold Bennett & Ian Hay, & St John Irvine, & Sir Owen Seamen,—in fact more literary people than I can count. I have met with wonderful hospitality in Scotland. At Edinburgh there were two thousand people to hear me & tickets unobtainable. I spoke also (without pay) to a big meeting of students at Edinburgh University & am to address the Glasgow students tomorrow . . . . . . The dear good boy had a cold but is well again. I have taught him to say, "Whats the finest country in the world? <u>Canada</u> Whats the best university in the world? <u>McGill</u> He & I give away pocketfuls of pennies to all the poor people & especially the ex-soldiers who play music on the street. The other day Stevie remonstrated; he said:

"If we give away our money, a penny and then another penny at last we'll have none & <u>we'll have to play the music</u>"

Please send that to George as he will appreciate it.

I told you that I had supper with Rosomond & her husband: such charming people.

Tell Teddy the Butlers asked very particularly about him.

E.V. Lucas is going to drive us in his car to Hambledon (you dont know who he is but all the world does). He has among 1000 other things written up the cricket of Hambledon & we are going into Bury Lodge to see some sort of "screen"(?) that is there with old cricket scores on it,—or something.

Next Thursday I am going to lunch ~~with~~ to meet Chancellor of the Exchequer (Sir Robert Horne) & to put him wise on the Income Tax  So you see I float right on the top scum here.

Tell George that at a Scotch dinner party (which is done regardless of expense) there is first a <u>terrific</u> grace & then the host says, the <u>very second its over</u>,—"and now would ye perhaps <u>like a little whiskey before your wine</u>."

George will get what I mean & can add it to his stories. Tell him that in Scotland their great fear is that there may come a moment, a single moment, when you have no whiskey in you:—

Thus:—

"And now before you go forth into the cold will ye not perhaps better take a small drop of whiskey—"

—or—

"And now before ye take your wraps off & sit down, had ye no better take just a small drop of whiskey.

or

"And now while ye're waiting on your taxi,——

or

And now before ye'll be lighting your pipe.

                                        etc. etc.
                                        endlessly

Perhaps to save time send this letter on to George: I've no time to write it all again

                                        y. a. son
                                        Stephen Leacock


*To Agnes Leacock*                      58 Romney St
                                        <u>but address</u>
                                        Care of Gerald Christy
                                        Outer Temple
                                        London
                                        [Late November 1921]

Dear Mother

The leaves enclosed are from the sweet smelling plant on the portico (verandah) at Bury Lodge: I drove down there yesterday with Mr E.V. Lucas and Beatrix in a motor: had dinner at the George Inn: I bought two rounds of beer for all the men standing round the bar & after dinner we went up to Bury Lodge & had a cup of tea & looked at the cricket screen.

We leave London on the day before Xmas: I have to be in Paris then for some time arranging the publication of my books in French & then home on a French steamer, due back on Jan 20. The good boy is at the seaside with his nurse The air there has done him such a heap of good that Bx thought it better to leave him there. I enclose a cheque for $10$\underline{^{15}}$ for Charlie to buy Xmas presents for the little Burghs and you. I have sent to Carry & Daisy direct. Best wishes for Xmas.

I meet such a lot of people here. I find I am much better known in London than in Orillia

> Y. affe. son
> Stephen Leacock

## To Gerald Christy[1]

Hotel St James et d'Alban
Paris
December 30 [1921]

My dear Christy

Bournemouth went awfully well. Pity they advertised it as the same lecture afternoon & evening. Still the house was good. Please send me the account when you get it. I want to get all my English accounts cleared up before I go & shut down my bank account.

My tour has been most enjoyable & most successful & I feel that I owe all sorts of thanks to you & Champion

> Very best regards
> Stephen Leacock

P.S. I leave here early on the morning of Jan 14: please send mail to reach here only on morning of the 13th: after that to McGill. Later on when it is finished send me a bill for postage.

> S.L.

1  See footnote 2, page 124.

## To Basil W. Willett

Paris
Hotel St James
Rue de Rivoli.
Jan 2 1922

Dear Willett

Enclosed to Bob Benchley.[1] Will you please read it over & if rates any action send it on to him in care of LIFE N. York or any other address that you have. The Preface shall follow in a day or so.

–best regards
Stephen Leacock

1    Born in Worcester, Massachusetts, Robert Benchley (1889–1945), humorist, drama critic, and film actor, graduated from Harvard University in 1913 and went on to become one of the outstanding humorists of his generation.

## To Robert Benchley

Paris. Jan 2 1922
But address McGill
University
Montreal. I arrive there
Jan 23

My dear Bob Benchley

Mr Willett ( John Lane London) has shown me your book. It is fine. They are asking me to write a preface which I am delighted to do.

If I were you I would cut the Declaration of Indep[ce] out of the English Edition: of four directors of the Lane Co not one had seen it in his life. I am quite sure that if you read it out loud in the English House of Commons they would mistake it for the preamble of a Tramways Bill.

Willett talks of rearranging the order of the "pieces" in your book to suit the English market. But I don't know that I see much to alter in that way Willett thinks & I agree with him that the parodies of stories at the end (which by the way are beautiful) would go better in England if they could be made general not particular: you see in England ① no one ever heard of the American magazine ② ~~three~~ there are only thirteen actual survivors of the readers of Harpers (but dont tell Mr Willett I said it as I am going to break out on Harpers myself) and ③ no one in England has yet realized that there is reading matter included in the Sat Evening Post.

But listen: you can generalise it quite easily like this

Our Magazines

&

What They Supply to Us

I    The Stodge Magazine: For the Use of Clubs, Country Homes, Royal Palaces = no subscribers under 60 years of age permitted

II   Our Success Magazines: ~~Found~~ Sold in ~~all& to~~ all young graduates, young clergymen, young men off the farm etc

III  Our Peoples Magazine—found in all Dental Parlours, Railway Waiting Rooms, ~~Aquari~~ Cafeterias Acquariums, etc etc subscriptions 70,000,000; advertisers 700,000,000

---

You see what I mean: The words are nothing. You can find better I'm sure

> with very best congratulations
> Stephen Leacock

P.S. This letter at 20 cents a word, works out at, —— but no, no, its all right. Dont think of it

## To Basil W. Willett

Hotel St James
Rue St Honoré
Paris
Jan 8. 1922

My dear Willett,

After a lot of thinking I have at last reached a decision about my next book It will be called:—

### MY DISCOVERY OF ENGLAND
### England Rediscovered

and it will be a (supposedly very) humerous account of all my impressions of England,—people, ~~audiences~~ gov't, London the Press,—all of it. You may have seen some of the stuff I've done in the London Sunday Papers which will give you the idea of the line that I mean. I will put in plenty of comparative stuff to make it sell in America. I arranged with Mr Wells of Harpers to do some stuff of this sort for Harpers & out of that came the idea. The stuff in the Sunday Papers & what I do for Harpers will have to be worked over. It will take a lot of work & when I go to McGill I shall be overwhelmed with college work but I will do my best to have the MS all in your hands shall we say in 2 months plus the mail time from Canada. I may do better. But it is only right & business like to warn you that I've such a lot to do at college that I may fail to get the thing done in time. But I think that humanly speaking you would be quite safe in getting a dummy ready & listing the book & getting John Kettlewell on the jacket. I can send you over enough words for the dummy & a (provisional) table of contents.

My idea is that this type of book will sell well wherever I've been lecturing & ought to sell in London well because of the stuff that I will put in (all good natured & no harm or libel) about the Press & the House of Commons & a lot of things.

You have still time to catch a mail here & let me know how this strikes you fellows in the office.

Best regards
Stephen Leacock

## To Agnes Leacock

[A Bord de "Lorraine"]
[le] 23 Jan [192]2
Monday

Dear Mother

We are still about 300 miles from New York I hope to get in on Tuesday late in the afternoon a fact that the arrival of this letter will indicate. We have had the most awful passage! storms all the way! I never knew what rough weather meant before. The waves swept the decks of the ship & one or two came down on the top of it like tons of bricks: few people at meals. Beatrix sick all the way; Stevie sick for 2 or 3 days then better & now though it is still rough quite happy. Tonight we may get under shelter of the shore (Rhode Island & Cape Cod). The ship is all coated with ice: . . . . we hope to land in Montreal on Wednesday & shall go to the Ritz Carlton Hotel till we can look around for a flat or house . . . I'll write from Montreal when I get time.

Y affec son
Stephen Leacock

## To Robert Benchley

McGill University
Montreal
Feb 6 1922

Dear Bob Benchley

Willett (John Lane England) asked me to do a preface.[1] Here it is. If all right please send it on to him. When your English edition is out I'll send it to E.V. Lucas & Seaman & Charles Graves. They'll recognize its quality at once

Best regards
Stephen Leacock

---

1　The preface to *Of All Things* (London: John Lane, 1922) consists of the following four paragraphs:

It is a very great pleasure to me to have the opportunity of writing a few words as a preface to the English Edition of Robert Benchley's first book. I have known and admired Bob

Benchley's work ever since his Harvard days, when he was one of the brightest ornaments of the editorial staff of the *Lampoon*. I do not think it any exaggeration to say that it represents American Humor in its highest and most cultivated form. Although cast in the mold of burlesque Benchley's work is the product of an educated mind. I do not know just what it is they did to Bob Benchley at Harvard, but they put a stamp upon his mind, or shall I say they knocked a dint in it—which fashions all he does. There is a literary flavour in his work, an underlying basis of culture and thought which lifts it, to my thinking, on to the highest level.

It is for this reason that I feel certain that Benchley's work will obtain in England an immediate recognition. English readers, the best of them, appreciate exactly that sort of thing. They like a kind of humour which depends upon a certain background of knowledge and scholarship rather than the cheap merriment of the illiterate. When they turn to the present work they will find precisely what they want. They will meet, for example, on page 183 a conception of spring and a feeling towards vernal equinox (see diagram) which will delight the heart of the Royal Astronomical Society.

In writing these few lines of introduction for an author whose work appears in England for the first time, I have a pleasant sense that what I do now will reflect favorably upon me in the future. My function is that of the discoverer of a new planet, which sheds a grateful illumination upon the reader's head.

Readers of to-day generally like to know something of the personal appearance and personality of a new author. If I were attempting in Mr. Benchley's case to track this curiosity to its source and kill it, I should say that Mr. Benchley's face is one in which a high culture and an excellent education struggle in vain against a native geniality. I should also, if I followed the standard models in this sort of thing, explain that Mr. Benchley is an enthusiastic believer in modern democracy and an ardent admirer of the constitutions of the United States which he challenges the world to improve. "Where," he said to me one day, swinging round in his office chair, his eyes flashing with enthusiasm, "should we get another like it." I should explain also—if I were attempting to write a preface as it should be done— that our author is a keen golfer, an ardent mountain climber, an insatiable ozone breather and one of the most daring ski-jumpers among the editors of New York. But as I don't know whether Mr. Benchley is or is not these things, but merely that he *ought* to be them, I will not certify to these facts. Instead of such assertions I will only state as the measure and indication of Bob Benchley's personality, charm, gift of conversation, ease of social movement, and so forth, that he is one of my friends. That ought to cover the whole case.

In gratitude for this preface, Benchley sent Leacock a copy of the New York edition of *Of All Things* with the inscription: 'To Stephen Leacock, who certainly <u>ought</u> to like most of the stuff in this book as he wrote it himself first. Gratefully, Bob Benchley.' The inscription is dated 'New York February 22, 1922'. For further information on the relationship between Leacock and Benchley, see Ralph L. Curry, 'Leacock and Benchley: an acknowledged literary debt', *The American Book Collector* 7, no. 7 (March 1957): 11–15.

*To John Lane*                    McGill University
                                  Feb 9. 1922

Dear Mr Lane

I must apologize for my delay: I have been overwhelmed with college work

I've sent on to Willett enough material of my new book <u>MY DISCOVERY OF ENGLAND</u> for the dummy & advertising purposes: I am working hard at it in every moment of leisure I can get and shall try to finish the material on April 1st. My college work is so heavy that I may fail in this.

Mr Frank Dodd[1] came up here & we had a long discussion: I have decided not to do anything definite about later books beyond my present contracts till I see how Dodd Mead & Co can get along together. But Mr Dodd writes very enthusiastically & I shall hope for fine results & satisfaction all round.

Very sincerely & with best family regards to Mrs Lane and yourself

Stephen Leacock

1    Frank Dodd (1875–1968), an American publisher and the grandson of Moses V. Dodd, the founder of Dodd Mead and Company, joined the family publishing business in 1897, becoming treasurer in 1916 and president in 1931. He conducted business on a personal level with such authors as Leacock.

## To Paul R. Reynolds[1]

McGill University
February 13/1922

Dear Reynolds,

Mr Powell dealt with me direct about that sort of stuff before I sold him two articles for a high price: I would see no reason for dealing with him and them through an agent. I communicated with him from England but as yet have nothing done.

On the other hand if I do that sort of thing and he does not want it I will put it in your hands.

T.B.Costain of the Saturday Evening Post[2] writes me re contribution and wants to see me. If you care to make a deal with him for a series of Burlesque Plays (not in dramatic form, but on the model of Behind the Beyond) to be done as soon as I clear off my "My Discovery of England", by all means do so. I could send some advance material—not much but a little.

Very sincerely,

1    A literary agent, Paul R. Reynolds (1864–1944) established the first literary agency in America and the first representative of British publishers in the United States in 1893. He handled a vast number of Leacock's humorous articles.
2    Thomas B. Costain (1885–1965), journalist and author of best-selling historical romances, was editor of *Maclean's* magazine from 1910 to 1920, during which time he met Leacock. In 1920 he became associate editor of the *Saturday Evening Post*. In 1939 he became an editorial consultant for Doubleday, Doran and Company. He resigned this position in 1946 to devote himself to his writing.

## To Houghton Mifflin

McGill University
Montreal Que.
Feb. 16/22

MESSRS HOUGHTON MIFFLIN & CO.

Dear sirs,

I have an idea in which I think there might be a good deal of money both for you and for me. I am planning to prepare a sheet or chart, to be entitled

"A student's chart of the progress of the modern world." I send you under separate mail a rough draft intended to show, not the precise contents or divisions of the chart, but merely the general plan on which it will be made.

The chart will begin at about the year 1750, representing the opening stage of the Industrial Revolution in England, or perhaps at 1776 to represent the beginning of the American Revolution. The exact date does not matter: what is needed is some period nicely in advance of the French Revolution and of modern industrial change.

The chart, as you see, is divided into columns. Down the first one run the dates; down the second one British political history; the third contains American political history; the fourth European political history; the fifth great economic changes; the sixth legislation and social progress; the seventh progress of modern science (with sub-divisions probably); the eighth has progress of modern literature; the ninth military progress, wars etc., etc., etc.

My idea is that this chart would cover a sheet of paper about two feet by three. It could be sold as a sheet at a very low price, or sold in the form of a little wall-map with a canvas back, or for the very rich you could sell it on gold plate.

I have found by experience that it is a wonderful thing for students to get a rapid comparative view of modern history and economics in chronological outline.

Please let me know what you think of this plan. If you care to go in for it and undertake it with me on a royalty basis I can prepare the material with great rapidity,

> Very sincerely,
> Stephen Leacock

## To Houghton Mifflin

McGill University.
Montreal. Que.
Feb. 18/22

MESSRS HOUGHTON MIFFLIN CO.

Dear sirs,

As an appendage to my letter of yesterday, I would like to suggest that if you prepare the chart you could fold it up and paste it into my "Political Science". The added value to the book would pay your overhead cost.[1]

> Very sincerely,
> Stephen Leacock

1  On 20 February 1922, W.E.S. of Houghton Mifflin acknowledged Leacock's plan for the student's chart, promising to 'write you as soon as possible in regard to it'. On 9 March 1922, he noted: 'We have submitted your proposal to our field men who are in a position to determine pretty accurately the demand for such material, and have not yet had reports

from all of them, so your chart is still under consideration.' Then, on 15 March 1922, F.S. Houghton replied:

We have now completed the consideration of the publication of the 'Student's Chart' that you recently submitted to us. We can see the value of such a chart if rightly used, by an instructor, but after consulting with our sales organization we regret to say that we do not think it would be advisable for us to undertake its separate publication. As you suggest, it should be published as separate sheets, perhaps blocked into pads or made up into a wall map. Either of these forms if published would be somewhat out of our line and could best be handled by some house that features such specialties.

We are accordingly returning the copy of the chart with our sincere appreciation for your giving us the opportunity to consider it and regret that we cannot undertake its publication.


## To Basil W. Willett

McGill.
Feb 25 (1922)

Dear Willett

Yours of the 9th Feb—Believe me I am far more interested than you in getting the book done by April 1st—working at it in every spare minute—but crowded with college work, committees lectures & engagements. Still I think I can do it. I have 20,000 words done out of 40,000. So go right ahead. Best regards to everybody at the office

Very sincerely
Stephen Leacock


## To Basil W. Willett

McGill University
Montreal Que.
March 8/1922

Dear Willett,

I write to you as representing the firm as I am not sure whether Mr Lane is in London.

In a conversation which I had on Saturday last in New York with Gundy[1] and Frank Dodd, Gundy raised the question that to his way of thinking my new book, "My Discovery of England" does not fall within our present contract, yours or mine, at all, and that I am free to dispose of it where I will. He bases this idea on the fact that our contract refers only to "works of fiction" or some such phrase.

I think, therefore, that at any time when we agree upon a new contract it would be better to substitute a more general phrase to describe the book or books concerned, and make it read "Works of fiction or humour or popular essays, but not to include works of scholarship,"—some such phrases as that,—

1   S.B. (Sam) Gundy was the wholesale and trade manager of the Methodist Book and Publishing House before becoming, in 1904, the manager of the Canadian branch of Oxford University Press in Toronto; he held the position until his death in 1936.

and indicate some one person or firm,—you or me or Mr Dodd or somebody who can decide whether a book of mine falls within the contract or not.

As to the present book "My Discovery of England" I have been taking it for granted that we interpreted it as falling within our existing contract. Indeed, I should have thought it atrociously bad faith on my part to have proceeded so far with it unless I considered it so included: and I am sure you would feel the same way. It is plain of course, that the only claim your firm has on the book is that of the present contract and the only claim that I have for advance and other royalties on the book is of a similar kind and that the only claim that Mr Dodd's firm has on the book is that of whatever rights he bought from the John Lane Company under the existing contract. It is obviously that or nothing.

Gundy's particular difficulty is one that can easily be cleared aside. The trouble is that he feels that in the present state of the Canadian market his advance royalty on five thousand copies is likely to press rather hard on him. This is a point on which I am incline to agree with him and in regard to which I feel sure that I offer some rearrangement that ought to prove suitable.

But I think it well as a plain and distinct matter of business to leave no doubt about the fact that this book "My Discovery of England" is considered by us to be one of those referred to in the contract. If it were otherwise I should feel myself badly treated in having been allowed to go so far under a misunderstanding and in such a case,—which I am sure is not actual and which I only mention for the sake of clearness and frankness,—I should not be willing to dispose of the book to your firm on any terms. I only mention this for the sake of clearness in our business relations and I feel sure that you will understand that there is not the slightest offence or inputation made.

Meantime, when we come to discuss our future plans, a point which Mr Lane has already raise in correspondence, I wish you could offer some scheme whereby I could deal with one house instead of with three. As I said to Mr Dodd, the three-cornered arrangement is very difficult to carry on. Take for example the present book. You and I both think that a humorous book on England from my pen at the present time is just what we want. I laid aside a more pure form of fiction in the shape of burlesque plays and burlesque motion-pictures to do it: and your enthusiasm over the idea has been a great help and stimulus. On the other hand, Frank Dodd feels that he would rather have started off with a book of fiction. So there we are. These are of course not insuperable difficulties but they are bothersome. I am certain that many writers feel as I do that their great need is to work under smooth conditions with a minimum of friction and bother.

I apologise for such a long letter. I trust that you will at once assure me as to the main point of it. When that is settled we can go on at our leisure to discuss future plans though I fear it will be hard to do anything until Mr Dodd has had a little more chance to see how he finds his side of it.

I am sending him a copy of this letter with the request that he will indicate his concurrence with the idea that "My Discovery of England" falls within our understanding of the terms of the contract. Gundy's contract as I recall it though I have not the text at hand, merely gives him the books given under the contract to the John Lane Company without any stipulation as to whether they are fiction or not.

Very sincerely,
Stephen Leacock


## To John Lane

[McGill University
Montreal]
March 31 22

Dear Mr Lane
You will be glad to hear that the <u>MS</u> of my new book <u>My Discovery of England</u> is posted with this by the mail on the <u>Olympic</u> out of New York April 1st
Please be very care about Owen Seaman's preface & see that he has a proof sent to him.
Of course I cant see the proofs. But in addition to the office reading I am engaging Miss Cook who worked with me in London to read them over. She saw a lot of the MS in the making & would detect any errors or discrepancies. I think that to save time she ought to read the proofs, if you dont mind, right in the office.
I am quite proud of the book & think we may make a big hit with it

Very best regards
Stephen Leacock


## To J. A. T. Lloyd

[McGill University
Montreal]
July 24 22

Dear Hogan
All that I could do at Cornell was done months ago & has apparently borne no fruit. They must be a pack of pups.
I'm glad you have got a new job: things must be tight as the devil in England: even here they're bad enough. I see Parkin is dead. Requiescat, or as we say in Spanish, let the earth be light upon him.

best regards
Stephen Leacock

## To J.A.T. Lloyd

Orillia Ont
July 28 1922

My dear Hogan

I had just written a line to you when I got your letter with the proofs of your admirable article in the <u>Fortnightly</u>. It is excellent As usual you are far too kind to me, but I think none the less of you for it. As I said I had written long ago & in the warmest terms to the president of Cornell. I fear he must be a skunk. Haultains claim on Cornell is so patent that there should be no doubt about it.

best regards to your wife
Stephen Leacock

## To Thomas B. Costain[1]

Orillia, Ontario,
September 2nd, 1922.

Dear Costain:—

My plan of writing burlesque plays and films has been known for some time to my publishers and others: and now, without any solicitation or action on my part I am offered definitely a very generous sum for the plays by a first class magazine.

How does this stand? You will remember that the best that you were able to say was that the Saturday Evening Post would <u>give every consideration</u> to the stories: but that Mr. Lorrimer (and I don't blame him) never buys a pig in a poke. You will realize, however, that in a sense this is no offer at all.

I have to return a definite answer to the other people at once. I gather that you would hardly think it fair to expect me to turn down a definite and certain offer for a mere probability and I presume that you would feel it only right to release me from whatever obligation there might be as between you and me for the submission of these stories. But I am taking no action definitely till I can hear from you.[2]

It would of course be quite possible for me to write burlesques for both you and the other people. But I take for granted that neither you nor they would want to run the same kind of stuff from me.

Mr. Tom Manon wrote me about doing short articles for the Saturday Evening Post: and I should like very much to arrange this by writing short stuff for the Post and placing the burlesques elsewhere.

Very sincerely,

1  See footnote 2, page 142.
2  Costain answered on 8 September 1922: 'I am sorry but there seems to be no way out but to let the other people have the plays. I cannot imagine any circumstances which would induce Mr. Lorimer to contract in advance for material, so clearly the other people must have the stuff.'

## To Archibald MacMechan

[McGill University
Montreal]
Oct 18 1922

Dear MacMechan

Young Henry Borden, one of our McGill graduates, is applying for a Rhodes Scholarship. He is one of the decentest boys I ever taught. I've sent a recommendation officially to the Secretary of the Committee. But if you are one of the people influential in this (as no doubt you are) please do what you can for Borden. He is just the sort of boy we ought to send to Oxford

Very sincerely
Stephen Leacock

## To Houghton Mifflin

McGill Univ'y
Montreal
Oct 31 1922

Houghton Mifflin Co

Dear Sirs

I am sorry to say that I do not see any way to accept your proposal that I should accept only a half royalty on the sale of my book in England & give you the other half. I am far too well known in England (as apart from any effort of yours) to make that necessary. Any firm there would be glad to give me a full royalty. Will you please look into this at your convenience. For all my other books in England I get a ~~ten~~ twenty per cent royalty including my <u>Essays</u> & my book on <u>Social Justice</u>. For my Political Science I will accept a ten per cent royalty on the English retail price (this is the same as the original U.S. royalty paid by you but modified by me in your favour. The modification to be in force until revoked by me).[1]

Very faithfully
Stephen Leacock

---

1    F.S. Houghton answered him on November 3, 1922:

> your suggestion that we should allow you a 10% royalty on the English list price is not feasible. We assure you that we have every desire to see that you get a maximum return on this foreign edition, but in view of the fact that our share of the return must take care of overhead expense, it would seem that the usual procedure was fair in this case. A part of an arrangement of this kind is that we send a set of plates to the English publishers at their exact cost to us, with the expectation that any royalty return that we receive from our share of the accounting will be the only profit that we have for negotiating these foreign sales.

*To Houghton Mifflin*

McGill Univ'y
Montreal
[undated—a few days after
November 16, 1922]

Messrs Houghton Mifflin Co
Boston

Dear Sirs

I am greatly obliged for your very clear & very courteous explanation of the arrangements with Messrs Constable.[1] I accept them most cordially now that I understand the circumstances

There is just one proviso that I should like to make. For two years I have been working on a book

Political and Social Theories
Of Modern Times[2]

I hope to complete it next summer (by July 1st) & had looked forward to submitting it to your firm as it is quite outside of the line of the publishers of my lighter work. I hope that in the case of this book, in view of the fact that my name is known very much better in England than in the States, you would be able without any prejudice from the present instance to arrange for simultaneous publication on a royalty basis in England & America. If you feel at all attracted to the idea of this book I should like to discuss it further.

Very sincerely
Stephen Leacock

1   F.S. Houghton wrote to Leacock on 16 November 1922, outlining in detail Houghton Mifflin's arrangements with Constable about the English publication of the second edition of *Elements of Political Science*:

We accepted their suggestion of a royalty of 10% of three-fourths of the list price because this is the customary arrangement for the foreign edition of a book that is printed and bound on the other side. As we have already explained to you in previous correspondence, it is customary in such cases to divide these royalties for foreign editions between the author and the publisher, as this seems to be the fair arrangement. In our more recent contract forms we include this provision, but the contract for your book in its original edition was made before we had developed this foreign business to any extent and, therefore, before the necessity for such a clause had arisen.

2   In the Houghton Mifflin files at Harvard University, there is a note, dated 1/24/20, that states about Leacock's proposed book: 'His colleague, Hemmeon, says this will be a book on Modern Socialism mainly.'

## To Basil W. Willett

[McGill University
Montreal]
Dec 24 1922

Dear Willett

As to the matter of <u>Saucy Stories</u> stealing an article <u>How to Live 200 Years</u>. This article is covered in Canada by a cast iron copyright which I hold. The magazine is circulated in Canada

But in a case of this sort there is probably no malice or fault on the part of the editor. Some scoundrel sold him the story & he took it in good faith. I have had this happen before

What I prefer to do is to ask the editor, since he used the article to <u>pay</u> me for it. The fact that he paid the other man is neither here nor there. Its his loss not mine.

Half of what he pays goes to you, as the article is in one of our books.

Send a copy of this letter to the people concerned & they'll see the point. Mer Xmas

Stephen Leacock

## To Basil W. Willett

[McGill University
Montreal]
Dec 24, 1922.

Dear Willett

<u>Re new book</u>

I am already some way into my new book <u>The Drama As I See It</u>. It is a set of 7 or 8 plays & films done on the model of <u>Behind the Beyond</u>, as if one sat in the audience, not in dramatic form.

<u>Harper's Magazine</u> have the first U.S. Serial Rights, <u>Macleans</u> (of Toronto) Canada, & for England I have sent the first MS to Moore of Christy & Moore Outer Temple who has been acting as my agent[1]

Would you mind calling him up by phone & arranging that he keeps his release dates in harmony with our book publication (Dodd Mead say middle of June). This may mean putting one or two pieces in the book that are not serialized or vice versâ

Please tell Moore that he ought to get a good price Harpers pay $750 each for the sketches,—contract length 3500 words. The first one completed ran 8600 words. Moore should get all the more for it. Harpers pay no more as their contract was made first

---

1   Leonard Moore (1876–1959) was one of England's major literary agents. He joined with Gerald Christy in 1912 to create Christy and Moore Ltd. Among his many writers were George Orwell and Ernest Thompson Seton.

My best regards to Mr Lane & to all the firm & my best wishes for the New Year

Stephen Leacock

## To Leonard Moore[1]

McGill University
Montreal
Jan. 2. 1923

Dear Moore

Yours of Dec. 21 reached me today. It will not be possible to delay the publication of the book beyond the time arranged by the Bodley Head. But I am asking Mr. Willett of that firm to discuss the date with you. I note that you expect to find difficulty in selling these articles. I am greatly surprised. Harpers pay $750. each for them. But if you cant sell them I am asking Mr. Willett to take them over from you instead of having you take them back to me, which would waste time. You may notice a lot of articles of mine now being published weekly in England. They were placed with a syndicate here early in 1921.

With best regards to Christie.

Very sincerely
Stephen Leacock

P.S. Herewith Play No. II.

1   See footnote 1, page 150.

## To Lorne Pierce[1]

McGill University, Montreal
11th., Jan. 1923

Dear Mr. Ryerson,[2]

I am very much obliged for your letter. I am pleased and flattered to be included in your Series,[3] and especially delighted to think—that I am to be dealt with by Peter MacArthur. I owe him a great deal of—kindness and encouragement when I was first starting to write, which I can never forget. I may say that it was— Peter MacArthur who helped me to bring out my first book. Up to the time of meeting him I had really only done short, casual stuff.[4]

Very sincerely yours,
Stephen Leacock

1   Lorne Pierce (1890–1961), publisher and critic, was editor of the Ryerson Press from 1922
    to 1960. He founded the Ryerson series The Makers of Canadian Literature in 1923.
2   This letter is incorrectly addressed; it should have been addressed to Dr Lorne Pierce,
    Editor of the Makers of Canadian Literature series, published by The Ryerson Press.

3    Twelve volumes appeared in this series between 1923 and 1941. The first four volumes
     appeared in 1923, and they were devoted to Isabella Valancy Crawford, William Kirby,
     Robert Norwood, and Stephen Leacock.
4    Peter McArthur published twenty-three of Leacock's humorous sketches in *Truth*, which
     McArthur edited from 1895 to 1897. McArthur wrote to Lorne Pierce on 19 January
     1923: 'If my memory serves me I met him (Leacock) only once, for about five minutes,
     in the billiard room of an hotel, about thirty years ago. Of course I had considerable
     correspondence with him when I was editor of Truth, in New York, but that correspondence
     closed twenty-six years ago.'

## To Ferris Greenslet, Houghton Mifflin

McGill University,
Montreal
15. Jan. 1923

Dear Mr Greenslet,

I am very much obliged for your letter.[1] I now enclose the Table of
Contents of Political and Social Theories of Modern Times. I'll send on a
chapter later.

I am only too sorry that you had not time to look me up when you were
in Montreal, but I look forward to your next visit when we must certainly meet.

Yours very sincerely,
Stephen Leacock

### POLITICAL AND SOCIAL THEORIES OF MODERN TIMES

CHAPTER I.

Preliminary. The Political Thought of Ancient Times.

II.

The Dark Ages and the Mediaeval Period.

III

The Origins of Modern Democracy and the Transition to Modern
Times. The Reformation. The Seventeenth Century. Divine Right.

IV.

The Enlightenment of the Eighteenth Century and the Social Contract. Rise of Modern Science. Natural Individual Rights. Rous-
-eau and His Age. The Economistes. The American and the French
Revolutions.

1    On 12 January 1923, Ferris Greenslet wrote to Leacock: 'It is the opinion of our educa-
     tional department that the book is not likely to have a definite text book use, and we gather
     this is your own view of the case. It becomes, therefore, a matter for the general depart-
     ment of this house to deal with.'

V.

The Counter Currents and the Reaction. Beginnings of the Historical School. Montesquieu. Edmund Burke. The Reaction After the
French Revolution. The German Idealists.

VI.

Laissez Faire and Liberalism. The Economic Basis. The Industri-
-al Revolution. The Wealth of Nations and the Classical Econ-
-omists. Bentham and Utility. Austin and Sovereignty (United
States) The Philosophical Radicals. John Stuart Mill.

VII.

The Other Side of Laissez Faire. The Problem of Poverty and
Socialism. The Visionaries. St. Simon. Fourier. The Humanitarians.
Carlyle. Dickens. The Socialists. Karl Marx.

VIII.

The Historical Movement of the Middle Nineteenth Century
and the Relation to the Inductive Sciences. The Historical
Idea Before the Nineteenth Century. Progress of Natural
Science.. Geology. Biology. Darwin. Evolution. The Historical
School in Economics and Political Sociology

IX.

The Decline of Individualism. Laissez Faire and the Working
Class. Rise of the World States. Cosmopolitanism and Imperialism.
Africa and the White Man's Burden. Green. Maine. The Break ~~Off.~~ Up
The Classical Economics.

X.

Natural Science and Social Theory. Biology and the Organic The-
-ory of the State. Economic Interpretation of History. Eugenics.
Rising Tide of Colour.

XI.

Social Reform and Social Revolution

XII.

Political Tendencies of Today.


## To Gerald Christy

McGill University
Montreal
Jan 20 1923

My dear Christy

Your partner Mr. Moore has sent me a statement of payments due to me for
articles sold by him in London. I send you a copy of it. You will note that he
deducts English income tax. I send you also a copy of a telegram (cable?) sent by
me to Mr Moore. I have been writing for English magazines for many years: no

tax is payable by me out of any cheque sent me by an English Editor except the Canadian Income tax which I always pay. If Mr Moore has found a way of mixing up the money due to me with the English law of agency that is merely an entirely unnecessary complication which would have the result of making me pay the tax twice over. In short I regret to say that I cannot do business on such terms. If Mr Moore instructs the editor to send me a cheque there is no more income tax on that than if the editor sent a cheque to Canada for pulpwood. On receipt of the cheque if I then send Mr Moore his commission there is then income tax to be paid on that, but it has to be paid by Mr. Moore, not by me.

Mr Moore still has certain writings of mine in hand. If he has sold them I shall be obliged if he will ask the editors to forward the cheques direct to me: if not I shall be equally obliged if he will hand over the unsold manuscript to Mr Willett of the Bodley Head, Ltd. or to any other representative of that company. I am writing to Mr. Willett to explain the matter to him. I have the most agreeable recollection of our dealings together which left me with a complete reliance upon your honesty and fairmindedness and I feel convinced that you will straighten out this matter for me.

Very sincerely
Stephen Leacock

## To Frank Dodd[1]

McGill University
Montreal
24. Jan. 1923.

Dear Mr. Dodd,

I have read with very close attention your letter of Jan. 11th., in regard to a contract for my future books. I am very sorry to say that I do not see my way to accept the arrangement that you propose. I cannot see that I have anything to gain by making a contract for three future books. In such a case I am bound and you are not; no matter what offer is made to me, I am no longer free to accept it. You, on the other hand, are free to do as you please. You imply, for example, that under such a contract you would be in a position to devote a good deal of ~~time~~ money and effort to pushing the sale of my books. You would very likely do so, but you would not be in the slightest degree <u>bound</u> to do so. If my books did not appeal to you you could leave them to languish and to take their chance of such sale as they might find for themselves, without expense or effort on your part.

Please understand that I am not here talking of what I think you <u>would</u> do, but merely of the contract that you propose, and the amount of advantage which it has for me.

1   See footnote 1, page 142.

I appreciate very much the friendly and encouraging spirit of your letter, and am much pleased to hear the good news about "MY DISCOVERY".

Suppose we leave the question of a future contract till we can discuss it together in a free and easy manner and go fully into the different aspects of it.

Very sincerely yours,

## To Frank Dodd

McGill University
Montreal
1. Feb. 1923.

Dear Mr. Dodd,

I wired you today that I am still perplexed about the title of my book. I dont like to call the book NONSENSE PLAYS or BURLESQUE PLAYS or any general thing of this sort meaning a comic collection. The book is not that. It is really like a view or picture of the modern drama, as seen always from the point of view of the immediate spectator sitting in the theatre. Please read in HARPER'S my NO. I. and you'll see what I mean. I want a title to reflect that Idea. I enclose a list that I have been thinking of, and I include in it your title of NONSENSE PLAYS.

Please ~~make~~ mark your first and second preferences on it, and get somebody whose opinion you value to do so the same.

Yours very sincerely,

Suggested Titles for Mr. Leacock's New Book of Plays and Films.

The Drama as I See It
Nonsense Plays
Where Thespis Walks
The Footlights and the Films
The Book of the Play
Pen and Ink Plays
Across the Footlights

## To Paul Reynolds

McGill University
Montreal
1. Feb. 1923.

My dear Reynolds,

I am awfully sorry that there should have been any misunderstanding between us in regard to my books. My impression was that I discussed with you what your commission would be in the event of my turning over the agency of my books to you. Indeed in my own mind I am absolutely certain that I said and meant nothing more than this, but unfortunately you got the impression from our conversation that I then and there turned over the agency of the books to you, giving you 10% of any increase that you obtained over what I now get.

In the case of the offer which you were good enough to send me, there is no harm done, as it is lower than what I now get and less favourable in every way than offers I have received in other directions. It is quite possible that I might in the future avail myself of your good offices, but until I do so definitely and in writing, I think that any further action in the matter could only lead to confusion.

I hope you are content to let it go at this but if you think that I have acted unfairly, please write and tell me so. I have appreciated immensely the way in which you have disposed of my magazine work, and the cordiality of our relations which I hope has not been disturbed.

Yours very sincerely,

## To Archibald MacMechan

McGill University
Montreal
8.Feb. 1923.

My dear McMechan,

I have been asked by a Toronto publisher who is getting out a series of Canadian authors, to write an introduction to the works of Haliburton.[1] I find it very hard here to get material about Haliburton's life. I have only the memoir for the Centenary, published by the Haliburton Club. Please get some one in your library to send me a bunch of stuff about him. If you dont know anything about Haliburton in Halifax, you dont deserve that three million dollars.

Yours very sincerely
Stephen Leacock

P.S. When are you coming to Montreal?

1   Thomas Chandler Haliburton (1796–1865) was a Nova Scotian judge and author. *The Clockmaker, or The Sayings and Doings of Samuel Slick of Slickville* first appeared in 1837, and its immediate success led to ten more Slick volumes between 1838 and 1855.

## To Basil W. Willett

[McGill University
Montreal]
12. Feb. 1923.

My dear Willett,

I send you under separate cover the MS of a little book I have just prepared under the title COLLEGE DAYS. It is made up of little essays and poems which have appeared in college papers. The three poems are topical, but all the rest is general; even the poems are, I think, fit for general reading.

This book is outside of any existing agreement now between us.

I shall feel most happy if you care to undertake its publication, but if not, I am assured of publication elsewhere. I wish this book to go through the press at once and appear as soon as possible.

> Very sincerely,
> Stephen Leacock

P.S. Please cable me at my expense without delay your decision about this book

## To Basil W. Willett

[McGill University
Montreal]
12th. April. 1923.

My dear Willett,

By this same mail, under separate cover I send you the complete text of my new book "OVER THE FOOTLIGHTS and OTHER FANCIES." You will have no time to send me proofs but Miss Grant Cook who has been working with me is going back to London in the middle of May, and is fully conversant with my ideas about the book. She will read the proofs, and will arrange with you anything that might come up in regard to make-up or other details.

Notwithstanding anything in our contract, I want to keep the dramatic rights in the material in this book, in so far as I myself might prepare anything in it for the stage. The reason is this: in order to get the book ready in time I have put into it several things which I had written to sell for the stage. There are various other things which can be turned into acting pieces with a stroke of the pen. I feel assured in advance that you will see the reasonableness of this stipulation.

You will notice that apart from the text of the book I send you also three pieces, namely, THE SUB CONTRACTOR, an Ibsen Play, Basilisk Vangorod, A Russian Play, and DAMNED SOULS, a (new style) Russian Play. These appear in the book, but are available for first British Serial Rights if used before the date of publication. Please hand them over at once to Miss Campbell Thompson at Curtis Browne's, and see that she understands clearly just when the limit for serial release is set. Miss Cook's permanent address in London is the Writers Club, Norfolk St. Strand. She expects to arrive about the 29th. of May. Please communicate with her.

> Very sincerely,
> Stephen Leacock

## To Basil W. Willett

[McGill University
Montreal]
16th. April. 1923.

My dear Willett,

I have just had your letters of April 4th. and 5th. I have cabled you "Publish Footlights First". I am not inclined to hold over the publication of the book on account of the possible serialisation of the different articles in England. I see no reason, none the less, why Miss Campbell Thompson should not dispose of the articles in one way or another—that is to the Sunday papers and weeklies, cut into two parts when necessary, if they are too long—before the date of publication in book form. Please tell her to see what she can do. The Norwegian play, and the two Russian plays, for example, are short enough for a daily paper.

Yours sincerely,<br>Stephen Leacock

## To the Secretary the P.E.N. Club

[McGill University<br>Montreal]<br>19th. April. 1923.

Dear Madam,

I am very much obliged for your letter inviting me to become an Honorary Member of the P.E.N. Club. I thank the President and Committee for the honour they do me. I regret that owing to the great number of clubs to which I now belong, and their various claims, I cannot widen the circle and add any more to the list.

I am none the less grateful for the invitation.

Yours very sincerely,<br>Stephen Leacock

## To Basil W. Willett

[McGill University<br>Montreal]<br>May 7 23

Dear Willett.

I cabled you today. "Cut out from Footlights book story called <u>Sack the Lot</u>." It is not suitable and is not in shape for use.

On Dodd Meads galleys I find a good many things to change. The copy was evidently not in good shape. I dont know whether the copy sent to you was free from the same faults. Please therefore have the MS changed as to the particulars involved in the ~~foll~~ instructions herewith.

I posted you an extra piece <u>The Historic Drama</u> (very important to include: it is the best in the book)

Very sincerely<br>Stephen Leacock

Instructions<br>Re Proof Reading of Leacock's<br><u>Over the Footlights</u>

(1) Change all such expressions as "readers of this <u>magazine</u>," "this <u>paper</u>" etc etc to "readers of this <u>book</u>".

(2)  all such references as "this season of 1921, or 1920 etc." to read <u>1923</u> or better, whenever possible make it the <u>ensuing season</u>, or the <u>season just past</u>" etc etc, some general terms

(3)  Cut out all signatures "Stephen Leacock etc)

(4)  Cut out altogether <u>Sack The Lot</u>

(5)  Please <u>first</u> in the book <u>Cast up by the Sea</u>

(6)  Put the Greek Tragedy as No IV

(7)  Put <u>The Historic Drama</u> as No VI

(8)  At the close of <u>The Faded Actor</u> insert the foll'g words
     To him, then, I dedicate this book. He will never read it. But that matters nothing. I dedicate it all the same.

## To Mr Blodgett

[The Old Brewery Bay
Orillia, Canada]
Aug 23 1923

Dear Mr Blodgett

I send you my signature at the bottom of this letter and enclose with it a much better one for your collection;—that of General Sir Arthur Currie, Commander in Chief of the Canadian army in the war & now my esteemed principal at McGill.[1]

Very best wishes
Stephen Leacock

P.S. I can write better than this but the weather's is against it.

1  Sir Arthur Currie (1875–1933) studied at his home-town Strathroy Collegiate, where he was one of Stephen Leacock's students. During the First World War he became the first Canadian appointed commander of the Canadian Corps. In August 1920 he became principal and vice-chancellor of McGill, a position he held until his death.

## To Sam Gundy[1]

[The Old Brewery Bay
Orillia, Canada]
Sep 4 23

Dear Gundy

Under separate cover I send the proof of college days. Please see that the preface is put at the beginning of the book & that the reference to Bruce Baron's father's jacket is cut out.

Please cut out the use of the word <u>Chapter</u> & indicate the sections only by number as the English sample herewith. ~~Please~~ Kindly return the sample

Very truly
Stephen Leacock

1  See footnote 1, page 144.

*To E. V. Lucas*                                    [McGill University
                                                     Montreal]
                                                     Nov 18.23 .

My dear E.V.

I may be the worst correspondent in the world but I'm the best friend. I not only read all the books that you sent me (such as the Hambledon book, every word) but all the things you write that you dont send me. Moreover I always boast of my acquaintance with you and impress people very much with the fact that I have drunk whiskey with you in a car for 80 miles. . . . Let me therefore hear no more complaints out of you, on the mere ground of not writing. . . . I almost came over to England last week to help Stanley Baldwin[1] win the election but had to decide not to as it was a little too much of a hurry? It's just possible I'll be there in June. . . . . . . I suppose you'd have no use for coming over to the United States to lecture, would you? I think you said you hated speaking.. I am in it all the time, I mean in share intervals, and in close touch with the people who run that kind of thing: if you'd care to look into it & see what its worth let me know. It's a hell of a job though;—I've just come back from Kalamazoo (see Lippincott's Gazetteer Letter.K] where as a part of my work in lecturing to the teachers of K. I had to attend a Baptist dinner party. . . By the way I feel that the word Kalamazoo ought to of use to you.. Thoughts on Kalamazoo,—without really knowing what it is, or where it is, but speculating as to what it must be like from what one hears of 3000 miles away of the United States eh, what? . . . go to it.

                                                     Very best regards
                                                     Stephen Leacock

1   Stanley Baldwin (1867–1947), Conservative British statesman, lost the election of November 1923.


*To Houghton Mifflin*                               [McGill University
                                                     Montreal]
                                                     Nov 18 1923

Houghton Mifflin Co

Dear Sirs

I appreciate very fully your letter of Nov 10. My new book Political and Social Theories of Modern Times will not, I regret to say, be ready till a year from now. I could, if you like, send some chunks of it to go into galley proof this winter. Or would that only be a nuisance.[1]

                                                     Very faithfully
                                                     Stephen Leacock

1   Ferris Greenslet responded on 22 November 1923: 'I don't think anything important would be gained by putting any parts of it into galley proofs at this time. We will put it tentatively on the schedule for the late Autumn of 1924.'

## To Peter McArthur[1]

McGill University
Montreal
19 Nov. 1923

My dear McArthur:

First rate. Fine. Excellent. Of course it is too flattering[2] but I don't object to that at all.

You have really made me seem quite an interesting character and I am correspondingly grateful to you. It adds one further increment to the gratitude that began years ago when you gave me the first solid editorial encouragement I ever had.

Very best regards
Stephen Leacock

1  Peter McArthur (1866–1924), essayist and humorist, wrote the first book on Stephen Leacock (1923).
2  This reaction is to Peter McArthur's book Stephen Leacock, published by the Ryerson Press in 1923 as part of the Makers of Canadian Literature series. The book consisted of a twenty-page biography of Leacock, more than one hundred pages of selections from his writings, and a forty-page appreciation of his work by McArthur.

## To Dr Alton Goldbloom[1]

[McGill University
Montreal]
Nov 23 23

Dear Goldbloom

My wife tells me that you expressed a certain reluctance to send me an account because I used to be your teacher.

It is very kind of you to look at things in this light & I appreciate it. At the same time I can not allow you to act on this very generous idea & request that in due course you will send me an account.

Very sincerely
Stephen Leacock

1  Montreal-born Dr Alton Goldbloom (1890–1968), a pioneer of pediatric medicine in Canada, graduated from McGill Medical School in 1916. He was appointed assistant demonstrator in pediatrics at McGill in 1921 after a period of study in the United States.

## To W. D. Lighthall

[McGill University
Montreal]
Dec 13 23

My dear Lighthall

My best thanks for your very interesting monograph on The Outer Consciousness.[1] I have just received it & look forward to reading it over a pipe of tobacco after my work

Very sincerely
Stephen Leacock

1    The pamphlet, *The Outer Consciousness*, was privately published by the author in 1923.

## To Christopher Morley

[McGill University
Montreal]
Jan 21 1924

My dear Morley.

I wouldn't think of asking money for such a kind favour as that. By all means print it. I'd like to see a proof. Somewhere in the essay "dep_o_rtment" is put for department.

Yours faithfully
Stephen Leacock

P.S. I read you here, there & continually & always like what you write.

## To Basil W. Willett

January 21, 1924.

The Bodley Head
London

Dear Willett,

Herewith a note on my proposed new book. I shall do my utmost to have the copy all done by the end of May: but I am badly crowded with other work.

I want to sell book rights only for British Dominions except Canada. I want to keep all second serial rights, picture rights, dramatic rights etc. I want as now on my other books twenty per cent and I think my advance royalty ought to be higher than on the other books: and I want to count thirteen books sold as thirteen and not as twelve. I hope that you can see your way to meet these terms and feel sure that you will accept them. Our relations have been so prosperous and friendly that I shouldn't like to have them disturbed.

It is my intention henceforth to sell my books one by one so that I remain free. But on certain terms, if you care about it, I am willing to place with you instead of this book alone, this book and my next two works after it (other than works on political science). I do not like, and have never liked counting thirteen books as twelve. It is quite out of date here. If you care to take it out of all my contracts I am willing to make terms for three books. I should appreciate very much your views on this point and hope that you can see your way to accept what I offer.

In any case I would like to take this occasion to assure you how much I appreciate the interest that the Bodley Head has always shown in my work and the cordiality of our personal relations.

With best regards to Mr. Lane and to your directors,

Stephen Leacock

### To Dr Alton Goldbloom

[McGill University
Montreal]
Jan 23 24

Dear Goldbloom.

With much pleasure I enclose a cheque for your account as rendered,—and may I take this occasion to say again how much my wife & I appreciate what you have done for Stevie.

Very faithfully
Stephen Leacock

### To Christopher Morley

[McGill University
Montreal]
May 9/24

My dear Morley

Your kind words,—in your admirable volume of Essays,—first made me blush and then break into tears.

I am not what you think I am. But after this I will try to be.

best regards
Stephen Leacock

## To Basil W. Willett

[The Old Brewery Bay
Orillia, Canada]
May 18 1924

Dear Willett

Yours of 28th April. I am very glad that you are going ahead with the
Garden of Folly without delay. I think I wrote to you that one item, viz. a part
of the Glimpses of the Future appeared already in College Days. Please cut that
part out (not of course the whole article). I wrote this before but thought it well
to say it again

I am sorry to say, but it would be of no use to get Miss Cook to read the
proofs as she was not working with me during the preparation of this MS. The
proofs will have to be read in the office but I have learned to have great
confidence in your people's work.

~~But~~ In the event of any difficulty please use the cable at my expense

Very sincerely
Stephen Leacock


## To Grace Reynolds

[McGill University
Montreal]
Oct 15 1924

Miss Grace Reynolds
Sun Life Assurance Co

My dear Grace.

It so happens that I want to get some one to work with me on half time at
$50$^{00}$ (fifty dollars) a month

If you want this job you can have it.

It would mean that you would work (ordinarily & usually) from 10 a.m. till
1 a.m. either at my house or at McGill. Sometimes I would want you to work
in the afternoon instead. My work only runs till June 1st but in the four summer
months I would see what I could do for you, either to get you a summer
position, or at any rate send you from my summer place by post enough work
to mean $25 to $30 a month.

The great advantage to you would be that matriculation would then be a
perfectly a simple matter.

I will call you up by telephone today & see if you can come up to my house
after your work today (I am not at McGill but at home after 5 today) & tell me
what you think

If you accept this offer you can begin as soon as your company permit it

Very sincerely
Stephen Leacock

*To Waitman Barbe*

[McGill University
Montreal]
October 24th, 1924

Professor Waitman Barbe,
Department of English,
West Virginia University,
Morgantown, W. Va.

Dear Professor Barbe,

It is a matter of much regret to me that I cannot accept your very kind invitation to lecture. I am sorry to say that I have so many engagements already that I can take no others for the rest of this college year.

With very sincere thanks.
Yours very sincerely,
Stephen Leacock

*To Paul Reynolds*

October 25th. 1924

Dear Reynolds,

Elser has done such admirable work for me that I had to say even the slightest word of objection.[1]

But I think it might be better sometimes instead of cutting things down to the vanishing point to see whether an article could'nt undergo the opposite treatment (applied) lengthened so that one part of it might make a whole article.

In the case in point (enclosed please return) the second Russian play has lost so much that it no longer gets over. The effect can't be got. It was already supposed to be highly condensed. One has to remember that the reader attributes tose articles to me and that my reputation is concerned. I admit that I am very commercial and like money but at the same time I have enough of the pretty vanity of a writer not to care to see things too much altered. In my opinion the Russian play I wrote is very good. But I doubt very much if it will stand the terrible cutting it has been given.

I should never grudge the time to add or subtract from anything that is sent to me.

Please take this up with Max Elser in such a way as to show fully my confidence in him and my appreciation.

I know of course that the difficulties of Syndicates mixed stuff are very great and that Elser surmounts them wonderfully.

Best regards,

---

1   Maximilian Elser, Jr (1889–1961) was general manager of the Metropolitan Newspaper Service, which he founded in 1919. The Service syndicated some of Leacock's humorous essays in American newspapers.

## To Frank Dodd                                November 11th, 1924

Mr. Frank Dodd,
Dodd, Mead & Company
443–449 Fourth Ave.,
New York, N.Y.

Dear Mr. Dodd,

I have to thank you for your very kind letter of November 6th.[1]

As to the little book called "Oh Mr. Leacock" I preferred not to read it.[2] This is a fad of mine, I never take any clippings or as far as I can I never read anything about myself. But my wife read the book and thought it very clever. Her only criticism was that the book contained so much matter of a general character where the humour belonged to the subject and not to me, that it was a pity to have lessened its appeal by giving it a pressing reference to me.

I should therefore wish that you would regard the publication of the book as purely business matter. I should think it very likely that the publicity would be very useful to me and if there is anything unfavourable in it, it wont do me any harm.

Very sincerely,

1   In a letter of 6 November 1924 Dodd wrote to Leacock regarding *Oh, Mr. Leacock*:

It seemed to me a particularly clever and friendly parody of your work, and Mr. Lane, while assuring me that you would have no objection to its publication, at the same time stated that you would prefer not to be connected with it in any way officially. I think it might be good advertising, and unless I hear from you to the contrary, I am going to assume that you wouldn't object to its being published here.

2   Carleton Kemp Allen, *Oh, Mr. Leacock!* (Toronto: Longmans, Green, 1925).

## To J.B. MacLean                              [McGill University
                                                Montreal]
                                                November 19th, 1924

Colonel J.B. MacLean,
The MacLean Publishing Company,
University Ave.,
Toronto, Ont.

My dear Colonel MacLean,

I am so glad to learn that you are going to reprint what I wrote about Randolph Jones in the Financial Post.[1] It was a disappointment to me that in the hurry of going to press the Montreal Star set up the article in such an undignified state and I am certain that in the Financial Post it will appear in a way more worthy of the subject with which it deals.,

1   'Randolph Ketchum Jones', *Financial Post* (Toronto) 18, no. 47 (21 November 1924): 10.

I agree entirely with everything that you say about the boy who is gone. He seemed, as you have said, destined to do great things for this country and your sense of his loss will be shared by ever so many people.

With best thanks for your kind letter.

Very sincerely,
Stephen Leacock

## To Paul Reynolds                                    November 24th, 1924

Paul Reynolds, Esq.,
70 Fifth Ave.,
New York, N.Y.

My dear Reynolds,

Of course I will be glad to see what I can do about touching up the College article. But I wont touch that at all for a week or so until I feel like it.

Here is another matter. I have to go down to Nassau in the Bahamas in the end of December to take my wife and little boy whom I am to leave there with my wife for the rest of the winter as he needs a change of climate. It has occured to me that I can easily put together an illustrated article on Nassau for a magazine or Sunday paper. The place has plenty of interest,—pirates, rum-runners, sandy beaches and palm trees, American plutocrats, British Government house, with champagne flowing everywhere like mud, it seems to me easy. I would write it up in a pleasant personal strain. I should think it would go very well

If you think well of this you might see what any of our editors think of it. I mentioned it to John Kennedy of Colliers when he was here in Montreal and he seemed to think well of it. I don't know whether Colliers would have room for anything very extensive but this I leave to you.

The steamship company and the Colonial Hotel people have been good enough to take a very warm interest in my going to Nassau and would very likely be quite willing to co-operate with you in placing an article.

I hand over these suggestions to you for what they are worth and if you can take any action to place them go ahead and do so.

Very sincerely,

P.S. The address of the hotel is as follows:—
James E. M. Donald, Esq.,
Assistant Manager, The New Colonial,
New York Office,
Room 202, 67 Wall Street, New York, N.Y.

## To Eugene Forsey[1]

The Old Brewery Bay
Orillia, Canada    [1925]

My dear Forsey

I was very glad to get your letter & to learn that your summer is being spent so well

As to whether you will take English or Economics, it is a very important decision to take & you must reflect well upon it. It affects not only your college course but your "hereafter". I think that in any case you ought to take graduate study and ~~econom~~ college teaching as your work. If you go on in economics there is no doubt that you can get a scholarship (fellowship) for one year at McGill. Then if you can manage two years at Oxford or Harvard & get a higher degree I should think that there is every reasonable hope that our department will have grown enough for us to make a place for you.     one )

Once started the rest is easy. And in Economics you ) can always pick up a few hundred dollars a year by doing writing, civil service examining & so on.

I mention this prospect quite prematurely ~~& ought~~ out of place so that you may be able to judge better what to do. But I make no doubt that your prospects would be equally good in English: at least I should think so.

And if you feel the <u>call</u> towards English follow it. But remember too that economics is also, as it were, a literary and philosophical subject. It need not be turned into mere <u>business</u> as the Americans are apt to do.

Still you've time to think it over

Very sincerely
Stephen Leacock

---

1   Newfoundland-born Eugene Alfred Forsey (1904–1991) studied philosophy, political science, and economics at McGill, winning a Rhodes Scholarship to further his studies at Oxford. Well known for his socialist views, he became a senator and was later named to the Privy Council of Canada.

## To Frank Dodd

February 12th, 1925

Frank Dodd, Esq.,
Dodd Mead & Company,
New York, N.Y.

My dear Dodd,

I am sorry to say I have no book in sight for spring or early summer publication. I am still hoping, however, that I may manage a book for autumn and you may rest assured that I shall keep you advised as to the prospects of this.

I am most anxious to see whether the sale of Nonsense Novels and Literary Lapses can stand up against the strain of the higher prices. If they do not perhaps you might try putting them back to $1.50. These two books after ten years of publication has such a continuous and steady sale in England and America that it looked as if they would become permanent properties of value, selling at a price which would give me a very decent return. If the price is cut to a cheap reprint edition all that I would ever get would never amount to anything much.

Very sincerely and with
best wishes,

P.S. We have all been deeply grieved here to hear of poor John Lane's death.

## To Paul Reynolds                February 13th, 1925

Paul Reynolds, Esq.,
70 Fifth Ave.,
New York, N.Y.

My dear Reynolds,
When I was down in Nassau I saw a good deal of Mr. A.C. Burns, the Colonial secretary. He is a very brilliant Englishman who has been for some time in the Diplomatic service of the West Indies, Nigeria and elsewhere, he has done some writing for Blackwoods. He told me that he was intending to write an article about the British West Indies, particularly about Nassau and the Bahamas and he asked me whether that kind of thing would find a market in the United States. I told him that the best chance for the kind of article he had in mind, which would presumably be illustrated, would be with one of the more dignified monthly magazines, such as Century or Harpers. I told him further that I would write to you and that I felt sure that you could get a much better chance of success for him than if he undertook to manage the matter himself. Burns showed me so much kindness in Nassau that I shall be more than pleased if I can do him some service in return, I shall therefore be very greatful if you will send me a letter, which I can send on to Burns, stateing that you will be very glad to look after anything that he cares to send to you. I repeat that Burns is a man of exceptional ability and interest and I should imagine that anything he would write would be well done. Incidentally I may say that he is the brother of Delisle Burns a very well known writer of Political Theory.

Very sincerely,

## To Gerhard Lomer

[McGill University
Montreal]
Mar 20th, 1925

Dr. Lomer,
McGill University,
Montreal, Que.

Dear Lomer,

I am sending down to the library three volumes of Pesch's National Economy (in German). I had intended to order a private copy for myself and a copy for the department. The book is excellent and I am delighted to have it in the library, but at the terrible price at which they turn the quotation marks into Canadian dollars, I cannot afford the luxury of a private copy. It occurs to me that in ordering for the library direct you might have had a discount on the price; In that case I will be glad to pay the difference and hand these volumes over to you. There are two more published and I think we ought to have them.

I think also that we ought to have a certain amount of new representative German stuff. Can you tell me if it would be possible to find out before hand what the quoted prices would mean in Canadian dollars.

Very sincerely,
Stephen Leacock

## To Mr Pollock

March 24th, 1925

Mr. Pollock,
Income Tax,
51 McGill St.,
Montreal, Que.

Dear Mr. Pollock,

I have to thank you for your courtesy in giving out to Miss Reynolds the necessary information about my income tax. I now enclose a cheque on the Bank of Montreal for $3,912.64. I note what you say about royalties paid to U.S. government. I will take steps to get from them a definite statement of what I owe for 1923 and I will pay it and get a receipt. The peculiarity of the situation is that this money is not payable by me, but by my publishers in New York and deducted from what they send to me. The publishers may object to reopening the question of the 1923 tax. But in any case I will keep you advised as to what happens.

Very sincerely,

P.S. In regard to the British income tax, the British government up to the present does not collect any tax on the royalties paid by publishers to authors outside the United Kingdom. The only British tax I have had to pay was in 1923 on certain transactions that went through the hands of Messrs. Christie & Moore.

*To Frank Dodd*                                  [McGill University
                                                 Montreal]
                                                 March 26th, 1925.

Messrs. Dodd, Mead & Company,
449 Fourth Ave.,
New York, N.Y.

Frank Dodd, Esq.,

My dear Dodd,

I want to ask you if your firm will for the future consent to forego any share in second serial rights of the books of mine which you took over from the John Lane Company. As you know the Metropolitan Syndicate have been selling these rights since January 1923 and have paid you <u>half and half with me</u>. Under this arrangement you will find that you have probably received more for second serial rights on the Lane books than you paid me in royalties on these same books. In other words I have lost heavily and had better not to have made any such arrangement. I did not of course foresee what you were getting.

We have come to a point now where it is very difficult to make any future use of these books without special preparation of the material by me, involving lengthening, shortening, revising, etc, etc, etc. It does not seem fair that I should be prevented from doing this and getting the money for it by your claims. I think you will agree with me that the fair thing for you to do would be to cry quits on any future claim on second serial rights in the volumes concerned.

I am not referring here to <u>My Discovery of England and the Footlights</u> which you published. Your second serial rights in this case rest on a definite basis and I am very happy to share with you. Nor am I referring to <u>The Garden of Folly</u> of which I reserved the second serial rights from the beginning. I should very greatly appreciate your acceptance of this proposal.

                                                 Very faithfully,
                                                 Stephen Leacock

### To Paul Reynolds                           March 26th, 1925

Paul Reynolds, Esq.,
70 Fifth Ave.,
New York, N.Y.

Dear Reynolds,

Herewith a copy of a letter to Frank Dodd. Please pry these rights loose. In the back of my mind is the idea that if Dodd says yes he can have my next book and if Dodd says no he can't. It would be rude to tell him this, but you might be good enough to see the firm and keep this idea up your sleeve. Do not of course show them this blunt letter. Please inform Elser.

Very sincerely,

### To Alf B. Bryn                             March 26th, 1925

Alf B. Bryn, Esq.,
Oslo, Kristiania,
Tostrupgaarden.

Dear Mr. Bryn,

I am very much obliged for your book, it looks very funny, but then all Norwegian looks funny to me. I am writing at once to the Bodley Head Publishers about your Norwegian translation and they will write to you.

Very sincerely,

### To Paul Reynolds                           April 9th, 1925

Dear Reynolds,

I am glad to say that I have arranged with Dodd that henceforth I own all second serial rights in all my books except only My discovery of England and Over the Footlights. Will you kindly therefore divide all of the next money between you and me as the arrangement is in effect now.

I am delighted at this as it now gives me a free hand to work on the old books, revising, alterating etc. I am sure that I can very soon get ahead of the release dates and then be free to sell the articles first and to do some longer ones and then cut them up into bits for Syndicate use

I am afraid that the Concordia College stuff would be too long for use by College Humour though I am glad that the editor spoke so kindly of it.

Your sincerely,
Stephen Leacock.

## To Paul Reynolds                                    April 11th, 1925

Dear Reynolds,

To avoid all error let me make it clear that payments to <u>Dodd Mead</u> have stopped <u>now</u> and that the returns presently one for March come to me. It is on this understanding that I am letting them have the bookrights in my next two books. I only mention this to you to avoid error. Verbum Sap.

Very sincerely,
Stephen Leacock.


## To Paul Reynolds                                    April 13th, 1925

Paul Reynolds, Esq.,
70 Fifth Ave.,
New York, N.Y.

My dear Reynolds,

I send you herewith, as under the schedule below, nine articles for Syndicate use. They are put together, as you will see, from articles out of books and magazines, but with various changes to suit them for Syndicate use. I am very much pleased and gratified with the energy and interest which Elser has put into this work. I will try to keep on sending original matter as well as second hand copy. But I think perhaps that you had better make sure about this Syndication. It would not do for the salesman to profess to be selling continuous original copy. Any mistake in that direction would do me very great harm.

What I want to do is first to get ahead of the current publication by the Syndicate and then do some longer articles which we can sell for much better money to the magazines and which after magazine use can be cut up into pieces for the Syndicate. For example I have written out the notes for an article called the <u>Appalling Growth of Seriousness in America</u> which will run to about 4,000 words but at least two chunks of 1,000 words each could be lifted out of it.

What I would like to do, then, would be to try as far as possible to send to Elser two new articles every month and rely on the revision of older work for the other two. I presume that it is better business for us to supply two articles a month of original matter and anyway if we didn't the supply of old stuff would threaten to run out.

Incidentally it must be remembered that with the best will in all the world a person may not be able to write two articles every month that would be worth while. My accumulated books are the work of sixteen years.

Very sincerely,

## To Paul Reynolds                    April 20, 1925

Dear Reynolds,

In view of our cordial relations with the International Mag Co and with MacLeans Magazine and because of the fact that I can't recall without hunting up a lot of papers whether I sold them U.S. and Canada rights or merely U.S. I will accept and cash the fifty which you send from them. As a matter of fact I had endorsed the cheque before I saw that there might be a mistake, but I will send it back if there is any I don't know whether you have followed this new law which permits Canadian magazines to force authors to give them their work. I have worked against it and given evidence against it. I am afraid that the result will be that American editors will fright shy of our Canadian work. In the present case as our Syndicate use the article there may be a row over the copyright. Please keep this letter in case I want later to show it to the MacLeans that the arrangement was not of my making.

Very sincerely


## To Paul Reynolds                    May 7th, 1925

Paul Reynolds, Esq.,
70 Fifth Ave.,
New York, N.Y.

My dear Reynolds,

I send you back herewith your letter and cheque for $180.00. I am sorry to say there has been a mistake here. I thought I had written to you already to say that I am completing this story and that it will run to four or five thousand words. I have it now well under way. In the literary sense I could not bear to have a piece of it substituted for the whole and in the commercial sense I could not bear to sell it for $200.00.

My own recollection is that I sent you this not as a completed story, but only as the beginning of a story in which an editor might be interested. I may say further that I have a very strong hope of doing not one story but a little string of them dealing with college professorial life. I have a great many notes, plans and characters. These stories when completed,——if they ever are completed,—— will make a volume. I do not want to prejudice the whole enterprise by breaking off a piece and thus spoil the prospect of selling the full length stories.

Please convey to the editor of College Humour my very sincere regret and throw on my shoulders just as much blame as your own kindly conscience will permit.

Best regards and continued appreciation of all that you do for me.

## To Paul Reynolds

May 8th, 1925

Paul Reynolds, Esq.,
70 Fifth Ave.,
New York, N.Y.

My dear Reynolds,

This letter is to introduce to you my young friend and former student Mr. Howard O'Hagan.[1] He graduated with honours in Political Economy at McGill three years ago and is just finished his course in law.

Mr. O'Hagan has been very much interested in Canadian Economic questions and has started to do some writing about this kind of thing in the Canadian press. His especial knowledge and interest lies in western Canada where he was born and brought up, and in the problems of immigration and development which are connected with it. He knows the country well and among other things has had experience as a guide in the Rocky Mountains. Last summer the Canadian Pacific Railway sent Mr. O'Hagan over to England where he gave talks on emmigration to Canada.

He is now fully equipped to enter on the pursuit of law and is able, if he wishes to do so, to go into a law office in Edmonton or some other western city. But he has a great notion that he wants to see what he can do in the way of writing along the lines of his own interests. He does not want to write snappy, journalistic stuff but articles with a certain amount of solid value. I am altogether with him in his ideas. My experience is that the thing which a young man does best is the thing towards which he feels a strong attraction. I have given O'Hagan a letter to John Kennedy of Colliers but on second thoughts I felt that I would like to go further. I know how willing you always are to be of use to my friends and I am proposing to O'Hagan that in the next few months he should prepare half a dozen articles dealing with the kind of stuff in which he is interested and send them along to you to see what can be done with them.

My own opinion is that there is a great deal of western material of very high magazine interest,—the migration question, the different aspects of Pacific trade, the whole business of the Japanese, the further settlement of the far north west, the oil resources of the MacKenzie valley and the political questions connected with the United States and Western Canada,—a whole lot of things which, with a proper presentation of facts and statistics and a proper background of economic knowledge would be first class material. There is a good market for

---

1   Albertan-born novelist Howard O'Hagan (1902–1982) attended McGill University, where he graduated with a BA (1922) in economics and political science and an LLB (1925), while editing the *McGill Daily*. Among his many literary works is his first novel, *Tay John* (1939), a classic about a Native North American caught between his Aboriginal heritage and advancing white society.

this sort of stuff in England. I know that Gwynne of the London Morning Post is crying out for this sort of material. I have written about it and talked about it with Amery, the present Colonial secretary. If any young man can make a hit with this sort of material he will find an open path in front of him.

O'Hagan also wants to write stuff dealing with the present development of education in our colleges. Here I do not feel on such sure ground. The field is there but I would not feel so certain whether he could do this kind of thing.

I should be ever so much obliged if you will let O'Hagan come into your office and have a real talk with you, not in a hurry but at full length and if you can arrange to have him go away and get busy and write up some stuff and send it to you to see what can be done with it I shall feel that he is getting a real opportunity.

Would it be of further use to him to go and see Max. Elser? Further more do you not think that if he sends you some articles of solid merit we might do something for him in London with the Quarterly or the London Times.

You can, I know, give him much better advice then I can about the length of articles and the technical details connected with them. In all of this, I would like to repeat I shall be ever so much obliged for anything that you can do.

Very sincerely,


*To Sigrid Enghardt*                    May 11th, 1925

Miss Sigrid Enghardt,
Tordenskjoldsgade,
Denmark.

Dear Miss Enghardt,
    I am delighted with your idea of translating <u>My Discovery of England</u> into Danish. Several of my books have been translated into various languages,— Swedish, Japanese, German, etc. As to the terms, there is no trouble about them. I will write to my publishers and ask them to let you undertake the work on the easiest terms known in the business.

Very sincerely,

## To the Montreal Trust Company                    May 18th, 1925

The Montreal Trust Company,
11 Place d'armes,
Montreal, Que.

Department of Wills & Estates.

Dear Sirs,

In connection with my estate which I have placed in your hands I enclose herewith a schedule of securities. When I get time I will send you the complete statement of my copyright interest. Meantime, I may say that they refer to a book published by Houghton Mifflin and Company, Boston and a long list of books published by the Oxford Press, Toronto, Ontario, Dodd, Mead & Company, New York, N.Y., and John Lane Ltd., The Bodley Head, Vigo Street, London, England, together with current second serial rights with the Metropolitan Newspaper service, 150 Nassau Street, New York, N.Y.

My estate also includes a life insurance policy of ($10,000) ten thousand dollars with the North American Life Assurance Company, agent F. Horne, Orillia, Ontario.

My estate includes further my house at 165 Cote des Neiges Road, Montreal unencumbered, papers and deeds in regard to which are with Messrs. Chauvin, Meagher, Walker, Stewart and Crepeau and my property at Orillia, Ontario (25 acres and a house) the papers in regard to which are in the hands of Frank Evans, Barrister, Orillia and Arthur Thompson, Barrister, Orillia, this property is also unencumbered.

I possess further half interest in a lot in Swift Current, the other half being owned by my brother Edward Peter Leacock of Calgary, papers in regard to this are in my deposit box in the Bank of Montreal, Stanley and St. Catherine Streets. I possess also a mortgage for ($15,000) fifteen hundred dollars on a house in Sutton, Ontario occupied by my mother Mrs. A.E. Leacock, and owned by my sister Dr. Rosamond Leacock of Calgary, Alberta. I have never taken any interest on this mortgage and I do not intend to take the principal unless my sister should become better off than I am. But until I execute a legal arrangement of this fact this mortgage remains, as it is now, part of my estate.

My current and savings accounts in Montreal are with the Bank of Montreal, Stanley and St. Catherine Streets and in Orillia with the Royal Bank.

Very faithfully,

## *To B.K. Sandwell*[1]

Orillia Je 2 1925

My dear B.K.

Many thanks for your letter which fully explains the most extraordinary situation. It is a great pity you ever left us but unfortunately there is no use in lamenting that. In our department we appointed John Farthing[2] as an extra man a year ago, and now, just two weeks before you were again a possibility, we appointed young Goforth[3] as a lecturer. So we are blocked for years. I think that it would be your best plan to join the staff of Saturday Night: this would I am sure, be very congenial work. I remember General Currie repeating with great gusto to a whole supper party at his house (last winter) some of your bright things about the <u>standards</u> of social life & I am sure that you have a wide public. You could still keep your eye open for an academic job. But it would be folly to disguise that fact that owing to the untoward things that have happened you'd have, as it were, to begin again lower that your proper place in seniority. I dont think it is worthwhile. If you can get a pretty good job with Saturday Night as a basis of operation for literary & journalistic work, take it. There is a lot of stuff in the way of economic articles dealing with Canada in relation to the U.S. & England & that sort of thing for which there is a steady demand, to say nothing of pure, or purer, forms of literature.

But in any case keep me advised of your plans & of course I will be of any use to you which is possible.

With best regards<br>Stephen Leacock

P.S. Write me at Orillia. Beatrix is getting along steadily though not so quickly as I had hoped.

1   B.K. Sandwell (1876–1954) was a student of Leacock's at Upper Canada College before graduating with a BA in classics (1897) from the University of Toronto. He taught economics at McGill (1919–22) and was head of English at Queen's University (1923–5) before accepting the position of freelance writer and then editor (1932–51) of the weekly *Saturday Night*.
2   John Farthing (1887–1954) was a member of the economics department at McGill.
3   William Wallace Goforth was appointed sessional lecturer in economics at McGill in 1925. He resigned from McGill in 1928.

## *To Paul Reynolds*

October 11th, 1925

Dear Reynolds,

Please suggest to Elser in the most friendly way in the world that perhaps when such very extensive revision is made as in the enclosed, I ought to see the M.S. You see there is no getting away from the fact that I am supposed to be the author of these pieces. And it is only fair to remember that I have a literary reputation to consider based on a great many years of very hard work. I doubt if there are many people who would allow an editor to reduce a 7000 word story to 1500 words without even seeing it and remain responsible to the public for the signature.

Perhaps if you show Elser this letter he will appreciate the point involved as we always agree so well.

As a matter of fact I had just written to him to see whether we could use these Winsome Winnie stories in instalments. If that is not possible and if they have to be shortened up in this way, would it not be better if I did the shortening.

Very sincerely,


*To Gerhard Lomer*                              [McGill University
                                                Montreal]
                                                October 16th, 1925

My dear Lomer,

Eayrs of the Macmillan Company[1] writes to say that he will be very glad to turn over the care and sale of the monographs to the library when his own active sale seems to be at an end. But he says that he would rather not be tied down to a definite number of months (you will remember that I had proposed three months), he would like to wait in each case until the active sale was over. In the case of any monograph that happened to make a big hit and sold well in the stores it would be a pity for all concerned to call them in too soon.

On reflection I see that Eayrs is quite right and with your approval I will tell him that we accept this arrangement, In every case sooner or later the custody and the residual sale of these monographs comes back to the library.

I am hoping that you can manage to take 350 of each monograph at twenty cents. For the ones sent you later on by the Macmillan Company you will of course pay nothing unless and until you are enabled to sell them.

If I can be of any help in getting this money I shall be glad to co-operate with you. The matter menas a great deal to my department. I want to bring out two or three of these little studies every autumn. I am willing if need be to pay the deficit this year but I am afraid that I cannot go on doing so indefinitely.

Very sincerely,
Stephen Leacock

1   Hugh Eayrs (1895–1940) joined the Macmillan Company of Canada in 1916 and became president in 1921, holding the position until his death in 1940.

## *To Grace Reynolds*

[Liverpool, England]
Fri. Nov 27 1925

———

My dear Grace.

You will have had from Dr Adami by this time my sad news.[1] I cannot bear to write of it. But it is necessary to send you word what to do about various things. And let me say again how deeply grateful I was to you & to the Goforths for helping us off. Give them both my kindest regards & to Bob also.

Very sincerely
Stephen Leacock

1  On 24 November 1925, Dr George Adami, the vice chancellor of the University of Liverpool, wrote to Grace Reynolds:

I have spent a very sad morning with Professor Leacock as it has fallen upon me to inform him that evidently during the voyage, smooth as it was, there has developed rapidly one of the common complications of cancer of the breast, namely the spread of the condition to the pleural cavity and the accumulation there of fluid, which, in its turn, has told upon the heart action, so that Professor Blair Bell dare not give his injections because Mrs. Leacock is not in a fit state to survive the after effects. It is a great distress to all of us to find that, after all, we are powerless to help.

Professor Leacock has asked me to write to you, as he is unable to write himself, so that you may advise his friends as to the state of the case.

## *To Caroline Ulrichsen*[1]

165 Cote des Neiges Rd
Dec 29. 1925

My dear Carrie,

Thank you very much for your letter. Stevie & I reached home yesterday. George met us here & has gone to Toronto to arrange for Beatrix's funeral.

With best love to you all
Your affe br
Stephen Leacock

1  Caroline Ulrichsen (1878–1961), née Leacock, married Jan Ulrichsen; they had three children, Barbara, David, and Dora.

# CHAPTER 6

## STEPHEN LEACOCK
# AFTER HIS WIFE'S DEATH

## 1926–1934

In *Last Leaves*, a posthumously published collection of Leacock's articles and essays, there is one telling commentary that reflects his mood during the years following his wife's death:

> The real adoring husband overtalks his wife, overdominates her, pays with unexpected presents for easy forgiveness of his ill temper, and never knows that he adored her till it is too late, because now she cannot hear it.[1]

When Beatrix died, she was only forty-six years old; Leacock himself was about to turn fifty-six. She had been relatively well until shortly before her death, and Leacock could not have expected her sudden and rapid decline in health. Now all the stability in his life was irrevocably altered, and he had never been so alone. Like the Victorian gentleman that he was, he rarely gave intimations of his deep feelings, and his letters contain little that reflects the great loss that afflicted him until the day he died. He had to continue his life, especially for the sake of his ten-year-old son, and so he threw himself into his work, both his teaching and his writing.

In 1926 Leacock enlisted the Macmillan Company's co-operation in the publication of theses written by his graduate students. On 26 April he drafted an agreement for a proposed series of monographs, the McGill University Economic Studies on the National Problems of Canada (series xv). Owning the rights to this series, the Macmillan Company was responsible for arranging and paying for the printing, binding, circulation, and sale of the theses; McGill paid the Macmillan Company fifty dollars for each thesis published in return for which the university received fifty free copies of each one. Although the series was under the

---

1 'Are Witty Women Attractive to Men?' *Last Leaves* (Toronto: McClelland and Stewart, 1945), p.4.

direction of W.W. Goforth, Leacock was very much involved in every aspect of the series, and when the Macmillan Company terminated their involvement in 1929 because of poor sales, Leacock continued to promote the series and had numbers 14 to 17 published in Orillia by the Packet-Time Press in 1930.

In 1926, Leacock also published a new volume of humour, *Winnowed Wisdom*, composed primarily of material he had written in the early part of 1925, before Beatrix's illness was diagnosed. Although the book was better than his previous two collections, it lacked the light touch of his earlier humour. He also contributed five articles to the thirteenth edition of the *Encyclopaedia Britannica*; he would later be asked to contribute articles for subsequent editions.

On the first day of May in the following year, trusting the advice of Dr Goldbloom, Leacock took his son on a trip to Europe. They travelled in company with Mr and Mrs Herbert Shaw, Mrs Shaw having been a close friend and confidante of Beatrix's, and Leacock's secretary, Grace Reynolds, who had also taken over the management of Leacock's Montreal home. After landing in Liverpool and spending some time in England, the group journeyed to France, stopping for a few days in Paris before travelling on to Biarritz, where they spent several weeks.

During this time, Grace Reynolds had become an important part of the Leacock household, assisting not only in the management of Leacock's household and business affairs but also in the care of Stephen Jr. Her decision to take a library course left Leacock again in need of a stabilizing influence. When the five returned to Canada, Leacock wrote to his sister Carrie, proposing that if her daughter Barbara was willing to come to Montreal to attend McGill and serve as his secretary, he would guarantee Barbara's tuition fees and provide her with a generous allowance. Barbara became Leacock's surrogate daughter, sensitive to all his professional needs and a constant companion at every stage of his life. She also distinguished herself academically, pursuing both a bachelor's and a master's degree. Until she became Mrs Donald Nimmo in 1937, Ba, as Leacock affectionately called her, was the new stability in Leacock's life.

After producing no books in 1927, Leacock returned to his pattern of publishing a volume of humour each year. But for whatever reason—whether it was the painful events of recent years or fatigue of his craft—Leacock's humour appeared to have lost its edge. *Short Circuits* (1928) and *The Iron Man and the Tin Woman* (1929) were relatively poor volumes, and even his next three books of humour—*Wet Wit and Dry Humour* (1931), *The Dry Pickwick and Other Incongruities* (1932), and *Afternoons in Utopia: Tales of the New Time* (1932)—though they contained some substantial pieces of comic levity, failed to produce the deft and robust humour of his earlier volumes.

At the same time, Leacock continued to undertake more serious writing, publishing *Economic Prosperity in the British Empire* in 1930 and *Back to Prosperity* —his plan to remove or reduce trade barriers within the empire—in 1932. He also published long studies of the two people he most admired, *Mark Twain* (1932) and *Charles Dickens* (1933). A total of ten books in this eight-year period proved conclusively that Leacock was still a major literary force in Canadian and international life.

Throughout these years, Leacock became increasingly close to Mrs Herbert Shaw, 'Fitz' as she was affectionately known, who was an untiring listener to his humorous diatribes and became one of his closest companions. She was also the hostess for many of the parties Leacock held at his recently built nineteen-room lodge, which replaced his original lakeside Orillia home on the same property. Leacock followed the growth of Mrs Shaw's daughter Peggy, with whom his niece Barbara formed a good friendship. His many letters to her about his Orillia property, where the Shaws also had a cottage, his use of her services in his research, and her frequent companionship gave her a central place in Leacock's world in the last two decades of his life.

On 19 January 1934 Agnes Emma Leacock died at the age of ninety. A constant source of stability and strength to the entire Leacock family, she was a woman of uncommon fortitude and perseverance, holding together her large family through times that were often good but were more often very diffficult.

## To Caroline Ulrichsen

Montreal
Jan 4 1926

My dear Carrie,

I don't remember if I wrote to you since I came home to thank you for your kind letter. Perhaps I did.

There are two things I want to know. 1st If David has any real holidays at Easter (a week or more) would he care to come up here. I'd make all arrangements & pay his way.

2nd This summer. I have to try to make a life around Stevie. Do you expect that you & the children could come up to me for the whole summer. Mrs. Hamilton will be keeping house. She was so wonderfully good in Liverpool that I want her to stay with me as much as she cares to. You don't get on well with her: But neither did I: I think you will find it different now.

Without you and the children I should feel doubtful of going: by a piece of bad luck the one summer when Peggy would have been of more use than ever, Fitz can't come as the Ardagh's want their cottage; Let me know about this when you can.

I have been hit so hard financially that at Xmas I did nothing. I shall hope presently see what I can do for Barbara.

y. affec. bro.
Stephen Leacock

## To Basil W. Willett                     Jan 9 [1926]

Dear Willett

It was so good of you to write. It seems such a long time now since first we met, that I can count you among my old friends, to whom my dear wife's death has made a real difference.

> With best regards & good
> wishes to all of you
> Stephen Leacock

## To Francis Paget Hett[1]                Jan. 12 1926

Dear Old Frank,

It was so kind and good of you to write. I am sure that both you and Alice have felt my dear wife's death very deeply.

I shall look forward to seeing you again. As far as I can make plans, my mother-in-law will help me with my Orillia house and my sister Carrie will come with her children. Orillia is so good for Stevie that I want to keep things going there.

You will be glad to know that I am starting a crusade here for the cure of cancer. You will presently perhaps hear some echoes of it in the press.

> Very sincerely,
> Stephen Leacock

1   Born in Victoria, British Columbia, the son of John Roland Hett and Letitia Martyn Sibbald, Francis Paget Hett (1878–1966) was friends with Leacock from their childhood days on Lake Simcoe and, like Leacock, attended Upper Canada College. A barrister and solicitor in England, he was the last private owner, with Hugh Sibbald, of Eildon Hall on Lake Simcoe.

## To Mrs MacDougall                       Jan 12 1926

Dear Mrs. MacDougall

My best thanks to you and Bob for your kind message. I realized how tender & kind was the feeling that inspired your letter. You will be glad to know that I do not intend to take this blow without a kick back. I am starting a campaign against cancer that will knock the hell out of it. You'll read all about it in the press in a day or two.

> Your old friend
> Stephen Leacock

## To Basil W. Willett

Montreal
January 25th, 1926

B. W. Willett, Esq.,
c/o John Lane,
The Bodley Head,
London, Eng.

My dear Willett,

I am sending you to-day the manuscript of my new book <u>WINNOWED WISDOM</u>. There will be no time for me to send you corrected proofs. But if you will send me galley proofs I will cable to you, at my expense, if there is anything wrong which needs correction.

The book runs almost exactly to 50,000 words.

If there is to be a sub-title under the main title <u>WINNOWED WISDOM</u> I will send it to you later.

Very sincerely,
Stephen Leacock

## To Gerhard Lomer

Jan 26

Dear Lomer
    (Re the Economic Monographs)
I am asking Goforth to hand over the monographs to you. You seem to be even harder up than we are. We'll have to leave over the questions of pay: the Govenors have paid a good part of my deficit any way.

Very sincerely
Stephen Leacock

## To Archibald MacMechan

Feb. 1.

My dear MacMechan

I was greatly touched on reading your letter in regard to my dear wife's death. Her loss has shown to me how greatly she was loved & valued & how many friends we had. She was so brave in her illness, so uncomplaining to the end, that I have learned courage from her. But it is a great help to receive a letter from an old friend such you have written.

With kindest regards
Stephen Leacock

*To Grace Reynolds*                    165 Cote des Neiges Rd.
                                       Montreal
                                       Feb 9 (1926)

My dear Grace

Mrs Hamilton has gone to Toronto & will not be back here this season.
My mother is ill & cant come (yet). Everybody tells me that I must have some
one permanently to look after Stevie.

At the same time the amount of secretary work that I have has fallen away
so much (now that I have given up so much of my work) that there is only about
2 hours a day at the most.

I would like to see if you would care to take over the work of looking after
Stevie. You could do my secretary work between $9^{30}$ & $11^{30}$ in the morning &
look after Stevie the rest of the time,—I dont mean every minute. He would be
with other children, or resting or out with me part of the time.  But there must
be some one in charge of him. I would make detailed arrangements with you
about days off & evenings off & all that sort of thing. You would of course live in
the house & would have to come to Orillia for at least the greater part of the
summer. At Orillia my sister Carrie is to keep house for me & the children all play
together so you would find it very easy. My sister's eldest girl is practically grown
up (she is 17 & very big & athletic so that she & you would be company for one
another. I need hardly say that at Orillia you would of course live as a member of
the family & not shut off with Stevie alone as governesses sometimes are.

In return for this I would pay you $70 a month (with board & laundry &
car fare) all the year round.

The objection is that it takes you away from your mother in the summer &
to a great extent here also

My difficulty is that I cannot afford a governess & a secretary both & it wont
do to have one person in the summer & another in the winter. But if you dont
like the idea I will try to think what I can do

No doubt you would be afraid that Orillia would be very dull for you but
if Barbara is there it wont be so at all

You had better send a copy of this letter to your mother & think it over

I shall be greatly disappointed if you dont care for the idea, but on the other
hand I can see that you might prefer not to take on this kind of job

                                       with very best regards
                                       & wishes for a good rest
                                       Stephen Leacock

## To Archibald MacMechan

McGill University,
Montreal, Que.,
March 20th, 1926

My dear MacMechan,

I am immensely interested (not of course financially) in a book which has just been published by the Bodley Head. It is called the Memoirs of Mrs Susan Sibbald edited by Frances Paget Hett (a great grandson). The Sibbald family were among the first settlers in my part of the country (the Lake Simcoe district of the county of York, Ontario). The wonderful old lady who wrote the Memoirs came out to Canada as a widow with several children, took up an estate, the most beautiful place I know in Canada, sent her boys presently into the army and the navy and to the East, where they all had very distinguished careers, and ended by founding a sort of local dynasty which still occupys a considerable place in our part of the world. These Memoirs, unfortunately, deal with what the writer remembers of things in England and Europe when she was a girl and a young married woman. I could have wished that she had kept her diaries and letters of her life in Canada. But even as it is I am told on all sides that Mrs Sibbald's diaries and letters contain a wonderfully interesting picture of the times in which she lived. As an old friend of the family and a very close friend of Frank Hett I want to do all that I can for these Memoirs, and I am sure that if I can enlist your interest, I shall have done a great deal.

With best regards and hoping to see you at the Royal Society.

Very sincerely,
Stephen Leacock

## To Sir Arthur Currie[1]

McGill University,
Montreal, Que.,
March 22, 1926

Dear Mr. Principal,

I enclose herewith a memorandum of the items of additional expenditure in my department which I should like to ask you to sanction for next year. You will observe that it represents a total of $2,200.00 over our present budget. I am very sorry to come to you again after the generous treatment which we received last year. But the growth of the work in the department is so great that what I am asking for here is only a minimum of what we could spend with great advantage if the funds were available. For example, our elementary classes in the second year in Arts, in Commerce and in Social Science now number two hundred and ten, to say nothing of the hundred and thirty-four students in Applied Science, and ought to have far more tutorial work than we can possibly

1   See footnote 1, page 159.

give them with our present facilities. In addition to this nearly all our senior classes are so large that the method of ordinary lecturing is no longer satisfactory by itself. In short we need from now on as many young men as tutors as the college finances will permit.

The other items for printing and publication etcetera etc also seem of great importance. We are most anxious to expand the graduate school into what one may might call an advanced national school of Canadian economics. We want to draw to us, especially from the West of Canada, young men who have taken courses in the junior universities and who would like to have the further advantage of a year of study in a great trading and commercial centre such as Montreal.

You will notice that there are certain requirements which I have written in red ink. I have put in the red ink merely for ease of representation. There are the things which I propose to finance with the help of friends and graduates without coming on the govenors for assistance.

I have included at the end a the publication of a quarterly xxxxxxx economic journal. I do not think that this can be accomplished until times are much better in Canada. But I should like to have it kept in sight as one of the aims of the department.

After you have had time to look through these items, I should like, at you convenience, to come in and see you about them.

> Very sincerely
> Stephen Leacock

## TWO GRADUATE TUTORS AT $500.00 EACH

In connection with the need for more tutorial work which I have mentioned, I should like to be able to appoint for next year two graduates who would at the same time study for the M.A. degree and help us as tutors in the junior and large classes. I am specially anxious to get two young men from the West of Canada in order to set up a connection of that kind from which a great deal might be expected in the future. I have already ventured to discuss this subject with Principal Tory of the University of Alberta and I may say that he met the suggestion with great enthusiasm.

## MR. GOFORTH TO BE AN ASSISTANT PROFESSOR
### AT $3,000.00 per annum.

As I have mentioned to you several times, I have been greatly impressed with the excellent work of Mr. Goforth and with the spirit and the enthusiasm which he brings to it. I have told him that from now on there will be in the department a lot of editorial work in connection with the printing of monographs which can only be done after the regular session is closed. We find by experience that after the men have completed their theses for the M.A. degree there is a lot to be done before their work can be put in shape for printing and publication as a monograph. I am very anxious to have Goforth ~~to~~ stay with us at a fee which will enable him to meet his living expenses [he has a wife and one child] and I think that if you can see your way to appoint him an assistant professor at a salary of $3,000.00 a year, it would then be quite fair to ask him to take over in return the work of which I speak. Goforth expects to live in Montreal during the summer months and this arrangement would mean that we always have somebody in the department who is on the spot to look after anything that needs to be attended to in the summer.

## PUBLICATION OF FURTHER ECONOMIC MONOGRAPHS
### $200

Last year, as you will remember, we published four monographs of which, for greater certainty, I send you copies herewith. These cost us a great deal of work and involved a deficit in money of several hundred dollars. But I have been assured on every side that they were well worth while. The London Times and the London Morning Post spoke of these things as a genuine service and in Canada they met with a cordial reception everywhere.

The Macmillan Company have been more than satisfied with their share in the enterprise and have made us an offer for the purchase of 350 copies of each of the monographs which we propose to publish this year. The titles of these new monographs are as follows:—

1. The Nova Scotia Coal Question. Eugene Forsey
2. The Pulp & Paper Industry & the Proposed Embargo. N. Reich
3. The Port of Montreal . . . . L. Tombs
4. the Motor Car industry in Canada _ _ _ _ H. Aikman

If we add to this the regular sales and the supply of copies at a cost price to the library, the budget for these monographs so nearly balances that there should be no greater deficit than fifty dollars for each one of them or $200.00 in all.

## RENEWAL OF THE MONTREAL MANUFACTURERS
### GRADUATE FELLOWSHIP $800.00 A YEAR

The money which was given to me about four years ago through the kindness of Julian Smith and various other members of the Montreal Manufacturers Association, and which enabled me to pay $800. a year as a graduate fellowship ( an enormous help in our graduate work) is now exhausted.[x] I propose to go and see Mr. Smith and some of my friends and get this money renewed for a few years until when times are better I can raise the necessary capital sum to make it a permanent endowment.

You will observe that this item makes no claim on the college finances.

[x] I find on enquiry that it will still run for one year.

<u>BOOKS FOR A DEPARTMENTAL LIBRARY</u>

With our installation in a new building and with adequate quarters for the work of the department I am most anxious to get together a departmental library of about 1,000 standard books in Economics. The aim is that our economic students may then look on the department as their headquarters where they may carry on the bulk of their work without distraction and without running back and forward.

I propose to get these books without adding to the annual budget. I have prepared and am sending out to our graduates in economics of the last twenty years a circular and a book plate which I enclose herewith asking each of them to send me a few books and particularly books which they used when they were at college. I have ~~prepared and enclosed a~~ written on the book plate ~~with~~ a latin inscription which will go in each book with the signature of the donor and will serve at one and the same time to commemorate the name of the giver and to get me the books which I want.

We shall also need charts, maps, pictures and other equipment. I will undertake to find the money for it.

## *To William C. Bell* (April 15, 1926)

Dear Billy

Best thanks for the Susan Sibbald Memoir. I have written to Macmechan (of Dalhousie University. He reviews for the Standard) & he is much interested. Send me a few of the circulars. Stevie will write when his parcel comes. It is very likely in the mail now.

> V. sincerely
> Stephen Leacock

## *To Dr Alton Goldbloom* [Prince George Hotel
> Toronto]
> ~~Wed~~ Tues. May 4 [192]6

My dear Goldbloom

I have just received a telegram to say that Dr Timme will see me on the morning of <u>Thursday May 6</u> but cannot give me a later date as he is going out of town.

I suppose this means that you can not be with us which I regret very much. But I will bring you back word what Timme says & will not do anything without your approval. Let me take this occasion to express again my thanks for your kindness & unfailing attention.

> Very sincerely
> Stephen Leacock

## To Dr Alton Goldbloom                May 11th, 1926

My dear Goldbloom,

I am so sorry that in the rush of college business I have not been able to see you to-day. Dr. Timme whom I saw in New York asks if you will be kind enough to send him Stevie's record. I am having XRays taken for Timme in Toronto. When he has all the material he is to give me an opinion. I will let you know what he says.

Very sincerely,
Stephen Leacock.

Dr. Timme's Address is:—
Dr. Walter Timme,
1 West 64th Street,
New York, N.Y.

## To William Wallace Goforth               Orillia, Ont.
                                            September 9th. 1926.

My Dear Goforth:

I enclose a letter from Mr. Eayrs with every word of which I agree. At a price of $1.00 the Monographs will not sell: the deficit will be so large that the enterprise must collapse. I could get the governors to pay it once but never again. We must get the costs down, 20,000 words is enough. You must cut Frisey's thesis. We can only bind in paper and can only afford last year's scale of things.

I am willing to put the price at 60 cents (if Mr. Eayrs consents) and to ask him to take 300 of each Monograph at 40 cents: we can sell to the Montreal trade (with return privilege at 50 cents). By that we get from Mr. Eayrs for each Monograph $120. and by selling 100 of each in Montreal we get $50. That will cut the deficit to a point where we can face it. I will consent that Tombs may have more words provided that he pays the difference and any number of charts and maps if he pays for them but not a different form.

Please lose no time in looking into this. We must remember that we are only judged by results, both you and I. Explanations of failure won't interest anybody a particle. Best regards and with no feeling of censure or trouble,

Stephen Leacock.

## To Hugh Eayrs

[McGill University
Montreal]
September 23rd 1926.

Mr. Eayres,
MacMillan Publishing Co. of Canada Ltd.,
TORONTO, ONT.

Dear Mr. Eayres,

Goforth, and I, and Lawrence Tombs have been discussing very fully the question of the selling price of our monographs. We find that nothing below 60¢ would be possible, owing to the greater length, better paper and binding, and considerably better contents of the new booklets. 60¢ would be a very tight squeeze, and it would compel me to ask the Governors to cover the deficit of $100.00 per monograph.

75¢, from our point of view is the best price. This would still mean that we do not cover our cost, and that the Governors would have to expend a little money to cover the shortage.

We are taking for granted that at 75¢, you would take 300 of each at 50¢.

Let me know whether you can accept this arrangement. We should leave to you entirely the price (between 50¢ and 75¢) at which you sell to the trade.

I need hardly say that of course we are open to further discussion, and will do nothing that does not meet your views.

Best regards,
Stephen Leacock

P.S. Please answer to Goforth, I shall be in New York for some days.


## To Mrs Wainwright

McGill University
Montreal
Nov 15 1926

My dear Mrs. Wainwright—.

I was so glad to get your very kind letter, which recalled to me so vividly the pleasant visit that I made at your house. I meant to send you a line after I had had a glimpse of your husband at the dinner in New York when he gave me best regards & good wishes from both of you.

It is so good of you to ask about Stevie; he is flourishing but still terribly small. Today I am taking him to New York for a (second) consultation with Dr Walter Timme & I feel sure that his report will be favorable.

If this reaches you in Liverpool do please see my dear friend Mrs Adami—or no doubt you have seen her already. She was infinitely kind to Beatrix in her last illness and a wonderful help to Stevie & me & I feel for her so much last summer when she lost her own husband, himself a very old friend of mine. The newspapers I fear put into quite a false light the little bit I have been able to do about cancer. It has only been to give some money & some time towards introducing here Blair Bell's lead treatment. But I fear that it looks like a blind alley. For the present there seems to be nothing for it but research & still more research.

If you will—answering your suggestion—send Stevie an English Xmas card I am sure he will be delighted.

> With best regards to you &
> to your husband
> Stephen Leacock

## To Dr Alton Goldbloom

[The Old Brewery Bay
Orillia, Ontario]
Nov. 23 1926

My dear Goldbloom.

Dr Timme found Stevie in excellent shape. He wants me from now on to get you to send a monthly report on <u>height</u> & <u>weight</u> & measurements. He ~~always~~ also wants a comment on Steve's heart & general health. There is a slight murmuring of the heart which Timme says is frequent in such cases & need not be a cause of alarm.

Please dont name any symptoms, any <u>heart</u> or anything, in Stevie's hearing as he grows very sensitive.

> Very sincerely,
> Stephen Leacock.

## To Basil W. Willett

165 Cote des Neiges Road
Montreal
(January 1927)

Dear Willett

The <u>Behind the Beyond</u> stuff is all right. I gave permission to Mr Clinton Baddeley, a Don of Jesus College, to go ahead with it at Cambridge (not for money) & to do what he liked with it for money in London paying us what he thought right. The advertisement is with it.

I dont think I'll have enough material for a book in the spring: I may, in the autumn.

> My very best regards to all
> of you
> Stephen Leacock

*To Miss Sommer*                                    [McGill University
                                                    Montreal]
                                                    March 14 1927

Dear Miss Sommer

As I am fifty seven years old I think I may safely give you my photograph, as long as you promise not to look at it but only to hand it on to the printers.

And I am delighted to let you keep the MS of mine, & I will keep your letter & put it away in old lavendar

                                        with best regards
                                        Stephen Leacock

P.S. To come down to business, I will tell Notman to post you a photograph.


*To Sir Arthur Currie*                              [McGill University
                                                    Montreal]
                                                    Mar. 17. 1927.

Sir Arthur Currie
McGill

Dear Mr Principal

I want to ask if I can keep on <u>John Culliton</u>, now a teaching fellow, as a sessional lecturer for two more sessions (1927–28, 1928–29).[1] After that Eugene Forsey will be available to come on the staff as already discussed by you an me in conversation.

I send you herewith a broadside sheet of the work on the department. The second year, in spite of the relief given, is still crowded. The honour classes of the third and fourth year are still partly joined. This makes some of the classes too large for proper advanced teaching. For example <u>Economics 10</u>, an advanced & difficult course has <u>46</u> students.

I would like to give Culliton $1500 a session & pay it between Oct 1 & May 1st. If I have to, I will drop <u>one</u> of the two graduate fellows granted last year as an annual feature.

If Goforth goes to China I can manage without him if I have Culliton & two graduate fellows. I enclose tables to show the changes in the budget. They are nothing.

                                        Very sincerely
                                        Stephen Leacock

1   John Culliton (1905–1963), a member of the Economics department at McGill and one of Leacock's most beloved colleagues, graduated with a BA from the University of Saskatchewan in 1926 and came to McGill to obtain his MA. He was appointed lecturer in 1927.

## To Sir Arthur Currie

[McGill University
Montreal]
May 18 1927

Sir Arthur Currie
McGill University

Dear Mr Principal

In the light of our conversation of last week, I understand that you are kind enough to allow us to add the name of Mr John Culliton (B.A. <u>Sask</u>. M A McGill) to the staff of our department as a sessional lecturer

In reorganising our work on this basis we assign some ~~14~~ 12 to 14 hours (as shown in the enclosed schedule) to Mr Culliton. We are all very appreciative of the help thus given to us.

Very sincerely
Stephen Leacock

This enables us among other things to undertake 3 hours a week all year of <u>Pacific Economics</u>. S.L.

## To Grace Reynolds

[Hotel D'Angleterre
Biarritz]
Sunday ~~May~~ Jul 3/27

Dear Grace

I got your telegram & your letter from Paris & your card from Cherbourg & was so glad that you got away with so little trouble. Mr Clark wrote & expressed regret that on that day no one was able to meet your train . . . so by this time you will be out on the ocean . . . Mr Clark said that he had put your name on their special list so that you will find friends . . . By the time you get this you will be quite settled down at home as if you never been away.

Write & tell me what Mr Glassco said & what plans you are making . . Dont forget to look in on the tenants & see if things are all right . . . Pay W$^{\underline{m}}$ Gentleman 5$^{\underline{00}}$ for May if I didnt do it & 5$^{\underline{00}}$ for June & charge it to me . . . . . . I've been cabling about Shawinigan it fell quite suddenly well below my selling point: I've got no answer yet . . . Stevie & I both miss you & find it very queer to have to do everything for ourselves. My dress suit, for instance, never came back & I realized it had been away four days & raised hell . . . . .

Give me all the news when you write: there are a lot of little things you were going to see to, & for the moment I dont think of them

with very best regards from
both of us
very sincerely
Stephen Leacock

## To Francis Paget Hett

[Hotel d'Angleterre
Biarritz]
July 18 1927

Dear Frank,

I'm afraid that I won't be in London: I may take the boat at Southampton (instead of Cherbourg) so as to have a day or so in Hampshire: but I can't manage the trip for London.

I gather from your letter that you & Alice will hardly be able to come to Canada this autumn.

But if I am wrong & if you are there in September couldn't you both come to me for a fortnight or so.

I am sorry to hear that you had to have an operation & hope that you are getting along all right.

I go home in August (I've been here all summer for Stevie's growth) & though my Orillia house is rented now I expect to get into it on Sept 1st.

With best regards
Stephen Leacock

## To Grace Reynolds

Hotel d'Angleterre
Biarritz
Wed. July 27 '27

Dear Grace.

Yes, I was surprised to hear from your letter that you are not going to get married. I thought it all settled. But on the other hand I have always felt that it is a wretched thing for people to get married unless they really & truly love one another & cant get on without one another. Short of that there is nothing in it. A woman needs to be at least twice as old as you are, in fact more than half as old as I am, before she needs to marry just to get a husband and a home.

Your letter naturally didnt give me any details and I couldn't gather whether you had made up your mind finally, so of course I cant give you any advice. But I may perhaps say this: I was to give you, you remember, a bonus of salary as a present to help you get married and of course I'll give you that just the same. With the salary that you brought home and with that you wont need to worry about the immediate financial aspect of things. Barbara is coming to my house & the secretary work of mine gets less then so that there wouldn't be any use in our thinking of your old job: it wouldn't be enough. But we will see what there is at McGill and if you work down town we can see what extra stuff there is if it is needed . . . . But there is no use trying to write all this in a letter. You can tell me all about it when I see you in Montreal.

The Montroyal only comes to Quebec & I go by train to Montreal but dont meet it as I may not take the boat train: I'll cable you up from the Ritz & you can have all my mail ready to bring down & if you are working you can leave a note at the Ritz to say when you will come there. I may need your help with some of my papers, especially the taxes.

Stephen Leacock

## To Arthur Thompson                    November 30th, 1927

Arthur Thompson. Esq.
Barrister,
Orillia, Ont.

Dear Arthur:

Yours November 28th, I wired you to-day, "Yes, let Watson make survey as in your letter."

Re Wilson. I'll give him $10.00, for an option on the property, as in your letter, good till July 1st, 1928, (next summer). The sum involved is too big to buy blind. He is an honest man.

Re Langman. If I buy there I want as high a dam and as big a pond as I can get by flooding back till I am forced to stop by coming to the road in the west. I'll give Langman $10.00 for an option, till July 1st, 1928, as in the agreement you drew plus all the extra land to flood and forty feet shore line at $25.00 an acre. Meantime I shall be obliged if Mr. Langman will return my $50.00, or else return forty of it and give the option just mentioned.

If, which I hardly expect, it turns out that Haglett and Moore will sell at $25.00 an acre, I'll come up to Orillia now, in the hope a speedy conclusion. The money involved is too big to be spent without accurate immformation. If they will not sell the whole matter must wait.

It is perhaps proper to say that the map made and sent to me and returned herewith is not (as I remember the agreement) correct and I do not accept it, in the case an option is purchased as in this letter, as discribing the land to be sold.

It substitutes a line drawn to the road corner of the fence for a line drawn to the nearest point of the fence. (see my corrections).

Please note that apart from this option it does not matter whether the line is or is not correct, or whether the agreement says this or says that, as the whole proposed bargain is off and my be replaced by a similar one, or by another one, or by none at all.

With renewed thanks for your care of my interest.

Very sincerely,

## To H.L. Draper

Orillia. Ont.
July 5. 1928

Dear Mr Draper

I am asking the Graduate Faculty to admit you to our school (to which I shall be delighted to welcome you) on condition that you do some summer reading (say, equal to 1 hour a day) on the <u>Govt of Canada</u> & on <u>Money</u> . . . if you have special areas in mind, I'll consider assigning other things: but you're weak in those

Also that you take 3 hours a week of <u>lectures</u> apart from seminar & thesis (Most students do this anyway)

. . . . If you accept this, write to me at Orillia for references to read: if you are anywhere near Orillia come & see me: and wherever you are, start & decide on a thesis (write to the Ass'nt Registrar for a printed circular) . . . . try to get a subject that will fit in with your proposed career & help to get you a position . . . . . . explain to me what you want to do in life . . . bank? journalism? college work? finance? civil service? . . .

Very sincerely
Stephen Leacock

P.S. I am asking the Dean to send this on to you if he approves. This will complete your business of application.


## To Kenneth Noxon[1]

[The Old Brewery Bay
Orillia]
Sep 1 1928.

Kenneth Noxon. Esqre
Wright & Noxon

My dear Noxon,

In sending you the enclosed order on my bank for payment of your accounts, let me accompany it by the expression of my appreciation of your work. I feel that I shall always be in your debt for your brilliant original plan of remodelling or rather rebuilding my house instead of merely moving and enlarging it.

You have made it a thing of great beauty and for me a source of pleasure and satisfaction for the rest of my life.

Very sincerely
Stephen Leacock

1   Kenneth Noxon, the first architect to graduate from the University of Toronto with a Master of Architecture, designed Leacock's rebuilt summer home in Orillia in 1928.

## To Eugene Forsey

[McGill University
Montreal]
Jan 10 1929

Eugene Forsey. Esq.M.A.
Balliol College
Oxford Engl

Dear Eugene

I sent you a cable (copy enc.) just before I got your letter . . . It is proving a little difficult to get the funds for Culliton to go to study in S. Africa & Australia & we would have a better chance a year hence. Therefore it would suit our plans better if you, without serious disadvantage to yourself, could stay in England another year. But your own claims come first & if this wont fit in with your plans you must of course come here & we will see what can be done for culliton . .

Very best regards
Stephen Leacock

P.S. I wrote a letter (officially) to Dr Martin (Acting principal) in regard to your appointment and he answers that as the matter does not effect the budget & only involves your taking Culliton's place, as agreed with Culliton, it is matter for the department. With this I think we may go ahead.

## To Mrs R. B. Hamilton[1]

Feb 24 1929

My dear Mrs Hamilton

I have just learned to my great surprise that last March you signed away your interest in the existing Pellatt trust in favour of a promissory note of Sir Henry Pellatt with certain shares in a company of his as collateral. You will understand that such a change in the nature of the trust introduces a grave element of risk and imperils Stevie's entire inheritance. A trust ought not to depend on the solvency or insolvency of any single man but should consist of real and definite securities of an absolutely first class marketable character. My lawyer Mr G.L. Smith of Smith Rae & Greer is looking into the matter to see what can be done to safeguard Stevie's interest and I trust you will see fit to accept whatever advice he gives you. The consequences of what you have done might be very serious . . . . .

Will you please communicate with Mr G.L.Smith & let him know whether you are willing to associate yourself with what he is doing or whether you do not intend to do so.

1    Mrs R.B. Hamilton was the mother of Beatrix Leacock and Stephen Leacock's mother-in-law.

## To Canadian Librarians

[McGill University
Montreal]
April 15th, 1929.

Dear Librarian:—

I wonder if you are aware that for some time we have been publishing a series of Monographs on National Problems of Canada. Associated in the publication of these is The Macmillan Company of Canada Limited, who have published these monographs for this department. I enclose a full list of the last and forthcoming series.

These monographs are prepared in our graduate school. They involve a lot of work, and contain information not obtainable elsewhere.

We think it very important for the Canadian Universities to carry on this class of work. It is, without exaggeration or rhetoric, a patriotic thing to do. We must not always lean on the United States for our research and our publication.

But such an enterprise needs support. I hope that you will see fit to ask your Board to give a standing order for this series to The Macmillan Company of Canada Limited.

Very sincerely,
Stephen Leacock.

## To Sir Arthur Currie

[Chateau Laurier
Ottawa, Ontario]
May 22. 1929.

My dear Sir Arthur

I am very glad, as we all are, to know that you are back with us: and I am sorry that I go from here (Ottawa–Royal & Economic Societies) to Orillia & shall miss seeing you on your arrival.

I am sending you by later post an extended report on the department to show what we have been doing. But please dont bother to read it till you have some leisure time, as there is nothing in it beyond our following along as we were. Only one thing I might call to your attention without delay. John Farthing has had a severe breakdown, mental we all presume, & I fear he is still far from well. I kept in touch with the Bishop by letter & telephone but I did not see John as it was evidently not desired. I felt sure that you would like to know about this. When the time came to make the budget I wrote & asked the board to give Farthing the increase of $500 to bring him to $3000. This as I recall it was entirely along the lines intended when he came to us, was it not . . . But the rest of the things I can keep till you have time. We had a wonderfully successful year.

> With very best regards to Lady
> Currie & to yourself
> Stephen Leacock

---

## To Gerhard Lomer

[The Old Brewery Bay
Orillia]
June 8 1929

Dear Lomer

Re <u>monographs</u> . . . . . All <u>sales</u> are made by the Macmillan Co.. please refer all orders to them. They sell to <u>libraries</u> as well as in stores. There are no free copies except to the advertisers . . The college pays a <u>subsidy</u> of such such a sum only a small part of the total cost: the rest is met by sales & advertisements. . We do not therefore wish the library to give any <u>away</u>. . If we supply you with ten of each I imagine that that will enough for casual use by readers in the library. I will therefore ask the Macmillan Co. to see that you get these . . .

They will send you a list of the publications up to date & if you will please mark down any of which you have no copies or less than ten copies & send it to them, I am sure they will be glad to give you the books & in future to send you 10 of each regularly.

Where they cannot supply them perhaps you can get what you want from those in the possession of the department, in my room in the Arts building. I am sorry not to be able to <u>exchange</u> them but the financing of these is a great difficulty & I am not sure that the series can go on. As it is I am having to offer a personal guarantee.

> Very sincerely
> Stephen Leacock

---

## To Sir Arthur Currie

[The Old Brewery Bay
Orillia]
Sep 16.29

Sir Arthur Currie
McGill

My dear Sir Arthur—

I send herewith a report on the work in the department of Economics, but before I discuss it, let me first say how glad I am that you are back again: René du Roure who is up here with me tells me that you are looking very well, and "right on the job" again.

I have made the report as short as possible as you know all about Goforth leaving & Forsey being appointed etc.

The great difficulty is with Farthing, but I gather from his letter that you would know more about his condition than I do as you have seen him. Our other difficulty is with the Macmillans printing of our monographs as it is hard to get the advertisements. I may get you to help me to persuade the Bank of Montreal & the Canadian National Railways to give us a lift.

I shall look forward to seeing you again at the end of the month.

Very sincerely
Stephen Leacock

## *To Agnes Leacock*[1]

165 Cote des Neiges Rd
Mon Nov 25 29

Dear Mother

Herewith a notice of Stevie's play . . . He is very well & the doctor says is growing quite satisfactorily . . . I want to send his outgrown things to some one: how old is Teddy's Dick . . . . . . Barbara is going home for Xmas but Stevie & I to Orillia . . . We go via Oshawa but I will bring him to Toronto to see you.

y. aff. son
Stephen Leacock

---

1   Attached to this letter was the following newspaper clipping:

PLAY "RED RIDING HOOD"
_____

Dramatic Story Acted by
Troupe of Children

A charming dramatic entertainment in the form of an up-to-date version of "Red Riding Hood" was given by Miss Peggy Shaw and a troupe of little friends at the home of Mrs. Herbert Shaw, 19 Redpath Crescent, on Saturday afternoon. The title role was played, with great charm by Miss Peggy Shaw. The part of the wolf, modernized into the wicked young Lord Wolf, was taken by Master Stevie Leacock, who displayed exceptional dramatic talent. Miss Marion Savage, as Janet the Lady's maid to Lady Hood, showed decided histrionic ability.

The part of Lady Hood, mother of Red Riding Hood, was ably presented by Miss Faith Lyman, while that of the Lady Dowager Hood, an up-to-date grandmother to whom her grandchild brings not butter and eggs, but pate de fois gras, was delightfully done by Miss Jean Scrymgeour, whose youth belied her powdered hair and antique gown. Master Francis Lyman did good work as Gaffer Gammon, the woodcutter, and Miss Peggy Cape made a brief but telling appearance as the maid to the Dowager Lady Hood.

The play was preceded by a musical rendering of "The Painted Doll," in which the following children appeared daintily costumed in character: Peggy Shaw, Sybil Shires, Ian Bailey, Pamela Wilson, Nora Bailey, Peggy Cape, Joan Stearnes, Marion Savage, Jean Scrymgeour, A. Scrymgeour, David Cape, Stephen Leacock, Faith Lyman and Francis Lyman. The stage management and production were the work of Captain Rene du Roure.

*To Hugh Eayrs*                          [McGill University
                                         Montreal]
                                         Dec 5 29

<u>Re my book</u>
<u>The Economic Integration of the</u>
<u>British Empire</u>

Dear Eayrs,

I appreciate & value very much your warm reception of the idea of my book.

Its length will be 80 to 100 thousand words  It should contain about <u>20 maps</u> of the same size as the page, bound ~~round~~ right in with the page. Tables also but they dont matter & they only cost the same as type.

Should be completed on May 24th . . .

I hope for a retail price as low as $2.<u>00</u>: I want to plan for a real "killing" & any price over 2.<u>00</u>.

I have written so far a good many thousand words & am working on it every day. I am engaging one of my colleagues Prof Culliton to work on statistical matter.

There will be no difficulty whatever in our arranging terms of publication. But what I am anxious for is that the book should have a good appearance & be put on the market with a "hurrah" . . . . when I get enough of it done so that you & Smith can feel that the conclusion is a certainty & have time to read some of the text & judge of its "appeal" we could almost start to put into galley proof perhaps?

. . . . . . . .

Further:—I propose to get entire control in Canada of all my books past & present (i.e. take them away from the Oxford Press to whom my lawyers are writing) so that if ever the time comes we can get out a complete addition . . . . <u>But</u> meanwhile McLellan & Stewart want to get out a Canadian Edition of Sunshine Sketches. I told them that I wanted the copyright of all my books to remain with your house & me, but that if they cared to get out an edition without holding an <u>exclusive</u> agency, of course I'd be very pleased <u>subject always</u> to the fact that you might not think it in your interest . . . . I said that I would leave it entirely to you: it is too small a matter to bother with . . . .

Dont you think that when Gundy lets go of all my books we might think about a cheap Canadian edition of the whole lot of them,—or of the best titles first?

. . . . . . . . . .

When are you coming down? I'll be in Toronto for a day on or about Dec 28, or 29.

                                    best regards
                                    Stephen Leacock

## To the Orillia Packet and Times                Jan. 20, 1930

Orillia Packet and Times
Orillia, Ont.

Dear Sirs:

In accordance with our previous correspondance I now send you the M.S. of the "Asbestos Industry in Canada" by G.M. Mendels with a view to your printing it as one of the monographs of the Department called the "National Problems of Canada" as per sample. It is understood that you receive $130 for 500 copies printed according to sample—the monographs not to exceed, for that sum, 20,000 words. Kindly look over the monograph sent and ratify this arrangement and if on your calculations it is found to exceed 20,000 please tell me what extra sum would be required.

Later I will propose to you when I see you at Easter a scheme for taking over the selling of these monographs—you to do the work of distributing and soliciting orders by mail: I to pay the postage and stationery involved in ~~your~~ in handling copies, proofs, return ~~postage~~ copies etc.—in other words you supply the labour and trouble and time, but not out of pocket expences postage and material: you to receive 10 cents per copy on all copies sold or sent to purchasers by you: retail price is to be 60 cents and a subscription price is 50 cents. Copyright to remain with the University or the author, not you: your rights only to a service and a payment. No proprietorship contract (as far as legally binding) to be between you and me, not you and McGill.

Very Sincerely Yours,
Stephen Leacock

P.S. Other monographs ready to follow: four a year   Kindly indicate extra charge per 100 after 500 and how long type will be kept before breaking up.

## To Hugh Eayrs                [McGill University
                                Montreal]
                                Jan 24 1930

Dear Eayrs,

My book is driving ahead. I have a stenographer typing as I go & one of the McGill staff engaged to work on statistics. I have every hope of finishing it on April 1st.

Meantime I want to get started on publicity . . I am having 1000 four page circulars (see form enclosed) printed here (red ink for main headings) with copious extracts—quite enough I know to sell the book in thousands. Naturally your firm name is not on the circulars <u>yet</u> but I will send you the page proof & then if all is satisfactory you can put it in...The cost is $20 and I pay it for the time being and you reimburse me if & when, & only when you pay my first royalties—ergo if the book is never finished you pay nothing

As soon as you see the circular you can see enough of the book in the extracts to judge of its carrying power & then we'll proceed to a contract. As I said in conversation I want 10 per cent on the first 5000 in Canada & then 20% and 10 per cent on the first five thousand in England & then 20% & ditto in the U.S. & advance royalty in a lump of $2500.<sup>00</sup>. I am sure from what you said that this will suit

I think the shape & form in which you have done Laurey's Export Trade would be just right & a retail price of $2.<u>00</u>,—not more as we want a wide sale.

> Best regards
> Stephen Leacock


## To Sir Arthur Currie

[McGill University
Montreal]
Feb 6 1930

Dear Mr Principal

To get further information on one or two matters concerning my department of which you spoke  I held a meeting of the members yesterday

I. In regard to <u>Human Relations</u> all of them would be very glad to assist in organising it. I have also written to Yale & Chicago for light: and I have consulted my friend (& yours) Captain Arthur Mathewson (Alderman) & he is writing me suggestions for lines of work.

II. <u>Mr Farthing & whether if he leaves to replace him by extra teaching tutors or by an appointment</u>. All agree that we can carry on for one more session so as to keep Farthing's place open another year. The department disagree with me in preferring (all of them) an appointment of a teacher rather than teaching tutors. I think they are wrong but of course would prefer to accept their views.

III. Commerce. In regard to what can be done to improve the work in Commerce with <u>Dr Hemmeon</u> & Dr Day[1] would like a chance to see you personally.

IV. I forget No 4 . . .

> Very sincerely
> Stephen Leacock

---

1   John Percival Day (1880–1949) received a doctorate from the University of St Andrews and joined McGill in 1923 as an associate professor of economics. He became chair of the department following Dr Hemmeon.

## To Hugh Eayrs

Please acknowledge
at once

[McGill University
Montreal]
Feb 13 1930

My dear Eayrs

By this same mail I send you proofs of circular of Economic Integr$^{n}$ of the British Empire . . . . I am most anxious to get things arranged and publicity started . . . Barring illness or accident I'll have copy finished April 1st——55,000 to 80,000 words—I submit that retail price $2.00 is best,—I mean not more: maps,—3 or 4 blue & yellow maps same size as page . . . several lists & tables made up of ordinary type & lines—If you follow all that is going on,—Lord Beaverbrook Baldwin, Lord Melchett, etc you will know that this is the very moment for this book. I hope that you can send me acceptance without delay. I can hardly wait for <u>letters</u> to & from England but no doubt you can get all needed authorization by cable. I gather that Sir F. Macmillan is in the thick of things. Send me word, the earliest minute possible, & indicate how you want the firm name put into the circular.

Best regards
Stephen Leacock

## To Frank Dodd

[McGill University
Montreal]
Feb 28 1930

Frank Dodd Esqr
Dodd Mead & Co. New York

Dear Dodd

I have your letter of Feb 20 and accept the terms named in it for a book of selections viz ten per cent to four thousand & 15 per cent after that. It is perhaps only fair to say that when I have a book to sell I think I can get 20% for it: but I may be mistaken. I am glad that you are interested in the idea of an autumn book but I am afraid I shall not be ready with one. I have some material that is very good but not much chance to get much more of it just now as I am terribly busy with a book on The <u>Economic Integration of the British Empire</u> which ought to be on the market by June if it's to have a good chance before the English elections.

Would there be any sense in a smaller book,—say 30,000 words at a cheaper price, timed to hit the Christmas market? or would that only lose the chance of selling a bigger one.

> Very sincerely
> Stephen Leacock

P.S. No. You make the selections since you know the public better

## To Frank Dodd                                     Mar 14

Dear Frank:

I am very glad to learn of your interest in my book on the Economic Integration of the British Empire. It is not a funny book but a book of imperial and world politics. Personally I should be most happy to let you have the book on a basis of 10% royalties on the first 5000 and after that 15% with a retail price suggested at $2.00 (the book will have 60,000 to 80,000 words and with the advance royalty left entirely to you to after seeing the full MS. . . But I am not free to act alone in the matter, my contract is with the Macmillan Co. of Toronto (Mr. Eayrs the general manager being an old friend of mine) and under it I am to have in Canada 10% on the first 5000 and then 20% and they are to get me the same in England, and they are to dispose of the book in the U.S. where, I have already told them I will accept 15%.

Their New York branch do not think there would be sufficient American interest in the book to warrant printing a separate edition and would only be willing to buy from the Canada and England, to which I would not consent. I think and Mr. Eayrs thinks that this is entirely wrong and that the back kick from the English market of the big sale which we expect would easily run an American edition. Personally I hope for great things; if the book gets out before the next general election in England I think it may make a great hit. You will notice however that I write to you with entire frankness. Unless Mr. Eayrs has already made an arrangement I would like him to offer you the book as the terms above and with a view to this I will send him this letter and ask him if the matter is still open, and if he approves to send it on to you.

In any case I am much obliged at the evidence of your interest.

> S.L.

*To Hugh Eayrs*                                [McGill University
                                               Montreal]
                                               April 14 1930

The Macmillan Co
Bond St. Toronto

My dear Eayrs
    Today by express I send you my book all complete, in triplicate, typed on 3
different colours of paper. Also three maps: as I dont understand the technique
of reproducing them I didnt make 3 copies of each. I can if it is quicker. But I
thought they would perhaps have to be redrawn by the printers.
    Do Rush the book & boom it. I spoke here at the Board of Trade on the
Integration of the Empire April 9 with huge success—The president wrote me
to say how ~~they~~ enthusiastic they were & that the members would be glad to
help to circulate my book as soon as it came out. Please dont let the maps hold
the book back . . . If it is printed in England I dont need to read proofs.
    Please acknowledge book by telegraph to Montreal & my niece will get the
message: I am going tonight to Orillia & will be there till Easter Monday

                                               best regards
                                               Stephen Leacock


*To Sir Arthur Currie*                         [McGill University
                                               Montreal]
                                               April 29 1930

Sir Arthur Currie
McGill University

My dear Sir Arthur
    I am sorry to say that I have not been very well for the last five days. I have
a giddiness which comes & goes & which makes it hard for me to undertake to
do anything at a fixed time.
    With your approval I will ask Hemmeon to act as head for the few weeks
left this term & I will come & go as best I can. In any case lectures are over &
I have hardly any work.

                                               Very sincerely
                                               Stephen Leacock

## To Sir Arthur Currie

[The Old Brewery Bay
Orillia]
May 14. 1930.

My dear Sir Arthur

I am sorry to say that I find it not advisable to try to get back to McGill at all this month . . . . I am getting on well enough but I get a bad spell every now & then when I find it troublesome to keep on my feet and when my 'cruising radius' is limited. . . I imagine I'll be all right in a month

. . . . I am much obliged for your visit to my house the other day: till you came I had been getting quite nervous but your talk was most encouraging . . . . Hemmeon sends word that everything is going along quite all right.

With sincerest thanks for your
kindness
Stephen Leacock

## To Sir Arthur Currie

[The Old Brewery Bay
Orillia]
(late May)

My dear Sir Arthur

By this same mail I send you a letter on college business. But apart from that I want to ask you to do a personal favour for me, or rather for some of my friends.

You are, I believe, ex officio, one of the directors of Trafalgar school. At present the number of applications for admission as borders is far beyond the accomodation. Two friends of mine Mr & Mrs Herbert Shaw of Redpath Crescent Montreal want to enter their little girl as a boarder next year and Mrs Shaw has asked me to write and get you to use your influence. Peggy Shaw & my little boy have been playmates all their lives, so that naturally I am much interested

Peggy is 12 years old, a bright sweet child, very artistic, and in excellent health

I believe that Mr Shaw is writing to Miss Cummings. But would it be too much to ask you to call her up on the telephone & I am sure that a word form you will settle it.

With best regards
Stephen Leacock

## To Sir Arthur Currie

[The Old Brewery Bay
Orillia]
May 26. 30

Sir Arthur Currie
McGill University

My dear Sir Arthur

I appreciated very deeply your kind letter: I am quite sure that I was wise in coming up here as I am getting well so fast up here that already I am getting back to something very close to normal. Whatever was wrong with me ~~was~~ is going away . . . . . Up here I am able to get such absolute rest with no noise of the street & do just as much or as little as I like. . . . Already I am looking forward to next year. I have only five more sessions at McGill and I intend raise hell in Canadian economics during the short time left to use. . . From the lists Hemmeon sends me I see that all the winners of graduate scholarships in economics in McGill are Jews, except one, who is a Jewess. . . . This is a serious drawback: they are clever fellows & excellent students but we cant get jobs for them because the railways, banks & commercial houses dont want them. My book on the <u>Economic Integration of the British Empire</u> will be out in a fortnight and I will send you the first copy off the press . . . Do find time, if you can, to read parts of it and if you are not too busy I'd appreciate very much if you, could write & tell me what you think of the general idea of it . . . . Again let me tell you how much I appreciate your kindness & solicitude, & how glad I am that you didn't catch me & put me by force in a hospital

with very best regards
Stephen Leacock

## To Macmillan of Canada

[The Old Brewery Bay
Orillia]
Aug 9. '30

The Macmillan Co
Toronto

Dear Sirs

I have been greatly disappointed to learn that your edition of my book is still not out.

I have been also surprised and disappointed to learn that so far as you know nothing has been done about an <u>A</u>merican Edition

At the present time my book is receiving great publicity in England, whole columns in the Post, The Times The Spectator, The Express etc.—quite exceptional

If I had been in your place I would have collected these, printed them as a circular and used them to start a large Canadian sale.

Messrs Constable & Co have been most energetic. I received a most enthusiastic letter from the Right Honorable L.S. Amery (of the former conservative cabinet) to whom they had evidently sent a copy.

No book, however good, can get started in circulation without energy and effort on the part of the publishers and I therefore appreciate very much what Messrs Constable have done to get reviews immediately on publication

What steps have you taken?

Very truly
Stephen Leacock

## To Sir Arthur Currie

[The Old Brewery Bay
Orillia]
Aug 31 1930

My dear Sir Arthur

By this same mail I send you a copy of my Empire book. I cant expect you to find time to read all the statistics & stuff of that sort but I am sure you will be interested I looking over the book.

I am sure too that you will be pleased that with Day's book on Banking & this on the Empire, the department is keeping its end up.

With best regards
Stephen Leacock

## To Basil W. Willett

[McGill University
Montreal]
Oct 4. 1930

B. Willett Esqre.
John Lane The Bodley Head

Dear Willett,

I have to make up some heavy payments this month & so perhaps you will excuse me if I ask you to send me my royalties now due. For some years past these payments,—no great amount unfortunately,—have been delayed for about a month and it hasn't mattered much to me. But I'd be obliged if this year you would send the money without delay . . . . so sorry to mention it. . . . . .

You may have observed perhaps that Constable & Co have a book of mine on Empire politics & if so I hope you will realize that this involves no disloyalty to the Bodley Head. Constable & Co published ~~this~~ work of mine of that class long before my connection with Mr Lane: indeed they have sold my books for 25 years.

> Very sincerely
> Stephen Leacock

## To the Editor of The Spectator

[McGill University
Montreal]
Dec 5. 1930.

The Editor
The Spectator
99 Gower Street
London

Many thanks for your delightful Xmas number: I was glad to see anything of mine in such good company .. Generally my bright thoughts lie column to column beside Uncle Wigglely and the Natzenyammer kids & Bedtune Stories . . .

> Very sincerely
> Stephen Leacock

## To Angus and Robertson[1]

[McGill University
Montreal]
14 December 1930

Dear Sirs,

May I send you my best thanks for giving me such pleasant and easy and idle reading as <u>Seventh Heaven</u> and Professor Murdoch's <u>Speaking Personally</u>. I say "idle" in the good sense to mean reading without tears or effort. Not long ago I wrote—but never completed—an article on Bad Language, most of which I see Professor Murdoch has now stolen from me before I wrote it. But it doesn't matter; I can read his instead of completing mine.

Your book business and contemporary press has great advantages over ours in your relative isolation. Here we get swamped by the U.S. Having said which, it being Sunday morning, I'll go out and buy the American papers.

> Very sincerely,
> Stephen Leacock

---

1   Angus and Robertson is an Australian publishing firm that published Nina Murdoch's *Seventh Heaven* and Sir Walter Murdoch's *Speaking Personally* in 1930.

## To Hugh Eayrs

[University Club of Montreal]
Dec 16 1930

H. Eayrs
Macmillan Co
Toronto

Dear Hugh

In regard to the Canadian sales agency for my books held formerly by the Oxford Press, Allen Lane suggested that as he is bringing out these titles in a cheap form we might arrange things thus:—

Your company to have the Canadian agency for these books and to publish them at one dollar each giving me a ten per cent royalty ten cents a book and undertaking to buy 3000 ~~titles~~ books distributed as you like among the titles and to guarantee me a royalty of $300⁰⁰ (three hundred dollars) payable on July 1st 1931 and after that whatever royalty might accrue but without any guarantee . . . If this will suit your company it will suit me & I will close it at that. Please answer to Orillia

> Best regards &
> Merry Xmas
> Stephen Leacock

## To Hugh Eayrs

[McGill University
Montreal]
Jan 2 1931.

Instead of old business I will write you a personal letter.

A few years ago I was making a very handsome income . . But I had to work for every cent of it . . I lectured all the way from Minneapolis to New York. I got $350 a lecture less commissions & expenses . . I can still have that if I want it. But it was too hard. I gave it up voluntarily . . . That took a big slice off my income . . . I wrote for the Metropolitan Newspaper ~~service~~ syndicate: that brought in a lot of money . . . but it was a hard strain to keep it up . . I gave up that, voluntarily, of my own will, to their regret . . I wanted a life with only ordinary work . . . With the syndicate work went all rights in England . . all second serial rights here . . a lot of money

. . My books, as you know, being a publisher, only bring in serious money in the first year of publication . . When I published them I took for granted 40,000 to 50,000 copies on their sale within 3 years or so . . But old books dont sell . . . McGill pays me $5500 a year . . . just that . . no more . . . I have lost in my investments as little as any body of sense would lose: but even people of sense have lost a lot, nominally in shrinkage & actually in dividends: read the quotations for,—well, for a lot of them—

Now,—what am I to live upon?

...Since John Lane took my <u>Literary</u> Lapses off his own bat, I have had offers to publish my books from most of the leading houses of ~~London~~ England & America ... I never even considered them ... The Macmillan Co of London refused my Empire book, the first publishers to refuse anything of mine since Houghton Mifflin after accepting my Political Science refused my Literary Lapses in 1909 ... that's 21 years ago ... Your house were the first ... they are the only ones who can say, 'we could have published Leacock's books but we dont want to' ...Your New York house refused to reopen a contract which has lapsed,—the first the only ones to do that: Houghton Mifflin have renewed & renewed an unfinished contract of mine,—no delay no uncertainty, and immediate answer .. Doubleday Page and Co twice renewed my still unfinished contract for a life of Dickens—a Canadian firm have renewed after 15 years a contract which I made for a book on the government of Canada—Your firm alone refused to renew .....

Then came these books .. Publishers said we want them .. I said I am legally free but have talked with Eayrs ... I told you that .. I got no answer ... Then came Allen Lane & I made you an offer .. You refused it ... I made the same offer elsewhere: They accepted it by telephone & offered to <u>improve</u> on it, but I said no, thats my offer take it as it is ...

The books are sold .. In God's common sense read this letter to <u>anybody</u> and ask if I am wrong ... and I am sure that there is nothing personal & no lack of friendship in this & nothing that prevents me from wishing you a happy new year

Stephen Leacock


## To Francis Paget Hett

[McGill University
Montreal]
Feb 7 1931

Dear Frank,

My warmest thanks. The book plate arrived today. It is delightful & quite carried me back to Orillia & made me also homesick to be in the boat & fishing.

I am writing to Miss Talbot today to tell her how much I appreciate her work.

... I do hope you will be out here next summer: I am planning a tremendous lot of gardening with fishing as my sole recreation,—and lots of it. I am going to try to get rights on the bit of the river above where we cut across the field so that I can walk continuously along the whole stream

...Yes, Fitz & Mademoiselle & Peggy are in Bermuda. They have taken a house the description of which sounds very charming: it is quite a large place with a garden & trees .... but still, give me old <u>zero</u>, every time; it's more seasonable ... It has been freezing here continuously since New Year's day.

Best wishes to both of you: I shall look forward to having you both at Brewery Bay some time.. You always come too late: July is really the best: longer days & better fishing: August is too hot & September carries with it a <u>whisper</u> of regret.

> v..sincerely,
> Stephen Leacock

## To Gerhard Lomer

[McGill University
Montreal
Feb 24 1931]

Dear Lomer

The books in the enclosed list were part of my grandfather's library. When he died in Genoa in 1887 these books remained packed up till now. They have been sent to my brother.

I notice a lot of interesting items and would be glad of your opinion.

> Very sincerely
> Stephen Leacock

## To Douglas McPhee

[McGill University
Montreal]
March 12 1931

Dear Mr McPhee

As soon as I can find the time I will complete, say, 3 country broadcasts & you can submit them to the same people as before . . . If they do not buy them I shall be glad to invite you to try to dispose of them or others elsewhere. What I should wish to do would be to prepare the broadcasts & leave to you the production into records and the sales. I should not wish to collaborate in authorship or have anyone else use the material of my books, as I think I could use it better myself . . In any case I am greatly obliged to you for your friendly and encouraging cooperation.

Please do not see Mr Prendergast until I first write to him.

> Very sincerely
> Stephen Leacock

## To Douglas McPhee

[McGill University
Montreal]
March 19. 1931

Dear Mr McPhee—

In further references to proposed sketches for broadcasting, I should wish to prepare them under the title of <u>Scenes from Sunshine Sketches</u> by <u>Stephen Leacock</u>.

If I worked under such a name as Libby Littletown I should be sacrificing all the accumulated asset of a fine copyright & working to create a Libby copyright

I should not care to sell more than 12 at a start for fear that the thing might not work out

On the other hand I should be willing to prepare six for submission which might be more satisfactory than only submitting one.

V faithfully
Stephen Leacock

## To Douglas McPhee

[McGill University
Montreal]
March 29 1931

Dear Mr McPhee.

On second thoughts I feel sure that one sketch will be enough for our present purpose.

If your correspondents care to buy the enclosed (Politics in Mariposa) I shall be glad to discuss doing more.

I am quite convinced that <u>Sunshine Sketches</u> is so well known to the educated public in Canada that it is an assett at the start.

This sketch is quite as good as I am likely to do and there is no need to look further. If it is not suitable to your correspondents I am much obliged you all the same & will sell it elsewhere.

Very faithfully
Stephen Leacock

## To Mrs Wainwright

[McGill University
Montreal]
May 21 1931

My dear Mrs Wainwright

You were good enough to say that when you & Miss Ruth drive up to Ontario in a month or so, you would drop in at my cottage & spend a day or two with me there. To which I answered come at any time & just send a telegram an hour ahead of you.

I am afraid that I have to alter the idea a little and ask you to write a week or so ahead as I may not be there. Circumstances into I need not enter, make it a little uncertain whether I shall keep my place going all summer or only part of it. I still hope to run it as usual but we all get these little jolts (see Stock Exchange quotations 1929–1931) & I have only had my fair share of them—

Naturally if I am there, there is still room for my friends. But write ahead.

> Best regards to you all
> Stephen Leacock

## To Hugh Eayrs

[McGill University
Montreal]
Je 2 1931

H. Eayrs Esqre
Macmillan Co. Toronto

My dear Hugh:

I am not throwing any doubt on the accuracy of your account but I wish you could leave it over a while . . . . .

For some time past I have been so little able to work & so many dividends are cut that at present my current income is shot to pieces and my desk a litter in unpaid bills. Selling out securities just now would seem disastrous . .

I shall hope later on to ask you to run up here: at present I am not awfully well & of little use to my friends

> Best regards as ever
> Stephen Leacock

## To Raymond Knister[1]

[McGill University
Montreal]
Oct 29 (1931)

Dear Mr. Knister,

I am very sorry that I have not answered your letter sooner—I just found it unopened on my desk this morning. I should like very much to see you, if you could come to McGill University any Monday, Wednesday or Friday at 4 o'clock.

> Yours sincerely,
> Stephen Leacock

---

1  Raymond Knister (1899–1932), writer and anthologist. His anthology *Canadian Short Stories* appeared in 1928, and his first novel, *White Narcissus*, appeared the following year.

## To Carl Goldenberg[1]

McGill University
Montreal
n.d. (1931)

Dear Goldenberg

I think you might consider altering this presentation to make it economic instead of politics.

If one grants that Germany was not responsible for <u>all</u> the war, it does not follow that <u>all</u> reparations should end . . . Personally I disagree . . . I am prepared to advocate cancelling reparations & war payments on the ground that we cannot collect them without economic harm to ourselves . . But I dont agree that we should cancel them <u>all</u> off entirely on moral grounds. The Treaty of Versailles was wrong but not so ~~long as~~ wrong as that.

I think your article would be better if it dealt not with what happened & what were & will be or would be the economic consequences,—not with this <u>moral</u> question

But of course it is your article not mine. It shows a wide acquaintance with material

Yours sincerely
Stephen Leacock

---

1    Carl Goldenberg graduated from McGill with gold medals in economics and political science (1928) and in law (1932), as well as a master's degree (1929). Of these letters he wrote: 'These two letters refer to an article I wrote in 1930 on "Reparations and the World Crisis". I revised it after receiving Leacock's criticism. He then sent it to the Journal of the Canadian Bankers' Association, which published it.'

## To Carl Goldenberg

[McGill University
Montreal
Dec 13, 1931]

Dear Goldenberg,

The article is first rate—I have sent it with a warm letter of commendation to the Editor of the Canadian Bankers Magazine—Now, as Mr Asquith said, we "wait and & see."

Very sincerely
Stephen Leacock

## To Basil W. Willett

[McGill University
Montreal]
Dec 20th (1931)

A. Willett
The Bodley Head
Vigo St.

Dear Willett,

I plan for the spring a new book—<u>Afternoons in Utopia</u>, to be made up of stories and sketches all turning on our economic and political future . . . . I send you a "blurb" herewith which will show you just what is intended.

Not <u>one</u> of the stories is written so there will hardly be time to get more than one or two of them in and out of magazines. But I won't wait. Life is too short. Now,—when can I have them done: I am crowded with college work and have one other book (80,000 words) to write at the same time. If I say <u>spring</u> and its <u>summer</u> does it matter much: or would you like to play safety and put the book on the second list of your 1932 stuff instead of the first? Tell me the last date possible for the earlier list.

With best regards and
Xmas compliments,
Stephen Leacock

<u>AFTERNOONS IN UTOPIA</u> is certainly a book of exception. All the world knows Stephen Leacock as a humorist, and the academic world is well aware of the existence of Professor Leacock the economist. The dual personality thus involved has been as frequent a subject of remark as that of the mathematical Lewis Carroll of "Alice in Wonderland". But it remains for "Afternoons in Utopia" to reveal its author in both personalities at once. These "Tales of the New Time" are not only laughable to the verge of tears but at the same time philosophical to the verge of perplexity. They are equally absurd and equal sound economics. In the tale called "The Band of Brothers" we get an idea underneath the mere fun of a serious indictment of communism. "The Doctor and the Contraption" is an amusing picture of the further progress of medical science. The final piece, "War in Utopia", gives us a reassuring picture of future war, apparently as innocuous as it is complicated, being conducted solely by dicrectional wireless.

## To Basil W. Willett

[McGill University
Montreal]
Jan 9 1932

B. Willett
The Bodley Head

Dear Willett,

I am glad to hear such good news of <u>Dry Pickwick</u>

You will recall that this book as originally proposed was to be partly reprinted from others, as was <u>Wet Wit</u> & <u>Dry Humour</u>, the American sister book. On that account I put the royalty low & cut out all advance royalty.

As it turns out, the book is all new stuff, just the same as any other.

I ask no change in the amount (percentage) of the royalty, but would you perhaps send me an advance on publication of whatever you feel the sales justify . . . Like all people here I find this a hard winter,—dividends cut & capital unsaleable, heavy taxes & low receipts. 'Hence These Tears.'

best new years wishes
Stephen Leacock


## To Hugh Eayrs

[McGill University
Montreal]
Feb 21 32

H. Eayrs. Esqre
The Macmillan Co

Dear Hugh,

I have your letter of Feb 17.

It seems to me that Messrs Constable have been guilty of a breach of contract which has had for me very serious financial consequences. But, apart from money, I cannot conceal from you my disappointment and indignation that the publication of the book should have been delayed till after the great tariff debate on the introduction of protection in England. The whole purpose of my hurried and desperate work on this book for the sake of which I threw aside everything else was to get it before the public in plenty of time in the hope that it might contribute to influence public opinion.

I understand from you that Messrs Constable claim that in the royalty payments on another book they made an overpayment. I regret to say that under the circumstances I can only view this in a business light and must ask them to send me a copy of the contract under which this overpayment was made and the necessary statements and receipts to establish it. I will also ask them to send me at the same time a copy of the contract, or of the documents which make a contract under which the book now in question (<u>Back to Prosperity</u>) is being published.

I have cabled Messrs Constable but they have not answered

> Very sincerely
> Stephen Leacock

## *To W.N. Defoe, R.D. Broadcasting*

[McGill University
Montreal]
Feb 22 32

Dear Mr Defoe

I shall be very glad to cooperate with you in the matter of a broadcasting program. What I should suggest is a series of ten minute talks under the title <u>Stephen Leacocks Stories</u>. I propose that these should be (in intention) short funny talks dealing with typical phases & incidents of modern life, <u>not</u> uplift talk about what is in yesterday's newspapers. At any time I shall be glad to prepare a few samples of these "Stories". Some will be based on sketches in my books, adapted to teaching & others new

> Very sincerely
> Stephen Leacock

P.S. All financial details we can leave for the present.

## *To Hugh Eayrs*

[McGill University
Montreal]
Mar 14 32

H. Eayrs Esqre
Macmillan Co

Dear Hugh,

(Yours of March 11). I am sorry there has been such a lot of trouble over these two Empire books. I am quite willing to pay whatever I may owe you & to pay without delay. But I think I am entitled to a clear statement of the agreements & contracts in regard to the two books.

You say that my "deal is solely with you for both books". In that case the delay of the English publication of <u>Back to Prosperity</u> (not even yet out), if it involves provable financial loss to me, is a matter not between me & Constable but as between me & you. I understood from our correspondence that time was the essence of that contract. I put off an interesting and lucrative contract with Doubleday Doran to complete the Back to Prosperity book.

All England has been humming with Empire-tariff debate for two months & my book is still buried in Constable's office. Everybody knew that when parliament met in February, free trade & protection, the new tariff bill & its empire aspects would be the major topic of interest for all the British people. If Constable had got the book out in January, by this time they would have sold thousands & I would have had the money. What am I to do about that? What redress have I got for that? Is that claim against you, or against Constable.

Now all I want is ~~that. A copy~~ this. That you will consent to leave the claim for overpaid royalties on <u>Economic</u> ~~Empire~~ <u>Prosperity in the Empire</u> outstanding till it is eaten up by royalties accumulated on <u>Back to Prosperity</u>.

Or else:—

That you will be kind enough to show to my Toronto lawyer Mr G.L. Smith of Smith Rae & Greer all the documents in the case, if he calls upon you,—namely constructive or actual contracts between your firm & me for each of the two books, & ditto between you & Constable & you & New York with statements of receipts & payments. He can then advise me whether or not my claim for delay of publication is of a nature provable in Law. You will realize that this request is most reasonable, as you could not collect from me in a court without establishing your claim in exactly this way. I repeat, my Dear Hugh, how much I regret all this fuss

~~very~~

Very sincerely
Stephen Leacock


## *To Caroline Ulrichsen*

[McGill University
Montreal]
March (1932)

My dear Carrie

I would like to suggest that you take the money which you will receive under Jim's will and the money which you have already and the money which you will receive if you live long enough, after mothers death and father's death and Charlie's death and put it into a trust fund of which you will only draw the interest but which you can leave by will as you like subject to Jan's life interest. If you care to do this, I will add to the trust fund—first: anything I get under Jim's will less $50 expenses incurred by me in connection with his funeral: also,—anything I get from mothers estate, if I survive her, less the mortgage held by the estate against me. Roughly speaking that means that I would give you something more than $1200 on Jim's estate & something ~~more~~ at least about than $1,000 on mother's estate. . You might in general terms and without legally binding yourself let me know within, let us say, a month whether you would say yes or no to this . . . . The money would go into a trust firm as approved for instance by myself & ~~your~~ ~~Uncle~~

George . . . . The details would be settled later . . . but you can say yes or no in a month and later on say <u>no</u> if need be before finally signing the agreement.

Your affec bro
Stephen Leacock

## To Charles Leacock                    April 10, 1932.

Dear Charlie,

As executor of Jim's estate your business is to pay to mother the money left her by Jim. You are not concerned with the division of mother's estate. It is mother's obligation to hand over the money received to her trustees: but it is not your obligation to do so. You might or might not know of the trust. If mother instructs you to do so you may pay to the trustees. Is this clear.

S.L.

## To William C. Bell                    [The Old Brewery Bay
Orillia, Ontario]
Je 22–32

W.C: Bell. Oxford Press.

Dear Billy:

My <u>Afternoons in Utopia</u> is all finished and sent to New York and England.

It is sold to Lane for advance £250, royalty being 20%: to Dodd for advance $1000; royalty being 15% up to 5000 copies and then 20%.

In Canada, Macmillan offered 20% with advance $250. & I refused it: McLelland & Stewart offered $300. and 20%, but wanted to make the retail price $2.25. I refused it. The book has not been offered to any other firm for Canada

I propose:—

You and I go in fifty-fifty, sharing the risk thus . . . .

We buy from England at say 50 cents, covering duty and freight

We get 90 days credit, I presume & buy, let us say, 2000 copies. We make the retail price $1.50. We sell to the book stores at $1.00? or $1.10? (to discuss)  We split the difference . . . . . .

You do all the selling and handling . . . . what about advertising?

. . . . I wish I could see 30 cents a copy in it for me . . . .

Please write me your views and then come up here with Charlie (anytime) and before we drop a line in the water, or take a single drink, we'll arrange it all and cable England; then I'll take you trout fishing.

best regards
Stephen Leacock.

## To Barbara Ulrichsen[1]

[The Old Brewery Bay
Orillia, Ontario]
July 13 32

My dear Barbara

I was so glad to get your letter as Stevie & I had been wondering how you were getting along & meaning to write to you. It must be wonderful to be over in England just now. There are not many things in life equal to a first visit there ... If you get stuck for money write or telegraph me ... Everything here is all right & quiet: your mother is well & granny drove over to Beaverton to see her ... My Utopia is all done & in galley proof .... finance is I suppose, no worse than it was but I haven't done up the accounts since you left ... Write & tell us, when you get this, how you like France & the rest of your trip .. I suppose it seems all too short

best love from both of us
your aff. uncle
Stephen Leacock

1   Barbara Ulrichsen (1909–93), later Barbara Nimmo, the eldest daughter of Caroline Leacock and Jan Ulrichsen, came to Montreal in 1927 to attend to Leacock's secretarial duties; in return, she lived in his home, and he paid for her McGill education. In August 1937 she married Donald Nimmo (1909–68), and although she moved with her husband to Detroit, then to Syracuse, and then back to Detroit, she continued to do secretarial tasks for her uncle. The Nimmos had three children: Nancy (b. 1938), Stephen Butler (b. 1944), and Joan (b. 1946). Blessed with remarkable organizational skills as well as a fine sense of humour, Barbara became Leacock's 'adopted' daughter.

## To William C. Bell

[The Old Brewery Bay
Orillia]
July 25    32

W.C. Bell. Esqre. Oxford Press.

Dear Billy

The delay over the Canadian edition of my <u>Afternoons in Utopia</u> is getting serious. When you decided that you couldn't handle it, I wrote Hugh Eayrs. But he's away ... To save time please act for me

Offer it to Eayrs, thus:—
No advance needed.
Royalty only 25 cents a book if sold at $1.50 ..... If sold at 2.00, royalty only 30 cents a copy up to 4000 after that 40 cents a copy

Dodd publishes in the middle of September in NYork: Lane in London simultaneous. If Eayrs doesn't want it, get someone else. Eayrs offered originally 20% with advance of $250 but I refused it. Now the time is so short that it is harder going

best regards
Stephen Leacock.


*To Houghton Mifflin*                    [McGill University
                                          Montreal]
                                          (November 18 1932)

Houghton Mifflin Co
Boston

Dear Sirs

A year ago a Canadian firm, The Graphic Co. Of Ottawa, proposed to get out an edition of Lahontan's Voyages. The translation they used was an old one of two centuries ago, very quaint & attractive. I wrote the preface & one or two special notes.

The company failed. The book never came out.[1] But in the course of the work I made a discovery, viz, that <u>Lahontan</u> was one of the great pioneers of American western exploration but his exploits were denied & his reputation ruined because he had offended the church I put this into a magazine article.[2]

I now send you under separate cover a copy of my introduction, notes, and of course the magazine article.

Would you consider publishing Lahontan with this material & illustrations . . . Please do not say <u>no</u> too rashly . . . Remember how with one word you refused the sale of a million books by me.[3]

With continued regards
Stephen Leacock

1  The book was published by the Graphic Publishers, Ottawa, shortly before the company failed. On 15 May 1932, Leacock transferred the rights to the book to the Macmillan Company on condition that the edition would be reset completely. Macmillan never issued the book.
2  'Baron de Lahontan, Explorer', *Canadian Geographical Journal* 4 (May 1932): 281–94.
3  An allusion to Houghton Mifflin's lack of interest in his first collection of humour.

## To Francis Paget Hett

[McGill University
Montreal]
Nov 19 1932

Dear Frank

I was delighted to get your book and am reading it with the greatest pleasure & interest. The "Memoirs" are full of a quaint charm. I suppose, in a way, it is what is called a book for "scholars" but some of it is too good for them .... In return for your Robert Sibbald I am sending you my Mark Twain: but I am not sure that your man isn't the best of the two

I should have written long ago to tell you how much I enjoyed your Iceland letter & pictures (Stevie of course is incorrigible as a correspondent) .. My best fishing this past summer, oddly enough, was at Sibbald's point. In a while it was excellent: I kept a boat there & drove over at least a dozen times .. Then the fishing seemed suddenly to end: but I am sure there will be enough of it left to coax you across the Atlantic in 1933

With best regards to yourself
& to Alice
Very sincerely
Stephen Leacock

## To H.A. Gwynne, Editor, Morning Post (London)

[McGill University
Montreal]
Dec. 2 1932

My dear Gwynne,

My old friend J.A.T. Lloyd writes to me about having discussed with you the question of doing some work for the Morning Post. He said that perhaps a letter from me (as I have known Lloyd & his work for so long) might be in point. If that is so, I can only too gladly commend him to you; we were closely associated for years when we were on the staff of Upper Canada College and I got to know Lloyd intimately and to value his brave and honest character. His literary work I have known ever since he first made his mark in Canadian journalism years and years ago. He writes with the trained and scholarly pen of a man properly educated, like ourselves, with a rock bottom basis of Greek verbs. Lloyd couldn't split an infinitive if he tried.

So I have sent him this letter with the request that he send it on to you if it is of any service to him. May I add that I am glad to write it also for the reason that it renews an acquaintance of which I have such pleasant memories of old.

With best regards
Stephen Leacock

## To the London Advertiser                    (January 2, 1933)

To the Editor of The Advertiser,—

I am well aware that your newspaper is a Liberal newspaper and has therefore often criticized things I have said or written in regard to politics. That is fair enough. But I do not think that you should, because of political differences, print such malicious stuff as the notice that I inclose, under the name of "book criticism".[1] It is only an attempt to inflict commercial injury. It has no connection with real opinion. It seems to me, if you don't mind my saying it, cowardly. Will you please print this letter?

                                        STEPHEN LEACOCK

1   On 10 December 1932, there appeared in the Letters to the Editor column a review of *Afternoons in Utopia*. The entire review reads:

MORE SPOOFING

'Afternoons in Utopia.' By Stephen Leacock; 240pp., Macmillan; $1.50

   Long ago Professor Stephen Leacock reduced his humor to a formula, so that it is now as standardized a product as a comic strip, and just about as subtle and witty.

   He was probably wise commercially, though some feel there ought to be limits to the number of variations on a single joke. His patronage began with the upper intellectual classes and has shifted the only direction possible—and far. The meat of his new book is simply an appeal to popular prejudices against whatever is intelligent in contemporary thought.

## To F. S. Allen                      [McGill University
                                        Montreal]
                                        Jan 21 33

Dear Mr Allen

Thank you for the courtesy of your discussion (yours of Jan 11)[1] of the Lahontan matter . . I agree it is hard now to take on anything so problematical

   I'll be glad to think over your further suggestions for later on.

                                        Very faithfully
                                        Stephen Leacock

1   On 11 January 1933, F.S. Allen of Houghton Mifflin wrote to Leacock:

We have given our most careful consideration to your proposed new edition of Lahontan's book, with Introduction and Notes, and are very sorry to have to report that under present publishing conditions it seems inadvisable for us to undertake the book. We have been much interested, however, both in your contribution and in the Old English translation that was reprinted by Thwaites in 1905, and we are glad to have had the matter brought to our attention. Undoubtedly Lahontan deserves more attention from readers today than he is getting, whether or not we can accept his account of his journey up the "Long River" as veracious in every particular.

This pleasant overture from you, together with the fact that some of your humorous writing has been included in Mr. Linscott's COMIC RELIEF, prompts us to make the suggestion that we might possibly be proud to be the publishers of one or more of your books in the field of humor.

With renewed regrets that we cannot see our way to publish the Lahontan book, we are returning the manuscript enclosed.


## To Vernon Knowles                                    Feb 6   (1933)

Knowles Mail & Empire

Thank you very much for your letter of Jan 31  I am sorry to say that I have since been informed, on what seems the best authority, that the review of my Afternoons in Utopia (offensive, malicious & the only one which appeared & therefore easily identifiable) was written by a man called Deacon[1] who is said to review for the Mail & Empire  Will you please had him this.[2]

S.L.

1   William Arthur Deacon (1890–1977), Canadian critic and essayist, wrote a series of critical and humorous books. He became the literary editor of *Saturday Night* in 1922, and resigned in 1928 to take up a similar position at the *Globe*. On 2 February 1933, Hugh Eayrs wrote to Leacock: "I finally found out that the London Advertiser review of 'Afternoons' was written by this man W.A. Deacon who reviews for the 'Mail and Empire' here and has a string of smaller papers as well. Of course, here in Toronto we're so sick by now of Deacon's lapses from taste every now and then, we take no more notice of him. He appears to have two vendettas, one against Englishmen and all things English, and the other against men of academic standing,—why, God only knows."
2   Leacock wrote to Deacon: 'Will you please tell me whether you wrote a review of my Afternoons in Utopia which appeared in the London Advertiser.' The letter was returned to him by Knowles.


## To G.L. Smith                                    March 3 (1933)

G.L. Smith Esqre

Dear Goldie,

In reply to your letter of Feb. 27 ult.re. Pellatt estate.

4.  I authorize you to:
1.  Obtain a copy of the will of the late H.M. Pellatt (ob. Orillia 1909)
2.  Form an opinion from it of the legal interest of my son in the estate.
3.   "    "    "      "   " of my right to act for him in the matter as his guardian at law.
4.  Whether he for himself is, or I on his behalf am, entitled to ask from the custodians of the estate an account of its present situation and disposition, without the consent of Mrs. R.B. Hamilton, mother of my late wife, who

at present enjoys the interest on a share of the original estate but without the right of disposal of it by will.

5.   If in your opinion I have the right on my son's behalf to call for a statement, without being under the necessity of showing my prima facie cause for doubt or suspicion but merely as the obvious right of a legatee,—

6.   Then will you kindly take whatever steps are necessary for such an enquiry and statement.

With best regards,
Stephen Leacock


*To Lyndon E. Abbott*[1]                McGill University
                                        Montreal
                                        Sunday March 5 33[2]

My dear Prof Abbott

I send you under separate cover a copy of the Canadian Geographical for May 1932 with my article on the <u>Baron de Lahontan</u> . . . As it is out of print I will ask you (which otherwise would be rude & stingy) to send it back later on. But meantime I'll try to get you a copy that you can keep. . . You will note, as illustrative of the large opportunity offered, that Lahontan's name is not in the Enc. Britannica . . . . . . . . The Minnesota (or Rivière St-Pierre of early maps) rises in the divide where the Red River on the other side starts for the "frozen sea" . . . . If my ideas are right Lahontan was the <u>first</u> explorer of central Minnesota & the first person to hear of the divide & the rivers to the frozen seas What is needed is

i.    Accurate physical comparison of the course of the Minnesota with the text, not forgetting that the (negative) difficulty about L. not mentioning the bend is entirely removed by the fact that Captain Carver (1767) never mentioned it. Yet he <u>did</u> go up the river.

ii    examinations of the Indian names by an expert

iii   times, distances & weather of these check up, I know

iv    the difficulty of the <u>bearded</u> Indians

v.    points of corroboration, things said not likely to be invented & yet contrary to what would be expected,—eg: "sailing" canoes,—the account of the Eskimo dress etc etc

---

1   Lyndon E. Abbott was a teaching assistant in the Department of Political Science at the University of Minnesota from September 1932 to June 1933. Leacock gave an address there on 1 March 1933; Abbott met him afterwards. 'I did not pursue Lahontan's explorations', Abbott later wrote, 'but the episode did stimulate me to read up on the various early explorers of the Minnesota Territory and adjacent areas.'

2   Leacock dated the letter 1932, though he wrote it in 1933.

vi. To me, <u>this</u> is the strongest: Lahontan's extraordinary truth and accuracy in all the rest of his journal: his scientific measurements: his <u>truthful</u> honorable mind. He was a gentleman. He didn't lie

Very sincerely

Stephen Leacock

Get a big map made—huge—get a meeting of the historical club or of the Minn. historical society—& go for it!

## To Walter Tasman Conder [1]                (late August 1933)

Dear Mr Conder,

May I begin by saying how greatly I appreciate your proposal that I might come to Australia next year to do broadcasting and lecturing. The obvious difficulty is that it would take me about 5 weeks to go and 5 weeks to return and thus my available time would be about 5 weeks in Australia. (Leave Montreal June 1st, arrive back Sept. 15.). Thus what would mean to you only 5 weeks of my services would mean to me 3 1/2 months of my time and earning power.

I should be willing to come for a fee of 500 (five hundred) Canadian dollars per lecture, with a proportionate fee for broadcasting when done separately from lecturing . . . and would be willing to do minor lectures, lunch talks etc. for such cut fees as we might arrange. But I should think it fair to ask for a guarantee that my receipts would cover the expenses of travel and hotels for myself, my little boy (I am a widower with one son) and my niece who acts as my secretary, and would also give me at least 1000 (a thousand pounds) sterling over this.

You will observe that from <u>my</u> point of view that is less than I could make at home in three and half months, especially as most of my expenses here would still be running. But I am sure that I need offer you no explanation to the effect that my proposal is reasonable.

If you cannot entertain it, would it be too much to ask you to cable to that effect.

In any case I want to thank you most sincerely. I was in Australia twenty five years ago, and I'd like to see it again.

Y——

1   Walter Tasman Conder (1888–1974) was general manager of the Australian Broadcasting System from 1933 to 1935.

## To J.P. Day[1]                                    October 4th, 1933.

Dr. J.P. Day,
Department of Economics & Political Science,
McGill University.

My dear Dr. Day,

In reference to Miss Savage's Ph.D. course, I understand,—

that Miss Savage has taken the B.A. degree in Economics & Political Science at McGill with honours and has taken the M.A. degree with one year of resident work,—

This gives her <u>one</u> year of credit towards the Ph.D. degree for which in all three years is required.

Miss Savage, I understand, has also completed <u>one</u> year of resident study 1930–31 under your direction at McGill, this year being devoted to work following naturally from the work done for the M.A. and planned for completion as Ph.D. work. Miss Savage now proposes to attend the classes of the London School of Economics with a view to further study along the lines already marked out.

If she completes this year of study she is therefore qualified to present for acceptance a thesis in the form of a book representing the result of the work done.

But it is proper to state that this thesis in the form of a book, in order to be accepted as a final qualification for a degree, must, in the opinion of the department, contain material which warrants its publication and which is of real interest, real value, and a real contribution to the literature of the subject. Without this, nothing else is of avail. If the thesis is only an <u>essay</u>, a survey, a summary of things already done, it could not be accepted.

On the other hand, a fair interpretation of what is meant by presenting a thesis in book form would mean that the college, if it approves and accepts the thesis, would use its best endeavours to aid in the publication, whether by a direct guarantee to the publishers or by indirect endorsation that would help the sale. But this aid is not given as a matter of <u>obligation</u>. The understanding is that the candidate is responsible for publication. I state all this at full length so that Miss Savage may be under no misunderstanding. The circumstances of her course during the last 12 months are, in my opinion, most unsatisfactory, and, in my opinion, seriously prejudice her chances for a degree. She abandoned her studies for one whole year 1931-32 without notifying us. She then reappears with an unexpected letter from England asking you to cable to her what work she ought to do at London University and what courses she ought to undertake.

1   See footnote 1, page 205.

She has had 16 months to think about this. In my opinion this is reducing the idea of consultation and guidance to an almost ridiculous degree.

I think, therefore, that Miss Savage must understand that her chance of getting a Ph.D. degree at McGill depends entirely on whether she produces a thesis which in our opinion is worth being published as a book and which she actually publishes as a book, with financial or other support from us, or without financial or other support from us.

Very sincerely,

I should suggest sending a copy of this letter to Miss Savage.

## To Herbert T. Shaw[1]

[McGill University
Montreal]
Oct. 5, 1933

H. T. Shaw
Anglo-Canadian Leather Co.

Dear Herbert,

Apart from the demand note held against me and originating from the loan I made to you, I am having to push my credit with the bank a good deal more, in fact to make provision for an overdraft of $5000.

For this the bank need more collatoral. I could manage it with other securities, but perhaps you would not mind turning over to the bank (Bank of Montreal, Guy and Sherbrooke St.) the 400 shares of International Pete and the 200 McColl Frontenac, the retention of which was the purpose of the original loan, as collatoral for me. This would mean that you would retain ownership of the shares indefinately, would receive interest, and could sell if you wished.

If you can do this will you please communicate with Mr. O'Brian, the manager of that branch.

S.L.

1    Herbert T. Shaw (1886–1971) was a graduate of McGill University, where he developed a lifelong friendship with Stephen Leacock, who presented the lectures that prepared Shaw for his career as the eventual president of the family business, known as the Anglo-Canadian Leather Company. He married Cherry May Fitzgerald (1888–1972) of Charlottetown, PEI, on 16 June 1915, with Stephen Leacock and his wife Beatrix as the best man and maid of honour. The Shaws had one child, Peggy (b. 1919). Although there were strains on their marriage, and they lived separate lives in Montreal after the stock market crash of 1929, they never divorced. After their separation, Mrs Shaw—'Fitz', as she was affectionately known— became a close friend and a research assistant of Stephen Leacock. Peggy married E. Kenneth Smith (1917–2003), who had a successful career as a physician, on 30 May 1942.

## To Herbert T. Shaw

[McGill University
Montreal]
Oct. 12, 1933

H.T. Shaw
Anglo-Canadian Leather Co.

Dear Herbert,

I understand that you have sold certain shares of Int. Pet. and placed the proceeds with Mr. O'Brien of the Bank of Montreal and that you have given him other shares with instructions under which he may sell them, and that the proceeds of these sales are to be applied against the demand note for $10,000 which I hold against you and which is locked up in my deposit box. I am leaving on the train and have no time to go and release the note and substitute a lesser one for your signature. But till I do so this letter can serve as a receipt against all moneys thus paid on the note, and as diminishing its amount by the sum thus paid.

S.L.

## To Grace Reynolds

Jan 25 1934

My dear Grace

It was very good of you to send me a note of sympathy over written death. I am sure you will realize what a loss it means to all her family, and I thank you for having written

With best regards
Stephen Leacock

## To Lillian Leacock

Jan 27 (1934)

My dear Lill

My best thanks to you & George for your telegram about mother's death. You know as well as anyone what a place she filled & how she will be missed.

With best thanks
Stephen Leacock

## To Margaret Burrowes                    Jan 27 (1934)

Dear Daisy

Thank you for your letter. I was very glad to see Billy & Dick at the funeral, especially as it was so long since I had seen him

> Y. affect. bro.
> Stephen Leacock

## To G.L. Smith                           Feb. 2 1934

G.L. Smith Esq.
Smith Rae, Greer

My dear Goldie,

I have to thank you for your letter in regard to winding up the Leacock trust of which you and I are the trustees, and in regard to mother's will of which you and I and my brother Charlie are executors.

I note that you suggest that we should now take the will to probate.

I am not a lawyer but, as I understand it, the trust and the will are two separate things. Mother's will does not in any way affect our disposition of the trust. We are called upon to divide up the property in a certain way: whether she left a will or left no will, made no difference.

I see no need to incur the legal costs of probating the will. All that mother had to leave was a little furniture and personal belongings, the commercial value of which would scarcely exceed the cost of probate. The only use or significance of what she left is for her children and grandchildren to divide it up, as affectionate remembrances from her, in accordance with her wishes as she wrote them. If we cannot divide these few treasured belongings without quarrelling, I wash my hands of it, take nothing and leave the rest to do as they like.

The trust is a different matter. There we must act according to the terms of the deed. I shall be in Toronto before long: can we leave it till then?

> With best regards,
> Stephen Leacock

## To Stephen Leacock Jr[1]                 Feb. 2, 1934

My dear Stevie,

As far as I have authority in the matter, I do not wish you to be confirmed until you have given much more thought to what it implies than you have probably done up till now.

---

1    Stephen Lushington Leacock (1915–1974) was the only child of Stephen and Beatrix Leacock.

Many people go to church, and quite rightly, because their doing so corresponds to a sort of moral need, a reaching out for something higher than themselves. They do so without thinking about the dogma taught by the church in its details, but only from a general idea that the church stands for righteousness.

But to accept confirmation is a very different matter. If you do that, you must express an honest and honorable belief, without equivocation, in a lot of things which I am apt to think you don't believe, and which, personally, I reject, —in some cases with contempt.

I do not believe that God made the world in six days, do you?

I do not believe that God created Adam and made Eve from one of his ribs, and put them in a garden and created animals, do you?

I do not believe that Joshua made the sun stand still, do you? that Elijah went up to heaven and Jonah lived in a whale? Do you?

Nor can I feel anything but horror for the jealous, vindictive slaughtering god of the old testament. To visit the sins of the fathers on the children is, to simple people, the last word of injustice.

Nor must any one tell you that the Bible does not mean this literally. It does. Nor did any one question that for centuries.

Now let us grant that the teachings of Jesus Christ is the most beautiful moral teaching ever known in the world. But let us ask,—without quibble or equivocations,—was Christ a man or a god? was he born in any different way from human beings,—was he? did he go right up to heaven,—physically and literally,— without mental quibbling about it,—did he? did he, in the plain sense of the word, turn water into wine? raise men from the dead? and walk upon the sea? Did he?

And are you satisfied that there is a place called hell where people burn in flames,—not a state of mind, but a place,—for ever and ever? and a place called Heaven,—not a state of mind but a place where people live for ever, singing and happy, without care for those in Hell?

Let no one, I repeat, tell you that you need not believe these things, that they are figurative only and not necessary to salvation. My dear old friend, Herbert Symonds, who christened you, tried all his life to think that, and couldn't.

Those who can believe these things are happy in the comfort of them, and die happy in them, as mother did, a few days ago . . . But those of us who cannot believe them must find our salvation elsewhere . . It is for you to decide. Unbelief is a burden, but the pretence of belief, hypocrisy, is death to all that is decent in you.

Your affectionate father,
Stephen Leacock

# CHAPTER 7

## STEPHEN LEACOCK
# TOWARDS RETIREMENT

## 1934–1936

After his mother's death, Stephen Leacock returned to his busy life in Montreal. As his secretary and loyal companion, his niece Barbara continued to watch over him and Stephen Jr, while Leacock pursued at a feverish pace his teaching and writing at McGill.

Leacock's serious writing was growing steadily in quantity and quality. In *Lincoln Frees the Slaves* (1934), a work that portrays Abraham Lincoln as a historical figure of deep humanity and great nobility, Leacock explored social causes and the results of the Civil War between the States. His own sympathy lay with the South, yet his passion for human liberty made him a devoted fan of the North. The consequence is a triumph of interpretative professional history. In the same year he approached liberty from a different perspective in *The Pursuit of Knowledge*, a consideration of the merits of a restricted curriculum compared with the advantages of a system of electives in creating the best-educated person. The book's subtitle best describes Leacock's progressive leanings in the debate: 'A Discussion of Freedom and Compulsion in Education.'

Between 1934 and 1936 Leacock published three important works on humour, beginning with *The Greatest Pages of Charles Dickens* (1934), a biographical reader and a chronological selection from the works of Charles Dickens with a commentary on his life and art. Each of the ten chronological chapters consists of an introductory commentary by Leacock with selected excerpts from Dickens's work. The following year Leacock published his detailed examination of the technique of humour, *Humour: Its Theory and Technique*. Relying on Dickens and Twain and rarely using his own writings, he argued that humour always evolves away from ridicule towards sympathy, achieving at its highest form a basic kindness towards those who seem to be the victims of the humour. *The Greatest Pages of American Humour*, published in 1936 and in many ways a companion to *Humour*, is Leacock's careful study of the rise and development of humour in American writing. Given his extensive knowledge of and devotion to the subject of American humour, this book is a well-researched and well-selected examination of the best examples in its field.

Also in 1936, Leacock managed two books of his own humour. *Hellements of Hickonomics in Hiccoughs of Verse Done in Our Social Planning Mill* was Leacock's announced farewell to economics, achieving its humour at the expense of both economics and political science. And in *Funny Pieces: A Book of Random Sketches*, he achieved humour of a higher quality than he had managed to produce for many years.

The final section of *Funny Pieces*, 'Personalia', contains three pieces on education that reflect directly on personal events that befell Leacock in this period. In 1935 the principalship of McGill University, left vacant since Sir Arthur Currie's death, was finally filled by Arthur Eustace Morgan. A man with no experience of a large university, he began to find fault with various departments, including the Department of Economics and Political Science. On 12 June 1935 Leacock received a short letter from A.P.S. Glassco, treasurer of McGill: 'Pursuant to the above Resolution, the Governors have instructed me to notify you that you will be retired from the University on May 31st, 1936.' Principal Morgan communicated the Governors' decision on 13 November 1935, and Sir Edward Beatty, Leacock's close friend and the chancellor of McGill, wrote to Leacock on 14 December to reiterate the Board's decision: 'For yourself, I am afraid that I have no sympathy. You have had a full life and achieved fame. Beyond that I do not see what reward any man can obtain.' After teaching at McGill for thirty-five years, Leacock did not want to retire, yet retire he did in 1936, thus succumbing to his fate in an action he never forgot or forgave.

In 'The End of the Senility Gang', one of the pieces in 'Personalia', Leacock begins:

> As a general rule nothing is in worse taste than to put personal or local matter in a book meant for the public. But this little volume of *Funny Pieces* covers such a queer scope and claims so much of its readers' indulgence, that there is no harm in making it a little queerer and its claims a little more exacting.

He then proceeds to discuss the senility gang: 'After I had been teaching at McGill University for thirty-five years the Governors of the institution, in a sudden passion of righteous anger against old men, turned out to grass the thirteen of us who had reached the age of sixty-five.' Leacock himself, as he proceeds to explain, was the first to be executed on 'the conviction of the notorious "Senility Gang", and the sentences of Chief Justice Sir Edward Beatty of last autumn.' With the 'execution' of the twelve remaining 'criminals', Leacock jokes, the university had managed to rid itself 'in time of the outbreak of senility which threatened it. As the Chief Justice said in his charge (paid for by the railway) to the jury: "This university will be lifted into a class all by itself, or held only by itself, and the universities of Mecca and Timbuctoo." ' Clearly, Leacock's retirement from the institution he regarded as his second home was a bitter blow not only to his honour but to his longstanding love for the university itself.

The final selection of *Funny Pieces*, 'I'll Stay in Canada', is Leacock's public reply to a British editor who had asked whether he could not come home to England now that he had finished his work at McGill University. Expressing his wish not to be far from the Americans (while managing again to express his bitterness over his forced retirement), he laments:

> The Americans come up here and admire us for the way we hang criminals. They sit in our club and say, 'You certainly do hang them, don't you!' My! they'd like to hang a few! The day may be coming when they will. Meantime, we like to hang people to make the Americans sit up.
>
> And in the same way we admire the Americans for the way they shovel up mountains and shift river-courses and throw the map all round the place. We sit in the club, fascinated, and listen to an American saying, 'The proposal is to dam up the Arkansas River and make it run backward over the Rockies.' That's the stuff! That's conversation.

In the end, it is his fondness for Canada that precludes a return to his place of birth:

> We are 'sitting pretty' here in Canada. East and west are the two oceans far away; we are backed up against the ice cap of the pole; our feet rest on the fender of the American border, warm with a hundred years of friendship. The noise and tumult of Europe we scarcely hear—not for us the angers of the Balkans, the weeping of Vienna and the tumults of Berlin. Our lot lies elsewhere—shoveling up mountains, floating in the sky to look for gold, and finding still the Star of the Empire in the West.
>
> Thank you, Mother England, I don't think I'll 'come home'. I'm 'home' now. Fetch me my carpet slippers from the farm. I'll rock it out to sleep right here.

## To Gerhard Lomer

[McGill University
Montreal]
Feb 9 1934

Dear Lomer

I feel very much honoured indeed to know that the Library School will prepare a coopererative bibliography of my work. . . If I can be of use, I'll be glad to. Those are translations of different books of mine into German, Norwegian,

Magyar and Japanese . . . None into French as René du Roure & I have reserved that,—& yet never done it . . But for Maurice Dekobra did a chapter on my work in his <u>La Rire dans le Brouillard</u>.

V. sincerely
Stephen Leacock

## To Barbara Ulrichsen                   Feb 8 1934

Barbara Ulrichsen
3869 Cote des Neiges Road
Montreal

Dear Barbara
    If you like to buy International Nickel (outright & not on margin) up to $400 I will guarantee you for two years, and my executors will be and are by this instructed to guarantee you, against loss by decline in value

y. affec uncle
Stephen Leacock

## To Francis Paget and Alice Hett        3869 Cote des Neiges Road
                                          Montreal
                                          Feb 22 34

My dear Frank and Alice
    Very many thanks for you kind letters about mother's death. I feel that to you & to all the Hetts her loss comes especially close: we were all so much together long ago
    It was a wonderful scene at the churchyard when we buried mother: deep snow & bright, bright sun & very still & quiet in the shelter.
    It did not seem sad at the time,—it was like a gathering of the family,—but now it seems so strange & sad all the time to think that she is gone . . . so I was glad to get your letter . . .
    I send you today a book I have just written on Abraham Lincoln: it is published in England also but in a badly reduced form as they could only use 30,000 words (for matters of economy & uniformity) . . . so I had to cut out about 8000.
    I shall look forward to seeing you both, I hope, up at Orillia.

V. sincerely,
Stephen Leacock

## To Mr Shirard

[McGill University
Montreal]
March 25. 1934

Dear Mr Sherard

Thank you very much indeed for your interesting letter. Somebody said that the Dickensian had not favored my book: but I never read reviews: it's a fool thing to do: so I hadnt seen what that particular damn fool said.

with many thanks
Stephen Leacock


## To Mr Markel

April 8 (1934)

Dear Mr. Markel,        N.Y. Times

I would like to propose to you that I do a set of articles for the N.Y. Times to use & to syndicate on

The American Humourists—each about 3000 words. Some years ago (1921?) I did a series for the Times on economic stuff.

I think people just now like amusing things & things that get away from controversy. I'd do these in a light style like the Artemus Ward piece. You could pay me whatever would be right for use in the Times & 50-50 for syndication, —or any other fair arrangement.

Something like this: (write out yet trying to find attractive titles).—or no— let me first indicate a few names: some would be grouped & some make an article by themselves.

Franklin & Washington Irving. Sam Slick . . . Max Adeler.—Petroleum Naseby . . Orpheus C. Kerr . . Mark Twain . . Josh Billings . . . O. Henry . . . Fun in Rhyme: Hans Breitner, Bret Hart etc . . .

S.L.


## To Mr Laurence

[McGill University
Montreal]
Ap 23 1934

The Editor
The Quarterly Review

Dear Mr Laurence

It is just possible that you know my name especially as I have had in my time the honour of contributing to the Quarterly . . I am the head of the department above . . .

I want to introduce to you the name of my young colleague Mr Carl Goldenberg. At my suggestion he is submitting to you an article on Recovery under the NRA

He is a very brilliant young man who took all the medals & honours we had to give & is now working on our staff . . He had been attracting wide attention by his speeches & newspaper articles on Recovery. I want to see him have a wider opportunity.

> Very sincerely
> Stephen Leacock

### To Francis Paget Hett

> The Old Brewery Bay
> Orillia
> Thur Aug 9 34

Dear Frank

I am so glad to hear that you are here . . I'll come over the first day that its cool enough . . Just now, terrible . . fishing here is punk . . but you might care to come back with me for a day or two anyway & see how punk it is

> V. sincerely
> Stephen Leacock

### To Hugh Eayrs

> [The Old Brewery Bay
> Orillia]
> Sep 17. 34

Dear Hugh

Herewith I send you a copy of a feature article I wrote in the <u>Times</u>. Please read it, not for pleasure but as a business duty. You will observe (I hope) the wonderful condensation and picturesqueness and the way in which the economic basis of our history is revealed (. . . If you dont, you're a nut). . . .

This will give you the ground plan for my <u>Economic History of Canada</u>, for schools & colleges. I propose to write it this winter to be ready (published) in time for the school session of 1935–36.

I append a rough outline of the terms I submit for your consideration. I think that if such a book got established it would have a fine market.

> Very best regards
> Stephen Leacock

Memo of Prof Leacock's
suggestions for terms of Publishing an
Economic History of Canada

(1)  The most important thing is to keep the price <u>low</u> .. The length of the book
will be partly governed by this . . . Please send a rough idea—how many
pages (or words) and what retail price . . . Can we get it to $1$^{50}$ (a book say
of ~~150,000~~ 120,000 words)

400 pages

(2)  Royalty: 10% on first 5000
15   on 5000–15,000
20   ......... after 15,000

_____

because if it ever gets to that it runs without further publishers effort (if you
prefer it, call it 25%!)

_____

(3)  no advance royalty, but a <u>guaranteed</u> royalty (3 months after publication) of
$400: the reason of this is that the authors expense in library assistance and
stenographic & clerical work will be more than that: for example, I spent so
much money on my Economic Integration of the British Empire that I
made <u>nothing</u> out of it.
Look it all over Hugh; as Colonel Sellers said, "There are millions in it"

best regards
Stephen Leacock

P.S. The more I think of that 25% up above, the better I like it


## To Mrs Herbert T. Shaw[1]                    (October)


Dear Fitz
Bert Little's Death[2]—On Thursday Mary sent me messages about coming
in for a cocktail but I didn't get her on the phone—I went to the Club at about
4 & saw the notice just up that Bert died at 2.30—so I phoned Barbara, because
I thought we could take the children, & met her on the street & we went to
Mary's house. But Allan McGee was there all ready & a man & women I didnt
know. I went upstairs & kissed Mary & sat & talked with her. She was making
no fuss & doing just what she should. She said that Ted Eberts was already

1  See footnote 1, p. 232.
2  Herbert Melville Little (1877–1934) joined McGill's Faculty of Medicine in 1913, becoming
an authority on gynecology and abdominal surgery. He died on 11 October 1934. Mary
Little (1884–1979) married him in 1918.

arranging about the body viewing & the funeral. Grace was out of town. They had sent for Pat. We talked and then I went away and in the morning I came back & Pat had arrived & I sat & waited. And Mrs. Turpin was there & people telephoning. Then Ted Eberts came and I drove with him and Mary & one of Bert's brothers and little Pat Little up to the cemetery to choose a grave. Pat had come down from Upper Canada College & just arrived but Berts body not yet. Pat had on only his ordinary school overcoat but he had a new dark one in Toronto so we telegraphed for it. In the cemetery we chose a lot with four graves. Mary had never been in the cemetery before. Then we drove back & they left me at McGill. This morning I walked down to the Cathedral for the service at 10. Ted Eberts & Allan McGee & Billy Turner had arranged everything. Mary had asked me to sit near her so I was in a pew just across from Mary & the three boys. There was a great crowd of people. All of the doctors & all of the governors. I drove out to the cemetery afterwards with Sid Little, the senator & Dr Peters & another man I dont know, but I didn't speak to Mary. I drove back with Ted Eberts and Grace, who had just arrived from New Brunswick. Yesterday Mary looked very much strained & broken & hadn't slept. Today she wore a veil but looked terribly tired. I shall go to see her tomorrow but not today—So that is that—I had an idea that money is all right but since I talked with Buster Reid a minute at the Club I dont know. If there is not enough.[3]

3   The letter ends here.

## To Sir Edward Beatty[1]                Nov 21. (1934)

Confidential                copy to Mrs Beatty

My dear Edward,

Herewith a typed letter to you as our chancellor.

I want to do all I can to help Mary Little, Bert's widow. She is left in very reduced circumstances. Presently things may be better, but just now she has to look about for supplemental means of support.

The idea outlined in my letter to you as chancellor is one which I think would be fine for McGill and of real help to Mary Little.

I thought at first of writing also to some of the Governors who were old class mates & friends of Bert's: But on second thoughts, I judged it better form and better business to write only to you.

S.L.

1   Edward Beatty (1877–1943), a lawyer, was appointed general counsel of the Canadian Pacific Railway in 1913 and became president in 1918. He became chancellor of McGill University in 1921, and was knighted in 1935.

## To Sir Edward Beatty

[McGill University
Montreal]
Nov (1934)

Dear Mr Chancellor

I write to ask if the Governors of McGill can see their way to vote five hundred dollars ($500) for the French department to use in establishing for this session ~~and~~ a place of assembly, club rooms for conversation & refreshment, for their students.

I will explain the circumstances.

My own status in the matter is that I have been for years closely associated with the French department. Professor Du Roure & I have talked for years of the desirability of setting up a sort of French Club, an afternoon gathering place for the students, where they can come together, take light refreshment and talk French & read French newspapers & journals.

I think that there is a special opportunity for this just now & what the department might hesitate to ask for itself I can fittingly ask for it.

Under circumstances known to you, Mrs H.M. Little is anxious to try to derive some revenue from her ownership of her house at the foot of Stanley Street, opposite the Mount Royal Club. She is setting up there a French Luncheon Club which will be self supporting from the fees paid by the members.

It has occurred to me that as Mrs Little has thus the premises and the services and the facilities, it would be possible to establish in her house at say from 4 to 6 every week day a McGill students ~~club~~ French group, under some such name as L'après-midi française.

The students could not possibly pay a fee to correspond to all expenses of premises & light & heat and attendance. But I thought that they could pay a small sum say $1$^{50}$ a month each to cover the cost of tea & toast or coffee and pretzels or whatever it is.

Membership could go automatically to all the honour students in French (especially to those who join in the periodical meetings of the Cercle français and the Société Française) and to any other students or members of the faculty or Board of Governors invited to belong.

Professor Du Roure assures me that he & his staff would gladly undertake without any remuneration whatever ~~the~~ such supervision & assistance as would be needed for the conduct of the activity of the club. It could also be used as a centre for little réunions, causeries and the meetings of the societies I have named.

I enclose $25$^{00}$ as a contribution to buy ~~maga~~ newspapers and magazines and will gladly undertake to ~~finance~~ meet any deficit on the ~~food~~ cost of the refreshments,—a most unlikely occurrence.

It seems to me that if the College pays Mrs Little say $100$^{00}$ a month for 5 months, the stimulus and opportunity thus given to the ~~practie~~ study of French would well repay it.

It would naturally be assumed that this plan is an experiment only, without presumption or prejudice for the future. But one might hope that it would serve to direct attention to the great service that in better times can be done by the establishment of a complete French residence at McGill

Very sincerely
Stephen Leacock

## To Allan Lane                              Nov. 25/34

My dear Allan Lane,

I was so sorry that I was out of town & missed seeing Richard.

I cabled you to say that my book <u>Theory & Technique of Humour</u> will be posted to you in M.S. on Dec 24.

If there is any money in it I have decided to go to Australia next June & July to lecture. I have often been invited but forget the names of the bureaus. Please find out if you can from Gerald Christie or somehow & cable me at my expense. I take it your interest granted as lecture tours help book sales greatly.

S.L.

## To Stephen Leacock Jr                  [McGill University
                                          Montreal]
                                          Mon. Dec 4 1934

Dear Stevie

Yours of Dec 1st—<u>very important</u> about your granny's money. When I signed the statement that I would acquiesce in the payment of <u>all</u> <u>the</u> <u>money</u> in the trust to your granny, I had in mind what I understood to be the case that she & you would be advised by me. Now I think perhaps it would be better to put about $5 000 into annuity and $5 000 at interest . . . thus would give from the annuity . . . 67.50 a month

  "  interest      <u>25.00</u>
      $102.00 "      "
      ————————————

Her way means that you get <u>not one cent</u> of the money left to her—now if anything goes wrong with my money you'd be badly off.

On the other hand if your granny is content with what I propose I can make up the difference in eggs, food, and residence at Orillia

In any case please wait till I come.

Very affect. dada
Stephen Leacock

Read the enclosed to your granny.

## To Mrs R.B. Hamilton

3869 Cote des Neiges Road
(Dec 4, 1934)

Dear Mrs Hamilton

~~I enclose a copy and~~ You will have seen a letter to Stevie. I dont think it would be right to take all the money for yourself as an annuity to die with you & leave Stevie not one cent when in reality all the capital belongs to him. Please re-consider it.

Y affectionately
Stephen Leacock

## To Major James Eakins

[McGill University
Montreal]
December 20th, 1934.

Major J. Eakins,

Dear Jim,

In connection with our conversations, I suggest a monograph of about 8,000 words (with appended tables and charts). This should be widely circulated and its contents syndicated also by newspapers in excerpts and partial reproduction.

It is no good to print such a monograph and <u>give it away</u>. What is <u>given away</u> gets <u>thrown away</u>. It must be done through the trade.

I would arrange with one of my Toronto publishers for a first edition of 10,000 copies. Let us presume that these would retail at 60 cents per copy. I would take 10 cents a copy as my royalty (16 2/3 per cent). If such a monograph were published without special aid to circulate it, it would only sell to about four or five thousand copies. My pamphlet called <u>Stephen Leacock's Plan</u> sold, I think, just over 5,000. This is not good enough for publisher and author. But if an edition of 10,000 at 60 cents is <u>guaranteed</u> then it is easy. <u>Guaranteeing</u> that does not mean paying $6,000. It means undertaking to see that $6,000 comes from somewhere, either the public or the guarantor.

I would need a further $200 to spend in hiring graduate students at McGill to help make charts and tables and convert units. This would be a great help to these boys both as training and financially and it lies near my heart to get them this sort of stuff to do.

Also: the publishers would probably say that charts and maps (requiring blocks) are an extra cost to be borne by the author and not by them: that would have to be carried by the guarantor: But it could be no great matter. Now:—no one buys a pig in a poke. . . . . So I send herewith two samples of the pig.

(1) A résumé of the ideas I propose to write: I will not, for any money, subscribe to ideas not mine.

(2) a <u>sample page or two</u> to show the style. I want it to be bold, striking, clear. If I am asked to do this work I will undertake to deliver the manuscript for approval (still without tables and figures, etc) within a month. If it is accepted the terms above stand (subject always to finding a publisher at 60 cents per copy for a 10,000 edition) For any edition past that, I would ask a royalty of 25 per cent: but that does not concern the guarantor. If the MS should be judged unsuitable by the persons interested, I should expect a consolation fee of $250.00 and the MS would remain in my possession.

Please submit these ideas where they may be acceptable and make it clear that I would not on any terms write to advocate what I dont believe, or leave out what I think essential. If I cant advocate a return to gold payment I would not feel interested in writing on the tax question.

With best regards,

## To Francis Paget Hett

[McGill University
Montreal]
Dec. 23. 34

Dear Frank,

Best Xmas wishes to you and Alice . . & Best thanks for the Nelson touch and for <u>Jutland</u>. I can't feel that Jutland is fair to Beattie and it is grossly unfair to Von Sheer by pretending that his object was a general fleet action with all the grand fleet. I think his performance wonderful! And his chasing Jellicoe away by the "death ride of the cruisers" & the destroyers while his other ships turned in their own length, so to speak! . . . It is simply comic (on page 202) to say:

"Experience had shown that the one way of escaping torpedo damage was to turn away from the approaching missiles so <u>that the ships sterns</u> were presented as targets" . . . That's a hell of a good way to get away from anything or anybody! But what does the other fellow then do to your stern?

"Jellicoe," continues the writer "turned the grand fleet four points (45°) away from the enemy . ." exactly and lost sight of them.

I have just finished a book on the <u>Theory & Technique of Humour</u> which I will send as soon as out . . . am going to Orillia for Xmas: wish you could be there.

Best wishes,
Stephen
(Leacock)

## To Adelaide Hett Meeres[1]

3869 Cote des Neiges Road
Montreal
Dec 24 34

Dear Addie

Merry Xmas! and to Charlie & the rest . . . Stevie & his Uncle Charlie went to Orillia on Sat night. Barbara and I leave here tonight & drive from Oshawa to Orillia on Xmas (tomorrow) morning . . . stay four or five days. . . . I enclose a poem which I read about Tingle at Lilian Capes house . . I see a letter for her from you in by mail (Sutton postmark): she's gone up to Ste Agathe . . . I've done a tremendous lot of work since October & not done with it yet . . If the roads & weather allowed it I could drive you over with whoever might be there for a drive & sleep at my house. . . yes, you're right about mother: I think of it all the time

George has been terribly ill but now pulling through

best love to you & all the
crowd
Stephen Leacock

1   Adelaide Hett Meeres (1882–1961) was the younger sister of Francis Paget Hett.


## To Robert Benchley

McGill University,
Montreal
January, 4, 1935

My dear Bob Benchley,

I am getting out a book called "The Greatest Pages of American Humour". I want to put in, say 2000 words of your own inimitable work, without my fee. This I can ask with a certain reasonable modesty as you will see by the plan enclosed that the book is not just a collection of excerpts, but is a critique of the authors and hence is good advertising. Please let me do this, or you might force me to pay for it.[1]

Very sincerely,

1   Benchley sent a telegram to Leacock on 11 February 1935: 'Anything of mine that you might want to use in your book was yours in the first place.'

## To John Murray                    Jan 10. (1935)

John Murray
The Editor
The Quarterly Review
London

Dear Sirs,

Years ago I ~~wrot~~ contributed once or twice to the Quarterly, and you may know my name.

I attach herewith an article I wrote a few weeks ago in the New York Herald: it was widely syndicated in Canada.

I would like to build on it an article called:—

### ECONOMIC SEPARATISM IN THE BRITISH EMPIRE

to discuss the present centrifugal forces. This includes, overwhelmingly, Canada and also Western Australia, Tasmania and in other aspects S. Africa. . . . . . . . . . . It all arises, as I see it and (as I discussed it in my book called The Economic Integration of the British Empire) out of the circumstances and ideas of the Laissez-faire period. . . . . It was not foreseen that political self-government would be an economic disruption. . . . . They took free trade and free intercourse, colonial and foreign as well, for granted. . . . . We are now reaping the results.

You cannot of course engage to use an article before it is written, and I am far too busy to write "on spec": the article I have in mind would not be of interest to the U.S. . . . . . . But if, in general way the idea strikes you, I'd be glad to do it and submit it.

S.L.

## To Russell Doubleday [1]              Jan 21. (1935)

Dear Mr. Doubleday,

My best thanks for your letter of the 16th. I am so glad to hear your continued interest in the idea of <u>Greatest Pages of Amer. Humour</u>. As to the matter of a royalty in advance, I am glad to say that it is of ~~my~~ no consequence to me . . . . But I think you might guarantee a royalty of $250 six months after publication. Otherwise the contract looks a little vague.

It will help me to a decision in the matter if you wouldn't mind letting me know how the prospect looks on my Greatest Pages of Chas. Dickens & how it is turning out.

---

1   American author Russell Doubleday (1872–1949) worked for his brother's publishing firm, Doubleday Page & Co., and retired as its vice-president and chief of its editorial department.

But I am most anxious to go ahead. This humor stuff is booming. I've just been out in Missouri & I was lecturing on Amer. Humour & I find the greatest interest. Please get busy & answer. Also, when are you coming up here for a pleasant Sun. to renew acquaintance.

S.L.

## To Frank Dodd                                        Jan. 22. (1935)

Frank Dodd.

My Dear Dodd,
    I have just returned from a week's lecturing on Amer. Humour & allied topics in the middle west where I met a wonderful reception by capacity audiences. Everywhere I go among the college I hear the same thing (as last Weds, at the Univ. of Miss.) that it is high time that Humorous Literature was studied as such in English courses. Perhaps you know that the sum of $5000 a year is already intended for a series of Mark Twain lectures on humor to be given in a perambulation from college to college.
    All this means that a book like my Humour, Theory & Technique would have a huge sale in the colleges with good advertising & a efficient salesmanship, —and stay there for years & years.
    But I am afraid that such a title as <u>Why Laugh</u> would kill such a chance. Please think it over. I posted you the M.S. over two wks. ago.

S.L.

1) The Theory & Technique of Humour
2) <u>Humour</u>: Theory, Technique & Samples.
3) <u>Humour</u>: Its Theory & Technique

## To Gerhard Lomer                              [McGill University
                                                 Montreal]
                                                 Mar 4 1935

Dear Lomer
    I am deeply sensible of the honour done to me in the preparation of a bibliography . . . In return, without waiting till I die, I am turning over the MSS of my books to the library: I thought, later on they might be of interest.
    I have ~~most~~ quite a few of them, and in pretty good shape . . I will bring down a sample when I next go to Orillia & will arrange with you about some kind of suitable case for each (made let us say with a back like a book) & I will pay for the cases . . . I probably have about 15 volumes

V. sincerely
Stephen Leacock

## To Hugh Kelly

[McGill University
Montreal]
March 13th, 1935.

Hugh Kelly, Esq.,
McGraw Hill Book Co.

Dear Mr. Kelly,

I am glad that you like my idea of a <u>Manual of Elementary Statistics</u>, <u>For College and Business Use in the United States and Canada</u>.

I think that all the books on Statistics (as far as I know them) are <u>overdone</u>. The author is so anxious to show that there is a real science of Statistics (which there isn't) that he fills his book with all sorts of pseudo-mathematical stuff which is of no real value. . . . . There is a certain equipment which is useful to all college students and the young men in banks and business houses and in journalism.

It consists in knowing:—

(1)    Introduction: Meaning and use of Statistics and development of statistical knowledge.

(2)    Where to find statistical figures

(3)    All the tables of weights and measures, and the units used in each big trade. For example many students would find it hard to get information about the world price of wheat because it is quoted in dollars per bushel, in shillings per quarter and nowadays by the metric ton.

(4)    Foreign Exchange: Mechanism and tables.

(5)    Index numbers and how to make them and use them and the chief ones in the world.

(6)    The presentation of statistics: Tables & charts: graphs
Charts and graphs in two and three dimensions and how to put them together.

(7)    Population and vital statistics and how they are gathered and counted, with expectation of life, annuities, etc. etc. . . .

(8)    Monetary statistics: money exchange
Interest on money, amortisation the statistics of wealth and how computed.

(9)    Statistical Fallacies
Slide

(10)   Statistical Forecasts and what they are worth     Probably Betty Porter

(11)   Mathematics by rule of thumb. Much use may be made of mathematics, especially of logarithms by people who use them only mechanically without the algebraical background. Logarithms are thumbed over every day by ships' captains who would fall dead at the sight of a quadratic equation.

I should propose to invite the collaboration of my colleague, Professor John Culliton, of McGill, who would help me to gather the material. All the writing involved would be mine. I should consider it proper to put his name on the title page. I should wish to urge that the price be kept as low as possible (say $1.00) on which I would expect 10 per cent up to 20,000 copies and after that 15 per cent, to be shared half and half between Prof. Culliton and myself.

Let me know if you feel inclined to go further. In any case best thanks.

Stephen Leacock

## To Russell Doubleday                    March 26, 1935

Russell Doubleday
Doubleday, Doran

Dear Mr. Doubleday,
(Greatest Pages of Am. Humor) I will bunch up Mark Twain into one large chapter of discussion and short quotations, which costs nothing, with a selected chapter from Roughing It and the Innocents Abroad which costs nothing as the copyrights are off and about 1400 words from Huckleberry Finn for which we have to pay. According to Harper's letter, the price will be $100. But I am now writing them, asking for world rights and explicitly indicating the passages wanted as per schedule herewith.

In regard to expired copyrights usable without charge, I must trust to you for the law, as you are on the spot and in business. I understand (from the World Almanac) that U.S. copyright even if extended to the fullest degree permitted expires in 56 years. This means that there is no copyright on Mark Twain's Tom Sawyer, Roughing It or Innocents Abroad. There is no copyright on the work of Bret Harte which I need: etc. As to O. Henry, I understand your firm has the copyright. I have already permission from Irvin Cobb, Bob Benchley and George Ade (all in writing) I am writing to the publishers of Ring Lardner, Montague Glass and Finly Peter Dunn, who are all dead. No one of them is indispensible. Therefore the whole cost of copyright is the small sum paid for Huck Finn. I am therefore going ahead at full speed; will make the book full length and cut it as required.

S.L.

## To Robert B. Pattison[1]

[McGill University
Montreal]
March 26 1935

Rev. R. B. Pattison
27 Linden Ave.
Ossining, N.Y.

My dear Bob
    Many thanks for your letter of March 19, which recalled very far away days.
No doubt the <u>Bible</u> outsells Dickens, but I never class it as a "seller" best or
otherwise . . . I am quite certain that Dickens would never had said that he got
his style from the (translation of) the New Testament: He had too much conceit
to admit that he got it anywhere . . Thank you for your family news: I am sorry
to say that my mother died in January of 1934, just over ninety years of age

with best regards
Stephen Leacock

1    Robert B. Pattison was a friend of Leacock from their early years at Lake Simcoe.

## To Russell Doubleday

March 27, 1935

Dear Mr. D.
    What about my doing a Greatest Pages of O. Henry? I could do it in a week.
I was, as perhaps you know his earliest commentator in England.

S.L.

P.S. In further postscript to my letter, I think that the publication of a Greatest
Pages of O. Henry might revive and boost the sale of the copyright you hold.
Think it over.

S.L.

## To Dr Charles F. Martin[1]

McGill University
Ap 15 '35

Dean Martin

Dear Charlie
    Dr Grant Fleming & Dr Ripley asked me to speak on the 26th at the
Ritz—Yes. gladly—but not as they suggested <u>half an hour</u>—I havent the
equipment. I will speak 12 to 15 minutes: of medicine: in the conquest of disease:

1    Dr Charles F. Martin (1868–1952) began his medical career at McGill in 1893. He was dean
    of McGill's medical faculty and was retired in the same year as his good friend Leacock.

of the need for faith in the profession on the part of those of us outside . . . Please tell some one to send me any good outline book on the history and progress of medicine. Very little needed . . I'll dilute it with economics

Very sincerely
Stephen Leacock


*To Barbara Ulrichsen*                                Orillia
                                                     Tues. Ap. 23

Dear Barbara,

I am telegraphing you this morning to say that I won't come back this week end. I feel all right as long as I am round here in the garden but the minute I get into Orillia on the side walks & in the noise I feel quite unsteady & disturbed. So I think I had better stay. I must turn up in New York for the big Cancer Fund meeting on the 15th[1] and so I can come to Montreal after that. Until then there is nothing I am needed for. Please notify Dr. Grant Fleming that I can't be at the City meeting—but not to make any fuss as though I were ill. You can pack up & arrange the house. When in doubt bring the things. Arrange for Ronald Latham to arrive via Toronto and we will meet him. I will take him into the house as it is so nearly empty. He won't mind it later, if people come, I put him up in the Y.M.C.A. for a few days.

You will be here when you are free. I feel quite lost without you to arrange things and accounts. I exchanged for a DeSo car—$600 extra & sent a cheque. Tell Tim to see that it is all right.

y.a.u.
Stephen Leacock

1   Leacock addressed the Cancer Control Committee at the Plaza Hotel in New York City on 15 May 1935.


*To Mrs Herbert T. Shaw*                             [McGill University
                                                     Montreal]
                                                     Tues (April 30, 1935)

Dear Fitz

That certainly beats everything I ever heard of!! I cant get over it! Thank of it . . .

Today I am sending you down some flowers on chance from your place— You ought to be here: I went in to get roses at the 5&10 & found that all their first stock is cleaned out; people are planting so early—But yesterday it turned wet & cold so perhaps the late stuff will do as well or better—I shall be so glad to have you back here! I am sending the car to Belleville for you for Tuesday the 7th of May at 2 something railroad time——I am going fishing tomorrow by myself as George & Charlie couldn't come up—Pat Little is coming for a Saturday-Sunday the first time he is free, either this week or next & Stevie & Kelly are to drive down & get him—I hope the flowers get to you all right— Your room is all ready for you with the fire ready to light & your things as you left them.

Stephen

## To J.A.T. Lloyd

(May 1, 1935)<br>(At a friend's house<br>overnight—cant find my<br>paper or envelopes—being<br>in Montreal for a day but at<br>Orillia for seven

Dear Mr Hogan

Your business—Russell Doubleday wrote Series temporary help up till they see how the one or two in the press work out—will be glad to consider the question of your Poe later. . . . the market here for everything is rotten—

Reminiscences:—Good old B.H. died two summers ago. . he had in old age made a great hit with paintings of Canadian ~~flowers~~ wild flowers . . his pictures now eager sought by buyers—

Bowwow Mills is still at U.C.C: just the same but as it were shrunk into himself—my son Stevie is 19 but very very small: he has a bright mind & is to matriculate into McGill, I hope this year—

I have a beautiful country place now at Orillia to which I could retire if I had money but I have lost so much of what I had like everybody else, & have so many claims upon me that I find it very hard to keep the place going—I am trying to make it support itself as a farm—

Forgot to post<br>Best regards<br>I enclose a picture<br>of my house<br>Stephen Leacock

## To Mrs Herbert T. Shaw

[The Old Brewery Bay
Orillia]
1st of May, '35
Trout Day

Dear Fitz,

I am presently going fishing which makes me think of you and wish you were here to come with me. After I wrote yesterday I packed a box of daffodils, hyacinths and a few violets and sent them parcel post.. they would have cost 75 cents to go by letter post and I was hoping that parcel post would get you practically as soon. I may send more today. It turned very cold last night but I had my 100 tomatoes covered with long wooden troughs & it never touched them . . . Did I tell you that I have Jones back? It seems he had no pension (on technical grounds): so I wrote to Hugh Guthrie Minister of Justice whom I know to urge him personally to get it right. I give Jones work from <u>8 to 12</u> each day "lawn, grounds & forests," with 50 cents a day and casual perquisites & <u>no contract</u> so as not to spoil his pension. I just said "leave it to me—I gave him 3 bags of potatoes (all his vegetables in future) and a load of wood & Stevie gave him a plug of tobacco. He has his own job & the <u>carpenter</u> <u>shop</u> as his Head Quarters so he is all right. . . . Your hotbeds are well covered & not hurt—flowers fine—must stop at once  I just remembered about eggs.

with love & to the little girls
Stephen Leacock

## To Mrs Herbert T. Shaw

[The Biltmore
New York]
Wed May 15
11:30 am

Dear Fitz

I got here at 1 in the morning after a 24 hour trip, pretty well all in all . . . but my Purdue visit & speech at the Literary Dinner of Purdue University was a real success.. This morning I got up at 8 & began the day by doing 1500 words of Ignoramus.. I am to see Mr Wheeler of the Syndicate this afternoon . . . If the stuff goes I can do it at odd times in the summer and if it doesn't go, it is nobler to try to work than to quit.. after I had done that I made up my speech for the luncheon of the New York Hospitals & the Cancer Committee at the Plaza Hotel. I am to speak on the <u>Conquest</u> <u>of</u> <u>Disease</u> & I am going as part of it to read out some notes that Charlie Martin gave me & give him credit for them. . . . I do hope you are coming to Orillia tomorrow: I was going to write anyway on the chance of it getting to you and then I realized that a special delivery stamp ought to make it a sure thing. I am due in Orillia at noon so that I'll be ahead of you .. I hope you come for your sake as well as mine for there will be such a lot to do ... In Indiana it was like summer with the leaves all out and quite hot in the day. I realize that at Orillia I get too absorbed in the farm & the other stuff fades out of my mind,—quite apart from any question of booze—though no doubt it all goes together ... I feel so sorry for George: I'll tell you all about it when I see you. Meantime, best love. It seems too good to be true that I may see you tomorrow: perhaps it is.

Stephen Leacock

## To Dr Charles F. Martin

[The Biltmore<br>New York]<br>May 15 1935

Dear Charlie

I had the most extraordinary reception & success here at the lunch of the Cancer committee .. In the course of my talk I said that I wouldn't try to rehearse on my own authority the progress & triumphs of medicine but would read from a script prepared for me by Dr Charles Martin dean of the McGill Medical Faculty.. I said that I was proud of our medical faculty .. I had a long honour rolls of names of distinction of which that of Dr Martin was only one. I said that I might recall the name of Dr Osler,[1]—doctor still to us & not Sir William,—and that of one of our graduates who achieved a sudden reputation fifty years ago under his professional name of Jack the Ripper [I suppose you know how it is practically certain that Jack the Ripper was on our rolls as Dr Neill Cream: I didn't give the name]—I said that all these men Osler & Martin & Jack the Ripper were working, each in their own sphere,—mistaken perhaps, —but with the same devotion to an idea . . . . . Now this may & may not get into the newspaper report & it may or may not get in right. But as it sounded it was good . . . I gave it a sudden serious twist by showing that even the abnormal forms of a thing bear witness to its power. Such a lot of the men spoke to me of you & of Eddie Archibald & the others,—more messages than I can transmit. Sir Gerald Campbell (of the Consulate) was next me & spoke of the wonderful work Penfield is doing & how much he appreciated having him in consultation at his wife's operation ... So I send you my best thanks for such a fine day.

Yours as ever<br>Stephen Leacock

1   Sir William Osler (1849–1919) was a professor of medicine at McGill from 1874 until 1884.

## *To G.L. Smith*                                   May 18, 1935

G.L. Smith
Smith, Rae & Greer
Toronto

My Dear Goldie,

I have to thank you for your letter about Mrs. Hamilton's financial affairs.

I may say in opening that my own financial position is greatly changed. My private income from investments is only about $300 a month. My Montreal house though I paid $25,500 for it and it is unencumbered, will for the present, if rented, bring in hardly more than the taxes and charges. In a year or two I must retire with a small pension and leave Montreal as I can't afford to keep the house. I am too old to go on lecture trips more than a year or so longer: I find the strain very great. My writing is about done.

So you will see that I am not in a position to do as much for Mrs. Hamilton as I would wish. Mr. Wilson told me in Toronto on May 16 that the estate was worth $10,000. It appears from your letter that it is worth $8000 only. This would bring in a revenue, at best, $400 a year or $33 a month. To give Mrs. Hamilton $100 a month I should have to pay $67 a month. I am not in a position to do it, nor would it be just to my son's interest for me to pay Mrs. Hamilton $700 a year for her life time in order to secure for my son $8000 at her death. The best I can offer is 50 dollars a month, $1000 a year in addition to the small moneys which she has of her own. You will note that in reality Mrs. Hamilton has no claim to the principal sum of $8000 at all, and any act of anybody in giving it to her without the consent of my son and myself would scarcely be valid. A little while ago when I understood that Mrs. Hamilton was penniless, I said at once that I would support her for life. When I understood that there was a little bit of money left of the estate, my son and I in order to secure it for her from the Pellatt estate signed a paper to consent to its being handed over to her. When we heard that the sum would be larger and would amount to about ten thousand dollars, I felt that it was worth a considerable sacrifice of current income on my part to secure this principal sum for my son. But as I have explained above, there is a limit beyond which I am not entitled to go. Nor would I be willing to have anyone else than myself as trustee of the money. I am far better qualified by my profession and my training and my experience to manage this estate than most people are. I would not think of paying $600 a year for the sake of a claim of $8000 on a sum managed by some one else and the investment or use of which I would be powerless to control except by a complicated or expensive legal process.

I would propose therefore that Mrs. Hamilton hand over the money to me; that I sign a paper in which I pledge her an interest on it and the succession to it if she outlives my son: the sum of $50 a month payable by me during my life and by my trustees if Mrs. Hamilton outlives me: the pledge that all investment and use of the money will be over a joint signature of my son and myself.

I hope that Mrs. Hamilton will see her way to accept this proposal as I have nothing else and nothing further to offer. I will send a copy of this to Mr. Wilson and a copy to Mrs. Hamilton. Meanwhile let me repeat my appreciation of your kindness in helping this matter to a settlement.

S.L.

## To Mrs R.B. Hamilton                    May 18, 1935

My dear Mrs. Hamilton,

I send you a copy of a letter I have written to Mr. Smith. The best I can offer you is, as I say in the letter, the interest on the money (about $33 a month) and $50 a month paid by me. I must be the sole trustee. If this won't do I must drop the matter. I am so sorry you couldn't have trusted me without bringing in lawyers and legal expenses. But you must now go one way or the other, either to the right or to the left.

S.L.

## To Mrs Herbert T. Shaw                    [McGill University
Montreal]
Orillia, Sunday
(envelope dated June 2 1935)

Dear Fitz

Barbara & Lou got back at nine oclock & Barbara gave me your letter . . I miss you here very much: it doesn't seem the same. . . . Still it wont be long. I hope you are better and I am sure you will be, but you ought to see a doctor and then as soon as he says you are only run down, you will feel grand . . . I went fishing with Doc. A yesterday . . He caught a trout. . . . . Your place looks fine: Gordon is weeding & everything seems in good shape. . . . . . . I leave this afternoon to go to Baltimore & get back .d.v. on Wednesday. I am sending you 3 broilers ~~about~~ on Tuesday & when I get back I'll see about sending eggs & asparagus & broilers etc all together

with love
Stephen

*To Mrs Herbert T. Shaw*                    [The Belvedere Hotel
                                            Baltimore]
                                            Monday 5 P.M. Je 3  35

Dear Fitz

    I just arrived here after 24 hours of travel or more counting the trip in the motor car (I left Orillia on Sunday at 1.30)—These journeys are hellers—but I mustn't complain. It is always fine when its over & I am on my way back. I seem to miss you very much this time and I'll be so glad when you come up to the Lake—after all it is only next week—Tonight I have to attend a <u>reception</u> (You know how I love a reception) and tomorrow I speak at a college convocation— It is sultry & hot here like August with us . . . On the way to Toronto I saw George who seems cheerful in a way though he is up against it in business . . He said that Ethel might live all summer—but her life is not worth much to her as she cant leave her bed—I forgot to arrange about broilers going to you but when I get back I'll see what they have done.—Goodbye for the present and be sure to write

                      with love
                      Stephen


*To Mrs Herbert T. Shaw*                    Orillia Wed
                                            2 PM

Dear Fitz

    Just back & just got yours of Monday & I am heartbroken that you are still feeling wretched—Do go & see a doctor & then you will feel well right away— all that that you <u>think</u> is only just ill health & run down & lack of vitality—a million dollar ~~inome~~ income wouldn't help—do please get medical advice & then in no time you will feel fine & life will all feel happy—This is just a line to catch the mail—I wrote from Baltimore.

                      With love
                      Stephen Leacock
                      Orillia


*To Mrs Herbert T. Shaw*                    [The Old Brewery Bay
                                            Orillia]
                                            Sat. morning Je 8. 35

Dear Fitz,

    I've been glad to get your letters. Your place is looking fine: you have no idea how things have grown since the real weather began. It is just wonderful here.. Yesterday I went up to Oro with all hands to build a barn. As it costs me a lot of money paying for stabling & a great loss of time taking the horses over half a mile night & morning, we began building at two o'clock and at half past five had the four sides done but then the rain came & stopped work. Today they can put on the roof & shingle stain it and make the door and its done.. I'll build you a little garage in a day any time (then all you have to do is to buy a car).

I had a nice letter from Mary (all in type writing which looked very formal). Do you know if she has any plans yet for the summer . . . I am sending you broilers on Monday. Eggs, I suppose not, as they are too cheap to pay express. I shall have about $60 worth of broilers of this first lot (more than that) and by the following lots about $200 probably with all the pullets left. My butchers bill is not <u>extinguished</u> as we have broilers and trout & we sell Hatley enough broilers to pay for the meat (I think)—let me see—say 10 a week at 60 cents, that's $25.00 a month—that ought to do it . . . Your peonies are all wired up,—asparagus not so good—weeds a great difficulty . . . if you care to let me use your extra land (beyond the poplars) I will "give you for it a kiss" and $5.$\underline{^{00}}$ . . . If so telegraph collect as the time is passing when I could use it.

> Love
> Stephen
> (Leacock)

Be sure to see a doctor & get well

## To Mrs Herbert T. Shaw

(Orillia) Thurs. Je 13 35
10 to 6

Dear Fitz,

Lou is to leave very soon so I send this by him. I shall expect you about 7 pm on Sat. & will have dinner for you & Peggy here. When I wrote I was thinking of you as arriving at midnight as before but of course this time you start early . . . Kelly ploughed up your ground. It was such a mass of grass that it was hard to get it out, & so he & I thought that the only thing that would grow is buckwheat so we filled it up with that. It will be fine for Peggy's hens & it will look beautiful . . . Your place is all lovely, everything at its best. I gave Gordon 4 melon plants & they are well started. Spinach ready to use.

I will put both your boats in the water on Friday & let them staunch up——It is so nice that you are coming & you will soon feel better; all that you think you think you dont think at all. It is just nervous exhaustion & will all pass away.

> Best love
> Stephen Leacock

## To Thomas H. Wilson                    June 11, 1935

Dear Mr. Wilson,

If you don't mind my saying it I do not see that your services are necessary in arranging Mrs. Hamilton's transfer of the money held by her as the legacy due to my son. Speaking again with great frankness I presume that you, as a lawyer, do not work without pay any more than I do as an author. If Mrs. Hamilton is willing to pay for your services I have nothing to say and will come to Toronto to see you. But all that I propose is that Mrs. Hamilton should transfer the money and securities held by her for my son on the terms indicated in the annexed document. If she does not wish to do so, neither I nor my son have anything more to say. I hope you will excuse what seems the bluntness of this letter. I have offered to Mrs. Hamilton at the time when I understand she had lost all her money, to keep her for her life: when I gathered there was a little money left, then my son and I signed it all over to her, though by rights she had no claim beyond the interest: when we understood that there was $10,000 left I told you and her that in order to keep this for Stevie, I would give her enough to bring her income up to $100 a month. Now that I learn that there is only $2,250 of cash and certain doubtful securities, I offer to add $50 a month to the interest if the principal goes to Stevie on the terms stated in the schedule. If this is not satisfactory, then as far as I am concerned the discussion is over.

Very faithfully,
Stephen Leacock

Schedule annexed.
Schedule to my letter to Mr. Wilson of this date:

I offer to Mrs. Hamilton the following plan:—

She will hand over to me the cash and securities left from the Pellatt estate of which my son is heir amounting roughly to something over $6000 cash and $2000 nominal securities and I promise to invest the money as I see fit and guarantee to her 5 per cent on it and $50 a month over and above it and if I die before she does my estate is hereby instructed and my son is hereby instructed to make the same payment on the same terms.

And if my son dies before Mrs. Hamilton then I, if I am alive, and my estate if I am dead, will give to Mrs. Hamilton the capital sum for her absolute disposal.

And in return Mrs. Hamilton will leave everything she has to my son, if he survives her, except only such personal keepsakes of no serious value as my son may consent to her leaving to other people.

On Mrs. Hamilton's placing the money and securities to my credit in any bank this arrangement goes into effect and I hereby sign it and my son signs it and my niece signs it as prospective guardian to my son and there is no need for any legal documents or law fees as this document is absolutely valid among honest people, and among crooks nothing is.

Signed          Stephen Leacock
                Stephen Leacock Jr.
                Barbara Ulrichsen

## To W.D. Woodhead[1]                    Orillia, June 29th. 1935

Dear Woodhead,

I have your further letter (June 27th.) about the question of Professor Plaut[2] coming to McGill. I quite sympathize with your difficulty in carrying an "action at a Distance". I think it bothered even Isaac Newton.

My feeling is that if the Principal, with a knowledge of the facts before him, wishes Dr. Plaut to come, then I or anyone else ought to give way. This is what we would have done with General Currie.

The facts are that I and my colleagues (excuse the latin) think that there would be no prospect at McGill for Dr. Plaut: if a vacancy occurs it ought to be met by rearranging the work and saving the salary: if a second vacancy occurs, it ought, in my opinion to be filled from the list of distinguished applicants whose names are already filed and include Canadians of high academic qualifications and experience and knowledge of Canada, and in one or more cases, honorable service in the war, or from similar new applicants.

There is, you remember, the consideration to be added that Dr. Plaut might be invited to teach in the school of commerce. This is outside of my province; and even in my own province, I presume that I have no authority in any real sense and that the Senate has full power to act with my advice or without it.

This surely leaves the matter as wide open as it is possible to make it.

With best regards,
SL

1   W.D. Woodhead (1885–1957) was a professor of classics and chair of the department from 1923 until his retirement in 1950. He was dean of the Faculty of Arts and Sciences from 1934 until 1936.
2   Professor Plaut was one of the German refugees who was on the staff of University College, Hull, England.

## To Mrs R.B. Hamilton and Thomas H. Wilson

Orillia, Ont.
June 29, 1935

Dear Mrs. Hamilton and Mr. Wilson,

I write to you together as you appear to be acting together as solicitor and client.

I have received a letter from Mrs. Hamilton in which she refuses my offer to act as trustee for my son's inheritance and to give to Mrs. Hamilton $50 a month. Mrs. Hamilton states that the money left to my wife and after her to my son, is all lost and that the money obtained for her by Mr. Wilson is other money got from the wreck of the Pellatt estate and not representing the legacy to my son. As to this I need only say that as Mrs. Hamilton had no claim except what arose from the life interest, this statement if it were true would indicate a quite illegal . .

Mrs. Hamilton has refused my offer. Let me repeat the substance of it. I proposed that Mrs. Hamilton pay over to me all the money and securities received from the Pellatt estate: that I act as sole trustee for my son: that I pay to Mrs. Hamilton the interest received on the money when invested and pay her, over and above this, $50 a month, payable by me alive and by my estate if dead: that if I fail to pay this, or if my estate fails to pay this then Mrs. Hamilton gets back the capital sum, all of it if she asks for it or part of it if she consents to wait and take interest on the rest.

Now consider the security behind this. My estate includes my Orillia property, an investment of fifty to sixty thousand dollars, unencumbered no debt: includes my Montreal house, bought at $25,000, unencumbered; investments in good securities bringing about $3000 a year, together with copyrights, a pension while I live etc. etc.

Now if Mrs. Hamilton's claim is guaranteed against this estate, as a first charge, any lawyer anywhere would tell her that the security is as nearly absolute as can be:

Mrs. Hamilton has written that she intends to keep the money for herself, thus depriving my son of the money which his mother always expected to come to him. This is a very serious thing to do. I am not going to fight it at law but I consider it a dishonest thing to do, and if it is done Mrs. Hamilton and Mr. Wilson will understand that my door is closed upon Mrs. Hamilton for ever. She is well aware that when I understood she was left penniless I offered to keep her for ever. This is now changed entirely and Mrs. Hamilton must ask herself just how much Mr. Wilson is prepared to do, and if her money gets lost, as it easily may since she knows nothing of investment, just to what extent Mr. Wilson is prepared to support her. It appears to me a very serious thing to cut an old woman of 80 years of age away from her natural support. If I do not invest the money, who does? And will he back it with a guarantee like mine?

Of course not.

My offer was refused and I withdraw it. I now substitute for it a similar offer but with $40 a month instead of fifty. If this is not accepted in a week, it lapses.

S L

## To R.B. Bennett

[The Old Brewery Bay
Orillia, Ontario]
July 17 1935

The Rt Hon R.B. Bennett[1]

I cannot tell you how very much I appreciate the honour you do me in telling me that in your opinion I would be acceptable as a candidate to the Conservative voters in this riding, and still more how much I appreciate the fact that your personal good wishes go with me . . . But my life has run for so many years in academic and literary ground that I feel I must finish in that furrow to the end . . But I would like to say that I shall be proud to give all the support of which I am capable to anyone who stands for the party in this riding with your personal endorsation.

It is my opinion that in the present division and distraction of parties there is a steady drift every day towards Conservative principles—towards your leadership . . We shall carry this riding for you on the platform that you yourself have built.

With sincerest regards in the personal sense, and humble duty
in the public,
Stephen Leacock

1   Richard Bedford Bennett (1870–1947), who led the federal Conservatives from 1927 until 1938, was the eleventh prime minister of Canada, serving in that office from August 1930 until October 1935. He was defeated by Mackenzie King's Liberals.

On 12 July 1935, Bennett had written to Leacock:

A number of our friends are extremely anxious that you should permit your name to be placed before the Conservative Convention in the constituency in which you make your summer home.

I need hardly say that I am thoroughly convinced that you could render very conspicuous service to Canada in the next Parliament. Your wide knowledge, your great reputation, and your disinterested approach to problems affecting the welfare of the country could not but be of the utmost value. Won't you favourably consider the matter, and thereby give great satisfaction not only to those who know you in the community in which you live, but to thousands who have read your books with pleasure, as well as to one who subscribes himself, with high esteem and regard.

## To the Traffic Dept, City Hall, Montreal

Oct 4th 1935

Dear Sirs,

I wish to call you attention to the very unsatisfactory and dangerous condition of traffic control at the corner of Sherbrooke St. and Guy-Cote des Neiges between the hours of 8:30 and 9:30 A.M.

The string of cars coming east along Sherbrooke and coming south down the Cote des Neiges is such as to the make a practically continuous line where they come together. One set moves forward with one light and the other with the other light. The pause of each light is enough to accumulate a new line of cars. There are at this hour a large number of school children and young people attempting the crossing.

There is need to station a traffic officer there. The lights merely act as a decoy coaxing people into danger.

Very faithfully,
Stephen Leacock

P.S. Enclosed an outline map.

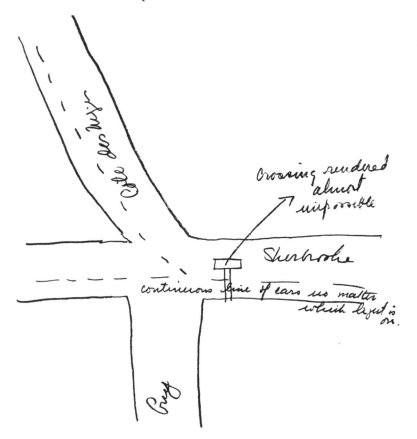

## To W. D. Woodhead

Oct. 10, 1935

Dear Mr. Principal,

I have to thank you for your kindness in sending the very accurate memorandum of the discussion of last Friday on Social Research.

To what was said, I should like to add that I did not sufficiently stress my opinion that, at McGill and under our circumstances, a closer grouping of Economics and Political Science with Psychology and Sociology might not be desirable. The studies of department connect naturally with French, for the obvious reason of environment and the connection with preparation for law, and with English, probably because students going into teaching like to know something of the economics of Canada. Personally I do not think that college Psychology is of any great value in Economics; and personally I look on Sociology rather as an open and interesting field for speculation and culture than as a disciplinary academic subject, capable of being utilised in a college curriculum.

But as these are purely personal opinions on a controversial matter, I have thought it best merely to show the letter to my colleagues without asking whether they approve or dissent.

Very faithfully,
S.L.

## To John Kelly

Oct. 20, 1935

My dear Kelly,

I am very much concerned to hear that we lost 145 chickens in a week. You probably understand as well as I do how much this means.

Will you please take steps to see 1) that all the fowls on the place are shut up at night in places where skunks cannot get them. 2) that you sell any potatoes or ducks or chickens or turkeys that can be sold. If potatoes can be used for chicken feed (boiled) with more profit than in selling them please use them that way.

I appreciate very much your work and Tina's but a very little figuring will show you that we could not keep on very long as we are.

But let us get through the winter as best we can. Keep the accounts in the form I showed you and try and keep the loss each month as low as possible and no doubt things will take a better turn next year.

Very sincerely,
S.L.

## To Frank Dodd                          Oct. 30, 1935.

My dear Dodd,

About books of mine in the Making:

1.  Napolean as a Naval Stratigist. Held up for the time being. Too much on hand.

2.  How soon can we start the next war.

    A satirical and humorous discussion of the chances of peace and war, with an undercurrent of serious appeal and warning. About 20,000 words: a lot of it rewritten from previous books—Have done it as a forty minute lecture before large audiences with great success. Held up because there will, may, be a naval war between England and Italy: if not, I will send a dummy as soon as the clouds clear away.

3.  My Life and Reflections. Contract offered me by English syndicate. But, I will only write it in my own way: nearly all reflections, very little life—and no personalia about people I have met which is the very thing they want most. I mean to send them as soon as I can a sample first chapter, à prendre ou à laisser. I will send it also to you. I don't think anyone in the States would syndicate it the way I want to write it.

4.  Funny Pieces. I have on hand quite a lot of odd sketches since my last bookful. I could have 50,000 words, I imagine, by next autumn. I enclose herein a dummy and a preface which I think you may like.

S.L.


## To Sir Edward Beatty                    Nov. 7, 1935

My dear Edward,

I am greatly obliged to you for sending me your London address. I had seen the digest of it in the press but was glad to have a chance to read it in extenso.

In my opinion the group of younger economists etc. of whom you speak will never have influence with the public at large unless you and other people of high position give it to them as a present.

There isn't one of them who can write a book, or a page or a line that can arrest and hold the interest of the public. There isn't one of them who can do anything to a public audience except bore it to death.

But let it be known that these young men are denounced by chancellors of universities, and it makes their political fortunes. People would couldn't read their dull books or keep awake at their academic lectures, will rally round them, will vote them into parliament. Left alone, they are quite powerless; as harmless as a wayside weed.

There are economists who can write but a single paragraph,—on the new deal or social credit,—and send it over a continent: whose thoughts go everywhere and whose spoken words can hold the student audiences of the greater colleges spell-bound and silent, till even the elms on the campus bend to listen at the windows. But these are not the men. And in any case, as I understand it, it is the policy of one great university at least, to turn these "real boys" out.

S.L.


*To Mrs Herbert T. Shaw*                    [The Biltmore
                                            New York]
                                            Fri 4 pm Nov. 8 '35

Dear Fitz

I got for Peggy just exactly the Encyclopedia—2 very fat volumes—not secondhand & not old—just fresh—quite wonderful—it set me back six dollars . . . I am waiting round here for some one to call at 7 to take me to the dinner of the Acadia College Alumni . . I wrote an advance "piece" for the Herald-Tribune & sent it over by messenger, so perhaps it will get into either the Gazette or the Star—please look for it—I thought you'd like to get this letter in the morning, eh what? and its nice to be able to write it—I heard yesterday (true or not) that I dont need to leave Montreal (my job) unless I want to—that will need a lot of thinking about . . I imagine that a certain person has done a lot of talking & nosing & consulting as to what is to happen & who to get my shoes . . . Frank Dodd (publisher) called here but missed me but left a letter, very enthusiastic, about my book for next autumn to be called Funny Pieces for which I sent him a plan and a preface . . . He says he will sign a contract as soon as I like & one for My Life & Reflections.. so that I have work enough for 1 year without needing any more . . Just before I left I got (via Bâ) a telephone invitation to lunch with Mrs Miller Sunday 16 17 to meet the Principal & Mrs Morgan[1] but I am already engaged & can't go . . . I imagine Mary is asked . . . I am to leave here tonight at 11:40 if I can catch the train & go to Toronto & then to Chicago . . . That will be a hard trip. I expect tonight to be very easy . . . I am due back by the late train on Tuesday evening but I wont call you up till next morning as it is too late & you might be asleep . . .

                                            Affectionately
                                            Stephen Leacock

1  Arthur Eustace Morgan (1886–1972) was the first principal of University College, Hull, before becoming principal of McGill from 1935 to 1937; he resigned from this position when friction developed between him and the Board of Governors. He later returned to England, where he became warden of Toynbee Hall, London.

## To A.E. Morgan

[McGill University
Montreal]
Nov. 19. 1935

Principal Morgan
McGill University

Dear Mr. Principal.

    I beg to acknowledge the receipt of your letter informing me that I have been retired from the active staff of the university, and to thank you,—my dear Morgan,—for the personal kindliness with which you write.[1]

Very faithfully
Stephen Leacock

1   On 13 November 1935 A.E. Morgan, principal of McGill University, wrote the following letter to Stephen Leacock, informing him that he and several of his colleagues would face mandatory retirement upon turning sixty-five.

[McGill University
Montreal]
November 13 1935

Dear Leacock,

    As I understand you are already aware, it has been decided by the Board of Governors that sixty-five years is to be regarded as the age of retirement of all university officers. Although it is true that the resolution of the Governors reserves to them the right in very exceptional cases to extend that period, it is the intention of the University to regard retirement at sixty-five as the normal procedure. This will be interpreted as taking effect at the end of the session during which the officer concerned attains retiring age, and for this purpose the end of the session will be taken to be the 31st of August, and not the 31st of May as was implied in the letter sent to you by Mr. Glassco on the 12th of June last.

    I have the pleasure of informing you that the Governors have decided to offer you an annual pension of half the average salary earned in respect of your office over the last five years, and for this purpose your salary has been taken as if it had been unreduced from the 1931 figure.

    On this basis, your half salary is $2,750 The amount due to you from the Carnegie Pension Fund is $1,105. The University will undertake to pay you the balance of $1,645, which will bring your pension up to the figure of $2,750.

    In making this communication, I wish to extend to you on behalf of the Governors a very sincere expression of gratitude for the work that you have done for the University during your long tenure of office. It is my very warm hope that you will enjoy many years of happy retirement.

Yours sincerely,
A.E. Morgan

## To Sir Edward Beatty

[McGill University
Montreal]
Dec 11. 1935.

Sir Edward Beatty
Canadian Pacific Ry Co

My dear Edward
(Yours Dec 6)—Yes I read today Underhills paper in the Forum. Those who have seen it agree with me then. It is written in a gentleman's hand which will get him nowhere: I will tell him this when I get a chance. I think, if you dont mind my saying so, that in your London address and perhaps elsewhere you do not clearly enough distinguish between political economy in its real sense, and the mere polemics of Canadian politics. A great many people spend their whole lives in working on such things as economic origins and history, and theories of things that have no connection with Canada. Such great men as Thorold Rogers and William Cunningham gave their lives to the history of work & wages and the evolution of industry. Your condemnation struck a whole lot of people of whom you ~~probably~~ possibly never heard: and who are hurt but cannot answer back. You said "With exceptions", but that means nothing; if I said "with exceptions, all Canadian bankers are crooks," how would Charles Gordon like it.

I wouldn't have written sooner but there seemed no use in it. Since I got your earlier letter I had one from the Principal definitely removing me from McGill: so that what I do or dont do, as a professor, is so nearly over that it is of no consequence. I feel deeply humiliated, not at Morgan's letter, but at the thankless and unfair letter which it ratified. I am at least certain you didn't write it

Very sincerely
Stephen Leacock

## To W.A. Irwin[1]

December 16th, 1935.

Dear Mr. Irwin,
Herewith my article, Academic Freedom in the Canadian Colleges.[2]
I am sure you will like it and I shall be very glad to have the honour of appearing again in Macleans.
But I need to say a word or two. The public rightly or wrongly insists of thinking that headings and sub-heads are part of the author's thought and composition. The presentation of this article is of great importance for my future

---

1   W.A. Irwin (1898–1999), diplomat and editor, became associate editor of *Maclean's* magazine in 1925, becoming managing editor in 1943 and editor in 1945.
2   'Stephen Leacock on "Academic Freedom"', *Maclean's*, 49, 3 (1 February 1936): 14–15, 38–9.

relations with the people among whom I have worked for 35 years, therefore, I should not want any heading or sub-heading to appear which I had not either written or approved. I am sure you will see how reasonable this is.

As to the main heading <u>Academic Freedom in the Canadian Colleges</u>, I wish very much to leave it as it is; it is dignified and proper and will be far more in the interest of your magazine than any more "popular" title. Leave it as it is and this article will be widely quoted in America and in England.

What you add on the opening page I cannot suggest as I dont know your <u>Make-up</u>. But please let me see it.

I was so pleased with your commendation of the part of the article which you saw that I am sure you will like the rest.

Very sincerely,
Stephen Leacock.


## To W.M. Birks[1]                                 December 18th, 1935.


I thank you very much for your letter and the enclosures which I send back herewith. As far as your correspondent's pleasant joke goes, I quite appreciate it. But I think I see in your letter an undercurrent of reality and I can't quite see eye to eye with it.

The idea seems to be that if a professor makes a speech outside the college, to people not connected with it, and says, "I am a socialist: capitalism is doomed", then he has shown himself unfit to teach in the college and ought to be disciplined. I dont see this. Socialism is not illegal. Its proposals are not revolutionary. They involve only parliamentary voting. Socialism is a beautiful dream, that can never be realized. But it invites the sympathy of many of the kindest and best minds in the world, (including my own) even when they cannot believe in it. In practice it is bound to fail. It is an error that dies in the sunlight. In the long run truth prevails on earth: and fools should be suffered gladly. Rich men always reach out for methods of repression and always will. But in the end righteousness wins. No professor has the right to press the propaganda of socialism on a college class: nor has he the right to press the propaganda of Christianity or of aviation or nudism or tariff protection. If he does so, he breaks his contract. But apart from that a professor ought to be as free as you are. There are and have been socialists in many of His Majesty's Cabinets in the British Empire, including the government at Westminster itself. There is no reason why

---

1    William Massey Birks (1868–1950), business executive and philanthropist, was a governor of McGill from 1910 until 1950. After graduating from McGill with a BA in 1885, he went to work with his father's firm, Henry Birks and Sons.

a professor should not be a socialist just as he might be a ventriloquist or a prohibitionist. But he must not start ventriloquism in his class-room.

But I think the present danger at McGill is all the other way. Many people are losing sight of the fact that a university in its first and foremost meaning is a home of learning, a place of thought, a repository of the wisdom of the past and a workshop of the wisdom of the future. It is made up of its books, its classes, its students and its professors, and the writings and thoughts that it inspires. This is a university. This is,—or should be McGill,—not its finances and its accounts and its investment of money. These things are necessary, but they are only a means not an end. It is the same as in a family: the money they have represents only a means whereby family love and family happiness can be achieved. They eat meat, they dont eat the butcher's bill.

Recently one of the McGill governors spoke to an audience of McGill students and was reported (in print in the Daily) as having told them that the governors were "responsible for what the professors are",—and responsible "for what they teach". Personally, I had always thought the responsibility for what we are rests with God Almighty. I know that responsibility for what we teach rests with the college Senate: if a professor were willing to teach for nothing the governors couldn't stop him. The governors for the most part do not understand the curriculum any more than we understand their business.

I have a son at McGill. I would rather have him hear fifty lectures on Socialism, than one lecture as derogatory to his father's profession as that address.

I would like to add this. I am able to write this to you because I am independent. Others are not so fortunate. But do you not think that if one of the oldest of the professors,—after 35 years of service, and after the receipt of all sorts of kindness and the enjoyment of the greatest liberty,—feels that the college is being wrongly treated, there must be ever so many others. May I in conclusion refer you to the words of,—or not, I wont quote it or you might say "the devil can quote scripture for his purpose".

> Very sincerely,
> Stephen Leacock.

*To* _____[1]                    (1935)

Dear _____

I have to thank you for your very kind invitation . . . Now that I have retired from work at McGill, I propose to give myself the long luxury of silence. I have always disliked speaking in public but felt that I had to do it as a matter of

---

1  This letter is a form letter Leacock prepared to use as a response to all lecture invitations he received at this time.

academic duty, now gone. Apart from two addresses long since arranged, I shall
never, please God, speak in Mtl. again. I enter into this very personal explanation
so that you will understand that in refusing your invitation I nevertheless
appreciate the honour you do me.

S.L.

## To Major James Eakins                                    (1935)

Major J. Eakins

Dear Jim

I was greatly disappointed not to be able to get together,—at what was very
short notice,—the group of men, mostly old friends, with whom I wanted to
talk about gold in New Ontario.

I have always been much interested in that country: as a matter of fact I am
to go up there early in July as the guest of the Ontario government. You will see
a track across it when I go

I think that there are big things coming in that country: and part of it
concerns mining, and concerns the sale of gold stocks

Since Roosevelt's currency legislation I see little danger of gold collapsing
in value. And if this danger is removed, the change of currency & prices that
goes with the depreciation of the dollar puts a premium on all gold mining.

But from the point of view of the investing public ~~all inve~~ the whole
situation turns on distinguishing between honest stuff & crooked stuff. Investors
are sick of crooks. But a great many investors—of whom I am among the
humblest,—are willing to put up money that they can afford to lose, in order to
have that fascinating thing called a "run for one's money". This is quite apart
from investing in absolutely good securities the savings that one dare not lose.
To old fashioned people it might sound like gambling: but it is not: it means
investing money, with open eyes, in a thing which quite frankly may be good or
may not. This, in the dull life of a person on a salary who sees the years reaching
in front of him, each like the one before, is a perfectly sensible thing. This is the
basis of the sweepstake idea.

Now, if it were possible to go to a Montreal broker & know that he was honest,
and his information very honest, there'd be plenty of money forthcoming for
investment in speculation chances on the new gold. As it is, one friends who are
brokers would not feel inclined to discuss with their clients new openings & stuff
newly prospected. They must leave the client to ~~the~~ blind chance or to the crooks.

If you can work out the basis for a new set of relations between the Montreal
security market and the clients anxious to put up money on the kind of risk I
describe, I think you will do a service all round.

Incidentally the more we prospect and scratch that new country the better it is for Canada.

I am sending a copy of this to one or two friends of mine who are interested. I am so sorry that I am to be out of town so much that I dare not to get into personal touch with ~~more than~~ any large group of people concerned

Very sincerely
Stephen Leacock

## To Adelaide Hett Meeres

[The Old Brewery Bay
Orillia]
Jan 5   36

My dear Addie

Your letter went to McGill & then came here & got buried under a mass of mail & I never got it till the day before yesterday—I have had such a sore foot & such a run-down feeling that I left all the mail tied up as it came from the letter box—My foot is practically better & I think I can put on a boot tomorrow —I've been flopping around in overshoes & huge shoe packs—However, I'm better & am only mentioning it as I thought you would wonder why I didn't answer . . . . .

Stevie & Barbara & I came up here 3 days before Xmas & George & Mary drove up ~~the~~ on Xmas Eve & that was our Xmas party. We all like Mary so much. I was delighted at their marriage & so glad they didn't wait. George is 58 & Mary is only 32 but it makes less difference than it might because George is very fond of social life and likes to go out & so Mary has lots of life and is not turned into being an old man's nurse. They seem very happy together. They have known one another for several years and I always felt when I saw them together that they were perfectly suited. Nobody speaks ill of dead people & I mustn't talk of Ethel but Mary is doing just what Ethel ought to have done years ago. They have a little furnished apartment in Toronto & Mary does all the work needed, which is nothing & ever so much nicer than pretending to have to hire a servant to cook an egg. Ethel always had to have money spent on her . . . . George & Mary went back after Xmas day & have gone to St Louis for New Years as the guests of George's boss . . . . . . As for me, my work at McGill ends in May & my salary ends on Sep 1st & after that I get a pension of $230$\frac{00}{}$ a month and that with what I have of my own puts me on easy street & I never need work again. But I wont have money enough to keep up this place & a Montreal house as well, as the taxes in Montreal are very heavy and the railroad fares up & down mean a lot of money. But I am going to live at least one more winter in Montreal & see how much I go behind in doing so. In Montreal I can work & write & make money & up here I cant do anything: in the summer it is wonderful but in the winter there is nothing at all. In Montreal between Oct 1 and Dec 20 I made enough money writing & lecturing to pay all my expenses & all the Orillia expenses,— & by writing I dont mean money from old books but writing new stuff—Then I come up here & do nothing . . I could never live here in the winter: I'd have to have some sort of little place,—rooms or something in Toronto & go up & down—That is for after I sell my Montreal house, which I can hardly do for a year or two as the market is rotten—But Stevie is at McGill and is so happy there that I want him to have at least another year . . . . . . Before I left Montreal I had from Frank the most delightful book as a Xmas present (a book on yachting off Scotland, wonderful stuff by a navy man)—I haven't written to Frank yet but I will . . . Sib sent me a copy of a Saskatoon paper with some cheering remarks about my leaving . . . . but McGill begins to seem all dead for me: General Currie's death seemed to change it all . . . . . The "farm" here goes along pretty well . . We had some wonderful turkeys, the last one 19lbs dressed—but I'm afraid that as a whole they meant a loss of money—We are selling a lot of eggs & I begin to feel that the place can keep itself . . . Our wood only costs us out-of-pocket $1.75 a cord & the same wood in Orillia (cut just beside ours) costs $6.50 split & delivered . . . . . Kelly smoked the hams & bacon a huge success. One ham of one big (16 lbs) just about pays for the cost of the pig,—very nearly: we pay $3.$^{00}$ for him The cats mostly scraps & home grown food . . . . . . Give my very best to Charlie and any of the family that are round. Perhaps you see (my) Charlie sometimes. He wouldn't come here for Xmas: likes Toronto better.

> With best & affectionate
> greetings for New Years
> Stephen Leacock

## To W.T. Conder                                    Jan. 11, 1936

Dear Mr. Conder,

I am sorry to have to postpone for the present the question of an Australian trip. Advice which I have received makes me feel that financial success would be very doubtful.

But as I am retiring from active lecturing (Being 66 years old) next spring, I am free to go at any time . . . If you care to write me next August and show a good prospect of going without loss I'd like to think of it. I would not care to do any broadcasting . . and I hate addressing audiences of more than 2000 people. I can talk to 1000 in a whisper. For some years I have only taken such lectures as come along unsought, not having time for more than 12 or 15 a year, so I hardly needed agents. When they intervened I paid 25% commission. Before the slump I had no trouble in getting $350 U.S. dollars a lecture for the bigger stuff and $250 for the small: none less except as auxiliary. Since the slump lecture fees are cut to pieces. I enclose a list of lectures filled and fees receive (I refused about twice as many again.)

If you could show me a reasonable prospect for my coming, covering my expenses as from Vancouver (they pay themselves with a Canadian lecture or two) to New Zealand, Australia, in Australia and via England to Montreal,—expenses including myself and my son, railroads and hotels (I never stay in private houses) I'll be glad to consider it. But of course other questions come in esp. at my age. The C.P.R. give the enclosed figures.

S.L.

Please understand that this is only tentative.

## To Marie Meloney[1]                                    Jan. 11, 1936

Dear Mrs Meloney,
    Please read this. A London Daily Paper asked me to answer the question why not come home. I'd like to see this appear in New York with you and please don't think it has no American appeal as that is the whole point of it as you will see if you've time to read it all.
    I'd have to arrange the release dates as the same: but that's easy. I'll cable them if you can use it stating when. They want to use it as soon as possible.

S.L.

1   Marie Meloney (1876–1943) was editor of the Sunday section of the New York *Herald-Tribune* from 1926 to 1943.

## To John Lane                          [McGill University
                                          Montreal]
                                          Feb 5 36

John Lane
The Bodley Head

Dear Sirs
    I have completed a book as in printed announcement of Dodd Mead herewith <u>Hellements of Hickonomics</u>. They publish Ap 1. I enclose a copy of the contract. The payment of 20% after 20,000 is accepted by Dodd but qualified by my consent not to push the claim if it works hardship. Please be certain to return contract.
    Dodd has U.S. & Canada book rights. Serial first rights are negotiated but not completed U.S. & England. In any case they are not to stop publication Ap 1. The MS runs to about 1200 lines of verse and about 4000 words of preface, of interleaf text and conclusion. But you can see for yourself as I am

sending the MS as I take for granted you'll be glad to publish it. I think it will make a big hit.

British bookrights & India & Colonies not Canada

I can offer it to you on the same terms as Dodd with this further proviso —no <u>advance</u> royalty but a return made & payment therewith 3 months after publication & thereafter every 6 months not every year.

Dodd has another book also of mine "<u>Funny Pieces</u>" (MS June 15) No doubt you also will take it

But This Hickonomic Stuff looks big. Please cable on receipt of MS.

Best regards & good wishes

## To A.E. Morgan                                      Feb. 13, '36.

A. E. Morgan, Esq.,
Principal, McGill University

Dear Mr. Principal:

In a note of Feb. 10, you are good enough to say: "I should be glad if you could spare me a little time to discuss the future of the department of economics". The Chancellor also in writing to me said a short time ago: "Your influence will be increased in some way by the fact that you are no longer a member of the active staff."

On the strength of this I thought it might be of use if I set down my opinion in a brief memorandum, as follows:—

———

The Department of Economics has suffered greatly from the financial stringency of the past few years. It has had to forego the services of outside examiners from other universities; it has lost various scholarships which it had from McGill and from private sources for graduate students, and, most of all, it has had to suspend the publication of the monographs on Canadian problems which were a chief feature of its work.

But for all this there is no remedy but time. With the return of prosperity, all of this will come back and I do not think it would be wise to reorganise the department so as to amalgamate it with others and destroy its distinctive character. It has to cover already a wide field. In Canada, of necessity, economics must be taught in its bearing on the Canadian environment, which is quite different from that of England. Many of us might wish that economics could be taught more as a philosophical subject and less as a practical treatment of Canadian problems. But that is not possible here and now. The public expects from us a kind of training which will fit young men for service both with the government and with the business enterprises of Canada. In my opinion, to unite economics with other departments would rob it of the success which it has had.

I do not see that it is necessary to make any new appointment in the department. I stated to the Faculty last year, before I had any idea that I was to be put out of McGill, that in the event of a vacancy among us, those who were left could easily close up the ranks and carry on. I think this still. It is possible to do this because the graduate school is much reduced in numbers and the other classes are capable of reorganisation with a view to economy of teaching.

The saving to the University effected by such a plan is very considerable. A part of my pension is paid by the Carnegie Trust and thus only a part of it has to be paid by McGill. The immediate saving is about $3,600. a year and ultimately $5,000. or a difference in capital account of $100,000.

It would seem to me that Dr. Hemmon, after his long, arduous and efficient service in the department for almost 30 years has a proper claim to promotion to the place I hold.

I am authorised by my colleagues, Dr. Hemmon and Dr. Day and Professor Culliton to say that they entirely concur in the views as to the department expressed in this letter. Mr. Forsey is ill but I have every reason to presume his acquiescence.

I have lectured at McGill since January 1901. I have been at the head of the department nearly 30 years. Its graduates have filled many important posts in Canada. The writings and lectures of its staff have been widely known and have influenced the public life of the country.

I thought therefore that my views might be of use in any decision to be made in regard to the future of the department.

> Very faithfully,
> Stephen Leacock.

## To Dr Charles F. Martin

[McGill University
Montreal]
February 15th. 1936.

Dean Martin
McGill University

Dear Charlie,

Herewith a memorandum. I sent a copy to the Chancellor. The Principal on my presenting it said that I have no right to submit it; no right to ask the opinions of junior men whose opinions were not wanted; no right to make a representation in writing by only by word of mouth to him.

His manner and language were very overbearing and quite unsuited to the dignity of his position or the privilege of mine.

Will you please see that my views reach the Senate: whether they act on them is their own proper business.

Very sincerely,

## To Dr Charles F. Martin

McGill University
Montreal
Feb 15. 36

Dear Charlie

I couldn't talk to the Medical Undergrad's Society because I have just refused our own undergraduate society in Arts on the ground that my talking is over. . . . . I see that the students are bound they will have you stay on. I am all for your doing so, and shall be only too glad if I can lend a hand . . . It seems to me that representation could be made without involving any bad feeling or censure

Very sincerely
Stephen Leacock

P.S. Please thank the students and tell them that I fully appreciate the compliment and that I carry still the warm recollection of my last visit to them.

## To Home University Library

The Old Brewery Bay
Orillia, Ontario, Canada
March 20.36

(proposing book of Humour)

It occurs to me that you might care to invite me to write a book for your series of humour. I hope I may with modesty take for granted that you know who I am and what claim I may have to look upon humour as my business. If you would care to have such book and it would interest you to do it, I would not care whether I got percentage or you try payment.

## To Dora Hood's Book Room

[McGill University
Montreal]
March 26, 36

Dora Hood's Bk Room
720 Spadina Ave
Toronto

I note in your list a volume of Lahontan's voyages with a notes by me. Please tell me who published this. I prepared it some years ago and was never paid for my work & understood that it had not appeared . . As the publishers failed. Strictly speaking this makes the copyright rather peculiar & the legality of selling it a little dubious . . But I may be mistaken as to the facts . . I'd be glad of any information

Very sincerely
Stephen Leacock

## To Charles Spearman

March 27, 1936

Chas. Spearman Esq.
360 St. James St.

Dear Mr. Spearman,
Mr. Bruck whom I had not seen before, suggested that I might preface a book jointly with you dealing with Gold and Mining. He proposed to print it at his expense and sell it at his expense by canvass to mining shareholders. Under the plan I was to do the smaller part of the book (about 6000 words up to 10,000 words on gold in relation to the Currency Standard and Legal Tender and Prices: you were to do much the larger part on the technical and geological aspect of Mining. Mr. Bruck was to pay to each of us a royalty, amount not discussed.
As it stands I am afraid I should not wish to take the plan up: it would give me no supervision in the way in which it was advertised, the way in which my name was used and the claims for it. But with a certain change I would be willing to consider it. Mr. Bruck might get a reputable firm of publishers to list it and print the book, a firm acceptable to you and me: they could sell it as they liked to the trade and pay you and me a royalty, but nothing to Mr. Bruck. They could supply him with as many copies as he cared to pay for at printer's cost, nothing to the publishers, and he could pay a royalty to you and me. They would easily accept this plan as it would guarantee all their cost. But I am sure they would ask, as I would, that all advertising matter and circulars etc. must be approved by them.

I should not want to do more than 6000 words, the subject doesn't need it. I should expect the same royalty for the book as you although you do far more for the book than I do; because my fifty years of hard work has fortunately given my name on a book a selling value by which you would benefit.

Will you take this letter as a basis of our conversation to-day?

Very sincerely,
Stephen Leacock


## To Louis Kon[1]

[McGill University
Montreal]
Ap 15. 36

Dear Mr Kon

I am immensely interested in knowing that there is to be a Russian edition of some of my work—pleased & flattered—Do tell me where to send & I'll gladly pay in roubles, or in bonds of the old Russian gove'nt of which I still hold 8,000 . . . When I get round to it I'll see what I can do in the way of making extremes meet by writing you a piece . . I suppose humour is common ground

Very sincerely,
Stephen Leacock

---

1   Louis Kon (1883–1956) was a Montreal communist who, for a time, worked with the Russian embassy in Montreal.


## To Mr Blum

April 19, 1936

Dear Mr. Blum,

I'd be delighted to act on your letter in regard to Leacock Madeira and other wines. I'd have to time to do so on a financial basis, but I'd like to promote the sale of wine that my family have made for nearly two centuries.

I think what is needed in Canada is a certain amount of advertising campaign to revive the use of such wines as Madeira: for example to send out an edition of the booklet my cousins circulate in England. I could help in this. Then someone on the spot and with good connections and credentials should get in touch with clubs and hotels. I found the situation here quite hopeless. In my Club (the University Club) I am one of the two surviving foundation members. Colonel Sullivan, the secretary, and the members were entirely willing to stock the wine and wrote to the commission and said so. They were told in answer that the Commission had no legal power to accept an order from a club: they said further that they had such a long list of wines in stock that they wouldn't add the Madeira to their list.

You see what that means you are up against: no need to dot the i's and cross the t's.

I am sending a copy of this letter and with it our letter to my brother George Leacock who is the President of the Moloney Electric Co. of Toronto. He has a very wise personal connection with just the people needed. In Canada everybody knows me,—and my brother George knows everybody.

It is possible that he might like to talk with you on a business basis. But I know that in any case he would be only too glad to lend a hand in a general way and help to get you a suitable agent. It would have to be someone with class: but there are lots of them.

I think my brother is good friends with Commissioner Odette of Ontario.

> Very sincerely,
> Stephen Leacock

### To Mrs Herbert T. Shaw

[The Old Brewery Bay
Orillia]
Ap 24 Friday

Dear Fitz,

It has been so cold and wet here that your garden seems practically just where it was—I thought there would have been some hyacinths or something to send with the roses that I sent, but there is nothing at all . . . Nor any ploughing or planting to be done. . . We must leave it all over for a fortnight at least. . . . the ice is not yet out of the lake. . . I got here as arranged from Buffalo & go on to Chicago on Sunday night & expect to be back in Montreal late on Wed night. . . It seems all queer to be here without your being at your place: I went over & walked all round but it is all just wet & rotten & I was almost glad you weren't here as you would have been disappointed—but a week or two & it will all be wonderful

> Stephen

### To Adelaide Hett Meeres

[University Club of Montreal]
May 2, 36

Dear Addie

I was glad to get your letter but sorry to have such poor news of Charlie— a wretched business as all internal troubles are—I had been told already about Uncle Martyn by George & Charlie—I was up at Orillia with Stevie for 2 days a week ago but it was all very cold & wet so no work to be done on the land. but a week from now I expect to go there more or less for keeps this summer though I have to come to Montreal at least once again—You must come over

when things are easier with you & when Barbara & Stevie & I are settled . . . I
am planning to do a lot of work, or have it done, on the garden & the farm. So
far it has cost a lot of money but I think it will soon run itself—I hope Frank is
coming over: the summer never feels right without him—I have seen George &
Mary (his wife) several times. Stevie & I like her very much. I forget if you know
her—Charlie (Leacock) I dont see so much of as he doesn't seem to care to
come to Orillia. Write me later on & tell me about how things are & whether
you can come over. We can always bring you.

Yours affectionately
Stephen Leacock


## To Gerhard Lomer

[McGill University
Montreal]
(May 19 1936)

Dear Lomer
    I should have seen you officially to ask you to accept this 40 or more volumes
of my works for the library in accordance with a gift made of my old students
. . . But if you wont accept them as librarian, keep them for yourself . . . There is
also a picture done of de Lall in crayon that I'd like to ask the library to accept
as from the same group . . I enclose a card: I wrote to Mrs Low & said I'd refer
it to you.  I know nothing of it.

Very sincerely
Stephen Leacock


## To the Canadian Pacific Railway

[The Old Brewery Bay
Orillia]
Je 1. 36

The Canadian Pacific Ry
Maintenance of Way

Dear Sirs
    Last year you were good enough to let me cut the hay from your unused
track bordering on my Orillia property. I'd like it again. I dont want the hay for
myself, but what is next to the same thing, for one of the men who work for
me, William Jones, a 4 years veteran of the war who has worked for me ever
since & is now 69 years old . . If he can have the hay I'll let him have my horses
& machine to cut it etc.

If you care to lease me this piece of track (it's about half a mile) for a nominal lease of \$1.$^{00}$ a year, the lease to expire instantly on notice, I will undertake to keep the sides of the track in proper order—As it is, your unused track & that of the CNR beside it are turning into breeding places for noxious weeds, caterpillars etc. and are growing up with shrubs. If you lease it to me I can make a real use of it for hay by killing weeds & putting on fertiliser.

Very truly
Stephen Leacock

PS. I would of course leave the track proper untouched

## To Mrs Herbert T. Shaw

[The Old Brewery Bay
Orillia]
Thurs. June 4, 1936

Dear Fitz

I am so sorry to hear that you are not feeling well, which will pass away with rest and cheerfulness; you ought to try and get acquainted with a humorist who could make you laugh. I took Walter Scott and the Doctor to Johnson's yesterday; water all mud, and high with rain; nothing biting; caught 2 by accident . . . I've been working terribly hard . . my Morning Post stuff ran to 6500 words, all done. A Mr. D——, former theatre man, is talking of my doing some popular "chats" on economics. So I have made out an abstract and sent it . . . am today getting up lectures for Detroit and New York—back on Sunday . . .

Stephen
(Leacock)

P.S. No eggs; Hens suddenly quit. I am <u>buying</u> them. . . .

## To Mrs Herbert T. Shaw

[The Old Brewery Bay
Orillia]
Tues. Afternoon 4 p.m.
(June 10, 1936)

Dear Fitz,

I shall be so glad when you come up. It is very hot today, so in all of a huge afternoon mail the only letter I opened is yours . . . I am glad that René is coming up to you for August. I think it will save his life, so to speak. He is foolish about his French money. I have tried to tell him so a hundred times . . . As he is to live in Canada his interest lies in dollars not <u>francs</u>; in Canadian prices not French . . . If the franc falls in gold value,—and it may crash at any time,—then in terms of dollars René looses heavily,—and he spends his money in <u>dollars</u> . . . It is true that if the franc crashes French prices will rise and <u>presently</u> French wages & salaries and also the <u>interest</u> on stock profits, but not the fixed interest on <u>bonds</u> & <u>fixed securities</u> . . . if René's money is in bonds & fixed securities (fixed interest, <u>rentes</u>) he loses out as the French bondholders did in the war . . . and even in common stocks he loses out because the fall of the exchange in terms of dollars is far quicker than the rise of French stock profits . . . add to this the danger of war & upheaval, losing all round.

The franc today holds still at <u>6 3/4</u> cents nearly. René could send a cable & sell everything & transfer . . . He perhaps does not realise that his broker's (his cousins) interest is exactly the opposite of his own . . . The broker's interest is to <u>invest</u> & re-invest and never leave the money quiet . . . as he gets a commission every time . . . and all brokers & cousins are human . . . to say that he re-sells at a profit is nothing: he may re-sell at a <u>loss</u> & that's worse than anything . . . René interest lies in investing in first class Canadian securities (common stock of high standing, gold of high standing & bonds of high standing); then he is all right as he gets his pay in our dollars & if our prices rise his money income (salary, even, presently & stock profits at once) rise with it . . . Do get him to see this—read him this part of this letter but not the sentence which follows which says that René hates to interfere with his cousin, to send a sharp straight order, "Sell out all my holding, buy dollars & transmit to my credit Bank of Montreal" . . . Do try to save him.

&ast; &ast; &ast; &ast; &ast; &ast; &ast;

Hooker's getting on fine. I keep track of what he does & have him come to me if he gets stuck for material etc. . . For example, he broke a pin in the wheel of the lawn-mower,—five minutes in our workshop instead of five days in Orillia. . .

Tell Peggy that I wrote to New York & asked Dodd, Mead how they liked our <u>Owl</u> & <u>Dog</u>. I'll hear in a day or two. Hatley sent a hurry-up order for 5 broilers at <u>25</u> <u>cents</u> <u>a</u> <u>lb</u> . . . I imagine a back kick from an appreciative customer—

Could you use broilers if we sent them not cleaned? They're all so busy here—or wouldn't they travel that way

I have been working terribly hard. This morning I wrote half an article to try on <u>Vogue</u> & will do the other half tomorrow . . . I have paid all plain expenses here so far (food & wages) out of articles & lectures . . . I wish you were up here. It is so nice & quiet you'd love it . . I've seen no Orillia people since I got back on Sunday morning . . .

Goodbye for just now
Stephen Leacock

P.S. I am sorry you're not up here just now

## To Carl Goldenberg

[The Old Brewery Bay
Orillia, Ontario]
Je 14. 36

Dear Goldenberg—

Many thanks for sending me your excellent article in the Fortnightly—first rate—I enclose a letter to the Yale Review .. But if you want to write steadily & regularly I think that perhaps a regular newspaper connection is better. The rate is lower, The glory is less, but the total return à la longue is more

best regards
Stephen Leacock

## To Fred Smith

[The Old Brewery Bay
Orillia, Ontario]
Je 22. 36

Dear Fred

I have been making a good deal of use of your farm instruments, for which I am much obliged

I would like this summer to make use of your two-horse mower (we've about 6 acres to cut): & the binder (we about 16 acres to bind) & of your sulky rake. Your disc is still here & we would need to use it again in the fall.

I would like to offer $15$^{00}$ as a fair price for this use that we are making & going to make of your implements. I enclose a cheque for that sum.

Also I would like to offer you $10$^{00}$ over & above this and buy your plough. The standard price new, of a two horse plough is only $20$^{00}$—$25$^{00}$. I enclose a cheque for $10$^{00}$.

Also if you care to sell me the sulky rake for $5$^{00}$ extra, over & above the other two cheques, I'd be glad to take it . . . I'd offer more but it will cost money to repair it. I enclose $5$^{00}$.

I hope you can accept all this as it stands. If so, just keep the cheques and initial this letter. If not, drive over with Lou & tell me why not.

In any case please let Lou fetch over the sulky rake.

V. faithfully
Stephen Leacock

## To William Kaye Lamb

June 25, 1936

Dear Mr. Lamb:

I was delighted to receive this morning your letter of June 19 showing interest in the Simpson problem and contributing your opinion that his letters do not show, as has been claimed, a progressive mental deterioration, a growing insanity, during the later period.

This has qualities of a real mystery. Just as in the better modern detective novels, the evidence and the suspicions swing first one way and then another. During the last few weeks I have received two or three well-considered letters, one of them giving not only the writer's views but also those of a number of other students, and these were all trending toward the suicide theory. In all these letters the signs of a growing mental disturbance said to be found in Simpson's later correspondence were mentioned and in some cases heavily relied upon as deciding between the murder and suicide views. Now come you on the opposite side, and that fresh from a reading of the letters.

There appears to be a chance for me to see the Ross letters in a manuscript which is deposited for eventual publication with the Macmillan Company of Canada, Toronto.

Don't bother to just reply to this letter but please write me if you think it likely that the Macmillan manuscript does not contain some of the letters which led you to the view that Simpson was stable and normal during the last few months of his life. And, as you say you will, please write now or later if anything new comes to your mind.

The book in which the Simpson study belongs is not being written just now. I am working on three others, which is enough. One of those is in galley, the others barely developing into manuscripts. What I am doing with the Simpson material for the time being is to write letters of inquiry and to gather material in other ways.


*To Hugh Eayrs*                                    [The Old Brewery Bay
                                                   Orillia, Ontario]
                                                   Aug 25. 36

My dear Hugh
    Yours of Aug 24.
    To increase a set of articles of 8500 to a book of 25,000 words, is not a matter of mere good will or intention. It cant be done without producing something else. The whole merit of my <u>Morning Post articles</u> (& I have been overwhelmed with congratulations) lies in the <u>pith</u>, the <u>condensation</u> the power of presenting much in little. A new book of 25,000 words would be an entirely different thing, less readable, less saleable & would need several months work, during which the market would be gone.

.    .    .    .    .    .

Now dismiss all idea of any fault or blame, of mine or yours or any bad will. Why not publish as a <u>pamphlet</u>?—the whole <u>merit</u>, the whole idea being that this is the <u>Morning Post Stuff</u> that made such a fuss.

Done in paper in good taste, with only 8,500 to print (200 per page, clear type)—sell retail at 50 cents with 5 cents a book to me—or if you like at 55 cents with five cents a book to me.[1]

V. sincerely
Stephen Leacock

1   Eayrs replied on 27 August 1935: 'We will do the little book in a brochure to list at 50¢, paying you 10%.'

## To the Town of Orillia

[The Old Brewery Bay
Orillia, Ontario]
Aug 27 1936

The Town of Orillia

Dear Sirs

I am asking Mr Arthur Thompson to request you on my behalf to reconsider the figure of my assessment for the year 1937. It has been raised from $6550 to $8500, an increase just short of 30 percent.

It has occurred to me that this great increase may be due to a misunderstanding as to my residence here. It has perhaps been thought that I am henceforth residing here all the year round, and hence will be receiving municipal services for the whole year instead of for five months as hitherto. But this is not so. I expect to live in Montreal for several years yet, and hence only to receive ~~the~~ here municipal services as extended to a summer resident.

May I remind you how very limited these are in the part of the town where I reside. I am beyond the reach of the city water supply, the city sewers, and sidewalks. To get electricity I had to build a quarter of a mile of line at my own expense and the same way with telephone service. I get no fire protection and no police protection of an immediate character.

I have always understood that when Orillia annexed the outlying land reaching to Atherly the expectation was that property holders in this district, receiving so little, would enjoy a lower assessment. But the increases in the past and this final increase of thirty per cent, brings the assessment in my case almost to the point where it extinguishes the value of the property. At the present tax rate, I could hardly obtain for my property, if rented for the summer, anything much ~~for~~ more than taxes and depreciation.

It is true that I have added a lot of stable & outbuildings to my property in the last two years. But these are larger to the eye than to the exchequer: the whole lot of them would only sell for a few hundred. Indeed the selling value of my property is probably a good deal less than it was five years ago.

But on the strength of these new sheds I would willingly accept an added assessment of $500,—to make a total of $7000. But anything more than that I should find it hard to pay.

I would ask the Council to consider the peculiar situation in which summer residents are situated. They pay already a full set of local taxes in their own town, and then have to pay on their summer property <u>school taxes</u>,—and never send a child to school, high school taxes, and taxes for months & months of winter services which they are not there to receive. The only way to make summer residence, in the form of property holding, a feasible proposition is to keep the assessment <u>low enough</u> to enable the proper holder to pay two set of taxes. It might be said that if summer residents dont like the conditions they need not come. But to take such a line is suicidal to the interests of the town. Places like Orillia with a beautiful lake district around them, should expect to draw a large and continuous profit for local trade from the existence of a great number of summer cottages and summer estates.

In my own case, if I may speak personally, I have spent in the course of the last thirty years thousands, and thousands and thousands of dollars in Orillia: and have steadily gone on the principle of buying in the town itself & never a cent outside of it that could be avoided.

But if this large expenditure is only a signal for higher tax burdens, it will become very difficult for me to meet the situation. I am now living on a pension and on an income for less than it used to be: my working time is drawing in. I should feel deeply sorry if the financial conditions imposed here, compell me to reconsider my situation.

V. faithfully
Stephen Leacock

# CHAPTER 8

## STEPHEN LEACOCK
# DISCOVERY OF
# THE CANADIAN WEST

## 1936–1937

In the fall of 1936 Leacock embarked on a lecture tour of western Canada, 'partly because he could not think of anything else to do and partly because it had the earmarks of turning into a triumphal tour for the retired man'.[1] Although he had never lectured in Canada for money, motivated by a kind of patriotism and donating the funds from his lectures to organizations such as the Canadian Rotarians and the McGill Alumni Clubs, he now planned to devote his energies to an exhausting series of public lectures throughout the West.

Having negotiated with McGill for the release of his son, now a freshman, from his studies in order to accompany his father, Leacock left Montreal on 25 November 'with two huge black suitcases plastered with bright red stars for "quick identification"'.[2] The trip, which took him to the land that had attracted all five of his brothers, was the most rewarding experience of his life, as Leacock was greeted enthusiastically by one audience after another everywhere he went. But the demands of the tour took a toll on him, and despite being overjoyed by the warm reception he received, he resolved never to lecture again. 'No more this season, and please God I won't need to lecture any more—wonderful success—all records broken, but it's hard,' he confided to his niece.[3] And Leacock would hold firmly to this promise: except for small gatherings of Ontario Conservatives or McGill alumni, he never gave another public lecture.

Though now retired, Leacock took no break from writing. When he returned from his western trip, he immediately started to write out the lectures he had given, beginning them as a series of articles for the Montreal *Star* and then revising them for book publication. The result, *My Discovery of the West:*

1   Ralph L. Curry, *Stephen Leacock: Humorist and Humanist* (Garden City, New York: Doubleday and Co., 1959), p.266.
2   Barbara Nimmo, 'Preface', Stephen Leacock, *Last Leaves* (Toronto: McClelland and Stewart, 1945), p.xi.
3   Ibid.

*A Discussion of East and West in Canada* (1937), was a balanced and sympathetic portrait of the economic situation and prospects for the future in western Ontario, Manitoba, Saskatchewan, Alberta, and British Columbia. It also earned Leacock a Governor General's award for non-fiction.

On 10 August 1937, Barbara Ulrichsen married Donald Nimmo, son of the editor of the Detroit *Saturday Night*. The wedding took place at The Old Brewery Bay, and Leacock spared no expense in arranging it. The ceremony was held out-doors on the magnificent lawns of his Orillia home. Although Barbara moved with her husband to Detroit, she continued to work for her favourite uncle, typing for him and visiting him frequently in the years following her marriage.

## *To the Editor of The McGill News*[1]   [Sept. 15, 1936]

Sir,–Data quite right, and the dates, too, if read properly. I gave my first lecture at McGill in January, 1901: a three months' course in Political Science to supplement the three months (October, November and December, 1900) just given by LeRossignol. The class in attendance was of the third and fourth year, hence some were Class of 1901 and others of 1902.

I came back next year, 1901–2 (all session), as a sessional lecturer in History and Political Science; and the next the same (1902–03). In the session 1903–04 I was made a regular member of the staff in the Department (as organized) of Economics and Political Science. I became head of it on September 1, 1908.

I never knew that my students went to Dr. Peterson in 1902 to speak for my permanent appointment, and I am touched at the recollections, I mean, the *thought* of it. It was only one of infinite kindnesses that have not ended yet.

Orillia, Ont.                                   Stephen Leacock

1   George E. Cole of Winnipeg, Manitoba, wrote to *The McGill News*:

Unless I am greatly mistaken, Mr. Leacock came to McGill to complete the year 1900–01, begun by Prof. J. E. LeRossignol who gave the first lectures at McGill in Political Economy. Dr. Leacock carried on in the winter term in Political Science with the class of 1902, probably among others. This was the first course in Political Science given at McGill.

The class of Arts 1902 was grely taken with the Leacock manner of teaching Political Science and did not hesitate to talk about him. Our enthusiasm brought us into conflict with Principal Peterson who wasn't greatly concerned about students' opinions of a new lecturer. Fortunately for McGill, it did not interfere with Dr. Leacock's appointment.

I feel, however, that Arts 1902 discovered Dr. Leacock at McGill and was the first to appreciate his inspiration.

Some time I hope to meet Dr. Leacock and tell him how graciously (?) Principal Peterson received a committee from Arts 1902 when on an errand of telling him what a good lecturer Dr. Leacock was.

*To Mrs Herbert T. Shaw*                    [The Old Brewery Bay
                                            Orillia, Ontario]
                                            Friday Sep. 25, 36
                                            1/4 to 1

Dear Fitz,

I just got back this morning from Sir William Mulock's place. He called for me on Tues at 11 with his daughter Mrs. Kirkpatrick, chauffeur & two maids —right on time or nearly—he said he was "<u>worrying</u>" about it—Drove to his place. It is 4 miles outside of Gravenhurst; a bungalow that he built last year (at 91) for convenience in fishing & gave it to his daughter—We got there just about 1 & he had me out fishing right after lunch—He fishes in the private lakes of the Beaumaris Club—we fished all Tuesday till 6—all Wednesday from 11 am till 5 & all Thursday ditto—lunch right in the boat—He hardly drinks anything at all (all George's stuff crazy)—Luckily for me I took no changes—I bought a bottle of the best rye I could get as a present & two quarts of Scotch for myself.—so I got along—Sir William forgets all about rye—He wanted some chess. I couldnt get a board in Gravenhurst. So I phoned Kelly to drive me up a board & men. Stevie came with him. Sir William insisted that Stevie must stay. So he stayed & had the sofa in the dining (living room) for 2 nights. We caught in all about 60 or 70 bass—Kelly drove up & fetched Stevie & me back this morning as Sir William wanted to fish & I couldn't stay longer—I wrote a poem on & for him in his album, which he is going to have put in the papers—It is sad that such a man should ever have to die . . .

Here all seems flourishing—there was heavy rain but no frost . . the reason why I go & come so fast from Montreal is to save money. I have to go on the first to get material for my Fortnightly Review article so I drive with Barbara & Stevie & Helen & that saves a lot of money & then I come <u>back</u> with Lou & that saves more still . . So if I get there on the first (Thursday) I shall expect to get away again on Tuesday the 5<sup>th</sup> & you could come with me & we can stay here as long as you are able—I have a lot to do & must come or waste money; but it will be fine & comfortable & I imagine Tina can "do" for us all that needs doing . . . I have such a mess of letters to answer that I cannot write all the news but it was nice to find letter from you on top of the pile,—the first I opened— & then I looked through for <u>cheques</u>—like hens eggs . . . I must quit . . I'll be so glad to see you again—I am much better & working terribly hard. The poem I wrote for Sir William is a corker—such good taste,—no <u>me</u> in it

                                            Stephen

## To Mrs Herbert T. Shaw

[The Old Brewery Bay
Orillia]
Sat Sep 27
12 noon

Dear Fitz,

I have been out all morning working on the building job; my hay barn looks quite like a Hudson's Bay Fort & I put up a flag staff on it and am buying a 25 cent Union Jack & sewing it into the corner of 20 cents worth of <u>Turkey</u> <u>Red</u>— thus saving buying a four dollar flag;—that makes the ordinary red ensign—I didnt hear from you today as I had half expected to: I hope you got the last lot of vegetables etc all right . . . My idea is to have Lou go down with a truck a little later & carry all vegetables, etc.—potatoes not ready yet & very little of yours ready—artichokes, carrotts etc. still to mature—I tried your plan of early picking of apples; picked 20 baskets & sent them to Toronto & was offered only <u>10</u> cents <u>a</u> <u>basket</u>! Kelly brought them back & Hatley paid 20 cents—I had a hard knock when I got my New York publishers returns.—My poor Hickonomics didn't sell at all!—However I can live all right on what I have and don't need to worry—But I was sorry; I had put such a lot of work into it. . . . However,—one must take the rough & the smooth—I have the furnace going; it is pretty cool outside but no real frost at night yet . . . I heard no more from René after his letter saying that he got back: he'll find it hard going—I have had the most terrific string of invitations to speak—what the hell do they think I am—politicians have to speak & people like Principals & Deans & new appointees—but my god! why should I! but I answer but what tires me is this silly notion of "salesmanship" & getting into personal touch! a man called me by long distance to invite me to speak at the Empire Club & went on & on & on— it was hard not to get mad about it. I expect to leave here early early early on ~~Thu~~ Wed—Thursday night—wrong—due in Montreal Thursday at 4 & go right into the house . . . I have to have a few days in Montreal for my literary work— I suppose Lou can sleep at your house & keep the car over there—He can of course put it in my back yard but it is so hard to go in & out

Stephen
Leacock

Best regards to Peggy; tell her I miss her; the orchard seems lonely without her knocking the apples down.

Stephen
(Leacock)

*To Mrs Herbert T. Shaw*

Orillia
Monday Sep 28
9.30 am

Dear Fitz,

I was at my desk at 4 this morning in the dark & wrote till I finished all my article on Social Credit (including reading up the material) at about 7:30—then I worked with the men & had breakfast and it's <u>now</u>—It rained all day yesterday—a regular down pour. Donald Nimmo stayed over & left this morning an hour or so ago—today lovely sunshine—great weather to work— my article on Social Credit that I just finished runs to 4600 words—they had said only room for 3500 so I have cabled again to ask for 4000 & I'll cut it down to that. When I get it done I'm going to start on a piece called <u>My Amazing Uncle</u> (about 5000 words on E.P.)—very difficult because I can't tell how much voice & mimic counts for in the E.P. stuff—But I mean to do it in my own way—It will be a part of a future volume of reminiscences—I am so glad not to have to give lectures at McGill! as a professor Emeritus I have my corner in the library & my right of access & my mail at McGill—it wont seem any different really . . . I hope I hear from you today: it is nice to get letters regularly just about nothing—Ill probably write again when I do—I begin to feel tired from working so long; what about Peggy's exam?

Stephen

*To William Wallace Goforth*

[McGill University
Montreal, Canada]
Nov 2. 36

Memorandum to Mr Goforth on My Western Trip

My dear Wallie

I thought it wise to set down the plan and scope of the lecture tour I am to make and the circumstances of its making

A great many people in Canada, of whom I am one, think that the relations of the East & the West in the Dominion are not quite as they should be. There is far too little sympathy and understanding.

It has been thought that if anybody as well known as I am lucky enough to be, with old pupils everywhere as the result of my 47 years of teaching and with friends everywhere as readers of my books, should make a lecture tour in the west it would be of service. I think this myself.

I should not propose to lecture only on economic and political subjects, but on educational and literary things, and should try to make the lectures a compound of wisdom and amusement, and to help to create an atmosphere of good will. I know that I can do this, lecturing in my own way and fashion . .

If such a tour had been planned with ample time and with advance agencies, the commercial results would be very high. But the tour being undertaken with very little time for organisation & hence with hardly any choice for local societies and committees, the commercial returns will be very small and it will be advisable in the case of colleges and college societies to give lectures for nothing

But I understand that certain people, feeling that the trip would do good, are willing to give very generous support to it so that I can disregard the difficulty indicated. I need only say that on such terms I shall be delighted to go, and entirely confident of my ability to do exactly what I have explained.

V. sincerely
Stephen Leacock


Western Trip
Itinerary

1936
Wed Nov 25 . . Leave Montreal
Th — 26    arr. Fort William 10.pm.
Fri 27. Sat 28    In Fort William ⎰lecture Canadian Club: Canada & the United States
                                  ⎱    "      McGill Graduates

Sunday 29.    Leave Fort William 820 AM: Winnipeg 7.45 PM

Mon Nov 30. Dec 1.2.3.4. Sat 5 ⎧In Winnipeg:
                                ⎪Address. Can. Club. Peace Order & Good Government
                                ⎨            University of Manitoba. Education by the Yard
                                ⎪
                                ⎩Women's C.C. . . . . McGill Graduates

Sunday Dec 6 leave Winnipeg 9:45 AM: Regina 5.55 PM

      Dec 7–8                    In Regina
                                    Address Canadian Club
                                    . Other Meeting  .

Wed Dec 9. leave Regina . . Arrive Saskatoon

Thurs. Dec 10. Fri Dec 11.    In Saskatchewan ⎧Address University of Sask.
                                               ⎨      (Recovery after Graduation)
                                               ⎩      Can. Club

Sat Dec 12 leave Regina arrive Edmonton.

Sun Dec 13 or 14.15.16.    In Edmonton.  Address <u>University of Alberta</u>
                                    Looking Back on College

                                    Canadian Club. <u>Debit or Credit</u>
                                    One other meeting

Thurs Dec 17 leave Edmonton Arrive Calgary

Fri Dec 18. Sat Dec 19. In Calgary. Address.  Board of Trade
                                    <u>Economic Separation</u>
                                    College & Can. Club?
Dec 19

Leave Calgary arrive Banff . . . Dec 20 In Banff (Informal talk Hotel)
                                    Dec 19

Arrive Vancouver evening of 21. In Vancouver   1 week (University. Can. Club & McGill

    Arrive      27 Victoria                    1    "     leave Victoria in January.


## To W.E. Gladstone Murray[1]                    Nov. 6th. 1936

Maj. W.E. Gladstone Murray
Ottawa

Dear Weg,

Continuing our conversation on broadcasting I have received further suggestions from New York about studio broad-casting, and am quite determined not to do any.

But here comes in another thing. I am to lecture in the West (Nov 26–Jan.6), clubs, colleges etc. . . some lectures on economic situation of Canada, others education and education.

I think some of these will be of interest: e.g. in Winnipeg I talk on <u>Peace Order and Good Government</u>, a plea for the Uniting of Canada . . and in Edmonton on <u>Debit and Credit, a talk on Hard Money</u> (by Daniel in the Lion's Den) . .

Now, of course, I don't want any money, as I'm paid already, but if some of these talks went on the air there might be a lot of people interested.

If there's anything in it I could send you my schedule.

                                    Very best wishes,
                                    S.L.

---

1   Canadian-born William Ewart Gladstone Murray (1893–1970), a student of Leacock's at McGill and World War I veteran, was the director of public relations for the British Broadcasting Commission (1924–35) before becoming the first general manager of the Canadian Broadcasting Corporation (1936–42).

## To George Leacock

Montreal
Nov. 36

Dear George,

I was very glad to hear that you are out of the hospital—I am sending you a copy of my <u>Funny Pieces</u>. You needn't read any of it except page <u>209</u> where your name occurs.

Now this,—

Charlie writes that he will come on as far as Fort William with me, but I have written to him not to do so as I have a terrible lot of work and I need to be absolutely undisturbed on the train to get up the speech I am to give . . . and at the hotel I have written ahead to say that I want to stay undisturbed in my room & see <u>no one</u>, not even the press. (I give them their stuff in envelopes)—now there would be no place in all that for Charlie.

I wrote him at Sutton and I wrote him at the Elliot House but will you please see that this word reaches him and without hurt or offense. I enclose also the itinerary of my tour and list of audiences. You will see that it involves a very heavy strain. Stevie and I leave here Wednesday evening Nov. 25 at 7.35 p.m.

Best regards to Mary and yourself.

y.a.b.
Stephen Leacock


## To Frank Dodd

3869 Cote des Neiges Rd.,
Montreal, Que.,
Nov. 23, 1936.

Frank Dodd, Esq.,
Dodd, Mead & Co.,
New York, N.Y.

Dear Dodd:

I am leaving on Wednesday for a lecture trip through Western Canada to the the Coast (November 25–January 18). I propose to write it up as <u>MY WESTERN EXCURSION</u>. I send you an advance notice of it.

I propose to publish it as a book on April 1, 1937. It ought, with proper salesmanship, to sell easily up to 5000 in Canada. . . . in the United States it wouldn't sell much but as a combined U.S. and Canada it should be all right. It is to contain a lot of light foolish stuff and a lot of solid discussion put in attractive form. . . . as a sample of what I mean I enclose a copy of my article in the <u>Fortnightly</u> Preview of <u>Social Credit</u>, which, in a rewritten form will appear in the book.

Several recent articles I have written about Canada and the U.S. have gone, quite literally and absolutely, all round the English speaking world.

Do not therefore think this book an impossible book though it may be, as I mean to write it absolutely in your way.

I should not ask any advance royalty or guaranteed royalty. If the book could retail as low as $1.50 I'd expect only 10 per cent. up to a sale of 10,000 copies and after that 20 per cent: if sold above $1.50 I'd expect 15 per cent. up to a sale of 10,000 and after that 20 per cent.

Please send me, if only provisionally and without committing yourself, your views on this.

Yours sincerely,

Encl.

P.S.—Please return enclosure: I can't get any copies here.


## To Barbara Ulrichsen

[Royal Edward Hotel
Fort William, Ontario]
1 pm Friday 27/36

Dear Barbara

Everything OK—train fine—on time—met by Mr. Duncan—hotel first rate—great comfort—everything per schedule.

You packed everything beautifully wonderful—the only thing that bothered me was about Wally Goforth. I was sorry I didn't see him and afraid I might have hurt his feelings by asking him too brusquely about the New York stuff, so I wrote him yesterday, Canada Cement Bldg., is that correct? If not & in any case please call him up and say I was sorry not to see him and have written him and that I hope to discuss later with him the question of my writings. Best love from us both.

y.a. uncle<br>Stephen<br>(Leacock)


## To Gordon Glassco

[Royal Edward Hotel,
Fort William, Ontario]
Sat Nov 28

Dear Gordon

We had a fine meeting here last night, a dinner at the Prince Arthur Hotel in Port Arthur, about a hundred graduates and wives and daughters. There are not enough McGill graduates in this town to eat in anything bigger than a lunchwagon, so we had to fall back on Toronto & Queens & such, & pretend that they were the same. We had 13 McGill graduates (the other one was sick) and 18 Toronto & 15 Queens & 6 Manitoba & 4 Western and some from Minneapolis etc to make up. It should be noted that bright young McGill graduates are needed in this district: they tell me here that the business connection with Toronto is much closer and it has gradually come about that jobs are filled from there.

Among the leading McGill men here, one of the best known is G.R. Duncan who is in Real Estate. He was in Applied Science in Lord Rutherford's day and was a demonstrator under Rutherford & Soddy, and took his first degree in 1901 and a higher degree later. Then there is Dr. Crozier a medical man of 1903 who spoke the thanks of McGill at the dinner. Dr. Macintosh of the class of 1894 is the doyen of the McGill graduates. Among the younger ones are several representatives of Commerce such as Frank Murphy of 1925, who is now in the family business as a coal importer.

I struck also one or two more doubtful cases of graduation from McGill. The barber who cut my hair here called me "Professor." He said, "I'll trim it a little full over the ear, eh, Professor?" and I said, "Yes, either that or trim the ear." Then, noticing that he called me "Professor", I said "Are you from McGill?" He answered, "Yes, sir, I left in 1913, came right here to Fort William, got a chair here in six months and have done fine ever since! Two other boys came at the same time & have chairs down the street!" That looked fine as academic advancement, three appointments to chairs in one and the same town! But afterwards, I didn't feel so sure. My ears were pretty well shrouded with towels. He may have said "Montreal" and not McGill. Anyway he & the other two boys, he says, are going back for a vacation "to see the old place" some say, so you watch for them and see where they go.

Stephen Leacock.

*To Mrs Herbert T. Shaw*                    [Royal Alexandra Hotel
                                            Winnipeg, Man.]
                                            Sunday, 10, P.M.
                                            Nov. 29, 36.

Dear Fitz,

Just arrived—We have a vast suite of rooms here—my trip is like a progress, or Pageant—we rode on a private car with Mr. Main, C.P.R. official and a Dr. Moody—a wonderful day—such easy rolling comfort—light blue sky— forests—scenery—frozen lakes—whiskey—around here—reporters—flashlight photographs—then 3 reporters and I got them up to the suite, because I remembered Morgan's rudeness and gave them drinks and we sat and talked— if they don't write it up kindly and nicely that's their business not mine—I did my part—.......I didn't get tired to-day because I ate nothing all day—it made all the difference—I find already western opinion very hostile to C.P.R. and Montreal—its like walking on stepping stones.

> Good night, I hope I hear
> from you.
> Stephen
> (Leacock)

## To George Leacock

[Royal Alexandra Hotel
Winnipeg, Man.]
Sunday night
Nov 29 36

Dear George,

Your letter was given to me here. Our journey has been like a Rajah's progress. I spoke in Port Arthur and Fort William—crowded tables,—many brought to Jesus.

To Winnipeg with Mr. Main in his private car (the Manitoba). You met him in Orillia with Charlie Jones on Old Home Week day. Lunch in the car—hot day.

Met by a battery of reporters. Ducal suite in the hotel—all hell—damn nonsense, but I shall stick in and see no one. The Free Press (Sifton) is anti C.P.R.—too bad—I gave interviews but I'll take care not to read them. (too much like an actor opening the paper)—Stevie is having a grand time. The gov'r general is here: just like his impudence—but I needn't see him and don't mean to—We stay here a week. Best regards to you both—many people speak of you.

> y.a.b.
> Stephen Leacock

## To Mrs Herbert T. Shaw

[Royal Alexandra Hotel
Winnipeg, Man.]
Mon Nov 30 36
5.15 PM

Dear Fitz

I got a letter from you this morning; so glad to hear—it is so nice to get letters—I am just trying to get ready & set to go out to a dinner & to my lecture—this job is worse than prize-fighting. there's no end to it—I will be glad when its over—I've avoided the world so far today; cut off the phone. Now I'm going out for a sort of walk on deck up & down & then to my lecture—My God! how can anyone stand what they call public life—The Governor General spoke here today in the hotel at lunch to the Can. Club—380 present—I hope

I beat his god damn record; that would do him good—He is here in the hotel again tonight at the St. Andrews Dinner—but I am in the Fort Garry the other hotel——. I got a Star on Saturday & saw that Howard Ferguson had got off a lot of platitudes.—Keep on writing.

Stephen<br>(Leacock)

## To Barbara Ulrichsen

[Royal Alexandra Hotel
Winnipeg, Man.]
Wed Dec 1. 36

Dear Barbara

I haven't heard from you but Mrs Shaw writes that Donald came & that everything is going on first rate . . . All the arrangements for us and the packing & everything has worked out wonderfully—I am just <u>swamped</u> with telephone & other calls & I said to Stevie "if Barbara were here she could do all this & you cant: it is good for you to know what you cant do"—and he said he understood.

It is just like a come-to-Jesus parade—I talked at the Fort Gary hotel & they said a little before the meeting this is the record for seats except for the Queen of Roumania—and a little later "this beats the Queen of Roumania", & later the Queen is no where—

Mrs. James of the University Women's Club has been phoning—about her meeting—afternoon hotel meeting,—about when I come,—& I said:

Mrs. James, if, as you say, all records are broken as to how many people hear the speech, what the hell does it matter whether I drink tea with 30 or 40 first? —could she understand it?—no. I have been very tired but I think I can now hit an even page of doing things—I had a telephone message (among 100 from "Mr. Sheppard" but couldn't remember who is that?—

y.a.u.<br>Stephen Leacock

## To G. Eric Reid

[Royal Alexandra Hotel
Winnipeg, Man.]
Dec 1

Eric Reid, K.C.
London Ont.

Dear Buster

I am lecturing in the West. At Port Arthur I addressed a dinner of 100 University graduates. It was a regular come-to-Jesus meeting. After my talk they all swore to lead a better life.

There are only about 15 McGill graduates in this town,—but they will form a branch of our Society.

Please write to <u>G.R. Duncan</u> of ~~Port~~ Fort William (Real Estate) & send him the constitution & the oath & tell him what to do . . . I am asking Gordon Glassco to send you a printed account of my meeting.

Yours in the faith
The Apostle Stephen
formerly
Stephen Leacock

## To Barbara Ulrichsen

[Royal Alexander Hotel
Winnipeg, Man.]
Dec. 1

Dear Barbara,

By mistake the hotel charged me & I paid the bill ($26.40) and so these cheques were sent after me.

Please deposit them

V.a.y.u.
Stephen Leacock

I telegraphed about Uncle Charlie. When he got a little out of health before, he used to go to the Orillia hospital . . . now, I suppose he can hardly afford it . . so I will pay the bill if he likes to go there.

I noticed a very stupid and insulting letter from the Philadelphia woman. I tore it up. It is difficult not to answer that sort of stuff in kind, but much wiser.

## To Mrs Herbert T. Shaw

[Royal Alexandra Hotel
Winnipeg, Man.]
Wed Dec 2

Dear Fitz

I've been trying to work on my book in my room this morning but its hard. I have had the telephone shut off by explaining that I am <u>deaf</u> & not going out because I am <u>lame</u> and refusing to see people because I am <u>blind</u>,—but even at that written messages & telephone numbers—of course its kind—but I'm tired—I was quite sick yesterday but I went to bed—I keep explaining that all I can do is to do my job—for instance among the numbers to call is Mrs Craig, Aubrey's sister, who is of course kindness itself but can she understand—no—I am going to call her & say I'll drive out in a taxi at 5 and see her but she'll say,— well! stay right to dinner! tired? lie down right here etc.—all very kind—The only letter I really liked was from the old Archbishop who said he was too old to come to see me! Hoorah! he's the stuff . . . I drove out at 5.30 & had a drink at Bogus Coyne's house (Upper Canada of 1896); Ronnie Counsell was there, Jack's brother. Jack he says gets no better . . . all these people are against the East . . they all think they're being robbed . . . I got a telegram from Calgary asking me to lecture on <u>Social Credit</u> straight out . . . I will if the Canadian Club could stand for it . . . I buy the <u>Gazette</u> & the <u>Star</u> (2 days late) and the Toronto <u>Globe</u> <u>& Mail</u> which looks pretty poor stuff so far.

### To Mrs Herbert T. Shaw

[Royal Alexandra Hotel
Winnipeg, Man.]
Dec 4 Friday

Dear Fitz

I spoke today at the Men's Canadian Club with a Manitoba broadcast—to myself I was nervous & constrained & it was hard—but I fell back on being a <u>professional</u> & pretending where I could feel—the crowd broke all records—it was at the Fort Gary Hotel—460 seats sold & then all sale stopped—it beat the Governor General who drew 360 with sales still open—only once before in history had they <u>stopped</u> sales—when the Prince of Wales came—& I think I got away with it—God knows I tried to—but you have got to be <u>rested</u> <u>rested</u> rested & I'm too old—but I <u>meant</u> what I said & I think it got over—I am going to see Irene Craig & then go to bed after tea & tomorrow I get a speech ready for the University Women's Club & then I'm done here—The University Women's Club have sold out the hotel again already—but I am too old for all this—but I have earned half the money that was put up—I do so want to be done—I will never, never again try to do this sort of thing—I just long to be still—I can do it and I'll get interested in doing it and God, it is 30 years too late—however—thats all right—I'm lucky to be here—

Stephen
(Leacock)

### To Frank Dodd

Royal Alexander Hotel,
Winnipeg
Dec. 5th. 1936

Frank Dodd Esq.
Dodd Mead Co.
New York City.

My dear Dodd,

Many thanks for your letter of Nov. 27th. about my proposed book dealing with the problems of West and East Canada and based on my present lecture tour to the coast, to appear under some such title as <u>My Western Excursion or</u> <u>My Discovery of the North West</u>.

I am sorry you don't see your way to accept what seem to me the very modest terms which I suggested, namely, <u>no</u> advance royalty and <u>no</u> guaranteed royalty and only 10% royalty if the book can be sold retail as low as $1.50, but 15% royalty if the book retails at or above $2.00, with an increase of 5% in the royalty if and when the sales pass 10,000 copies.

I realize that the book could not sell widely in the U.S. and that of course you have no idea of what publicity I am receiving here, but I am sorry that I could not let the book go on those terms. I shall therefore see if any first class publisher will take in on those terms and if not I will publish it myself. Let me repeat that I fully understand your position as to what is for you unknown material is unknown territory.

Very sincerely,
Stephen Leacock.


## To Mrs Herbert T. Shaw

[Royal Alexandra Hotel
Winnipeg, Man.]
Saturday Dec 5, 36.

Dear Fitz

I didn't hear from Montreal today but I may later—Gordon Glassco sent me a copy of the McGill Daily of Dec 2 with my "piece" in it about the McGill graduates with "Chairs" in the barber shop at Fort William—I hope you saw it & what is more read it—Mr Aberhart passed through Winnipeg & was asked by the press what he thought of my view that the conservatives would presently beat him & he said They <u>cant, theyre all dead</u>"—not bad, I thought—Today I lecture to a big meeting Womens University Club, again at the Fort Gary & again all available seats sold out & all records broken—I am not afraid of it as I have it all ready & though I was sick yesterday I am better today & not eating any lunch—my work will be over in this town at 6 o clock & then I drive with Mr Main of the CPR who took me in the private car & my old friend Charlie Macpherson at Mr Main's house—that will be easy & pleasant & Ill come home at 9.30 & pack up for Regina—Do give me all the news—I see the Star & Gazette here every day but I dont suppose I'll get them in Regina & Saskatoon & Edmonton.—The talk here is all of the <u>King, King, King</u>,—nothing else— oddly enough I had a letter from London (Nov. 23) asking me to write up the coronation—I answered "just let me know who's being crowned & who the woman is & I'll write it," but then I tore it up! Stu Hett wrote from Prince Albert but I dont go there—I spent 1/2 an hour with Irene Craig—hadnt seen her for 7 years or more—she & her husband run a repertory theatre . . .

Affec.
Stephen Leacock

## *To Mrs Herbert T. Shaw*

[Hotel Saskatchewan
Regina, Sask.]
Sunday Dec 6, 1936

Dear Fitz

Just arrived here on Sunday evening after a day on the train from Winnipeg—25 below outside but alright inside especially as we had a compartment—a long journey from 9.40 AM till 7 PM (6 Regina)—given a vast suite in the hotel which seems pretty empty—I talked to 500 women yesterday at the Fort Gary—a lot were turned away; I felt <u>fine</u> & not a bit nervous but they seemed <u>heavy</u> as hell—I said at the start—"I have been received in Winnipeg all the week, to my great humiliation, with <u>open laughter</u>,—even at the university. I do hope etc. etc." and they were like Miss Baker "<u>How could he dare!</u>"—& took it wrong—It didn't matter as I felt A.1. & didn't give a damn & did my stuff beautifully—I cant say how glad I'll be to be back—I had an invitation to go to Newark New Jersey to lecture in January & I have just written "never again!!!"—Jesus Christ—of course—its wonderful to get it all—but I have worked in 1888


## *To Mrs Herbert T. Shaw*

[Hotel Saskatchewan
Regina, Sask.]
Regina Monday morning
Dec. 7, 36.

Dear Fitz,

Your last Winnipeg letter missed me there & has just come . . .—Yes as you say—King, King, King—I made a good joke in Winnipeg. lecturing on coming verse; I quoted:—

> The Queen she kept high festival in Windsor's lofty-hall,
> And round her were her gartered knights and belted barons all,
> There fed the noble Wellington, there drank the gallant Peel
> While at the bottom of the board Prince Albert carved the veal"

"Part of the humour of <u>that</u>," I explained, "is in the contrast between the pomp and formality of royalty and the <u>quiet domesticity of the British Royal Family</u>," . . . . I paused & gave a mock sigh and then repeated . . . "<u>The quiet domesticity of the British Royal Family</u> . . . and said

> did I hear a silence?
> did someone drop a pin?
> No? all right we'll go on

Very cold here, 40 below yesterday, today <u>warmer</u> only 20 below—I talk at 6 to the <u>Women's Can. Club</u> ... I am going to try to write parts of my Regina speeches for the press as I find that reporters just make a hash of humour, taken on the fly like that—I see in today (Monday's) paper the first confirmation of the idea that the King has gone "batty"—Mr Baldwin says "The King's <u>health</u> wont allow & so & so"

We are again in a palace (see the picture, in a huge suite of rooms, 3 bathrooms 2 bedrooms & a sitting room—I talk here twice tomorrow but its not a strain like Winnipeg—give me all the news: write each day  your letters even if sent wrong follow instantly as the C.P.R. <u>officially</u> knows my route & looks after it all—I am going out now to a department store to buy detective stories to read

Stephen<br>Leacock

## To Mrs Herbert T. Shaw

Regina<br>Tuesday 8

Dear Fitz

I enclose 2 Regina clippings—<u>Please keep them for me</u>—dont forget—they & others as that's all the record I have—I started pasting them in a book but it was too like an actor & I had to stop—<u>Read</u> them you pig & see the joke about taking Aberhart in the rear——Last night I spoke at the Women's Can Club—<u>all</u> women; not a man—much like an Orillia audience in calibre—I spoke to them of <u>Love</u> and love stories—an old friend of mine blew in just as I was dressing & said "If you are going to talk to these western women on <u>Love</u>, just wait till you see them and the words will die on your lips."

He was right. But I told them of how much the <u>accentuation</u> of the word <u>love</u> meant & told the story—of "<u>love, Reen</u>" (Orillia telegraph girl)——Today I talk to the men's Club at noon on <u>Brotherly Love Among the Nations</u>, with a Saskatchewan broadcast—the broadcast is a bitch of a thing—It means that I have to keep getting new stuff—this place only over laps a little with a Winnipeg broadcast but wipes out Saskatoon—I must get to work—I got up at 6—its about 20° something below—outside all dead—not a soul moves here in the night—not a soul, among 60 thousand people.

love<br>Stephen<br>Leacock

## To Dr Charles F. Martin

[The Bessborough
Saskatoon, Sask.]
Dec 11 36

My dear Charlie

Your medical friends have been most kind . . McKusker of Regina especially
a host in himself. The 'Medical' Faculty seems the only one at McGill to retain
a hold on the West . . The Arts men are far less in evidence especially now when
there are so few livery stables.

We had a great McGill dinner at Regina,—with Sir Frederich Haltain &
other notables as extra guests. There had been a graduate society in years past
but it had become as someone said "as dead as Moosejaw"—It is now to be
resurrected

But McGill is slipping in the West: not enough continuity of contact. What
are needed are half a dozen scholarships each year for brilliant postgraduate
students. McGill ought to be the West what Oxford was—once, to all the
Empire. But it isnt. Even the medical men are the last generation, not this.

Very best thanks for all
your kindness
Stephen Leacock

## To Mrs Herbert T. Shaw

[The Bessborough
Saskatoon, Sask.]
Friday Dec 11, 36.

Dear Fitz,

. . . . . I had a wonderful meeting at the college—never saw anything like it
in my life—then a lunch   I was very tired—then I lay down then a dinner,
a quite distinguished company, President Murray of the college (a real man)
Mr. Brockington of the Broadcast (Bill May's second), Judge Turgeon Royal
Commission sitting by Sir Charles Gordon, Judge Maclean sitting by something
else, Col. Ralston ex-minister of defence at Ottawa, Dr. Collingwood a professor
at the college and various others—cocktails & water—apart from an odd word
nothing about the King—out here I gather he makes them tired, just tired—
Regina papers carry a lot of the bitter angry stuff against Mrs Simpson.——
Then I went on to a sort of little club or circle (couldn't refuse) very tired but
not sick as I drank nothing—today resting up for a big meeting tonight at which
I am going to talk just foolish stuff & explain that the occasion demands it—I'll
be so glad to be done—Its all I can do to hang on—my stomach is going back
more; but I can stick it out next week & then its easy—next week I talk straight
Social credit—there's no harm in it—as they see it. It just sounds like being an
Oddfellow or Knight of Pythias—a man told of going with a commission to see

Aberhart & Aberhart told them beforehand he could only give them 15 minutes. When they got there he said, "Now gentlemen, I want you to kneel down & pray"—They prayed for 13 minutes (or <u>he</u> did), then he rose & said, now gentlemen what can I do for you—Tell René that I hear here at first hand that Carleton <u>Stanley</u> is a ghostly failure—(René will be interested)

These western towns are on a huge plan—all streets 100 feet wide—they cover miles & miles with 40,000 people in Saskatoon—but it seems far, far away—I saw here a man to whom I said goodbye in <u>Dec. 1888</u> when he & I were fellow teachers in training in Strathroy, He's at the college here——

> best love
> Stephen Leacock

## To Mrs Herbert T. Shaw

[The Bessborough
Saskatoon, Sask.]
Sat. Dec 12.36

Dear Fitz,

After my lecture last night I went up to a room for a drink or two with about a dozen men—Colonel Ralston & Prof. Swanson & bank managers etc. and they talked (not very long) of the King & expressed nothing but a sort of quiet contempt & especially for his broadcast. I must say it seemed to me God's awful. "<u>He will follow with profound interest our fortunes</u>".—oh! will he! "if at any time he can be of service"—oh, thank you—"his brother had what was denied to him a wife a home & family". Christ! he could have had 50—let him leave that talk to poor little bastards trying to save up to get married—the one wish seemed to be that he'd go away & stay away—also they seem to agree that the whole King–Simpson business would last a year.

. . . My talk last night went over fine & was broadcasted for Saskatchewan. I have now done 1/2 of my job, at least.

## To George Leacock

[The Macdonald
Edmonton, Alta.]
Sunday, Dec 13 36 noon.

Dear George,

I post you from here a box of cigars that they "give" me in Regina: I can't smoke them I'd have sent them sooner but I couldn't get any string. I am not dirty enough to call them a Xmas present. I'll send one later, or not send one but these cigars are not one. We got here this morning. Stevie got in touch with Peter who is spending the day with us. They are off together. I have met with a wonderful reception—crowds and crowds, and broadcast and everything. I stay in my room all I can. I'll be glad to get back—Then I'll be done for life.

I had various telegrams and letters from U.S. about writing about the King but said no. In two years he and Mrs. Simpson will have parted or will be in Hollywood.

I'll send you from here the speech I mean to write out and do up brown, if I write it out and do it up brown, on Social Credit.

> With best Xmas wishes
> to you both
> Stephen Leacock

P.S. I meet a lot of people who know you.


## To Barbara Ulrichsen

[The MacDonald
Edmonton, Alta.]
Sunday Dec 13/36

Dear Barbara

Stevie had a fine time in Saskatchewan. Dr. Murray (President) offered to send to the hotel a law faculty student to take him out & in spite of Stevie's strenuous attempts to get out of it, he came and they had a fine 2 days seeing everything. Today Peter came at once after breakfast when we got here & they had all the day together. Peter has exams to get ready (Tuesday and following) but can come back & forth & they seemed to be arranging some sort of supper party for a group of friends.—I am so glad as Stevie was terribly happy but as it were just living in the room—I like to do it but it is not natural for him. The success of my trip has been just overwhelming & I am sure I can stick it out. I am ever so much better today and not sick at all. It's purely a matter of strain. Today I wrote interviews and got them all set for tomorrow. In another envelope I send a letter for Maclean's for you to copy and send on.

Tell Jack[1] when you see him that I now understand what they mean by Social Credit. There is no doubt they will all vote for it. It means voting for Jesus as against T.B. MaCauley. That's how it sounds to them; The plain honest people against the money oppressors,—that's how they see it. It's not economic theory at all.

> y.a.u.
> Stephen Leacock

---

1  John Culliton.

## To Mrs Herbert T. Shaw

[The Macdonald
Edmonton, Alta.]
Monday afternoon
(Dec 15)

Dear Fitz,

Here I am right in the Lion's Den—all ready to fight the lions—everything heated up to fever point—I am to speak at the college tonight broadcast—twice tomorrow & a big talk on Social Credit on Wednesday at noon, broadcast over the province—I enclose some clippings & I'll send some more from the other paper—I went up (—at that minute some bastard called me up—Christ I think I remember them as butting in on me at Orillia—Christ I'm not high hat but Jesus I don't know them—)—I went up to Sid Woods for cocktails at 1/4 to 1 & spent half an hour—a little talk of the King—say, he has bust things up hasn't he—The monarchy fits us & we need it but the effect is very great.—I have been sleeping half the afternoon & now I am having tea & soft boiled eggs in preparation for tonight—I wish I had heard from you today

Stephen

## To Mrs Herbert T. Shaw

[The Macdonald
Edmonton, Alta.]
Tuesday Dec 15 36

Dear Fitz

I didnt hear from you yet here—last night big meeting at college but I was pretty tired—yet it got over but I was sort of light headed & felt nervous—afterwards a reception at President Kerr's house, quite a lot of people—today I rested a lot & felt almost normal—went and spoke at the college on the present situation of economical science to a student group of a hundred or two,—went fine—I enjoyed it—now resting to attend dinner of Varsity Alumni—I now know a whole lot about Alberta & social credit etc etc—sent a night letter east to see about sending a long despatch—this province is all right—the whole thing is just a foozle—tomorrow I talk here with a broadcast on Social Credit—I've had publicity in _tons_—pictures, interviews, photographs—and I now know all about it—but naturally dont write it in a letter—I enclose for Peggy an Alberta prosperity dollar; tell her not to spend it—to keep it as a _curio_—later it will be worth easily $5.00—I got it as change with a pair of rubbers—notice the little stamps on the back—the man who sold the rubbers got it in Dec. 2 & had (or should have had to put on stamps) but I said to hell with the stamps I'm sending it to a little girl in Montreal as a curio—The "scrip" is all over

*To Mrs Herbert T. Shaw*                    [The Macdonald
                                            Edmonton, Alta.]
                                            Friday morning Dec ~~10~~ 17
                                            1936
                                            10.30 A.M., getting ready
                                                to leave for Calgary

Dear Fitz

I got 3 letters all together from you! Just think of it! It seemed like being home again—I agree all about the King & The Royal Family: Jesus, I'm sick of the little bugger & of Mrs Simpson & all their doings—It's amazing how little the Kingship seems to count, as long as there is a king. Little Edward, I think, has killed all personal allegiance

I sent the <u>Star</u> by this mail a full text of my Edmonton speech & a lot of facts to publish with it—please look for it—one part read:

<u>"You may also state it as my opinion that any talk ~~of~~ about the sanctity of a contract to pay high interest to an Eastern Loan Company or insurance Company gives a Western man a pain in the leg, or even higher up. I am not saying that the Western man is right but only saying where he gets the pain.</u>" Please look for that & let me know of it, & if the speech appears . . .

Last night I spoke at a dinner of the Women's Press Club & the Canadian Authors, about 40 (& talked on <u>Comic Verse</u>)—I felt pretty sick after it but went right upstairs & fell asleep & felt better—This morning I wrote letters for 2 hours (answering the mail is a heller) & started to get packed up—My God! I wish it was over—But I'm doing it to the king's taste; every last obligation, every last civility . . . . I was invited to go to a semester (half year I suppose) & teach in a Tennessee University (no), to come here for a week to the University of Saskat. (no), to lecture at Williams College (no), to speak at the American Banker's banquet (no)—no—no—nothing,——I speak in Calgary twice tomorrow & Medicine Hat <u>once</u> on Saturday—then it gets easy—It has been so nice to get your letters; it seems to keep me in touch.

                                            best love
                                            Stephen Leacock


*To Mrs Herbert T. Shaw*                    [Hotel Palliser
                                            Calgary, Alta.]
                                            Calgary Friday Dec 18 36

Dear Fitz

I had a vast meeting here & talked on Social Credit—400 there & 200 turned away—broadcast Southern Alberta—Jesus it was eloquent! I am all for the west. I spoke again at 3 pm to Women's Can Club on Fiction——and tonight again to college graduates—you have no idea what I have done here; The wisdom of being 67 years old & hating to make a fuss or quarrel . . . I am angry with McGill for putting me out—what a slight—the bastards! wait till I get back.—I was quite sick last night but going fine tonight—hard to eat—those buggers, bastards to dare to write me two sentences and put me out—but wait, by God, wait I always waited like an Algonquin—wait & wait & wait & then— —I leave at 7 am for Medicine Hat & speak to a public meeting—then a train to Vancouver—I wish I heard program but I cant till I get there—I cant tell you how these people here hate her like Sir Chas Moron,—they just go crazy and turn anything from the Bank of Mount-Jail—all appear in the paper—that is the strength of Aberhart—Christ he did it—even though they themselves lose on church funds etc still he did it!! & I am the only buggar who can see all that— you because I have come fresh from there here—I wish you were here & I could talk instead of write because writing sounds exaggerated—But when I think that the life of this country is in the hands of those miserable bastards—good god!—This for instance, tonights paper—Christ! That drives them crazy!!!


## To Mrs Herbert T. Shaw

[Cecil Hotel
Medicine Hat, Alberta]
Sunday Dec 20 – '36

Dear Fitz,

Just finished up my Western trip as far as the prairs prairies are concerned & off now, thank God, at five o'clock this afternoon (in an hour) for British Columbia—great meeting here last night, the Quota Club "Sat down 200,"—such clattering of dishes & running of help,—just like Orillia—songs, piano,—and my "address" went over with a whoop! You've no idea! Then I went to some one's house for a drink; this morning two men took me out for a drive; very wonderful—all about here on a big scale—

time


## To Mrs Herbert T. Shaw

[Hotel Vancouver
Vancouver, B.C.
Tuesday Dec 22
9 am

Dear Fitz

Got here last night—10-30—usual battery of photographers, reporters—I enclose a report—British Columbia is quite unconnected with Canada; its another place; its somewhere else—My God! The desolation of the prairies! snow & blizzard & emptiness—little lonely houses without a tree—& from that you wake up in the gorges and slopes of the rockies—deep snow & trees all buried like Christmas trees & all of it so snug & then you get here & Christ its London! just exactly London in December—rain & a little wet snow coming & going & the smell of the sea—Canada!—god there's <u>no</u> connection—I have to speak today at a big meeting then it will be easy . . . I was quite sick in Calgary but getting better now every day—oh my god am I sick of it—I have finished arrangements for my book so I'll be busy when I get back (late)

## To Mrs Herbert T. Shaw

[Hotel Vancouver
Vancouver B.C.]
Dec 22 36

Dear Fitz

I cant tell you how wonderful this place is—outside is a slightly wet, misty night just like London—just exactly—being near Xmas time the "Waits" on the street are playing that Christ was born on Xmas day—a fact quite incredible in Saskatchewan—today before having to speak I got a taxi man to drive me to where the end of the town runs to Stanley Park, runs to the open ocean. There is no snow—bright sun & big trees & ferns & grass—steamers going in & out & a multitude of little yachts & motors at anchor & across the bay mountains with clouds & mist—it has <u>no</u> connection with Canada—

I said today:

Gentlemen, before I speak I want to pay my tribute to the wonder & beauty of this city. I had not known of it. No one ever told me. If I had known it, I would not have waited sixty six years to come. I would have been <u>born</u> here. You have here mountains that recall Scotland, vast trees that emulate Australia, a harbour and a coast that matches the Riviera & with it all & through it all the soft wet wind from the sea, that carries with it the breath of England. I know of no city in Canada that can compare with it, with the possible exception of Moose Jaw, Saskatchewan,—which I have never seen—

Wed. Morning

I was tired & stopped there. Thank God! my job is now easier & easier—I dont have to do a thing till next Monday in the way of speaking, & I can work on my book—I am going out to Stanley Park for a walk by the sea till lunch, the first real walk I have had (if I have it) since I left Montreal———I was much interested in all your news about Peggy's and René's play etc.—I get the Montreal Star here & the Gazette but they are 5 days old when ~~come~~ they come—There is much less King–Simpson stuff in the papers here than in the Star & Gazette—one day the King was not only off the front page but clean out of the news. What the Bishops mean is that he shall <u>not</u> get an English divorce because they claim (though they dont say so) that he's not legally entitled to it. The Simpsons, when he met them, were man and wife. The rest came after: and was all fixed up—a continental divorce would prevent her from using an <u>English</u>

title as Duchess of Windsor  This is too late I realize for Merry Xmas to you. Perhaps I said it before at any rate Ive been thinking it—

> Best love and to Peggy
> Stephen Leacock

## To Mrs Herbert T. Shaw

[Hotel Vancouver
Vancouver, B.C.]
Later. Thursday

I am just lost in wonder over this beautiful city—it is beyond words—all the "business section" (see Orillia) is close up together like London or Paris—fine shops, continuous streets, even sky-line—and then there is the harbour & docks & beaches, (not bitches as René would call them) & the sea & the ships coming in and out of the park——

Afternoon

Fred Laing (Gordon's brother manager of the Bank of Montreal) gave a lunch for me,—about 20–25 men at the "Vanc" Club—all the notables—on request I made a speech—making speeches Monday at big dinner of Board of Trade, Shipping & God knows what—Broadcast province—I am going to make it funny if I work all night at it—am invited by mayor & everybody everywhere—also sick at the stomach a good deal—feel sick—yet I thought of coming home a week earlier by shifting a speech—Ive nothing from Jan 6—to Jan 13 but I guess I'll stick to the job—have completed all arrangements for syndicating my account of the trip

Tell Peggy god bless her—her card arrived today but I havent seen it as Stevie has gathered up all the cards & is going to put them up in our bed room for Xmas Day—& we have a pint of champagne & I am not going out or working but just sticking in the hotel—The management sent me up a huge basket of Chrysanthemums,—like Madame Patti—

> best Xmas love to all of 'yez'
> Stephen

## To Mrs Herbert T. Shaw

[Hotel Vancouver
Vancouver, B.C.]
Xmas 1936 6 pm

Dear Fitz

Stevie & I went out this morning & walked all round Stanley Park along the sea wall most of the way—it is all wonderful—ferns & green grass & trees thousands of years old & the sea & ships going in and out—we walked over 2 hours

—then we had a pint of champagne & then dinner—I just can't get over the charm of this place—tomorrow I have one or two engagements & a drive with an old friend on Sunday—lecture twice on Monday & on Tuesday take the boat to Victoria—I got Peggy's card & was delighted to get it—I am sending her & you a couple of chinese trinkets, I haven't yet just decided what.

Meantime Merry Xmas & Happy New Year.

Stephen Leacock


*To Barbara Ulrichsen*                     [Hotel Vancouver
                                            Vancouver, B.C.]
                                            Xmas 36

Dear Barbara

Merry Xmas to you & Donald & Harry & Margaret & the baby if, as I presume, you get this in Detroit.

Stevie & I had a nice Xmas = shut off all phone & visits = went for a two hour walk by the sea around Stanley Park: Then a pint of champagne in our room: dinner & a sleep.

This place is the world's greatest wonder; the streets are all together and continuous in the town itself which makes it like London or Paris: the climate is England: the harbour full of shipping & crowded with yachts & motor boats: great mountains with clouds across the bay: broad beaches all sand with ocean tides & beside the water trees 200 years old, and then the Pacific Ocean.

You can form no idea of the success I've met with—more than one could imagine & everywhere broadcasted, to the surprise of each city to any extent they like without charges. A few more and I am done—I was pretty sick each day but getting better now.

I am sending to you at Cote des Neiges—an express packet of odd chinese trinkets (there is a wonderful market for them here) & you can then keep your own & give and post the others as marked. Stevie's <u>Santa Claus</u> was accepted & published by the Winnipeg Tribune Dec. 19 & copied here in the Xmas edition of the News Herald.—He is sending you a copy when I get extra ones from Winnipeg.

Best love <u>and</u> New Year
wishes from both of us.
Y.a.u.
Stephen Leacock

*To Mrs Herbert T. Shaw*                    [Hotel Vancouver
                                            Vancouver, B.C.]
                                            Mon. Dec 28  36

Dear Fitz,

It is 9 am—I've been working an hour & now going for a walk and then in for a big day—two speeches both on a big scale. Womens Canadian Club in the ball room here at 3 pm & a big dinner of the Board of Trade at 7.30 with a British Col Broadcast—but I can do it—not a quiver of an eyelash—but when its over Ill be glad & then off to Victoria by boat tomorrow—an old friend of mine & his wife took me for a long motor ride yesterday, along the bay & all about—this place defies all description & all pictures.

I hope I hear & I do hope youre better.

                                            Stephen
                                            (Leacock)


*To Mrs Herbert T. Shaw*                    [Hotel Vancouver
                                            Vancouver, B.C.]
                                            Tues (Dec 29) 9³⁰ am[1]

Dear Fitz,

Just leaving for Victoria by boat—snowing—wet snow and I see below zero in the west.

Last night I fairly eclipsed myself—huge dinner of the Board of Trade—all Vancouver government, church, bench, bar,—I was the only speaker—present Mr. Aberhart—I met him here in the morning, as I said in my last letter & dared him to come to the dinner & he came. I said the talk would be religious, as near as I could make it, and I took a text:

1st. Book of Kings, Chap. 13 verse 27—"And he said saddle me the ass. And they saddled him"——God! how they roared! Even Aberhart—I spoke half an hour—two broadcasts going I don't know where—. . I have hardly eaten for days. But in Victoria it will be different.

I hope to hear from you when I get there—Happy New Year by the time you get this

                                            Stephen
                                            Leacock

1   Leacock erroneously dated the letter 'Jan 9'.

*To Mrs Herbert T. Shaw*                    [Empress Hotel
                                             Victoria, B.C.]
                                             Dec 30  36
                                             <u>My Birthday</u>

Dear Fitz

As Peggy would say, "Where do you think I am now? In Victoria—" (You remember,—What do you think I am now? a reporter)—came over by the boat yesterday Tuesday—left 10$^{\underline{30}}$ am got here 3.$^{\underline{30}}$ pm. This hotel is,—well, look at it— vast. I dont have to speak for 5 days & so I can get to work—I enclose some clippings to show Mr Aberhart at my banquet and Jerry McGeer and others—also interviews here—Please keep the clippings & give them back to me—Please read the one about my appearance & my birthday—I was so glad to hear from you after many days of silence—you will have got heaps of letters of mine stored up at home—But I am sorry you have been ill—rest, rest—if you can—its nothing but nerve fatigue & yet that is really one of the wretchedest things that are

*To Mrs Herbert T. Shaw*                    [Empress Hotel
                                             Victoria, B.C.]
                                             Dec. 31./1936
                                             4$^{30}$ pm

Dear Fitz

I got a letter from a New York syndicate for an article this morning so I sat down & wrote one & got it all done & sent—funny stuff about lecturing, picked out of scraps I'd done in papers—I felt "real good" after I'd ~~one~~ done it— nothing like work & sticking at it. Then I went for a taxi ~~riole~~ ride for half an hour as I was too tired to walk, cold beef lunch at 3, a sleep & now going for a walk before its dark.

This place is a flood of sunshine like a bright cool day in our October— yesterday Captain McMurray of the CPR coastal fleet took me for a drive (2 hours) wonderful scenery round here—tonight big dinners etc. in this hotel but I am not in any.

                                             <u>Happy New Year</u>
                                             Stephen
                                             (Leacock)

## To Mrs Herbert T. Shaw

[Empress Hotel
Victoria, B.C.]
New Year's Day
1937

Dear Fitz

A few "voids" (yiddish for words) as a New Year greeting—last night there were huge doings here but I was sick (not very, just a little) & didn't see them—this huge hotel is a local resort as well as a general—but its no damn good; no liquor except in rooms—Today bright & snappy & just about freezing; no snow, all sunshine—I took a long walk yesterday afternoon round the park along the sea (to get rid of not feeling well)—The scenery is wonderful—The town has an old look, like Charlottetown though its only about 70 years old anyway—Vancouver has taken all the trade—I've been working very hard; stuff for my western book & other stuff—I dont speak till Monday but when I do it will be big audiences & broadcasts & the first speech is all brand new & to be made up—I shall be glad when I hear again from you: If you see René tell him that I got his new year's greeting card & was pleased to hear from him  Tell Mary that I am always just writing to her & never do; once I wrote to her but the letter got so clever that I used it in a newspaper instead. Tell her I will write to her when I get home . . . By the way I am due to arrive on the <u>morning</u> of Sunday 17th of January and I take for granted that you will be tired & not want to see me or anybody early in the day—So I will arrange instead to have you join me at the Club at say <u>12 noon</u> for cocktails as it is Sunday & you cant stay to lunch. Ask René & Mary to come too. It will be nice to see everybody (my few everybodies) again

Happy New Year
Stephen
Leacock

## To Frank Dodd

Victoria, B.C.
Jan. 2, 1937.

My dear Dodd,

Please note enclosed. I have lectured from Lake Superior to Victoria in a blaze of front page publicity and broadcasts over every province. I have never seen any attempt to use the opportunity to sell my books.

Take an instance:—In Calgary the crowd of applicants for tickets to a lunch talk I gave on Social Credit was so great that they took the largest room in town, the Hudson Bay Building dining room, and at that turned away two hundred. The speech was broad-cast; it was a wild success.

Every one who heard it, in order to get out had to pass through the Hudson Bay store which has a book stand. There was no placard or notice of my books at the stand and not one in the stock.

Take this:—The C.P.R. owns most of the hotels including this huge palace. Everyone has a book stand. I am such a friend of the railway that they give me a whole suite of rooms for a minimum rate and where the regular service was not very good sent a private car to haul me 500 miles. In their hotels I have given speech after speech. At the Vancouver Hotel to huge crowds with broadcasts each time. <u>Never</u> have I seen a book of mine on a book counter in a hotel. To ask would have been to have.

Take this one. <u>Never, never</u> once have I seen an advertisement of my books in a paper. When the front page was all filled up with my pictures and interviews and reports the opportunity was obvious to put in an advertisement for my books.

I am sure I need not dot the i's and cross the t's of all this.

Very sincerely,
Stephen Leacock


## To W.J. Healy

[Empress Hotel
Victoria, B.C.]
Jan 4 '37

W.J. Healy Esqre
The Provincial Library
Winnipeg, Man.

My dear Tim

I was terribly pleased to get your letter—it came just at a pleasant time when I was able to sit down in comfort after finishing a talk here & light a pipe and enjoy it. . . .

I am afraid that both you and I have dropped into that pleasant retrospect of the past, that is the mark either of great minds or of small ones, I forget which—if you still remember your Latin (I cant forget mine) the phrase is "laudator temporis acti"—

But I take a great and increasing pleasure in looking back to the old days

I didnt get half time enough to talk the other night and now I dont know when the other half will be filled in . . . I was so pleased at your mention of my Stevie's writing: he has done quite a few small pieces & I take care never to say a word until they are <u>done</u> . . . I am sure that his trade will be that of "letters" in one shape or other

Since I saw you I have wandered on & have met such a lot of the men we used to know—. . . . in a way I knew more than you did as I taught school for 10 years & that means I have old pupils all over the place—and damn old some of them look—one thing, Tim I find funny about them & I must write up is their mistaken memory of things that they think happened and that didnt happen

Today after the meeting a little old clergyman came to me & said (which was correct) my name is so & so (he got that right), I graduated in your class & the thing, he said, that remains in my ~~my~~ mind ~~Is~~ is <u>our little whist club</u>, which you & I joined in the same year, You remember?

I said—Our Whist Club!!  Can I ever forget it!!!

But I never played whist in my life.

best & warmth<br>Stephen Leacock

P.S I was so taken up with writing to and about you that only in the post script do I revert to thanking you for the picture of E.P. (which I shall frame) & the very interesting family souvenir in the form of his letter to Moncreif

## To Mary Leacock

[Empress Hotel
Victoria, B.C.]
Sunday Jan 4 37

Dear Mary,

It was so nice of you to call us up this morning—The telephone is just too wonderful: I never get over it. In two weeks we shall be (please god, or not) back in Montreal. The trip would have been fine if I hadn't been more or less sick every day but it is making me well, so it is well worth while.

I see such a lot of "fellers" who know George. The kind of man who is sure to know George is about 5 feet 9 inches high, fairly stout, well dressed but a little untidy! smells a little of whiskey & seems to know everybody around the hotel & the town. I see such a man come in and I say "Whoof! he knows George!"

This place is wonderful but hell it is too far away—it is not for us—it is for the people on the prairies.

When I get home I shall never work again—just do what I like & write what I want to and <u>never, never, never</u> lecture or talk or go to anything. I only need about 6 friends and I have 8 right now.

Stevie joins in affectionate regards to you and George. I shall have to be in Toronto as soon as I get back & I'll see you both then.

y.a.b' l<br>Stephen Leacock

## To Barbara Ulrichsen

[Empress Hotel
Victoria, B.C.]
Jan 5 37

Dear Barbara,

I have just written to Margaret (Burrowes) to come down (if she wants to) on Sat. Jan. 16 for a week of typing . . She is to write & tell you if coming & you send her expenses, (return fare, chair, meals, tips, taxi)—There will be far more than you can do alone.

I had the most marvellous success here with a talk yesterday on Economic Separation in the Empire,—they laughed & cried, just about: never was anything like it they said . . . I put a lot of work into each speech & never a note.

I am much better especially as here one can walk—no cars to matter, no snow, the sea right here to walk beside.

We are due to leave Vancouver on Jan 13 & arrive Montreal Jan 17. If any question comes up of newspaper interviews say you are quite sure not giving any: for U.S. please say that you will refer to me. I do not intend to say gratuitously that I wont lecture, but to refuse each offer merely saying sorry that I cannot meet their terms and of course not willing to haggle.

y.a.u.
Stephen Leacock

## To Dr Charles F. Martin

[Empress Hotel,
Victoria, B.C.]
Jan 7   3[7]

Dear Charlie

This town is eagerly waiting for you both, & the Canadian Club looking for you, personally, with a book . . At a McGill dinner last night I told them that your were indefinitely delayed . . . at Hollywood.—

. . . What I am really sorry is that I shall just exactly miss you: leave for home on the 12th . . .  No, Charles, I cant talk to the Medics, thanks all the same,—not to them and to no one—For me, as I told a newspaper the other day I go from this trip to retirement and my farm and from there I dont move at all till I go straight to Westminster Abbey . . . (as a matter of fact I'll live in Montreal in the winter: but the other sounds better & sound, to me, is everything)

Best New Years to you both

Stephen Leacock

## To Mrs Herbert T. Shaw

[Empress Hotel
Victoria, B.C.]
Thursday Jan 8 37

My dear Fitz,

In regard to Kipling's poem & Sudbury, the facts in the case have been misunderstood. The verses that the Sudbury people used were <u>not</u> written by a local poet: they are 1/2 or rather 1/3 of a poem by Housman. The Sudbury people made the mistake of thinking that they would carry their meaning without the <u>title</u>, or the context & without the first half. They fail to do so. But taken as a total I think that opinion might properly be divided—

Today I spoke to the Rotary Club in this hotel on Peace & War at lunch— Gladstone Murray phoned from Victoria & said he must see me presently about national broadcasting.—But I cant do it—He had, I am glad to say, heard good things of my broadcasts—

Tonight I attend a little dinner of U.C.C. "boys" in the Club & make a speech—tomorrow a big meeting of Teachers of Victoria, but all I want is to get home. I can live now on what I have. I will work no more. I will write, but I wont work . . . . . I walked today twice (for an hour & ~~four~~ for 2 hours) along the sea! What a climate! I've been writing it up for my book—I wrote 7000 words. I am fascinated with my book & I'll take no dictation, no back talk— nothing, by god nothing from anybody—I am trying to get 15,000 words ready for the first two days I am at home.

--------

I'm so glad you said about John Lyle. God forgive me I couldn't make out who it was—Thought it a telegram from a school mate of Stevie. Now I will see that Stevie sends him a nice long night letter in reply.

Jack ~~Consell~~ Counsell who said he was coming here has not been heard of—Billy Bunting is in a hospital at Vancouver—Last night we had a big McGill dinner—I'll be glad to get home. I do hope some <u>bastard</u> asks me for an interview from the <u>Star</u>—I sent them fine stuff on Aberhart & I believe they didnt use it.

## To Mrs Herbert T. Shaw

Empress Victª
Sat Jan 9 37

Dear Fitz,

I had a letter from you yesterday (Peggy shooting at Orillia—shooting what, not said—well, well, shooting . . .)

Last night I spoke here to the Victoria Teachers, my last talk in Victoria— one left on the mainland & then done—Today all I have to do is to talk with General Sir Charles somebody about General Hornby's plan of immigration; then ~~talk~~ lunch with Colonel Urquhart to talk of his life of General Currie (he'll never finish it) & then drive with Colonel Wilby and have cocktails with Captain McMurray—the point is that in Victoria <u>colonels</u> are as thick as methodist ministers in Westmount———At the Upper Can College dinner the other night <u>one</u> half were colonels—& one colonel hadn't any dress clothes—so the chairman, with what I thought awfully good feeling, himself just wore a plain suit so that Colonel So: & so wouldn't feel hurt—

Today it is snowing hard & down in the States below it has been below zero—Victoria, as you don't know is not in Canada but in the U.S. in point of latitude—The U.S. is 15 miles away across the Juan de Fuca Strait and surrounds the town. The mountains are the Olympic Mountains—snow capped—Me for a walk.

Stephen
(Leacock)


*To Mrs Herbert T. Shaw*                        Empress Victoria
                                                Mon Jan 11. 37

Dear Fitz

I just got your letter (said by you to be your last on the trip, as it must be)—and this even by the air will be my last as the or . . . . . (I stopped for dinner  cant see what the hell I was going to say.

Today is my last day here as we leave on the 2 o clock boat tomorrow for Vancouver, stay overnight lecture at the University on Wednesday at noon & take the Montreal train home—Stevie & I spent today in going by train to Nanaimo, up through mountains on a railway that makes the Niagara Gorge look flat—half an hour for lunch at Nanaimo & then back at 5—early dinner & packing up & writing—I am writing, writing all the time as my book is sold by telegraph—Frank Dodd wouldnt meet my very modest proposal ~~& so to his great~~ and, with Hugh Eayrs offered lower terms—So I wrote very modestly, "quite understand etc etc, I will see what I can do & if need be publish it myself etc etc"—Then, by Jesus, I sold it by telegraph on my terms to Houghton Mifflin and I have just had the <u>delight</u> of receiving a telegram from <u>Dodd</u> offering to take the book on my own terms and am now telegraphing back "So Sorry book sold"—Christ! It feels good—Hugh Eayrs had grown to think I was an easy mark! . . . . . . I hope to arrive on ~~Saturda~~ Sunday morning & will phone you when I get in & see what you say—I am writing to René & to Mary (now) to ask them to join me for cocktails at 12 noon Sunday and anybody can lunch with me who is kind enough to—I have as I say been <u>writing</u>, <u>writing</u>  I am to

Stephen Leacock and
Stevie sailing on Lake
Couchiching, *c.* 1930.
(Photo: Olive Hett Seale,
courtesy Peter Sibbald
Brown)

A gathering of friends
at Agnes Leacock's home,
Bury Lodge, in Sutton,
Ontario: (*top, left to right*)
Adelaide Hett Meeres,
Alice Hett (Mrs Francis
Paget Hett), Stephen
Leacock, Fitz Shaw;
(*bottom, left to right*)
Charles Meeres, Agnes
Leacock, Francis Paget
Hett. (Photo: Olive Hett
Seale, courtesy Peter
Sibbald Brown)

A postcard
from Stephen
Leacock to
Frank Hett,
showing the
Leacock home
at The Old
Brewery Bay,
Orillia, 1928.
(Photo courtesy
Peter Sibbald
Brown)

Frank Hett and Stephen Leacock at Leacock's trout pond near The Old Brewery Bay, 1932. (Photo: Olive Hett Seale, courtesy Peter Sibbald Brown)

Fitz Shaw, Stephen Leacock, and Frank Hett on a fishing excursion to Leacock's favourite trout stream, 1933. (Photo: Olive Hett Seale, courtesy Peter Sibbald Brown)

Sir Arthur Currie became principal and vice-chancellor of McGill University in 1920, following a distinguished career as commander of the Canadian Corps and key military strategist during the final 100 days of the Great War. Currie had studied under Stephen Leacock during the latter's tenure at Strathroy Collegiate. As an administrator at McGill, Currie was well liked and respected by Leacock, and the two men maintained a friendship that lasted until Currie's death in 1933. (Photo courtesy of the McGill University Archives)

Critic and essayist B.K. Sandwell remains best known as the editor of *Saturday Night* magazine from 1932 to 1951. Like Currie, he was taught by Leacock (in Sandwell's case at Upper Canada College) and maintained a close friendship with him. His tribute to his mentor and friend (reprinted in the Epilogue) was broadcast nationally on CBC Radio following Leacock's death in 1944. (National Archives of Canada, PA-172614)

Agnes Leacock, *c.* 1930. (Leacock Museum Archives, PL–134)

Barbara Ulrichsen, graduate of McGill University, 1931. (Leacock Museum Archives, with the permission of Nancy Winthrop)

EMPRESS HOTEL
VICTORIA, B.C.

Canadian Pacific Hotels

Dec 30  36
My Birthday

Dear Fitz
    As Peggy would say, " where
do you think I am now? In Victoria "
— ( you remember, — What do you think I
am now! a reporter) —— came over
by the boat yesterday Tuesday —
left 10³⁰ am got here 3³⁰ pm
    This hotel is, — well, look at it —
— vast. I don't have to speak
for 5 days so I can get to work
—— I enclose some clippings to
show Mr Aberhart at yr banquet

A letter from Stephen Leacock to Fitz Shaw, one of more than three hundred Leacock wrote to one of his closest friends.

Stephen Leacock with his great-niece Nancy Nimmo, feeding Leacock's chickens at The Old Brewery Bay, Orillia, 1941. (Leacock Museum Archives, PL–054; Photo: Yousuf Karsh)

Shortly after gaining notoriety for capturing the definitive wartime image of Winston Churchill, Canadian photographer Yousuf Karsh visited The Old Brewery Bay to take a series of portraits of Stephen Leacock. This one shows the scholar and writer at his desk in the sunroom, where he composed many of his books and articles over his lifetime. (Leacock Museum Archives, PL–053; Photo: Yousuf Karsh)

have all the book done by May 1ˢᵗ with maps & charts & figures. I think it will be fine. Anyway I'll like it—

I'll be so glad to see you,—even to hear you

> Stephen
> Leacock

## *To Frank Dodd*

3869 Cote des Neiges Road
(after 17 January 1937)

Frank Dodd Esqre
Dodd Mead & Co

My dear Dodd

I am just back from the west and find your letters of Jan 11 & Jan 12—So sorry that we didnt get together on my Discovery of the West. Houghton Mifflin & Allen are to publish it  Please dont send the jacket as I have myself designed one—So far from ~~not~~ wanting to stop your publication of my future books I offer you one right here & now as follows:—

I have now finished & done with lecturing for ever (except that I have 3 engagements to fill in the next six weeks. Philadelphia, Harrisburg & Watertown) —after that,—never—though my desk is still kept full of invitations. But I'm done with it & I dont need it financially, so I propose to publish my humorous lectures under a fair title not misleading anybody to think its anything else, the title being something such as:—

HERE ARE MY LECTURES

or

LECTURES THEY LAUGHED AT

etc.

something to bring in the word lectures. The length would be about 60,000 words but easily lengthened or shortened to any extent. Now, you can have that book on a ten per cent royalty, no advance, no guarantee, U.S. & Canada, royalty rising in U.S. to 15 per cent if and after 5,000 copies sold in U.S. & ditto in Canada—As to England I've just heard that the Lane firm has gone under which leaves my English books in the air, as they owe me back royalties for, I think, over 2 years as I didnt press them—that gives me back automatically all my copyrights & prevents sale of stock till cleared—Hence I dont know where I ~~came~~ am on English rights in the ~~fiction~~ lectures book—The Western book English rights are sold—But if you'd care to take the Lectures Book I'd be most pleased ~~tha~~ Would have it ready for you as any other book,

> Very best regards
> Stephen Leacock

## *To Sir Edward Beatty*

[McGill University
Montreal]
Jan 21. 37.

Sir Edward Beatty
Canadian Pacific Ry.

My dear Eddie,

I have had it in mind to write you some notes as to what I saw in the West, dealing with McGill University, & with the Railway, & with the situation as to money, debt, & social credit.

I have to leave tonight for Philadelphia & I am informed that you are very likely leaving for Winnipeg on Saturday.

So I want to send, if I may, an advance notice about <u>McGill in the West</u>.

. . . . . . . . . .

It is my opinion that McGill has lost & is losing ground in the West, not by anybody's fault but because of the change of circumstances.

Years ~~old~~ ago our medical school supplied all the best doctors. They are still there, alive or buried.

For many years (1907–1915) we carried on all the work of the two senior years in Arts for Alberta & British Columbia. Of necessity that came to an end.

At the present time all the older & best medical men out west are McGill. But the new generation do not know Joseph.

We cannot try to draw undergraduates from the west. Their own colleges are first rate. But we ought to draw <u>graduates</u> who come for a year or so to McGill & then go back.

Such people are worth more than I can tell you to our College. Each one is a living, breathing, enthusiastic representative of McGill.

We ought to make McGill the Athens of Canada, a place to which people send their sons for a year of graduate study. We dont want students who propose to come East & stay east. We want boys who come here & go back.

I suggest we offer graduate scholarships,—each one needs: $1000, that is, $800 maintenance & $200 for transportation & fees.

I propose that we ask our McGill societies ~~to ne~~ to nominate them for us,— begin modestly one in each province,—and suggest that presently when the west comes back, they will try to duplicate the offer with a second scholarship for them,—my train is just about to go & I cant develop the idea further.

I enclose my cheque for $200 and will give as much each year for five years in the hope that some other "fellers" will get as enthusiastic as I am—

My best regards
Stephen Leacock

*To Percy Cudlipp*                          Jan. 24, 1937

Percy Cudlipp Esq.
Evening Standard,
London, Eng.

Dear Mr. Cudlipp,

I am delighted to know that you are publishing "My Fish Pond."

I have just come back from a tour through the West to British Columbia. I lectured everywhere, I saw everybody, and I know everything. I am proposing to write up the ideas arising out of the trip for publication in twelve weekly instalments, beginning with the 13th of March. I am arranging with the Miller Services (Andrew Miller's Syndicate of Toronto) to handle these articles in the Canadian and American press. I really think that they will create great attention. The central idea will be to show that the provinces and the Dominion are falling apart in a dangerous way. The provinces have turned into little kingdoms. They own nearly all the public resources; they carry enormous budgets and enormous debts. Each fights against the other. They begin to talk of the inter-provincial balance of trade, and to penalize imports from one to the other. All clamour for dominion help. All ask money without responsibility.

The country is rapidly being "Balkanized" in the economic sense. The Dominion is committing hari-kari. Soon it will become only a weather bureau.

Meantime the things most conspicuous count least. Alberta's Social Credit is merely social suffering. It will not end in a social overturn but only in the general reduction by force of funded debts and the formation of a new progressive people's party, powerful by their ignorance and often able to achieve the impossible by not knowing it is so.

. . . . . . . . . .

I propose to send you on the heels of this a printed sheet showing the titles of my twelve chapters with typical samples of their contents. You will see that I have tried to call in humour as an auxiliary to argument.

I will send you also in typewriting the full text of chapters one and two.

Now at last I come to the point. I hope it may be possible for you to use these twelve articles, sent in weekly releases, in the STANDARD. If so, I leave the price with confidence to yourselves, but if you could not use them all but could take some of them, please cable at my expense what proposal you could make. If, unhappily, you can use none of them, I will ask you to be kind enough to pass them on to Mr. John Farquharson, 8 Haley House, Red Lion Sq.

I send you this long letter in advance so that you can have time to reflect on it,—I am afraid, perhaps, time to sleep on it.

Very sincerely,
S.L.

## To Napier Moore[1]

3869 Cote des Neiges Rd.,
Montreal, Que.,
Jan. 27, 1937.

Napier Moore, Esq.,
Editor: <u>MACLEANS</u>, Toronto.

Dear Mr. Moore:

I have it in my mind to write an article:—

### THE LINGERING SHADOW OF PROHIBITION

It will show that, although prohibition is gone, it still casts an evil shadow in the senseless and vindictive and unprofitable restrictions that have taken its place.

In our hotels, beautiful as palaces, the sale of a glass of beer is a criminal act. In our golf clubs men gather in some dirty, below stairs wash room and drink out of flasks,—surreptitiously violating a law that they will not openly oppose even by signing a petition,—and they themselves men of place and position, lawyers, doctors, judges.

In comfortable clubs, equal to the style of Europe, men drink water and chew celery,—why! because they love water and adore celery? Oh no! Because they are all afraid to speak and say "This regime is dishonest. What is right in our homes, must be right here."

Now comes the Nemesis. What they will not do for honesty and honour, they will have to do for money's sake. If we don't change our law, our tourist business will wither and die on its stem. Our restriction system grew up and flourished because <u>by contrast</u>, it was liberty itself: the contrast with an American State jail and life imprisonment for the third time law, as in Michigan.

Now all is changed. The tourist in Europe and in the States finds a law that coincides with his own idea of morals. In Canada he must still walk in the shadow.

I mean to attack this and would like to enlist your support to the extent of printing an article. Naturally you won't buy it till you see it. Address me at Hotel Vancouver, Vancouver. As to the pay I leave that entirely to you. I'd offer to do it for nothing but you might accept the offer and that would be a heller.

Best regards,

---

1    Napier Moore (1893–1963) was a Canadian journalist and the editor of *Macleans* from 1926 until 1955.

## *To Sir Edward Beatty*                   February 4th, 1937.

<u>Memo on the Railway Problem</u>

Sir Edward Beatty,
Canadian Pacific,
Montreal.

My dear Edward,

I send you herewith a broadside sheet of the articles I am syndicating about the West, not that you should have to read it, but to introduce what I want to say. I had to leave out the <u>Railway Problem</u>: but I am putting it with great emphasis in the book that follows the articles, and also the <u>Immigration Problem</u> on which I spoke much. I'll make Mr. Howe's childish performance sound as funny as it is.

But the trouble is that no one in the West thinks about the Railway Problem. They shovel it off on the Dominion government and don't give a damn how much is spent or less.

The thing needed is to make them see that the railway problem helps to keep the West poor. The way to make them see it is to get it into the agenda of the coming Duncan Commission for the West. Incidentally they need <u>economists</u> as technical experts in the comission to help draw up questions and consolidate answers. I'm not talking for myself. I wouldn't have time. But men not altogether from the West,—I think, for example, that Harry Angus of the University of B.C. and Swanson of Saskatchewan would obviously suit everybody. But if with them were two men from here it would prevent the commission from seeming loaded to the muzzle before it begins. I think of Professor John Culliton of McGill who came from Saskatchewan and is very popular there and Wallace Goforth of Montreal who took his M.A. at McGill after the war and is now probably the best technical expert in the country. I thought I would like to suggest this in good time and ask you to pass it on if you see fit.

With best regards,
Stephen Leacock

Postscript: In answer to your kind personal enquiry, I may say that I still have to lecture at Harrisburg and Buffalo and after that I mean never to talk in public or attend anything public again,—nor to bore busy and important people with letters as long as this.

## To Margaret Burrowes                    Feb. 6th. (1937)

Dear Daisy,

I am afraid that I cannot wait any longer in regard to Margaret's coming as I have to make up my mind. If she is not to be here I can use the room for Lou and have him work on the house (painting and oiling and driving the car.) So I am writing to him to come and he will be here I expect for some time. But I will pay for your maid in any case and if I need Margaret in a hurry perhaps she can come down.

Meantime I want to ask whether or not Margaret could come to Orillia when I go there for the summer, that is on about the last of April. I would give her expenses, including golf and amusements and extras and the typing guaranteed at $20.00 a month and perhaps running to more. Please think this over and let me know in lots of time. If you do not wish her to come I must make other arrangements which are difficult to alter once they are made.

S.L.


## To Margaret Burrowes[1], daughter of Margaret and William Burrowes

[McGill University
Montreal]
Feb 8 37

Dear Margaret

A letter of mine to your mother crossed yours to me.

I am afraid that I didnot make it quite clear what I meant. I hope that you can come to me in May, & if you can, I will pay for your mothers maid <u>now</u>, till you are earning money with me & could pay all or part. But I am just afraid that I couldn't manage to pay for the maid if you are not coming either now or then. You had better think it over . . see what you can do.

I will go further. It is most likely that Barbara will get married this summer. If she does I offer you her place, but not to do any secretary work as I can do all that myself except in crowded times. I would give you, not what Barbara got while I was at McGill & had all the McGill work & I had no time to do my own accounts, but the lower rate that she was put on when my salary was cut to a pension, namely, all expenses & all extras of transportations (amusements etc to a great extent but not by contract) and $20 a month. I could also give you the typing to do though that would probably next year only mean $10.00 a month.

If Barbara does not get married I could have you stay just the same & do the typing with a guarantee of $20.$\underline{^{00}}$ a month.

---

1   Leacock's niece, the daughter of his sister Margaret ('Daisy').

In either case I would pay for one course each term at McGill

No doubt you can make up your mind about this matter within a reasonable time.

Your affectionate uncle
Stephen Leacock

## To the Magazine Digest

[McGill University
Montreal]
Feb 8. 37

The Magazine Digest
Toronto

Dear Sirs

In reference to your unauthorized use of an article written by me the matter turns not on what you would pay for such an article but on the penalty for breach of copyright. This as you know is a very different matter. But I do not wish to push matter to extremes. Without prejudice to copyrights, I will be content with a payment of $100 $60⁰⁰. This is exactly what much less than a Digest publication paid for the right to print a summary, shorter than yours, of my article <u>My Fish Pond</u> namely a $100 in the Atlantic before Xmas: and the London Standard for the same £20 (guineas)

These facts are easily verified. I am authorized to say that if you make this payment the (London) Fortnightly is satisfied to set aside any ground of complaint they made have had.

Nothing in this proposal is made to preventing further use of this article or to permit your further use or sale of it.

V. truly
Stephen Leacock

## To Lord Atholstan[1]

Feb. 20th, 1937

My dear Lord Atholstan,

I enclose herewith a printed broadside announcing a set of articles written by me after making a lecture tour to the West.

I should like very much to see them appear in the Star and I understand that the syndicate which handles them has been in negotiations with your staff about them.

1    Lord Atholstan (Sir Hugh Graham, 1848–1938) was a Canadian publisher who owned the Montreal *Star*.

The Toronto Globe and Mail are to pay $40 a week for the use of them in Ontario (outside of Ottawa and Fort William). But as far as I am concerned I should feel quite safe in leaving the price to you if you could use them for the Star with sole rights in Quebec. To me it is not so much the money that counts as in having the articles read by my friends.

You have in the past extended such a kind welcome to my work that I hope you can do so again.

Very sincerely,
Stephen Leacock

## To Andrew Miller                    Feb. 20th. 1937

Dear Mr. Miller,

I am getting my niece to send you some stuff for publicity,—but I really think that all Canadian papers know who I am and will buy or not buy from the Broadside,——In any case all I can do is to <u>write the articles</u>. I appreciate immensely the work you are doing but as far as I am personally concerned I find it very harassing to have to take a lot of fuss over what means very little in money: my only concern is with the <u>articles</u> as <u>thought</u> and <u>art</u>. All the same, I repeat, I appreciate your work. I have written to Lord A. via Archibald, which I think better.

Very sincerely,
Stephen Leacock

## To George and Mary Leacock          Feb 28.37

Dear Mary & George,

I was "to" Harrisburg in Pennsylvania (lecturing) & passed through Toronto & phoned & they said you were away for 2 weeks . . . when I got back here I found your letter from the hospital—It will do George a lot of good. I wish he could cash in when possible on the Moloney shares & limit his connection to 2 big sales trips a year across Canada & live on the farm—expenses would be mighty small—Its only an idea in the clouds to think of—Times are going to be good & business fine in 1938 & thats the time to cash in on prospects.

I have to lecture in Buffalo on <u>Tuesday March 9</u> and arrive with Stevie on that morning in Toronto, change trains; return from Buffalo next morning arriving <u>8 am</u> & change for Orillia stay in Orillia one day & night & return on

Thursday evening Toronto for Montreal. If you & George could come up with us that would be fine & I could, if you prefer it have Kelly meet us with the car & pick you up at Aurora

Y. a. b in'l<br>
Stephen Leacock

P.S. Buffalo is the last lecture I have accepted: unless I got poor I shall take no more: have refused a lot.

## To Andrew Miller

[McGill University
Montreal]
(March 3, 1937)

Dear Mr Miller

Here is a plan that may relieve your finances—Suppose you offer to <u>American</u> newspapers a series of short articles of 1000 words each under such a heading as

Notes on Western Problems

as

Shared by the United
States & Canada

Blurb:—

Professor Stephen Leacock after a recent tour of the West to the Pacific Coast prepared for the Canadian Press a series of elaborate articles, as indicated in the enclosed broadside sheet, on Canadian western problems.

Dr Leacock has now condensed such of these discussions as are of American interest into short digests of 1000 words, under headings as follows

I    The St. Lawrence To the [··]
II   The Wheat Problem of the World Can Production be Restricted
III  Gold Mining & Gold
IV   Social Credit  Failure or Portent?
     Will it spread South & East
V̶

Now, you could try out that idea with no expense beyond a little typing & I'll give you 50-50 if you get anything & turn out the articles to use as soon as Canadian release allows—<u>only</u> in U.S.—Of course I wouldn't write any of them till we had enough orders to justify it—on the other hand a <u>cheap</u> price might bring orders

Stephen Leacock

## To Real Estate Department, Canadian Pacific Railway

3869 Cote des Neiges Road,
Montreal.
March 15, 1937.

Canadian Pacific Railway,
Real Estate Department,
Windsor Station.

Dear Sirs,

I have been informed that your railway is selling the track between Medonte and Lindsay.

A piece of this right of way was cut off my Orillia property. I had no choice in the matter, the railway having the right to take it for a public road.

I am most anxious to buy it back again. No doubt you will at once recognise the priority of my claim. I would not have _sold_ this land, as a bad use of it would ruin my property. The railway had the right to take it to build a railway but it wouldn't seem quite fair to sell it now for uses that might rob my remaining property of its value. I will take occasion to call on your department for discussion.

Yours very truly
Stephen Leacock

## To Mr Shirard

[McGill University
Montreal]
15/3/37

Dear Mr. Shirard

I have your letter of March 3. I am so sorry if in sending back the book your publishers so kindly sent to me I did anything wrong. I assure you I didn't "toss it back in contempt;" I sent it by the post. Publishers often send me things as no doubt they do to you with the expectation that I will be interested & will write a note about the book. But I am sorry to say that your book apparently dealt with what Mr Harris said about Mr Wilde etc. etc. and I havent the faintest interest in any of it. Write something else & I'll be delighted.

Be reasonable. If I sent you my <u>Elements of Political Science</u> you couldnt read the damn thing.

You now write and tell me that Sir Edward Sullivan says that Mr Harris book (which I dont know) on Mr Wilde (whom I never saw) is <u>an outrage</u>. What if it is? It just too bad. So is Easton Mears book on President Harding.

I am so sorry if I did wrong in what I thought the sensible thing to do: send back to the publisher an expensive book of no use to me.

Very sincerely
Stephen Leacock

## To Carl Goldenberg

[McGill University
Montreal]
Mar 20 37

Dear Goldenberg

Thank you ever so much. These look to be documents of extraordinary interest & value.

I can take about 1 page of your economics, dilute it with 20 gallons of talk and about 60 drops of pure humour & sell it anywhere as Extract of Canadian Patriotism. Thank you

V. sincerely
Stephen Leacock

## To Percy Cudlipp

April 2, 1937

Dear Mr. Cudlipp,

My best thanks for your letter of March 17th and for the Standard with the Fish Pond in it, admirably made up.

We never see the Standard here and I haven't been in London for ten years and had forgotten your form and space and I see now I've been sending you the wrong stuff,—burlesque instead of humour. The Atlantic have bought the U.S. rights with the Two Milords (one of the pieces I sent) I expected it would be too broad for them (I mean too burlesque) but right for you, but I got it backwards.

So now I try you with another piece "While You're at it, or Expert Advice on How to Throw your House to Pieces." I wrote it ten days ago and the U.S. rights are bought by the Commentator, a New York magazine. I see they rewrite the title in their letter of acceptance as Disown Your Own House, which is very good. The interest of the piece lies in the House rebuilding movement which rages in the U.S. and here. I think you have it too.

I hope you can use this but it doesn't matter.

S.L.

## To P.P. Howe

April 2, 1937

Dear Mr. Howe,

I cabled "Your letter fully satisfactory. Please go ahead as indicated."

This means, does it not,—that: Old books as in your letter and back royalties payable only to extent indicated in your letter.

Funny Pieces: goes ahead as under Lane contract.

Hellements of Hickonomics: You publish it on a 10% basis, or don't publish it at all. I shall not offer it elsewhere, but if you don't want it and another publisher asks for it, I shall let him have it. That's fair enough, isn't it?

<u>My Discovery of the West</u>: You can have this on the same terms as Mr. Allen has Canada, (15% rising to 20% after 10,000 sold. This book might do well in England as the political and financial people will be interested in the serious side.

<u>Here are my Lectures and Stories</u>: (Short title on back <u>Lectures and Stories</u>) This book will be all right. You can have it at 10%.

But these 10% are just cut rates on special things. I had with Mr. Lane 20% and £200 advance. By consent as times fell off we reduced it to 15% and £100 advance. I should hardly wish to offer any new humour book at less.

One other point: I think it would be reasonable to make up royalties every six months, as Lane did for twenty years and pay within three months of date computed. I am too old to wait a year for anything, even money.

S.L.


## To Frank Dodd                              April 20th. 1937

Frank Dodd, Esq.

Dear Dodd,

My best thanks for your kindly letter. You will be glad to know that I have completed all arrangements to stay with the new John Lane Co. They will go ahead with the Funny Pieces and My Discovery of the West. I am sorry that you are not publishing the Discovery. I think it may do well. It was very difficult to syndicate it owing to the length of the instalments, but it is running now in its ninth week (of twelve) and seems to make a hit.

I thought Houghton Mifflin were publishing it but they decided that it was too Canadian plus British and not sufficiently American. And now I don't know what Thomas Allen is doing about American rights but I gather he has placed them.

If times get really good again will you please think of binding up my humour books (only those, not histories and essays) into a set as Stephen Leacock's Humour. You see if you have quite a loose stock of ones that don't sell now, the cost of them is only the cost of binding and I should expect that one could make up a handsome binding for about 40 cents and sell a set of a dozen volumes at 25 dollars. Please think it over. I might try it out myself (I mean at my own risk) for a small Canadian edition.

S.L.

## *To the Magistrate of Brockville*     (May 3 1937)

A Humble Prayer
  to the Magistrate of Brockville

I desire to acknowledge my guilt of the charges set forth against me in the summons to appear before the Magistrates Court at Brockville. I enclose herewith my cheque for $19.00 in exulpation of my guilt.

And I desire to say:—

That I am fined because I permitted my driver Lucien Pelletier to drive my truck without flares. I never in my life heard of flares till now. Neither did Pelletier. I had no notion that a truck must carry flares. Nobody told me. There is no obligation laid on the man who sold me the truck to tell me about flares. There ought to be but there isn't. The province ought to issue a circular notice of traffic requirements and have all dealers issue them along with sales.

It is not possible for me to read over the Ontario statues regulating traffic and the various cases and precedents that interpret them.

I am well aware of the legal principle that <u>ignorantia legis neminem excusant</u>. But I claim that it belongs with a great deal of our law, such for instance as the doctrine of common employment, which the complexity of our industrial life has rendered obsolete.

Ignorance <u>does</u> excuse, at least to the extent of imposing on the government the obligation of giving a reasonable chance to know the law.

I did not know of flares.

Now what comes next? There may be a dozen more obligations and limitations?

Lou Pelletier speaks French: shall I be fined in Ontario for that? My truck is painted green. Is that legal? Or is it too Irish? I have no idea.

I am a member of the Church of England. Does that disqualify me from using a truck in Ontario?

In what direction can I look for light? What remedy have I except to move back into the province of Quebec, where they temper the administration of the law with the saving grace of common sense and where a penitent tear blots out a fine.

With which I commend the magistrates of Brockville to the consideration of his gracious majesty whose name they so wrongly invoke.

Given at our Old Brewery Bay
At this our Orillia
This 3rd of May 1937.                    Stephen Leacock

## To Francis Paget Hett

[The Old Brewery Bay
Orillia, Ontario]
June 1.37

Dear Frank,

So glad to get your letter but sorry that you won't be out—fishing rotten here, but season lovely & I am building, planting, ploughing,—5 3/4 men working,—that is 5, and old Jones 1/2 & me 1/4. The John Lane stuff must sleep. They are to ~~pl~~ published for me my new book <u>My Discovery of the West</u> & others later. I have done a lot of writing since I returned—Barbara gets married this August to Donald Nimmo of Detroit, son of an old friend of mine Harry Nimmo who died recently—all my friends are dying. Dont do it. Stevie well and at McGill in Honour English.

Best to yourself and Alice
yours as ever
Stephen (Leacock)

P.S. Ask them to raise me to the peerage: I have had so many honorary degrees & the other day a Gold Medal, that the peerage is all I need. Tell Eddie Peacock to tell Amery to tell Stanley Baldwin to tell Neville Chamberlain that I would accept any peerage from a Duke Sinister to a Baron Scavenger.

## To Mrs Herbert T. Shaw

Orillia
Sunday Je 6  37

Dear Fitz

I was glad to get your letter. I think René is deplorably rude not to send a word of answer to an invitation as open & cordial as what I sent—Everything looks lovely up here—Peas just coming into flower—Ive been getting up at daylight and writing hard for hours every day—I got a cheque three days ago and absent mindedly tore it up, $200, threw it in the waste paper basket—luckily I had ordered that no one but me must ever empty them—So after a search elsewhere I found it & gummed it together—Dr. Ardagh came over & we drove to Jordan's (the pond) to see what is being done—car stuck—I started to walk for home for some help—he got it going & caught me up—of such small news my life is made—I got a request from the US to do an encyclopedia life of Dickens 2000 words for $200—Say! Its like picking up the money. I can do it in one day—<u>But</u> the letter has been kicking round unopened—so I am redoubling system on the mail and bringing the box up here— I had a letter from Lilian but I cant read her writing—all I could see in it was 'rum' and 'love' and 'fine time'—but that covered it—I'm going to get to work. I am writing (try to remember) a new book for the

HOME UNIVERSITY LIBRARY SERIES
called
HUMOUR & HUMANITY

---

Stephen

P.S. <u>My Discovery of the West</u> is out & looks fine. I'll have a copy to send

## To Mrs Herbert T. Shaw

[The Old Brewery Bay
Orillia, Ontario]
Friday. Je 11 37

Dear Fitz

Just got your letter in pencil written on the street: I was so glad to see that you said that Dr Morovy says everything is all right: I am glad: now all you have to do is to get <u>general health</u> & then you be fine, as I am getting to be. My stomach is getting so damn well that I cant stop eating! I'm back 10 years & still moving back . . Today at lunch we had whitefish caught by Kelly plus our own asparagus spinach, potatoes! All off the farm. I was up just at daylight & writing I'm doing 2000 words a day—Dr Ardagh came over this morning & talked an hour or so—no special news—wanted me to go pickerel fishing but I said no— Ill wait for herring—The weather is ideal but getting a little dryer—I hope to hear from René that he is coming up. Dot comes on Sunday for a week & George & Mary may come tomorrow for overnight & Sunday—Now I'll go & have a look at my peas,—I look at them about 4 times a day. Ill be glad when you come.

Stephen

## To P.P. Howe

[The Old Brewery Bay
Orillia, Ontario]
Je 14.37

Dear Mr Howe

I have received your letter of May and have not yet had time to read over the contract which no doubt is all right

But I have cabled at once in regard to your suggestion that you would ask Lord Tweedsmuir to write a preface. That would never do. My friends would all think it (I mean my friends in Canada) a great mistake for me to solicit a preface from the Governor General or allow one to be solicited in my name. I once met Lord Tweedsmuir about 15 years ago or rather I went to see him on business, he being there with Nelsons publishing firm. That is the only time I ever saw him in my life. Nor would it seem to me, as a Canadian, proper for the Governor General of Canada to write a preface to a book dealing in very precise terms with all sorts of controversial questions of Canadian politics, unless he made it so entirely colourless and non-committal and so explicitly withheld any concurrence of opinion that it would be of less than no value

Suppose I stagger on alone for a while yet.

Very truly yours


*To Tresham Lever*                                    [The Old Brewery Bay
                                                       Orillia, Ontario]
                                                       June 21, 1937

Sir Tresham Lever, Bt.
Thornton Butterworth Ltd.
London.

My dear Sir Tresham,

My book for the Home University Series, Humour and Humanity, is finished. I am sure you will be well pleased with it. It runs to 50,000 words as exactly as can be. I expect to post the manuscript to you by the end of the week.

There will be no need to send proofs to me, if I may take for granted that you find no need to delete, add or alter anything. I see no reason why you should. The book is written in a vein to give no offence to anyone in religion, literary or political grounds. It brings in plenty of American interest as is natural since I live in America. I repeat, I am quite sure you will like it. It has been to me a great pleasure in the doing, and I am still grateful for your ready acceptance of the idea.

Very faithfully,

# CHAPTER 9

## STEPHEN LEACOCK
# ALONE AGAIN

~⌐

## 1937–1939

After helping to arrange Barbara Ulrichsen's marriage to Donald Nimmo, Stephen Leacock returned to his work as an independent scholar, continuing to publish articles and books while overseeing his son's education at McGill. His publication, in the fall of 1937, of the collection *Here Are My Lectures and Stories* was further proof both of his retirement from the lecture platform and of his continuing work as a writer. The volume includes his 'Frenzied Fiction' lectures as well as a very good piece of reminiscence, 'My Fishing Pond'.

In the same season he published a second volume on his theories of humour, *Humor and Humanity*. Here Leacock expresses clearly his own philosophy of humour: 'The essence of humor is human kindliness,' he wrote in the preface. 'It is this element which has grown from primitive beginnings to higher forms: which lends humor the character of a leading factor in human progress, and which is destined still further to enhance its utility to mankind.' But it is in the book's opening sentence that he gives his now classic definition of humour: 'the kindly contemplation of the incongruities of life, and the artistic expression thereof'. Still bitter over his enforced retirement from McGill, Leacock sent a copy of *Humor and Humanity* to his friend Dr Gerhard Lomer, with the note: 'This is the fifth book I have published since I was retired (as useless).'

In 1937 the Royal Society of Canada conferred on Leacock its Lorne Pierce Medal. Although he had never been very active in the Society, Leacock appreciated the high honour. The citation stated:

A sane economist, an authority on Canadian history, a critic and essayist of international repute, a lecturer of magnetic personality, a teacher who has profoundly influenced many generations of students and, above all, a writer and speaker who is the incarnation of humour, Stephen Leacock has won for himself a unique place in the Canadian scene. Adding lustre to the staff of McGill University for thirty-four years, his genius has been acknowledged with honorary degrees from Brown

University, Queen's University, his alma mater of Toronto University, Bishop's College, Lennoxville, and his own university in Montreal. Author of many books on many subjects, he has illuminated with clear thinking and pungent phrase whatever theme he chose for his pen. Generous of his time and talent in helping many good Canadian causes, he has contributed greatly to the growing reputation of Canadian letters.

A further accolade came in 1938, when Leacock won his Governor General's award for *My Discovery of the West*, a recognition in part that Leacock's gift lay equally in his ability to explain in lucid language intricate social problems and in his ability to do so with humour. At the same time, Leacock continued to receive invitations to speak to both public and private audiences. He turned down an invitation to join the staff of the University of British Columbia. He was invited to give a series of six or eight public lectures at Harvard University; he turned this down, too. He was urged to make a tour of Russia and also a tour of Australia and New Zealand; these requests he refused. He had retired, and this fact gave him an easy response to all such invitations. He had a second excuse, in that his health was not as robust as it might have been. He was hospitalized in 1938 for prostate surgery, the length of his stay lasting longer than he intended, and his letters indicate that he endured a long period of recovery. And so he was content to split his time between Montreal, where he monitored his son's education, and Old Brewery Bay, where he continued to write tirelessly.

At the beginning of 1939 Leacock moved into Montreal's Windsor Hotel, which he found well suited to his needs. On his return in the fall he decided to give up permanently his Côte des Neiges home, though he would retain the title to the property until his death. His world was becoming smaller, his circle of friends now including only his close friend Fitz Shaw, his niece and her husband, his son at McGill, his colleagues from McGill, and his publishers.

In the preface to *Model Memoirs and Other Sketches from Simple to Serious* (1938), Leacock noted somewhat apologetically: 'I am aware that parts of this volume may be found offensively serious, and can only plead the influence of advancing years.' But the true source of his occasionally sombre tone is readily apparent in his final story, 'All is Not Lost!', which begins with the statement, 'I was just starting out trout fishing one day last week when I saw from a headline in an afternoon paper that war in Europe was just about a dead certainty— anything within twenty-four to twenty-six hours.' The story concludes with his hope that 'this, our actual world, would be as good as the bright world of imagination if we would only let it be so. Everything is there, the smiling abundance of our unrealized paradise, the good-will toward men that all men feel and none dares act upon. It is all there for the asking, if we can only cast aside from the gateway the evil spirits of fear and apprehension and distrust which keep us from our kingdom.'

On 10 September 1939 Canada declared war on Germany, as Leacock had anticipated. The Second World War would prove to have a debilitating effect on the senior scholar, who lamented its ruinous devastation and suffering until the end of his life.

## To Barbara Nimmo

[The Old Brewery Bay
Orillia, Ontario]
Sep 7. 37

Dear Barbara

Your freight—It seems to weigh under 600 pounds—railway freight rate, about $4.50 to Windsor, Ont.—truck rate I am finding out, probably less—if the stuff is packed well enough to ride in my truck it can ride in any other truck—

Cost in my truck—gasoline for 660 miles (1 1/2 a mile) = $9.90 Kellys meals, say 5 at 50 cents = $2.50,—1 cabin say 1.50 cents = total $14.00—under the circumstances there is no sense in sending the truck

I will pay truck charge if there is a service, or railway charge, if not. If things need re-packing I will have it done.

Special Items. The cedar chest can go by express at $1^{\underline{20}}$ a hundred  If I add Kelly's time 2 days, even at the rate I pay the other men that means $20^{\underline{00}}$ for my truck and about $6^{\underline{00}}$ by freight or truck—Please write me as to what to do— The apples potatoes etc. are nothing. A few cents buys in the Detroit market all I would send

Your affec uncle
Stephen Leacock

## To Barbara Nimmo

[The Old Brewery Bay
Orillia, Ontario]
Sep 13 37

Dear Barbara

[Yours]—I will fix your freight so that it will be all right

First—I will have it so crated that it can travel by any means of conveyance.

Then—I will send it viâ Strathdee Transport if they go direct Orillia–Windsor (Coville dont)—if not via Can Nat'l—

And. I will pay for it. The chest: you couldnt get it in the car?

Next. Is it possible to send you viâ express—a hundred pounds of fowls & vegetables etc. What happens?

I didnt go to London—I only seem to get better slowly. I miss your help very much. There seems such a lot to do.

Best love to Donald & yourself.

y.a. uncle
Stephen

P.S. If you & Donald get time any time to drive up it goes without saying that you can load your car with chickens turkeys apples (the winter ones are going to be great)—if you have a butcher you might ask him if he would put things in cold storage & you could take half a dozen chickens & a couple of turkeys at a time. The <u>ducks</u> have turned out wonderful

## *To Barbara Nimmo*

[The Old Brewery Bay
Orillia, Ontario]
Oct 2 37

Dear Barbara

(1) Send me amount of Windsor truck & I'll send a cheque. It came to more than railway apparently.

_____

(2) Encycl. I'm glad your doing it. Write to Bank of Montreal, Royal Bank & Nova Scotia & ask to be put on monthly mailing list for their monthly survey—ask for back no's since Jan . . Wrote C.P.R publicity & asked for their <u>Agricultural & Industrial Progress Bulletin</u> (monthly)—These will give you economic . . . . . I say more when I've seen Culliton

_____

(3) Typing. Yes. See enclosed to know what its about. <u>Bell Syndicate Series</u> If you can make <u>3</u> it will be far better  I had no 1. ready to send & then at the last minute saw that 1500 words was the limit. I'll send tomorrow. No need to send them back one by one but keep a list . . They may sell or may not but <u>you</u> take rights. I've had $100 anyway.

_____

For the encyc. if you can do it will I'll only take $10: that'll give you $40, & with typing & odd stuff I hope it will mean $20 a month . . We'll try anyway . . . my finance is bad, so I am trying to start all over & pay with my pen for current living

_____

(3) Yes. Go to Orillia & get me all my <u>humour books</u> & ship by freight to the Hotel. I forgot them & no one else can pick them out. Include my own humour—In return take as many chickens apples (but <u>not</u> the ones reserved to keep till 1938) and anything else you can carry away . . Arrange with Kelly to send you a turkey for US Thanksgiving—couldn't he ship it to Windsor

_____

Hotel fine—We have a little suite. I suddenly & terribly missed my study in the early morning—esp. as theres no morning sun—. . but that's nothing as long as I can work————. I have more than I can do . .

y.a. uncle
Stephen Leacock

When you want to do some <u>real</u> work you can make a book of <u>College Selections</u> & I'll go on the title page with you so as to sell it . . . e.g. . . . The English Humorists . . . or Essayists or something—You can have all the money.

## *To Barbara Nimmo*

[Mount Royal Hotel
Montreal]
Oct 11. 37

Dear Bâ

Yours from Orillia—Best Thanks—you're <u>sure</u> about the coat? I'll buy one & not buy a suit. I'll pay your $8<u>00</u> & current stamps & typing a little later—Keep it as an <u>account</u> . . For the moment I can only issue cheques that have to be . . if <u>you</u> get stuck let me know

Please <u>Rush</u> my Bell Syndicate typing as there is some other typing coming right along—Please note the enclosure. Short title <u>Lighter Prose</u>—you & I will make the abstract—I will then get a <u>dummy</u> made with <u>printed</u> title page & contents . . . & typed Chapter Heads. You will take it to Publishers & try to sell it <u>on my name</u>, not as writing it <u>all</u> but a lot of it You can have all the money

y. a. uncle
Stephen Leacock

COLLEGE SELECTIONS
FROM THE
<u>LIGHTER PROSE</u>
OF
ENGLAND & AMERICA
1400–1900
*Satire, Irony, Parody, Humour*
an introductory Essay and
with ∧ historical & Critical Notes
BARBARA NIMMO & STEPHEN LEACOCK

## To V.C. Clinton-Baddeley[1]

[Mount Royal Hotel
Montreal]
Oct 17 37

Dear Mr. Clinton. Baddeley

Thank you very much for your letter of Oct 7.

My records are in Orillia. But my recollection is that I gave you the right to make a play out of <u>Behind the Beyond</u> and I did not give the sole dramatic and broadcast rights to it. Such a thing would not have been reasonable. <u>Behind the Beyond</u> was a very valuable copyright with very considerable prestige & your offer, as I recollect it, contained no guarantee at all corresponding to the exclusive & permanent rights in it. You are mistaken in thinking (I quote your words) "It is significant that in many years no one over here ever arranged plays from your stories." Among others Charles Hawtrey did, at the Empire Theatre in London.

If the record is silent, the rule of what is reasonable should prevail. But if you have a definite written record of a substantive contract with me (It is quite possible as I was careless in such matters and my memory cannot reach over 27 years & 40 volumes), that shows my recollection is wrong & then of course the record prevails.

No doubt it can be reasonably straightened

V. sincerely
Stephen Leacock

1   V.C. Clinton-Baddeley (1900–70) was a British writer, actor, and editor. In the 1930s he adapted some of Leacock's comic pieces for the theatre.

## To Barbara Nimmo

[The Canadian Political
Science Association]
Sunday Oct 18 37

Dear Barbara

Your typing,—machine, work, & execution & handling my writing,—is beautiful. Much better than I can get any other way—I'll send all I can—Keep track of postage (use air mail where it helps) & material etc & I'll send a cheque when I get a few—I have heaps of work, but my strength is low & working hours (for real ideas & expression) very few . . . my feet are not well yet—I'm like Brownings Grammarian————Keep thinking of the <u>College Selections</u>—I dont think poetry can get in. I'll write an introduction "On the Study of Lighter Literature"—If you & Don come to Orillia at Xmas, you could bring your Cambridge History of Modern Literature————The idea will be to stop chronological in time to avoid copyright—i.e. end with the 19 cent Humorists (era of Dickens & M Twain—No living authors

The way to go to work would be to make a chronology of what is lighter prose, & then divide & cut into appropriate groups e.g.

> Queens Annes Essayists
> Addison Steele etc
> They're a division
> also Goldsmith, Sterne
> Charles Lamb & his crowd
> etc.

y. a. u.
Stephen Leacock

## To P.P. Howe

Mount Royal Hotel
Montreal, Que
October 25th, 1937.

John Lane the Bodley Head,
London, England

Der Mr. Howe,

I enclose a copy of a letter to Mr. Clinton Baddelay. I sent you a cable letter in the same sense. That settles that.

Broadcast and dramatic rights in my books. My records are at Orillia. You will find that in some of my books the publishers have part-rights in dramatic and other uses. In some (later books) only British book rights. Please therefore check over any payments made to me and see that they conform to contract.

But I cannot expect you without charge to negotiate such rights when you draw no advantage. In such cases I will be glad to pay you 15 per cent.

You make a great mistake if you think other people could adapt my work as well as I can. It stands to reason I can do it better.

When adaptation or recasting is wanted cable me deferred at my expense what length of broadcast (or what number of words) and out of what book. I will do it within 48 hours.

This puts my new book Here are my Lectures in a new light. It is one continual broadcast needing only cutting to length. I offered you the English book rights and said that I realized you might think the book uncertain. But if you like to take it I will add to it 20 per cent of Broadcast British rights. If I send you the MS. edition due November 15th, is that soon enough—If not, cable for a MS.

Yours sincerely,

P.S. Please make out a list and memo of rights if you have the contracts. If not, I will make it out from Orillia later.
P.P.S. 12/18/9 Cheque received of 2/6 on outstanding claim—many thanks.

## To V.C. Clinton-Baddeley

Mount Royal Hotel,
Montreal, Canada.
November 18th, 1937.

V.C. Clinton–Baddeley, Esq.,
63 Peel St., W.8,
London, England.

Dear Mr. Clinton-Baddeley,

Thank you very much for your letter of November 8th and enclosed cheque. From the text of it and from my own recollection, and from the common rule of reason, I can see no justification for any one thinking that I sold out all dramatic and contingent rights in Behind the Beyond or in anything else. Behind the Beyond is a broadcast as it stands. The only question is to what extent, if any, it must be shortened to meet the exigencies of available time. But that, for me who wrote it, is a simple matter. I propose therefore to undertake the preparation of that and other things of mine for broadcasting. I am writing Mr. Howe to that effect.

Very sincerely,

## To Barbara Nimmo

[Mount Royal Hotel
Montreal Canada]
Mon Dec 6. 37

Dear Bâ

I send you a cheque for your account, certified at the Bank: I find that best as it keeps immediate track. . . .

As Xmas comes on Saturday that means a Sat–'Sun' Holiday & so I hope you & Don will be able to spend Xmas with us. I shall have René with us, and, I hope, Uncle George & Aunt Mary . . . Owing to the hard times all Xmas presents, given or received will be restricted at my house to 25 cents

I made a mistake about some typing that I had that could have waited & sent it to Mrs Simons: the ordinary stuff, I've done quite a lot, is in too big a hurry. But after this I hope to have some. I'll send tomorrow or next day one file of letters for you. (about the money that Jack and Hector Charlesworth were going to pay & didnt)

Let me know about Xmas

y. a. uncle
Stephen Leacock

## To J.A.T. Lloyd

The Old Brewery Bay
Orillia Ont
Dec 28 37

My dear "Hogan" Lloyd,—if you can still stand for your old name—I was so glad to hear from you & very glad to know that the kindly review of my book in the Times was from your pen—I have a book out in New York & Toronto called <u>Here are My Lectures</u>: I think it is making quite a hit but the English edition will not be out yet for a month or so: I will ask Dodd Mead to send you an advance copy and then if you care to get a review of it early on, it will be a fine thing for me—Books have to get a hearing right away

. . . . . I have not much (personal) news to give: I was "retired" by & from McGill a year & a half ago: spend my time now in writing & up here in the country. . . . Mrs Willie Grant (he died as Principal of U.C.C.), who was Maud Parkin has come to McGill as head of the Women's College (Royal Vic. College)—We have a new Principal Dr Lewis Douglas,—his family were in U.C.C. in my time but before you . . my best New Years wishes to you & your wife. Do write again.

V. sincerely
Stephen Leacock

## To Barbara Nimmo

[Mount Royal Hotel
Montreal Canada]
Jan 6 '38.

Dear Barbara

The cheque came along with very pleasing promptness. I send you your forty + 50 cents to cover the exchange. As Canadian funds are up I think that will do it. If not I'll send the rest in stamps. . . . Is the enclosed bill (Milne) correct as far as you know? . . . Hope you & Don were not the worse for the drive. We had a cold trip to Oshawa that kept Stevie in bed a day—is well now. . . . no other news

y.a.u
Stephen Leacock

For your information I may tell you that it doesn't matter whether we want the baby to be a boy or a girl—whichever you get you will wonder that you could ever have wanted the other . . I spent months in dreaming of a daughter, and forgot it in one minute & couldnt even understand it.

## To Barbara Nimmo

[Mount Royal Hotel
Montreal Canada]
Friday March 11. 1938

Dear Barbara

I send you today under separate cover registered 3500 words to type 2 copies. There's no hurry as it is only No 1 of a series of <u>Model Memoirs</u>. I shall not send any of it out till I have at least three—Registered mail is very slow so theres no need to use it provided you keep 1 copy, MS or type, till ~~I hear~~ you hear that I have the other . . one page (9) got left out. I enclose it

. . . . . . . . . . . . . . .

I hope you are getting on all right. Every one hear talks of you & sends messages. Uncle George is sailing for Europe (England) on the Europa March 19 (Mary too) . . . Stevie & I go to Orillia April 13th

Love to yourself & Donald
y.a.u.
Stephen Leacock

## To E.G. McCracken

Royal Victoria Hospital
Montreal
April 6 38

Dear McCracken

I am in hospital convalescent from an operation of March 23, doing well, but I fear there is no chance of my being able to join you so early as the eleventh——Buster Reids death came as a terrible shock: I was looking for him in Montreal just at that time. Such a sudden and sad death must keep his life all the brighter as a memory and example for us . . . Please tell all the boys how sorry I am not to be able to come

with very best regards
Stephen Leacock

## To Barbara Nimmo

Roy. Vic. Hospital
Apr 24 '38

Dear Barbara

I have been thinking of you a good deal while I have been ill, but writing was difficult. But now for the first time, I am up & in my clothes & can write . . . All the news I've had of you sounds fine & I am so glad that you are keeping up your health & that your mother is there——Later on you will be able to come to Orillia & you can either have your own old room with the bath room & the room next it (Stevie's) cut off and turned into a little suite, or what no doubt you will prefer, the boat house. . . . I will add to it at the end of the kitchen a simple wooden bedroom so that you can have a maid there & I will put in, discreetly hidden a little outdoor closet draining away properly, so that having the maid there doesn't disturb the privacy of your upstairs . . with that, and a telephone, I think you would be as all right as at the house & much nicer for you & Donald. . . .

I hope soon to be able to go to Orillia . . I am still having XRay treatment but I am told that there is every hope of a complete & final recovery. . . . Stevie is up at Orillia now. He went up for the weekend with David Spielman a college friend. Mrs Hamilton was to join them in Toronto: they arrived Friday noon & get back Monday (tomorrow morning). Stevie's exams begin on Thursday & last a week but I hope to go on to Orillia three or four days ahead of him. My God, it is good to be up again . . . I am a poor patient: no courage: no nothing: so it goes hard with people like me. . . . Yet as I say, its great to be up . . I am planning to write already . . Fortunately a lot of last years & last winters work brought in various cheques so that when its all done I wont be so far from top side up . . Your Uncle George leaves on the Queen Mary on May 4, due New York I presume the 9th. No doubt they have sent you cards

> Best love to you both
> y.a.u.
> Stephen Leacock

## To Carl Goldenberg

R Vict Hosp
Ap 28 38

Dear Carl

Best thanks for your note— I hope soon be out of here as a re-conditioned 1938 Model of a Professor, 4 cylinders . . . Good luck to your Inter-provincial labours

> V sincerely
> Stephen Leacock

## To Barbara Nimmo

The Old B B
Orillia Ont
May 3, 1938

Dear Barbara,

I arrived here safely last night with Mrs Shaw and a nurse. I hope to be soon* well

. . . . I was so glad to get your letter which came here yesterday (all about the paper etc . . . Dont worry over anything. When you are well enough you & the baby can come here & this is your home, for Don too, as often and as long as you need it . . . So that even if everything went wrong with the paper it would only mean a period of waiting & looking round for Don, without the least anxiety as to how & where you are to live . . . . . I will fix up the extra room in your boathouse because it is in my own interest anyway. You see, if anything happened to me, the boat house must be rented anyway & it would rent much more easily with a maids room . . . But no doubt things will not come to any such pitch: I only mean that you & Don never need worry while I'm alive and have Orillia.

The place looks lovely here. I never saw it as good: and Kelly has everything in wonderful shape.

I shall be hoping for your good news . . Stevie is still in Montreal with exams . . . I missed you terribly when I had to go to the hospital: everything in confusion . . .

> Best love to you both
> y. a. u
> Stephen Leacock

## To Barbara Whitley[1]

[The Old Brewery Bay
Orillia, Ontario]
May 4. 1938.

Dear Miss Whitley

I am so glad that you are going to collaborate with me in Radio monologues. I have not all my material with me yet but I enclose material for 3 from which you can judge what is meant.

I will (with your approval after you've seen these) write to Major Murray & suggest the plan. Dont be afraid of it. You have the talent for it & ought to do it . . It will take some time to get things going as just now Major Murray is away and in any case it takes <u>weeks</u> to arrange programs, especially if Major Murray were to give us a "<u>national hook</u>-up" as he has kindly done for the radio pieces of mine now running on Fridays. They are records made before I was ill.

> with best regards
> Stephen Leacock

1    Barbara Whitley was a young Montreal actress when she starred in many of Leacock's plays for radio.

## To Barbara Whitley

[The Old Brewery Bay
Orillia, Ontario]
May 10 '38

Dear Miss Whitley

That's right. I've written at once to Major Murray. I'm afraid that he's away but I expect that the next move will be that he will ask you to go & see <u>Mr</u>

<u>Stadler</u> (in charge of <u>CBM</u>) & Mr. Stadler will try out your voice & perhaps ask you to do a piece of script: no doubt if Major Murray is to be in Montreal soon, he will see you himself—

Radio talk is different from acting in that <u>tones</u> are everything (there are no gestures to get over . . . Too much of it might spoil acting, but a little is a help

V. sincerely<br>
Stephen Leacock

P.S. I am expecting Peggy Shaw up here this weekend, so if you get this in time, call her up & tell her all about it

## To Mrs Herbert T. Shaw

[The Old Brewery Bay
Orillia, Ontario]
Tuesday May 10th

Dear Fitz

You'll be glad to know that I am feeling fine—I got great sleep last night by the simple idea of going to sleep in my clothes after dinner as I used to do when I was well (altogether, with adjournments) I got 9 hours,—& oh, say! You should have seen me at 6 oclock (Daylight S) ought of doors snuffing the fresh air . . . Today it is cloudy & half wet so Lou is setting out tomatoes & cabbages: you ought to be here There would be a lot to do in your garden—You ought to let me plough up the end part & put in it some kind of ~~snuff~~ stuff of which you could take the best to Montreal & leave the rest for hen food . . . . Kelly & Tina[1] leave overnight on Wednesday & so will be due at your place about noon on Thursday. I think that Tina is going on (with her sisters husband to Three Rivers,—her sister has been ill) so I dont think that she'll be with you—But I dont know——It's such a pity you're not here today; such a lot you could do . . I'm not going fishing till you come but I'd like to go the first day you feel like it; I'm quite back in it It is such fine exercise & absorption . . . . . . The billiard room is in fine shape: I am keeping Rowe an extra day to paint the walls & benches & trim it up generally. . . . Still waiting for good news from Barbara; too bad it wasn't on Peggy's birthday I found out that after all I forgot to enclose her letter so I will put it in now. I'll hear from you I hope this morning, so perhaps I'll get time for a second letter. Kelly & Tina are to go in after lunch

Stephen

1   See footnote 1, page 390.

*To Barbara Nimmo*                [The Old Brewery Bay
                                   Orillia, Ontario]
                                   Orillia 10³⁰ am
                                   May 10 38

Dear Bâ

Just got your good news & more delighted than I can say[1]; I have wired it on, as sent by Nancy, to Mrs. Shaw & asked her to telephone Montreal friends. I am so glad.

Your affec uncle,
Stephen Leacock

1    Nancy Nimmo was born on 10 May 1938.


*To Mrs Herbert T. Shaw*           [The Old Brewery Bay
                                   Orillia, Ontario]
                                   May 21, 1938

Dear Fitz

I heard from Barbara today: Baby (Nancy) wonderful—still in hospital; Don not allowed in for fear of infection—looks through glass—The paper still in doubt. I gather it is to be sold if any one will buy it. It looks like hard times ahead but Ba can come here and live here for nothing—

This morning I wrote a long letter to the New York Times and explained that I had planned a series of articles on education (to make a book later) and gave the ideas and part of an opening chapter and headings for others—and suggested that if they said yes I would do six chapters for them to look at (if they thought it likely)—so if it goes through that will give me a lot to do—I had Jones plant 12 ferns in the bush to see if they act—today I did quite a little bit of light gardening myself—planted 20 feet of long scarlet radish seed (from Montreal) and planted a big row of lettuce 2 feet wide for turkeys and hoed up the cabbages in the early garden—the farm with Lou is running fine—the hens lay enough eggs to buy all the food for all the poultry—cows and horses on pasture, cost nothing, and never again—Hatley sells asparagus at 7 cents a bunch (13 pieces) i.e. roughly 2 pieces for a cent (I bought one bunch to learn) at that rate my garden will give $5.00 worth in May and June . . . I am keeping quite a lot of early stuff for another garden;

. . . (Trout) Johnson wrote in answer to my letter that the bull is to be put on a chain in a yard—so your fears were well grounded—Aubrey may come tomorrow so that the cook is trying a cold meat pie . . . Today we tried Irish stew but it was more Irish than stew—the (dumplings) like gobs of dough— When you get this you'll be all full up of bridge and golf and evening dress and conversation about Chechoslovakia; but believe me a talk on pigs has more body to it and touches real life much closer

Stephen (Leacock)

*To Barbara Nimmo*

[The Old Brewery Bay
Orillia, Ontario]
Sunday May 22.38
7 am. Ideal Weather,—
wonderful, all sunshine
& early birds & blossoms.

Dear Bâ

I was so glad to get your letter—I hadnt realize that you are still in hospital—I am so glad the baby is such a fine child—do you propose to say "Baby" or begin with "Nancy" right away . . . I send you $18$\frac{00}{}$ but have to date it June 1st as I am trying to avoid overdraft. I was doing fine with finance till illness hit me down, not quite so easy just now—up here I've being going into it closely in a way neither you nor I had time to—For instance I find that from May 1st to May 15 we served 333 meals (Lou & Albanie eat here, 2 maids, Stevie since May 8 & Mrs. Shaw & Peggy part time) and that they cost 17 cents each for outside supplies —but as many things represented "stocking up" to start & as inside supplies increase greatly (broilers, vegetables) I hope to get down to close to 10 cents: at an average of 5 people per meal (when Lou & Albanie go back, that is 1$\frac{50}{}$ a day or 45$^{00}$ a month,—one can run a latitude of 45 to 60,—. . . . Similarly the fowls, eating by the measured pound of food of which I know the cost are running at about a little over $15$^{00}$ a month: but the hens lay not far from 50 cents a day (20 cents a day cash rest we eat), so that the hens are very nearly feeding the 225 broilers—as soon as planted food comes in I'll have all the hens & their eggs for nothing . . . . I shall be anxious to hear what happens about the paper. I hope that Donald finds a buyer . . . But as I said before always remember that you can at any time come & live here & all expenses vanish & Don has time to look round . . . Apart from that I suppose you both plan to come up with Baby presently . . The boathouse is quite undisturbed, but, listen,—I must make a noise like "books & study" in it,—fill up the shelves & go & read the newspaper there,—then out of the kindness of my heart I clear out of my "study" when you & Don come——no doubt you guess why—stop & think—if not the solution is that I want the income tax inspector to think what a decent fellow I must be to give up my working premises for my niece's holiday—you see at present I have a $750 exemption for "working library premises": that would expire last Jan 1 unless I go back to my house . . . But in my 1937 return I put down working library premises Montreal & 2 Orillia (& a note that they too excluded, as they do, the Montreal one . . . But as yet I haven't seen the boat house—The outer wharf is smashed flat & floating but the house looks beautiful—but you & Don may prefer to have your old room here, bathrooms & Stevies room for a maid, & keep the boat house for fun & entertainment . . . . I have been getting better & hope to God I stay that way for 30 years . . I hate to think of it . . I have begun writing again last week & even light gardening: my back is easily tired & I cant stoop without difficulty & at times in the middle of the day I have to sit still for 2 or 3 hours but in spite of that I surprise everybody at the way I get well .... George & Mary came up both fine & very interesting about their trip—Stevie has been interested every minute about the Baby, as I was, but he never writes & is too young to realize that people want to hear: nowadays if the Queen had a baby I'd write "Dear Queen, this is great news—" but young people dont understand that

> y.a.uncle
> Stephen Leacock

## To Mrs Herbert T. Shaw

[The Old Brewery Bay
Orillia, Ontario]
24 of May Tues 1938

Dear Fitz

Just got your letter (10.30) & settle down in my library with a fire to answer it—It rained all day yesterday & today raw & cold with a high wind & occasional flecks of sun—great stuff—Lou a holiday & nothing to do with it—the two maids going home for midday dinner & back in the evening—Albanie on guard & I sent word to Rowe to come over & set out cucumbers & tomatoes great big plants in cages in the barnyard garden—I had Lou cover it with 8 inches of old manure all over it & a load of sun—it is warm & sheltered & ought to grow wonderful stuff—Aubrey gave me a <u>basket</u> of wonderful asparagus on Sunday so I cut what I had here this morning a pretty good cutting & sent it with the girls to Brechin as their family garden hasn't got it ... I've been working well & so I feel cheerful. This morning I sent away to New York the plan for my book on education & suggested (to the Times) that they let me do six articles of 3000 words each without any <u>pledge</u> that they will buy them but merely an assurance that they think it the kind of stuff they want ... if they say yes & if I do the articles I will use part of the money to shingle stain the barnyard buildings & put ~~cub~~ cobblestones in the barnyard ... Charlie, as I said, has been very crazy . . . I made a plan to have him go into the hospital here but George by phone says no, that on receipt of my letter he will only curse & swear & fly off somewhere else—so there is nothing I can do; I have no money to look after him. . . . George & Mary turned up on Sunday at 4$\frac{30}{}$ just as the Morphy's left at 4 pm ... but then there were no maids in so I made them a cup of tea & had to let them drive back without dinner—George said that Carrie said that Don Nimmo said that they they were only putting the paper into receivership because the present partners couldn't agree on terms of sale to an outsider & one man ~~hange~~ hung out hoping to be paid extra—apparently under their incorporation deed a mere majority cannot <u>sell</u> the concern. . . . It seems that Barbara had a very hard time

but that she & the baby are now well. . . . Yesterday in the middle of the rain;
drizzle a lot 3$\underline{30}$ pm some one came in a car & blew & blew outside the house—
no one went so at last I did—I saw a car with people & thought it for the
maids—so I turned to go back—Then some one called—It was Chris Beaton
& her sister Park Scott & another—imagine sitting there blowing blowing
blowing & not getting out—<u>I aplogized for not being able to ask them</u> in. & let
them go. Did they really think I was such a bloody fool as to suppose they
<u>wanted to see me</u>—!! Let them buy their own drinks,—but imagine by God the
nerve of blowing! blowing! blowing!

— — — — — — — —

I am so glad that René may come up with you—That will be fine if he can
. . . I expect tomorrow to move back the matting into the billiard room & I
propose to get Swinton to make a cushion for the window seat . . . In any case
<u>you</u> hurry up & come. The garden idea is at its height & lots to do all the time—
It still seems cold to put plants out but if the ones I put in your garden fail I still
have more in reserve—

Stephen

## To Barbara Nimmo

Old Brewery Bay<br>Orillia Ont°<br>May 28 1938

Dear Barbara

Keep this letter as a business document. Your letter of May 26th tells me that
the Income Tax people demand from you $21.65 for 1933, $19.15 for 1934 &
$22.43 for 1935.—in all $63.23. I had previously promised, & still promise, to
look after this. But at present I am short of ready money. If you care to let it slide
for, say, 3 months more, I will be responsible for what it slides to. If you care to
pay it out of your savings I will be responsible for it with interest at 3 percent (I
presume that at least equals your savings rate) until I pay it and this letter can be
held binding against my estate & is binding also on Stevie as accepted by his
signature and I herewith append a demand note jointly from us so that in case
of emergency you can cash it, and in case of forgetfulness or disagreement you
are safe-guarded

y. affec uncle<br>Stephen Leacock

Signed as indicated above

Stephen Leacock Jr

- - - - - - - - - - - - - - - - - -

Orillia May 28 1938

On demand we jointly and severally promise to pay to Barbara Nimmo (Mrs Donald Nimmo) at the Bank of Montreal Guy & Sherbrooke St Montreal the sum of $~~$63.23~~ with interest at 3 per cent till paid.
$95.93 S.L.

Stephen Leacock
Stephen Leacock Jr

## To Barbara Nimmo

Orillia
May 28. 38

Dear Bâ

The income tax is OK . . They couldnt <u>collect</u> it as the US govt doesn't collect Canadian taxes, nor vice versâ, but they could & would forbid your entry. So I guess it has to be paid.

I could pay it, but I am trying to accumulate a little available lee-way in the next month or two so as to avoid all overdrafts. I just got by this month. June will be easier. But you realize that if need be I can send you a cheque at any time . . . . I hope that everything is going on well—George explained to us the situation of the paper as he got it from your mother and it sounded as if the chance of a favorable sale was good. I suppose your summer plans are still a little vague & depend partly on the question of Don's holidays. I havent been into the boathouse but imagine that it is in good shape . . Stevie is always going to write to you & never does . . . . I am trying to get started writing but it's hard going: on the other hand I have had time for the first time to try to get this place running on a proper basis. Love to you all

y.a.u.
Stephen Leacock

## To Barbara Whitley

[The Old Brewery Bay
Orillia, Ontario]
May 31 38

Dear Miss Whitley

I received your letter—am so glad to hear how interested you are—I sent your letter to Major Murray, underscored in red the part that you couldn't write him as girl to girl about your going away—& asked him to write and fix everything. He will.

In regard to the text of broadcasts,—change & alter as you like—I didnt look over them closely—turn "readers" in something equivalent in the first person

For example
In the one about roughing it in the bush, the lady speaks to the butler and he answers "yes ma'am"—this changes in radio monologue with—"you say, yes,"—and then on she goes

I told Major Murray not to consider my part in it—If you cant get over with <u>mine</u> you can with your own—mine are only useful that as my name is very well known it makes it a reasonable thing to do—same with you (when you are nearly seventy, ~~and~~ that sounds the wrong way but no doubt you can see what I mean

with best wishes
Stephen Leacock


## To Mrs Herbert T. Shaw

[The Old Brewery Bay
Orillia, Ontario]
Thursday Je 9 38

Dear Fitz

I hope you went to Prescott  Movry & didnt neglect it—a little done now may save a lot of trouble & now that you are getting so much better in every kind of way   it is the right time for getting better still—so go now if you havent ... It is just 1 pm & is my tired time & today for cussedness I seem to hit a very tired streak, so I'll rest—I wrote quite a little sketch today on my third <u>Memoir</u> called "<u>So This is the United States</u>" & got along fine with it—and also started putting together some little stories of about 200 words each to see if I can syndicate them,—as <u>Stephen Leacock's Stories</u>—they are partly taken out of old stuff & partly done new—I also superintended Lou & Rowe trying to make the horse lawn mower work—it had occurred to me that what it needs is <u>more weight</u> piled on it to give it power, which has turned out to be right—it cuts the tennis court like a billiard table but of course it cant work (& isn't meant to) in long grass—on a lawn like yours Lou could cut with it at a rate equal to three Pauls at once. It is lovely weather but a little cool & all your place looks fine. I saw ~~pa~~ Paul about the door shutter. I have not heard from Rene but expect that he'll telegraph and come tomorrow   as you notice my hand is cramped with writing but I guess you can read it.

Stephen

## To E.G. McCracken[1]

[The Old Brewery Bay
Orillia, Ontario]
June 10 1938

E.G. McCracken
183 St George St
Toronto

Dear McCracken

I am glad to see that we are to have our meeting at Hamilton and I enclose my cheque for dinner though I cant play golf—You may have heard that I had an operation last winter & was in hospital March 22 to May 1st . . . I am better now but not yet in quite normal shape. But I will drive to Hamilton in time for the dinner &, if the boys will excuse me, leave again about 9³⁰——I hope to have with me Professor René du Roure and as he is a McGill professor I presume it is in order to bring him to the dinner as my guest & so make my cheque to cover two places . . It seems so sad to think that poor Buster cant be with us

Best regards
Stephen Leacock

1    E.G. McCracken was the founding secretary of the McGill Society of Ontario.

## To Barbara Whitley

[The Old Brewery Bay
Orillia, Ontario]
Monday Je 13 '38

Dear Miss Whitley

I was so glad to hear from Major Murray that you are to go "on the air" for 6 successive broadcasts weekly beginning early in August . . he asked me to arrange a length of <u>14 minutes</u> . . easily done . . . Please send me copies of the broadcasts I sent you (I will of course pay for the typing) and mark how long each takes you as it stands & I will lengthen or shorten accordingly—I cant remember whether I sent you three or four—nor quite which—as soon as I hear from you I'll send you the rest of 6, all cut to 14 of your minutes . . . I'm so glad you are to do this. It will be a fine start for all sorts of work of yours later

Very sincerely
Stephen Leacock

*To Barbara Nimmo*                    [The Old Brewery Bay
                                      Orillia, Ontario]
                                      Tues. June 14 38

Dear Barbara

I think it would be much better for you to have your old room anyway—
You can have Stevie's with it as he has moved down with me & you can have
the bathroom to yourselves—The boathouse would never do except in the very
hot weather & all the wharf (coils, stones, everything) is smashed into a tangled
mass making all bathing impossible—I cant fix it till the hot weather . . I am
sorry the situation about the paper is still so uncertain. I hope it will clear up
but of course I need hardly say again that you can come & live here as long as
you like if you hit an interruption between this editorship & a new job . . Still
will hope it wont be long before the paper is settled & you & Don can come
together for a holiday . . . I am getting better very fast now & writing a lot. René
is up here & Mrs Shaw & Peggy are coming (to their own house) the day after
tomorrow George & Mary were here on Sunday, both very well. Your uncle
Charlie blew in & out, seemed much better

                                      y.a.u.
                                      Stephen Leacock


*To Barbara Nimmo*                    [The Old Brewery Bay
                                      Orillia, Ontario]
                                      Je 24. 38

Dear Barbara

In making your arrangements please count on my supplying you with a
little nurse maid for Nancy to sleep in the room next you & have nothing else
to do—I didnt mention it sooner because the financial outlook was pretty
cloudy, or at least uncertain. But one or two extra cheques have come in my way
by May & so I can with great pleasure supply the maid to Nancy as my first
present to her, the first I hope of lots. I will have a partition door put up & that
will cut you off with your own bath room & towels & laundry & the maid
beside you—The moment the hot weather came I realized that your own room
is far better than the other end, always cool & fresh . . . . . . . Let me know how
things go & remember that you & come up here & Don can come & go during
the unsettled interregnum & there is nothing to worry over . . . . Rene was here,
just gone . . talked of you & Don very often but hasn't written . . . he & Stevie
were laughing over being the only people not to write, yet really the people
immensely interested . . .

I've not been very well, but merely nearer to mental depression: heavy
illness takes its toll but I mean to get out of it.

Let me know about your plans. This house is all yours as soon as you want it, & it will be a great help to me to have you here——I have two excellent girls as maids, quite exceptional from Britain,—sisters, of a family of 9 sisters & 1 brother—it is their younger sister I can get for you .. the great advantage is that then they will <u>all</u> be available all the time. I spoke to Mary the older one about the idea & said that I would not speak definitely as you might prefer plans of your own but I wanted to know if she thought her sister would be suitable & would come. It all seems on

> y.a.u.
> Stephen Leacock

## To Barbara Whitley

[The Old Brewery Bay
Orillia, Ontario]
July 2. 1938

Dear Miss Whitley

Fine! I was just writing to you when I got your letter. I'll raise Mrs Eiderdown to 14 minutes & send you 3 more one of which is called <u>John & I or How I nearly Lost My Husband</u> & two more that I'll select . . . . Chop & change anything as you like because the more you suit it to your own feelings & ideas the better you do it . . . There is a beautiful piece of mine just coming out in the Saturday Evening Post (I read the proofs today) called <u>My Victorian Girlhood</u> by Lady <u>Nearleigh Slopover</u> that would be just the thing but I dont know whether the necessary rights will be clear in time for use in your series of six . . . Watch for it (I'll send you a copy anyway) & if you fancy it I'll see if I can get the rights .. I'll get the new stuff ready as soon as I can . . . I have various other enquiries for radio stuff . . . I am sure you can succeed and you will find that doing work as the fruit of one's imagination is above all other kind

> Very sincerely & with best
> wishes
> Stephen Leacock

<u>P.S.</u> On second thoughts Lady Slopover is in a different vein .. Keep it to do by itself.

## To Barbara Whitley

[The Old Brewery Bay
Orillia, Ontario]
July 4 38

Supplementary: this is the Second Letter
Dear Miss Whitley.

I enclose <u>John & I</u> or <u>How I nearly lost my husband</u>: it counts, as I reckon it to 3000 words; that in 14 minutes is about 210 words a minute; I dont think you speak as fast as that. So it will probably need shortening but you can easily do that

There seems a little confusion about length: you say that Mrs Eiderdown (not enclosed; I am keeping it to lengthen it) runs 5 minutes; that sounds correct as it is under 900 words. But you say that the Wrong Woman can all be done in 14 minutes—yet it looks like 4000 words—But you can if need be shorten it to 14 minutes—

I will lengthen out Mrs Eiderdown to more than double its present length. That will be one monologue: The Wrong Woman is another: John & I another: and I will expand a little sketch that I have into a monologue called Miss Maisie Beattit Enters College and I'll dig up, or write another, to make six Tell me, when I send you my Victorian Girlhood how what you think of it as No 6,—can you imitate a very firm, very autocratic voice (English) of a lady of sixty? I can, ever so easily so I am sure you can. If you could do that so that the voice itself is a treat, then it might be good business to use the story—its just a nice length—I would write & ask the Post for permission, even if we had to announce it as from the Post

. . . (So you wrote in a thunderstorm! & such a firm hand to . . . no radio will frighten you . . .

> Very sincerely
> Stephen Leacock

## To Barbara Whitley

The Old Brewery Bay
Orillia
July 5 38

Dear Miss Whitley

Herewith Mrs Eiderdown with enough material to reinforce her to 14 minutes—You will see that the style is more easy & broken—because its written as talk—you will notice also that I put in "my dear"* as if to a fellow-female listener—as you did in your monologue in the Morgan Hall

Decide which piece you wish to begin with & you have in hand 3,—Mrs Eiderdown—The Wronged Woman & John & I  I will send you Maisie Beattit as soon as I write it—Let me know how you get on

> Very sincerely & with
> best wishes
> Stephen Leacock

Put it in elsewhere if you like

## *To Barbara Nimmo*

The Old Brewery Bay
Orillia
July 6. 38

Dear Barbara

No plan of mine, except the plan of getting ill again or dying, shall interfere with you & Don bringing Nancy to Orillia . . . But no doubt you are right in the plans you are making . . . Your room will be ready at any time & I can get a little maid at short notice . . . . I hope everything is going on all right: but in any case dont worry over finance: Don is young & your life just beginning & Don has lots of ability for all sorts of work so that as long as you see your way ahead for the time being the future is all right—While I am here or alive you neednt worry about the question of bread & butter  But on the other hand perhaps the outlook for selling the paper may be brightening & things looking up—Write & give me the up to date situation

News here:—

Kelly is back in Montreal working in the Cote des Neiges Road house—Tina in N. Brunswick with her mother & expected here in a few days—Lou here leaving for the mines next week—the place running like clockwork—we put in 11 tons of hay without a drop of rain—gardens, poultry,—all in apple pie order. Uncle Charlie comes & goes & is back to (his) normal—

y.a.u.
Stephen Leacock

## *To Barbara Nimmo*

[The Old Brewery Bay
Orillia, Ontario]
Wed Aug 3 38

Dear Barbara

I have been wanting to hear from you & hope that things are going well & that you & Don & Nancy will soon be here . . . but in any case write & tell me all the news & what the prospect is for Don getting settled again . . . Not much news here . . I had rather a bad time with neurasthenic depression but I think that it has gone,—for a spell anyway. Apart from that everything very quiet & pleasant. Tonight Peggy Shaw has organised an open air entertainment & I am to help with it . . had invited Uncle George but he is not well,—used up by his western trip just over . . . Uncle Charlie, I am sorry to say, seems very batty . . but as he has written me off I see nothing of him.

Do write, & do remember that if trips are not just right for the moment for Don's future, at least you can have this place & while I am alive nothing very much can happen to you & though job needs waiting for, time goes

y. a. uncle
Stephen Leacock

## To Barbara Whitley

[The Old Brewery Bay
Orillia, Ontario]
Tuesday Sep 6. 28

My dear Barbara

Again I was absolutely prevented from hearing you (last Saturday)—But I heard on all sides glowing accounts of how well you did the monologue.

I am so sorry that your mother doesn't want you to go on. But that is case where outsiders have no right to advise . . . I don't expect to be back in Montreal (apart from a visit of a day or so) till rather late in ~~August~~ October but I hope that when I come, you & your mother will lunch with me one day at the Club . . And meantime I shall be all ears & attentions to listen to you next Saturday . . . I gather from what you say that the two monologues you are to do of your own will follow at the same day & hour. But be sure to let me know if they are put on a a different hour . . . .

with very best wishes
Stephen Leacock

## To Mrs Herbert T. Shaw

[The Old Brewery Bay
Orillia, Ontario]
Wed  8 am
(September 13, 1938)

Dear Fitz

I didnt hear from you yesterday which perhaps helped to give me a sort of slump down, and I wasnt so well in the night but I'm up & trying to snap back & get away from depression & realize what a fine recovery I've made—Duck shooting is tomorrow & Kelly's going out at 3 in the morning; if he gets enough I'll send you a couple by express. After he gets back I am going with him to Oro at 10 to 12 to get thimble berry bushes & there are ducks there too—so your chance isnt so bad—I read the NY Times a good deal yesterday (Weekly Record) & for the first time I begin to fear that there <u>may</u> be war—crazy though it seems. If so what in hell is England to do,—and still heller, Canada—Kelly is going in with messages & a bank letter & will take this. I'll write later today

Stephen

## To Barbara Whitley

[The Old Brewery Bay
Orillia, Ontario]
Sun Sep 18 38

My dear Barbara

My best congratulations—I was delighted to listen to you last night . . You have a wonderful gift for the technique of radio—But I mustn't say too much or you'll be disappointed at giving it up: but the way to look at it is that, in a sense, all art is one, and the same gift will show itself in writing or other ways— Gladstone Murray called me up a week ago & spoke with great praise but the line was working badly & I cant quote his exact words, but he spoke with enthusiasm

I shall look forward to seeing you: I dont get back till about the tenth.

With best regards
Stephen Leacock

## To Mrs Herbert T. Shaw

Orillia  (Sep 19  38)

Dear Fitz

I was glad to hear from you—I always am—and I miss you . . . The European situation is this; please remember that I said it. England wont any longer make war over any European frontier—the German in Chechoslovakia will be given autonomy & may join Germany—France wont make war without England— Hitler will be told that if he says 'Colonies'—that means war at once. I havent been well but I think is just nerves. It hits me early in the morning but I get out of it—I am sure nothings wrong—We are making asparagus and I have bought 50 extra roots to make a bed at your place. Tell me at once where—the roots come on Friday & we must make the bed—answer so that Ill get it ~~Thursd~~ Wednes. Be sure. I'll be so glad when you come—I am so glad Peggy is getting busy: if she wants to do commercial stuff I will write people about it

Stephen Leacock

## To Mrs Herbert T. Shaw

Tues. 8$^{30}$ am
(September 20, 1938)

Begin here
All the figures of accounts below are
just for myself: you needn't read them

Dear Fitz

That was a nice long letter you wrote on Sunday—fine—& such a lot in it—Ill be so glad when you come—I havent the paper yet for the war news. Rene talks of nothing else. You'll hear him. He goes down today—I am trying to get over my slump, ever so hard, and I think Ill crawl out of it. Its just <u>fear</u> that gives me a nerve collapse in the morning. But I get out of it—I dont know how I'll live in the city with no out-of-doors each minute,—I hope at the Windsor, with a car to the mountain twice a day if need be   I think I will walk into town this morning & get the paper to see the news. England wont be in any war and I dont think France will either; and thank God the chance of Canada being in looks pretty damn small . . . . . I am making ~~an~~ the asparagus bed—It costs money but that kind of money is well spent—Its the <u>current</u> stuff that bothers me,—gasoline, gasoline gasoline,—Food cost an awful lot in August Don & Barbara & Rene—Hatley net bill was $145<u>00</u> instead of $98 as in July— and with that our own eggs & vegetables & fowls—butter cost $14<u>00</u>—The washing costs a lot of soap—Still I had the money to pay for it all, if I take the summer as a <u>total</u>, but for example in the month of September by itself I shall have spent at Orillia about $800 and my income in that month as it comes in looks only about $675; but in the autumn months, October November & December, my income in sight would be $800 a month and expenses would be only about $700—$600 in Montreal & $100, or less, at Orillia. Kelly & Tina & Albanie get each month a total of 21 for Kelly, 20 for Tina, 15 for housekeeping, 2 for cigarettes, 65 cents for paper & 3<sup>00</sup> Albanie,—in all $62<sup>65</sup>—Taxes are over & above this & mean after deducting   Troops rent about $100 a month. There's nothing in all that that I ought to worry about, especially as another year at Orillia I can have only 1 ~~made~~ maid just use a car for little trips & have Jones for 4 hours a day for garden & house work—I write all this out as a way of not worrying about it. Moreover if I get busy & keep writing I chase the wolf miles away from the door . . . I found on turning over the sheet that it had writing on it already—just a bit of one of my articles of the summer. I will be so glad when you come up. The bed is being put out of your room today and the roof mended (I think its done) & I'll have fires lit ~~evey~~ every day or so to get it all well aired I must quit & either walk or drive to town to get a paper

Stephen

P.S. The mushrooms passed off again—but last night heavy frost there will be lots in a day or so & meantime we can take mushroom walks anyway

## To Barbara Nimmo

Orillia
Tues Sep 20 '38

Dear Bâ

Just rec'd your letter; sorry to hear that so far things are still unsettled—But the horizon can & will change soon—and I am sure that neither you nor Don are silly enough to start to worry ahead of time . . . . I'm having the cucumbers done up for lunch—meantime give me an address in Windsor where I can send a box and I will send you by express 2 chickens 1 duck and enough apples & garden stuff to make up 100 pounds—All that only costs me $1⁰⁰ to send & when you get it there you can unpack it & sling it into the car and there'll be no duty—at least so I suppose—If easier I could send 2 boxes at 50 cents each— let me know if you can get the stuff in without objection & I'll send it

I am so glad Nancy is so fine. Everybody fell in love with her here—Stevie goes down on the 28 & Mrs Shaw comes up & if she does I'll stay another week but I cant stay alone, as my nerves are poor. Finance is tight but I will send you that 90 something anytime you get stuck & I'll hope soon to send typing. I've not been quite so well but soon I expect to be writing a lot

> Love to Don & yourself &
> Nancy
> y.a.u.
> Stephen Leacock

## To Mrs Herbert T. Shaw

Sat Sep 24 (1938)
¼ to 8 am

Dear Fitz

Your kind sweet telegram came yesterday. I cant tell you how I felt towards you for sending it. My nerves had been getting me beaten in spite of all I could do & your message lifted me up—and now with the morning comes the news of Andrews death[1] and the awful war news, as I gather from Kelly—I'm going in with him at 8 for the papers—Ill send this later with a special delivery—I feel just overwhelmed at Andrews death . . . and the war,—surely to God it won't come

1  Sir Andrew Macphail.

## To Barbara Whitley

The Old Brewery Bay
Orillia, Sunday Sept 25

Miss Barbara Whitley
4339 Westmount Ave
Westmount

My dear Barbara

Your "visitors day" last night was just splendid. I am sure everybody has been telling you so—You should do it on the stage & since you dont like professional stuff do it at McGill with an imaginary baby & an imaginary nurse—Monologue work on the stage is wonderful stuff . . . I used to be great friends with Eric Sale (he's only been dead 3 or 4 years, so perhaps you remember his name—he did wonderful stuff & it will interest you to know that he got all his effects, slowly almost painfully with ever so much work—I shall look forward to seeing you when I come back; I am practically certain that Stevie & I will live in the Windsor Hotel . . . let me say again how much I enjoyed the monologue . . . the only objection is that radio after all is limited,—its for blind people—By the way I've lectured sometimes, particularly in London to Blind People—I mean as a humorist to entertain them—there is, I found, a trick in it—your voice must never stop—a stop is like a sudden chill so if you are asked to entertain them at any time remember to keep a sort of current of tone or undertone going all the time.

> With very best wishes
> Stephen Leacock

*To Barbara Nimmo*                      Windsor Hotel
                                        Montreal
                                        Oct 15 1938

Dear Barbara

I am so glad that I am to be Nancy's godfather, really ever so pleased & only sorry that I cant be at the Christening . . in such cases you have a proxy (not foxy) godfather, I believe . .

I'm glad that the customs packet turned out so well: I expect to go to Orillia in a week & I'll send another . . . . I hope that you & Don are not worrying over the present dull outlook: at your age of life & with your health if you can see your way ahead for two years (as you easily can) you dont need to worry: by worry I mean of course worry: one may take thought & make efforts but worry is different . . .

Stevie & I have wonderful rooms in the Windsor, on Dorchester St, full of sun beginning at sun-rise & lasting till toward noon—a huge sitting room 24 × 18—Finance is tight but I can carry it. I go to Orillia on a definite basis so that there's no feed to buy for poultry or anything, $75⁰⁰ a month covers wages & house keeping money & Alb ($23 + $21 + $3 + $15) with $13⁰⁰ for extras——and in return Tina does my washing for the cost of express & the place is there for Xmas—My income, I mean, pension plus investments, wont cover the present rate of expenses while Stevie has to be at college but I am still earning money with writing & that makes the difference——Everybody here always asks of you & they all seem to have heard of Nancy & are delighted to hear what a fine baby she is . . . .

Best love to both of you I'll write from Orillia

> y a u
> Stephen Leacock

## To Barbara Nimmo

Windsor Hotel Montreal<br>Tue Oct 25. 1938.

Dear Barbara

I have just got back from Orillia. The rings are in the bank box . . . if any were stolen they were junk. . . . . .

Kelly is leaving for Orillia with the truck & I am telling him to send you each week a box with 2 chickens 1 doz eggs & apples & vegetables to fill up—I forget if you took away jam: if not write to Tina & tell her to put <u>jam</u> in the box

Till Xmas I am a little tied up for money & trying to get together a balance to clear my taxes: but after Xmas I hope you can lean on me a little & I'll try to get work that you can do for me . . . . My health has been too uncertain to feel sure of things but I expect to be better able to tackle things . . . Meantime even this little item of a weekly box of stuff will come in for something

With love to you all<br>
y. a. uncle<br>
Stephen Leacock

## To Barbara Nimmo

Windsor Ho.<br>Montreal<br>Nov 29 38

Dear Bâ

Herewith enclosed Britannica assignment—They pay $50—I'll give you $40 & Jack Culliton $10 & nothing for me—

You dont <u>write</u>—merely get the material in your own words—to correspond with what is there and <u>what is new</u>—I will get Jack to look it over & verify & I'll write ɏ it & you can type it for nothing—you should have it back here without fail by <u>Dec 3</u> & I'll get it to the editor by Dec 15——Dont worry if cost of postage seems high—I can look after that all right—I am so glad these odd bits of work are available—If I were in better shape I could do more. And I think I am not ill, only nervous, and ought to be all well soon . . I'm so glad the Orillia box comes in handy . . . Above all dont worry: things will take a turn soon

love to yourselves & Nancy<br>
Stephen Leacock

## To James Keddie[1]

[The Windsor<br>Montreal]<br>Dec 4 1938

Dear Mr. Keddie

Thank you very much for your letter of Nov 29. I'm so glad the book titles idea worked out so well

—Yes, the article you suggest is just the kind of thing I'd like to write

—I remember when I was a resident boarding school master, an overindulgent rich parent in speaking of his over-indulged rich son whom he was leaving at the school, said to me.

"Jimmy, of course, is a boy you can lead but cant drive."—

I thought to myself, "oh, cant I? Wait till you're off the premises & we'll see" . . . .

Indeed the article you suggest is just the kind of thing I'd like to tinker with when I go up to my country home for Xmas,—

I had some articles in the Times (N. York) on education & I am to expand them into a book for next autumn & so I am interested in doing all sorts of education stuff just now

best regards
Stephen Leacock

1    A Scotsman by birth (b. 1907), author and publisher James Keddie (Jr) worked for the Bellows-Reeve Company.

## To Barbara Nimmo

[The Windsor
Montreal]
Dec 9, 1938

Dear Barbara

Yes, do, by all means come on Friday—that will be fine—Stevie & I arrived on the noon train today & the house is nice & comfortable & will be all right for Nancy & we can have a fine Xmas together & talk of what to do next. I'm sorry that things are not opening up yet, but dont worry: it will be all right

best love to you all
y. a. u.
Stephen Leacock

## To Mrs Herbert T. Shaw

(Dec 19 38)
Monday morning
8 am

THIS COMES FIRST—IT WAS THE POSTSCRIPT TO THE LETTER I TORE UP

Postscript
A little later

——Im sorry I didnt write a more cheerful letter but Ill send it anyway as you always understand. There is not much news here. Dr Ardagh came in last night. Played a string of billiards: the table is fine with new lights & the shades painted white . . Barbara & Don & Nancy are due to arrive on Friday night by motor & will stay for a week; so you'll see them. The weather is soft and beautiful & the house as warm as anything. I'll be so glad when you come and it will make me feel all right. I'll write again. I haven't been over to your house as the snow is very wet; not frozen snow . . I hope Mary is better: give her my best and tell her I was asking. She has done so much that she needs a rest . . and I hope you are over your tiredness. I shall expect a letter today and that will be fine

Stephen

Monday
10 am

Second Part

Dear Fitz—I felt so low a good part of yesterday & for some time in the night that I wrote a grumbling letter & afterwards wrote a postscript to it & then later tore it up. I know it is all <u>imagination</u> that I feel. I half wished I had phoned David & got him to say so. It's mental help I need,—just cursed sensations that I create myself—I'll be glad when you come up

## To Barbara Nimmo

Orillia Ont.
Dec 19. 38

Dear Barbara—

As we are all so hard up I'm afraid we must reduce Xmas to a minimum: so I only enclose a mere mite,—\$3$\underline{^{00}}$ for yourself to get some stockings or if you still have lots, any other little thing to wear, \$2$\underline{^{00}}$ for some trifle for Nancy, & 1$\underline{^{00}}$ to spend on Don, 50 cents on Stevie & 50 cents for me—I'm sure you'll understand. Finance is all right with me but tight: and only all right as long as I can work: and of course just now you & Don should spend as little as you can— So I'll expect you towards Dark on Friday—The road is open across the track & is better than the first turn by the lane especially if new snow comes.

In haste
y. a. u.
Stephen Leacock

## To Mrs Herbert T. Shaw

The Old Brewery Bay
Orillia, Ont.
Wed. 2 pm   Dec 21   38

Dear Fitz

I had such a bad time for 2 nights that I nearly telegraphed & telephoned you . . . I know that it is only broken nerves & imagination & I am doing all I can − − − but mental illness is hard to fight. I wanted to ask Dave Mackenzie to send me two or three words of reassurance. I <u>know</u> that I am only made bad by fear, & apprehension & I <u>know</u> that it is just craziness—all my physical symptoms are better than they were six months ago—far better—and mostly better than before my operation. But my mind seems in danger . . So I meant to send you a special letter & also telegraph you to speak to David—You see I have no pains, no stoppages, no illness—and if I have to get up again & again & again it is only because fear is keeping me ~~aweek~~ awake – – – so this morning I got up & walked,—with no fatigue at all,—to Orillia & round town—& I think I can be better tonight—but if need be after this letter comes to you Ill phone you. I'm so sorry & so ashamed—it's all only fear & mental disease—but it's hard. I'll be so glad when you come up & I shall try to be all better by then

I dont know when René is coming but I suppose about Saturday. Kelly is fixing up your outside door today: I decided you'd rather have it closed up altogether to keep out draft. I am getting cannel coal for your room and I think it will be warm & nice. The weather is beautiful—mild & soft

Edward Ardagh came out last night & we played billiards & I told him I wasn't awfully well but that there was nothing he could do except give me his company. I'm sorry to write this way—when you are here I'll feel better: The billiard table is just beautiful and it will be a treat to play endless games.

Stephen


## To Barbara Nimmo

[The Windsor
Montreal]
Jan 10. 39

Dear Bâ

The Bank will send you by this mail a Detroit draft for $30<u>00</u>. This is $10<u>00</u> for the caning article and $20<u>00</u> on the back pay due in 1938 when the income tax account, which was part of your salary was sent to me. It is understood that all & every payment I make to you either in cash or back pay or in goods supplied or for maintenance has been & is to be in future free of all income tax either US or Canada: so that if now or in future these payments of cash or maintenance lift your income into reach of taxes, I am to reimburse you for the amount of tax you have thereby to pay.

So you had better keep a copy of this letter & later on you will send me a statement from your books of everything in 1938 including these $20 tax instalments as the account was not rendered till then & so they belong in there. Better send me a typed copy of this letter from my file . . . send me word how things are going. love to you all

y. a. u.
Stephen Leacock

## To Barbara Nimmo

[The Windsor
Montreal]
Mon Feb 20 39

Dear Bâ

You recall that ~~I~~ idea of an article on <u>self expression</u> of children as damn nonsense—see if you can get me reference to books (up to date) or magazines— I dont need selections or passages just names of books if there are such—I sent you more stuff for Miller didn't? . . I've done a lot of work this winter: my health has threatened to go wrong once or twice but apart from that things are all right financially & I am moving slowly ahead, indeed at quite a pace. I mention it so that if you are worried over finance you will be less so if you know that Orillia will be there to fall back on. This month my account is a little tight but any day it will loosen up & I'll send an instalment plus typing money—Write & tell me how things are with Don? Anything doing yet? and Nancy?

Best love to you all
y. a.
Stephen Leacock

## To E.G. McCracken

[The Windsor
Montreal]
Feb 18 39

Dear McCracken

Best thanks for your note about the meeting of the 20th . . . . But I cant come as I am down here for the winter, my son is still at McGill (3$^{rd}$ year) so I spend the college session in Montreal . . . Later on I'll sink onto the bosom of Ontario for practically the whole year

best regards to the boys
Stephen Leacock

## To Barbara Nimmo

March 3, '39

Dear Bâ

Herewith 2 stories. Im so far ahead that from now on you neednt send to Miller direct.

What about your house? Do you get rid of it at Easter. You certainly are very courageous & are not letting yourself be beat. I hope things will soon turn—If you planned a 2 or 3 week visit to Orillia at Easter would that ease finance . . . I expect to go there on April 7 and I think that as a matter of economy I must then stay on for good. In that case I shall engage 2 Harrigans (Gertrude & Irene at $20 & $15) and the house will run easily & if you're there that will give extra help for Nancy. Let me know what you plan about your house.

> best love to you all
> y. a. u.
> Stephen Leacock

P.S. No need to send the Miller sketches flat. He has to reproduce them.


## To Donald Nimmo

[The Windsor
Montreal]
March 26 '39

Dear Don

Yours of March 23—I quite agree about going ahead without ~~furth~~ additional expense—that is, there is only printing & postage—Yet I suggest this,—print another six & keep on sending them by mail to the best (selected) paper in each city—no return stamps they can throw them away—you can if you like write on them, "no return or answer required"—they may succeed in getting over and a very few sales cover costs—If later they caught on we could run the back numbers as new ones—It would be enough to send to, say, 50 papers—a 1 cent envelope & 2 cent stamp is only $1$\frac{50}{}$ a week or if its a 3 cent stamp 2$^{00}$ a week—six weeks of that is $12$\frac{00}{}$—I can stand it—The printing is $10, I think you said

It will be too bad if you lose a lot of time over this for nothing but a worse thing to lose is hope—These things happen in literary work.

Consider this. When a man called Epstein (Publisher's Press Montreal) undertook to syndicate my <u>Nonsense Novels</u> as I wrote them, he printed the first one <u>Gertrude the Governess</u> and sent 1000 copies to the U.S. & <u>didnt sell any</u> . . Ultimately we got $35 each for the series; when I did the second series I got <u>$1000 each</u> for them—so you see literary merit & even effort dont always win—Meanwhile hang on with real estate, . . . . The only thing that seems to me hard luck just now for you is that you are not free to come up & down to Orillia,—which I ~~dont~~ didnt expect to be a condition of a commission job. Love to B & N

> y. a. u.
> Stephen Leacock

## *To E.G. McCracken*

The Old Brewery Bay
Orillia
April 10 39

Dear McCracken

Yours ~~with~~ received & read most sympathetically  I will write to Lewis Douglas: we are excellent friends

In regard to functions: this is what I think

> Men like a good time
> They like a drink
> They like women to be in it
> They dont want it to cost too much
> They dont want <u>long speeches</u> & heavy stuff.

I suggest in each of the three places Hamilton London & Toronto <u>a McGill Smoker</u>, at some place where the cost can be kept low—a good plan would be if any one rich enough to have a big house would let us come there & <u>pay</u> for <u>our own liquor & refreshments</u> = an <u>informal</u> programme. Advertise "There will be no set program & no long speeches, but an informal ~~& impromptu~~ evening of college songs & impromptu ~~stunts~~ stunts & talks . . . ."

There should be a <u>guest of the evening</u> but he must understand that he is not to make a speech—just a couple of words—we could arrange behind the scenes for McGill music & songs . . . I will be glad to be the guest of the evening at Toronto if you care to have me—in spite of what you might think, <u>dont</u> have the three smokers on three successive nights—I know that would ~~to~~ allow one & the same guest at all three but I dont think that helps much—set the dates tentatively & ask Lewis Douglas to come to <u>as many as he can</u> & you'll see he'll come to one.

Talk this plan over, of a McGill Smoker, with the other boys & if you like I will write a circular letter for you . . . . . . I wont write to the Principal until I get your answer.

I have to add in postscript that my health is still uncertain: I am all hell part of the time & the rest all in. But I am sure I could come to Toronto

Suppose you write Gordon Glassco for a list of Ontario undergraduates at McGill & we can circularize them specially

Also, get him to mark the names of any that have done <u>stunts</u> in the McGill shows (lots of them have) & we might get a little act or two done at a smoker . . . The main idea <u>is a big time, lots of booze, women & cheap as Aberdeen</u>

Best regards
Stephen Leacock

## To Mrs Herbert T. Shaw

Orillia, Wed 11 am
Ap 12 39

Dear Fitz

I've written a huge mass of letters to catch up & now the damn things are done I can write to you . . . The weather is queer—thaws all day—snows at night—4 inches yesterday, all gone and then 2 inches last night. Kelly is working on the green house stopping the drip of water where the roof meets the side. Jones finishing my shelves and going to shellac them. Albanie doing chores— bright sun but a hell of a lot of snow still. I did a little writing this morning but can't really get at it till the library etc. in better shape. I can't keep track of it. The Pontiac deal is taking a little time as the Ottawa man won't combine with the Orillia man. I think I can sell the DeSoto for nearly $300 and if I can, I can buy a new car but there's no hurry for a few weeks as the roads are awful and when the frost starts to go out of the Oshawa road (Beaverton and Brechen unpaved) it won't be usable till some time in May. I look forward so much to your coming, when you <u>do</u> come, your room is all ready.—nothing in it but the usual furniture . . no storage or junk. The new ham (the last pig) has turned out a success which means 4 pigs this year. The hams alone have been worth all the pigs cost to buy and feed. I think I'll send for a taxi and ride into Orillia with the mail, especially as I have 2 books in the customs. Freda McGachen is applying for a post at Queen's (Dean of Women) and I have written most warmly in her behalf as I am sure she could do that sort of thing just right.[1] (Perhaps her application is confidential). Morning mail not in yet.

The new staff is tackling Irish stew. When you come you must show them how to do it with lamb. Food is going to be a cheap proposition in this small house (hold) with eggs and butter for nothing and milk for nothing and still enough bacon for three weeks . . . morning mail in but nothing more to answer, thank God! Your letters come in afternoon. I hope I get one today. Give messages to Mary and René.

Affectly,
Stephen Leacock

1   Freda McGachen was in the Department of English at McGill. She later became head of the Montreal *Gazette* Library.

## To Daniel C. Marsh
President, Boston University

[McGill University
Montreal, Canada]
Ap 19. 1939

My dear President Marsh

I cannot tell you how very greatly I appreciate the honour which you suggest on behalf of Boston University. Unfortunately an illness and a serious operation of last year has rendered my health extremely uncertain and prevents me from undertaking so long a journey or incurring the strain involved even on such an honorable & agreeable occasion.

I need hardly say with what regret I find myself compelled to forego the conspicuous distinction proposed

Very faithfully
Stephen Leacock


## To James Keddie

The Old Brewery Bay
Orillia
Ap. 22 1939

Dear Mr Keddie.

Here we are. I wasn't sure whether to use the title <u>Who Canonizes the Classics?</u>—or <u>The Books we call Classics</u>, or to put them together,—<u>Who Canonizes the Books we call Classics?</u>

But I leave that to you: I wonder if you agree with me about George Meredith being gone to oblivion? Yet I once read his books one after the other—students at college now, outside of special classes dont know his name

with best regards
Stephen Leacock


## To Mrs Herbert T. Shaw

Sat April 29 1939

Dear Fitz

That was nice of you to go all the way down to post the letter—and the result was that I got the letter & so was so glad to—you neednt be a bit worried over Peggy & the war—I've come round again to the idea that there wont be again—Hitler can talk & talk, but thats all—Of course I will miss Peggy but after all it's a short trip & you'll enjoy the idea of her going over – – – I got a letter about a McGill Society of Ontario meeting in Toronto and I am settling on <u>May 10</u>—but it only means that I have to go down in the afternoon & back that night or morning train—if I knew when you might come here I'd fix the date to fit    as it is I thought best to let it go at the tenth and if you're here I'll leave at 3 pm & back late at night—A north west wind arose & blew away all the ice—so now it will be warm—last ~~nigtt~~ night Doc. A. came out & he & I played billiards—he played much better than before & it was quite a good game, first at 60 ~~to 100~~ on a hundred & then a fifty point game at 30–50. He won both times,—very close . . . I was at your place today and the dark blue hyacinths are wonderful—nearly out—I dont remember them before—Street was late with your trees as his brother was taken ill & went to hospital but as the trees were still all right, Kelly put them in yesterday—today I had Jones & Albany & the horse, clearing up litter & turning it into light wood—they cleaned up all that dirty place where the ducks were – – – today I bought 4 pigs ($20⁰⁰). I told Kelly that Pig No. 4 must be all mine—up till now I take half the ham & half the bacon & he takes the rest & theres nothing in it for me—but Pig 4,—both hams and all the bacon and all the pork will make it different—I wrote nearly a whole article this morning & so I feel better about work – – I expect to finish it tomorrow . . . Be sure to write—it is nice if you write in the morning after your breakfast, just as if I had come in from my walk & you were talking to me—I hope that Paule Tétrault[1] is all better again: give her messages from me. I may have to send her a rose yet—I wish you were here. We could go fishing at Johnsons. Kelly may go tomorrow—but as have no car I cant go & anyway I dont want to just yet – – – –

Affectionately<br>Stephen Leacock

1    Mr and Mrs Tétrault were friends of Leacock. Their son Claude won a scholarship from McGill to study in France.

## To Mrs Herbert T. Shaw

Orillia Sunday Aft<br>Ap 30 39

Dear Fitz

– – – A lovely bright day but pretty cold wind off the lake from the Northwest—ice all gone & the lake looks itself . . today I did no other work than finishing adding up my income tax; it takes time, though at the end there not much of it compared to the big times. But I'm entitled to deduct all typing & paper & taxis to deliver manuscript & God knows what & I'm so sick of trusting to the tax people to accept a reasonable average that I do it all out . . . no particular news . . if you had been here we'd have gone trout fishing but I think Ill wait till you come—Day light savings began today, thank God—Its so hard for me not to get up that I welcome it—next week will be the first real start at gardening but the ground still seems as cold as Xmas—

I forgot to send you the shares I bought for your birthday. Tim has them. I'll get them & post them—they're only worth $20⁰⁰ now & I think you'd better sell them & have another birthday—I miss you so much up here but at any rate you'll be here soon for a visit & I hope to have the Pontiac perhaps within a week & can send it down . . . . . . . I'm writing in the sun galley—The afternoon sun makes it warm & the house is cold. It's looks lovely outside—I'll walk this letter to the station mail . . Be sure to write: I shall expect to hear tomorrow

> Affect'ly
> Stephen Leacock

## To Mrs Herbert T. Shaw                    Mon May 1 1939

Dear Fitz

Two letters from you,—Friday & Saturday—together this morning I opened them together to get the dates right & then read them as one volume— I'm so sorry you were tired: but you have no idea how well & full of pep you seem most of the time—but tiredness, utter tiredness is pretty gods awful—

Today bright clear cool—I made myself work to do an article on golf for The New York Times as the editor had written again—so he will pretty well have to take it—It was <u>forced</u> but I did the best I could & ended up with the story of the girl & the lost ball—as changed by you—so at least I worked. Today being the first of May I am trying to make a new start but my mental condition is poor—in spite of every effort I make—I ought to realize how nice it is that I am here, and as far as doctors say, am well: think of the poor devils who try to think they are well <u>in spite</u> of what the doctors say—I'll be so glad when you come—I told you that I have to go to Toronto to arrange a McGill meeting on the 10th—back same night Im glad I'm going as I see that at once it gives me something to think about without looking forward years at a time

Today Kelly is grafting trees—Jones getting my little early garden ready— Its still pretty cold—only 50 this morning—but it would be nice weather for you to work in—did I mention (yes I did) your wonderful blue hyacinths. I never saw them before—Let me know if you want a few rows of early stuff for eating in June—

x  x  x  x  x

I took an hour or so & walked round & supervised Jones & Kelly & then had a sherry at 12—I find it's better than whiskey for the middle of the day . . . I wish you were here—today, in the last two or three hours has turned beautifully warm, just right to garden——I am waiting now for the MS I wrote to come back via taxi & then must go in again via taxi to catch the mail—I'll write again later but it wont catch this mail—no word yet about Pontiac car—I'll send for it as soon as I hear

> Affectionately
> Stephen
> Leacock

## *To Mrs Herbert T. Shaw*                    Tuesday May 2   ¼ to one

Dear Fitz

Cool bright weather—but it never seems to be warm. Kelly has a cold & work stopped. Doc A came out & played billiards—but kind 'o wrong as I had fallen asleep—but I woke up & played—no particular conversation. . . . The motor people promise my car for this week: if Kelly is well he will get it on Thursday or Friday, so you can "lay to that" except that I have to use it on Wednesday to go to Toronto—Mr Cracken just telephoned to ratify the date— I am to meet him & one or two others & arrange a meeting – – – I didn't write today. I do hope I can soon: especially as finance is a little tight because of buying the car & taxes:—though the standing expenses here are not heavy & it looks as if living at Orillia with the Lodge & the farm could all be done easily without working any more & just using what I have—but it's lonely: I wish, I mean I hope you'll be up soon & then it will feel different. I wouldnt want to stay here in November unless you could come & go . . . still thats far away.

Fishing. I think I'll send Johnson a cheque for $10, because even if there are no fish we like to drive up now & then—its part of our life – – – I didn't get a letter this morning but I expect to this afternoon. You have become a wonderful correspondent. The way to be it is to just get the habit of having pens & ink & paper at hand & write anything or everything.

By the way are the King & Queen passing <u>Orillia</u> or are they? Nobody seems to know. They are said to be passing <u>Rama</u> but that might just mean going to Toronto, Washago & passing east of Rama. I was saying to Walter Wood that if they dont come through Orillia but go viâ Medonte or Washago (the only two alternatives) they will come at night & he might get a bus load at $1.00 a piece to go and see the royal train pass . . . I,—as Paul Lafleur,—used to say,—am thinking of planting a tree to commemorate the year & day – – – Your gold stock I think is a lemon: I'll send you the shares: better sell them: its too slow.

Affecty (affectionately)
Stephen Leacock

## *To James Keddie*                    The Old Brewery Bay
Orillia
May 5 '39

Dear Mr Keddie

I am so glad that my article on the Classic books appealed in just the right way . . . As to the Dickens idea, I'd like to do it when the time comes & to make it not only and simply an outline as to who Dickens was & what he did,—but, as it were, an introduction to a world that to young people is very long ago,—

stage coaches & Xmas fires, exuberant sentiment roaring laughter, colours & contrasts long since gone, & bounded by 'foreign parts' and ending in open spaces that must have seemed infinite—I think the reason why some young people dont read Dickens is that they haven't caught this atmosphere, and similarly I think that once they have caught it Dickens is with them for ever—

—I'll be glad to do such a "piece" any time you care to have it . . .

with very best regards
Stephen Leacock


## To Barbara Nimmo

Sunday May 7

Dear Bâ

This is just a line for Nancy's first birthday (May 11.) & best wishes & love from Stevie & me—I am sending her a little trifle by mail but want to be sure of this letter getting there in time. It seems wonderful to think of her as a year old,—no doubt trying to stand up & soon trying to talk—Write & tell me the news—I'll send a letter later about business

y. a. u.
with love to you all
Stephen Leacock


## To Mrs Herbert T. Shaw

Tues May 9. 39

Dear Fitz

Best love for Peggy's birthday tomorrow . . I'm sending her a little trifle but it will go by next mail as I cant get it off by this—

Rain—drizzling—I worked (wrote) all morning on my education book—I'm like Old Balt when he didn't know if he was "hright—er—wrong"—I just go on—

—Tomorrow I go down to Toronto to the McGill Society and—I shall stay all night—Mrs Hamilton didnt come up here yet but may come up then overnight—I havent heard from her whether she wants to come—but its nothing to me & its company for Stevie—I had my foot in hot water for an hour this morning as I wrote—I've neglected my gout too much—and I am trying to cut down further on drink by having only sherry in the middle of the day—Each time I try to feel well something goes wrong—and it's not easy going and I wish you were here as it is lonely up here—I am going to try physical work in the garden—Barbara's Nancy is 1 year old: I am sending her a little silver

locket with room for a photo in it—other news,—let me see—nothing much—
Do let me know about sending down the car but I realize that wont be till after
Peggy leaves now—

> Affectionately
> Stephen Leacock

## *To Mrs Herbert T. Shaw*
Orillia Tuesday 6 pm
(May 10, 1939)

Dear Fitz

It was nice this afternoon to wake up from sleep (I'd had lunch very late:
chicken croquettes & asparagus & beer) & find your letter . . . After reading it I
called our Mr Jones in conference and arranged about your garden, namely
thus—that on the day, which ever it is, that Kelly leaves for Montreal, Jones, your
Charlie & my Albanie will get the horse & harness & get your place all ready to
plant . . . I have a lot of seed & you can get right at it with Jones at your service.
The only adverse possibility is heavy rain, because that wont stop you & Kelly
in the car but it would stop the garden stuff . . . You never saw such growing
weather as now   warm rain all morning and then a heavy hot sun all afternoon.
The asparagus in my big field (in the trench) all jumped up in a row,—all in 1 day
it seemed to me—peas & everything moving like blazes—<u>but</u> I see already that
things in the glass house are so slow at first that out of doors things just about
catch up to them

I drove in at 1 oclock & posted the mail: I do that each day. It is a nice little
break & doesn't interfere with Kelly's work—one thing you will enjoy here is
the unlimited cream,—for me no damn good . . I am going over to your place
now to take a look . . what did you think of the Duke of Windsor broadcasting—
I see no sense in it,—what can he say? only generalities—or do you think it did
good—Peggy's trip sounds longer than I thought—it is hard for you to be
without her for so long, but after you have been up here for a little it will seem
as if she were just coming back & want to go back—except at first . . . . I'll be
so glad when you come up—even the first time—I am trying to get well. Today
I wrote a lot of stuff and I hope to keep writing & then I always feel that even
if I am sick later on when I get well the bills will be paid . . . Keep on writing .
. . I do so like to hear what happens—I mean just this, just that . . . Is Claude's
scholarship announced yet?

## *To Mrs Herbert T. Shaw*                Orillia
                                          Sun May 14  39

Dear Fitz

It's the dead hour,—5 oclock on Sunday afternoon—always feels so dead here as I am not like you, I <u>cant</u> work in the garden on Sunday—cold last night—The glass house just got by—if it turns warmer I expect to start planting things tomorrow—Kelly expects to leave Thursday morning—he went today in his motor boat lake trout fishing in Simcoe—not back yet—but other people are getting a lot of fine trout – – I did quite a bit of odd gardening yesterday & the day before—and I'm sure it does me good—but its disheartening to keep getting a set back just when I feel I am started—Up early this morning (sunrise) & did a lot of papers—finished a chapter of my book & got it ready for Barbara & wrote part of a book review (a new book on French Canadian literature)—but Sunday is dull. The other days interest me because the men are working, especially Jones with whose work I am concerned—I got Mr Rowe to go up to Oro and get me thimble berry bushes at 5 cents a piece—40 of them, fine big ones away ahead of what I could have got from market gardeners—Kelly dug them in where the strawberries used to be—At your place, all fine. I told Charlie to uncover the aspargus bed & scratch it lightly with a rake but not too hard—If it keeps dry it will be hard to work the ground— but its not nearly as bad as mine – – I'll be so glad when you come up . . . . The place is running nice & easily. The liquor is costing a way below my estimate & so is Hatley's as I have all the milk & butter & eggs for nothing. One thing you'll like is the cream, beautiful stuff—all you want—Mrs H.[1] goes back to Toronto today. She is 84 and lives alone . . it seems difficult. I'll get this letter into the mail tonight & it ought to reach you tomorrow but I guess it just may or may not—the train gets into Toronto with just time for the Montreal mail—I do hope that Hemmeon and René have got Claude Tétrault settled—They ought to do it <u>before</u> the exams—no doubt they have—Is Mary perhaps coming up? You said no more about it except that she might or might not—it would be nice company for you on the trip apart from the pleasure of having her here – – – – – The weather seems queer: it was cold last night & this morning—now turning warm as the evening goes on—I've no furnaces & the house is half comfortable and half not – – I've had Jones & Albanie tidying up all the outer yards—it begins to make a big difference. I intend to have this place in a month or so as tidy as a new pin & get some pleasure out of it

Affectionately
Stephen Leacock

1   Mrs Hamilton.

*To Mrs Herbert T. Shaw*                    Orillia May 17 (1939)
                                            Wednesday

Dear Fitz

It is seven thirty (D.S. time). Yesterday I worked quite a lot out in the garden in the big field—ideal weather & the ground there just right—I have marked out 24 rows of stuff each 150 feet long with the seed measured into it by ounces—Onions take 1½ ounces for ~~16~~ 150 feet and cost 15 cents for 1½ ounces. Beans go 100 feet to a pound and cost 18 cents a pound, or 25 cents for one of my rows—Its all done like that. Then I went rock bass fishing in the boat, just myself from 6:30 to 7:30—so you see how well I must be getting & I read an Edgar Wallace instead of going to bed—but theres the hell of it—the room got cold—I took a whiskey & soda at 11 & a second one later & then I got all upset inside & had a wretched night—but I stuck it out—I drop back into fears & abysses so easily that the only plan is to keep fighting against it—my foot bothers me & I'm careless about hot water for it & my medicine.

—It got quite cold at night; it hadnt seemed possible but it did. I hired Mr Rowe for two hours (75 cents) to make a third man at the saw & they gathered & sawed up kitchen hardwood for the Lodge & here for the rest of the month. After paying Sarjeants prices it is fine to see it pile up in the yard—well,—I must have another cup of tea & get at my book: I'm behind time on it & the least little laziness more might knock it out for autumn – – I hope you'll be just getting ready to leave when you get this. My best to Peggy & good wishes to her & Julia for the trip—sorry I couldn't present them at Court . . Suppose I give Peggy a personal letter to the Duke of Connaught asking him to take Julia & her out for a whirl some night . .

                                            Affectionately
                                            Stephen Leacock


*To Mrs Herbert T. Shaw*                    Wed. 31. May  39

Dear Fitz

Another beautiful day—you never saw such weather as <u>since you left</u> . . . I was over at yr place last evening, (to get asparagus)—it looks all correct—grass growing already—am arranging about ~~. . . hen~~ hens—white wyandottes but I wont actually put them there till the day you come . . I've got ready a huge mail this morning—cleared up my table—been busy since 6 am . . drove into town & back with Walter & did a list of messages—Kelly is working this afternoon at your place—oats—We got all our potatoes in yesterday . . . Doc A. came out for billiards last night . . King & Q <u>not</u> stopping at Orillia . . I'm just as glad. I wont go to Washago. I hope to hear from you this afternoon; I wish you could be here now . . the weather is just heavenly & it all looks so lovely – – melons arrived from Montreal: planting them today—I corrected & posted my Humour piece . . my God! it is good   I've decided to put it & similar pieces of last winter into my new book <u>Too Much College</u> so that the title will be

<u>Too Much College</u>
& Other <u>Kindred Essays</u> on Education & Humor

That means that I needn't <u>pad</u> the book—I've enough stuff right in sight—The book will carry me through next winter

must stop as Walter is to come for the mail & I have to get the salad before lunch

Affect'ly
Stephen Leacock

## To E.G. McCracken

Orillia Je. 1. 39

Dear Punch

Herewith your letter with added suggestions—All your ideas are just in line with what I think . . . . .

I send a page or two of appropriate thoughts

Best regards
Stephen Leacock

<u>McGill Nights</u>

A university, like an old soldier, must never die. Nor must it even gently fade away. It must keep on.

If it has a glorious past, it must see to it that it has a glorious future. If it has trained many of the leading of the country now growing old, it must see to it that it trains the leading men still young.

This obligation lies on all of us. A college cannot live on bricks and mortar and equipment. Gifts of money, however generous, can never take the place of the greatest gift of all, the affection and enthusiasm of the college graduates

This must be kept alive. The strongest light burns dim if left untended.

Our "McGill Nights" are instituted with a view to keep this lamp of learning trimmed & bright so that its light can reach the furthest graduate, and illuminate alike the record of the past and the unturned pages of the future

Stephen Leacock

*To Mrs Herbert T. Shaw*                    Sunday morning
                                           Je 4 39

Dear Fitz

I wont try to write a long letter as I had a rather mean night; I think I got a chill. It discourages me for a little and I had been trying so hard not to get into a nervous state & to go on working no matter if I felt a little off. It is difficult . .

I am terribly sorry to hear of poor Angus's death. I hadn't known that he had anything wrong as he is athletic & always looked well—With the news of it comes this terrible submarine disaster, just when from the radio we gathered all saved & yesterday at near Orillia (on the Brechin road) a terrible motor collision worse than the Pinkertons The driver at fault (dead) was I understand a worthless young brute, already in 9 accidents great or small & <u>never</u> with his wife but with other peoples . . I only <u>hear</u> that. I know nothing.

René should have <u>advertised</u>. I kept saying so. But he kept saying that that was <u>their</u> business, whoever <u>they</u> were. I said go to the Principal & say that the school cant get pupils without advertising & plan an attractive circular—& send it all over . . . But he wouldn't see it . . . I am afraid that when he says he is watched it is true

George & Mary & Dot & Harry came up last night & are here now asleep. I went to bed pretty soon after dinner as I wasn't feeling so good & they went down to play billiards . . . . I'll stop . . Its hard to shake off the effects of a bad night. You see I get frightened. Yet I realize its only a condition of nerves as I get better with every effort I make but I'll be so glad when you'll be back here

                                           Affecte
                                           Stephen
                                           Leacock


*To E.G. McCracken*                         Orillia
                                           Je 7

Dear Punch

This is an idea in regard to our honorary degrees:—

Each recipient has as part of his letters his McGill degree, for example, B.A, then the letters <u>M.SO.</u> (McGill Society of Ontario,—and the rest are individual & for himself & different each time,—& always calculated to Please not to hurt

For instance, if we confer a degree on Doug Ross it could read Douglas Ross, B.A. M.S.O. H.B.C. (<u>Hard Boiled Conservative</u>) You could arrange a <u>ritual</u> & I will arrange with printers some black letter old type "parchments,"— Degrees can be proposed to the Committee (that is to <u>you</u>) at any time & a batch accepted, say, for the autumn meeting & duly conferred—Not given except to members of the Society in good standing & the <u>real meaning</u> is that they have done & are doing good work for McGill in Ontario—Send this idea to other fellows & let me talk of it at Kitchener

best regards<br>
Stephen Leacock

## To E.G. McCracken

Orillia Je 12 39

Dear Punch

I expect to arrive in Kitchener about 1 hour before dinner & to bring with me <u>René du Roure</u> & my son <u>Stephen Leacock Junior</u>. "Stevie" is a fourth year undergraduate in Arts & therefore I believe eligible for membership with us. I enclose a cheque for 3 dinners & 2 golfs—Stevie & René will play, but merely expect to have a short game to themselves before dinner, so they will not be included in any handicap or arrangement & need give no trouble to anyone . . I'll pay my membership & Stevie's (if admitted) by separate cheque later

In the "announcements" of which your circular speaks you would like me, would you not, to talk especially of our plan for "<u>McGill Nights</u>"

. . . . I have a long way to drive home so I am sure that no one will mind if I start off at 9.30 (Kitchener Time) 10.30 our time . . .

I expect to leave here at 1.PM (D.S.T) and get to Kitchener about 1 hour before the dinner

Best regards<br>
Stephen Leacock

## To Mrs Herbert T. Shaw

Monday Je 12. 11<u>30</u> am

Dear Fitz

I didnt write yesterday as I wasn't feeling so good. George & a friend called Tommy Lyons drove up & had dinner (not Mary) & went back about 5 . . . . It is so nice to think that you will be here soon. I expect René at noon tomorrow & then so after that you will be here & the summer begins. I gave your note to Tina. I haven't got your hens yet but I think I can get white wyandottes from Hamilton (same man as sells the day olds)

Today pretty cool—almost cold—Jones planting my garden (at that point your letter arrived: about the Mozart concert: Saturday letter) . . . . . . . . . . . certainly he (you know who) has got himself into a great mess . . I'll be glad when you come, Fitz; I'm not ill but I seem to live in fear & each time I beat it down some little discomfort starts, a nothing in itself & it gets me down again— Still I am trying to keep on the job. My writing has run low but doesn't quit . . .

I am going to write to Mary (Leacock) & see if she & George would like to come up on Saturday night & I'll make it a sort of dinner party for your arrival . . The herring fishing will have begun & so George can go fishing on Sunday morning. Your place all looks fine—not a single peony is out yet in either place—they are just due to start any hot day after a rain—but the great mass of them wont be out till after you come—I'm glad to hear that Mary & the boys are coming: I suppose Pat has to work. Mary will love it up here as she can get a real rest & the boys are just in time for the herring fishing . . . I got Mr Rowe over her today to fix up the maids bedrooms better. Close up the hall entrance that looks so dirty and put a door from room to room. I have a door & the wood that comes out makes or nearly makes the partition. It will give a chance to keep that end of the house decent – – – 12 o clock blowing—Jones will come in for his beer—but not for me yet as I want to write a bit first . . . It will be fine to see you. I'll be looking for to it. Wont write again as it couldnt very well catch you.

> Affectionately
> Stephen Leacock

## To J. A. T. Lloyd

> [The Old Brewery Bay
> Orillia, Ontario]
> July 29 '39

Dear Hogan Lloyd

I was glad to get your letter—The rescue stuff didn't amount to much in reality except as a high class piece of navigation—the kind of thing we'd have done easily enough on the <u>Iverna</u> when we sailed Lake Simcoe . . . . . . .

I hope you are keeping pretty well All our crowd are getting so damned old: I walked past 50 & 60 as if they weren't there,—just mile-posts.—but my illness last year got me . . . . . Poor old Bowwow died a year or so ago & Somerville this summer . . . But there's no use turning a letter into an obituary . . . . . . .When you write as I hope you will tell me first how you are & how you are getting on . . and then what you are all thinking in England about the chance of war. I cannot believe it possible. Seen from here it looks as if the English people are determined to fight rather than give way or anything,—have called Hitler's bluff—and as it is called, & as they are in earnest, there will not be war Hitler's only hope will be sudden & sensational victory: anything like initial defeat would knock him to the bottom of the pit . . . But then of course from over here we only see things at a distance . . . .

> With very best regards both
> to you & to your wife
> Stephen Leacock

## To Frank Dodd

August 29th. 1939

Frank Dodd Esq.
Dodd Mead and Co.
New York, N.Y.

Dear Dodd,

I send you by to-morrow's mail the complete copy of <u>Too Much College</u>: be careful that the customs make no delay.

The book as sent you contains nicely over 50,000 words of which a little over 37,000 words are <u>Too Much College</u> proper and the rest supplementary essays in education and humour. As a matter of fact if you thought it better business I could send you a few more thousand words but my own opinion is that the book will stand or fall on the college part. I understand that under our contract you are buying the book rights for the U.S. and for Canada, and paying royalties from the U.S. in U.S. dollars and for Canada in Canadian dollars.

I understand further that all rights other than these belong to me but that if your firm submit a bargain for selling rights on a percentage basis in any part of the book, I should be very glad to go in on it on reasonable terms.

If I remember rightly you are to pay me on publication such royalty as you feel your sales prospect justifies.

Very sincerely,


## To Tina Kelly[1]

(September 1939)


MEMORANDUM FOR MRS. KELLY FROM PROFESSOR STEPHEN LEACOCK

Dear Tina,

It is proper to explain to you what arrangements I am able to make in regard to your future.

I give you herewith a cheque for fifty dollars, as for the month of September and October and I propose to continue to give you twenty-five dollars a month until May 1st, 1940 when I should hope to be back at Orillia and might replace this arrangement with some other plan whereby you might at that date return to the Lodge. But the future is so uncertain owing to the war and to my advanced age that I cannot be sure of my income, or of my residence here, or of anything else beyond that date. I can only say that I should expect to go on with

---

1   Tina Kelly, born Tina Pelletier, left her employment as a housemaid in Montreal to marry Irish-born John Kelly (1900–1939). When John lost his job, Leacock employed both of them at his Orillia home. John fell asleep and died at the wheel of his truck on 6 September 1939.

these payments for at least a year from now unless some other plan replaces them more to your advantage.

I regret to say that I am afraid that there are very few assets left to you from poor Kelly's estate. But we will do the best with what there is. Unfortunately certain debts come first.

There is $250 due to the bank for the truck. I will pay this.

There will be about $200 to pay in connection with Kelly's burial and various items that go with it for medical services and other things. There are, I presume, a small amount of outstanding bills. I will look after all these subject to the conditions below. There is on the other hand the pile of cordwood all of which I understand belongs to Kelly except six cords sold to me and paid for. This wood ought to increase in value as it gets drier and especially so on account of rising war prices. I propose that you leave it here and later on, according to circumstances, I will sell it for you, but not without your consent in writing for any sale made.

I regret to say that Kelly's insurance policy has been marked void by the company. I am trying to see if they will pay something but I fear it would not be much.

There is also the chance that the C.P.R. may consent to make a payment. But I do not think you would be wise to bring a suit against them. I propose to lay the circumstances before them and see if they will make a payment not by legal compulsion but by free will. I fear that in any case it would not be much.

If by unexpected good fortune payments were made to you by the Insurance Company and the Railway which amount together to more than a thousand dollars I should expect you out of the surplus over a thousand dollars to pay the funeral costs as above. But I am afraid there is very little chance of their being as large as this and very likely they will be nothing at all.

If after going to Three Rivers you find that you would prefer to go home to your own people for the winter I will pay your travel expenses down there, and if circumstances make it ~~possible~~ feasible for you to come back here in the spring I will pay your travel expenses back.

I propose to leave here at the end of September and to engage a caretaker for this house and for the Lodge. But I do not wish you to leave in the Lodge any small articles of value and I cannot in any case be responsible for the safety or the condition of anything you leave in as much as war time conditions will greatly increase both the risk of theft and the difficulty of finding any one in a position to look after property. I can only say that what you leave will be as safe as my own belongings but no safer, and I take no responsibility and give no guarantee.

I had hoped and expected as you know to give Kelly the east corner of the property to build a house on. This conveyance was not made and with the present arrangement the proposal lapses, unless you wish it otherwise and would rather have the land than the considerations above. I could not offer both.

But as the conveyance carried with it no right of sale it would be of little value to you and even if a right of sale were given all that you could now get for it would probably be less than the money due on the truck to say nothing of the other sums in consideration.

I had left to Kelly in my will,—and it so stands in it,—the sum of two hundred and fifty dollars. I had been compelled to reduce this from five hundred as left in an earlier will because the fall ~~of~~ in my own resources made it necessary. But as the will reads it was left to Kelly only if he survived me and not to his heirs.

I propose to change this sum to three hundred dollars to be paid to you in twelve instalments of twenty-five dollars a month, so that if I die before you the monthly payments to you would go on after my death. But as it is not possible to do everything at once I cannot for the moment draw up the necessary papers and hence leave the bequest in this document as an instruction to my trustees and heirs in complete confidence that they ~~will~~ would fulfill it.

But this bequest will not be made if it turns out that the moneys that may be paid to you by the Insurance Company and the railway company amount to a thousand dollars or more, not if the monthly payments have already lasted a year.

Nothing in this memorandum is to be held as meaning that I am convenanting to pay Kelly's debts, and nothing in it is to be understood as forming any kind of contract of what I <u>have</u> to do, but only as an expression of my intention of doing what I can.

On the other hand nothing in this memorandum is to mean that the things mentioned here are all that I might do, or that the time indicated is the limit during which I would do anything. All that would depend on your need of help and my ability to give it. In the critical time in which we are living it is not possible to say more.

# CHAPTER 10

## STEPHEN LEACOCK
# THE END OF THE WAR

## 1939–1944

With the outbreak of the Second World War, Stephen Leacock turned his attention to writing his thoughts on the 'God's awful' world situation. 'To stress the value, both to the British Empire and to all the world, of the continuance in despite of wars abroad, of that international peace and good will which now unites all of English-speaking North America,' he penned *All Right, Mr Roosevelt* in the late fall of 1939, as a response to the manager of the Canadian branch of Oxford University Press and his request for a pamphlet on 'Canada and the United States Neutrality'. Leacock found himself in the same position he had been in at the outbreak of the First World War, recommending that Canada and the United States manifest their longstanding international friendship by uniting in these troubled times.

In the same fall he also published *Too Much College*, a bitter and detailed criticism of colleges and their failures. For this careful examination of the subject, Leacock had asked all the major schools in Canada and the United States to send him their course catalogues, and after making an examination of all of them, he wrote critiques of teaching methods and other curricular matters. The sad effect of college courses, he concluded, was that they were training people to do, not to know: 'College is meant to train the mind, not the thumb.'

In 1940 Leacock returned to the situation affecting the world, focusing again on the importance of international co-operation. In the preface to *Our British Empire* (issued in the United States as *The British Empire*), he explains his reasons for addressing this topic:

> I write this book in the hope that it may be of service in the present hour. It is a presentation of the British Empire, not for the pageant of its history but for its worth to the world. The Empire is united not by force but by goodwill. It means co-operation, not compulsion. In it we live as free men.

> The link of our common history, the bond of our common language, the identity of our outlook hold us closely with the United States. With France, the long record of bygone wars that once divided us is now but a common glory. In the hour that is, we share that comradeship in arms which faces a common danger with a united endeavour. Through these associations we may see a vision of a world at peace.

And in the book's conclusion Leacock issues his earnest wish: 'The world needs an unwritten union of Britain, America and France. This will set up a standard to which all honest men may rally.'

The war is an unremitting theme of Leacock's final letters: 'the war, the war, the war, . . . What we all have got to do is to keep busy doing something—one can still hope for the unexpected. . . . it is hard, isn't it to keep normal?' Like his contemporary Lucy Maud Montgomery, Leacock was painfully conscious of the devastating effects of a war in Europe, and he was bitter about his own inability to contribute constructively to the war effort. And so he continued to write.

In 1940 Leacock accepted an offer from Samuel Bronfman of the House of Seagram to write a history of Canada, titled *Canada: The Foundations of Its Future*. '[T]here is no doubt', he wrote in the preface, 'of the value to our country of such a record of the history and the life of its people as this book was designed to be by those who collaborated in planning it.' The final manuscript was vetted in September 1941 by the poet A.M. Klein, who also provided an introduction on behalf of the House of Seagram.

In December of the same year, Thomas B. Costain, a good friend who had recently been named editor of Doubleday, invited Leacock to contribute a book on Quebec City for Doubleday's series of books on famous North American ports. 'In view of the research work you did for your recent history, I imagine that you could approach the task without feeling it would be too onerous,' Costain wrote in a letter to Leacock. Leacock suggested that Montreal would make a better subject, one reason being that the local sales in Montreal would be vastly superior to those in Quebec City. 'Therefore,' Costain replied with assent, 'we bow to your superior judgement in the matter and want you to do the port of Montreal for us.' The result was *Montreal, Seaport and City* (1942), arguably Leacock's best historical book. Leacock himself boasted to his brother George that he had finally achieved a mature, serious style at a time when he might be just past writing good humour.

Leacock seemed to defy that assessment of his humour with the publication later that same year of *My Remarkable Uncle and Other Sketches*. The collection opens with one of his finest pieces of humour, his autobiographical sketch of his famous uncle, E.P. Leacock. The volume contains Leacock's only serious short story, 'The Transit of Venus', which follows the travels of a college professor and his ultimately successful courtship of one of his students. Also in 1942 he published *Our Heritage of Liberty: Its Origin, Its Achievement, Its Crisis* with the subtitle, 'A Book for War Time'. Written in response to R. W. Bardwell's request that Leacock write on 'the common ties of people living in a democracy and what we need to preserve it', the book, ultimately published by Bodley Head in England, reviewed the history and the accomplishments of democracy. For its American publication, Leacock relinquished royalties on the first 500 copies to enable Dodd, Mead to print the book, which promised limited sales.

During this time, Leacock's personal world was becoming increasingly constricted. Orillia, he wrote to Mrs Shaw in 1940, 'is lonely and depressing. . . . but I have no home life in Montreal.' Although he was still close to Barbara and was concerned about her welfare as though she were his own daughter, he was separated from her by geography, and they remained in contact almost solely through their letters. Stevie graduated in honours English in June 1940; following a year teaching English at McGill, he headed down to Toronto in 1941 to work for the publicity firm that also employed Henry Janes, a son of Leacock's friend Charlie Janes of Orillia. And Leacock's close friend from McGill, René du Roure, died suddenly in the fall of 1940 at the age of sixty. He had sought to enlist in the French armed services, just as he had done in the First World War, but had not been accepted because of his age. Leacock maintained that René's grief over the collapse of France was one of the contributing factors to his premature death. Leacock's home in Orillia, once the centre of his family and social life, was now a very lonely place for him, and writing was his only way of staving off his increasing loneliness and depression: 'I get depressed up here now', he wrote in 1941, 'till I get busy and work.'

Leacock's health was also not as robust as it had once been and became a matter of growing concern. He had been hospitalized in 1938 for prostate surgery; two years later he had an operation on his throat. But though his weakened condition persisted, it did not diminish his determination to write. In fact, Leacock, already a prolific writer, produced five new books in just two years, between 1942 and 1943. In addition to the three books that appeared in 1942, Leacock in 1943 published *How to Write* and *Happy Stories Just to Laugh At*. The former is a critical analysis of the art of writing. As Leacock wrote to Gerhard Lomer, the book 'is like a favorite child to me because I wrote it purely to suit myself with no eye on editors or sales to the public'. The latter Leacock described as 'a book of little stories,—not essays, but sketches each of which is a story'. The volume contained eight sketches under the title 'Mariposa Moves On', as well as fifteen other stories.

Early in 1944 Leacock was finally incapacitated by his failing health. His throat was causing him considerable discomfort that made it extremely painful and nearly impossible for him to swallow. As his condition worsened, he had difficulty making himself heard. Cancer, the cause of his wife's sudden death, was now stalking her husband. He made arrangements for Barbara to publish a posthumous volume, which would be entitled *Last Leaves* (1945). His social treatise *While There Is Time: The Case Against Social Catastrophe* would also be published that year.

On 27 February 1944, Leacock drove down to Toronto to enter the hospital for preliminary tests. On 16 March he had an operation for cancer of the throat, but by that time his condition had advanced beyond recovery. Later that month Leacock suffered a relapse, and on 28 March, he died.

### *To Mrs Herbert T. Shaw*         Orillia, Wed Sep 13  1 pm

Dear Fitz

Lou went over & put up the shutters etc. & I understand that the plumbers "did their stuff" as we say in vaudeville—I'll go over later today—It has turned out beautiful weather—The place seems so empty now that you are gone,—and Peggy—not that I see her much but when she is here things seem moving—I've been thinking of your journey & hoping there's no delay with those damn ~~tyr~~ tires—I listened to the war news at noon & still feel as if it could all be over very soon—be sure to get in touch with René & give him my message—tell Paule Tetrault that Claude at Poitiers is probably safer than in Montreal and that as a centre of study it has been going ever since Charlemagne in 800 AD started a school—

I am arranging to have Mrs Tunney "put down" tomatoes etc—(sounds like an insurrection)—so if you want anything 'put down' off your place let me know—Lou went to Barrie & sold $3⁶⁰ of bottles—That makes $10⁰⁰ altogether—I am living in bottles till further notice—Be sure to write—I miss you so much here & shall be waiting for a letter

> Affectionately
> Stephen
> Stephen Leacock

### *To Mrs Herbert T. Shaw*         Orillia
                                                 Thursday Sep 14 39

Dear Fitz

I hope you are safely settled at home by this time & not too tired—I am just leaving for Sutton to fetch Charlie & so I am writing in a sort of hurry; in fact I've been hurrying round in Orillia today trying to see about selling the tires from Kelly's truck & about bringing down the wood that he owns up at Moonstone. I'm getting Mrs Tunney to put down jam half & half . . in the pauses of other things I'm trying to get start~~ing~~ed writing again  Be sure to phone René & let me know how he is .. It seems pretty dreary up here now but yesterday I worked out of doors practically all day & then read & slept on the sofa till the war news at 11 pm .. Its hard to know how it looks. It depends on the great air battle coming over the big cities when the Germans begin it—If the Germans are beaten at that its all over—I didnt go fishing—I couldn't find the energy—as you see I cant even write a letter—I'll just send this & hope to add to it by the same mail

Affectionately
Stephen Leacock

*To Mrs Herbert T. Shaw*                    Orillia Sunday Sep 17  39

Dear Fitz

Your two letters (one of Thursday & one of Friday) came together on yesterday Saturday afternoon. I was so glad to hear. I'd been a little nervous of a breakdown & delay—Your letters made the war seem much nearer than it does here .. it is god's awful isnt it .. one simply has to think of it as short or it would be too terrible to think of it at all—As to the person you write of (I never put names in a letter) he must really chuck a trace or go under—what he ought to do is to offer special French classes for men in training in the McGill contingent and likely to go overseas—that sort of thing is humble but it all counts—There is a lot to do here before I can get away. I still have not heard about Tina. I went yesterday to Sperin's place where Kelly's wood is & got it all arranged with him & signed.—I broke off there for a special radio bulletin: Polish gov't moving further west. It looks bad for Poland & then the real war begins – – – It was terribly hot here but today cool & almost cold—I am trying to get all the wood cut that I can—I am hoping that Tina & Albanie can live here with only $25⁰⁰ a month in cash for Tina plus $5⁰⁰ for Albanie, provided I can give them wood & vegetables & milk & eggs & butter & electric light—money is tighter & tighter— Dodd sent me the jacket for my book: Peggy's drawing was too late so I am afraid he wont use it at all—the jacket he sent is awful (a picture of me!—oh Jesus! but it's too late to kick or to cave—I expect to send you two ducks next week—I killed 2 but they are too small. I am having the pigs killed this week—I am trying to close it all up so that I dont need to come back & dont need to worry about this place—your place is all right—Sir Richard Tute sent for his MS!—but Barbara had posted it. I wrote to her and she answered that she was absolutely sure of it.—I dont seem able to write to you so as to get over: I just put little scraps— I do hope that <u>he</u> tried to get on his feet—There would be no good his coming & its too late anyway—Pity that Douglas is a "neutral": it seems all out of keeping: that the head of McGill cant attend meetings, cant address the stoodents!

Affectionately
Stephen Leacock

## To Mrs Herbert T. Shaw

Orillia
Monday Sept 18 (1939)

Dear Fitz

I have just come from the inquest on poor Kelly . . Town hall.1:30 pm "whereas in the name of the King it has come to our notice that John Kelly . . . now well and truly swear" all seemed very tragic . . But there is no doubt that Kelly was just driving straight ahead with his mind elsewhere. It was a clear day & the bell & whistle both going. The heavy part of the truck was thrown 65 feet, Kelly's body 150 feet & the debris reached more than 50 feet further . . . The doctor (Parkes of Coldwater said that every bone in Kellys body was broken – – – I heard from Tina's sister that she is not coming back this autumn and is not well. I am sending Albanie home to N Brunswick with a ticket to allow a stop over at Three Rivers. He and Alfreda leave tomorrow (Tuesday) night & get to Montreal Wed morning at 6:10 & Albanie goes on at 7.55 to Three Rivers. I am getting Jones to look after the place for the winter & sending Tina $25$\frac{00}{}$ a month till next spring—I hope to come back Sep 29th & go the Windsor. Tell me this,—if I drive in my car, ~~I~~ what could I do with it when I get to Montreal?

But that's all for this place. The war news looks so awful that it dwarfs everything else . . . But I worked all morning on an article on <u>Humour</u> for the Encyclopedia Britannica, which seemed to me good going, as I was not very well . . . I think I will teach at McGill: they are sure to need me: the inquest proved to me that I can't attend meetings—Yesterday ~~Jim~~ Jimmy Eakins came through—he is & has been back & forward to Oshawa—special work—has quit his business & with it his income. He told me what he is doing but it is confidential & mustn't be written down—it is fine of him to give up the fine stuff he had—he seemed pretty glum but on the job   Please try to get René to see that if he will <u>teach</u> at McGill, special classes, for medical, field ambulance men, all sorts of people, needing overseas French in a hurry—that is the very best thing he can do. Do you know if Day is back. I dont like to write to Hemmeon—but they are sure to be stuck—but I dont like to butt in.

Affectionately
Stephen Leacock

## To Mrs Herbert T. Shaw

Orillia Tuesday
Sept 19/39

Dear Fitz,

I am planning to ~~come~~ drive down on the 29th Friday, the car to leave here at 5 a.m. & arrive at 6 p.m. I will bring down 3 ducks cleaned and anything else you say & especially some big pots of ferns. I'll come into Montreal the back way & so to your house & leave the car there for the night, as my Orillia driver couldn't navigate in Montreal. I will send most of my stuff by freight and have lots of room in the car

Tina is not coming back, so I am sending Albanie home today & Alfreda leaves too. Jones will sleep at my house & look after the place. The Lodge can stay unoccupied till next summer.

Poor Tina's illness cost $50 for nurses & doctors. I am swamped with bills but I can buffet my way through when I get working again.

The war news seems so terrible, if it really means a long long war. God knows how people can stand it ... I'll try to arrive sharp at 6 so that you can be sure to be in & then I'll taxi down to the Windsor & get settled in.

Affectionately
Stephen Leacock

*To James Keddie*
The Old Brewery Bay
Orillia Ont Sep 20 39
but after Sep 28, McGill
University or
The Windsor Hotel
Montreal

My dear Keddie

My best thanks for your letter & cheque. I am concerned to hear that you are still under par: I know well that feeling of only getting through half of what you want to: still, those of us who feel that way have still lots of energy ..

Dickens & the world in which he lived—Nov 1 .. 2000 words,—right! It will be a pleasure to do it.

The war—the war—its hard not to think of it day & night .. Things look terribly bad at present I never thought it would come .. I didnt believe it could last .. now it seems here to stay

Very best regards
Stephen Leacock

*To Mrs Herbert T. Shaw*
Orillia Sept 21 Thurs
1939

Dear Fitz

This afternoon I got two letters from you together (Monday & Wednesday) & I was glad to get them—sat down in the library & read them through .. the war, the war, the war, .. what we have all got to do is to keep busy doing something—one can still hope for the unexpected—we'll know within two weeks what the air attack will mean. If it can be beaten I think the submarines will not be difficult . . . it is hard, isn't it to keep normal . . . today there was a garden party at Billy Johnson's (Poffo Poffo) . . 25 cents . . . red cross . . . about 300 there . . including Mrs Ardagh . . . Stevie & Mrs H went . . Mrs Turnbull was there, plastered . . . . . . that suggests—I wont name him, but what damn nonsense it is . . . if he should only get his feet on the ground—put on an old uniform & go on the platform to talk to French veterans—& be reported in the U.S. press & help to make ~~up~~ public opinion for us . . . . . I must get him to do it when I come – – – Charlie left today: I was sorry: I get nervous at night . . .

– – – – – – Jones came in at 6 & the radio started news & we listened—it is hard to see what is happening—but I think that Russia will take as much of Poland as they want & then leave Hitler what they feel like leaving to him—and if he kicks they'll say "let's ask England & France"—also—The east section of Poland would just about as soon be with Russia—I note from the radio that Russia is sending in speakers, pictures & propaganda for Sovietism—Hitler cant do that with his end of it . . . . I am hoping that Aubrey & his family will come up overnight on Saturday: I keep, so to speak, going to pieces when the working day is over, I mean <u>mentally</u>—I feel all the time so preoccupied & depressed about these young boys going to war—you see 25 years ago it was a sort of huge world adventure—but see Philip Gibbs in your last New York Times; he said it all so well that I dont need to try to repeat it . . . I am glad that Peggy is keeping so busy and active: she will always find lots to do . . . .

Dont forget that I am hoping to arrive at 6 on ~~Thurs~~ Friday: I think I'll bring 3 ducks: I must kill the damn things: too much bother to keep them & then some more a week later—if you think of it tell me what else to bring thats any good—tomatoes? cabbage? I've no celery & no onions—apples, you have enough

Affectionately
Stephen Leacock


*To Barbara Nimmo*                              Orillia. Ont.
                                                Sep. 24 39

Dear Bâ
    Herewith about 3000 words Enc. Britannica <u>Humour</u> . . . I need an exact count. The <u>long</u> paragraphs are used to save space. On page 14 I tried in vain for an example. Please leave 2 lines. Stevie & I go to Montreal by day train Friday: so send this to <u>Windsor Hotel</u>. Keep a copy & you can send it non-registered

. . . . . . . . . .

I haven't written as the war has made things too depressing . . and poor Kelly's terrible death . . I will try to send ducks etc per express this week. There is so much to do I am swamped. Kelly owed the bank $250, his funeral & incidentals cost $150, I spent $50 on Doctors & nurses for Tina. Kelly's insurance had run out a week before he was killed. Apparently he drove straight into the train with the mind elsewhere—The wreckage was scattered to 200 feet from the spot . . . . I went out at once but thank God the police had already moved Kelly's body . . . . . I am giving Tina 25 a month till next spring

    . . . . My hope is that the war will be short . . . that central Europe will blow up . . . if not God knows what . . . . Write and let me know how things are . . Love to you all. How's Nancy? . . .

y. a. u.

Stephen Leacock

## To Mrs Herbert T. Shaw

Orillia
Mon. Sept. 25

Dear Fitz

    As I said I hope to arrive at 5.15 on Friday—Steve & I will dine at the Club as I dont think it quite sport to leave him the first night to eat alone—So perhaps you'll eat with us & bring Peggy; in any case I'll phone you & drive up & bring your ducks. I'll be so glad to see you

    Eddie & Graham blew in today on their way down & we talked for half an hour or so (no drinks: then so sensible: none of us wanted them so we didnt have them) . . Graham thinks that the war will go on & on . . . . . I felt so mean this morning that I am afraid my letter was no good . . . I've been working all day since (except 1½ 1 hour sleep & feel better)—am going into Orillia for books at the public library tonight . . . I'll be glad to go back . . . I had Jones & Rowe & Dannie saw up wood & pile it in the basement. I have enough for Xmas (say 10 days) & for all next spring . . . and enough food for all the animals . . . and apples & jam & vegetables till July . . . I had a letter from the Christian Science Monitor about an article on Humour in Times of Depression, which is just like giving me money . . . I shall devote the winter to paying off all this accumulated debt & I really must try to do something real for the war . . . if McGill will let me teach that will be fine, if not I have another plan for lectures giving the money to some good war charity . . . I'll be so glad to see you . . talking is so much better than letters—I have ploughed up your garden . . . The flowers are just too lovely & the beans worth taking in—I went over today

Stephen

## To James Keddie

The Old Brewery Bay
Orillia Sep 28 1939
but just leaving for
Montreal, address c/o
Windsor Hotel Montreal or
if you forget it, McGill
University is always good

My dear Keddie

Herewith I send you the article on Charles Dickens & the World He Lived In . . It has been a great pleasure to write it . . I think it is good . . . It is more than 3000 words but do please try to use it all as artistically it hangs together in proportion . . . but if it has to be cut I can cut it . . of course no extra pay is needed for extra length that you didnt ask for . . . . The war is just a heart break here . . . all these young boys around us to go to that . . . The only hope is that Germany may crack up & go to pieces . . . I am afraid the U.S. will not go into it . . and how can one blame them . . one almost writes that the Black Death had destroyed Central Europe . . .

I'll be glad to hear from you

Very sincerely
Stephen Leacock

## To Barbara Nimmo

[The Windsor
Montreal]
Sat Oct 14.39

Dear Bâ

You might write & let me know how things are going, & especially how war conditions are affecting your outlook? It has been worrying me a little to think that perhaps the war may bring all real estate, for the moment, to a standstill . . . . or is it possibly, the other way?

. . The war will bring to the U.S. great industrial activity . . among other things that will boom is journalism & all sorts of trade, house & advertising papers . . Does this connect with any possible shift of activity in whole or in part, for Don . . . If things are rotten, do you & Don think at all of trying for an opening in Canada?

Please let me know what the outlook of it all is . . . If all clse fails, you can beat a retreat to the Orillia trenches & sit tight there—let me know—& whether you are worried . . and what is what . . as long as I am here you & Don needn't worry too much . . . I'm so glad to hear that Nancy is coming on, so fast, and walking . . .

y. a. u
Stephen Leacock

## To Arthur B. Thompson                    Oct. 26. 39.

Arthur Thompson Esq.
Barrister Orillia

Dear Arthur

Please have me represented at the Court of Revision as enclosed (Oct. 31). I bought from the CPR and from the CNR the two strips of abandoned track intersecting my property.

The assessment previously levied on these was based on their value as railway tracks and railway sidings. When put out of this use they became waste land of no use to anyone, too narrow to build on and with no complete access from outside. Their value there was away below the assessment, indeed they had no particular value except to me and to me only a precautionary value lest someone should buy them as a nuisance to resell to me at a forced sale.

I represented this to the railway companies and they fully admitted the point and each company sold the land to me at $50 an acre,—the C.P.R. $161$\underline{^{00}}$ in all, and the CNR $122.00,—a total of $283.

But if this is the cash value it is still too high for assessment value on land beyond the reach of town water and facilities used only in summer, but taxed for schools etc. on an all the year round basis. I wrote a memorandum on this point to the town council a year or two ago, urging them not to drive away Summer residents who spend plenty of money in town by taxing them in Orillia for facilities for which they already pay taxes elsewhere. The council very kindly accepted the argument and left my assessment alone.

I now submit that an increase of assessment of $200. to cover these two purchases is enough. The previous assessment has lost its meaning. The sales price proves full commercial value. I think the assessment should fall below that.[1]

> V. faithfully
> Stephen Leacock

P.S. Please present this letter intact to the court.——

1   In a letter to Leacock dated 13 November 1939, A.B. Thompson wrote: 'they decided to accept your proposal and fix on the increase in your assessment for the Railway lands at $200.00 in all, instead of the larger amount that had been suggested.'

## To Mrs Herbert T. Shaw                 Orillia Wed Dec 20 1939

Dear Fitz

I am so sorry that you and Peggy are not coming up to Orillia I asked an extra person chiefly for Stevie's sake, though I like his company & his being here would meant a lot for getting work cleared up that otherwise I couldn't do. I am sorry you dont find him very acceptable to you but really it is not as if it were a case of some personal enemy or hostile woman . I had no idea that you would cancel your plan on that account. Mrs Hamilton is ill and cannot come, and Donald and Barbara are people you get on with, to say nothing of René. It seems wrong to object to one extra person when it means a lot for my work. I hope that you will change your mind and I will have the car ready to meet you and Peggy at Oshawa as soon as you send word. I did not know anything was wrong in Montreal. I was not at all well and have not been well here. I am within ten days of seventy and what I have left seems short and running to an end & I think of death all the time, and have no courage to face all the pain and illness that must precede it. I had lots of courage for poverty and work but none for this. So I have no heart for wrangling over things that occupy young men & girls. It's all too far back. I hope you can come. The railway fare is of course my Xmas present, and you and Peggy will be ever so welcome here

> best Xmas wishes to all of you
> Stephen Leacock

## To James Keddie

[The Windsor
Montreal]
Jan 6 40

My dear Keddie

Happy New Year to you! Though, Heaven knows it looks gloomy enough, at large.

Herewith a correction for our Dickens. I have just read the latest Dickens book, Dickens and Daughter (Gladys Storey 1939) The writer was a friend of Mme Perugini, Dickens's daughter Kate and companion to her in old age. The book contains family details which I never saw before and which I am sure were not, many of them, hitherto in print. In particular it tells what happened to the Dickens family after Dickens's death.

It enables me to correct an error which doesnt matter in answers but which ought not to be repeated in Little Journeys. Most writers have spoken as if John Dickens (father) lost his job. It appears not. But whether he drew pay even while in prison I cant find out. So I use safe language. They finally pensioned him off (after the prison on £145 a year . . .

Mrs Storey also gives the true account of Dickens's separation from his wife,—which, with your sanction, can I do not propose to reproduce. Dickens went crazy over a young actress, had an affair with her, from which was born a child which died in infancy . . . While the affair raged Dickens bundled his wife off. Mrs Storey quotes Dickens's daughter as saying—"He did not care a damn what happened to any of us". . . .

But a thing that has slept for nearly a hundred years may well rest longer. After all it is only Mrs Storey saying so . . . . To put it in a child's book would leave a mean stain on its best page.

best regards
Stephen Leacock

(Please confirm) leaving out this supposed proof of Dickens's rottenness to his wife. It sounds bad enough even as I wrote it

## To Barbara Nimmo

[The Windsor
Montreal]
Th Jan 11. 40

Dear Bâ

Herewith 10⁵⁰ to cover 9.10 + exchange . . . I was wondering if you could give me some help on my British Empire book—figures, not only empire but world—There's one chapter on the 'wealth & resources of the B Empire which bristles with them—could you work in a reference library, say two hours a day—You see you could be ~~check~~ working on Chap II while I finish the others—The work is checking not finding material in Encyclopedias—U.S. Govt publications —League of Nations etc—I'm afraid to let the figures go without some one else looking over them—Say $50 for a month of two hours a day not Sundays—What could you do with Nancy? What would that cost? . . . You see, Culliton is too busy, in fact it was hard for him to find time for the enclo . . . I could get one of the Library girls of course—but then it's a pity to pay them when you might enjoy doing it & getting the money.

Best love to you all

y. a. u.
Stephen Leacock

## To Charles Leacock

[The Windsor
Montreal]
Jan 23. 1940

Dear Charlie

You will receive from the Bank of Montreal, Guy & Sherbrooke Sts, a demand note to sign for $550⁰⁰. I will endorse it to the bank at interest of 5½% per cent. The bank will then transfer in my name $550 to my credit at the Bank of Nova Scotia, Sutton, and from this sum I will issue cheque to pay your telegraph account $36⁰⁰ your telephone accounts $104⁸⁰ and others as listed by you and also enough money to repay to the Bank of Montreal the interest they charge against me and also enough to send you $20⁰⁰ a month, beginning as soon as the money is in the bank at Sutton. I will also undertake to pay your taxes ($31⁰⁰ a year more or less, and the interest on your mortgage $27⁵⁰ a year more or less.

In return you will make over to me by endorsation each of your interest cheques from England as received. If the money is more than enough to look after the changes mentioned above I will refund you any balance that is due, once every six months. If the money is not enough to cover the charges above including the $20 a month and the interest on the loan on the mortgage and on the taxes, I will carry the difference as a debit against you until further notice holding against it the securities mentioned below

In return for my doing this and as a security against the loan from the bank of Montreal and other advances you promise, and hereby in endorsing this letter as accepted you do promise, that my various claims under this arrangement as a first charge against both the interest and the principal of your English remittances, a first charge against your Sutton property (except for the first mortgage of ~~500~~ $400), a first charge against your personal property and your estate and against your inheritance to be received from TM Leacock's estate when father dies and against any other inheritance or assetts whatever. And you further promise that in the event of your receiving any legacy on fathers death, or in any other way you will apply it first to extinguish the debt due to me as above, and if there is any money left over after the payment of this debt and your $400 mortgage you pledge yourself to hand it over to me for investment in a ~~terminable~~ life annuity in your favour.

The plain meaning of this letter is that I am advancing money to pay your debts but that neither I nor my estate are to draw any profit from this. And if any doubt arises as to interpretation of this arrangement I promise, and you also promise, to accept the decision of George (George Leacock) as legally binding.

Your affec. bro
Stephen Leacock

I hereby accept the arrangement made in this letter

Charles John G. Leacock


## To Mrs Smith

[The Windsor
Montreal]
Feb 1   40

Dear Mrs Smith

Your letter of Jan 2 only reached me yesterday . . I was away in Orillia in the early part of January & the letter went there & missed me & by some delay which I dont understand only turned up last night . . I am so sorry for the delay in answering such a charming letter . . I send you herewith a signed copy of Mr. Roosevelt & I'll be delighted to autograph anything you care to send here . .

I also enclose a page of manuscript. I have found that people like to see authors manuscripts, and I suppose that after writing 40 books I can begin to call myself an 'author'.... It's a term I've always avoided. I had a friend long ago who wrote one book, and then always referred to himself as an author, as if it was his trade & designation,—he would say, "an <u>author</u> generally likes a pipe first thing in the morning,"—meaning that <u>he</u> did .... But I find that I am very glad to own a page of MS of O'Henry (I have it framed) & so, within my degree, hand out manuscripts. This bit of copy is a page from my new book to appear this spring, <u>A Presentation of the British Empire</u> .... I dont often have to change what I have written: when I do, I tear the page down to keep it from the others. Hence the tear in this.

with repeated regrets for delay<br>Stephen Leacock

<u>P.S.</u> I noticed afterwards a lot of scrawled writing on the back of the page & managed to decipher it .. It's the kind of note I scribble, not to forget a sudden idea. I cant read the first 3 lines but the rest is a piece of a broadcast that I did for Barbara Whitley to deliver (one of a series of three). The ~~BB~~ CBC are waiting for 'share air' for them. This one is called <u>Mrs Vanguard enters the War</u> I hope you'll hear it, I dont know how long before they use it

S. L

## *To R. W. Bardwell*[1]

[The Windsor<br>Montreal]<br>Feb 15. 1940

Dear Mr. Bardwell

I have to thank you for your very kind and interesting proposal. I think that I could make a home run hit, or, to use a more British metaphor, a shot between wind and water, with a pamphlet on

LIBERTY

Nearly a hundred years ago John Stuart Mill wrote a monograph on liberty, which became one of the world's books. It was translated into every European language. Patriots quoted it from a thousand platforms. Soldiers carried it in their knapsacks, and exiles in Siberia hid it from their guards.

It was the inspiration of the Europe of Mazzini and Kossuth, and of the England of John Bright. America accepted it as an exposition of principles already written into the Constitution.

1   Richard Woleben Bardwell (1889–19??) was an American editor and educator. While working as the educational editor with Row, Peterson Company (1939–42) he suggested to Leacock the idea of the pamphlet *Our Heritage of Liberty*.

But the passage of a century has smeared and dimmed the page and crossed it with corrections written in the hand of time. In our altered world Mill's negative liberty would mean little more than liberty to starve,—for bread a stone. Under our industrial circumstances, to leave the individual to his own exertions, would leave the weak to be trampled everywhere by the strong. The ideal of liberty, that there should be for each some province or his life and thought where the state must not intrude, is unchanged. But the application is as much altered as is our civilization itself from that in which Mill lived.

I think it would be a wonderful thing to follow out such an enquiry, without bias, rather searching for truth than stating it. Such vital problems as those connected with the social control of conduct,——the dogmas of the eugenist and the probitionist: the problems of the social control of industry,— the dogmas of socialism, and of collective regulation greater or less,—the old deal and the new: and at the summit the newer dogma of the totalitarian state annihilation the very foundations on which Mill stood,—all this presents a wide field, undermined with controversy and smouldering still in places with the ashes of old quarrels.

To make it a proper text for the young it should be made more of inspiration than of precept and dogma. The aim should be rather to present a vexed problem in the proper attitude of approach, than to offer solutions and panaceas to remove it.

I'd like to try it.

As to the financial terms I presume you would offer such and such a royalty with a certain guarantee. No doubt there would be no trouble about that.

But I am afraid I should wish you to go a little further. This kind of monograph written at this length and in this way would be of little use for any other kind of publication than what you suggest. If you found that you could not use my manuscript, a thing that might happen for a variety of reasons, I could make no use for of it except to submit it to other publishers for the same kind of purpose, which I should not want to do.

I would suggest that if I undertake to prepare a MS of say 15,000 words on Liberty, you in turn would undertake either to use it as stated, or if compelled to return it as unsuitable to give me such and such a sum (no great matter) as a sort of consolation cake,—what the lawyers call a "solatrium",—only in their case they take a lot of solacing. Their tears die hard.

V. sincerely
Stephen Leacock

## *To Charles Leacock*

Windsor Hotel
Montreal
Feb 18   40

Dear Charlie

Stevie is going up to Orillia for two days at the end of next week. I'll go too if I can but I am not certain . . . He expects to leave Toronto on Saturday morning, arrive Orillia at noon & stay over till Sunday night train for Toronto. He will stay the night in Toronto with Mrs Hamilton & return to Montreal by Monday day train.  If I come this schedule may be altered but thats the essential

Stevie would like it if you could come too, going to Newmarket by bus & getting the Sat. morning train. If you can, I'll send a cheque to cover all your expenses. Danny Bernwell is at Orillia, living in the back of the house & he will do all the work and the cooking. I hope you can come Send me a line right away.

I hope you are making plans to work your place in the summer

y. a. b
Stephen Leacock

P.S. In due time remind me of that note. There is only one out now

## *To Barbara Whitley*

[The Windsor
Montreal]
<u>Sunday</u>. Feb. 18 1940

Dear Barbara

I have this morning just started scribbling notes for a monologue
<u>Miss Rush leaps on Leap Year</u>

Miss Rush, that's you, is (or are) a rushing, voluble girl, talking ten to the dozen—no old maid type about her—but she's just made up her mind that's she going to snap up a man and snap him quick, it being leap year day (Feb 9) . . . She is sitting talking in a little upstairs sitting room, to a friend <u>Anne</u>, who has just come in . . ~~she is put~~ . . I make it an upper sitting room so that being in it she can hear any one come into the hall below . . . When she is talking to Anne she is waiting for a man to come,—a man to whom she has sent a "<u>love token</u>" . . . Presently he comes

I'll get it all to you in a few days—

Your affectionate Godfather
in the spirit
Stephen Leacock

## To Barbara Whitley

[The Windsor
Montreal]
Feb 23 '40

Dear Barbara

Peggy told me you liked the MS of the broadcast—so I'm very glad—Alter, change, shorten, lengthen use it as you like .... Remember a <u>text</u> is only a start .. there remains <u>voice</u>, <u>expression</u> feeling,—& in radio, all sorts of side devices to break the monotony that ensues if one seems to be <u>reading</u> .....

with best anticipations
Stephen Leacock

P.S. You broadcast a 7.45 .. Therefore make the girl say he's coming at <u>8 oclock</u>, then the hour of the action is the actual action of the hour, do you see .... ! !
P.S. I think the voice of a person puffing a cigarette is distinctive ... but not too long.

## To Barbara Nimmo

[The Windsor
Montreal]
Mon Feb 26 40

Dear Bâ

I should have written sooner but I was waiting to see—it turns out that I can't send The Empire book stuff as it needs so much consultation as to what goes in or not .. For a ~~long~~ lot of it I have to put things in if I can get them and if not, not ... Culliton has done a little and Mrs. Shaw is working on it a great deal .. I've been working awfully hard at it

I dont expect the <u>Too Much College</u> money for nearly, or quite a month. But if you need money I can send it on at any time. There is no trouble about exchange control in payment of an account or debt for services ... I am so sorry that things are slow and hope they will pick up. We must try to find some odd work you can do both for the money & for the interest. I'm so sorry that The Empire book was a flop in that respect

I enclose a story that Stevie wrote which was in the Standard last week— He has chicken pox & is staying in this week but there is no infection from reading this letter or the enclosure as he didn't touch either & in any case I understand that the virus of chicken pox dies fast. Best love to you all

y. a. u.
Stephen Leacock

## To R. W. Bardwell

Dear Mr. Bardwell

Your letter is fine. The financial terms first rate and I am glad to accept the proposal (royalty with guaranteed advance).

I would like to discuss a little further the question of just how young the young people are who are to read the monograph. You remember how W.S. Gilbert speaks of a "not too French French bean". I would suggest <u>not too young</u>. A book which one hopes to place in the schools must be young enough for school children. But I think in this case it would be better to have in one's mind the top class in the highschool, the senior pupils, so that the book could also be used in first year college, and read by people wanting to 'get wise' . . . . If I do it well enough it will have a wide circulation and never stop. I shall go at it with the greatest interest and naturally prefer a royalty basis.

At present I am just getting to the end of a book on the British Empire which I am doing at high speed, as specially of use and, I hope, help in war time. But even using time to finish that I should hope to get at this pamphlet before the end of March. But it would take a little doing to get it right . . . You might let me know how many <u>words</u> your 48 pages is. I'll write as many as ever you'll print, but I can cut it like a tailors coat to just whats wanted if I know before hand.

Very sincerely
Stephen Leacock.

## To Barbara Whitley

Dear Barbara

Thank you for such a nice letter,—. . I had been meaning to write to you . . The 'technique' of your last broadcast monologue was just <u>fine</u> . . Major Murray (I often see him) was talking of you with enthusiasm

When I get time (I am just buried, under the British Empire (a book I'm finishing)) I want to see you to talk to you about imitating <u>voices</u>, not necessarily to present two characters at once but to convey the idea of <u>age</u>, a peculiarity . . . When I was your age I was (almost) as gifted as you, and I could imitate all sorts of voices . . . It was quite a stunt . . I could imitate Professor Clark of Trinity College preaching & blowing his nose as he did it, . . and old Canon Cayley trying to say 'Ye are spies' and lisping so much that he may it sound 'Yeth pies' & they thought he was saying <u>Yes Boys</u>,—as the text of his sermon . . . How I wish I'd gone on with it . . But I had no nerve & no help . . .

However thats not the point. All I am trying to say is that <u>you</u> should develop your talent, because it is so well worth developing.

also very faithfully
Stephen Leacock


## To Barbara Nimmo

[The Windsor
Montreal]
(March 1940)

Dear Bâ

Here is what we call (in Montreal) a <u>ballon d'essai</u> . . . . If you see fit, please send it to four or five big educational publishers . . . If we get a contract I will write the book both the general introduction and the notices of the authors— You will prepare the material. I will take as my share 5 cents a word for what I write but nothing until you have had $500 from the royalties. After the royalties have paid you $500 and paid me 5 cents a word, then we share half & half.

You could do it all at home with your Nancy on your knee.

. . . . . . . . . .

Yesterday I finished and posted my <u>Presentation of the British Empire</u>, 75,000 words of which only 12,000 were already written when I came back here after Xmas . . . I have a contract for a school monograph <u>Liberty</u> in 15,000 words (Patrick Henry did it in a choice of two)—and I am working on <u>How To Write English</u> (a little book): Dodd will take <u>A New Survey of Economics</u> as soon as I will write it, and I have quite a lot of sketches that with future ones will make a book of selections called

<u>THE LIGHT SIDE, THE BRIGHT SIDE,—</u>

. . .

So you see I am busy . . . Your selections we could do & finish by July 1st ready for autumn . . Second thoughts,—write to a good many publishers & ask for their lists: see postscript. Keep track of postage & stationery expenses on this from the start

Best love to you all
y. a. u.
Stephen Leacock


P.P.S. Ste & I to go Orillia April 12

## To Mr Greenway

McGill University
Ap 4 1940

Dear Mr Greenway

I can sympathize entirely ~~from~~ with your point of view but I cannot see any way around the difficulty. What you are advocating is that the Canadian edition of my British Empire should ~~come out~~ not merely wait for the British edition but come out a <u>month after it</u> and two months after the American: or even longer, more likely three months.

I have the most eager hope for the value of this book in helping to hold American sympathy. It is more important in the States than at home, because with most of us it is preaching to the converted. There it may call sinners to repentance or at least ~~least~~ keep converts from sin, and strengthens faith already there. I have written it at high speed under a great strain: I have prepared with the publishers a circular of about 2000 words of extracts. I propose to send these all over with letters. No American publisher would think of arresting all this on the threshold. If he did, at any rate I wouldn't. Nor can I let the U.S. edition appear 2 months before the Canadian. That would make the importation of my book on the Empire illegal in ~~The Empire~~ Canada. The big U.S. book reviews of the New York Times, Herald etc go all over Canada,—more than any single Canadian publication. I hope to get a full page of the Times with illustration. It would be out of the question at such a moment to have my book not only not on sale, and indefinitely not on sale in Canada, but <u>illegal</u> as a order from New York.

The war time situation means that our mail is seldom less than 3 weeks in coming & often more.

Much of the book, such as the sections on Ireland and the war are of a current interest for U.S. readers that cannot wait

I am sure I need say no more except to express my regret at a situation that arises solely out of present conditions

Meantime I send you cordial thanks for the advance cheque for Too Much College & wish you as good luck with it as Dodd has had.

I send today the MS of The Empire. I sent the N.Y. edition 5 days ago. But in that case I was able to send it with ~~corrections~~ additions still to be made on galley proofs. With you there will be no time for that, so I had to keep it till the MS was complete

very s
Stephen Leacock

*To Frank Dodd*                                    [The Windsor
                                                   Montreal]
                                                   Ap 4 40

Dodd Mead & Company

My dear Dodd
    Yours of April 1st—Everything fine—I have to clear up one or two odd
jobs (articles delayed): then do the 15,000 word monograph on <u>Liberty</u> of which
I wrote: then I can get busy on <u>How to Write English</u> (I am making ~~it~~ notes of
it all the time.) . . . If it's a little book selling at a dollar I presume that 10 per
cent is all you could manage. On the other hand I'd like to keep it <u>cheap</u>—no
huge compendium about it—I want something that ordinary students can buy
& will buy for its own sake—
    But I'll expect to have it done on October 1st

---

<u>College Readings in Humor and Satire</u>[1]. I'd be glad if you would talk of this
with Messrs Crofts. The idea would be to get this book on the market early
enough in 1941 for booking it into classes for the 1941–42 session. I dont think
it could be ready for this session,—no time at least to sell it. I enclose a
Memorandum in regard to proposed contents
    Best thanks for the excellent cheques: you have certainly handled <u>Too Much
College</u> in good shape

                                        Very sincerely
                                        Stephen Leacock

P.S. Yes I'll do a <u>new Survey of Economics</u>, or hope to, as my main work after
<u>How to Write English</u>. It's all in my mind: as Zola once said, "It's finished, I've
only got to write it

                              Memorandum
                                   on
                    D$^r$ Stephen Leacock's proposed book
                    <u>College Readings in Humor & Satire</u>

This is meant as a full size college book, to cost the most that students will pay
but not more. My experience of such a price is that it is about $3$^{00}$. The book
would cover enough ground to serve as a text for the usual college course which
extends over 3 months & includes anything from 25 to 50 lectures. The Readings
would be drawn from English & American works only, from the earliest times
down. The special features ~~for~~ on which I should hope to make the book widely
popular would be the discussion of the <u>background</u> of humor & satire in the

---

1    This book was turned down by the publisher, who felt that the book would not find a
     large enough market.

social life of each period. This would take the form, first, of a general introduction, on a fairly comprehensive scale, entitled The Place of Humor in Literature; and secondly, little introductory essays, as a preface to each selection, or each section, intended to ~~elecit~~ elicit great interest in what is to come. This was the plan followed in my Greatest Pages of American Humor (Doubleday Doran) which has had a good & continuous sale. In the work under discussion I should wish to carry this plan a little further . . . .

In order to show what is meant by this environment or period writing I enclose a discussion of Charles Dickens's world & art, with certain passages marked as illustrative of the method.

Naturally the whole value of such discussion turns on how well it is written, & what ideas it embodies. I may add perhaps ~~that~~, without immodesty, that the way I do it is 'not half bad'.

I should use this plan as the means of bringing the comparison with foreign authors, e.g. Cervantes, and Molière whose influence could not ~~b~~ well be left out.

I think that a flat 10 per cent royalty would be fair but the money arrangements are easy, if there is faith.

Stephen Leacock


## To R. W. Bardwell

[The Windsor Hotel
Montreal]
Ap 5 40

Dear Mr Bardwell

I am delighted to accept the Liberty contract—you will note, I trust without the least offence, a clause I added to "mak' siccar" as they say in Scotland. It wont prevent my being only too glad to receive your editorial advice about anything that you think can be changed, altered or omitted with advantage

I am just done with my Empire Book of which I spoke. I have two or three odd articles to write (delayed). I expect to go to the country (The Old Brewery Bay, Orillia, Ontario on April 12th & have this monograph done, barring illness or other delay, in a month


## To Mrs Herbert T. Shaw

Orillia
Sat Apr 13 / 40

Dear Fitz

Still winter up here though there is a lot of bright sun this morning, plenty of snow in the bush & a lot of ragged snow round the edges of everything— lakes frozen—tremendous ~~snow torm~~ snow storm on Thursday night in Toronto & all up here—It is now 8 am    I've been up & busy since 6 but not out of doors yet – – had to relight the furnaces & start to unpack etc. There are a million things to do. It feels so different than Montreal with <u>nothing</u> out of doors. I havent seen your house yet—I'll go over later—not much question of gardening yet—except that it is the best to prune trees. We arrived safe & sound viâ Washago. Charlie got on at Beaverton & Walter Woods met us at Washago. Jones on deck. The two girls (the Crannings had cleaned up the house & today they move in for good.)—I have not unpacked my books yet as I want to get things straight a little before I try to work. I had a radio put in & it picks up Berlin as easy as nothing. It must be expensive. I dont think I'll buy it but I will rent it till I get to understand about radios. Jones has a couple of hot beds started but I havent seen them yet—I miss you very much and wish you could be here gardening alongside   Do come when you can & stay <u>here</u> not in your house— tell me what Rene says about his party—& tell me all the news—I cant write much of a letter yet till I settle down

> Yours affectionately,
> Stephen (Leacock)


## To Mrs Herbert T. Shaw

Mon Ap 15 (1940)
11³⁰

Dear Fitz

I've been super-busy all morning trying to get the Lodge ready—plumbing all to the bad & everything to do. I find that a whole lot of my pictures are there, some that I never, never could have given to Tina & that must just have been moved over from the house—also a regular <u>raft</u> of books, all sorts, including presentation copies from authors—I took the books back, 2 wheelbarrows full, but have left the pictures. Its hard to get things into shape here. It all seems dirt and litter—still, it gives one things to do all the time. Stevie & Charlie are going away tomorrow & I shall be alone here—but theres lots to do out of doors & things to write if I can get at it

Dodd Mead have sent the proofs which means I may have to get you to get information and telegraph it. By bad luck my freight is not here: meaning I have no encyclopedia & ~~not~~ only some of the guide books. It is still sort of half winter here. Yesterday cold & blowing but today getting milder. I got your letter of Friday & was glad to hear. The postman brought letters to the house this morning. I'll send this in by Rowe as he is taking the car in 'to the bull' so to speak, before starting to Peterborough to meet Tina & her brothers. The war news in this morning's paper looks good, but it's so hard to know just what hold we have on Norway. Sweden of course will be forced in. It's god's awful when you think of it. If only it could end before our own boys go.

> Affectionately
> Stephen Leacock

## To Mrs Herbert T. Shaw

Orillia
Tuesday Apr 16  40

Dear Fitz

I've been reading proofs of 'our' book—chapter I only, but it took a lot of time as I had to hunt up a few things . . . Tina and her brothers arrived about 9 pm. Tina started to cry but I spoke to her seriously & pointed out to her what a lot was being done for her . . . a nice home & five or six people working away to make it comfortable. I had Mrs Tunney get it all clean: bought some flowers & had the furnace & fires going. This morning she seemed much better. She has much lots to do—a house & garden & flowers all her own & her two brothers with her. Robert is a fine feller—I took to him immensely. Stevie & Charlie leave today . . . There is plenty to do but I find it hard not to be depressed with the terrible war news—all Europe will be in hell in 2 months

The weather today is real spring for the first time—Mr Rowe is fixing the plumbing of the glass house—Jones carpentering on hotbeds—not possible yet to dig or plant out of doors. . . George blew in for an hour yesterday . . . he had come up for an Orillia funeral . . .

Affectionately
Stephen Leacock

## To Mrs Herbert T. Shaw

Wed 3 pm
Orillia
(April 17, 1940)

Dear Fitz

I got 2 letters from you at once just now—Monday & Tuesday—I was so glad to hear;—I always am—today especially as I am alone & have been since Stevie & Charlie left yesterday. Stevie is staying over in Toronto and Charlie has gone on to Sutton—I feel as you do about the war. It's just too goddamn awful. Our only hope, for the boys sake, is that it will be so awful & so swift that it will blow the lid off in three months. It looks as if all Europe would go to war. I have got the paper yet as Mr Rowe didn't bring it. He is putting in the plumbing in the glass house) . . I hope to put the tomatoes in it on Friday & to plant cucumber seeds at the same time. The weather today was beautiful spring. It is lonely and depressing here: But I have no home life in Montreal & here there is out of doors to go all day long . . . I read more proofs today & am posting them . . . . . I enclose a letter from Dr Coats Dominion Statistician. You can tell Paule about it but dont part with it. Tear it up. Dr Coats is not supposed to make private recommendations, but I gather from his letter that he sent on a pretty friendly recommendation . . . as to the person of whom you write, I agree it is hard to do anything by, with or for him. And yet he cant last as he is. I tried to speak to him & he got mad. You, or someone might give him hell . . . I am going to walk in with letter & then walk all the way back, or else blow myself to a taxi . . I haven't started writing yet as the proofs take all my time & it is hard to get the energy & hope to do anything in the face of such news . . . I do hope you will come soon. It will be nice when you do. I cant go to your place through the bush but I'll go this afternoon by the lane

Affectionately
Stephen

### *To Mrs Herbert T. Shaw*

Orillia
April 18  40
Thursday

Dear Fitz

I went over to your place this morning (snow practically gone from the lane but the bush still impassable—everything fine—except the (south) gate knocked down—but the butt of it was all rotten anyway—apple trees <u>wonderful</u> & the cherry tree—your tied up shrubs ought to be untied & the climbing rose pulled up to place—I will not touch anything till you authorize it. The grass looks good. Garden all in a mess of mud—couldnt touch it for a week—today was wet, dirty, & drizzling so I had the staff here on indoor work, cleaning and painting the workshop and putting the hot water in the kitchen range—I cant quite understand the works on the radio I ordered, so I get my news mostly from the papers—things look critical—I imagine that thousands & thousands of Canadian boys will be going—especially if Holland is invaded—that will mean a need for men, trained, half trained or not trained at all—it all seems terrible—and I am afraid that the Germans have a hold on Norway difficult to shake . . As opposed to that I bought six geraniums for a dollar ten days ago & six more today—so as to make the sun–gallery a little more livable. It is nice here in the day when the men are working, but lonely in the evening—having no home life is poor stuff, but I have none in Montreal & at any rate it is nice to eat ordinary meals that don't cost 1$\underline{^{50}}$ per plate per person. I am hoping to hear from you today. You & the printer (proof) come together—I went to the boat house yesterday & knocked a hole in the ice (it is soft) & fished—could see perch but they wouldn't bite—quit now: going in with Mr Rowe to post this

Yours affectionately
Stephen (Leacock)

## *To Mrs Herbert T. Shaw*

Orillia Thursday Ap 18 (1940)
3$^{\underline{30}}$ pm

Dear Fitz

Your letter of Wednesday just arrived, made me feel sorry to think of how wretched you were feeling . . try to realize that it is only a depression because of the mean weather and the war; you are really all right & better this winter than ever in years & years . . . but it is hard not to feel crushed by the war. The only thing is to try to jolly ourselves with the idea that it will somehow crash & break. Goddamn the Germans—they're a poor lot . . . a mass of proofs came with your letter but I haven't opened them yet . . . I'm so glad I got that book finished when I did . . . I would never have done it here. I think that next fall I will close this place up with boards & not come to it in the winter & just pay a care-taker. I am disappointed with Tina: she doesn't seem to realize how much has been done for her . . It will no doubt be better if she goes away.

I think that unless somebody does something for Rene very soon it will be all over with him . . I think that you and Paule Tétrault should make an appointment with him & tell him that you are sure that McGill can keep him. I tried to talk with him but he got huffy right away . . . I wish you were here . . hope this place hasn't run out on me but it seems poor stuff being here . . I am having the men clean & paint the work shop and after that I'll keep on painting & fixing. It is all so shabby & so half complete . . . George said I ought to spend about 1500 dollars & fixed it all up . . I cant do that but I will spend all I can. I bought linoleum for the kitchen & I am going to buy some for the billiard room . . . I do hope you will feel better . . . I wish you could come up.

Yours affectionately
Stephen Leacock

## *To Mrs Herbert T. Shaw*

Orillia
Mon Ap 22   40

Dear Fitz

I am just going into town to post my <u>index</u>. Worked at it since 6 am & it is now half past eleven. It was a big job. I worked hours & hours on Saturday & Sunday . . . I am so sorry you are not feeling well especially as it seems to make you so depressed. I wish you could be up here . . The good thing here is that there is plenty to do out of doors. This year I find I can do a lot of work; gathering wood & all sorts of odd jobs . . But it is lonely at night to be here alone. I have got the glass house planted & hot beds & today planting some peas out of doors—The ice is still in the lake . .

The war news, thank God, looks better, that is, with such rapid movement there's good hope of a real smash up & end of Germany soon. I dont think they can stand defeat: They've no allegiance to Hitler except for ~~hours~~ success: not for himself: & the minute the success goes the country will blow up − − it's wonderful what they are doing but it is terrible to think of the loss

Yesterday I got Mr Rowe to drive me to go to dinner with George & Mary at Aurora (midday). But the car blew up at Barrie & I had to leave it there & hire a taxi back for Rowe & me. These motor people are all crooks. The car was sent in & inspected by the Pontiac man & although Rowe told him that it had heated up a lot in going to Peterborough the man said it was all right. The Barrie man, in 10 minutes,—as soon as it was cool enough to look at,—showed us that the engine water pipes had a crack

. . . . . . . . . . . . . . . . . . . . . . . . . . . . .

I am much concerned with what you say about René. Don't you think that you & Paule might arrange to see him & tell him of his position . . . Tell him he cant stay at McGill as things are

Among the deaths at Orillia is that of poor DeVere Wilson (of the Oro farm)—died 2 or 3 weeks ago . . . I hope I shall hear from you. I must go or I'll be late.

Yours affectionately
Stephen (Leacock)


### To Mrs Herbert T. Shaw

Friday 8³⁰ am
Orillia Apr 25. 40

Dear Fitz

Now that will be fine if you and Peggy can drive up in the first week in May—On short notice I will get your room ready with 2 beds & also upstairs Barbara's room that Peggy can have if she prefers it & perhaps she might care to ask little Barbara . . . also I can get in your phone at a day's notice . . but it will need a day . . I am afraid I expressed it wrongly about Stevie & Mrs Hamilton . . I only meant that when Stevie was away it was lonely here & it would be specially nice to have you come . . I didnt mean not come when he was here . . . Mrs Hamilton is not coming, and I'm afraid her coming & going anywhere will be restricted as she is not well,—she is 84 or 85 and seems breaking, which hushes animosity . . I had Jones unpack~~ed~~ your shrubs & the peach tree. Your apple trees look wonderful . . Also he put up the rambler-rose . . and I had Albanie rake leaves and burn them only on the drive . . The others not burned on the lawn but out on the garden . . Also Jones raked off the long flower bed . . . There is nothing more to do till you come as the earth is too wet and cold to dig, let alone plough or plant . . The ice is still there & makes everything late . . in my orchard we could dig on the high side, but only the day before yesterday . . my home garden I cant touch yet so you are right up-to-date except for a hot bed . . I was going to put in stuff & then remembered that the hot bed is now <u>asparagus</u> . . but if you like I can make one <u>in a day</u> & have it ready for you to plant . . I have your covers and it only needs four boards . . so let me know: I wont act till I hear from you . . . . It's hard to know what to think of the war . . it is terribly critical . . if the Germans can <u>take</u> Normandy by superior air power they can threaten England, but if we can take it then we've got Germany tight . . perhaps the sheer high speed of the war now may end it sooner . . I didnt go into your house . . it all looks all right except the gate post . . You can have Albanie all the time you're here & then have time to look round for a boy later

Yours affectionately<br>Stephen Leacock

## To Mrs Herbert T. Shaw

Sat 10 am<br>May 10  40

Dear Fitz

Happy returns for Peggy's birthday—it <u>is</u> today, isn't it . . . I got your two letters of Wednesday & Thursday together yesterday. The terrific war news seems to blot out everything − − but I am hoping that it means that the war may be short. The Germans <u>may</u> win an advantage but all they can do is to turn a short war into a long. As things are we <u>may</u> <u>win</u> a short war, a thing impossible while the deadlock lasted, and we must win a long war, since now all the outside world, U.S. & S. America is with us . . . but if we can beat the Germans in Holland then we go into Germany.

. . . I saw your young Charlie over "talking with Robert" in my orchard & sent him back with a reprimand . . He put in your six rosebushes, 3 in the upper bed & 3 in the lower  I couldnt remember the instruction . . You said something of getting a shack on your last day here—if it doesn't connect with me it is none of my business . . but if it is part of "what people are saying about me" (your version) it seems unfair to listen to it and believe it . . It's quite cold or almost today, bright sun but hardly a pleasure to work out of doors . . I've been up at daylight each day & wrote another article, shorter, only about 1000 words yesterday & today . . too bad about Rene . . but I wont write him . . I am sending Peggy a little remembrance by this mail.

Affection'ly<br>Stephen Leacock

## *To Mrs Herbert T. Shaw*                    Orillia Mon May 13   40

Dear Fitz

I think that, in a way, the war looks more hopeful. Some one is going to win it, as far as Central Europe is concerned, in six months. If that is <u>us</u>, then its all over. If not, then it's a long & slow war of years & years before we win. If I were Mary, I'd feel better about it than since it started . . . .

It was cold & rotten & has turned out beautiful now. Mrs. Ardagh & Maud & Marjorie have just been here (1.30 pm. I am waiting to go to town with Mr Rowe)—they have made a start today. I wrote a great big memorandum for them, all about costs & methods. I think they have struck a good thing—they are ever so much interested.

George & Mary drove up yesterday (Sunday) but it was cold & raw so Mary stayed here with Stevie & George & I went to Johnsons (7 trout) but too raw & cloudy for fun. . . . . I am working as I havent worked for 20 years . . up with the sun or before it & a lot done at my table before the men come . . It is nice here to have something to do. Thank you for calling up Stevie. He went to Quebec with George & so he would not, perhaps, have been there when you called the first time. I wanted to get something for Peggy connected with "Art" but I couldn't find anything here so I have written to the Art Emporium and told them what to send.

I expect to go to Montreal the day before McGill Convocation (Peggy will know when that is)—I shall get Mr Rowe to drive Stevie & me & come back the day after Convocation. I hope you can come up before then. Did you say anything to Marjorie about driving down? I didnt like to, in case you hadnt . . but I should think she'd like to go & the car is here

> Yours affectionately
> Stephen Leacock

## *To Mrs Herbert T. Shaw*                    Orillia  Tues
                                              May 14   40

Dear Fitz

I'm up with the sun & working till the war news at 8—The whole fate of the world for some years is being settled right now—It doesn't mean anything that the Germans over-ran the Northeast corner of Holland—The Dutch never meant to defend it—it is absolutely ~~liv~~ cut off by the Zuider Zee—but we cant tell yet about the rest—moving from the Hague looks bad

•        •        •        •

My work this morning will be answering letters for 2 hours—the damn things accumulate all the time . . . I want to ~~state~~ start writing on my pamphlet 'Liberty' but so far nothing done. Mrs A. & Maude & Marjorie came out for a few ~~minutes~~ minutes yesterday—Dave Parkes ploughed the ground—harrowing today—I want them then to work out costs by boiling up sealers in water; (A) over electric (B) over bought wood,—edgings etc . . . . . It is beautifully mild weather with perhaps rain . . I hope that Peggy will like the present. She ought to get it with this   I mean same time.

Affectionately
Stephen Leacock

## To Mrs Herbert T. Shaw

Monday June 5

Dear Fitz

I'm up early & just going to work but the war makes it hard to keep going—I feel sure that Italy is coming in & that the Germans will consolidate & hold all the channel ports and I dont see how the French can stand them back—Yet Aubrey Morphy (I saw him coming through) feels differently about it; he says the Germans have lost too heavily—will be checked along the Somme & the Aisne, & held and then slowly pushed back just as last time . . . The next few weeks ought to show us . . .

Yesterday was, in weather, Gods own day; just too beautiful . . . Your place looks fine: Charlie has cut the grass . . . I cut asparagus & gave it to Tina (with enough of mine to help out) for Sunday dinner; but I only cut the big ones & let the thin ones go . . .

It all looks beautiful here, but the war takes the heart out of it . . I miss you very much indeed & the place doesn't look the same either without Peggy flying around . . . I haven't heard from George,—no doubt at races . . . Aubry busy all day no Saturday holidays & hard work Sundays . . . he says orders are British with British money, <u>but</u> the Canadian gov't collects a <u>sales tax</u> on the stuff supplied to Britain—& there's a duty on anything in the States even if it cant be got in Canada—isn't that a heller! . . . I am pretty well decided to go back into my ~~hay~~ house and quit all <u>farming</u> here . . . It would be cheaper to leave Montreal but my roots are there & my heart. Fitz you just <u>must</u> speak to Rene: quote me. Say I said he would lose his job.

Affectionately,
Stephen
(Leacock)

## *To Mrs Herbert T. Shaw*

Thursday Je 6  40
Sunrise

Dear Fitz

Yesterday I'd got very low spirited over the war—later the evening news (last night a little better) . . Churchill's speech was brave but awfully depressing . . . & his absence of all reference to General Weygand, or to the French except that we must fight alone if need be . . . I felt that that he meant that the French army was gone, couldn't hold off the Germans . . . They began to yesterday . . . My god! the needlessness of it all . . . the contrast with the peace & beauty here & Europe ruined by a gang of criminals & a nation of gangsters . . it's hard to keep from being depressed all day . . . the remedy is duty & work . . . this morning I am up early to try to write, to begin in earnest my pamphlet on Liberty . . . a fit moment for it . . .

•　　•　　•　　•　　•

Local stuff . . Your place looks fine . . . I only cut any asparagus that it is big & leave the thin ones . . . I give it to Tina . . I finished planting one acre of potatoes—15 bags cost, outside of the labour on my own place already contracted for is:—

| | | |
|---|---|---|
| 15 bags @ 1.00 | — | 15.00 |
| fertilizer | — | 5.00 |
| Ploughman——————— | | 10.00 |
| | | 30.00 |
| add 1.00 for paris green | | 1.00 |
| | | 31.00 |

All the rest is with my own labour till taken up & sold hence,—outside cost— 31.00

Now as to what one would get

A very poor crop is 4 to 1　　= 60 bags

A very poor price is 25 cents = 15.00

　　　　　Loss　　　　= 31–15 = $16

A moderate crop is 7 to 1　= 105 bags

"　　"　　price is 40 cents = $42.50

　　　　Profit—　　　　$11.25 (if you don't count home labour)

A proper crop, to expect if well done is

10 to 1　　———————　150 bags

A pretty good price is 60　= $90.00

A fine crop is 15 to 1　　= 225 bags

" fine price " $1.00 a bag　= $225

———————————————

Counting home labour at 30 cents an hour means so far four men for 12 hours = $14.40 and as much again before I'm done with it . . . or $28.80 home wages. This makes a total cost of $60.$^{00}$  At present I am getting off my place per month, for my house use:—

| | |
|---|---|
| Ice | 7.50 |
| Milk & cream | 10.00 |
| Butter | 6.00 |
| Wood | 5.00 |
| Vegetables | 5.00 |
| Eggs | 4.00 |
| 2 ducks to eat | 4.00 |
| (some later) | |

$41.50

You won't read all those figures but they ease my mind . . now I must get some tea & get shaved & get to work . . . I'm so glad you are coming on the 16th—not so long now . . . The peonies will be just out – – all flowers gone now . .

> Affectionately
> Stephen
> Stephen Leacock

*To Barbara Nimmo*                          Orillia Ont
                                            June 7 40

Dear Bâ

Please write me your news & when coming & for how long & what time Don can get . . . . The war looks terrible . . I am afraid for the French army & Paris . . . then a sort of beleagerment of England by air . . . I was in Montreal for Stevie's convocation . . Opinion was low. Best love to you all

> y. a. u.
> Stephen Leacock

P.S. As far as one dare look ahead I have quite decided to go back to my Montreal house Oct 1 . . . My heart wearies for it . . . That will mean that you & Nancy can pay a visit . . . You could help us with installations.

## *To Mrs Herbert T. Shaw*                    Je 11  40
                                        Tuesday Evening 8 pm

Dear Fitz

Just been listening to news (7.57) & before that news—and news—and on the whole I think it's better—it means that the French & ourselves are in it together, with or without <u>Paris</u>—which is a wonderful & heroic thing of the French—if its taken it will be <u>empty</u>, & so the French bulletin said—will be burned down, if need be—As to Mussolini, world's prize skunk, he's our best asset—we can destroy Italy & the menace of it will stop Hitler idea of killing out England with gas from high altitudes—I feel as if the people in England feel <u>better</u> with Italy in, than they did—the miserable bastards can bomb <u>Malta</u> but it is bomb proof naval centre with a population with 10 Italians to one Englishman —meantime we can cut off Libya & let 200,000 Italians die of thirst, and leave a bunch more to Ethiopians in Abyssinia who have seen their women & children killed with gas bombs—if they get a chance they wont leave an Italian alive—we are doing it: they are. It seems possible now that the whole god damn combination may burst up in fragments if their French attack fails.

·      ·      ·      ·      ·

I learned this afternoon that you are not coming tomorrow. Tina said that she had made a mistake about what your maid said & that you are coming on Monday—but that means <u>Sunday</u> night doesnt it—It's disappointing but it wont be long & you'll be here—your peonies are just <u>almost</u> out but not quite—I was expecting you'd see the first of them − − − − −

Photographers and newspaper men (3) of them from the Toronto Illustrated paper (New World) came up & took pictures of this place for a feature article— 2 of them had been in Germany in 1933–34,—all over on bicycles—at that time ever so many people, they said, dead against the new Naziism . . . I took them to Johnson's (on their way home) to get photos of fishing—I caught quite a few fish, in fact quite enough to make it worth while—more than we have caught for a long time—they fished but only got 2 or 3—

·      ·      ·      ·

Its been hot & muggy . . I have been finding it impossible to write, because of the war-crisis—but in a sense everything is duty—poor Norman Rogers, what a terrible death—but at least his name will go on . . . The weather has been muggy & hot, but the country looks wonderful—everything growing visibly . . I havent seen Maud or Marjorie or been over to their garden, though I have through yours which is fine—grass cut again & everything shipshape—Tina says your new maid is cleaning everything up; so it will be easy for you when you come . . I'll be glad when you are here: you dont get as downhearted about the war as I do . . . by the way the chief photographer, a most artistic young man, fastened on Peggy's picture, not the new one    I mean the little one she did as a kid & that we call Ste Eustache and asked who did that? & I said a little girl of about 10 did it when she began to draw & he said it was extraordinary—& I could see he meant it . . . I'm going to blow myself to two taxis to go to the library for a book

Affectionately
Stephen
Stephen Leacock


*To Barbara Nimmo*                                    Orillia. Je 20 1940

Dear Bâ

Yours Je 12 . . . . I am writing to the Bank to send you $28$\frac{40}{}$ U.S. . . . To save me a lot of hunting round please send me a memo of this acc't—original sum & succession payments about $90? wasn't it? . . . & I paid so & so & you say its now $58.24? . . . . Middle of July? . . first rate . . I'll get a little maid for Nancy . . I had to let go the two sisters I had here (Rita & Theresa Cranny): They were charging things to me in Orillia without authorization

I have a new girl coming from Tina's home . . & I have engaged Tina for $15 a month to come in for about 4 or 5 hours a day & to cook both the and dining dinner . . meaning that I feed Albanie & Robert for their chief meal . . Tina also gets $15$^{00}$ for washing & $36$\frac{00}{}$ crash for board of Albanie & Robert so she does well, especially as there is damn little to pay for them as she gets their big meal & all milk, butter, eggs & vegetables . . . . . . . This year the cow gives me all the milk & cream & butter needed . . . the hen yard only costs 10 cents a day for food—that's for hens ducks, chickens & a cow & we get about 6 or 8 eggs a day: I get $7.$\frac{50}{}$ worth of ice per month, wood about $5$^{00}$ in summer & soon vegetables, berries & all that . . . .

But even at that it is hard to carry all my expenses . . especially now that the war has come in this terrible fashion . . It is awful~~ly~~ . . one thinks of it all the time . . There is no hope for France . . I wouldnt say it in print but the hope for England seems low . . The only chance is this: Germany perhaps, indeed very likely, cant invade and conquer England without using gas & bombs dropped from a great height, irrespective of military targets . . The English will do it in return when desperate . . ~~great~~ whole cities-full will be killed by both. Their short distance will give them a four or five to one start . . but even at that both will have to quit . . That in the long run will be better than straight conquest as of France . . . that crazy Maginot line, with a big ~~w~~hole at the side of it . . . . It's hard to work . . The place looks beautiful . . Uncle Charlie is batty as a bug & I am afraid he has cashed his English money & not paid it over to my account as arranged . . . .

I hope business will pick up . . It will fine to have you all here presently & Nancy will be a real treat . . I cant remember who it was I had as maid for her last year

y. a. u.
Stephen Leacock

P.S. I'll post you an <u>Empire Book</u> as soon as my next packet comes. I only had six & only 1 here

## To Mr Napier                                       Orillia, July 20th, 1940.

Dear Mr. Napier:

I understand from Mr. John Bassett's letter and from our conversations at my house, that your corporation proposes to prepare and distribute a presentation volume dealing with the development of Canada. The book would contain about 60,000 words with suitable illustrations and, possibly, tables of reference. The central thought would be a picture of the past that would carry the hope of the future; a vision not only of what our country has been, but what it may rise to, if we live up to our ample opportunities.

Such a volume would be intended not only as bright and interesting reading, but as carrying with it an inspiration for its readers. The intention would be that your corporation in publishing the book would earn the gratitude of the Canadian public; that what you would accomplish would be a service far wider and more worthy than a trade advertisement, and more to be valued than a mere personal present. What you would aim to secure would be a book that would be appreciated, talked about and sought after for its own sake.

I should be glad to be associated with such an enterprise. Such a picture of our country's history is one that I have long wished to present. It should show in its foreground, the passing lights and shadows of romantic history, the adventure, the exploration, the long years of conflict in arms, that make up our wonderful history of Canada; but behind all this the truer and deeper colours of the background would reflect the life of the people, the brave adversity of their pioneer days, and their gradual emergence into the plentitude of our industrial power. Seen in this light what we think of as the business and economic life of the plain working day of the farm and the factory, becomes the main strand in the tie that holds us to the past and draws us towards the future. Reading such a book the business man might reflect with pride, "I, too, am part of that."

. . . . . . . . . . . . . . . . . . . . . . . . . . . . . . . . . . . . .

Such a volume could not be overhastily prepared without injuring its chance of real success. I think that your corporation would be wise to calculate that the earliest date at which their volume might be in the hands of their friends would be the first of May of 1941. That season of the year is always recognised with us as one of the most propitious moments of publication. The summer languor has not yet dozed the reader off to sleep, while the recollection of last year's books has grown dim.

. . . . . . . . . . . . . . . . . . . . . . . . . . . . . . . . . . . . .

I gather that a very considerable edition would be presented to the friends of your corporation; that a certain smaller quantity of books might be specially bound up as an <u>edition de luxe</u>, but that the main edition would be in the ordinary form of the bound book that appears on the market at from two to three dollars a volume. The general make-up of the book, I feel certain, would be such that any writer might be not only willing but proud to associate his name with it.

. . . . . . . . . . . . . . . . . . . . . . . . . . . . . . . . . . . . .

The book would contain, I understand, as an addendum, a special chapter showing the part played in the industrial life of this country by your corporation since its inception nearly a hundred years ago. This chapter would not be part of the material signed by the author, but he could, of course, prepare the composition of it from material supplied by the corporation. This would be so handled as to fit into, and refer back to, the historical picture developed in the book itself.

. . . . . . . . . . . . . . . . . . . . . . . . . . . . . . . . . . . . .

The further suggestion has been made,—and I think it admirable,—that there might be added a brief chapter presenting the chief episodes of the development of your corporation, as a matter of the living memory of a person old enough to recall them as personal recollection. Such a chapter under some such title, as "I remember," would, I think, form a fitting tail-piece or <u>envoi</u> to the book.

. . . . . . . . . . . . . . . . . . . . . . . . . . . . . . . . . . . . .

If I undertook the writing of this book, I could begin work on it a month from now, and finish the manuscript,—God willing,—on March 15th, 1941, thus allowing six weeks for making the book. The illustrator could work with material currently supplied, and finish his part in the enterprise as soon as the writer, or even sooner.

. . . . . . . . . . . . . . . . . . . . . . . . . . . . . . . . . . . . .

The financial terms are a matter which I think it better to leave to written communication. I would ask you to attach a proper value to the use of the my name,—an asset, which, such as it is, has taken 70 years and 50 volumes to secure; but, if I may say it, still more to the interest I feel in the subject and the capacity which I may have to present it. You must, of course, take into consideration that such a work requires a wilderness of reference and research work over and above the composition itself. It is obvious that this book, if I undertake it, would engross the great bulk of my time, till its publication.

. . . . . . . . . . . . . . . . . . . . . . . . . . . . . . . . . . . . .

On this basis, I am certain that you can make me an offer. I would prefer not to engage in any higgling; I feel assured that what you might offer would be reasonable, and would represent the most that you felt your corporation could properly give as a compensation for the services performed. To such an offer I could give an immediate answer. The hundred and one minor details that arise in such connection could easily be settled later.

With best hopes for our working in collaboration,

Very sincerely,
Stephen Leacock.

## To Charles Leacock

Orillia
Aug., 9th. 1940

My dear Charlie,

While there is still time I wish you would try to get better control of yourself, and to make financial arrangements to carry on. If you do not do this none of us can be answerable.

I still have a small balance of the money you borrowed and from it could still give you $20 a month for three months beginning now, and perhaps Teddy or one of the others could then give you $20 a month for three months by which time your dividends are due. You would agree to pay the dividends into my Sutton account and receive them back at $20 a month and thus have regular means of support. Teddy, or any one else advancing the $60 needed could have the same security as I have against your property and anything you inherit and could rank ahead of my claim.

I am sending copies of this letter to Teddy and to George and to Dot. Beyond this I can go no further.

Your affectionate brother,
Stephen Leacock

## To Barbara Nimmo

3869 Cote des Neiges Road
Montreal
Sat Oct: 25  1940

Dear Bâ

Stevie wrote about poor René's death.[1] It was all terribly sad. He could only have lasted a few months at the best, or even weeks . . .

I now send you a clipping about Dr Day who seems to have played a fine part. We have no later intelligence of how he is getting on . . The principal is

---

1   René du Roure died on 15 October 1940. Friends maintained that his heartbreak over the German occupation of Paris played a significant role in his death.

taking some of his lectures. If they had <u>asked</u> me to I would have done it but after the way they acted last year I didn't feel inclined to make an offer & get a rebuff again . .

I am terribly busy with my big contract for a <u>de luxe</u> book on Canada which the Seagram Distillers Company will distribute as a gift book . . I've done nearly 10,000 words. Ive a lot of other stuff but it is hard to get the crony[2] . . . Write & tell me how Nancy is & how Don is getting on & all the news. Vote for Roosevelt. Its life or death for us. Wilkie once elected will do <u>nothing</u> for us & its hard going . . What about Xmas. I dont want much to go to Orillia but I think Stevie is very keen on it & so he will go. How do you feel about it. If you & Don & Nancy were sure to come I'd be more anxious . . Uncle Charlie is 'out' of the jug. George paid his debts 280.$^{.00}$ & started him up again at Sutton. I wanted him to go to Orillia. At Sutton it will start again

> y.a.u.
> Stephen Leacock

2   The term *crony* here appears to be a shortened form of *chronology*.

## To Barbara Nimmo

> 3869 Cote des Neiges Road
> Montreal
> Nov 10  40

Dear Barbara

I am very pleased & proud to know that David is in the air force: I must write him. It will help you better to understand how we feel about Mr Roosevelt . . I see that General Dawes has said, in effect, that England cant win. It looks as long and weary business, years & years . . an awful prospect for boys going into the war, but thank God they don't see it that way.

I am sorry to say that I cant manage Orillia this Xmas. The railway cost is too much. Last year, you see, it cut my room rent of 4$^{00}$ a day & that offset the fare. But this year I'd have to take Stevie & me & Tina & still keep the furnace man going & the coal bill . . . So Ive given it up. I may have to go to Toronto & back for a McGill meeting but that will be just before Xmas

Best love to you all.

> y.a.u
> Stephen Leacock

*To Barbara Nimmo*                                   3869 Cote des Neiges Rd
                                                     Montreal
                                                     Nov 15. 40

Dear Bâ

(Yours of 12)—Please type enclosed & send one copy to my ~~our~~ old friend
Harry Bruce (once of Beaverton),—H.A. Bruce, Riedesel Ave. Cambridge
Mass.,—The original & one to me—Bruce writes that he is doing a book on
the psychology of writing & asked my help. Hinc illae—if you know what that
means. If not, ask Donald,—or Nancy—We must talk of Xmas later—If you
drove to Toronto & if the weather was really open you might all drive on here
& I could pay for you & Nancy to go back in the train to Toronto so that Don
would be able to drive the car ~~whether~~ weather or not. Finance is naturally tight,
especially as no money from England and as I am putting all my work on a book
not paid till its done & not very much in the way of casual articles—But my Too
Much College did so well that it has carried me along—We are very
comfortable in the house & I find it much better for work . . But the war
shadows it all . . All those little boys who were at Selwyn with Stevie are in the
army now—its sad to think of it, and hard not to think of it

                                                     y. a. u.
                                                     Stephen Leacock


*To Barbara Nimmo*                                   3869 Cote des Neiges Road
                                                     Montreal
                                                     Jan 22 41

Dear Bâ

I reenclose the cheque—very nice of you but I couldnt dream of it—especially
as I make enough from books & articles these days to cover all ordinary expenses—
So glad to hear of Nancy's progress. Never let her go too fast, but I think that
learning things by heart, without effort, strengthens the memory—I wish I could
get some regular work for you to do with me. I am nearing the end of my Canada
book and have 2 others in sight but they dont so much lend themselves to library
work—Humour, we'll see—Uncle George & Mary were here yesterday at lunch
—Mary's first time in this house—They are so happy about their refugee children
—no special news—The war begins to seem god's awful here—
Do you hear from David?

                                                     love to you all
                                                     y. a. u.
                                                     Stephen Leacock

## To Mr Greenwood                                March 5 1941

John Lane The Bodley Head

Dear Mr. Greenwood

I have been laid up for 3 weeks or more,—bronchial cold plus gout, a fine combination which works in relays . . . Hence my correspondence was cut off.

I cabled you that I would do a book in the British life & thought series. I was not quite sure from your letter (and how in Heaven can you fellows collect your minds to write at all!) just what the volume was intended to cover & whether that had been thought out, but I am so keen on a particular volume as indicated by the enclosed title cover & enclosed memorandum that I am sure it would be just right and do a lot of good You may have written in a contrary sense about a different kind of volume. If so please reconsider, or take two. I gather the volumes are of 25,000 words. I could do the one I want to do in six weeks after receipt of a cable. Ergo on receipt of this letter please send me a contract (I am sure the terms are all right) and at my expense send ahead a cable telling me to go ahead. Deferred cables are only 9 cents a word so you say an awful lot without it costing more than a round of whiskey & soda at the club.

> Best wishes
> Stephen Leacock

P.S. I join with millions overseas in our continued marvel & admiration at what is being done "at home". We are glad to call it that again.


## To Mrs Herbert T. Shaw                          Orillia Ont
                                                   May 8  1941

Dear Fitz

The enclosed will show you why you didnt hear from me—my head was tired, I suppose, when I wrote the address. The office sent it back,—on general principles,—as my name wasnt on it and they didnt open it

Today Lou & Valmont are over at your place ploughing; it will take all today & tomorrow but the harrowing is nothing & so whenever you come you will have everything ready to plant,—the ground is in beautiful shape . . I will have the grass cut with a horse-mower. We cut mine yesterday but the knives were not sharp—I am still struggling with masses of unpacking freight & express & books & trying to get tidy & in order. So far not able to start literary work. Yesterday I got Lou to drive me to Johnsons & we fished from $4\frac{30}$ to six thirty or less. I got 8, Lou none—so that place is still all right . . I have a radio on & get the war news (two daily papers) more regularly than in Montreal. It looks terrible & yet it is plain that the U.S. will be in the war . . That must in the end win but my God! how long first! . . I remembered Nancy's birthday & set a small cheque as a proof of remembering it. Later I may try to give her something really good . . . will write to you tomorrow

> Affectly
> Stephen Leacock

## *To Mrs Herbert T. Shaw*          Orillia, Friday 12.30
                                      (May 9, 1941)

Dear Fitz

You asked about poetry about music:

I   Poetry about Music
    "The Lost Chord"—a poem about music set to music . . . distinguish this from 'The Lost Cord', of your last year's wood, somehow vanished.
    ——— ———

II  The poem: Thérèse, Thérèse . . . (I only recall it dimly; the little hands (of the girl now dead) at the piano
    ———

III Many poems turn ~~of my~~ on music
        Dryden: Alexander's Feast (keep this clear from Alexander's band).
        Gray.    The Bard

In fact all lyric poetry is poetry & music together. As for example the Marseillaise, composed as words and music together . . . There is much more to be said . . . but it will keep . . . I am getting ready to go to Toronto (McGill meeting) by car with Lou expecting to return late tonight − − I seem to get nothing done, because there is so much to be done . . . I had an article to write $100 (Banking, New York) . . . dead line May 12 at New York . . it looks up the spout . . but I can start something else . . . Let me know of anything you want done at your place . . My asparagus in a (relative) frost.—winter killed, I guess; a lot of it again

> Affectly
> Stephen (Leacock)

## *To Mrs Herbert T. Shaw*          Orillia  Thursday
                                      May 22  41
                                      12.30 noon

Dear Fitz

I hope you are feeling better . . . Your letter of Tuesday which I got yesterday made me feel quite concerned . . . but perhaps you got overtired or overdone . . . . Today I got up early & to my desk. The Toronto Magazine called the New

World asked me a piece on the U.S. for a special number & I wrote it all this morning about 1300 words & corrected it & sent it in to type & expect to get it off today . . . Another magazine called Think Magazine (New York, a house magazine) wrote to me for an article on U.S. & Canada & I'll do that (I have till June 15) So I am having a run of magazine articles that are paying expenses, even the huge wages bill here . . . . I sent over to Mrs Small. she is much concerned with the idea that the British case doesn't really reach Washington . . . but I think she's mistaken—She wants to sell her two Orillia places . . would sell Invermara at a sacrifice . . Will probably not be here this summer  Going to be with her sister (Mrs Bort) who is not well but cant be in Canada . . She says the Duke of Windsor doesnt drink a drop (I dont believe it) & that he seems enslaved by Mrs Simpson . . I had little time to talk of Nassau . . . After I left I drove down with Ansell to fish at Johnsons . . . hot, hot . . not a bite . . . I am still planting . . your place is all done except the potato patch & I'll leave that till you come . . . I am hoping you will turn up for the 24ᵗʰ . . I like it here while I am busy in the day in working & planting but otherwise,—it is lonely . . . I hope Mr Evam will soon have something . . I got a packet of stuff about the book including queries & what look like the dummy.

> Affectionly
> Stephen (Leacock)

## To Mrs Herbert T. Shaw    Orillia. Fri May 23 (1941)

Dear Fitz

I got a letter from you by the morning mail—none yesterday—I've been getting quite anxious about you not feeling better . . . really depressed . . I get depressed up here now till I get busy & work . . . I did what I think was a fine article yesterday, as I mentioned, called Uncle Sam, Good Neighbor, for the New World, Toronto . . 1600 words, all in one long sitting . . . .

Lou is going over to your place this afternoon for what he calls "lill' job" that you gave him . . . also water the pansies . . You'll be delighted when you see the peas in your middle garden, . . rolled flat as a pancake, clean, neat & symetrical . . .

An hour ago I got a letter from Bâ that they are to arrive this evening so I am turning on the staff to get the rooms aired & ready & ordering food.

I'll be so glad to see Bâ & Nancy & Don . . . its lonely here & I can't work after midday meal

The war is terrible isn't it . . oh my God! the French! I wish we could recognize anything, anybody & call it France & call Vichy, Vichy & keep on saying Vichy is not French . . The French in Vichy are under German control . . .

I hope you will be coming soon . . . and I hope Peggy will pick up & be feeling better . . We must definitely get her started on some art stuff because she has the talent and the energy and only needs a first start . . . I'll hope soon to see you

Affect'ly
Stephen Leacock

## To Mrs Herbert T. Shaw

Orillia
Monday May 26  41

Dear Fitz

I was over at your place this morning. grass all cut; the blue flower, those, out in full and some tulips. The peonies about to bud life size . . . still too dry to do anything—rain threatens & never comes—The war: I think that the U.S. will now get drawn in but it is sad to hear Bâ & Don talk of what much of American feeling is—if the U.S. naval power comes in we can hold the North Atlantic & the British Isles and North America <u>forever</u> and that means even if it is years & years: but its all hell to realize how helpless we are for want of fighter planes and that David Barbara's brother was here in his flying uniform: he's turned into a fine boy: at Brantford just now & knows nothing of when he goes over . . Ba & Don & Nancy arrived Friday evening & left Sunday afternoon. They will be back about July 12. Bâ is certainly fine the way she manages to make life bright on so little . . .

Affect'ly
Stephen Leacock

P.S. Your place looks ready at a minutes notice

## To Mrs Herbert T. Shaw

Orillia May 27  Tues  41

Dear Fitz

The news that the Bismarck is sunk makes the world look a whole lot brighter . . and the rest of the news on the whole is pretty good . . . I got 37 lbs of potatoes & 2 lbs of multiplyers & Norman, I believe has planted them all . . . The weather is muggy & heavy . . a little rain last night night but everything very dry . . . I enclose an enthusiastic letter from the Editor of the New World (please return it or keep it for me) on my article Uncle Sam, Good Neighbor. I wish you were here to read it to (perhaps you dont) . . . He sent $75 a very big price for Toronto . . . This muggy weather has stopped my work but I shall get at it hard on the first cool day . . . There's an awful lot to do here. barnyard &

buildings all in bad shape, fences rotten & the house needs all sorts of things. so it is an all day occupation to supervise it all . . . I'll be glad when you come up . . . I hope it will be soon . . . If there is anything you want done let me know . . Lou has dug up the flower bed and the place looks fine . . Your seeds are all up in great shape. They were planted on <u>May 12</u> the same day as mine in the glass house & are up nearly or quite as fast . . . My God, that Bismarck was a menace. That damn thing loose in the North Atlantic. Thank God they got it.

Affect'ly<br>Stephen (Leacock)

## To Mrs Herbert T. Shaw

Orillia  May 28<br>Wednesday<br>1 pm

Dear Fitz

I'll just scratch off a line while waiting for Albanie to start to town & then on to Barrie to get a hog—one of mine that was smoked & cured there—The news looks first this then that . . . once the U.S. is in the war, locked in, tight in, <u>really</u> in, then its all right . . . and Roosevelt with his clever <u>emergency</u> has, I think, made a situation where they can & will sink German ships & so presently get a <u>declaration</u> from Congress . . Get that and the world is ours. There was a demonstration here last night B.W.V.F. (fund) & I understand speeches & street dancing etc . . & George Drew . . They asked me but I couldn't do it . . Instead I went fishing with Lou & caught 11 trout & got Ansell to come back & dine & eat them. I hope you are coming soon—Its all right here while I am working in my study or busy on this place, but not so good the rest of the time . . I see we sunk a French Tanker, escorted by an Italian war ship . . my god! What a nation!!! if the war ever ends other nations will have their pride & their graves, but the French,—nothing.

Stephen Leacock

## To Mrs Herbert T. Shaw

Orillia  8.30 am<br>Thursday May 29  41

Dear Fitz

Such a beautiful, beautiful day! It just seems a heartbreak that there can be war . . . but now thank God after Roosevelt's speech I regard the end of the war as certain . . . long or short, Germany is lost . . especially because all the enslaved people will take heart. I see the French fired on & killed British bombers in Syria. . . .

I am up early and full speed at work . . books & farm . . just starting in to see Hatley about storing my two hogs, who lost their life in the abattoir in Barrie were there cured & smoked & now lie in the cellar, ruddy & brown in death . . . I now have 273 pounds of meat for a cost of 36.$\underline{00}$ (hogs cost \$10$\underline{00}$ for the two: ate 4$\underline{00}$ summer food bought and \$9$\underline{00}$ winter food bought), that is 13⅓ cents a pound . . . Ham being 45 cents & bacon 40 cents & even pork 29 I come out away ahead. . . .

Jack Drinkwater came over and drank whiskey last night . . . I've arranged to fish on his place . . . I hadnt known till he told me that George Drew is our sitting member in the Toronto Parliament . . Bill Finlayson gave up his seat to him.

> Time
> Affecly
> Stephen Leacock

## To Mrs Herbert T. Shaw                    Orillia Ont June 2  41

Dear Fitz

I've used up so much time in writing the enclosed letter to Jacques Chabrun. I sent it to you as of course I wouldnt like to post it without your approval & Peggy's . . . What I want to do is ~~the~~ to get him to say to Peggy, go to it,—send me the pictures & I will deal with them. (. . . . then she can get busy & feel happy & win out even if it means a little delay . . . I didnt write as I half expected you for Tuesday—now it seems to be Thursday—I shall be away on Wednesday & Thursday—. . I was up at daylight and working hard at my new book the one called How to Write . . . I'm so late with it, it means hustle . . . I'm glad I have to do . . . The war is such a dead weight of depression that without work one couldn't live . . .

My God, my God, those bastards . . . & the French (I mean the dirty ones,— say, they've done more against us, in handing over their navy & their colonies & their air force to the Germans than the Germans themselves ever could have done.

About Mary. What is she going to do? How is she fixed? What does she want? I am concerned about her. Can one be of any use to the boys.

> In haste, affectly,
> Stephen Leacock

## To Barbara Nimmo

Orillia Ont
June 2 1941

Dear Bâ

I am soon to hear what you say about your mothers finance. This is what she should do. Take such capital as she has left and put it into ~~her~~ an annuity. Let us put it, including what she may get under fathers will,—or rather grandfather Leacock's will,—at $3,000. She is 62. This works out at $20 (about $20) a month for life .. Present health is of no consequence: The worse the risk the better the annuity . . . A person (in old age) with $20 a month is an utterly different proposition from a person with nothing: can easily find a home with relations on a tolerable footing: has enough to pay board with a little pocket money over

The other side of it is that an annuity leaves no legacies,—nothing for you & David & Dora—But all you will get as things are going now, is little & perhaps nothing . . . . As to the money to come from England there cannot be much . . . George is in touch with Mr Vincent of Ryde who wrote to him & so he could properly write and ask him in a general way what the estate amounts to,—or on second thoughts I'll do it myself,—and enclose it,—and you can read it, return it to me & I'll send it on

I hope your mother will take this advice . . . Best love to you all: I'll be so glad to see you all again .. I still haven't framed Nancy: I must have it ready for her

y. a. u.
Stephen Leacock

## To Thomas B. Costain

The Old Brewery Bay
Orillia, Ont.,
June 2, 1941.

My dear Costain:

Your letter brought me most pleasant recollections of our association and work together in the past. . . . I'd like to see you anytime you pass this (Orillia) way.

About the book, Here's the difficulty. I've just finished a Canada book which stresses very much relations with the States. I did it for the big corporation (The Distillers) to distribute as a guest book. It is done de luxe with a lot of illustrations but apart from the form of it I really think that as a history of Canada it is very good . . . . . . . I hope that when the Distillers are done with their presentation I may get the right to publish a commercial edition . . . . . . . But my own publishers (Dodd Mead) have been interested in this book from the start and have told me (without seeing a word of it) that they feel they would make a good sale with it. So naturally they have first call.

Now I could and would like to do a book on historical relations of United States and Canada (or rather, British America) in spite of the existence of Keenleyride's five books but the bother is that phrases and words and ideas would so intertwine that the two books would have to be in with the publisher for fees of copyright difficulty. So I'd like to think about it.

Very best regards,
Stephen Leacock.

## To Barbara Nimmo                          Orillia Je 3  41

Dear Bâ

In further reference to your mother's affairs

Please find out for me:—How much is the <u>interest</u> & principal of the Beaverton mortgage . . . .

How much ought the Beaverton house to rent for, if rented, (a) furnished (b), un.

I take for granted that the house cant be sold even for the amount of the mortgage

Might it not be possible for your mother, if the Beaverton house will bring in as rent any surplus over the interest on the mortgage,—to move into Dot's house in Sutton & pay Dot the rent now paid and with the annuity of which I spoke & the excess of one rent over the other be able to make things meet especially if I could manage to give her a small amount per month, while I live and work. She could also have all the wood needed from Charlies farm,—I have advanced him $1050 for nothing but curses & ingratitude,—& from here supplies of vegetables preserves & all sorts that would cut expenses to very little—There is great danger that if nothing is done and if I die soon enough your mother will be in a very precarious position . . . So you might get busy

A fixed place to live, a fixed income, even if small—these are wonderful things.

y. a. u.
Stephen Leacock

## To R. W. Bardwell                          The Old Brewery Bay
                                              Orillia Ont
                                              Je 23, 41

Dear Mr. Bardwell:

I have given very conscientious thought and work towards the revision of the <u>Liberty</u> pamphlet, and I find it very difficult to work on the lines you suggest. I think the MS is excellent as it is, indeed first class, and only needs here and there the insertion of a lighter touch . . . . . . . It is hard to touch a thing up after the fact; it is like putting paint on a finished picture.

As I recall it you were to give me a 10% royalty of which you paid an advance of $275, which sum however was to be paid, and was paid, irrespective of whether the MS suited you. Nothing was said about the copyright, and whether if you paid $275 and did not care to publish the MS it would remain suppressed. The essential meaning of the contract was that I being a very eminent and successful writer of long experience and wide reputation (you will forgive the terms) could not be expected to submit a MS at your suggestion of such a full length as 15,000 words without some guarantee that my time would not be wasted. The flaw in the contract was that it didn't say what would happen if you didn't like the MS, whether you would then return it with thanks and regrets having paid $275 for the first chance to publish it, or whether you could count $275 a loss and burn the MS forbidding any other publication.

Under the circumstances I suggest that I pay you $100 (U.S.) and take back the MS and take a chance on what I could do with it.

My idea would be to alter it a little on my own hook and in my own way to make it, here and there, a little louder and funnier, and then see what another publishing house might think; and if it again didn't suit, I'd take the enterprise as finished with no ill-will about it and with every appreciation of your courtesy and patience and the compliment of your first suggestion.

Very sincerely
Stephen Leacock

*To Charles Vincent*

McGill University, Montreal
(permanent address)
but please answer to summer
address
The Old Brewery Bay
Orillia, Ontario
[June 1941]

Chas. Vincent Esquire
Solicitor:
Ryde, I.W. England

Dear Mr. Vincent,

I am a son of the late Walter Peter Leacock whose estate, as under a will of my grandfather, Thomas Murdock Leacock of Oak Hill, Ryde, I.W., I believe you are administering.

I had not seen my father since the autumn of 1886. I understand that your family have long been solicitors to the Leacock family and that you are fully conversant with the situation in regard to my father's estate.

Several of the presumptive legatees are far from well off and would like to have some idea of what the estate under present conditions amounts to, and whether and when and to what probable extent, legacies can be sent out to Canada.

As the senior living member of the family in America I thought I would ask you to send me such general answer to the above questions as might without prejudice be possible. My permanent address (in this world) is McGill University, Montreal, as I was a professor there for 36 years and now professor Emeritus. I give also the address of my house in the country at Orillia.

Very faithfully,
S.L.


*To Francis Paget Hett*    The Old Brewery Bay
Orillia Ont. July, 13 '41

Dear Frank,

I was so glad to hear from you. If Squadron Leader Shechan turns up anywhere within range I'll be more than glad to try to get him up here. . I've been thinking of you very much lately because the bass fishing has been simply wonderful and I keep contrasting the quiet peace of fishing on the Lake here with all that you fellows are doing over there. . I go out mostly with a friend of mine, a disabled veteran of the last war, unable to be in this, and naturally we talk of nothing but the war news,—till we get a bite. I do hope I live long enough to see the war over and to welcome you back here . . . This morning I heard Churchill, wonderful stuff . . . he's the greatest man England ever had before or after Alfred the Great . . . . the trouble here is that there is no way of getting into the war . . . for ordinary people—we can get as mad as we like but theres no one to kill . . . all around is peace & plenty and quiet, all the beauty & goodwill of Canadian summer . . . heavy taxes but the 'good times' pay for them . . the people are better off than they were . . . I haven't seen any of your people or the Sutton people this year . . . My brother Charlie was very ill, with a heavy operation, in three sections & so he has been, & still is in Toronto & I havent been over to Sutton . . . My sister Carrie's daughter Dora, is to be married in the Lake Shore Church on August 2 and so I expect to go over there for that . . . . . I have worked all winter very hard, that is, as hard as one can at 71 and am getting into better health . . but I cant travel any more and have to get to bed with the birds . . Do find time to write me a letter if you can, & tell me more of yourself and what you are doing.

With best regards to Alice &
to yourself,
Stephen Leacock

## To R.T. Ferguson

Old Brewery Bay,
Orillia
July 26, 1941

R.T. Ferguson, Esq.
Distillers' Corporation
Peel, Street, Montreal

Dear Ferguson,

I am sending you by express on Monday the Canada volume with such small revisions as are still needed marked in the text and the index. It is certainly a handsome book, beautifully bound, with striking illustrations, and the printing seems to me a splendid piece of work and a credit to the country.

I would like to repeat my suggestion that at the very start of your distribution you send 200 <u>de luxe</u> copies to England, to leading people noted for their imperial interest, such men as the Rt. Hon. L.S. Amery and Sir Edward Peacock, both very old friends of mine, and Lord Beaverbrook etc., etc. I would be very glad to help you with the selection of this list.

It would also be highly proper to send copies to all persons still living whose names appear in the text, or whose books are quoted, as for example Sir William Mulock, General McNaughton, Vilhjalmur Stefansson, Mr. Guy Ross etc. etc. A glance at the index would make it easy to compose the list.

I am also anxious, as I mentioned to you, to obtain from your corporation the right to the copy right of the book (text and maps, not illustrations) for use, let us say, six months after your presentation distribution begins. This would be in no way interfere with your continuing to print and circulate the book for as long as you liked on a basis of free presentation not of sale.

For this privilege I would pay a thousand dollars ($1000). My idea would be to get a publisher to bring out an ordinary book-store edition, plainly bound. He might, if he wished, try to buy from your corporation the right to use certain illustrations from your book. I should propose to make certain changes and omissions. I imagine that if I had asked to reserve this right at the start your corporation would have been willing to grant it on fairly easy terms as I should not think you would wish to get out a commercial edition under your own name, thus <u>giving</u> the book to some people and selling it to others,—a very doubtful way of seeking good will.

I should propose to pay the $1000 on the publication of the book which would mean that if I failed to get a publisher I would of course be released from the obligation. Under ordinary circumstances I should, of course, find no trouble in getting a publisher for any book of mine, but this case is a little peculiar as a publisher might hesitate to get out a book already widely circulated as a gift.

In any case I should be most anxious to have your corporation consider this proposal as early as possible, because I should need even now all the available time to get the book printed and on the market without being too late.

With best regards to Mr. Bronfman and to yourself and your associates.

Very sincerely,
Stephen Leacock

## *To R. W. Bardwell*                                    Aug 5 (1941)

Dear Mr Bardwell—

By all means go ahead along the lines you suggest: it is most kind of you to undertake the work—naturally I couldnt, in view of my 40 vol. of pub. works, give anybody carte blanche (words in italics, please) to write stuff for me to sign. But I dont see why any such difficulty need arise as I gather you leave the main current of the writing unchanged except here & there to simplify it.

But I beg you, in spite of your opinion, to leave the opening as it is: after all, all the world is a Rotary Club[1]

S.L.

1   Bardwell had written to Leacock: 'I am sure that you won't take offense when I tell you that the new introduction is too much like the typical beginning of a Rotary Club after-dinner speech.'

## *To Charles Vincent*

(Aug 6 1941)
Address:  Oct. 1–May 1
            3869 Cote des Neiges Rd.
            Montreal
Address:  May 1–Oct. 1
            The Old Brewery Bay
            Orillia, Ont.

C. W. Vincent, Esq.
4, St. Thomas St.  Ryde, I.W.

Dear Mr. Vincent,

Thank you for your letter of July 4 in regard to my father's estate.

I note that you say that my share (net) of the estate is about £740. Please invest this for me in war loans of the British Government, and please re-invest any accruing interest until further notice in the same securities.

I am sending to my surviving brothers and sisters a copy of this letter, with a copy of your letter and with the advice that they each write to you the same instructions as above. I make exception of my brother Charles J. Leacock in regard to whom I will write you later.

I gather that for many years your father and you have administered the affairs of the Leacock family and I am grateful to you for services rendered, and for more to come.

Very faithfully,
Stephen Leacock

## To Frank Dodd

The Old Brewery Bay
Orillia, Ontario
Aug. 7, 1941

My dear Dodd,

I am sorry to say that a month of unbroken hot weather has made work on my book How to Write slower than I had expected. But I shall keep on and try to make it How to Write Faster.

Meantime I would like to call your attention to the fact that I have a number of pieces not yet in books, some of which have had wide publicity. These will presently, I hope, appear as a book of selections ... But I think it wise at my age to make provision for other eventualities, although I am at present in excellent health and have done more literary work in the last twelve months than in any before.

I suggest that you make a contract with my niece, Mrs. Donald Nimmo, 716 Forest St. Birmingham, Mich., under which in the event of my death you give her a ten per cent royalty on a book to contain sketches of mine not yet in the books, such fragments of autobiography as I may leave, and a memoir to be written by Mrs. Nimmo to give the plain outline of my life, with such references to, and quotations from personal material in my books as may elucidate the memoir without going so far as to make it mere repetition. I enclose a memo of the title and an explanation.

Best regards,
Stephen Leacock

P.S. The copy right on my published works is a part of my general estate and does not belong to Mrs. Nimmo. But under my will Mrs. Nimmo has the copy right in all unpublished MS and the book rights of all magazine and serial matter.
P.P.S. It would be understood that the essence of this publication is celerity. My niece would not write and advertize for letters etc. etc. All that means delay. Interest fades. Lots of time for that later on if my Life were worth it: but I don't think it would be. There was nothing to it.

## To Charles Leacock

Orillia, Ontario
August 27, 1941

Dear Charlie,

I suggest that you take advantage of Teddy being here and our being all together to make a proper disposition of your money and property.

I trust that you put all you have under trust, the trustees to be your three brothers and the senior partner of Smith, Rae and Greer:—

—that the senior partner of Smith, Rae and Greer be paid the usual percentage fee on income handled and of course for the making of the trust: that the other trustees be not paid:—

—that you recognise certain claims as first liens on your property and income,—viz.(a) payable to Stephen Leacock $500 represented by a demand note raised at the Bank of Montreal (1939) with your signature and his, for the sum of $550 of which you received and spent $500:—(b) the sum of $500 raised on a joint note of Stephen Leacock and George Leacock at the Bank of Montreal (1940), all of which was transmitted to you by George Leacock and spent,—(c) various sums in cash from George Leacock in 1939, 1940 and 1941 amounting to . . . . . . . . . . . in all,—(d) various sums in cash from E.P. Leacock in 1939, 1940, 1941 amounting to . . . . . . . . . . . . . . in all.

I propose that in view of this indebtedness and in view of the possibility of future illness on your part, that:—

: you hand over all your property and income and real estate to the trustees, to include the capital and interest left you under father's estate, and the fixed income you now receive from Mr. Vincent and whatever equity you have in the principal it represents:—

: that your power to dispose of this equity and any other property by will be limited to the disposal of only such part of it as has not been expended or pledged on your behalf to the trustees:—

: that the trustees undertake to pay the current interest on the notes above until such time as your capital under father's estate can be moved from England, and that the trustees will then repay as above the loans and accumulated interest and set the rest of the capital to your credit:—

: that whereas your fixed English income now reaches to $250 a year, and the interest receivable from father's estate to 1% of $3250 (that is $32.50 per annum), and should on re-investment amount to about $100 a year:—

: and whereas your real estate at Sutton carries a mortgage charge of $19.30 a year, and taxes of $34.00 a year your trustees would feel able to pay you $25 a month payable regularly on the first of the month and undertake payment of your taxes and mortgage interest

On these terms your three brothers, or the survivors of them, would promise to do their best, but without legal obligation, to give you an income of $25 a month, over taxes and mortgage charges, even if the war should obliterate or diminish your English capital or render the transmission even of its interest for the time being impossible I suggest further:—

: that under a revocable power of attorney from each of your three brothers, the senior partner of Smith Rae and Greer can transact all business of the trust with the signature of any one of the brothers indifferently

: that provision be made for ~~the survival and~~ substitution of new trustees among your relatives in the case of your surviving all the old ones,

: that ~~a general~~ consent on your ~~part to the plan above as in general terms will be followed~~ part and on the part of your brothers to this plan in general terms will be followed by an invitation of Mr. Larratt Smith to draw up the deed of trust in detail, and such advance of money as you need can be at once supplied

Your affectionate brother<br>Stephen Leacock

The trustees shall have power to see fit to him for capital value of the money receivable from fathers estate after payment of debts as above, into an annuity in your name.

## To G.L. Smith

The Old Brewery Bay,<br>Orillia, Ont.<br>Aug.30, 1941

G.L. Smith Esqre,
Smith, Rae and Greer,
Toronto, Ont.

Dear Goldie,

I enclose herewith a proposal in outline for a deed of trust in regard to the property and funds of my brother Charlie. The deed has been seen by my brothers George and Teddy and by Charlie himself. All of them consent with the utmost good will. I enclose a written note to indicate Teddy's consent as he left for Winnipeg last night. But Charlie and George are here with me and indicate their consent by signing this letter.

We hope that you can undertake the work and the duties indicated and shall be greatly obliged if you do so.

Very sincerely,

## To R. W. Bardwell                    Oct  4 (1941)

Bardwell

I am sorry to say that in moving from Orillia I have mislaid the orig. MS & typescript of Liberty

If possible please send me one  I am in much concern about the MS. I am afraid I cannot consent to sign my name to whole paragraphs which I did write and do not approve  I enclose for example page 2. I never wrote a word of this: dont like it: and cant sign it: it is not my style and not my thought. So I suggest that you send me the first typescript and I will make as much use of your revision in eliminating and in altering as I can consent to do within what I think the individual province of authorship. If you can use this please do so. If not kindly share the loss of time and effort with me by letting me pay you $100 & publish the MS elsewhere

## To Mr Schofield                    [3869 Cote des Neiges Road
                                       Montreal]
                                       Oct 10 1941

Dear Mr. Schofield

Thank you for such a nice letter . . . . I am glad to think that I have made, as you say, so many people laugh.

I remember once a big boo of a self-important woman (God knows who, I didnt know her but she thought I did/must) meeting me in a store said . . . "You've done more than make me <u>laugh</u>: you've <u>made</u> <u>me</u> <u>cry</u>." . . . . I thought "Thank God for that."

Very sincerely
with best wishes
Stephen Leacock

## To R. W. Bardwell                    3869 Cote des Neiges Road
                                       Montreal
                                       Oct 12 1941

Dear Mr. Bardwell

Thank you very much for your letter of Oct 7 & the <u>Liberty</u> MS . . . I now propose to give it a further revision, thus:—

Avail myself of the excellent suggestion of your New York editor and add some stuff in the way of <u>positive</u> statement of what free democracy has accomplished for schools, etc . . . .

Also in discussing socialism ~~give~~ and showing that it wont work, do more justice to its <u>inspiration</u>.

. . . Revise the form of printing so as to allow of side notes & thus convey a lot of information in brief space with indication of sources of reading etc. This means a lot of certain minds, and gives the book an added value.

. . . I should wish also to alter the title to indicate more body of contents, thus:

OUR HERITAGE OF LIBERTY
*A Survey of its Origins, and History, its Achievement,*
*its Present Danger & its Future Completion*

It is my opinion that such a book should not be too juvenile . . it should find many readers among young intelligent minds in & out of colleges, and among all people restless & perplexed by the war.

. . . If you do not want to publish it in England I would be glad to. If it is judged in certain quarters to be of use in helping national spirit, as I mean it to be, its circulation will receive help. That is what happened to my recent British Empire. It did poorly in the States. In England they saw to it that it did well.

Very sincerely
Stephen Leacock

P.S. I send you as illustrating the make-up I propose, a section of my new book on Canada now in the press. Please return it. I've no copy

## To Barbara Nimmo

[3869 Cote des Neiges Road
Montreal]
Oct 26 1941

Dear Barbara

This is for you to sign, and to act on at your leisure. I hope a long leisure,— to carry it out

Observe what it means. Under my will as my literary executor you get all my unpublished manuscripts and the book rights on articles etc not yet in books. This includes all material even if in preparation for the press, as now, unless it is actually completed and in the publishers hands ready for the press as far as the writing is concerned. For instance, I am now preparing, under a contract, (Dodd) a volume of sketches to be called My Remarkable Uncle and Other Sketches. . . Once this is done & packed up for Dodd it becomes mine or part of my estate . . But if I dont finish it, it would be yours. Similarly in future. Keep this letter so as to preserve the plain business sense of what is meant. Best love to you all,

y. a. u.
Stephen Leacock

## To Barbara Nimmo

3869 Cote des Neiges Road
Montreal
Nov 6 1941

Dear Bâ

I've written to the Director of Public Information (Ottawa) to send you the monthly summary called <u>Canada at War</u> . . . Let me know if he does it . . . The war certainly looks bad just now . . and I am afraid that the U.S. is still a long way off it . . . . Teddy's Peter is to sail in a week or two . . expects to pass through here . . . I have news Uncle Charlie back at Whitley . . Stevie & I dont expect to go to Orillia at Xmas . . it costs too much . . & for me there is so little there at Xmas with Rene & Edward Ardagh gone . . .

Best love to all three of you
y. a. u.
Stephen Leacock

## To R. W. Bardwell

3869 Cote des Neiges Road
Montreal
Dec. 1. 1941

Dear Mr. Bardwell

(Yours Nov. 29). That's too bad. Please send the M.S. back as soon as possible . . . You paid me an advance of $260 but I lost a great deal of time in repeated revision and money out of pocket in repeated typing.

I suggest that I get a publisher or publish it myself . . . If I get a publisher I will give the first hundred dollars I get as royalties, and after that, when I have received a thousand, but not till then, I'll give you the next $160 . . . If I publish it myself I will give you the same sum,—as the first $100 over cost, and the first $160 after a profit of $1000.

Please let me have the M.S. without delay.[1]

Very sincerely

1    The manuscript was returned, Bardwell writing to Leacock: 'I regret very much that we are not publishing books for the college or adult level.' *Our Heritage of Liberty* was published by John Lane the following year.

## To Frank Dodd

3869 Cote des Neiges Road
Montreal
Dec. 3. 1941

Dear Dodd

Yours of Dec. 1 in regard to cutting one item out of the <u>Uncle Book</u>.

I enclose herewith a short piece (<u>The Mathematics of the Lost Chord</u>). written since, which can be used if more words are needed to fit the space as planned.,

My own opinion is that the more words in a "funny" book the better. People buy them by the pound and look to see if there's enough.

Best regards
Stephen Leacock


## To Mr Schofield

[3869 Cote des Neiges Road
Montreal]
Dec 4 .41

Dear Mr Schofield

I am so sorry if my letter hurt your feelings: I am afraid that you took in quite a needless sense . . now try to see it a little differently: I am an old man, 72 in three weeks: I get a great mass of mail . . I cant afford a secretary and dont want one. I have a lot of work. I have all I can do, & more & not strength enough for it

So I have to answer letters as best I can, as I did yours. I hardly remember your letter in detail but I think it was to ask me to use my influence to have you give a lecture in the English department: if I could have answered in detail I would have explained that to do so, especially on such grounds, would have been quite contrary to university etiquette. What could I know of you, that they didnt? What proof of your ability had I that they hadnt? . . So I mostly wrote, as far as I remember . . "I am sorry I cannot do what you wish . . . . ."

Consider this. All the year round I receive manuscripts some small and some bulky with the request, that seems so reasonable to the writer, that I will ~~look~~ read over the MS and say what I think of it and suggest how & where to publish it . . . I have long since learned to answer back in a set polite form to say that I have no time to read MS & that if I did it would not help, since gratuitous criticism merely offends, and since I am not connected with a publishing house and the publishing houses always insist on reading for themselves & take no one's say so.

If I read all such MSS it would take a large part of my time to do it . . But I am sure the senders never understand it

. . . . .

Now I may be mistaken about your letter. I think it was that. But I kept no record

So I hope you will understand. And if it wont hurt your feelings let me, at 72 (almost), offer you a little advice .. never bother to ask favours or help from anybody: it's not worth it. Stand on your own feet or fall or walk as best you can

> with this & with my best wishes
> Stephen Leacock

## To Barbara Nimmo

3869 Cote des Neiges Road
Montreal
Dec 10 1941

Dear Bâ

I rec'd your Encyc. stuff but have no time to get at it now—I will put it away till after Xmas—I expect to stay here—also Jack Culliton—send us anything to supplement it & we will get it ready just at New Years—Be sure that I have a copy of <u>Mr. Yust's frame</u> (scheme)————The war is very terrible— especially today's news of the loss of the Prince of Wales & the Repulse & U.S. at Hawaii—awful—

But I cant believe the Japs can stand up against our superior technical skill . . .

I'm working hard & very tired .. sorry I wont see you at Xmas .. I'm glad you're in your house & Nancy better

> y. a. u.
> Stephen Leacock

## To Mary Leacock

Dec 12  1941

Dear Mary

I get so used to the B.B.C Broadcast with a digest of the news before it gives it in detail that I'll put my letter that way . . . . . .

PROFESSOR LEACOCK NOT COMING TO TORONTO—— UNCONFIRMED RUMOUR THAT HE CAN'T AFFORD IT—STEVIE REASSURES PUBLIC: WILL VISIT TORONTO, AURORA, & OSHAWA. —MONEY NO OBJECT.

In other words Im afraid I'll have to stay here . . I find travel more and more unwelcome and I have, like everybody, such a lot of extras just now—on the other hand I <u>may</u> come.—if I do I'll just get on the train when I'm ready & send a telegram & be at the Royal York for a couple of days & of course come out to your house but not to sleep—Stevie will spend some time in Toronto with his Granny Hamilton but says that he would like to come to you for Xmas day, as Granny eats with <u>Mill</u> (ask George to fill in details) . . . Stevie is writing you about his time of coming . . . He also goes to Oshawa. . . .

As to Charlie I'm glad he's settled down . . . I wrote George about him a week ago but found the letter unposted & sent it on to (Aurora) I think, yesterday.

I've been getting through a lot of work. There is an article of mine called <u>Christmas 1941</u> to come out in The New World (Toronto) in their Xmas issue. Please read it especially the part about the people in church . . I am also asking the editor of <u>Banking</u> (New York) to send to George a copy of the last number with an article of mine of on Price Control . . . I expect my next new book to be out in January (MY REMARKABLE UNCLE AND OTHER SKETCHES) and my Canada book in February. I'm asking the Distillers (They publish it as a gift to friends) to send a copy to George . . . I hope to have two more books out before summer, . . . so you can see I've been working and am getting very tired . . I'll be glad to see George when he comes . . With love to all of you in which Stevie joins.

Stephen Leacock

HOUSE VOTES UNANIMOUS LOVE
That is the end of the Broadcast.

*To Thomas B. Costain*                           [3869 Cote des Neiges Road
                                                 Montreal]
                                                 Dec 22 1941

Dear Costain
That's fine . . terms first rate, and I cant tell you with what pleasure I shall go at this work on Montreal . . I have lived here 41 years and always have been deeply interested in the past and in the historical background.

Very best Xmas wishes<br>Stephen Leacock

## To Barbara Nimmo

3869 Cote des Neiges
Jan 7  42

Dear Bâ

I am today completing & sending to Mr Yust the material for the book <u>of</u> <u>the Year</u> viz

Canada in Sections
Biog. Coleman
Coldwell
Drew
Conant

And getting Cooper (via Culliton, enlisted air) to send

Canada & the War
Yukon
Alberta
Saskat
and biog. Bracken

---

That completes Book of Year

Send me any notes of yours left over, they may come up as proof reader

Main Encycl.

Send me any notes you have on any part of it and any documents etc I may have sent you. That completes it as far as you are concerned. Except that I will send you articles to type & send back to <u>me</u> not to Mr Yust. You will get no money for the typing but you shall have another 200 U.S. if when and as I get it . . . I am going to do over all the provinces properly: the material is not in your reach

y a u
Stephen Leacock

## To Francis Paget Hett

[3869 Cote des Neiges Road
Montreal]
Jan 14 1942

Dear Frank

It was such a pleasure to get your letter today that I must answer it right now after reading it while the pleasure is still warm around me—and the recollections it calls up—fishing, The Brewery Bay, trout, —why, —<u>sure</u>, as they say in the States—we'll live, I hope, to get lots of it . . . Let's say that the war all cracks up this coming summer—you'll be out here, I'm sure, as soon as ever it's over & there's a room and a bath, or at least a room and a boat waiting for you & Alice . . . I ~~eat~~ ate up all your news, crumb by crumb but looked in vain for any general opinions, ~~a~~ I suppose that over there in England you've little time for general opinions & have to keep on doing your job (in your case about 5 jobs) day by day . . . but I noted what you said "all work & no play" . . . I can give you perhaps home news of your family better than your own as I had a long letter from your niece, Queenie's Margaret, —in which she told me of a great Xmas gathering at Eildon Hall with Uncle Martyn still going strong. She is on the editorial staff of a Toronto illustrated monthly The New World, for which I wrote a Xmas 'piece'. That led to the correspondence. She writes a very charming letter: I dont think I've seen her, or not since she was a child but I think you will remember her from her coming over to England . . . I saw very little of Sutton & of your side of the Lake last summer . . . I went over to Duclos Point once or twice but only once or twice as the bass fishing was so good in our own lake & right near my own point that I didn't need to go . . . But I saw Addie & some of the others at the wedding of my niece Dora (one of Carrie's daughters) which was held at the Lake Shore Church, with the wedding reception at Beaverton afterwards—It was a lovely summer day & the Church & the church yard & the Lake looked as they always look,—just too wonderful . . . "everybody" was there but so many of them I hardly recognized them as I had not seen them for years . . . . . There is but little news to send you from here in a public sense as no doubt you know from the papers what is doing in Canada . . . so far the country keeps wonderfully prosperous and active in spite of the war taxes: so far there is no real burden: food & too much of it,—people just over from England feel almost sad to see the wasted food, the heavy helpings uneaten, the butter left on the plate . . . no real sacrifice as yet, but perhaps that only means more reserve power for the Empire . . For myself, at 72, I dont seem able to be of use: I cant go to meetings any longer, or make speeches . . cant do anything . . . except a little bit of writing but it isn't really needed: there's nothing to persuade . . . I work a lot at writing, all the early part of every day but I dont last after about noon . . . I did, among other things, a tract of 20,000 words on Liberty,—which would have revived all the Empire,—only it is such an awkward length,—more than a pamphlet & less than a book,—that my New York publishers say they cant afford the to bring it out— John Lane may do so & if so you'll get a copy in due course . . . I thought of you much all through the Hong Kong crisis and disaster. It must have seemed more than familiar to you. I do hope the English papers wont get the idea that the Quebec Rifles were French Canadian—If they do, please correct the statement, not in print but to your friends. Of the officers the one or two French Canadians were fellows who had been at the R.M.C at Kingston, practically English . . The men were recruited in the Eastern Townships (English) & in New Brunswick (Scotch Irish & English). Their names read like a parish register from Surrey or Ayrshire . . . . . . . . I'll be glad when the war is over (I cant live on any other idea) & when you come out again. One's old friends keep falling out every day. René's death was terribly tragic,—and before him Dr. Ardagh of Orillia . . . I didnt go to Orillia this Xmas: it didnt seem worth while. Stevie is, as you say, on the staff

of McGill, or if not quite that, in the graduate school with tutorial work to do
. . . He has slowly grown past five feet by a fraction & is getting broader &
stronger so that soon he wont have to think about his size. Naturally he feels it
now . . . A man who came back a day or so ago from ~~England~~ service in England
(medical at Birmingham) was telling me all about it. It's a hard time: I don't see
how they can stand it so well: there is no doubt the British people (including the
U.S. British) are the only people in the world . . . I hope you'll write again soon
& especially give me your general idea bout the "duration" & with hope enough,
I'll get the fishing rods ready . . . My best wishes to you both for a year happy
beyond expectation.

Stephen Leacock

## To Rosamond Leacock Edwards

3869 Cote des Neiges Road
Montreal
Friday Jan. 23. 42.

Dear Dot.

I wish to make provision whereby Charlie shall receive from the trust $25.00
each month. I enclose a cheque for $25. as for Jan. 1st and will send another on
Feb. 1st . . . If no money has yet been received from England for Charlie on
March 1st., April 1st. and so, I will ask George and Teddy to pay one month each
and then I will pay two months, i.e., I pay as much as the two of them . . . But
these payments are only needed till English money arrives.

He will receive from Mr. Vincent, as before, his money from Uncle Charles
estate, and from now on about 11 pounds a year less taxes from fathers estate.
I do not know what the new taxes will be as compared with what he paid before.

But I think his English money should give him $25.00 a month all the time.
The money received as rent for his place more than pays the charges on it.

This makes him all right for the summer; also, he can live with me at Orillia
all summer, or as much of it as he cares to, with no expense of any kind for
anything.

While he is with you the case is not quite so easy. I suggest that he pays you
out of his $25.00 a 'token' payment for his board at $3.00 a week . . . This will
barely off set your out of pocket cost but it will act as a contribution on your part.

Meantime while he is with you I will send each month, and I enclose now
a cheque to Charlie for $5.00 to help his personal expenses. This you understand
as J.R. Stephenson said, "I am giving to Crow." It has nothing to do with the
trust.

I enclose a copy of this letter for George and one for Teddy.

Enclosed is a letter and documents to sign for our English money. Please
execute, circulate and return.

I enclose a letter to Goldie Smith. You had better go to his office.

Your Affecte. brother

P.S. Enclosed further printed copies of <u>A Letter on Conscription</u>.

## *To Dodd Mead and Company*

[3869 Cote des Neiges Road
Montreal]
March 9

Dodd Mead & Company

Dear Sirs

Herewith the signed contract for <u>Happy Stories, Just to Laugh At</u>
I have already over 40,000 words complete or practically so and hence feel assured that I can have the full MS ready August 1st barring anything unforseen. This would allow for publication Oct 1st but not earlier than Oct 1 to allow for any magazine commitments that might interfere . . I will even ask you to leave the date of publication open as between Oct 1 and Oct 31: in case I get caught with anything valuable delayed beyond expectation in magazine use. I only expect to use a portion of the copy this way . . . I have every expectation of all copy clear of magazine use by Oct 1st.

I enclose a suggestion for publicity work similar to what I did with Doubleday Doran on my book <u>Montreal</u> . . . It is not an essential part of the contract except that without it I should hardly care to keep the clause about the next two books . . but I am sure it would be in both your interest & mine

Very sincerely
Stephen Leacock

Professor Leacock's proposal for Promotion work on Canadian Edition in
Montreal, Ottawa & Toronto: can be accepted or not

I propose either directly or through Mrs H. T. Shaw, my research secretary of some years back who has worked on this kind of publicity,—

i    To compose and print at my expense and circulate at my expense an announcement circular of extracts from <u>Happy Stories</u>, with comment,— not less than 2000 words, 4000 copies
ii   To take special steps to send the circular to prepared personal lists
iii  To take steps to obtain special quotations from the list in certain journals
iv   To interest certain departmental and large book stores personally in the sale
It would be difficult for me as the author to do this "boosting" entirely in my own person but Mrs Shaw will act under my advice.

I shall expect for this a special payment over and above any other royalty of ten cents (10 cents Canadian) on each copy sold in Montreal Toronto and Ottawa

Stephen Leacock

## To Lucien Montreuil

[3869 Cote des Neiges Road
Montreal]
March 28    42

M. Lucien Montreuil
Ecole Supérieure de Commerce
Quebec

Mon cher monsieur Montreuil,

Je vous remercie bien de votre aimable lettre du 26 . . Je regrette de vous dire que je ne suis plus à McGill: on m'a, dirais-je, mis à la porte—(histoire de vieillesse) il y a six ans.

Mais j'ai toujour quelques numéros de la Série dont vous parlez, que je vous envoie gratis avec mes compliments. Quant aux autres, je demanderai à M. Hemmeon, professeur en chef actuel, de vous en envoyer s'il y en a toujours à McGill . . . Malheureusement la Série, victime innocente de la dépression, fut terminée, il y a dix ans.

Recevez monsieur l'expression de mes sentiments les plus fidèles

## To the Bank of Canada

[3869 Cote des Neiges Road
Montreal]
Ap 11. 1942

The Bank of Canada
Ottawa

Dear Sirs

I write to ask for official information in regard the permission to bring out from England a sum of money, some £6,000, representing a legacy of the year 1940 and at present in Trust in England.

The circumstances are. This money was in trust in England, since many years, the annual interest being paid by the trustee Mr Charles Vincent of Ryde I.W., to my father, the late W. P. Leacock. At my father's death in 1940 the money under the trust was to go, and has gone, still in trust, to his eight surviving children. Instructions were sent under joint signature of all these eight, authorizing the trustee to keep the money invested till further notice in British government securities and to reinvest the interest as it accrued.

This was done.

Later on, the eight persons concerned sent a request to the trustee asking him to send out to Canada the entire principal, if permitted, or a part of it, as permitted or at least the interest as permitted. The trustee writes that he is not permitted to send either principal or interest This is contrary to information given by a local bank in Montreal who say that they constantly receive such funds

The persons concerned are under the impression that the trustee is misinformed

Will you please send me an official ruling as to whether:—

(a) the Government of Canada permits the importation of such funds,

(b) whether, as far as you know, the British government does, or does not, forbid the exportation of sterling funds under the circumstances described

I may add that there is no question of bad faith, no doubt of the identity of the parties, or the existence of the legacy, and least of all of the good faith of Mr Vincent, the trustee, who has managed the affairs of the Leacock family for fifty years

Very faithfully
Stephen Leacock


## To Mrs Herbert T. Shaw    Orillia Friday  Ap 24  42

Dear Fitz,

If there is any part of the book of which you have two typed copies please send me one . . I cant find

Atlantic Steamsters under sail (Samatian stuff)

Come Up on the Mountain

French & English (you have that, I think)

McGill

I am trying to get a whole set of extracts for New York. But its hard. My papers are in confusion & I cant get time both to sort & write & not so awfully well . . . still, I'll stick to it . . The book, so far, cut into extracts looks fine. This is a rush to get it off by Walter. I shall not come down to Montreal till I get the book into final shape for completing it there. I didnt want to travel alone but luckily it turns out that Stevie for quite other reasons has to go to Montreal, otherwise it would have seemed extravagant to take him . . . The weather here is beautiful. If I didnt have this damn book I'd work out of doors all day . . . Did Peggy get the books from New York (Dickens & American Humour) . . . Did the Gazette send you Canada? They promised to do so. They sent me 2 and I sent one to Costain

Time. Walter
Affectionately
Stephen Leacock

## To Mrs Herbert T. Shaw

~~Mon~~ Tues.  Early Ap 28
Orillia

Dear Fitz

Next Monday barring a counter order I will get your garden ready & plant half of it, leaving the late things for later

Tell me if anything else

The season is wonderful,—two weeks ahead

Shall I send flowers by express? or have you plenty?

Tina is seeing about Norman versus Tumney. I doubt if you'll find ~~ayn~~ anyone this year unless he's pretty small—or not till after school

Yesterday I worked as I did 35 years ago—planted 33 little hills early potatoes with manure under & black mould over in my glass house—I planted 18 cucumber sods, and three rows of peas each 125 feel long. I have 4 rows in now  a total of 500 feet—Jones & the horse made the trenches but I did nearly all the rest, put in manure etc

The leaves are nearly out—I also wrote a piece of Montreal & signed 100 <u>Canada</u> books.

Has Mr Evans sent you your copy? Answer. If not I'll send one from here

Tina reports you are very well & very busy with the wedding.

If you get time I'd be infinitelly obliged if you would call up Mr <u>Bermingham</u> (Wilder Bermingham, Bleury St) and jolt him up on my house. Tina said he said he thought he could rent it, but he seems to fall asleep.

Say to him that you are speaking for me.

Ask him please to advertise at my expense. Tell him to cut it down to where he can rent it, but not to doubtful tenants. I will put in an ice box & any other things reasonable. It was advertized and then he seems to have dropped it. Grace Reynolds & her mother called him up about it while I still had at a high rent, and I told him that I very much preferred to rent it to strangers as it hard to collect rent from people you know. Then some other people got in touch with him & thats all I know. I'll be glad if you could get him on the job – – – – The conscription returns (so far last night) mean French Canadians solid against Conscription. That ends it. Mackenzie King has brought out in lurid colours the division of the country . . .

Be sure to answer my questions:
① The two dollars,
② The garden,
③ Sending flowers

I rec'd the extra piece about Banking & Currency—

Affec'ly
Stephen Leacock

*To Barbara Nimmo*                    Orillia Sunday May 3 42

Dear Bâ

Herewith with love to Nancy for her birthday ten U.S. dollars (11⁵⁰ Canadian)
. . . . Write and tell me all the news & how you & Don are getting on. We left
Montreal on April 14 as I was not awfully well: I have to go back for a few days
to complete my book and shall time it for Peggy's wedding May 30 . . . It seems
impossible to complete it but I guess I can make it if I have luck: the publishers
are anxious to get it out in the summer

Stevie is here. George comes & goes. I expect him & Mary to pass through
today (from Gravenhurst) . . Charlie wrote yesterday from Whitby that he could
come so I telegraphed him to come . . . Dot I haven't seen . . . . The season here
is wonderful but the war makes the world hell.

y. a. u.
Stephen Leacock


*To Mrs Herbert T. Shaw*                    Friday 7 p.m.
                                            (May 3, 1942)

Dear Fitz

Just come back from your garden where I have been planning the planting.
I think you need plenty of potatoes & winter vegetables in bags for Montreal. I
have 1 lb of sets ready to plant & 2 lbs of multipliers and heaps of other stuff.

I expect to plant your garden on Monday & mine on Tuesday. Of course I
have a lot of side stuff in already . . . It is early but if it freezes I can replant . . .
I will cut your grass with a horse . . I expect a boy to weed the flower beds
Monday & Tuesday.

I cut a dozen bits of asparagus in your place, as much as in my big bed. Your
new rows . . not a sign of any in your old patch. As I have heaps, more than I
can use  I only cut yours for cuttings sake, but if you think better let the plants
alone this season, Ill do so: yet if I cut it now you'll have a lot at the middle of
June, and if I dont cut it you'll have none.

Last night torrents of rain—& storm. George arrived at 2 p.m in the thick
of it. I knew he was coming. He went off trout fishing this morning but I
wouldnt go as I was sure there would be none.

I worked on the Book for several hours . . got the chapters sorted & the
words counted and wrote 1000 words (no good) . . but thank god I had written
advance chapters near the end & so the book wont seem to fall off. My hope is
to get to Montreal a couple of days before Peggy's wedding & finish the book
in the library . . . I dont feel quite solid enough anyway to travel sooner with

confidence . . The last trip was not so good. The young military officer who came over to see me the other day, newly from England (no need for names) said:—1) The Russians tell the English <u>nothing</u>: no officers or technicians stay in Russia,—thank you & good-bye   2) invasion of Europe regarded as impossible.  3) American planes & tanks very inferior & disappointing . . . This for what it's worth. Yet Russia looks good . . .

I will send Mr. Bermingham 12$\frac{50}{}$ as soon as I can remember it . . . (I've done it: put cheque in envelope with letter & told them to call you up.)

Affectionately, Stephen
Stephen Leacock


P.S. It's a queer life here, just mucking round in the mud.


## To Francis Paget Hett

May 7, 1942
The Old Brewery Bay, Orillia

My dear Frank

I have just rec'd your letter & read it with immense interest and I know by experience that the time to answer a letter is right <u>now</u>.

. . My God, what a contrast!  Here am I sitting in my study at The Brewery Bay (incidentally, though, it is eleven oclock and I've worked here since exactly daylight)—but apart from that, here I am,—outside, all the beauty of the loveliest spring I ever remember,—except that its raining like hell . . the grass, the flowers, the lake and profound peace & safety . . the contrast with the hell those brutes have made of the world. My sorrow is not so much for the soldiers as for the conquered, downtrodden people—starved and beaten & shot as hostages . . . . I dont think we ought ever to make peace with the Germans: just military rule, ours over them, decent, or theirs over us, brutal . . .

Peter Leacock (Teddy's boy), is as you say over there in the artillery . . . whereabouts unknown just now

David Ulrichsen, also, Carrie's boy, over there flying.

Stephen Leacock Burrowes (Daisy's son) is in the overseas army here but not yet left

Harry Bergh (Maimie's son) the same

My Stevie is unfortunately out of it but has grown so well in the last year that soon he may be able to do some service that doesnt need much physique

Oddly enough I was just going to send you when I got your letter (and have now packed up to send you) a copy of my new book <u>Canada</u>. It is beautifully bound & illustrated. It's a gift book presented to their friends by the House of Seagram, but you wont mind the slight ~~smell~~ smell of Canadian Rye . . The publishers ~~had~~ have your name on their list as your book (Georgina) is quoted as an authority (see p. 114.) but I thought I'd like to send you one personally out of the advanced copies that they sent me . . . I send you with it in the same parcel the Atlantic Monthly for May, in which I discuss the Universe.[1]

I have done an awful lot of work this last six months: partly by instinct, partly because I had to, as my pension & what income I have wont begin to make the two ends meet just now . . . . Among other things I've done a moving picture which some day may move . . . and I am just finishing at high speed a book on <u>Montreal</u>,—it's a really beautiful thing . . . history, geography & life in general . . . . 120,000 words, begun in January & I passed 101,000 this morning . . . It will be out, I trust, in August . . . It rather laid me out and so I came up here for a weeks rest and am here still . .

The Canadian plebiscite, as you no doubt realize is rotten—<u>all</u> the French voting against conscription . . . when it says, Quebec 100,000, yes, 800,000 <u>no</u>,—that 100,000 is the British—same in New Brunswick, etc.

There will be no conscription here . . So far the country carries the whole burden, economic & financial, with great ease . . . what a lesson for peace time . . . how much we might have done and must still do

Tell Alice I look forward to having you both here at The Old B.B. before so many summers are gone,—let's make it 1943 . . . I went through a mental struggle about trout fishing & gasoline—decided no fishing—then the devil suggested, "well, you may as well pay your small annual sum for rights on the stream, anyway, that's not gasoline" . . so I did that . . . "you don't <u>need</u> to go at all," said the devil . . . My own idea is that at any rate I can go now & again with George who has a car & has to drive thereabouts for business . . . We meant to go on May lst, but there had been such floods of rain that I didn't go—George did, doubting my word, and caught nothing. Some afternoon soon I'll go with the devil in the form of a hired taxi-man burning gasoline. . .

Queenie's Margaret sent me a form to fill in, advocated the air for her, or her for the air. I filled it. From her letters as an editor-in-training she seems very clever. . . .

Its still raining. But I am going out into the garden to ~~stick in~~ stick in pea-sticks, just the job when it's wet. Our Mr Jones whom you remember is fixing the ice-box, and our Mr Yvon is holding the tools. Yvon (French Canadian, brother to Mrs Kelly) is a new arrival, just a kid, as the boy on the place. That is the outdoor staff and indoors Mrs Kelly and a woman in, 3 times a week, to clean & help. . . . . The personnel are, or is, only Stevie & me. Barbara coming up in June. George comes & goes very often. He has adopted 2 little girls for the duration: it has turned out very expensive as he sends them to a lady's school in Barrie but he's very good about it.

·  ·  ·  ·  ·  ·

1  'Common Sense and the Universe', *Atlantic Monthly* 169 (May 1942): 627–34.

Very best regards to you both. I was so glad to hear & shall keep your letter, —I was just going to say, to read to mother,—as I connect her memory so much with your family,—but I'll say to read to George & the rest. Mother never seems really gone, though.

Stephen Leacock

## To Mrs Herbert T. Shaw

Orillia
Thursday ~~Ap~~ May 7  42

Dear Fitz

Rain! Rain! Rain! "Reverend Thompson"—no chance of gardening till Thursday. I haven't even planted my little early piece. I have a boy coming to see me about weeding your flower beds while Jones & I are doing the planting on Saturday (he'd be under our eye

Important!

I have written Costain (am writing) that I will send him the book in the best shape I can about May 24 and they can start galley printing while I am still working & can correct galleys & add things

So when I come to Montreal I will be working on galley correction & addition. This means I need <u>all you have</u> MS & type, except the chronology, right away by express C.O.D. . . . I'll send you what I need in the way of questions when I have plays. I will send the typing or part of it to Barbara as it is coming too fast now for the time you have. I'll send her all of it if you wish. The loss of time by mail is just the same Make the ~~chornog~~ chronology cover the same space that 3000 words (in print would cover. Then I call it 3000 in my estimate

Affectionately
hurry
Stephen Leacock

## To J. A. T. Lloyd

The Old Brewery Bay
Orillia, Ontario
May 9–42

Dear Lloyd

I was glad & more than glad to hear from you . . I have often wondered how you are getting on—Πῶς ἔχεις, as we say in Greek—& how old age uses you— Your letter was interesting & kind indeed in its references to me, but you said nothing of yourself. Write another . . . I understand that the publishers are sending you a book of mine on Canada: you will perhaps be interested in what I say of Goldwin Smith & the Toronto of his days—I am here at my Orillia place (see enclosed Exhibit A, and working very hard—my pension & the income left

after the depression dont quite fit to what seems the unavoidable expenses of life
. . . So many of our friends of the old days have dropped off that there seem
hardly any left that we connect with . . The war seems to overshadow everything
it's just God's awful: I hope we never make peace with the Germans: just beat
them & let them stay beaten under military rule (decent but authoritative)
        . . . you must be sure to write to me

> Best regards
> Stephen Leacock

*To Mrs Herbert T. Shaw*                     [The Old Brewery Bay
                                             Orillia, Ontario]
                                             Friday May 22 '42

Dear Fitz
    This morning I got up at 3 a.m. & started work and at 11. the book was
finished—now I've only to check & revise  That's nothing—thank Miss Gray for
her fine work, just right the real touch—The rest I can manage—Jack Culliton
is to come up here ~~Satu~~ tonight Friday, not for that, but for a visit, and with his
help I can dig up what I want—one little thing you can do, or rather Ken can
do, what a queer phrase <u>Ken can</u> (the routine idea of Peggy's future admiration
for him) ——it is this—. I have a reference in the chapter called <u>Come up on
the Mountain</u> to people looking down from the Look out & saying that the
nearest houses "must be only 300 feet below"—What about <u>300</u>. ? —It's just a
sort of anyhow figure . . From the pavement of the crescent to belly-height over
the balustrade. Tell Ken anything within six inches will do.

> Affectionately
> Stephen Leacock

*To Thomas B. Costain*                       Orillia, Ont.
                                             May 26th, 1942

Dear Costain,
    I am sorry to say that I think the Port of Montreal would not be a good
title. It is too restricted, too specialized. There is an admirable book under that
title, copyright by McGill University, the <u>Port of Montreal</u> by Lawrence Tooms,
1925. It is just what the title means, a splendid technical study of the Port. A
book under the title would therefore be misleading, bought by the wrong
people with the wrong idea, who would then swear at me for persuading them
to buy something quite different from what the title suggested . . . . Montreal
was not a sea port at all under the French Regime and not in any large sense till
the steamboat days . . .

Moreover the announcement of a book on the <u>Port of Montreal</u> would catch the censor's eye at once. As a matter of fact I have carefully avoided details of the river, but on the face of it, it would be just the thing for a submarine or aeroplane operating on the river. Even if it got by, as it would on inspection, it might be held up for inspection and cause delay.

I suggest:                    Montreal
                    <u>City and Sea Port</u>
with Montreal as the title and <u>City and Sea Port</u> below.

Very best regards,
S.L.

## To Mrs Herbert T. Shaw

[The Old Brewery Bay
Orillia, Ontario]
Mon Je 8   42

Dear Fitz,

I am disappointed that you cant be here this week but it will at any rate give me a chance to get your place a little better—It has rained so hard that we couldnt cut the grass even with the horse mower —and the horse mower got broken & we lost 2 days—a lot of the stuff planted will have to be done again— the only good things are the tulip sets. but all gardens are hopeless so so far— Your peonies are beautiful but not out yet—I sent Jones to put wires but found out today that he only knew of the peonies in front of the house & thought he had done them all—

I have been working desperately to get the book done but still some days from the end. Jack Culliton is helping me. Its a hell of a big job.

The war news for 2 or 3 days looks less good but I still hope for big things this summer. Germany will burst up if we can only keep up the bombardment − − I am so glad to hear about Peggy & Ken—It all sounds fine. Mr. Ferguson said that you came down & saw the picture—it's fine isn't it—and Lomer will put it into the McGill Library half way up stairs − − Charlie is here. Dot drove him up on Sunday. He seems very well but looks very old. He is fixing up the boat house for himself as he prefers a place of his own—You must have had an awful time packing up the house. Are you all right for gasoline? The regulations here are the devil—No taxi man can carry any parcels from town except with the presence of the owner of the car. Hence I cant get my newspaper or anything from Hatleys (except by Hatley in the afternoon)—Thats no great matter but it does matter that he mustnt call for a parcel, laundry, Liggetts or anything. I've written a letter for the controller here to send to Ottawa & Liquor can only be got in a round about way. I went fishing at Johnsons with Jack Culliton in Paul Copelands car but apart from that I cant go as taxi men may not drive more than 15 miles—I think I have 2 not-bad tires at Jones's which you can use—I'll be glad when you come up & get settled in—The little boy Lloyd (I forget his surname can work for you at 15 cents an hour as much as you like

Affect'ly
Stephen Leacock


## *To Thomas B. Costain*

[The Old Brewery Bay
Orillia, Ontario]
Je 7 1942

Dear Costain
    Everything fine:—

<u>MONTREAL</u>
<u>SEA PORT & CITY</u>

The book is all done but I find that revision is slower than I reckoned. I hope to post it all to you last week. Now I fear I cant get it off till the middle of this coming week,—say Wed or Thursday June 10 & 11. On the other hand I am trying to make the revision so complete that proof reading can be rapid. It will be safe for you to reckon that I can read all the proof in three days (apart from the time of the proof sheets in transits—no doubt you can send me two sets . . I look forward very much to the humour book: I'll write about it soon

Best regards
Stephen Leacock


## *To S.B. Putnam*[1]

[The Old Brewery Bay
Orillia, Ontario]
June 27 1942

Dear Mr. Putnam
    I must apologize for my delay in answering your kind and most interesting letter—But my moving up to my country place for the summer threw my correspondence out of gear . . Your letter got buried . . . but it remained in the front of my mind as I had read it several times . . . . I had never read that very striking passage of Arnold Bennett's and am glad to know it: I knew him slightly; in fact he was very kind and hospitable to me when I was lecturing in London twenty years ago . . . Twenty years,—what changes! When we thought there couldn't be any more and that we had seen it all . . I suppose that you, as I do, live a good deal in the past and like to read over old books and the description of days that you remember or that are only just beyond the reach of

1   S.B. Putnam, a former resident of Montreal born in 1855, had written to Leacock from Boston on 29 March 1942 saluting him on his treatment of old age.

memory. I find,—I dont know if you do,—that the world looks very different in looking back on it ~~that~~ from what it seemed at the time. I think here especially of England. I was born in Hampshire in 1869 and lived my first six year in England, brought up in all the traditional ideas of the time,—the church, the gentry, the labourers,—"do my duty in that state of life into which etc. etc .." Of course I couldn't see how utterly embedded in "class" and "caste" was the whole of society, like a fossil snake in a stone ... I look back now with wonder, and condemnation, of the utter complacency of the English Victorian point of view towards poverty, and the misery of the slums .. as if it was all right .. as if the poor were a different sort of being ... They are, in a sense,—knocked out of the shape they might have had .. except the children .. social reform can not start with the idea that all people (grown up people) are the same: unfortunately they are not. Most of them, or at any rate many of them are badly damaged ..

I think very much of such things as no doubt you do .. and more than ever in the stress of war

I'm afraid I've inflicted a long letter.

> With best regards
> Stephen Leacock

## *To Thomas B. Costain*

> The Old Brewery Bay
> Orillia
> July 1 42

Dear Costain

I quite accept the terms suggested for the Humour Selections Book.
For the title:

I think it should be straightforward and indicate a book of readings, not a book of writings. But it needed just sound like stock-in-trade

I have been considering

> – HUMOUR I HAVE LIKED –
> MY CHOICE IN HUMOUR

Something of that sort.

Also;—

I would like to put a preface on the general topic of the growth of a sense of humour ... and put little essays of say 1500 words each before each selection ... such a model as Chesterton's Dickens Prefaces .. Also you might consider a chapter called,—MY ESTIMATE OF THE WORLD'S BEST JOKES ... I would be good sales stuff.

> Best regards
> Stephen Leacock

## *To Thomas B. Costain*

The Old Brewery Bay
Orillia, Ontario.
July 6, 42.

Dear Costain

Still answering your July 6,—
Montreal . . . Whatever you do we must keep that charming jacket outside. Get
it in also if you can for permance. —

Map of River as suggested on page 2 of your letter, first rate.

---

Illustrations. Sending you by express

Albums
Maps
Curios

---

In a separate letter I will discuss the Anthology.

Best regards; everything fine.
Stephen Leacock

Sent by express from Dʳ Leacock
to Mr T B Costain <u>Doubleday Doran</u> N York
July 6

1.  Album <u>Old Montreal</u>. Illustrations by <u>Charles Simpson</u> a fine artist. C.P.R.
    would surely give permission or you could commission Simpson

---

2.  Historic Montreal. Henry Morgan & Co. Out of print. please return. Write for
    copy to Cleveland Morgan, c/o Henry Morgan & Co, old friend of mine

---

3.  Growth of a Great Port. Out of print. McGill Library copy. They are
    clamouring for it back. Dont send it to them. Send it to me

---

4.  Tercentenary Historic Map 1942. Right of reproduction by request to
    Tercentenary Commission, cf City Council, Montreal  But you might
    think it exactly the wrong thing, since on sale in the shops . . . send it
    back <u>with no delay</u> . . I need it for proofreading . . copy can be bought
    from Burton's book store, St. Catherine St. Montreal

---

5.  Paper money of first railroad—rare & valuable

---

6.  Reproduction of map at the conquest 1759

---

7.        "          "   "   when Montreal a city (date of map 1835)

---

To follow (best of all but mislaid) Molsons Brewery Centenary Volume (1935) of pictures

Suggestion

My friend Mr. Stanley Coristine of the University Club has a marvellous family album of old photographs of old buildings, some surviving some not. If you thought it likely you could use such things, I am sure he would risk sending it by express registered & insured for your inspection. See his name in the preface

*To Thomas B. Costain*                    The Old Brewery Bay
                                           Orillia, Ont.
                                           August 12,42.

Notes for a sales Plan
_____

of
Professor Leacock's <u>Montreal</u>
in
Montreal
____

My dear Costain

I feel that a sales campaign started in time and well conducted could effect a great sale of this book.

This needs some one on the spot, of local credit and consideration.

The things needed are;—

1st. In this book a very complimentary discussion, far more than a casual reference, is made to the firm of Henry Morgan and Co. the first historically to move "uptown" (see opening pages of Chap.) . . . These people are the biggest in Montreal. The head of the firm Mr. Cleveland Morgan is one of the leading men of Canada and a long-time friend of the author of the book. The Morgan Store would find the book a wonderful "<u>ad</u>" for themselves. They have a huge book counter business.

I suggest that some one sees "Cleve" Morgan and gets him to place a record order before the book is even on sale. I can't do this myself. Noblesse oblige. "Infra dig." Not the thing."

<u>Next</u>.

There is a whole chapter on McGill. I suggest that we ask the <u>McGill Daily</u> to give a whole broad side sheet to the Book, entitling it

## L E A C O C K   L O O K S   A T   M c G I L L

I suggest that we have this copy all written up in advance, and given to our representative in Montreal, to show to the Editors of the Daily.

I suggest that this copy be written by Major Gladstone Murray, the general manager of the Canadian Broadcasting Corporation. He was the <u>founder</u> of the McGill Daily, 1912, and they will print every word he writes.

Gladstone Murray and I are friends of 30 years standing (I taught him) and are thick as thieves. We are under so many obligations to one another that we couldn't refuse one another anything. As a matter of fact I could write the copy myself, if he's too busy, and show him where to sign, but that's not the kind of thing I would say in a letter, so I won't mention it.

I am very closely associated in recent work with the Montreal <u>Gazette</u> and I think that if they were approached with special review copy, and naturally some liberal advertising they could enormously help the book.

I am, and have been for years, closely a friend of the C.P.R. having written much is their favour, apart from personal friendship with the just out-going president Sir Edward Beatty (since we were at school together) and other heads. The chief of their publicity is Murray Gibbon, an old friend of mine who gave me great help with this book, in spite of the fact that he himself is doing a book on Montreal. It was by his good offices that I was able to get the photograph of the <u>S.S. Samatian</u> of 1876 which I hope appears in the book. If it does, I wish you would insert in the preface at the point indicated on the proof, words as follows

I am greatly indebted, as I have been on many previous occasions to my old friend Mr. Murray Gibbon, of the Canadian Pacific Railway Company, not only for actual material supplied from his ample resources but for advice and suggestions supplied by his ample brain.

I think you had better put that in anyway, The C.P.R., through Mr. Murray Gibbon control an enormous publicity of newspaper inserts. Our representative should get material ready and get in touch with Mr. Gibbon.

Two Montreal Hotels, the Windsor and the Mount Royal, receive in this book very flattering mention, excellent "ads". I am on terms of great friendship with both as I lived in the Mount Royal one winter (1937–38) and in the Windsor two (1938–40). I learned in this residence of the great sales-power of "the girl at the counter." Take that sales power and multiply it by X, representing an approach to the management, and you can sell books like hot cakes.

It is obvious that the large stores of Montreal (Burton's, Eaton's, the Poole etc.) with the use of my name which I cannot make myself . . . .

So much for what can be done, and this is only a part of it, by a representative on the spot, one could start a sale of this book, like the gush of water from a stricken rock. But I can't strike it myself.

Now the best person to do all this, as a sort of proxy for my doing it, is Mrs. H. T. Shaw whose name appears in the Preface and who did all the library research work on the British Empire and Canada. Her husband is one of the leading business men in Montreal (head of the Anglo-Canadian Leather Company) and it fortunately happens that her husband's sister is married to Mr. Cleveland Morgan of whom I spoke above. This intimate family connection would not only spell volumes but sell them. Mrs. Shaw has a wide connection in Montreal and knows everybody. She would be able to take over this agency, and, I am sure, make a success of it . . . I suggest that you should pay her such and such a per centage on sales in Montreal with a consolation guarantee of at least so much. I will be very willing to pay 15% (fifteen per cent) of whatever you pay her as I am certain that I would get it back in royalties.

I am sure that if this book is handled properly we can have a great sale for it in Montreal. The thing is, to start everybody talking about it, and all at once.

With that I leave it with the sole regret that you can't come up here and discuss it with me at the end of a fishing rod.

Best regards
Stephen Leacock

## *To Thomas B. Costain*

The Old Brewery Bay
Orillia, Ontario
Aug. 26. 1942.

Dear Costain

### Re Montreal sales

While I am here and can get cheap printing done under my eye I propose to get out a circular (four sheets, one fold) with a notice of the book and extracts specially selected to appeal in Montreal; in all 2400 words of type with headings. I can get 5000 copies for $26.00—if I need so many. Postage $2.60 and envelopes about $4.00———I propose to get Mrs. Shaw to make out a social list and send the circular to them. She can get her friends to let her use the Women's Canadian Club and Junior League List and her husband's connection down town will get her the stock exchange lists and such (picked over for the purpose).

I am running the heading across the top.

STEPHEN   LEACOCK

---

Looks at

MONTREAL

---

Then comes a blurb of 100 words and then the extracts.

I propose to put across the bottom the imprint—

Doubleday Doran and company
Publishers. New York
On sale at all Montreal Book stores

---

1st. Is there any objection to my using your firm's name? Is the name McLelland and Stewart Toronto on the Canadian edition?

Is yours there also? I would not wish to put only a Toronto firm on a book for sale in Montreal (bad effect; less prestige)

2nd. I suggest that Mrs. Shaw receive 25 cents a book on all Montreal sales of which 15 per cent,—call it 4 cents—is charged against my Canadian Royalties. I hope you can let me have a decision (I have no contract with McLelland and Stewart) as soon as possible as I want to get to work on it.

Best regards
Stephen Leacock

## To Walter Yust [1]

The Old Brewery Bay.
Orillia. Ontario.
September 8, 1942.

Dear Mr. Yust,

I shall be very pleased to undertake the revision of the Britannica Canada articles. Some that are purely historic (e.g. Acadia) will need no change except to check up new bibliographical authorities (published since). For all the towns, districts, etc. There are the changes indicated in the new census (1941) population now available; manufactures, etc. still going through. I will write to Ottawa for advance bulletins. I will also write to all the city and town clerks as in the enclosed sample. I expect to farm out the articles to my niece Mrs. Nimmo, Professor Culliton, etc. (see later postscript as to articles by authorities). I shall give them the pay for the articles but all the articles will go through my hands . . . The war has brought to all the towns so many changes (air-fields, training schools and munition plants, etc. etc. that it will be a little difficult to settle what goes in and what ~~goes~~ not . . . But if I send you a sample or two to look over you can judge better.

You will note that I expressly say to the City and Town clerks that I do not know how much material the editors can use . . . or else the devils might get sore if they sent a lot of stuff you couldn't use.

Best regards,
Stephen Leacock

P.S. There will be the question of new towns, as conspicuously <u>Noranda</u> and the mining towns. Also, extra space for all articles dealing with the development of the North West Territory.

I find some difficulty in computing the question of remuneration, and think it better to add a note. I understand that you are to give me five hundred dollars for general editorial services. I understand this to mean looking over the articles and marking the places where they have to be cancelled, brought up to date, and marking the places where they have to be cancelled, brought up to date, increased by new material; doing this work myself or assigning it to other people; where it is thus assigned, checking it over so that I am responsible for it; making suggestions for entirely new articles. All this if it is entirely satisfactory.

In addition to this I receive two cents a word for any article I write, e.g. as I have just written a comprehensive book on Montreal and as your present article,

---

1    Walter Yust, an editor with the *Encyclopaedia Britannica* (Chicago), replied to this letter on 16 September 1942: 'Your general outline of your method of procedure would indicate that it is a good one. You will receive $500⁰⁰ for your general editorial services. You will receive in addition for any writing or revising the following: 2¢ a word for Class 1 (brand new), Class 2 (entirely rewritten), Class 3 (serious revision). You will receive $5⁰⁰ per page for Class 4 (minor revision), Class 5 (trivial).'

though by a high authority, seems inadequate in length and wanting in certain aspects I should like to write an entirely new article based on my own researches.

The difficult question, however, is the rate of pay applied to articles in which the revision still leaves them very largely intact. To pay two cents a word for the whole length of the article would be ridiculously too much. But similarly to pay two cents a word for the mere additions which, slight in themselves, involve reconsidering and testing the whole article, would seem too little.

Will you therefore at your convenience send me a memorandum as to what you think would be a proper plan. To help you towards this I send a classification of the articles with some notes on what they mean.

S.L.

## To Barbara Nimmo

[3869 Cote des Neiges Road
Montreal]
(Sept 8, 1942)

Dear Bâ,

I am posting you today my book <u>My Remarkable Uncle</u>.

My writings not yet used in books include:—

a)  2 articles <u>Atlantic</u>: one about 4 years ago called Through a Glass Darkly . . 4000 words. One this May, Common Sense & the Universe 5000 words.

b)  About 20,000 words of a book <u>How To Write</u>: MS round my study

c)  A story <u>Mirage</u> about 12,000 words, now submitted to Fox Films for a moving picture: duplicate MS round my study

d)  Articles with Jacque Chambren, Agent, 745 Fifth Avenue New York

1)  Health & Happiness, sold to a Woman's Magazine . . 2,000 words

2)  My Short Theatrical Career                    1,000    "

e)  Article <u>Hochelaga</u>. Enclosed                    2,000    "

(not yet reported on)

You will observe that that makes quite enough for a volume.

To make a memoir of, say, 5000 words as a preface, you only need take my books and use extracts, not long enough to get tiresome, thus:—

My uncle lived on a farm six years (quote Sunshine Sketches—Quote as essay No. 2 Remarkable Uncle

My uncle taught at Upper Canada—Quote My Memories & Miseries

My uncle was at Chicago . . . Quote (incidentally I wrote a piece for their something centennial & kept no copy . . .

To arrange all this is as sensible as life insurance. If anything happened to me & if you & Don got this book ready for Dodd within six weeks & wrote him

that it was coming it would be worth at the least 2000 dollars & perhaps more
. . . So from now on I'll try to get you copies of each thing published & you can
file them

> Best love
> y.a.u
> Stephen Leacock

## To Mrs Herbert T. Shaw

Orillia. Monday Sep 21  42
10.30 am

Dear Fitz

I just got your letter from Montreal about Troop, money etc etc. . . . . I wish
you had phoned Ottawa when you got my letter or gone to Tim O'Brien . . .
no doubt Herbert can get leave to send you more money & my cheque can wait
ready for you when you come back. . . . I'll be glad to hear all about Boston . .
This minute I am waiting for a taxi to go into the Packet office with the circular
of Montreal which I got ready . . I have been terribly busy & will be . . I had to
fix up the encyclopaedia & a lot of things . . It's a damn nuisance Barbara being
in Detroit . . . write & tell me all about Peggy's place, and the living room &
which corner the sofa is in,—a letter like the ones that Peggy writes . . If there
is any way of sending you money on account (I mean on your account with me)
I can easily do it as I got some royalties from England and have plenty to pay
you in advance all you need . . . It turned wet, wet, wet here after you left. . .
today fine and cold. Charlie is here & very well and very quiet . . I have
everything very comfortable for him. Your place is all O.K. . . This in a hurry.
will write soon

> Affectionately
> Stephen Leacock

## To Mrs Herbert T. Shaw

[3869 Cote des Neiges Road
Montreal]
Th. Oct 1  1942

Dear Fitz,

Just back & found a letter from you at the house—later will get away at the
Club—It seems crazy that the Royal Bank wont let you have money . . . . I called
up Tim's bank (just here in the letter) and asked if I could just send my cheque
payable in Montreal & you cash it there so that the person there merely had
funds in Montreal . . . . but he said no, it is all blocked . . not allowed

It looks beautiful around Montreal . . far different from Orillia . . but I found
the journey terribly tiring—I had dinner with Dot (her husband at work & not
present) & took the 11.15 pm train—

I hardly know when to expect you but the time seems too short to write—mail very slow—I dont expect to go out till the afternoon—Poor, good old Judge Greenfields died 3 days ago—buried yesterday—81 years old . . We shall miss seeing him in & out of the Club . . . By the way the Club now <u>closes</u> at 9 on Sat. Sunday & Monday & all members not living in the Club must leave the building—We shall have to go to pictures earlier—other nights 12 pm & Thursday only 1 p.m. .

I wrote to Costain re my new book of selections of Humour to be done with little essays in between—you may recall that I took a lot of discussion as I didnt want it to look like an autobiography—I worked out a plan & this morning got a letter from him of great enthusiasm—so I shall go right ahead & you'll find your part of it more agreeable than historical research . . . I am calling the book

<u>READ IT WITH ME</u>

*A Digest*

*of*

*The World's Best Humour*[1]

———

It's <u>not</u> arranged chronologically but according to the way a person naturally reads humour as one grows up from childhood. Then <u>SECTION I</u> is called

<u>DAMN NONSENSE</u>

. . . . (little essay)

1. Alice Walks in Wonderland

———(little essay)

2. And <u>is followed by Mr Ogden Stewart</u>

. . etc etc

I am going to make up ~~and~~ a hand ~~made~~ written Dummy when you come back . . typing is no good for that kind of thing . . . hand printing   I mean like this . . . the kind of thing that Peggy does so beautifully – – – –

Affectionately

Stephen Leacock

1   This book was never completed.

*To Thomas B. Costain*          [3869 Cote des Neiges Road
Montreal]
3 Oc. 42

Dear Costain

I'm delighted to hear that you may be up here soon. My plans are—to stay here till middle April (say ~~15~~ 14th) & go to Orillia to arrive on the 15th.

This is conditioned on my having all my material ready (or at least marked out) for my literary work when there . . . If you come here before then I will put you up at my Club (the University Club) & we shall be able to discuss all sorts of things, as well as any immediate business under most pleasant auspices— Orillia not so good as I may be living a little bit à la Robinson Crusoe owing to the domestic help problem. I shall have there my housekeeper & my old standby Sargeant Jones, now standing by at 75 years old . . But I'll be delighted to put you up anyway. I'll look forward to hearing from you

> Best regards
> Stephen Leacock

*To Thomas B. Costain*                    3869 Cote des Neiges Road
                                          Oct. 6, 1942

Dear Costain

Yours of Sep. 29 re the book READ IT WITH ME is just right . . . I'll send the contract as soon as I get it unpacked. My luggage went astray.

I think I can make this a very distinctive book . . . I am making up a preliminary dummy of it which I will send along. I want to put as much of myself into it as modesty will allow . . There are various points of which a few words stolen from your busy day would help.

Total length—I presume about 300,000 words 1000 pages,—or is that too big?

I hope to put in a section called MY OWN HUMOUR—SELECTED AND DISSECTED—

---

I aim at putting only those things which really amuse,—so that people laugh loudly or smile deeply.

---

I want the book to introduce to American readers British humour they didn't know before, —and conversely

---

I wish to make some of the sections to consist of a lot of little bits, strung together on a theme or central idea.

---

Your suggestions about 'funniest things,' 'best jokes in the world.' etc. etc. are exactly along the line I have in mind.

---

Re material.

As soon as my luggage arrives I will send you a list of the Anthologies and collections and single authors which I own,—a pretty wide range,—unfortunately I find that McGill offers very little of this material (Anthologies and Collections), hardly any in fact.

---

When I send you the list you can perhaps help me with other material.

---

As far as I am concerned we could expect to publish early in 1943, all well, and this, I presume is as early as you would wish to.

---

Very best regards
Stephen Leacock

P.S. Re Montreal. Mrs. Shaw is busy on the special lists being got ready for sending out the circular at the very time the book reaches Montreal . . . they will go out in successive volleys.

### *To Thomas B. Costain*    3869 Cote des Neiges Road
Oct. 8, 42.

Dear Costain

(Our Book, READ IT WITH ME) . . . I am at it, and absorbed in  it . . . but with various points to discuss.

1. Material . . McGill very poor; <u>no</u> anthologies . . . I send a list of what I have . . . Help me out all you can.

2. Very important and bearing on the contract . . . I want to make this book as much British as American especially as I propose to strike hard the note of our common speech and kinship . . . indeed I shall make our humour seem the salvation of the world, and our book the bible of it.

. . . <u>But</u> . . . reading the contract it sounds as if for a purely American book not published in Britain, or only as a remainder. If you don't want to risk British publication leave it to me; make the rights solely for U.S. and I am sure that I can get a straight 15 per cent Royalty In England with no trouble . . . my present sales there and status make it easy . . . As to Canada, I think I ought to get 15 per cent on the Canadian retail price as I do with all my Dodd Books . . . Canada has never been a cut market for me, only the "colonies and India" . . . I looked back to your letter of Dec. 16 and noted with a jolt that you speak there of only 7-1/2 per cent in Canada on the Montreal book . . . I'd forgotten it; like Harry Graham when the sense of England's shame (at invasion by the Germans) almost put him off his game . . . But thats rather different . . . This new book is cheap to make, just paper and ink no illustrations and overhead all covered. . . If there's more in it than I understand we can easily discuss it. Meantime I wish you would think of raising the contract to make it.

1. English edition left to me, —or you do it, directly or indirectly, printing or exporting sheets,—I get 15 per cent of English retail price in English currency (remainder terms for India and Colonies).

2. Canada,—left to English publisher or terms revised. I am sure that there is nothing in this to cause any trouble or disagreement. I have such faith in this

book that I know it will be a big hit. I am not calling it an autobiography but want to make it in every way a sort of personal contact with the reader.

. . . . . . . . . . . . . . . . . . . .

3 Investigation of copyright. Information wanted. If I want to know whether the copyright in such and such a work has expired,—what do I do? Will the copyright department at Washington answer such inquiries . . . Is there a sub-office in New York? . . . Can your office with no trouble find out such things?

. . . . . . . . . . . . . . . . . . . .

4 I am staging, with Mrs. Shaw's help, quite a flourish of publicity when the Montreal book hits Montreal . . . All social "lists" of clubs etc. are jealously guarded against wolves in author's clothing, to say nothing of naked wild beasts like publishers,—but we are finding back doors into the fold . . .

. . . . . . . . . . . . . . . . . . . .

5 I send you by mail to day a large photo of myself by Karsh of Ottawa, who has made a great reputation . . . This copy is a present for you, but I want you to consider the picture for use either on the jacket or as a frontispiece and I can easily have Karsh send a second one . . . I don't know if your house care to use photograph-jackets,—I mean authors' photos on jackets.

. . . . . . . . . . . . . . . . . . . .

6. There are some more things but you'll be glad to hear that I can't think of them.

> V. sincerely
> Stephen Leacock

P.S. List of anthologies by separate mail.

## To Barbara Nimmo

[3869 Cote des Neiges
Montreal]
Oct 8. 1942.

Dear Bâ
    Ency. letters rec'd for signature, will sign & post

_____

    Please send me all the Encyc paste-ups. I can use them first and return them to you, partly done & your work indicated

_____

    Enclosed a preliminary digest of Memoirs to be written either me or by you . . . If by you, you could use a great deal of <u>quotation</u>
    Type a copy & return original

_____

Very busy. Stevie in graduate history. Uncle Charlie with your mother &
going with her to Harry Bergh.

y. a. u.

Stephen Leacock

Material Towards
a
Memoir
by or of
Stephen Leacock

TABLE OF CONTENTS

1.  Preface
        (Articles & Essays as below,—put <u>Mirage</u> last)
2.  Sketch of Life—made chiefly by quotation. (Dodd Mead only publishers to
    think of, as they control copyright matter of sketch of life: John Lane
    England)
        Memoirs of Stephen Leacock or Memoir
        <u>Material available</u>
2.  A skeleton account of my life, largely done by in articles, or abridgments of
    articles, which are more or less autobiographical. e.g. Childhood in
    England (put in <u>The England I Remember</u>).
    Farm days—put in material from <u>My remarkable Uncle</u> and better from
    <u>My Discovery of the West</u>
    Also various items passages etc. about pre-motor car–horse & buggy
    days
    Upper Canada as a boy   use article Gentlemen in My Remarkable
    Uncle.
    Upper Canada as a teacher—use my Memories & Miseries as a School
    Master . .
    Chicago—use article contributed to a Chicago memorial volume of
    '41 or '42. The type script & MSS is somewhere round
    Lecturing at McGill—there's a lot of stuff.
    English trips—see MY DISCOVERY OF ENGLAND
    My Disc of England
    Lecturing etc etc etc

    Material to insert not yet in books:
    Mirage (My moving picture of the Man. Boom Days—Print it as it is
    copyright is still all mine.

Commonsense & the Universe
                        Atlantic 1942
Health & Happiness              ⎱ Sold by Jacques Chambrun  Not in
Blacking out the Consumer  ⎰ books—use MS or type script not print
(The England I remember), but this should go in holus-bolus as above.
Use original text. Magazine cut the end.
Remaking the World (sold to Pan American Syndicate. Oct. 1942
J Walter Thompson New York  The agent concerned, & for his firm the
correspondent Miss Estelle Platt
Are Witty Women Attractive to Men Oct 42 magaz rights ~~Book~~ sold
to Vogue (Jessica Davis, correspondent)
    Also I have written a great number of articles in the last 10 or 15 years on
economic and political subjects,—Barron's Magazine, Commentator, etc. . . .
These were ephemeral—but contain a lot of stuff that could be consolidated
into a chapter—Random Thoughts, to pick out all the plumbs
    Memo for you (Bâ) not to go to Dodd.

### Available Pieces
The Transit of Venus. A story about 6000 words that appeared in a Ladies Home
Journal about 1917–1919. Try the McGill Library Memoir . . . . . . . 6000
Business of Growing Old (Three Score and Ten) see original full MS . . . 2500
My Remarkable Uncle . . . 2500
Cricket for Americans (Atlantic) . . . . . 1500
Get me other MS from the cases: some are not good enough.
Migration–Quarterly Review . . . . . 5000
The Canadian Pieces (Come to Canada etc. etc.)


## To Town Clerk, Pictou, N.S.

McGill University,
Montreal, P.Q.
Oct. 10, 1942.

Town Clerk,
Pictou, N.S.

Dear Sir,
    I am commissioned by the Encyclopaedia Britannica to make a revision of
their articles dealing with Canada. Among these is one of 60 words dealing with
your town, of which I enclose a copy. I should be greatly obliged if you will
indicate the changes necessary in regard to population and other statistics and
will add any which you think of interest and advantage in regard to newer
manufactures etc., and concerning war developments in air-fields, camps and
plants. I do not know how much space will be available and hence am not

authorized to say how much the editors can use, but I am sure that they will want to use all they can.

Yours sincerely,
Stephen Leacock

## To B.K. Sandwell

[University Club of
Montreal]
Oct 13 1942

My dear B.K.

I cannot thank you enough not only for putting my pictures[1] in Saturday Night but for the charming way you wrote them up—Everybody here stops me on the street to talk about it

This adds another debt to the long outstanding account of gratitude that I owe to <u>Saturday Night</u>.

I remember as if it were yesterday instead of being 48 years ago when they first published my Pathology of Clothes[2] & gave me a standing with the Medical World I have never lost . . .

What kind of standing, I am not saying.

Sincerely yours
Stephen Leacock

1   The pictures are the photographs Karsh took of Leacock at The Old Brewery Bay.
2   'An Outline of a New Pathology' appeared in *Saturday Night*, 8 December 1894; Leacock's 'Half Hours with Poets' had appeared in an earlier issue (4 November 1894).

## To Thomas B. Costain

3869 Cote des Neiges Rd.
Montreal Que.
Oct. 16. 1942

Dear Costain

Herewith the concluding paragraphs of the preface of <u>Read it With Me</u>. Please read them. The idea is to strike the note, —A BOOK TO READ ALOUD, as part of our publicity.

Best regards
Stephen Leacock

. . . I can form no better wish for this volume than that it should turn out to be the kind of book which people bring home and read out loud in the family. It is a peculiarity of humour that it is best when shared with others; there is more of it when divided; with laughter one and one make four or five. This is most true of the humour that is really funny and which can stand the crucial test of whether people laugh at it. The best of such humour is apt to be universal in its appeal so that people of all ages can share the enjoyment of it. There is nothing in it that a school boy cannot appreciate in a flash, and his father if you give him time. I think that the main part of the humour collected in this volume is of that kind. All the world can laugh with Mr. Pickwick, sit chuckling in the main-top of the Mantelpiece with Captain Recce, get education across Mr. Dooley's bar and laugh it off with Bob Benchley. They say that even the Sultan of Turkey used to read Mark Twain, especially the piece about <u>Cannibalism in the Cars</u>, which he read again and again.

Let this be then, I hope, a book especially for reading aloud at home. I don't expect, or even desire, that it should replace the reading of the family prayers; but I feel that after reading it people would turn all the more willingly to pray.

Stephen Leacock

## To James Keddie

[3869 Cote des Neiges Road Montreal]
Oct 19  1942

My dear Mr Keddie

Your letter telling me of your father's death was forwarded to me from the hotel and reached me this morning. I cannot tell you what a deep shock of grief it brings to me.

Your father and I knew one another at first only through business relations, —and pleasant and harmonious they were,—and then through the personal correspondence which we carried on for years, and which came to be a feature and a factor in my life as I am sure it was in his . . . It was with the greatest pleasure that I used to settle down in my study chair to read the latest of his bulky letters,—and the bulkier it was the more I liked it . . We wrote in the plain straightforward way only possible in such an interchange of letters, about what we thought of this new world that seemed to overwhelm us in our old age . . . . All that he said I valued and if I am spared to try to help piece things together later it will serve me in good stead . . . He was just the kind of man whose tempered wisdom and personal knowledge of the old country and the new will be needed to keep us together.

Feeling thus I can realize what a great blow this sudden berevement must be to you and to all those he leaves behind . . You must please accept and convey to them the expression of my deep and lasting sympathy.

Very sincerely & tenderly<br>Stephen Leacock

## To Gordon Glassco[1]

3869 Cote des Neiges Road,
Montreal,
Oct. 20, 1942.

Gordon Glassco, Esq.,
Secretary, McGill Society of Ontario,
Montreal.

Dear Gordon:—

I have sent the Bursar $25.00 to add to our Loan Fund balance of $125.00 and I ask him in return to send me $150.00. I propose to give this to Mrs. H. M. Little to help her with the college expenses of her sons. You will recall that I wished to do this last year, but when we offered the money to Michael Little he refused it on the ground that he intended to enlist for overseas service and did not wish to incur the chance of leaving a debt of honour for his mother to pay if he did not come back. He has since completed two years at McGill and enlisted. His oldest brother Pat, already enlisted has, as you know, been posted as missing.

The third boy Brian is now at McGill. I am quite sure that if a loan were offered him directly he would feel that he ought to follow his brother's example in refusing, as he also intends in due course to enlist for overseas. I wish therefore to give the money to Mary Little personally, to help her with Brian's expenses now, and those of Michael when he comes back to McGill, and to do this as a small recognition of our Society and of what her late husband, himself from Ontario, did for Montreal and McGill, and in recognition of the devoted service of her sons.

I have talked this over with Fred Ker who has sent you a letter of corroboration. He promised to speak to Punch McCracken of whose hearty concurrence I feel assured. But I would be greatly obliged if you would write to Punch and send him copies of the correspondence. I need hardly say that we should treat this whole matter as confidential and not for general announcement.

Very faithfully,
Stephen Leacook

1   Gordon Glassco was the executive secretary of the Graduates' Society of McGill University.


## To Thomas B. Costain

3869 Cote des Neiges Rd.
Oct 28, 1942.

Dear Costain

Everything sounds (yours Oct. 20) all right about the book. I'll gladly acquiese in the arrangement suggested (paragraph 2), viz, same net price on Canadian sales as on U.S. . . . Arithmetic is not quite right in as much as the U.S.

tax is neither here nor there being deducted from my tax to Ottawa, whereas under this arrangement I still have to pay tax . . . but we can let that go . . .

An important point is that this tax is agreed all round to be only temporary to conserve exchange. It could easily be removed or lowered to what it was, even apart from the end of the war. It may not be in force when the book comes out. I suggest a clause recognizing that (as appended) and one limiting your interest to book rights only, and only to U.S. and Canada. We can leave the British market out for the present and talk of it later.

If all that is suitable please go ahead with the contract and we'll have it all settled . . . I am working at the book with great pleasure,—I think I can make it a book that ever so many people, ordinary people and not literature bugs, will want to read at home.

> Very sincerely
> Stephen Leacock

The present contract covers only book rights in the United States and in Canada, and not book rights in the United Kingdom, Colonies and India, nor does it cover any other rights other than book rights.

The present arrangement putting the authors royalties on sale in Canada below 15 per cent of the Canadian retail price is based on the existence of the present high Canadian tariff on import from the United States a temporary measure for the conservation of American exchange in Canada; with any substantial lowering of this tariff the arrangement will end and the author receive 15 per cent on the retail price of the book in Canada.

## To Thomas B. Costain

3869 Cote des Neiges Rd.
Montreal
Nov. 6, 1942.

Dear Costain

At last your novel arrived and got safely cleared through the customs. Owing to your kind dedication they charged me no duty at all . . . I am reading the book with the greatest interest especially as it is, apart from other things, a treasure of history. I will send you more detailed thanks later on.

My six copies of <u>Montreal</u> arrived—It looks fine, beautifully made . . . Mrs. Shaw is busy with circulars of which she is sending out about 1000 on selected lists and Henry Morgan and Co. (the big store) are sending out 3000 with their November advertising. Mrs. Shaw is also sending out circulars to all the big Canadian Book stores and Canadian papers.

Yours of Nov. 4, re Anthology Book <u>Read It With Me</u> you speak of expensive material. I presume this means expensive copyright to pay for. But I understand that for the U.S. there is no copyright on anything written before

1886 (fifty six years ago). This gives me free Chap.I. Lewis Carrol. Chap.II. Gilbert's Bab Ballads. Chap.III. Pre-Highbrow America (Jas. Russell Lowell-Artemus Ward, Josh Billings. Bret Harte. Max Adeler etc,—) all stuff before 1886. Chap.IV. Pickwick. Chap.V. Other Dickens' stuff. Chap.VI. Mark Twain's Sketches. Chap.VII. Huck Finn. Chap.VIII Alphonse Daudet. Chap. XI. J.M. Barrie (Nicotine). Of the later authors I think I can get permission to use all I want, for England:—

E.V. Lucas, Harry Graham, Chas. Graves, Fanstey, A.P. Herbert, Maurice Baring. etc. And with U.S.:—

Bob Benchley (he gave it before) George Ade, Irvin Cobb, Mr. Dooley (Estate). etc.

My intention is that what I can't get for nothing I don't use. It is worth while as publicity for these books e.g. John Kendrick Bangs,—to be revived and brought to notice—There are only one or two like Ring W. Lardner that I would rather pay for than go without.

This book is not <u>an</u> anthology, it is <u>my</u> anthology,—what I have liked—so it means nothing if I leave out stuff.

I note the contract as first drawn makes these permission fees chargeble to my account, as far as the account goes. If too large they might clean it out.

I'd be glad to get this point cleared up to avoid all future difficulty, and especially to prevent any idea that so and so or such and such ought not to be left out. I hope we can get it all fixed and a clear track ahead. Please get your people to report on what is said above.

Yours sincerely
Stephen Leacock

## To Thomas B. Costain

The Old Brewery Bay
Orillia, Ontario
(Nov 19  1942)

Dear Costain

My best thanks for your very kind letter about <u>permission</u> to reprint. Im afraid that you have been put to a lot of personal trouble about this matter. You and I could have settled it all over a "cup of ale" (as your Elizabethan friends would call it).

It is a perplexing situation but I think I see how I can arrange it quite satisfactorily.

In the first place we have an irreducible minimum for the book in the chapters on all the earlier humour beyond present reach of copyright claims which happily includes not only Charles Dickens but all the writing of Mark Twain which I would wish to include. To these we can add such authors (dead or alive) whose copyrights are held by your firm as discussed in our Montreal conversations. These fortunately include O Henry and, I imagine, various other stuff. To this we add the large chapters on <u>Punch</u> and the <u>Punch</u> people for which I am certain to get a blanket permission. I have already full permission from A.P. Herbert. Over and above these are the general chapters of foreign humour (so far I've only put in <u>Alphonse Daudet</u>. The comparative chapters on the World's Unconscious Humorists, the discussion (humourous and satirical of Ancient and Mediaeval Humour) and the chapter on Shakespeare my own Humour. Beyond that again I have full permission formerly given by Bob Benchley, Irvin Cobb and George Ade which I am sure can be renewed. So there is quite enough in that to make a book anyway as the book from the start has been regarded not as an attempt to select the world's best humour but as a purely personal discussion of the things that I have read and admired and invite people to read again with me.

The difficulty of the plan proposed by your permission department whose point of view I fully appreciate, is that it calls upon me to write the book first and then ask permission to print it. But suppose the permission is refused or that the price demanded is so high that the expected return will not justify it? What am I to do? If I refuse to pay I have wasted my time and compromised a lot of material that might be otherwise useful? Indeed it might easily mean the choice between a considerable financial loss or a large waste of time and loss of useful writing.

You see, at present a lot of the book consists of notes, scraps, memoranda, suggestions of lists of quotations to hunt up etc. Your permission department say that they can't ask for a blanket permission but must have all quotations complete, page, verse, even the words of small references. You see exactly what this would mean to me.

But I think I can easily get round it all. In the case of authors where permission is necessary I will myself write and explain that I am getting together a book of chapters on the humour I like and have liked best and that I want to put in an essay, entirely laudatory and all to the good, on such and such an author and select, say, 5000 words of his work to quote. I will do this on my own and without any reference to your firm, indeed there is no reason to mention it. If they care to give me the permission without any fee in this general way I will be delighted to act on it. But if not I can do without it. In the latter case I will put in a general chapter on my admirations of today, solely in essay form with quotations and brief references but with no reprinting or any sustained story.

By this means your permissions department will not need to bother any more as all the material will either be free of copyright anyway or set free by the general permission for me to use it.

Best regards

## To Thomas B. Costain

3869 Cote des Neiges Rd.
Dec. 5, 1942.

Dear Costain

Everything fine. I enclose the signed contract, and a specimen letter.

1. Re the contract. Note the title <u>Read it With Me</u>, and I want to add a subtitle,—<u>The Humour I like Best</u> . . . You will remember that I thought any such title as <u>A Biography</u>—or <u>Autobiography</u> would be a virtual, though not a legal, infringement on my contract with Frank Dodd for an Autobiographical book after the war . . . undoubtedly any "biography" title would hurt his sales of his book.

2. Re permission. I suggest that when I obtain permission in general and gentlemanly terms, you follow it up with a letter like the enclosed which contains the kind of brutal language that publishers and lawyers use. You will then get an absolute safe-guard and I will have one already.

.        .        .        .        .

I hope we are now all set for a real start . . . I am a little tied up with Encyclopedia Britannica work just now . . It's low pay for the time it takes but I like it, . . . but I want to get it all done with and then go full speed at this humour book . . . As soon as I hear definitely I'll write all the permission letters . . . Perhaps it would be better to leave the English edition to your management but we can talk of that later.

Very best regards
Stephen Leacock


Mr.————

We are very glad to learn from Professor Stephen Leacock that you have kindly consented to allow him to use certain selected material from your writings as a part of the subject matter of the book Read it With Me which he is preparing for publication by our house. We understand that Dr. Leacock has explained to you that this is not so much an anthology in the ordinary sense as a discussion and quotation,—and a eulogy of those chapters in British and American humour from which he himself has personally derived amusement. His request, we believe, rested on this basis.

Dr. Leacock now tells us that the passages from your work which he wishes to quote and to discuss, consist of;—


We understand that you grant us permission to cover all editions published in the United States and Canada and open market for copies produced in the English language other than in the British Empire.

We should be glad of a word of ratification to prevent any possible error.

*To The Editors of Queen's Quarterly*      3869 Cote des Neiges Road
Dec. 12, 42.

The Editors
The Queen's Quarterly

Dear Sirs
   I want (I have long been wanting) to write an article on <u>Geography</u> and its conversion to <u>Geographical Science</u> . . . This is purely an educational topic but I think I can manage to give it a certain public appeal, at any rate to all people entering boys and girls at college and to all people inside college struggling with the expanding curriculum, the new sixteen puzzle.
   The thesis is as follows. Two separate problems here join in one solution.
1. Matriculation (a fixed test, anything outside of which "doesn't matter") killed school geography, reading out loud, reciting poetry, speaking distinctly and those simple things that meant so much in the plain education of 80 years ago.
2. Every arts course finds itself in a dilemma about a list of subjects of which every educated man ought to know something, of which no educated man can ever know a great deal, except as a specialist in one of them.
   Such are geology, biology, astronomy (in its simplest form), anthropology and evolution in general . . .
   All of these are Geography in the old sense of gee (hard as in gin) sorry—I mean hard gin. These together could make a new <u>Geosophy</u>. If I dared to coin a word, or without coinage,—Geographical Science. This as a comprehensive matriculation subject, two years of high school, would give to all students of all college subjects (history, English, economics, languages, philosophy). the basis,—or solid earth,—that they now lack. If you think it sounds suitable I'd like to write an article of about 2000–4000 words

Yrs. sincerely
Stephen Leacock.

*To Dorothy Parker*[1]      3869 Cote des Neiges Road
Montreal
December 17, 1942

Dear Miss Dorothy Parker:
   I have a great admiration for your work—see my eulogy on it in my book "<u>How to Write</u>" just out, or just emerging, from Dodd Mead (they're sending it to you).

1   Dorothy Parker (1893–1967) was an American satirist, poet, and short-story writer.

I didn't quote you in that book as I had no permission but I want to do so in the new book of Doubleday Doran described in the accompanying general letter.

Receive, as the French say, the expression of my most perfect consideration.

Stephen Leacock

## To Mrs Herbert T. Shaw

[3869 Cote des Neiges Road Montreal]
Wed Dec 23–12³⁰ noon
(1942)

Dear Fitz

This I hope will reach you in time to say Merry Xmas to yourself & Ken & Peggy—I stayed in this morning till noon & ~~tra~~ tried to write my <u>Apology</u> for <u>The British Empire</u> & got a little way with it and will try to finish it tomorrow (excuse bad writing as my hand is very shakey) . . . I am going to the library now to get some books as it closes from 5 oclock today till Monday morning—I met Arthur Chipman for a minute this morning in my little before breakfast walk and he told me that several "fellers" at the club comparing notes had all said that there is not a copy of our book available—everything depends for you on how many they were able to get before the supply stopped but surely it ought to mean 1000 copies, in other words $100 for you, ~~pul~~ plus 5 per cent of my 30 cents a copy = $15⁰⁰ a total of $115————we'll hope so. I think I will lunch at the club & then walk back here and stay here,—if I can enough good books.

Dont you think that if you get time it might be a good thing to go into the Boston Public Library & get some idea as to whether a person could find good accommodation for working at making notes on books—you see, when you go later for a longer visit if I had some work where you really could make notes, partly in the library but <u>only</u> partly, and also by taking books out, then I could send you U.S. exchange as easily as I sent it to Barbara . . . . . . . . . . . . If you get time when walking on the Common go & look in at the little old cemetery round the corner from its far end

I see that by accident I used a sheet with a letter on the back. You'll have to return this piece—or no—I'll copy it again (stop) .͟. . . it's copied, so it doesn't matter—

Affectionately & with best Xmas to you all

Stephen (Leacock)

### To Mrs Herbert T. Shaw

3869 Cote des Neiges Rd
Montreal
Thursday Dec 24 42
(9.30 AM)

Dear Fitz

Just going out for my walk—I've been working hard on my <u>Apology for the British Empire</u> and think I can get it done—Meantime I was cheered by getting word from <u>Barron's Magazine</u> that the gold article (revised) is now O.K. & will soon be used . . . Yesterday I lunched at the Club but found there were so many there that I came home & stayed home the rest of the day and evening. I dont suppose I shall hear from you till Saturday—I imagine the mail is terribly crowded —but I shall be waiting to hear all about Boston—the weather here is all mild again, so no doubt it will be even milder there with you—I havent yet called up Mary but I bought a bottle of Scotch to take & Tina called up from Duxbury to make sure that the turkey was there—the Russian news is great isnt it—but that cursed treatment (this morning's paper of people in Czechoslovakia) makes me want to kill every dirty German—

Affectionately
Stephen Leacock


### To Mrs Herbert T. Shaw

3869 Cote des Neiges Road
Montreal
Xmas 1942   3.30 pm

Dear Fitz

Merry Xmas!

A kind of a dull one here so far. I got up and worked at my <u>Apology for the British Empire</u> & got it where I hope to finish it tomorrow. Since then a little walk breakfast & have sat around here. I must now get shaved and dressed up in the whole armour of God & go to the Club and then over to Mary's . . . Jack Culliton had dinner with me on his way out . . . feeling much elated. He is a pilot officer R.C.A.F. in uniform (as soon as he can buy it but he cant get any for the minute). Reports for duty Lachine Air Port Dec 29, dismissed over New Years & then, is part of the force, two weeks at Lachine & then on, he has no idea where. is booked for overseas & whatever. His uniform costs $300, the government giving him $150, but he doesn't mind debt any more being satisfied. He's a good fellow. He met me before dinner at the Club & we had a drink with Arthur Chipman & Charlie Davis & then to my place in Charlie Davis's car & Jack went away after dinner with a whole arm full of parcels to give at different houses & wishing he had his uniform, even an air overcoat.

I heard on all hands that our Montreal ran off the market. Burton only sold 400: could get no more . . . as I have had $1000 advance on it I mustn't reckon too much on whats left. . . . I asked her if she had heard from you. But no,—as we say in French . . .

I shall soon expect to hear from you. Mary phoned me this morning that Mike was only arriving this (Xmas) morning . . . dinner at 7:30

Again best New Year wishes to you all

Your affectly<br>Stephen (Leacock)

## To Mrs Herbert T. Shaw[1]

3869 Cote des Neiges Road<br>Montreal<br>Thursday Dec 30  42

Dear Fitz

My! My! Great is the power of work! I have, as you know, to do an article on <u>Toronto and Montreal</u> for Macleans & it seemed hard going, but I've been thinking & thinking like hell and now at last I've got it well started & find it quite fascinating to do . . started at 7 this morning & just quitting now at 25 to 10.

Your letter of Dec 28 (Monday) got here this morning & I just got it now— went down & got the letters when I quit work . . I see you stay there till Monday. I wasn't going to answer your letter till I saw that as I fully expected you back sooner. But this will easily reach you—Yesterday I asked Mary to lunch at the club & we had quite a nice talk especially about her doing work for the Montreal. She talked about the Dutch people but I never put intimate remarks in a letter . . She had not heard from you & wanted to know when you were coming back but of course I didnt know—I had finished yesterday my <u>Apology for the British Empire</u>. I do hope I can get it published and that it can be published without cutting it too much . . Mrs Simons was to have it ready for today . . . I got a telegram from Jim Eakins asking me to lunch at the Club today. I don't know how long he is to be here – – – Try to remember: I wrote a letter to Doubleday Doran (Costain & Miss Hulse) about the <u>Read It</u> book . . about getting <u>permission,</u> a sort of big circular letter for them to copy and send on . . I've had no answer. Did it get sent. Please keep it in the top of your mind . . . I'll forget it again. Work seems piling up from when you get back but I guess you'd prefer it that way. It's much nicer to have enough to do . . . I am afraid that Jones has fallen down on my chicken stuff and I am thinking about closing my Orillia place (as a farm and just using the house. I might give Jones the two cows and the horse instead of <u>Jan</u> <u>Feb</u> <u>March</u> & <u>April</u> wages . . . and then not hire him

---

1   Attached to this letter was the public notice: 'Emeritus Professor Stephen Butler Leacock, B.A, Ph.D., Litt.D., LL.D., D.C.L., Montreal; 73 today.'

... I guess I could do the work ... I'm thinking about it ... At Orillia if I bought milk and eggs & scratched up the garden for myself & just cut a pathway through the grass ... I don't know ...

I'll stop & go for a walk

> Affect'ly
> Stephen Leacock
> Lord Whitaker[x]

[x]I can't get over being in an <u>Almanac</u> along with Mohammad & Jesus Christ

## To W.A. Irwin

[3869 Cote des Neiges Road
Montreal]
Feb. 5, 43.

Dear Mr. Irwin

Yours Feb. 1st .... That's fine ... The enclosed little cutting (which please return as I shall use it in our article) gives you my general idea ... But just to avoid all misunderstanding I'd like to say that what I mainly want to write about is the <u>Future of Canada</u> ... it fits in, of course, with world democracy and security etc.... but I want to lay a minimum stress on how to deal with Europe ... and a maximum on what to do at home ... Here all turns on our vast assets ... our future is a totally different problem from that of Great Britain ....

I can hit 3,500 words to a syllable, knowing it before hand; time 3 weeks at longest ...

> Best regards
> Stephen Leacock

P.S. Your office sent to ask at what date I had cashed your cheque for $80 (article <u>Come up on the Mountain</u>) I answered I never recieved it. But I got $125 for <u>Toronto Montreal</u>.

.    .    .    .

I have throughout this article made no account of what is to be done with Germany, and what done to secure peace in Europe after the war .... That's another topic, but I see no difficulty in it ... Peace should be guaranteed by a League of Nations, in which would be all the free, allied nations. But only the British Empire and the States and Russia would vote, although all the Latin American republics could talk, like the Porto Rico delegates in congress. The Chinese could smoke and watch. Security would be guaranteed with a gun. Germany would be disarmed and prevented from making anything that could fire, float or fly. But beyond that I would treat Germany with the greatest leniency. I would hang, leniently, all the criminals and brutes. I would leniently take twice as much property as the Germans stole from conquered people. Beyond that I would ask nothing except that gangs of German labour,—on bed, board and one beer,—should rebuild broken cities. After all that I'd give them each a long pipe and a copy of Kant with beer out of a hose and a choice of Wienerschnitzel or Kielersprotten,—and then come back after a hundred years and see what they had turned into . . . or no, make it two hundred.

But in any case never trade with them, as that way lies false interest, treachery and war.

## To Dorothy Duncan MacLennan[1]

[3869 Cote des Neiges Road Montreal]
Feb 15 43

Dear Mrs MacLennan

Thank you very much indeed for your note . . I'm sorry to say that I only glanced at the Gazette. I hate reading anything about myself: if it's bad, it hurts my feelings: if it's good, it's never good enough . .

And I am afraid that I cant be of any use to you to get a copy of ~~Montreal~~ Canada; I have only one copy and I am sorry to say that I have parted with all control of the book.. But I feel sure that if you wrote and asked Mr Sam Bronfman of the Distillers Corporation (Peel St) for a copy he would send you one at once. My especial thanks for what you say of my <u>Montreal</u>

best regards
Stephen Leacock

I might take occasion to say that I think <u>your</u> Canada book is just the thing. I have widely prescribed it . . . and it needs no—needs no Samuel Bronfman—

That begins to remind me of a pocm, the one, the original & real one in the Mounted Police as the Riders of the Plains

. . "They need no sculptured monument,
No panoply of stone,
To blazen to a curious world
The deeds that they have done;
But the prairie flower blows softly
And the scented rosebud trains
Its wealth of Summer beauty
O'er the Riders of the Plains.

So with your book

It needs no Samuel Bronfman
It needs no Sherriff Scott

---

1  Writer Dorothy Duncan MacLennan (1905–57) was the first wife of novelist Hugh MacLennan.

To make a book that has a look
Of something that its not.
For every page is charming
And every chapter filled
With simple truth disarming
All thought that it's distilled

Very sincerely
Stephen Leacock

## To Frank Dodd

[3869 Cote des Neiges Road
Montreal]
Feb 18, 43.

My dear Dodd

I have been doing such a lot of writing lately with so much success with it that I'd like to make plans a little ahead, as far as the nature of the times, and the chances of life permit one to do so.

I am chiefly interested in getting out a book of little stories,—not essays, but sketches each of which is a story; so much of the material is ready ~~and~~ or half-ready that I can feel humanly sure, on the terms above, of having the MS complete for publication on Oct. 15 . . . That is to say, all in your hands August 1st.

I want to put the book out under a ~~hapt~~ happy, catchy title with the word Stories in it . . . so that it will mean Stories to make people glad, to take people out of themselves, who read them . . . We could use the phrase Stories for Happiness as a stop-gap title.

Total length . . . about 60,000 words. You take as usual U.S. and Canada Book rights, but no other, at 15 per cent U.S. for US sales, 15 per cent Canada for Canadian sales . . . I have enough of the stories absolutely done and finished, and first rate . . . to know what I am talking about

_____    _____

Others still. What's next for Canada? (the Development of Canada from now on). To be ready 3 months after the close of the war, but not before March 1944.

_____    _____

Recollections and Reflections: six months after that.

_____    _____

. . . I have also under construction a large book Geographical Science, planned and edited by me, but only a part about 1/6 written by me . . . an illustrated edition, then an educational edition. This needs, I presume, a college house.

very sincerely
Stephen Leacock

# PREFACE

All the stories in this book have, or are meant to have, one element in common. They are not true to life. The people in them laugh too much; they cry too easily; they lie too hard. The light is all false, its too bright, and the manners and customs all wrong. The times and places are confused.

There is no need therefore to give the usual assurance that none of the characters in the book are real persons. Of course not, this is not real life. It is better. They say that sunshine can draw even the crookedest elm tree straight. Let it be hoped that there is enough sunshine in these pages to draw straight a little of the crookedness of real life.

Stephen Leacock.

*To Barbara Nimmo*                         [3869 Cote des Neiges Road
                                            Montreal]
                                            March 1 1943

Dear Bâ . . . .

The Bank sent you today $200 U.S. . . . There will, I hope, be some more encyc. money coming to you but I have to wait till all the work is done & I get my editorial fee . . . Things press rather hard just now . . . But I shall hope to be able to send some more presently . . There will be no more typing or any work to do as the typing now is just for short lists & broken pieces

So David is in Ireland! He's certainly seeing a lot of the world. I am hoping that the war will end as rapidly as the blitz conquests opened it . . . . It is terrible . .

Love to you all.
y a u
Stephen Leacock

*To Thomas B. Costain*                      3869 Cote des Neiges Rd.
                                            March 2, 43.

Dear Costain

My best thanks for your recent letter about 'Montreal'. I am glad that it is selling so well and I hear nothing but good of it locally . . . and though I never take clippings I have been sent some really wonderful reviews . . .

As to our other book Read it With Me in which I am greatly interested I begin to be afraid that we had better assign the completion of the M.S. for the end of the summer instead of the beginning.

Two reasons:—

I. The very complicated procedure of which I am informed by Miss Hulse as necessary under publishers' custom for securing permissions is bound of itself to make delay . . . I do not wish to incur cost in this matter. In fact in these days I can't. Hence I would hardly care to use any material, or much material, for which I have to pay, let alone to sign up a sort of indefinite bill of costs . . . No doubt you see just what I mean . . . So it will be better if I move along a chapter at a time getting permission as I go . . . That of course involves delay.

II. The more I work on the book the less I am inclined to hurry it, instead, inclined to try to write all my sections of comment to make them really first class things . . . This takes time.

As a matter of fact a third reason is that I find my working energy limited,— I've just so many good hours in the day.

I presume that as nothing has been definitely arranged about printing the date Oct 1st. would suit you as well as July 1st. (this no doubt might delay publication till new years)

I haven't written to you personally for so long, at any length, that I've had no chance to tell you how much I've enjoyed your book—You've got some striking scenes and episodes but best of all is the feeling of having moved back into the atmosphere of another century. Many people will have told you that it must have meant a lot of work but I am wise enough to see that it meant years and years of play,—of feeling round with the history of a bye-gone time for its own sake without the idea of writing it up.

Best regards
Stephen Leacock.

## To Frank Dodd

3869 Cote des Neiges Rd.
March 9, 43.

Dear Sirs

Herewith is the signed contract for Happy Stories, Just to Laugh At.

I have already over 40,000 words complete or practically so and hence feel assured that I can have the full M.S. ready August 1st. barring anything unforseen. This would allow for publication Oct. 1st. but not earlier than Oct 1. to allow any magazine commitments that might interfere . . . I will even ask you to leave the date of publication open as between Oct. 1 and Oct. 31; in case I get caught with anything valuable delayed beyond expectation in magazine use. I only expect to use a portion of the copy this way . . . I have every expectation of all copy being clear of magazine use by Oct. 1st.

I enclose a suggestion for publicity work similar to what I did with Doubleday Doran on my book Montreal . . . It is not an essential part of the contract except

that without it I should hardly care to keep the clause about the next two books
. . . but I am sure it would be in both your interest and mine.

> Very sincerely
> Stephen Leacock

Schedule to contract for <u>Happy Stories, Just to Laugh At</u>
Professor Leacock's proposal for promotion work on Canadian Editions in
Montreal, Ottawa and Toronto; can be accepted or not

———————————————

I propose either directly or through Mrs. H. T. Shaw, my research secretary
of some years past who has worked on this kind of publicity,—

I.   To ~~complete~~ prepare and print at my expense and circulate at my expense
     an announcement circular of extracts from <u>Happy Stories</u>, with comment,
     —not less than 2000 words, 4000 copies.
II.  To take special steps to send the circular to prepared personal lists.
III. To take steps to obtain special quotations from the list in certain journals.
IV.  To interest departmental and large book stores personally in the sale.

It would be difficult for me as an author to do this "boosting" entirely in
my own person but Mrs. H. T. Shaw will act under my advice.

I shall expect for this a special payment over and above any other royalty of
ten cents (10 cents Canadian) on each copy sold in Montreal, Toronto and
Ottawa.

> Stephen Leacock[1]

1   In a letter from the firm dated 22 March 1943, Leacock's book was accepted.

## To the Atlantic Monthly

3869 Cote des Neiges Rd.
Montreal
March 19, 43.

The Editors
The Atlantic Monthly

Dear Sirs

I have it very much in mind that I would like to write this spring an article
of 3500–4000 words under the title <u>"Greek"</u>,—just that <u>"Greek"</u> . . . Not a
funny article except as far as even a serious article may be illuminated with an
attempt at humour.

In war time the constant preoccupation, the burden and anxiety of war gets too much even for those who are only spectators to be able to tolerate it without some attempt to turn one's mind elsewhere . . . Otherwise I would not suggest just now a topic that has waited 2000 years and can ~~weight~~ wait longer.

More than that,—The war and the prospect of what is to follow makes us reconsider and rejudge all the phases of our social life and culture, including our education and our literature . . .

So I want to examine the place that Greek has had, still has, and deserves to have or not to have in the future; to estimate its value in education as a purely disciplinary subject, and the value of Greek literature,—its historic place and what it means, or does not mean, now.

I wish, above all, to cast out affectation and the pedantry of scholarship and judge things properly.

I am one of the few living people (there cannot be many of us) properly qualified so to judge; I mean,—people who spent years of their life, and the best hours of their day, in learning Greek, and yet who have no vested or professional interest in it,—not professors or teachers of Greek, or writers of text books or historians of Greece, or interested in Greek as clergymen, able or nearly able to read the new testament . . . (The little bit of Greek that the Divinity student learns today is no great matter; he begins Alpha, Beta, Gamma at college and wouldn't know the verb if he met it on the street . . . . I do not want to seem to denounce Greek or "de-bunk" Greek but I think the value of Greek literature,—in itself and apart from history,—is greatly over-estimated . . . I do not believe that the plays of Aeschylus are anything more than primitive, or if the word is too strong, early, drama, comparable let us say to Miracle Plays . . .

.    .    .    .    .    .

I hope you could consider such an article as <u>likely</u> to fit in with your plans . . . I'd send it to England but I fear that even old friends of mine like the <u>Quarterly</u> would be horrified . .

Frankly, in my opinion the "great classical scholars," the Bentleys and the Jowetts, were just great bags of sawdust . . . How little they could really know of Latin as compared with people who spoke it every minute and wrote and scribbled it on wax . . . Do you that Plutarch who lived in Rome for years and years and lectured in Greek on philosophy, said that he could never really read or speak Latin fluently indeed never read the chief authors till in his old age . . . Where would an Oxford professor be beside that.

Yours very sincerely
Stephen Leacock[1]

---

1    In a letter of 24 March 1943 Edward Weeks, editor of *The Atlantic Monthly*, accepted the article: 'Yes, yes, yes! Indeed I do want that essay of yours.' The article never appeared.

## To Barbara Nimmo

Montreal
March 20. 1943

Dear Bâ

Please regard this as a topic all of itself and virtually a codicil to my will &
I will make a formal one later.

My nearly complete book <u>Happy Stories</u> is certain to make money; certain
for $10,000 and perhaps more. It is incomplete but Mrs. Shaw has all the notes,
materials and directions needed to complete it, even if it had to be done right
now. I therefore make it an exception in regard to your inheriting any MS or
literary material of mine not in the publishers hands and give this jointly, half
and half with Mrs. Shaw. Once complete and in the publishers hands it becomes
part of my estate if I am alive when it is given to them. You will forgive the
rather cheerless topic. I think it necessary in view of what I hope is the very
great money value of the asset,—all there, if looked after, all lost, if neglected. I
am asking Mrs. Shaw to copy this and send it to you and with it a copy of the
contents to date. She knows all about it and together you could write a preface
& complete anything incomplete.

y.a.u.
Stephen Leacock

## To Mrs Herbert T. Shaw

3869 Cote des Neiges Road
Montreal
Wed March 24/43

Dear Fitz

I have just read in the morning paper the news, utterly unexpected by me,
of Eddie Beattys death. It comes with a great shock: he had always seemed like
a person who goes on forever—I will send you the paper with his picture & a
full account. It seems that he had had <u>several</u> operations—presumably he didnt
survive the last as he died in the hospital—I had got up early to make an effort
to get ahead with the Encyclopaedia & was working at it till the morning paper
came—which quite upsets me for work so I think I'll go out and take a walk
instead.

11 a.m. I have just phoned and arranged to go & see John Counsell at the
hospital. Mary going with me. He had asked about my coming, it seems, & said
he would like to see me, so we are to go at 12.30 ... I got your letter of Monday
by this morning's mail. It must seem funny for you not to be in your own house
but the breakfast stuff sounds a great improvement .. I didnt get much work
done this morning—so I shall go out now & walk to the Club—I've no stamps.
I must remember to post this ... A letter from Dodd Mead gives me an extra
10 cents a copy (for publicity work) on all sales of <u>Happy Stories</u> in Toronto,

Ottawa & Montreal—and I will contract it on to you—that should be worth, let me see, say 500 copies next autumn, that $50.00 . . . that ought to come in just right—if the book makes a hit it would double that.

affectionately
Stephen Leacock


## *To Mrs Herbert T. Shaw*

3869 Cote des Neiges Rd
Montreal
Friday Ma 26  43

Dear Fitz

Yours of <u>Wednesday</u> here this morning  I note that it takes 2 days nowadays . . . This morning I walked up the mountain my first trip I think of 1943—its all snow up there, dirty flat snow but still snow—in fact winter. I walked down the loops & into Cedar Avenue by the fire-hall—in all an hour as I went pretty slowly – – – since then Encyclopaedia, town after town—I'm through the alphabet as far as Halifax but it's a long way still to the <u>Yukon</u> . . . I must hurry & be done with it; there is no interest left in it and I want to get at other things

I planted 3 boxes of onions about 6 or 7 hundred seeds in good earth bought from McKenna. I soaked them in water (in the bath) box earth & all & now all I have to do is to keep them warm and moist & carry them to Orillia— I'm wanting to get there. I feel below par here & I am sure I'll be all right & can work out of doors . . . Dot writes me that David Ulrichsen is promoted to be a FO flying officer . . I don't just know where he is—the war looks tough, doesn't it. Still, Germany is just living on millions of slaves; if they ever get a chance to rise you'd think they'd kill all the Germans—I hope they do.

I dont seem to have much news as my day just follows a routine  I walked to the Club yesterday afternoon, for the walk, & back in a street car—talked with Gilbert Jackson (former professor at Toronto)—I could send you typing but I imagine you would just as soon ~~not~~ let it pile up . . . The stuff I'm doing now is not <u>typed</u> as it is either ~~corrected~~ done by correcting the original print, or by using the typed material sent me by the town clerks . . Its about 12 & I shall read till one or so & then later go to the library & the Club . . Eddie Beatty's funeral is today, but I dont go to them as it is hard on me to stand round & wait and walk. . . . Say a cheerful word for me to Peggy

Affect'ly
Stephen (Leacock)

## To B.K. Sandwell

[3869 Cote des Neiges Road
Montreal]
Sunday March 28 1943

Dear B.K.

My best thanks for your letter & for your praise . . as one gets old praise gets sweeter . . especially from old friends

I am just finishing & hope to finish tomorrow & post to you on Tuesday a story of about the length of the last one. I hope you'll have space.

I read, with appreciation, all your stuff on the social outlook . . . things are pretty tangled, arent they! . . You recall the American Patriot who was willing to "sacrifice a part of the Constitution, and if need be the whole of it, to save the remainder" . . . That's where the moneyed interests of Canada ought to be now

Best regards
Stephen Leacock

## To J.E. McDougall [1]

[3869 Cote des Neiges Road
Montreal]
April 1, 1943

Dear Joe,

I hope you may by chance have seen the compliment I paid you in the Queen's Quarterly of last week—in reference to your That will be all for today . . a phrase that will always stay with me,—till I reach it

Meantime if it suits your leisure I wish you could come to the University Club on Tuesday next at 5 PM. to meet with me & Mrs Mary Little of Montreal. You met her once before at a broadcast of mine. She—and I,—want to talk with you of certain ideas that might work in with what your people are doing.

Best regards
Stephen Leacock

P.S. It is hard to get me on the phone, so leave a message.

1   Joseph Easton McDougall (1902–1992), while a student at the University of Toronto, was one of the founding editors of the humour magazine The Goblin. In its first issue of February 1921, Leacock wrote the lead article, 'A Sermon on Humour'. He also contributed 'The Faded Actor' (January 1923) and 'See The Conquering Aero Comes!' (March 1928). The magazine's original literary editor and book reviewer, McDougall became its managing editor in October 1925. The magazine moved from Toronto to Montreal in the summer of 1929, its managers hoping to secure lucrative liquor advertizing; however, the stock market crash of 13 September 1929 forced McDougall to close down the magazine in the spring of 1930. In Montreal, where he had a successful career in advertising, McDougall became friends with Leacock, meeting him first in the winter of 1933, when he invited Leacock to do a series of radio broadcasts.

## To R. T. Ferguson

3869 Côte des Neiges Road,
Montreal.
April 2nd, 1943.

My dear R. T.,

In regard to a possible French Translation of <u>CANADA</u> I think that if it is done we ought to make the work of translation as outstanding in its success as we like to think the book is in other respects,—its art work, its manufacture and its literary quality.

Now translation is a very delicate and difficult matter. In the case of poetry is it quite impossible and in the case of literary prose it is very hard to make a translation that carries the real spirit of the original. It demands not only a really idiomatic knowledge of the language to be translated <u>from</u>, but more than that, an idiomatic initiative, in the language to be translated into. It is possible for anybody ~~of~~ with a fair knowledge of a foreign language to make a translation into a language that is their own which, in a sense, conveys the meaning, which contains no grammatical errors but which loses,—does not even attempt to reproduce,—the fine points of significance, the little touches of humour, of double meaning, of poetic significance.

In addition to this there are many words used in plain and ordinary English and in plain and ordinary French which seem to correspond but which do not. I will take an example the ~~subtitle~~ title of our book,—CANADA—<u>The Foundations of its Future</u>. Now anybody who thinks that the the French for that is "Les Fondations de Son Avenir", either does not fully appreciate French or does not fully appreciate English. "<u>Les Fondations de Son Avenir</u>" would mean if you like "<u>The Excavations for its Future</u>," or it would mean "<u>The Foundation (act of founding: not a physical thing) of its future</u>" . . . . But the English word plays double, it means <u>Fondations</u> and <u>Fondements</u> at the same time. I will write on a sheet as a schedule to this letter a set of phrases that I will select (with no great deliberation, for I have not time for it) from our book <u>Canada</u>,—phrases which require skill, good literary practice in translating. I will set beside each a <u>wooden</u> translation into French which is no good. I will not offer, or not now, an attempt at real translations but I will leave that to any proposed translator of the book as a test of dual knowledge of the languages and power to imitate a French phrase.

If this book were properly translated it would score a great hit and the schools could use the two versions as exercises for their pupils.

Very sincerely,
Stephen Leacock

## To Mrs Herbert T. Shaw

[3869 Cote des Neiges
Montreal]
Mon April 12 43

Dear Fitz

I was glad to hear you over the phone & find that everything was going well with Peggy and Sherry: Did I get it right, Sherry? not Chérie¹ . . . I had a long day yesterday—arranged a lot of things with Costain. In the afternoon he came to Mary's house with me. he comes from Brantford and Mary had lived there & they knew a lot of people . . . among others asked,—"What became about Elsie Creighton?" Mary said she lives next door! (Mrs Leggatt)—Queer wasn't it?

I finished in the last few days a huge article on Gold (5000 words) but I had about 1500 of it left over from Barrons. I am trying to get packed up—it's a heavy business. Mail not in yet. I may write later.

Affect.
Stephen

P.S. I had a letter from an old English soldier in Calgary . . he lived as a child just beside Gad's Hill where Dickens had died 7 years before he was born. His father and grandfather were joiners and undertakers, made coffins & carried out funerals and did a lot of work for Dickens building the little "Chalet" where he worked & other things. Dickens got a lot of stuff about coffins & funerals from them . . . The old soldier had served all over hell. He wrote (from Calgary) that he could only ~~liv a~~ live a little longer. I wrote and asked him if I might publish his letter & give him any money I got

Affect'ly
Stephen Leacock

P.S. Your letter (Friday) just in . . seems so queer . . of course nothing had happened

1   Peggy and Ken's first child, a daughter named Sherry.

## To Mrs Herbert T. Shaw

[3869 Cote des Neiges Road
Montreal]
Tues Ap 13   43

Dear Fitz

Up early for a long day so I begin well by writing to you . . . Yesterday a heavy day. I did writing & letters & went & had my hair cut & joined Costain & Murray Gibbon for lunch. Costain had had a second interview with Mary (Monday) about a little picture book done by a Mrs Boswell & put in her hands as agent. She sent it over to the Club to Costain & he was so taken with it that he went right over to Mary's house & they had a long talk about various things & I think that it will mean that Mary will do publicity work in Doubleday Doran Books. She sounded jubilant over the phone. No doubt she'll tell you about it

Here's a funny thing. Costain told Morgan Powell of the Star that he was here to look for novels, especially young writers. Powell put that in the Star. So the telephone began to buzz for Costain. But one young girl was given Sam Coristine instead of Costain . . . and she said "You're at the University Club aren't you" and he said Yes. And she said "I've got something to show you . . . and he said . . Who are you? . . and she said Oh that doesn't matter. You dont know me. I'm just a young beginner but I'd like to show you what I can do and I think you be interested . . . etc etc You can carry it on . . It broke when she said <u>Manuscript</u>. I introduced Costain to Coristine & they "had a laff" over it . . . Being packing up . . . . endless letters to write . . all sorts of stuff . . but glad to get away. When I get to Orillia it may be difficult to post letters. I expect expect of course to write you every day but you may get 2 or 3 together . . There is no postman to collect letters & I doubt if there are taxis . . However I'll see. I sent for garden seeds yesterday & am taking 20 pounds of peas to plant as soon as I can. At your place I will see if I can put them in with a spade alongside of the asparagus so as not to prevent ploughing

I ought to get from you a letter since the birth of Miss Smith. Be sure to explain her name—Cherie, or Cherry, or Sherry, or Lizzie. I am so glad that Peggy is picking up so quickly . . I suppose you'll wait till a week or so after she goes to 7. A. Walnut & get here round May 1st & visit Orillia a week or so later and then back to Montreal—but no doubt all very vague.

Affect'ly
Stephen (Leacock)

## To Mrs Herbert T. Shaw
Orillia (not yet but soon)
Apr 14 Wed. 1943

Dear Fitz

What a weather! About 3 inches of snow in the night—still falling and a raging wind—real winter and cold!

I sent a note to the Post office yesterday about my address & they acted so promptly that I got no mail this morning . . . but it is a fault on the right side & I'll look forward to hearing from you at Orillia.

I had a long day yesterday & went to bed at 8 oclock. Was at Mary's with Joe McDougall for about an hour as an introduction for them. She will later go

& see him in his office . . Charlie (Leacock) sent word (very abrupt) that he is not going to Orillia. Stevie is to stay over in Toronto to see about work at Henry Janes's office. I dont know what will come of that. So when I go up there will be only Jones and Tina—But at least it will be cheap and I can get the early garden & chicken stuff done. I wrote 1500 words yesterday for McGill Centennial Volume for Number of the News 1843–1943 (first lecture given)— and am going to do for the government some <u>Leaflets on the Loan</u>—(300–400 words each. I did the first this morning—I couldnt think of any radio stuff so I wrote Ottawa that I would do that instead

Time
Stephen (Leacock)

## To Barbara Nimmo

The O.B.B.
Orillia
Apr 16  43

Dear Bâ

Glad to get your Syracuse letter & know that you are there; I hope Nancy is better . . . I arrived here with Tina yesterday leaving Stevie in Toronto till the weekend: he may get work with Henry Janes. Uncle Charlie was too busy looking after Henry Bergh to come; Harry is not ill but he needs help in the house as both boys are in the Army.

—Here it is mid-winter; lake tight frozen—snow, wind—everything dirt & mud. sun gallery god's awful no decent wood—Jones is here but he can do less in more time than anyone else. everything is leaking, smoking, breaking & no beer

But it all seems easy to me as I have called off literary work for a week or so, & as beside what I was doing this stuff is nothing

Peggy's Baby—I dont know what she to be called. In phoning to Mary Little & me, Mrs Shaw seemed to say "Sherry". Thats what we call her & I said you mean "Cherry" & she said "no Sherry"—If she has a boy he can be called "Bitters"—new joke, I hadnt thought of it

y.a.u.
Stephen Leacock

P.S. Uncle George would carry that joke further & talk of a mother who called her first two children Sherry and Bitters and the next two Whisky and Soda

## To Mrs Herbert T. Shaw

Orillia Friday
Ap 16  43

Dear Fitz

I got a Wednesday letter of yours today so that shows that the "Communications",—as they say in Tunisia,—are not cut.

I wanted to get to your place (its just noon as I write) but hell! its all deep snow & water & a bitter wind and snow storm. Such weather never was—they are still cutting huge blocks of ice on the Lake & fishing out on the ice—I have bought some coal—but meanwhile the best I can get is 56 degrees of heat in the big room & freezing in the sun gallery. I've been working outside—my god! what a mess Jones made of the hens. I lost 100 worth over a dollar each. I saw at once that the burlap was too worn & thin to keep out the cold. "All I had" said Jones  Jones realized it was put too low down—So did I when I saw it—I said Jones if you had written and asked for 50 dollars to hire men to make the house warm! You'd have got it—. I have to let it go at that. The greenhouse at the Lodge is blown flat & the other a wreck of broken glass—but I can fix it all & get it all straight as I have nothing else to do. It's fine, as I say, big Janet of Kootenay—you ought to be in it

X X X X X X

You must keep Peggy, as they say, "fed up"—in your mother's day they used to make calf's foot jelly & such things—give her some of that. I can quite see it is impossible to make plans, but what I will do is to try to get your place ready in shape for whatever use you want to make of it . . . I am going to drive into town & see about a liquor permit. I cant get beer until the 29th . . . do shopping—come back & work in the dirt – – I have a lot of letters to answer so I am not quite free but I am letting the rest go. I was so tired mentally that it is fine to be here and not have to write. I'll tell you what your place is like when I get there—

Why is Baby called Sherry? Is it a family name? or have I got it wrong? Do you like it? I'm sure you do & Peggy must or you wouldn't have it: but at any rate whatever name you give a baby it soon seems the sweetest name in all the world—so it doesn't matter. I only meant,—who is, or was Sherry? Is that in your family or Ken's . . Please return the enclosed

## To Mrs Herbert T. Shaw

[The Old Brewery Bay
Orillia, Ontario]
Sunday
April 18/43

Dear Fitz

Sunday 8 a.m.—have been up & fixed all the fires & the furnace (I do all that not Jones) and listened to the news.

. . . I had hardly finished my lament about the wood when Providence gave me a lesson—The bad weather suddenly began to go the sun came out and thawed most of the surface snow and all the wind dropped! the fires burnt, the sun gallery thawed: and Jones & I found a heap of huge buried wood blocks that will run my open fire a week and tomorrow  Dave Parks will come. I had no intention of taking any of your wood: the difficulty was that Jones <u>had taken</u> <u>some</u> before I came up. I told him not to take any more

Stevie came up yesterday & goes to Toronto again on Thursday. He is trying out some work in Henry Janes's office that will mean being partly in Toronto & partly here

I arrived here on Thursday morning and have not been off the place except in a taxi in & out of town on Friday getting out & in again at the liquor store and Liggetts. I think I can <u>get</u> practically all messages done by telephone and by Tina going in. I think Hatley will only need to come twice a week—possibly three times—

I managed to get through the swamp to your place. The snow was two feet deep on the swamp path but frozen so hard that I walked on the top of it. Your place looks <u>fine</u>—all snow gone from all the lawn & garden. Everything neat & clean & tidy. Jones said that Dave Parks promised again & again to come last fall to plough it and never came. But it doesnt matter. I'll get it ploughed now with a tracter and then dig the best parts after that – – – I havent bothered with Payne yet as no one could possibly dig out drains till the ground thaws some more

Affc.

Stephen

PS. I got 5 bottles (26 1/2 ounces) of Scotch from Barrie. That's all I am allowed for one month. Be <u>sure</u>, <u>sure</u>, to bring your registration card and <u>if lost</u> then get from your bank a form of application & send it to Ottawa for a new one. If you have that you can get 5 bottles at once, in one day,—without that, <u>none</u> <u>at</u> all.

I forgot to bring my tankards. Just saw them on the shelf too late. I didn't like to trust them to freight. If you have room in your freight bring them. If not I'll get Alfreda  she is in my house to send them, but I hate to trust them that way

## To Mrs Herbert T. Shaw

Orillia Apr 24  43

11 a.m.

Dear Fitz

Just finished working at my desk, since seven, and now going out to work out of doors. Mending, or rather remaking a stone-boat to haul wood & manure . . . My leaflets are great stuff. The last one 1200 words. I've averaged one a day ~~and I~~ or more and I have two in my head already to put on paper. They are all little stories of Mariposa, laid in the Barber Shop and they will add 10,000 words to the <u>Happy Stories</u> book which is now finished all except writing one story that is in my head & fixing up Damon & Pythias and the moving picture story (that was) <u>Mirage</u>. I'm writing to ask Dodd to see if he'd like all the <u>MS</u> by July 1st.

You'd better authorize me to go ahead & get in your telephone & light & drain & get the cleaning done (leaving the shutters on). It is <u>impossible</u> to get anything done here except at long notice. If you wrote & said coming in 3 days it is hardly likely I could have everything ready & quite ~~prob~~ possibly nothing ready. Be sure to answer Go ahead. Indeed I think I'd better go ahead anyway

— — — — — —

I had no mail yesterday so I am hoping for a letter for certain by now . . My hand is shaky with writing.

Fine weather at last. Best love to Peggy. Give her the enclosed snowdrops for Baby bedside table

time
Stephen

P.S. I reckon you dont need more U.S. money. Am putting $50 monthly salary of May 1st in your account with Tim . . If you need this, let me know <u>separately</u> I will send to Montreal railway expenses of you & Dorothy, or of you without Dorothy

## To Thomas B. Costain

[The Old Brewery Bay
Orillia, Ontario]
May 1 1943

Dear Costain

I meant to write to you anyway to say how much I enjoyed your visit, and that I hope that some permanent contacts may arise out of it . .

Meantime ~~ago~~ another reason for writing has come up. You spoke of a certain proposed biography. Dont touch it. It might prove all wrong. It happened that just after you left I got very direct information via Ottawa . . Such a biography, if things turn out <u>one</u> way would be a huge success . . But you have to wait till the ways part, otherwise it would look awfully out of place.

Stevie is much interested in getting his MS (15,000 words or so of it ready to send down to you but is delayed by having taken up some publicity work with a Toronto firm.

He had another encouraging sale of one of his (sensational) stories a fortnight ago and is ~~fell~~ feeling very good about literature in general. He is coming up here for the week end & I'll see how long he'll be in getting his ~~story~~ novel (the sample part of it) ready to send.

Meantime an old friend of mine Dr A.G. Morphy of Montreal, one of Canada leading specialists in mental disease writes that he has completed a book Forty Years of Medical Practice & asked me what to do about publishing it. I at once suggested that he send the MS to you to have a look at. He says that it deals with <u>fact</u> not fiction. It might be interesting

> V sincerely
> Stephen Leacock

## To Mrs Herbert T. Shaw

[The Old Brewery Bay
Orillia, Ontario]
Sat  May 1 43

Dear Fitz,

Such weather! After the ice went out on Thursday the weather back to wild rain all yesterday & last night fierce storm, from the northwest & bitter cold. The furnace died out with wet wood. I've been up since daylight now (6:30) trying to get fires going & to warm the house—still cold as charity.

Jim Aikens arrived Thursday night & spent Friday with me. He is optimistic about the war being over in a year. His son Jimmy is still instructing at Aylmer but may go over soon. His wife is expecting a baby in a month or so . . He slept all morning & I slept for half the afternoon so I didnt see much of him but enjoyed our talks by the fire. We went down in the rain & fished off the wharf—cold stuff—no fish—got wet

Today is May 1st & I must go back to my books & begin each day with book-work till ten or ~~lel~~ eleven as I used to—its the only way to get through

Sun well up now in a clear sky  By noon it will be a warm day  About Peggy's verses. Youll have to consider the best plan to do. I see that it is a great handicap that they should be for <u>college stuff</u> which just now is as dead as a loon. A college boy fooling around with girls is not a heroic figure. I suppose he couldn't <u>shift into uniform</u> for say the last three pictures with the verse a little reconstructed. But how on earth could Mike find time or interest to do it. I think that Mary (who will very likely be acting as agent for Costain in this and that might take them to McClelland & Stewart (when McCl. next comes to Montreal) & discuss with them the possibility of a Canadian edition of how many? and of what if any guarantee? . . . with good publicity they could sell as Xmas stuff——but my fixed judgement is that the theme needs reconstructing in the light of war interest. I've forgotten the text so I can say just how & where. It would be easy for Peggy to make a turn in the ~~argumnt~~ argument—turn the boy into uniform & the girl into a Quack (CWAC—Canada Army Womans Corps) without that I don't see it . . . It is hard luck because its nothing against Mike's verse or Peggy's pictures—just the bad luck of what is timely & what isnt

Liquor: The ration is out again. each permit is good only for 3 bottles (26 oz) ~~or~~ a month,—or two of forty. This is hopeless for me as random visitors always drink that much in my house in a month. So be sure to get all you can in Montreal & bring it ~~into~~ in your valise . . . Beer is cut to a little more than a pint a day (36 pints a month). It is getting near time for 7 am news . . . also I am getting so ~~bold~~ cold sitting here Ill have to move . . . Dont dream of coming here without all the notice you can give.

Affect'ly & to Peggy & the Baby

Stephen (Leacock)

## To Mrs Herbert T. Shaw

[The Old Brewery Bay Orillia, Ontario]
Sun May 9   43

Dear Fitz,

Rain, rain! after the lovely day Friday it rained all night & knocked out all question of ploughing. But I know it will be all right

Tomorrow (Monday) I am going to get Jones to help me take the shutters off your house & carry out mattresses into the sun & I'll light the fires & clean it up myself. It looks pretty clean anyway. Payne fixed the drain. The whole trouble was a clog of grease from the kitchen sink  The drain is now O.K—be careful to use a fine wire sleive in the sink—I've an idea you'll be here in no time & I'm looking forward to getting things ready

On Friday just as I'd finished work & laid a fire in the big room in drove George Drew & I had a most delightful hour with him over a couple of scotches. After I'd cooked & eaten my supper Paul Copeland drove over & drove me to his house where there was also a Captain Osler and we talked for an hour or so and Paul drove me home.

Today I began work early & hit up nearly 2000 words of Canada & the Sea. It's nice stuff to do. I sent the $50$\underline{^{00}}$ as salary on the idea that if you do less one month you do more another so it works out the same. There will be plenty of typing waiting for you & I am pretty little flags in the <u>Sea</u> MS for you to pick up . . . My hands get tired with so much writing. I am writing you in Montreal as a letter today wouldnt get to Boston till Wednesday (very likely) & you'd be gone—At your house be <u>sure</u> to bring all my MS. I have no copies of them— bring type & MS both

Affect'ly

Stephen (Leacock)

*To Dorothy Purdell*[1]

[The Old Brewery Bay
Orillia, Ontario]
May 22 1943

Dear Miss Purdell

(Your telegram and letter of May 20th.) . . . I am so sorry you have to go to the hospital, even for what sounds a minor trouble. I wish you, in the words of the English criminal courts, "a good deliverance."

I'm delighted with what you say about <u>Mirage</u>. The situation is changed, (but I think favorably) by the fact that the story will be published along with others next October in a book called <u>Happy Stories, Just to Laugh At</u>.

Any arrangement about pictures would have to accent this publication. But no doubt that helps instead of hinders. Some of the other stories in the book would lead themselves to picture making with infinitely less expense than <u>Mirage</u>. One in particular, <u>Pawn to King's Four</u> involves only the noise and racket of a hotel rotunda for two minutes and the peace and silence of a chess club for ten . . . This apparent contrast and the tragic stuff that follows in the basis of the picture. When the proofs come out I could send them to you to see if you would care to ~~I should~~ act as agent about them.

Meantime I am very pleased to extend the agency for Mirage which you are good enough to feel interested in, for a year from the date of this letter and ~~for t~~ under the conditions implied in this letter. But any offer made would have to be ratified by me for acceptance. <u>Mirage</u> would be very expensive to do properly. What you had better try for is a payment for an option good for one year after the close of the war (United States) in return for cash down.

Unfortunately <u>My Remarkable Uncle</u> won't do, as that is a reference to an actual person, an uncle of mine. Mirage (as said in the preface) says good-bye to him at the outset.

Best wishes
Stephen Leacock

1   Dorothy Purdell of Twentieth-Century Fox Films Corporation (New York) wrote to Leacock on 20 May 1943 're the request to renew my assignment of acting more or less as your agent'. She added that she was going into the hospital to have her tonsils removed.

*To Barbara Nimmo*

The O.B.B.
Orillia Ont
May 31 43

Dear Bâ

I am so glad, more glad than I can tell you, to have you & Nancy come up in the beginning of July for a month & I shall hope that Don can come later— I am so used now to doing the house keeping that you won't have to bother with that. But I ~~have~~ expect to have plenty of typing & odd work that would keep you busy and earn a little money for you all the time. I will do my best to get a suitable little maid for Nancy (subject to your ratification when you see her). Apart from that it is all easy. At present Stevie is working in Toronto on publicity work with Henry Janes & with the Associated Screen news—He comes for week ends—I hope, in his interest, that it lasts—let me know if you know of any little girl of Beaverton or Sutton that we could get for July,—or will you perhaps write to your mother about it . .

y. a. u
Stephen Leacock

P.S. I hope to post the first section of <u>Canada & the Sea</u>, tomorrow—

## To Mrs Herbert T. Shaw

[The Old Brewery Bay
Orillia, Ontario]
June 11   43

Dear Fitz
My hand is so tired with writing that its hard to write. I got your letter of Tuesday (you were not well) this morning. I hope you are better. Of course you have an awful lot to do & an awful lot of [···] to do just now
—I hope you got the asparagus eggs & rhubarb that I sent yesterday. The weather is just wonderful. I told the postman to hold letters on and after Monday
—Your place is all right. I go over each day. Garden needs hoeing.

Affectionately
Stephen Leacock

P.S. Dora (Bâ's sister) has a baby girl (Judith Ann: name given in the paper) born on June 9. "Both well" I just saw it in the paper.

## To Thomas B. Costain

[The Old Brewery Bay
Orillia, Ontario]
Aug 12   43.

Dear Costain
Herewith provisional table of contents. It is based on a total length of 250,000. I will keep sending a memo from time to time on exact permissions needed: it would greatly help if I could get permissions, as indicated, to quote so many words Best sales talk is that the book is purely <u>personal</u>,—it is what Stephen Leacock liked and read from childhood up and likes to read again and talk over. It is not in any way an attempt at an anthology. About 50,000 words

of the book are actually written by the author. Your slogan seems A.1. and I know by experience how appropriate your jackets are

You will note that everything is <u>provisional</u> & <u>average</u>. I want to make each chapter like a pleasant happy talk in itself, attractive to read.

Now I must go and pick beans.

V. faithfully
Stephen Leacock


## To George Stewart

[The Old Brewery Bay
Orillia, Ontario]
Aug 25. 1943

McClelland & Stewart Publishers
Toronto

Dear Mr. Stewart

I receive today from Doubleday Doran my royalties on Canadian sales on my <u>Montreal</u> up to May 1st 1943. But they did not include the special payment of 10 cents a copy on sales in Montreal to be paid to Mrs H. T. Shaw (1272 Redpath Crescent) for special canvassing etc. I presume therefore that you will look after this either directly or by sending me a cheque to pass on

Best regards
Stephen Leacock


## To Harry C. Clarke[1]

[The Old Brewery Bay
Orillia, Ontario]
Sep 20. 43

Dear Mr. Clarke

I have just finished the article, <u>Can we Abolish Poverty in Canada</u> I am sending it to be typed, which is a difficult matter in Orillia . . and will get it off by the first mail possible . .

I put an awful lot of work into it . . I know too much about it . . It may be too long . . but I'll send it as it is & will put with it some abbreviated passages to substitute if need be . . . But I think that people who think will think there's something in it to think about . . .

Best regards
Stephen Leacock

1  An editor at *Maclean's* magazine in Toronto.

### To Mrs Herbert T. Shaw

[The Old Brewery Bay
Orillia, Ontario]
Friday (Sept 23, 1943)

Dear Fitz

1/4 to 12—am in a rush to drive in with Dot & post mail & get my hair cut. The barber may close at 12—I got your letter of appreciation of the mine. I am hoping it may turn out a wonder; I <u>know</u> about it but I dont think many people know what it really is. It took a jump from 40 cents to 70 and is stuck now at about 65—but behind it is a most extraordinary story—it is not the gold that in it—no—hush -sh- it is something else. The mine merely happens to <u>own</u> it. Ah-ha!

I am writing in my new library. It just doubles the capacity of work—a flood of sun in the morning & warm as toast and the huge table. I've been working hard & have just finished one and posting the <u>Abolition of ~~Povet~~ Poverty</u>. I wrote over 5000 words but it reads fine to me. I shall now go full speed ahead at a set of articles for the Financial Post under the title:

<u>The Outlook for Canada</u>

8 articles,—20,000 words. Im going to try to do it in a <u>month</u>. I have your old Labatt again today cutting the grass off my annex garden.

time
Stephen (Leacock)

### To Harry C. Clarke

[The Old Brewery Bay
Orillia, Ontario]
Thursday Sep 23. 43

Dear Mr Clarke

Herewith the article on <u>Poverty</u>. I have put a tremendous amount of time on it but in spite of that I think it is all right. I believe it will really interest people,—but the first hope is that it interests <u>you</u>. You will see that I have indicated how it can be cut down to a great extent with a minimum of editorial trouble.

Best regards
Stephen Leacock

### To Mrs Herbert T. Shaw

Orillia Friday
Sep. 24 (1943) 1 pm

Dear Fitz

Dot left at 10.30 this morning which makes it seem lonely here: it is lonely at night anyway—I sent you today quite an express box: 2 chickens & beans, tomatoes beets carrots & a few real apples (off the trees)—I am struggling now with the proofs of <u>Canada & the Sea</u>. I hadn't really opened the packet & I find there are real proof sheets in it. I forget where you said the <u>maps</u> are. Mention it. I'll probably find them but mention it anyway.

Have you any flowers or any that you get free? If not I'll send some next week—

—It is very nice to get your letters each day—that & the postman & the mail is the feature of the morning—Now I must see about lunch—

Affectly
Stephen Leacock

I think Mary's idea of renting the upper house is fine—like getting money for nothing—They work while she sleeps—See Cascara Pills

## *To Barbara Nimmo*

3869 Côte des Neiges Road
Montreal
Oct 18   43

Dear Bâ

(Yours re Encyc)—Dont give it a thought. There's hardly any of it this year—just the annual stuff & I find I can get all that out of the New Year Gazette. All except the <u>Political</u> changes & I will get some one at McGill to dig those up & take half & half and that will leave just nicely enough to buy a silver mug. Later on when you want work of that sort we will dig it up—But dont bother about it now.

I am back here. Stevie living at the National Club Toronto and doing awfully well. He has the knack of writing just the kind of stuff that publicity people want and is interested in it.

Tina is at Three Rivers. Her sister has been ill & needs help in the house. I hope she'll be back in 10 days or so

I am very busy as I have been asked by the <u>Financial Post</u> Toronto to do 8 articles (8 weeks) on Canada and I want to do them in 4 weeks. I had a sore on my lip that needed electric treatment, just nothing. If it doesnt heal I'll have it treated again—

Uncle Charlie is at Sutton reported doing very well & quiet—I offered him Orillia but home is home—a poor thing but mine own (the man who ~~set~~ said that, said it all)

I hope everything is going along well, and I am sure it will—we seem to live in a world of new babies,—everybody has one but me.

y. a. u.
Stephen Leacock

## To Barbara Nimmo

[3869 Cote des Neiges Road
Montreal]
Sat Oct 30. 43

Dear Bâ.

Ive been wanting to write to you but I've had a rather bad week with a touch of some sort of flu with little energy to do anything—now passing off—but I wanted to say how delighted I am at your latest good news—any of the combinations are good & the one you get will seem best. I've heard little from you except indirectly by Mrs Shaw but it all sounds good & I gather that Don has settled into his job & likes it—I'd be glad to hear more about it. I understand that your mother has gone to Toronto and the Beaverton house is closed & Uncle Charlie, I hear, is alright & well looked after in Sutton. Dot & I have arranged things for his comfort with Mrs Prest . . . No news here, especially as I've been pretty well shut into the house—haven't even unpacked my boxes—

I feel that the war will blow up about next March & that will make a sort of new start (I wont say a <u>new deal</u> as Don hates it) . . hard to say what will happen—up here certainly a radical wave will sweep the country—but it wont sweep away Orillia & I have a vision of you & the children up there next summer.

y. a. u.
Stephen Leacock

## To Alvah Beatty

3869 Cote des Neiges Road
Montreal
Nov 11 1943

Dear Beatty,

Under separate cover I send you the revised and completed proof, with all insertions and complete side-references for <u>Canada and the Sea</u>. This is as far as I can go till I get the page proofs

I make the count of words in the text (exclusive of headings and sub-headings) as just over 37,000. But you had better have that checked over as you will remember that the rate of pay was 5 cents a word and so we need a reasonably correct count (There was also flat $100 extra for out of pocket expense. I send you also the maps but of course they have to be redrawn by a draftsman with proper instruments and on the scale the printers want.

I'll be glad to get in touch with the draftmen & printers

I sent you already a list of suggestions for pictures of ships & would be only too pleased to talk them over with you and Riordon if he is to draw them

I think this will make a beautiful little volume as an introduction to the War Volumes that follow

Best regards
Stephen Leacock

## To Cleveland Morgan[1]

3869 Cote des Neiges Rd.
Nov. 14, 1943.

My dear Cleve

Fitz told me that you had been turning over in your mind the question of some form of memorial publication to commemorate the rounding out of a century of business by your grand old firm. I got interested in the idea and (quite unsolicited) began thinking out a plan of a monograph. As the idea developed I went further and (still unsolicited and without any responsibility on your part) have written out a Preface which from the nature of it will make clear to you the plan of the whole monograph.

I think that such a monograph if well supported by research would be of great service as a contribution to Canadian history. It would be of great value if it presented,—from contemporary quotations of each epoch,—a successive view of the course and kind of business, of money and prices, of the variation in the cost of living and the rising standards of comfort and luxury of three hundred years. Such a document would be eagerly welcomed in every Canadian College and in every Canadian library, and I think that it would earn new credit for the reputation even of so established a house as yours.

I have in mind illustrations in part of the city in its various stages as depicted in the preface and in part more intimate illustrations of the first and later homes of the firm, together with minor insets and inserts of oddities of historic interest,—early money and such.

Very sincerely
Stephen Leacock

1 Frederick Cleveland Morgan (1881–1962) was the director of Henry Morgan and Company and sometime president of the Montreal Museum of Fine Arts.

## To Cleveland Morgan

3869 Cote des Neiges Rd.
Nov. 26, 1943.

Dear Cleve

Following on our conversation I got from my friend Mr. Arnold Evans some preliminary figures of costs of paper, press work and binding for a memorial volume. Mr. Evans is an advertising agent (see Telephone—Arnold Evans and Company) and works especially in conjunction with the Gazette Printing Co. He did a lot of the work for my Canada.

I got rough estimates for a volume of either 10,000 words or 20,000 words with a variation of from 3000 copies up to 20,000 copies and variation from paper binding of the best class (technically called Spanish Leather) to a leather and buckram binding as in my Canada (blue edition.)

Apart from art work and author's fees and costs of distribution the schedule runs like this;—

Very sincerely
Stephen Leacock

Book of 10,000 words, 64 pages, Spanish leather,

| | |
|---|---|
| For 3000 copies . . . . | $1,100 |
| "      "      "    (in two colours) | $1,400 |
| of type: see | |
| Canada | |
| For second 3000 copies add | $600 |
| and so on. | |

---

Book of 20,000 words, 128 pages, with cover of as Blue Canada (which is first class—

| | |
|---|---|
| 3000 copies . . . . . | $3,000 |
| next    "      "    . . (about) | $2,000 |
| And so on. | |

With type in 2 colours about $600 extra.

---

P.S. This I am sure is plenty for you to go on. There is presumably no art work involved (independent drawing and painting). Reproduction of cuts from photographs, prints and maps cost (approx) $20 for each full page cut. A book of the kind discussed would seem to need at least 1/5 of its pages in cuts, i.e. for 64 pages, a dozen cuts ($240)
For 128 pages 24 cuts        ($480)

---

All such things as appendices etc. are extra but of small amount. The figures quoted include the agent's fees as the printer and binder pay them, but the fee for the writer is a separate matter.

If you care to get further estimates and have one or two dummies made Mr. Evans will be glad to come and see you about it. There is no charge for this. I told him the whole plan was only tentative. I mentioned your name to him but only confidentially (to him, personally) and asked him to deal with the printers and binders as from me.

Best Regards
Stephen Leacock

## To Barbara Nimmo

3869 Cote des Neiges Road
Montreal
Nov 26    43

Dear Barbara

I take for granted that you will by this time have heard the sad news that David is missing[1] . . . George wrote to tell me yesterday and I have been greatly distressed and thinking of it constantly since. There are no details yet. There is always a chance that a plane has merely broken down temporarily and gets home. In that case we hear of it within a few days. After that there is little hope of good news till a Red Cross message can report prisoners of war. That can be within a <u>month</u> but most likely about two. There have been as you know ever so many cases of delayed information.

I should think it would be better for your mother if she came down to you right away & so had plenty to think of & to do. If money comes into it let me know and I'll send anything you need

.    .    .    .    .    .    .

Now, as to Xmas. I am sending you on or just after December 1st $20 in U.S. funds: $10 for a Xmas present to you: $2$^{00}$ for a present for Don,—call it a neck tie,—and $8$^{00}$ for Nancy. Of this $2 is—genuine Xmas present and the rest is her deferred money that I forgot all about. sale of beans & tomatoes after you came—call it $6.$^{00}$ but I think there will be more yet when I see Hatley's September account . . But meantime it makes a total of $10$^{00}$

.    .    .

I am enclosing the inscription for the book and very glad to do it. With best love to you all, and best sympathy over this anxiety

y. a. u.
Stephen Leacock

---

1   David Ulrichsen, Barbara's brother, disappeared in this flight. His body was never recovered.

## To Barbara Nimmo

[3869 Cote des Neiges Road
Montreal]
Wed Dec 8    43

Dear Bâ

I've been laid up in the house with a cold since Saturday & have found it hard to write even letters—I got the bank to send $22$^{50}$ U.S. to you I cant remember if I wrote you as to the distribution of it,—the "break-down" or "spread" as they call it in business. Break down $10 for yourself and spread 8$^{00}$ for Nancy and scatter 2 for Don & the other 2$^{50}$ is for a present for you to send to Sherry Smith c/o Peggy whose address you have. If I forgot to mention

Sherry & you have broken it all down on 1204 Harrison St Get the present anyway & I'll send 2⁵⁰ more. I am sending something to Dora's baby but will have to address it c/o Dot as I have no address.

You will have had what further news there is of David which certainly contains hope. If he and the rest were last reported over the Atlantic Ocean off Portugal they certainly were not in the Berlin bombardment and might be picked up or washed ashore: if picked up by a fishing boat without wireless it might be some time before they report them. The report was sent to your father from Ottawa: I didn't get it directly but only as repeated over a telephone by Major Powers sister

> y. a. u.
> Stephen Leacock

## To Mrs Charles F. Martin

3869 Cote des Neiges Road
Montreal
Dec 9 1943

Dear Mrs Martin

I am so sorry to hear of your continued illness,—not as a matter of disappointment over the prospect of the pleasant dinner party, as I couldn't have been in it anyway but for your own sake. You must be having a wretched week of it. I can sympathize all the better as I have been having much the same. All I am fit for is to sit in my room and read such works of devotion as The Expanding Universe and the Nature of the Atom, both full of Consolations.

Best wishes for a speedy recovery

> Stephen Leacock

## To E. G. McCracken

[3869 Cote des Neiges Road
Montreal]
Dec 20   43

My dear Punch

I was glad to get your card . . . . I was all set to come up to Toronto (ticket reservations) & hoped to get in touch with you and some of the brethren as a feature of my trip . . But an attack of flu has knocked it all out: I am getting over it now but not quite up to taking a journey . . much disappointed . . I only came down here in the middle of October & what with a two weeks cold at the start and then this damn stuff 2½ weeks I seem to have seen nobody . . But I hear that Gordon Glassco is better and am glad of it. Fraser Keith says you are keeping things going in fine style.

> Best regards
> Stephen Leacock

## To Barbara Nimmo

[3869 Cote des Neiges Road
Montreal]
Dec 20. 43

Dear Bâ

I think we can confidently feel a lot of hope about David. I asked an airman & he told me that all the bombers are fitted with automatic floats and rafts— and in that part of the world with warm water and mild wind people could float round, or be picked up by a no-wireless boat or be stranded and landed,—so that indefinitely it might be a long time before people, even quite safe from the very start could send any report home . . .

. . . . . .

Thats a real present, the Worcester sauce . . . I've had none for months & months & then only one bottle that Jimmy Eakins got from the Hudson's Bay Co . . . . . . .

I am sorry to find that I cant go to Toronto for Xmas; I've had flu and it just hangs on & on and at my age it makes one feel very weak, almost like an old man—Stevie was to go to the Morphys for Xmas but perhaps he'll come here instead . . .

. . . . . . .

I enclose a picture of Nancy as used this week by the <u>Financial Post</u> of Toronto in illustrating a series of articles I am doing on <u>Canada</u> . . I think I shall have more copies (as I send for some when I saw Nancy's picture & if you like I'll send you some more . .

## To George and Mary Leacock

[3869 Cote des Neiges Road
Montreal]
Thurs Dec 23 43

Dear George & Mary

I am sending you a globe for Xmas, if I can get one expensive enough—the idea is that it is great ornament in a house. . But if I cant get one I am sending you a book of cartoons which is a nice thing for a drawing room table. I am sending books for the girls. But if I cant do any of this generous stuff unless I can get out, and today looks a below zero heller. . anyway I'll send it later. I forget whether you have a globe in your house but it is all right even if you have as I know some one else I can give it to,——an old retired professor who lives in a country house & has always wanted one in his big room.

I wrote a very funny story lately and sold it to The New York Herald Tribune. If you buy their Sunday edition watch for it in the magazine section called <u>The Week</u>. I'll send you one anyway when I get it. It is called <u>Living With Murder</u>, and is so funny that I am encouraged to go on writing. I also did a piece (for no pay) for a military magazine of the Officers Training Camp at Brockville called '<u>Generals I have trained</u>. It turned out so good that I shall try to sell it in spite of their use of it . . .

It is bitter cold here . . taxis are very hard to get . . so I mostly stay in . . . I am arranging to write a little booklet, called,—

<u>WHILE THERE IS TIME</u>,—

<u>THE CASE AGAINST SOCIAL CATASTROPHE</u>

It will be put over (if I get it done as I want to,) in a big way.)

So sorry I cant be in Aurora . . Best Xmas wishes to you all

> y. a. b.
> Stephen Leacock

## To George Leacock

3869 C. des Neiges Road
Xmas Morning
1943

Dear George,

Your letter and the presents (just right) arrived this morning—tobacco exactly what I wanted. I'd been dribbling along on one little packet after another —always dry

Stevie arrived this morning & he and I will eat Xmas dinner here and he will take 2 or 3 weeks holiday.. He has hopes of getting into the MacLean Publication Company so if you have any influence there please use it. <u>Mr Spearing</u>, editor of <u>Bookseller and Stationer</u> (a MacLean publication) talks of giving Stevie regular work so if you know any of the MacLean people in any of the enterprises please see if you can get in a useful word. . .

> y.a.b
> Stephen Leacock

## To Napier Moore

[3869 Cote des Neiges Road
Montreal]
Dec 25 1943
(otherwise Xmas)

My dear Napier Moore

I want to ask you to do me a favour, or rather a favour for my son Stevie (Stephen Leacock Jr.) . . He is a graduate of McGill in honour English & has done quite a lot of sporadic writing and has for nearly a year past been in Toronto working with a publicity firm, with very considerable success.

He has been brought into contact with your organisation by doing some work for Mr. Spearing and the suggestion has come up that this connection might be regularised to put his work on a definite footing.

I think this would be excellent for Stevie and that he would do such work singularly well. He has an unusual talent for writing smooth attractive prose and has done well with random short stories and sketches.

But you know as I do that if a person wants to <u>write</u> as a life profession there is nothing like a fixed definite connection to bring out whatever talent he has.

You recall no doubt the saying of Admiral Fisher, "There's nothing like favoritism,"—meaning nothing like having the power to push a good man into a good thing ... Thats the sense in which I ask my favour

> With best Xmas wishes
> Stephen Leacock

P.S. I dont know Mr Spearing except by correspondence but I'm sending him a copy

## To R. T. Ferguson

Montreal
Jan. 1944

Memo to Mr. Ferguson
From Stephen Leacock

Herein the essential points in our arrangements for the Book <u>While We Have Time: The Case Against Social Catastrophy</u>;—25,000 to 30,000 words, the first printing of 20,000 copies of which 10,000 to be sent out free with the writer's compliments ... individual and 10,000 placed on sale at as low a price as may be with the profit to the bookseller, as much as may be. This edition bound in paper. 'an edition in a good cloth binding with a price only as much above the other as the binding compels it to be. Book is for Canada only. Copyright for the United States and U.K. remains with the writer. The book is based on the memorandum indicating the title and contents and beginning with the words "I call this piece of writing etc" ... and on the articles written by me for the Financial Post of which the later chapters cover the same ground as in the book and will be used in it partly by quotation, partly by re-writing and expansion. The MS is to be ready by Feb 1, 1944, but there is no penalty for delay until April 1, 1944 after which you and your associates can refuse to use it and call for the return of money advanced to me. I am to receive 10 cents a word thus; $500 on Jan 1, 1944 and $500 on the completion of the MS whether accepted for use or not and the rest payable only if the MS is accepted for use at a date not later than 2 months after the receipt of the MS. If the MS is not accepted I keep the $1000 already paid and have the rights and other uses of the MS. All the MS or any part of it can be used by you and your associates as you see fit for serialization in Canadian newspapers, with or without a fee. All money for serialization is yours. It is evident that the complete text may contain a good deal of matter that goes outside of the limits of the memorandum mentioned above,—in part the illustration material and for the touch of humour and for reference to certain minor topics without which the main subject if not complete as notably French and English harmony and inter provincial harmony, without which a complete view of Canada is not possible. The goal of the discussion is the vast opportunity offered——


## *To Barbara Nimmo*

[3869 Cote des Neiges Road Montreal]
Wed Jan 12   44

Dear Barbara

I was so glad to get Don's telegram saying "Barbara and son are fine" . . . So we mustn't think any more of what might have been but be glad of what is; you & Don have a son and Nancy has a brother and I have a grandnephew.

I shall look forward to hearing from Don as to how you are getting on & no doubt you will write when you can. I have passed on your good news to Mrs Shaw & through her to Freda McCracken & Jane & Norah Sulliton et al . . .

We have been having first bitter cold & then record snow here: a very tough winter and as taxis are impossible to get at the house when you need them it hard to get out and get home. Give my love to your mother: it must be fine to have her there Best love yourself and to Don and to David-Donald as I presume his name is

y. a. u.
Stephen Leacock


## *To Barbara Nimmo*

[3869 Cote des Neiges Road Montreal]
Jan 18 1944

Dear Bâ

I hope everything is going well. As soon as you feel like it you must write & tell me all about this wonderful boy. Nancy will be delighted to be able to play the part of nurse, philosopher and friend. I suppose that you & your mother are not able yet to think in terms of the summer but I hope you will be able to come to Orillia for a real holiday And if it would be difficult for your mother to run her own house I'd be only too pleased if she cared to come to Orillia for part, or all, of the time. But no doubt one cant make plans so far

I have not been well but hope to be out of the woods soon & by good luck Stevie is here just now and can stay on for a while as his boss, or associate, Jack

Chisholm of the Screen News is in Montreal just now anyway so that Stevie can be here while he is. Im glad as I have found it very lonely here when not well . . . . Barbara Dinnick who spends the winter with her sister in the Laurentians has been at Fitz's house for two days looking very well—Wilf, her husband is in England . . . . I have not been able to go about much this winter & so I seem to see nobody and hear no local news . . . If you cant write get Don to send me a line.

> y. a. u.
> Stephen Leacock


## To Barbara Nimmo

3869 Cote des Neiges Road
Montreal
Sunday Jan 23 '1944'

Dear Barbara

I am so glad to hear that the boy is to be <u>Stephen Butler</u>: that carries through to my grandfather's name and the Butler is also part of David's name. Fitz told me about your prompt dealing with the doctor's which jolted him 8 ounces in a day (or 182 pounds a year). By this time you will probably be at home again and Nancy will have a wonderful time—Write me more news when you feel stronger . .—. . I have not been very well so I wont write a long letter. Love to Don & Nancy & wee Stephen

> y. a. u.
> Stephen Leacock


## To Barbara Nimmo

[3869 Cote des Neiges Road
Montreal]
Sun. Jan 30 '44

Dear Bâ

I send you a wire to ask you to keep the nurse as ~~Mrs Shaw~~ Fitz had mentioned that you were doubtful of it . . . I send $25$^{00}$ at once (Tim's bank is to post it: Ive sent them an order) which is all the rules of exchange allow me to send offhand: let me know how much more it is and I will send the rest as soon as the bank allows it . . . I am ordering a mug for Stephen. I cant go down town to get it but what I want is only a plain pattern so it can easily be got . . anyway ~~Mrs. Shaw~~ Fitz can get it as easily as I can. I thought of putting on it the names to show the origin of the combination Stephen Butler not meaning that the Butler comes from <u>me</u>, as that is taken after David . . . I mean I dont want to <u>hog</u> all the names and I am sure your mother wont mind . .You can ask her. . The customs duty is sixty per cent so I thought I will keep this mug in Canada till you come—but as I have not yet ordered it and if you or your mother feel like taking the trouble you can try it there or no, they wouldnt let me send the money

Best love to you all,

> y. a. u.
> Stephen Leacock

### *To Cleveland Morgan*

> 3869 Cote des Neiges Rd
> Montreal
> Thurs Jan 27 44

Dear Cleve,

I am sorry to say that I am a very sick man but with good fortune I may round a present corner and go on for a good time, perhaps years. Meantime the doctors say that it is good for me to keep up such work as interests me without fatigue. At present I am working to finish a small book on <u>The Case Against Social Catastrophe</u> which may have a wide national influence. But when it is done I dont know of anything that would interest me more than the work we have planned. I'll let you know how things look a little way on from now

> best regards
> Stephen Leacock

*To George Leacock*                         Feb 1  44

Dear George
    Your letter is so kind. Dot will tell you all about it . . I think it would be
better perhaps not to come down just now though it is good of you to offer to
. . The doctors here know all about it. I have written Dot. She will show you my
letter. It is wonderful to have Stevie here & he is so fine & he has lots of work
to do here & of course I try not ~~to met~~ to let this put him to the bad: In fact I
dont let it do so . . . The queer thing is that I am much better. I am now eating
so easily, more & more the last three or four days that I realized this morning
that, by gosh, if no one had told me I had any trouble in eating, I wouldnt have
known it myself. Sometimes I hope that right as I am I could hit up eighty.
    As to quantity I ate as my breakfast (after bread & milk on getting up):—
1 large prune with juice
1 four small bits of bacon
1 boiled egg
1½ slices of brown bread & butter
2 cups of coffee
in other words enough for anybody . . . Now I think the doctors here are
thinking that with strength & luck this trouble can be held off & delayed &
treated with radium,—I hope,—I wont say—anyway a long time
    I've told Dot all about. Its the mental side that is hard to hold up, to keep
from thinking of it all the time . .
    If I go on eating as easily as now and as much it will mean a lot . .

                                        y. a. b. & love to both of you
                                        Stephen Leacock


*To Cleveland Morgan*                    [3869 Cote des Neiges Road
                                        Montreal]
                                        February 5 1941

My dear Cleve
    My best thanks for your kind letter. I am getting on very well both in health
and in my present work, and look forward to a serious commencement of our
Merchants of Montreal in about 3 weeks. Already I've a bit of notes, plans and
marked quotations I think we can make of it something very distinctive, something
never done before

                                        best regards
                                        Stephen Leacock


P.S. Apologies to Bessie for my delay in sending the cheque as enclosed.

## To George Leacock

Sat Feb 5

Dear George

Thanks for your fine letter about the <u>Blitz</u> article. I've written to the Editors to send you half a dozen copies—I'm so glad you liked it

I am doing my best to keep going—and my ability to eat is ever so much greater and I am eating enough food now for anybody to do with and am gaining strength—I was terribly run down before Xmas (November and December with cold & flu)

I am working every day & it has turned out that Stevie has more work to do here than in Toronto and of course I help & advise, and dig it up for him . . He may run up to Toronto for 2 or 3 days at a time a little later.

Love to you all

> y.a.b.
> Stephen Leacock

## To Barbara Nimmo

[3869 Cote des Neiges Road
Montreal]
Sunday Feb 13　44

Dear Bâ

I was so glad to hear via Fitz that Stephen is picking up from his stomach difficulty. Once he gets started he will go right on. I note that you write long letters to Fitz all about the "home front" for both of you (Peggy's family & yours) and of course she shows me all the letters so that's really writing to both of us . . . I am not well now & that makes one depressed & so I dont write to you as much but I like hearing it all . . I will presently send you material for a full family tree ~~of~~ on the Leacocks side via your grandmother reaching to 1740 something—meanwhile here is where Stephen's name comes in Stephen Butler Nimmo—s. of Barbara Nimmo—d. of Caroline Ulrichsen (Leacock)—d. of Agnes Leacock (Butler)—d. of Stephen Butler—s. of Mrs Thomas Butler * (Hester Lushington, married.1797)—daughter of <u>Sir Stephen Lushington</u> & with him you connect into Burke's Landed Gentry & go as far back as you like You have Lushington alone going to the 1400's and the Stephen running back . . —This Col. Thomas Butler appears in Burke but only as marrying Hester Lushington . . I have never managed to trace the Hampshire Butlers into the peerage (Marquis Butler of Ormonde) or the Landed Gentry—But I think they may connect up not via Hampshire (they have only been there 200 years) but via something Park (Oak? Park) Kent

> y. a. u.
> Stephen Leacock

## To Fraser S. Keith

3869 Cote des Neiges Road
Montreal
Feb 19. 44

Dear Fraser

I sat down to explain that the state of my health forbid me to write more than a couple of sentences,—but I found that like all professors I could'nt be brief if I tried

Dont lose this: theres no copy: it's right off the pen, the only way to write things . .

Stephen Leacock

## A Message to the Graduating Class of 1944

Stephen Leacock

You are going out from McGill into what is commonly called the "rude world" under very special circumstances and at a very critical period. For just at present the world is particularly rude, and it is going to be the work of you and your generation to try to make it better. Make a real job it it in the best traditions of honour, courage and decency.

There are great tasks in front of you and you will learn as you set your hands to them how great is your debt to the *Alma Mater* that has equipped and trained and inspired you to cope with them. A college is a queer place, full of freak characters and odd activities, with alternating aspects of drowsy inefficiency and alert effectiveness: a queer place, but it gets there just the same. If all the world did its work as well as the college does, then the world in the words of the old song "would go very well then." You are a product of the college: see to it that what you do justifies what the college has done.

You carry away a parchment—keep it. In the time being its utility is small although even now you can use a McGill degree as constructive evidence of mental sanity, barring any direct evidence to the contrary and even now you will find that your degree is accepted practically everywhere as absolving you from any test for illiteracy except as a mere matter of form.

But as the years go by your McGill parchment will take on a deeper meaning and will seem to breathe forth from the wall on which it hangs a magic wealth of memories, of wistful regrets and abiding and justifiable pride. It will serve to remind you that you have not really left college: no true graduate ever does. In the first eagerness of life's struggle the college seems left behind and but little thought of: but as the years pass and the foreground of life loses its colour and its interest in favour of the deeper background, your memory of college will rise before your mind in an outline as deep and firm as that of some ageing picture which a garish illumination confuses and a softened light revives.

There is a Latin motto which says that wherever we go we still carry with us our affections for the things we leave behind. I will not attempt to quote it, the more so as there seems to be a Latin motto for all the best things we ever want to say. But take it to mean that in going out from McGill your fellowship in all that it means remains unbroken.

### To Cleveland Morgan

3869 Cote des Neiges Rd
Montreal
Feb 23 1944

Dear Cleve

The circumstances of my illness make it still uncertain how much I can do & what not. So I will ask for a little more time before giving up the hope of tackling our <u>Merchants of Montreal</u> this spring. I imagine that if you had the MS all complete by August 1st that you could easily put it through the press for autumn publication. As I would only need, say, two clear months to do it there is time yet

Best regards
Stephen Leacock

### To Frank Dodd

3869 Cote des Neiges Rd.
Montreal
Feb.26. 1944.

Frank Dodd Esqre.
Dodd Mead and Company
New York.

Dear Dodd

I am sorry to say that I am leaving here to day to go into hospital in Toronto with much uncertainty as to how long. I am therefore turning over various unfinished literary business to Mrs. Herbert T. Shaw   1272   Redpath   Crescent Montreal, who has been acting as my research secretary for some years.

1. We spoke of an autobiography book with the title <u>Recollections and Reflections.</u> That title has since been copyrighted and used. I propose to call it

<u>MY MEMORIES</u>
<u>AND WHAT I THINK</u>

WITH A SUBTITLE <u>My Earlier Life</u>. Since one volume won't cover it all.

I have completed and sent to Paul Reynolds Jr. 599 Fifth Avenue New York about 7 thousand words of a first instalment. He is to see if he can sell magazine rights in it as a unit with or without any more of it.

The magazine title suggested is;

## MY MEMORIES
## FRAGMENTS OF AUTOBIOGRAPHY

I hope to go on with the book, if I am able to, while I am ill and to send it to you if and when the M.S. reaches (whatever is the lowest limit of book publication? . . . 30,000 words?) and if I am able to, carry it up to a full book length of say about 65,000 words. I propose our usual terms of a 15 per cent royalty on the U.S. and Canadian edition paid on retail price and in the money of each country; no other rights except these book rights; and under the circumstances I would ask an advance royalty of Five hundred dollars "$500. U.S.) provided always that the M.S. are assigned to Mrs. Shaw (as above) and the contract should carry the clause that payments are to be made to her. She will carry on the correspondence with you from this point.

.        .        .        .

2. Another book. I have just completed ready for the press a small book 32,000 words under the title

## WHILE WE HAVE TIME.—
xxxxxxxxxx
## THE CASE AGAINST SOCIAL CATASTROPHE

The Canadian rights have been sold to the <u>British Federation of Trade and Industry</u> at whose instigation it was written. Their agent is R.F. Ferguson, Suite 222. Rogers Building, Vancouver. B.C. .

They will be interested in getting out a large Canadian edition and will therefore give away a great number of copies over and above what they sell.

But I am sure that there is room for a U.S. and a U.K. edition and so I write to you first about it. It is true that the last quarter of the book deals with the development of Canada (the earlier part is universal) but it especially concerns the migration of population and capitol from the U.S. and the U.K. and therefore might find a wide public.

Mrs. Shaw could send you the M.S., or if you did not mind waiting till after the Canadian edition was out she could send you a copy (perhaps) of advance proof. You could buy sheets, or unbound copies, or bound copies from the B.C. Federation (as above) if you saw fit. Probably a good bargain.

The U.S. rights in this book are assigned to Mrs. Herbert T. Shaw (as Above) and all correspondence about it from now on should go to her. I hope you can handle this book. I think it might make a real hit, but as there is a certain doubt I am advising Mrs. Shaw to accept a ten per cent (10%) royalty as fair all round.

With best regards and recollections and hope for

many things yet.
Stephen Leacock

## To R. T. Ferguson

3869 Cote des Neiges Road
Montreal
Feb. 26, 1944

R.T. Ferguson Esqre.
British Columbia Federation of Trade and Industry
Suite 222. Rogers Bldg.
Vancouver, B.C.

Dear R.T.

I received yesterday your kind and sympathetic telegram and greatly appreciated it. I am to leave today to go into hospital in Toronto with much uncertainty even at the best as to how long. So I am getting Mrs. H. T. Shaw of 1272 Redpath Crescent Montreal who has for some years acted as my research secretary to look after various current matters and she will therefore answer the letters I now expect from you.

But one side of the matter I may take up now. As no doubt you remember, you and your associates have the copyright only for Canada in <u>Social Catastrophe</u>. I am writing to New York to see if a purely U.S. edition not sold in Canada can be arranged. In such a case, I am telling my publisher, plates, or unbound copies, or even bound copies, might be had from you under terms advantageous to you and to them. A similar arrangement could be made for the United Kingdom. Please note that the copyright for the U.S. and the copyright for the U.K. are both assigned by me to Mrs. Shaw.

> Very best regards and
> repeated thanks
> Stephen Leacock

## To Mrs Herbert T. Shaw

Natl Club Toronto
5 to 10 am Sunday
Feb 27  44

Dear Fitz

Billy Turner came in time & drove me down & took me right into the car, endlessly kind—The train (car) was mostly empty—passengers later station— I slept well—felt like getting out in half dark at Toronto—here to the club— (7 am) slept a little—Dot phoned—she will take me to see Wookie at the hospital at 11.30 am (that is in an hour or so) just for a talk & meeting. I asked her over the phone if Wookie means to go right on & she said he <u>doesn't</u> say is waiting for the first operation—I go into the hospital tonight—any time before bedtime—Xrays tomorrow—preliminary operation right away (Dot thinks Tuesday or Wednesday)—Dot is to come here at eleven o clock. The rest of the day I spend as I like—I must give Dot your letter. I neednt say I miss you or wish you were here—I needn't say words—the few said the easier to go right ahead. So I spend time dreaming that Jacques Chambrun is sending you glad news of the 100,000,000 people, or that Paul Reynolds has made a 4 bag hit or that Dodd is just crazy of Social Catastrophe or ~~Stew~~ Springer has leapt to $10$^{00}$ a share. Do you realize that any of these things is possible, or all of them altogether—I ate a good breakfast—I have good hopes & I am sure you have. If you are talking to Billy tell him how deeply I feel towards all his kindness & sympathy & what a wonderful help it has been.

> Affectionately,
> Stephen
> Stepnen Leacock

# EPILOGUE

*Stephen Leacock died on 28 March 1944. Adelaide Hett Meeres, who was with him as he died, recorded in a holograph note:*

> *He died from cancer of the throat—in Hosp. 'Give me my stick' he wrote 'I am going out to No Man's Land. I'll face it.' And he went, but he did not shrug his shoulders and there was no twinkle in his eye this time. Death is a serious thing, not to joke about.*

*Leacock wrote his comment out, for he could no longer speak. The man of compassion and wit was silenced by cancer and death.*

*In accordance with his wishes, Leacock's body was cremated, and the ashes were taken to Saint George's Church at Sibbald's Point on Lake Simcoe. The Most Reverend Derwyn Owen, primate of all Canada and an old friend of Leacock's, had come from Toronto through the snow to assist the local rector in performing the last rites. There, on 31 March, under a bare umbrella elm, where his mother and his brothers Jim and Dick had preceded him, Leacock's ashes were interred.*

*In the days following his death, obituaries for Leacock appeared in major newspapers around the world. The following tribute was published on 30 March in the* New York Herald Tribune:

## STEPHEN LEACOCK

What an urbane, delightful and many-sided man he was! Stephen Leacock, surely, was the First Citizen of Canada, and for something like forty years his luminous mind, playing with history, literature and the foibles of humanity, gave us a consistently excellent brand of humor. From his early 'Literary Lapses' and 'Nonsense Novels' down to the stuff written just before his last illness he kept to a remarkably high level. It was intelligent humor, buttressed by sound scholarship and lightened by a spirit that was at once gay and grave. He was the master of the sly twist, the unexpected but logical turn of thought, which at its best reveals truth in seeming incongruities. He depended upon no tricks of word or phrase or style—but the Leacock touch was always there. He did not write as a mere 'funny man', for none knew better than he the essential tragedy of human beings; he knew, moreover, that 'the saving grace of humor' is often only a sham, and that only a fool can laugh in the face of horror. War and disease and death and cruelty—no, he did not find them amusing. And yet he was able to say that 'civilization's best legacy, thus far, is the world's humour.' And of this he once said:

> It helps to supply for us, in its degree, such reconciliation as we can find for the mystery, the sorrows, the shortcomings of the world we live in or, say, of life itself. Consolation is hard to find. You recall perhaps the haunting verses, written years ago, that ran, 'There, little girl, don't cry.' They have broken her dolls, yes, and later on it will be her heart that is broken, but, 'there, little girl, don't cry.' It is all that we can say to one another.

Stephen Leacock was, for many years, a distinguished professor of economics at McGill University. To some it always seemed odd that an expert on the dismal science should have been able to turn his hand with such felicity to the writing of humor; unusual it was, to be sure, but hardly astonishing when one considers the rich facets of the man's mind. He was a first-rate historian and biographer. He was one of the finest of modern parodists. He was a lecturer of extraordinary charm. He was wholly devoid of pretense. He hated brutality in whatever form he found it (most of his considerable fortune went to the fight against cancer, from which his wife died) and he did not find anything amusing in the world's present mess. He had both courage and humor, but he never confused the two. He left a splendid legacy for all of us—and not all of it is a laughing matter.

*On 2 April, B.K. Sandwell, Leacock's friend of fifty-three years, delivered a tribute that was broadcast nationally on the CBC radio network. It was published as a small pamphlet entitled 'Stephen Leacock: An Appreciation', 'Reproduced by Gladstone Murray with the permission of B.K. Sandwell and the C.B.C., as a humble tribute to the memory of Stephen Leacock from a pupil and life-long friend':*

Today is the second of April. Less than a hundred miles north of the Toronto studio where I am talking to you are the two joined lakes of Simcoe and Couchiching. In all the little bays and harbors round those lakes, men have been spending this Sunday afternoon in their boathouses or at their moorings. They have been looking over their sailboats, testing the running rigging, getting out the tar brushes and the paintpots, making ready for the hoisting of canvas for the summer of 1944. They do it every year on the first Sunday in April, if it's an early spring. They've been doing it today in all the little bays round Simcoe and Couchiching, except one.

Old Brewery Bay is about a mile out of Orillia. It is on the neck of land between the two lakes, where the great railway lines run through on their way from the Georgian Bay ports to Montreal. In Old Brewery Bay Stephen

Leacock's boats rest undisturbed in the boathouse, and in the room above it his unfinished manuscripts lie on the table where he wrote the 'Sunshine Sketches of a Little Town'. For on Friday the ashes of Stephen Leacock were laid to rest in the churchyard at Sibbald's Point, at the other end of the larger lake, and his tremendous laughter will never again be heard across these waters that he loved.

I find it hard to think of Lake Simcoe without Leacock. I have known him for fifty-three years. In all that time he was the most alive man that I ever knew; and now he is not alive any more. He was a man who did everything with terrific gusto, who had a zest for life in all its phases. The only thing he didn't show much gusto in was the thing he was doing when I first met him. I was a fifth form boy at Upper Canada College, in Toronto, when he arrived there in 1891 as a house-master and began to teach me French. I don't mean that he wasn't a good teacher, for he was. He had a keen appreciation of the literary qualities of the French language, and he imparted some of that appreciation to me. But the truth is that he was teaching school merely to get enough money to take a post-graduate course, and he regarded us schoolboys as pestilential little nuisances— which we were. The only gusto he showed at that time was when he caned us; there was none of that sickening 'this hurts me more than it does you' air about those transactions. In later life I often heard him maintain that the modern way of bringing up children is all wrong. He held that the world will eventually return to the good old nineteenth century method of making them learn by licking them when they don't. Perhaps it will.

We boys had a considerable respect for Leacock in those days. This was not due to his skill with the cane, because there were other masters who did better. It was due to our knowing that he was already getting little humorous sketches accepted by New York periodicals. These were the days when he was writing the famous 'Boarding-House Geometry', with its 'All Boarding-houses are the same boarding-house' and 'A bee-line may be made from any one boarding-house to any other boarding-house'. All through his life the best of his writing was always material which he had first built up in conversation; and we would hear him telling the other house-masters the first rough draft of things which ultimately became classics of Canadian humor, such as 'My Financial Career', the sketch you remember in which he describes how he was so overwhelmed by the magnificence of the bank that he deposited fifty-six dollars and immediately drew it all out again. Last year my own paltry account was moved from a humble little branch, which was closed for shortage of help, to the head office, and may I confess that I never go into that marble palace to draw out my weekly eleven dollars pocket-money without feeling exactly as Stephen Leacock must have felt? Of course millions of other Canadians have felt just the same way, but nobody ever put it into words except Stephen.

However, between his salary at Upper Canada and his earnings from his pen, Leacock soon made enough for his Ph.D. course at Chicago, and that was the end of his school teaching. He and I turned up almost at the same time in Montreal about 1901. He was a professor in the Political Science Department at McGill University, and I was the morgue reporter and dramatic editor of a Montreal daily.

Leacock, speedily became mildly famous as the worst-dressed professor in Montreal. This was not due to any pose or affectation or even to general care-lessness. It was simply that he refused to be careful about things which in his opinion did not matter. Clothes in his opinion did not matter, unless you wanted to shine in 'society', which he certainly did not. There is still a caricature of him in the University Club in Montreal; it shows him with his hair rumpled in all directions, his tie on one side, his gown hanging in ribbons, his trousers baggy, the hanger-loop of his coat sticking up behind his neck, and a general air of hav-ing slept in what he had on. Yet he was not in the least absent-minded. His was the carelessness of a locomotive engineer, who knows that he has a big job to do and gives it all his attention, and doesn't have to bother about clothes to keep up his social position.

For a long time Leacock wrote only on history and economics. He went round the world as an investigator for the Rhodes Trust. It began to look as if he might become just a university don, and the 'Boarding-House Geometry' might come to be regarded as just a juvenile folly, to be lived down by forty years of textbooks and lives of Baldwin and Lafontaine. And then, about 1910, he con-ceived the idea that perhaps these lively sketches written in the 'nineties might bring in a little more money if they were turned into a book. It was entirely his own idea. He asked me about it. I told him that nobody in Canada had ever made a cent out of a book of humor, and that even if he was lucky enough to make a few dollars out of it it would ruin his reputation as a political economist. Fortunately he paid no attention to me, and he, Mrs Leacock, and my wife went on rummaging in dusty files for forgotten contributions, and these were turned into the first or Montreal edition of 'Literary Lapses'. That edition consisted of a thousand copies, and sold at seventy-five cents. It was produced at the author's risk and was actually a success; and it is now quite rare.

1910, the year of 'Literary Lapses', was the year in which Mark Twain died. There is much in common between Mark Twain and Stephen Leacock. So it was not surprising that, with Mark Twain dead, publishers should be looking for somebody to take his place. John Lane, the English publisher, then at the apex of his career, was one of them. He read 'Literary Lapses', decided that the English would like it, nicknamed Leacock the Mark Twain of the British Empire, and set about producing an English edition. It was a success, slow at first but gaining momentum. From that date Leacock the humorist stepped ahead of Leacock the economist, and never gave way again. After all, the world is full of economists, and humorists are as rare as Kangaroos in Iceland.

But before Leacock really knew how successful he was, an event occurred which was very fortunate for Canada. The managing editor of the Montreal Star at the moment was Edward Beck, an English-born and American-trained journalist with all sorts of enterprise and a very sound judgment. Leacock and Beck were the closest friends I had, and I owe more to them than to any other people in the world except my parents and my Greek professor. I never repaid the debt to them personally; one never does. But I think I squared myself to some extent with Canada and the world at large, because I brought them together, and the result was a commission to write the 'Sunshine Sketches of a Little Town' for the 'Montreal Star' and a syndicate which included my present paper, 'Saturday Night'.

'Sunshine Sketches' is the one completely Canadian book of Leacock's enormous output. It was written out of his experience of life on an Ontario farm and in an Ontario small town, the town of Orillia. It was written for Canadians; Leacock was getting what he then regarded as a good price for just the Canadian rights, and he did not bother about the outside market; and that was a condition that never happened again. So he emphasized all the specially Canadian elements of the subject. You remember the political catchwords of the Imperialists and the Canadianists in the great election campaign. You remember the excursion on the Mariposa Belle, in which everybody participated because it was a community affair, but social lines were clearly drawn; 'All the young boys and the toughs and the men in the band got down on the lower deck forward, where the boat was dirtiest and where the anchor was and the coils of rope. And upstairs on the after deck were Lillian Drone and Miss Lawson, the high school teacher, with a book of German poetry'—'Gothey', Leacock thought it was—'and the bank teller and the younger men.' And you remember Canon Drone and the building of the big new church and the tearing down of the old one and the question of what was to be done with the stone from the old one. First it was to be used for a Sunday-School, but the new big church took all the money. Then it was to be reverently fashioned into a wall that should stand as a token. But eventually 'it was laid reverently into a stone pile, and afterwards it was devoutly sold to a building contractor and, like so much else in life, was forgotten.'

All this is the very stuff of Ontario life. It has the warmth of the Ontario summer sun and the smell of the Ontario soil fresh turned in the spring. They tell me that the Government is worried about the Canadian troops who have been so long away from Canada, for fear they may be losing some of their Canadian-ism, their feeling for their old home land. Well, so far as the Ontario men are concerned, the answer is easy. Get a few hundred thousand copies of 'Sunshine Sketches' and scatter them around the Canadian forces, and they will dash out from their encampments, demolish Herr Hitler in a couple of weeks, and be back in Ontario in time for the spring seeding.

The secret of Leacock's style is that it is talking raised to the highest power. I have already mentioned how all his best work took shape originally as anecdotes told at the dinner table. It never reads like the work of a man with a pen in his hand looking at a sheet of paper; it reads as if he were talking to you, and rather expected you to interrupt.

And the secret of Leacock's thought is that he was a very *wise* man. He knew a great many facts, but he also knew their relative importance, which many professors do not. A man who is funny without being wise is just a buffoon. A man who uses his fun to convey his wisdom is in the line of the great comic writers from Aristophanes to Moliere to Mark Twain. There is more wisdom in one of Leacock's funny books than in the whole of 'Canada and Its Provinces' in forty-eight volumes. Leacock admitted it himself. The day will come when every advertising man will read Leacock's 'The First Newspaper' and know what advertising really is. The day will come when every professor will read his 'Homer and Humbug', and learn that 'The classics are only primitive literature. They belong to the same class as primitive machinery and primitive music and primitive medicine.' But by that time Leacock himself will be a classic, so they will not mind.

# APPENDIX

## Agnes Leacock: A Memoir

*Agnes Leacock wrote the following memoir between April 1914 and November 1917. The transcription is based on George Leacock's copy, which, like the few others known to exist, comes to an abrupt ending at the bottom of page 11.*

56 Rose Ave., TORONTO—April 1914.

As my children often ask me to tell them about their English relations and my own early life I will begin by a kind of family tree. First, of my Mother as I know least about her ancestors—in fact, nothing except that my maternal grandfather, John Linton, was a stock broker—office near 2 Royal Exchange Building, London. He lived in a large house in Clapham with a walled garden. I only saw it once—quite a good sized place. He drove to the Exchange with his own horses every day; and was what was I suppose would be called a rich man. He left 100,000 pounds—half to his widow (her maiden name was Ker) and 10,000 pounds to each of his children. There were five—Uncle John, my mother, Aunt Emma Bradley and Aunt Esther Linton. There was another I feel sure, but can't remember though I knew Uncle John; he lived at Balham, died there and I stayed once or twice with my aunt and cousins—3 boys, Henry who was in the Exchange, and the twins, Joe and Sam. I don't know what became of them, they would be old men now 67 or so anyway. Aunt Esther, "Ettie" I called her was a very loveable woman. She died when I was about 14; at Bath with inflamation of the lungs. Aunt Emma, my godmother, I knew well, stayed with them at Cheltenham several times, 19 Royal Parade. The girls and boys went to the different colleges there and afterwards Emma married the Reverend Carl Berle, Master at Malbro College. I stayed with her there. Her half brother Granville Bradley was then Head Master of Marlbro; later Dean of Westminster. Fanny married my half brother John Palmer. My children know all about him and then his cousins, Charlie and Carrie Palmer. The other Bradleys married well. Herbert, Dean of Merton College, Oxford is still my trustee. Andrew was Classical Master, Liverpool College—I think retired. Johnnie was drowned at Oxford.

That is all I know of my mother's people except my grandmother, old Mrs. Linton, who lived at Retford. My sister Carrie and I stayed there with her when I was eight years old. She had a pretty country house with a large garden leading to the river. I remember she was a kind old soul and gave me presents, among other things a prayer book, which I still have.

I was only four years old when my mother died—can just remember her at Soberton taking me to church; my father carried me home and he used to take me out riding with him, on my Shetland pony. I had a box saddle and he had a leading rein. He used to take me to the school on May Day, May 1st, carried me at the head of all the school children with their garlands to church. I suppose it was before the service they showed their garlands. My mother had the pennies ready to give them at the vicarage. That was one of the things I always remembered, how my father, and afterwards my Uncle Charles and Uncle Thomas used to change 10 shillings into pence, ready for the school children on May Day.

Some of the garlands were beautiful—primroses and wild hyacinth and cuckoo fruit mixed with moss; and some were just two or three flowers tied on a stick and carried by little tots of three years old, but everyone got a penny until the 10 shillings ran out!

I said I was four when my mother died, but remember that was when we left Soberton—I was five when she died. I remember the village quite well, old Farmer Twynham whose farm was close to the village and where I went by myself and was given apples and cakes, and two or three other farms, the Diebers and Kewels and my father's friends, clergymen, Mr. Hume, our Rector—he lost his son years after on the "Captain"—all drowned; and Mr. Dusantory, Mr. Dallas, Mr. Colpoise and the Kepples. Captain, afterwards Sir Harry Kepple lived near us and was a great friend of my father's; the Brooks, clergymen too, William Henry, clergyman of the adjoining parish and Isaac from the Channel Island. Nearly all my father's friends were Irish—my brother "Tim" was Thomas Adair after his brother, Mr. Colpoise or some old Irishman.

We went to Southampton about 1848. My father was given the living of Holy Trinity Church, it was in what was then a very crowded, low part of the town, but we lived, what seemed to me, a long way from the church. At Soberton the church was just across the road, up a little lane, but at Southampton, we lived at 10 Cranberry Terrace, nearly a mile, I suppose from our church—it was almost country after you got out of the terrace where we lived. About six months or so after we went to Southampton my mother died. All the memory I have of her there is how she took me everywhere with her and dressed me herself, though I had a nurse. We have no picture of her, but I remember she was a good height, not a big woman at all, with brown curling hair and grey eyes. Perhaps I should not remember this—but for another memory—one day my father came to the nursery and took me in his arms and carried me to their room, sat me on the bed. My mother was there, but I didn't at first know her—her beautiful hair was all cut off. She looked at me without speaking and turned her face away. Some one of my sisters took me away and told me mother was dead. I really didn't understand the meaning of the word and was terribly angry a few days after when they dressed me in black. I tried to tear my frock and screamed for my mother. They had to send me out of the house until the funeral was over. They took her to be buried at Soberton. Poor mother, it does not seem much for me to know of her after her five year's devotion to me.

Now I will begin about my father's family and where I've explained all relations, take up my story from where I am leaving off—about March 1849.

Well dear old grandpapa and grandmama Butler were then living at Bury Lodge. Grandpapa came over from Ireland when quite young to Sharbro' Castle in Kent. He may possibly have been born there, but I can't be sure if he came as a very young child or if it was my great grandfather who came then. My grandmother, Hester Lushington, was one of Sir Henry Lushington's daughters, Oakham Park in Kent (or Surrey) is where they lived and the baronetcy dates back I don't know how far. Lady Onslow was one of grandmama's sisters; Mrs. Chamberlain another; Sir Stephan L_____, Dean of the Court of Archers, her brother; also Sir Henry (after the old father died) he, or his son Henry lived at Titchbourn when I remember him; the place belonging to Roger Titchbourn who was lost so long no one, or very few knew him when he came back.

Titchbourn House is in Hampshire, a drive from Bury Lodge.

Grandpapa Butler had no relation to my knowledge except George Butler, his cousin, who lived at 6 Brunswick Terrace, Brighton. We used to stay there always for Easter. George Butler was lame from falling from his horse out hunting, but he was a very good looking man, with such bright blue Irish eyes. He was very kind to me, used to give me half a sovereign always when I went there and presents of different kinds, and used to have me down to late dinner before I was "out" and had parties on purpose for me. Aunt Fanny (she was really only my cousin) had been a beautiful woman; she must have been nearly fifty when I knew her, but still very good looking. She was a Gambier before she married George Butler; and my Aunt Hester, also married a Gambier (Admiral Fitzgerald Gambier) so we were doubly connected with them. Aunt Hester was my father's only sister. They, she and Uncle Fritz, had no children; lived at Anglesey Terrace near Gosport—I forget the number (9, I remember it now). I knew the house quite well. The Norris' lived next them. Mrs. Norris was Uncle Fritz's sister. We always called her Aunt and Willie, Cousin. My children have, some of them, heard me talk of Willie Norris; he went into the Rifle Brigade. By the way, he married another cousin, one of the Burrards, maybe that is not how it is spelt—look it up in the Peerage. Lady Burrard was another of grandmama's sisters. Willie went to the Crimea (same as my brothers) and had his arm shot off, all sorts of wounds and bruises and came home well again, took measles from his children and died in a week. Besides his sister, Hester, my father had two brothers, Uncle Thomas, Colonel 53rd Regiment and Uncle Charles, Vicar of Calterington–Hants, when first I knew him—later Vicar of Portchester afterwards, Newchurch, Isle of Wight, where he died.

Uncle Thomas married Arabella Dacres, Admiral Dacres eldest daughter, and he, Admiral Dacres had seven daughters. Aunt Fanny Kirwan is the only one my children know about. Harry Kirwan's mother, my real cousins (of course, Harry was not my cousin at all). Of Tom, George, Belle and Dora Butler, I need not write of them now, as their names have been familiar to all my children always, because from the time my mother died I frequently stayed with my Uncle and Aunt. They lived then at Hook Cottage, Blendworth near Horndean in Hampshire about three or four miles from Bury Lodge, where the old people then lived. Often too, my father would drive from Southampton to Bury Lodge and take me with him. He had to have two curates because of the hard work he had done. At Soberton he had college lectures during the week and prayer meetings and went among the Gypsies on Soberton downs. There was a regular camp there and a Gypsy family named Stanley who attended our church. My father christened their babies, one of them was named Maryanne after my sister. And losing my mother just when the children by his first wife were needing care, told on his health. I am afraid that he had quite a lot of trouble and expense with my half brothers and sisters. I will write of them later.

Anyway, soon after mother died he had fainting fits and then, one terrible Sunday, I saw him carried down from the pulpit in a fit of Epilepsy. He often had fits after that. He knew his life would not be a long one and he wanted me to be at home with my Uncle and Aunt and cousins that I might not be going to them a stranger. Dora was his godchild, she was just a baby when he died and Belle was about three, but Tom was nearly as old as I was, about a year or so younger and George three years younger. We were always the best of friends. I always loved out door life and boys' games and my father had taught me Latin so I could learn with Tom. But before I tell of my life with my cousins I must go back to Southampton in about 49 and 50. It must have been then we begun going to the Isle of Wight so often for change for my father. The Leacocks lived at Oakhill, near Ryde and Mrs. Leacock's mother, old Mrs. Young lived at Westridge—a beautiful country home about 2 miles from Ryde, Mrs. Young had been a friend of my mothers. She (mother) used to live at Benbridge, Isle of Wight, it was there she and my father were married—and the Youngs were old friends of both of them. The Youngs and Leacocks belonged to our church then. It was not till about that time Mrs. Leacock and some of her sisters became Romanists—it was quite a grief to my father—he had been Charlie Leacock's Godfather. The Leacock boys John and Charlie used to go to school in Jersey and the Channell Island boats came in to Southampton late in the evening, so they stayed with us the night on their way to and from school for the holidays. Mrs. Leacock sometimes came over from the Island to meet the boys and stayed with us too, once or twice. She brought Peter—that may have been another time—he was not at school.

Now I should tell you about my sisters and brothers—my mother was a widow—her first husband a Mr. Palmer a wine merchant, he only lived a few years. John, Charlie and Carrie were my half brothers and sister. My children will remember Uncle John, he was a surgeon in the Navy—for years staff surgeon in the Pirkenhead at Liverpool, (I think it was the Birkenhead—the Hospital ship any way) and he married his cousin Fanny Bradley—Charlie is still (at the date April 1914) living in Australia, Kedron, North Sydney. Carrie died at the age of 30 or thereabouts. She was the sister who took special care of me—she was very lovable. I missed her badly, I was 16 when she died in Bath, she was buried at Soberton, by our Mother. I was at Bury Lodge at the time and went to her funeral with my Uncle Thomas. She was the only one who died comparatively young, I had three Butler sisters; Maryanne (afterwards Mrs. Douglas of Orbiston, Lancashire); Hester Caroline (Sissie) Mrs. Christie and Kate (Mrs. Parry). My children know about their Aunts and Cousins. Two Butler brothers, George Stephen and 'Tim' Thomas Adair. George was in H. M. 17th Regiment in the Crimea, invalided after the war, went to British Columbia and married Fanny Brett, who lived in Portchester and went out to George after he had bought his farm. George died about the year 1885 of consumption. Tim, Thomas Adair—was major in 101st Bengal Fusileers through the Indian Mutiny; got Victoria Cross for swimming the Goomtee under fire and holding a fort, forget the name. He was about 21 at the time.

That is all the relations. My Father's first wife was Maryanne Thistlethwyate of Southwick Park in Hampshire, 5 miles from Bury Lodge, we often went there as her brother Tom and my uncles were friends. I forgot to mention my brother Tim married first Annie Buckley, an Irish girl, very young out in India. My children knew her—she and Tim stayed with us in Toronto when Dot was about a year old. She died a year or two later. His second wife was Annie Davidson. Her father was master of a College in the Isle of Man and her Uncles merchants in Montreal. Dot knew her, we stayed with them at Hill Farm, near Bury Lodge where they were living when Dot and I were in England. Annie died just a year after Tim—can't remember what year.

Having gone through all the relations as far as I can I suppose my personal experiences come next. They will probably be very disappointing as only a few events outside my own early life come to my remembrance.

My first personal recollection is of the Shetland pony running away with me; in the light of later days I don't think he did run away, but this is what happened—my father rode a great deal about the parish and by the time I was three years old (my sisters and brothers in the school room) he thought it time to teach me. The Shetland pony, "Sheltie" by name belonged to Maryanne, given her by old Mr. Young (your great grandfather, Mrs. Leacock's father). A box saddle was got for me and I was strapped in and taken with my father, "Sheltie" on a leading rein. After a day or two of this it occured to me I would like to take

* Charlie died April, 1916.

an independent ride and while my father was talking to some old man we met and not attending to me, leading rein loose, I shook Sheltie's reins and having no whip gave her a hard pat, and he nothing loath, started off. He probably was only going a good canter—but even now I can remember that though my small heart pounded with excitement the devil of mischief entered into me and an open gate gave me a chance to turn in and hide myself and Sheltie behind a haystack. Of Course, my father found me almost directly. I have no remembrance of any punishment—at most I was four years old. As we left Soberton then we moved to 10 Cranbury Terrace, Southampton, my father was made incumbent of Holy Trinity Church. Cranbury Terrace was almost out of the town. We had a nice garden. I could soon get out into the country, but the church was right in the town in the slums and a hard place to work, for my father, very different from his country parish. He had a curate, an Irishman, Mr. Wilde, married, some children—I don't remember much about them—only that he was lame and really not sufficient help for my father. In that crowded parish there was so much to do; and my father's health was beginning to fail. First he had fainting attacks and then Epilepsy. He would not give up work, but had a second curate, James Carson, Irish too, and such a nice fellow—young, good looking and good company, I thought, for he used to play with me any time he was waiting to see my Daddie. One night I coaxed my sister into letting me go to a missionary meeting with them, and as I always went to bed at 7, of course, I could hardly keep awake, in fact, probably went to sleep as all I remember was Mr. Carson carrying me home—though nearly ten years old I was very small and he was a fine tall young man.

I used to go to Miss Preston's Day School, quite near. A little boy in our Terrace went too. At first we were taken to and fetched from school, but soon we discarded our escorts and went alone. I had some cousins living in the same square as my school; Herietta and Agnes Lushington. They and their mother were at that time living with old Lady Prescott, then grandmother, and I often went to lunch and play there. Their father was Franklin Lushington. I think he was in the Navy and away at that time.

One thing I forgot to mention, before I was 5 I took the whooping cough from the little boy next door, Bobbie Wade, Old Captain Morsby's grandson. Bobbie had it badly and I used to mock him. My mother told me not to or I would have it myself, which I certainly did. By the way, Captain Morsby was commander of the Ripon, the troopship. Later on he took me and my sister over her. Reading Sir Robert's life, I see he sailed to India with Captain Morsby.

I had a very happy childhood, though practically an only child, my sisters and brothers being so much older. I had several little friends in the Terrace and was sent to Miss Preston's Day School when eight or nine years old, so that I might have companions. Every morning before breakfast I went to my father's room to learn my text, and on Sunday the collect. When my father was not able to go to church he liked me to memorize the sermon for him. Once an old friend, Mr. Dusantory, came to preach a missionary sermon. Someone put a 7 shilling gold piece in the plate and the clergyman put in a 10 shilling piece instead and gave me the 7 shilling as it was a curiosity then, not being issued any more. I had that gold piece for about 50 years—one of my children had or lost it.

We often went to the Isle of Wight in the summer, one year we went to North Wales. The train journey always made my head ache—I must tell the reason why. One summer at Sea View, Isle of Wight, my nurse made me a swing between the front door posts—we used to rent that house nearly every summer—the Midlanes. Well, one day my sisters had gone to Ryde, three miles off and there was just my father, me and one maid at home. My father was resting upstairs and I went to my swing and called the maid to start me. She gave me a high swing and went off to the back garden to talk to her young man. When she came back to me again I was on my back on the door step, unconscious. The first thing I remember I was up in father's room very sick. It happened my brother John arrived. He was then just passed for a surgeon and he sent at once for Dr. Bloxam, in Ryde. It was about three weeks before I knew much that went on; the rest of the family went back to Southampton. Carrie and John and my nurse stayed with me till I could be moved. I had concussion of the brain—that was the beginning of my headaches and delicacy. They had to be very careful of me for a long time. I couldn't eat butter or pastry or rich food of any kind and train journeys always upset me—that trip to Wales for instance I was sick before I got to Chester and at Oxford too, the first day, but remember going over to the colleges after. Worcester was my father's college. We went to Bailiol and others and to see the Marlye's Memorial.

We stayed at Festimog in North Wales—it was there we met Charles Kingsley. My father knew him. He used to ride a sturdy little pony and put me on it sometimes. The Lushingtons came there that summer too; I forget which except Alice and Uncle Stephen.

We went to Bethgitart too. My sisters climbed ~~Tuoroden~~ Snowdon; but my Dad and I stayed down at the hotel and walked to Gellacts grave; it has an iron railing round it, like a person's. He deserved it better than some human beings deserve remembrance.

The last year we went to Sea View I was left at school when the family went back to Southampton. The school was at Nussenden House near a church (St. Thomas?). Mrs. Moore was the head of the school. There were not many girls. I did not like being there at all and tried to run away, but was caught by Mrs. Moore herself coming in from the back garden just as I was going out. However, soon after that I went home. On the 5th of November I was at the schoolroom window watching for "Guy Fawkes". The boys used to carry a dressed up Guy Fawkes down and got pennies for firecrackers and bonfires. Instead of the boys, I saw our servant coming, I mean one from home, my family were at Guildford then, and the servant had come for me. She told Mrs. Moore that my father was dead, but didn't tell me—only that I was wanted home. On Ryde pier we met Edward Scholfield (he married Peter's Aunt Isabella Young). I knew him very well, have often been out on his yacht. He asked what I was doing out of school. The maid said something while I was chattering to him, and he kissed me goodbye and said, "poor little girl", so I felt sure something was wrong at home, and when I got to the house I saw the blinds down—didn't need to ask—my sister Sizzie opened the door and told me. I was very heartbroken for my dear father was so good to me and I had been so much his companion till I went to Mrs. Moore's. It happened the day before; only Maryanne was with him. Carrie was visiting one of my aunts and Sizzie and Kate had gone out for the afternoon when he was taken ill—one of his bad fits of epilepsy; he hadn't had one for nearly a year, only fainting fits and they hoped he had got over them. He was 52; at least, he would have been in February.

My brother John was on his ship in the Hebrides; he came to us. He was only my father's stepson, but very fond of him; he had never known his own father. Carrie came home too, but the others, George in the Crimea and Tim in India, could not come. He was buried at Soberton

September 5th, 1915.

It is a long time since I have written anything but letters, and a great event has taken place. My first Leacock grandchild was born on the 19th of August, Stephen's boy. He and Beatrix have been married a long time and this longed for child has taken up all my thoughts of late. I hope very soon to see him; at present he and his mother are in the maternity hospital, and it's not much use for me to go to Montreal till they get home to Cote des Neiges, as one can see so little of people in hospital, but Stephen writes often of the boy and he's a chip off the old block I'm sure—like Stephen and my father. He is to be called Stephen Lushington.

Now to go on with my history; after my father died Aunt Belle came to Guildford to take me to live with them. She and Uncle Thomas and my cousins were living then at Hook Cottage, Blendworth, about three miles from Bury Lodge, I think.

Tom was a year younger than I but he was a big strong boy (like our young Charlie Sheppard) and I was a small delicate girl. Tom was clever too, up to me in everything, but I was up to him in outdoor sports. We were great chums as the others were much younger. George was about eight I think, Belle five and Dora three. They were all in the nursery so were Tom and I for breakfast and tea, but we had dinner downstairs, and were allowed to go out by ourselves, and were great at bird's nesting, cricket and working in the garden.

I have been looking back to see if I have said anything about seeing the troops off to the Crimea in 1854 and I can't see any mention of it. It was not much I could record, only my sister taking me to the dock at Southampton to see the regiments embark. It was a bright enough pageant in those days, troops in scarlet and gold or blue and silver; flags flying in the town, bands playing. In spite of the crying wives and sweethearts it was a brave enough show to a child and all I pitied were the poor horses. But I saw them come back—writing of my cousins, Tom and George, reminded me of it. Uncle Thomas called us one morning to come down quick; there was a regiment back from the Crimea marching through Horndean, about a mile from the cottage. Uncle Thomas had George with him; Tom and I ran on and I dropped my shoe in my hurry, hadn't waited to button it.

They were just coming down the street as we got to the Seymours and we climbed the gate posts to see better. About half of them had their heads bandaged or their arms in slings; their hair and whiskers long and they looked so thin and ragged it was enough to make one cry.

A year or so after I went to live with my Uncle, Grandpapa died and then we all left Hook Cottage and went to live at Bury Lodge with dear old Grandmama. She was so good to me. I think it must have been a trial to her having all of us children to live in the house with her after the quiet life she had with Grandpapa. They were such a nice old couple—about 80 when I remember them best. Grandpapa was middle height, not a big man any way. He had quite white hair and very blue eyes and Grandmama was quite small, walked very upright. She wore a cap of course and black silk dress and mittens and satin, sandled shoes—she was quite a picture. My "Daisy" is like her in face—very like her—but, for all she was such a little woman there was a dignity about her which I doubt my Daisy ever attaining to! She and Grandpapa drove to church and always got out at the bottom of the hill leading to the church and walked up arm in arm, and the old coachman, Pratt, used to leave the horses and dogs—they always went—at the inn and follow with the other servants. I am afraid Tom and I were rather ill-behaved in Church, but that was after Grandpapa's time of course, I used often to stay there before he died with my Father. When Tom was 12 he went to Rugby. I was going to school too, at a small private school in Kent, kept by two ladies by the name of Stables, Hazledon House, W. Cranbrook—that was the address, but Staplehurst was our station. One of my Uncles used to take me to London and Miss Stable met us there and took me and several other girls back to school with her. I am afraid I was dreadfully backward and I know I was terribly homesick for some time, but I made friends after a while. One special friend Grace Pierpoint was afterwards Stephen's Godmother.

The School, Hazledon House, was quite in the country. In an old scrapbook of mine you will find a pencil sketch of it with the girls in their crinolines walking in the drive. There was a large kitchen garden which we were not allowed to go into, but there was a large front garden and field in which we walked or played and nearly every afternoon went for walks in the country, beautiful woods and hop fields all around. In the Autumn we always had some walks in the hop-gardens to see them being gathered in, for all I know it may be done by machinery now—then the poor people and Irish laborers and their families picked the hops with long canvas troughs, like hammocks and they were carted to the vast houses to be dried. No harvest fete is more picturesque than a hop garden—the trailing vines on their long poles; the pickers, men, women and children, variously clad and speaking various English and Irish dialects; besides the afternoons in the woods and hop fields. One of our great pleasures was going to church, literally going, as I don't think any of us especially enjoyed the actual service. We drove six miles in large covered vans; the reason why—Miss Stable didn't consider that in any nearer Church the unadulterated Gospel was preached. Our parish church was, I suppose, Cranbrook only a mile or two away. We sometimes walked there to do a little shopping but the doctrine preached by the Rector was not approved by the dear old ladies, who, but for their narrow-mindedness in that respect were really good kind women and much liked and respected by us all. The church we did attend was in a village called Headcorn. The clergyman, Rev. Henry Scovell, some of his belongings lived in "America" as we then termed any part of the States or Canada, I am not sure he was not born there himself. He had a wife and two children, Harry and Lucy. Harry was about 14 at the time I am writing of—we used to take our dinner in the Vans in fine weather and eat it in a house near the vicarage and after dinner the Misses Stables went to see Mrs. Scovell and some of us were allowed to play in the garden with the children—I wrote 'play' without thinking—of course no kind of play was allowed on Sunday. We walked about and sat under the trees and no doubt talked more nonsense than if we had been playing ball or croquet. I happened to go very often to the Vicarage for this reason—we had to write notes on the sermon, it came very easy to me to do it, but the doctrines Mr. Sewell preached, a modified Calvinism, didn't appeal to me and I either left out pieces purposely or altered the sense, so I used to be called into the study and talked to, reasoned with, but never convinced. When I was 16 I left the school. Many years afterwards I met Harry Scovell by accident in St. John's Hospital, Meyor Street, Toronto; his wife was there at the same time I was.

Well, I mustn't go on writing so much of the old school days or I shall never come to an end. One sad event though stands out in my memory, or rather two events, I took diptheria and nearly died when I was 14. The school had to be broken up till after Easter and I was sent home to Bury Lodge as soon as safe to travel. They couldn't have me in the house on account of the children, so Uncle Thomas got rooms at their farm for me for two weeks. He and Tom used to come and talk to me through the window. No one took it from me then but on my return to school one of the girls who slept in my room took it and died in three days, before her parents who lived in Yorkshire could come. Her name was Sarah

Broderick. I suppose in those days fumigation was not properly understood—the infection was still in the room. Later that term another girl died from inflamation of the lungs. She was an Indian girl, daughter of Mohun Lal, a Rajah of Delhi, he mother a Circassion, died when she was three and she was sent to Miss Stables then and was going out to her Father that summer—she was buried in Cranbrook churchyard.

I think it must have been about this time I spent the summer with my sister Carrie, Aunt Ester (Linton) and a cousin Louisa Winchin at Bournmouth.

May 25th, 1916. I shall have to hurry over the next years of my life or will never finish the record. I was at that school about four years, left for two reasons—to go to a finishing school near London. Also I had been criticizing the doctoring of Mr. Sewell (looking back I see I referred to that). I went to Miss Everetts, Lyrington House, Clapham Park. My friend Grace Pierpoint was there too. I spent one Easter with her at her father's parsonage, Southbourne, Eastbourne. It was the year the Prince of Wales married the Princess Alexr. of Denmark—10th of March—all the towns were decked with flags and arches, and we went a country walk with other girls picking primroses and flowers for the church. There were some connections of mine living near Eastbourne, the Gilberts and a Mrs. Carew, I don't remember much about them. Some of my holidays were spent in Devonshire with the Kirwans, Mrs. Kirwan was Aunt Belle's sister. The other children came to Bury Lodge the year of the 2nd Exhibition 1862. May was 3, Hyacinth 2 and Harry a baby in arms born March 13th. We went to London for the Exhibition and stayed before going at the Misses Doeres at Godalinney. I stayed there several times with Aunt Belle. Later on my holidays were often spent in Scotland with Mr. Douglas. I stayed at school until I was 19; after then often in Devonshire or Scotland. The Kirwans had moved from the parish I first went to stay in, Peters Moreland, and were at Butler Mills, near Clovelly. It was a lovely place and I used to ride a lot with Mr. Kirwan—it was all historic ground—Clovelly, Bedeford, Barnstable, Torrington and about all Appledon and Northan. When I rode to the golf links Mr. Kirwan played golf, I amused myself on the beach—watching the bar Tennyson has made so famous. I often think of it, especially when I read his hymn:

> "Sunset and evening star
> And one clear call for me
> And may there be no moaning of the Bar
> When I put out to sea."

This is as much as I wrote before my operation May 29th, 1916. It was like "Putting out to sea" for me. I hardly expected to see this side again but I hoped to see my Pilot face to face when I had crossed the Bar.

July 6th, 1917.

I wish my cousin Tom was here to help me as to dates—I am terribly mixed. However if I record events a year or two one way or the other won't matter. There is no one, except Tom, who could correct me; my own sisters and brothers are all dead; Carrie and John buried at Soberton, Hants; Charlie in Sydney, Australia; Maryanne Douglas died in the Isle of Man, but was I think buried in the Dean Cemetery, Edinburough, beside her husband. I never knew where Issie Christie was buried, I think at Kensal Green, George at Victoria, B.C.; Tim in a cemetery near London, Tom knows where—all divided in life and death— though a very affectionate family. There is one other living who remembers about our young days—Fanny Palmer. I spent several Christmas holidays with Mr. Bradley and of course, always kept up correspondence with them.

October 20th, 1917.

I feel inclined to miss a few years and go on to my married life—but suppose that would not be right—though I cannot remember things as they came. 1862 is where I left off—I stayed a good deal with the Douglases at Orbiston, near Hamilton. I was there when the old Duke died and went to his funeral, my brother-in-laws grounds joined the Hamilton Palace grounds—a Roman Bridge dividing them. There was a Cavalry Regiment quartered at Hamilton, 3rd Hussars and I had a good time as the officers were often out at Cribiston and we went to different fetes at the barracks. Major Howard Vyse was in command and Maxwell and Walker were two of the Subalterns I remember best. One year that I was there Tom came up too and we went about a lot and had a good time. It was I think early in 1866 that Robert Douglas died in Edinburgh in March, 16 Amstil Place. I was there at the time and stayed with my sister and the children two or three months after and then went first to Bury Lodge and in June to the Isle of Wight with Uncle Charlie to Seaview. One day we went to see the Leacocks—they were old friends of course and I saw Peter then for the first time since we were children. He came over to Sea View every day and late in the evening when Uncle Charlie thought I had gone to my room I went out in Peter's boat with him. We were engaged before the summer was over and married privately and later at All Saint's Church, Norfolk St. London. I can never think of it without sorrow and shame for deceiving my kind good uncles. It was Uncle Charles I was staying with—he went to the station and took my return ticket to Waterloo Bridge for me little thinking I was going to meet Peter and be married to him. They had nothing against his character, but he was not quite 18 and a Roman Catholic and going to the Colonies. They had not then decided where. I never saw my Uncle again for several years; he was then rector of Newchurch in the Isle of Wight and I went with Stephen, then a baby, to stay there; Peter came for a day or two—he was never asked to Bury Lodge, but I went there with the children before I left England.

November 25th, 1917

I see I have skipped all together too much—that summer at Sea View in 1866 when I was engaged to marry Peter, Lucy Patterson was with me. Uncle Charles took a cottage right on the beach at the end of the sea wall (I have a sketch of it somewhere) and it was just below there that Peter brought his blue boat. Sometimes there was another boy, Stephen by name with him—that was when Lucy was with me. We often spent the day at Oakhill (the Leacock's home) and went to the Youngs at Westridge for croquet and stayed to dinner late in the evening. Westridge is a beautiful place, lovely old gardens and woods. It belongs to Peter's uncle, James Young, who Jim was called after, and Alecia, his wife was very kind to me. She was a far away connection to Lady Alecia Erskine. Her sister, Margaret married Franklin Lushington, my father's cousin; there were two children, Johnnie and Alecia and Somerville Hay, Alecia's boy by her first husband, Captain Hay. Sommerville Hay was about twelve I think and was with us a good deal. Johnnie and Alecia much younger—she was a very pretty child with lovely hair. We called her "Missie" and my Missie was very like her.

Well to go on—that year my sister Kate came from Calcutta with her three children and an Indian "Boy" nurse. They were at Porchester and I was with them a good deal and Peter used to come over there—it was only a short distance, I think a half hour by train from Portsmouth, with the boats running all the time it was so easy to get backwards and forwards. Kate was going back to India in a short time. Before Christmas she went to London. My sister, Maryanne Douglas was in London then, Oxford Terrace. I went up the 16th of December to stay with her. Strange to say, I remember very little about that Christmas except that Kate and Weston Parry went to Calcutta, leaving Frank and Rosamond with a clergyman's family, Mr. Pound, and Cecil with me. I had left him at Bury Lodge to go and see my sisters. Then Peter came to London just after Christmas and we were married at All Saints Church, Norfolk Square and took rooms in Burand St. Russels Square and booked our passage to Natal. It was March before the vessel, the "Burton Hatter" was ready to sail. Captain Warren, a kind, nice old man—I think he was a Methodist. We had prayers on board, always on Sundays and some evenings. We had terrible rough weather in the Bay of Biscay, battered down—but both Peter and I were good sailors and as soon as they would let me I went on deck to watch the huge waves dashing over the ship. There were only two other first class passengers going over—Thomas Norman, going out for his health and Mr. Fawcett. We were friends with both, especially Norman—I felt so sorry for him. I had an Irish maid, she was very pretty but not much good. It was a long voyage, twelve weeks. We saw flying fish and all the usual sea sights and were becalmed crossing the line. We sighted the Bluff of Natal a week before we landed. It was the only really wearysome part of the journey—as we would appear to be quite close to land and have to put out to sea again, because there was not the proper tide to cross the Bar.

I remember I nearly cried with disappointment after about the fifth trial. When at last we got in we couldn't land from the ship—the Kaffirs and coolies came out in boats and we had to be taken ashore by them. I had my dog, Tou, a black retriever with me and he was frightened at the Kaffirs and tried biting their legs. It was hard work getting from the quay to the town—deep sand—we sank with every step; and there was no way there except walking and the Kaffirs carrying our luggage. We went to Natal House, I forget the proprietor's name—will add it if I think of it. Had to wait there several days for a waggon to take us to Pietermaritzburgh. We went about the town (to church on Sunday) and saw banana fields and cactus hedges, but it was not easy getting about except just in the town where the paths were trodden hard—it was all sand and very hot, but all this was 52 years ago, now it is quite different. Stephen went there on the Rhodes Commission and brought me pictures of the town—quite modern.

Well we started for Maritzburgh about the first week in June in a waggon with fourteen oxen, a Dutch driver and Kaffir boy, Peter and myself, Eliza, my maid and the dog. The waggon was full of our luggage with mattresses on top of the boxes for me and the maid. Peter slept under the waggon and the men outside. The first stop for the night was at Pine Town. I remember feeling nervous about sleeping there as there were no other white people, just Kaffirs and coolies, but they must have been unusually honest for I left my opal ring on the washstand, and after we had started one of the coolies came running after us with it. It was the second night that we slept, as I described, in and under the waggon, the third night we were within a mile or so of Maritzburgh when the sun went down, and the driver wouldn't go on; he outspanned the oxen and neither persuasion or threats were any use. They will not travel after dark because there [*the memoir ends here*]

# INDEX

*Page numbers in italics denote letters written
by Stephen Leacock; unitalicized page numbers denote references.*